HDL Chip Design

A practical guide for designing, synthesizing and simulating ASICs and FPGAs using VHDL or Verilog

Douglas J Smith

Foreword by Alex Zamfirescu

Doone
Publications

Cover graphic: designed using ModelView from Intergraph Software Solutions.
Interior design: Doone Publications.

Package STANDARD & package TEXTIO reprinted from IEEE Std 1076-1993 IEEE Standard VHDL Language Reference Manual, Copyright © 1994 by the Institute of Electrical and Electronics Engineers, Inc.
Standard logic Package STD_LOGIC_1164 (IEEE 1164) reprinted from 1164-1993 IEEE Standard Multivalue Logic System for VHDL Model Interoperability, Copyright © 1993 by the Institute of Electrical and Electronics Engineers, Inc.
Standard synthesis package NUMERIC_STD (IEEE 1076.3) reprinted from IEEE Draft Standard P1076.3, dated 1995, Draft Standard VHDL Synthesis Package, Copyright © 1995 by the Institute of Electrical and Electronics Engineers, Inc. This is an unapproved draft of a proposed IEEE Standard, subject to change. Use of information contained in the unapproved draft is at your own risk.
The IEEE disclaims any responsibility or liability resulting from the placement and use in this product. Information is reprinted with the permission of the IEEE.

Doone Publications

7950 Hwy 72W #G106, Madison
AL, 35758, USA
Tel: 1-800-311-3753
Fax: 256-837-0580
Int. Tel/Fax: +1 256-837-0580
email: asmith@doone.com
web: http://www.doone.com

FOREWORD
. . . .

The EDA industry is an increasingly challenging area in which to be working. I work at VeriBest Incorporated and have been in the EDA industry for many years, and I am fully aware of the books that are available. This one, however, is unique as it deals extensively with both VHDL and Verilog in a comparative manner and includes many graphic examples of synthesized circuits. Doug Smith, also of VeriBest Inc., has been mastering the valuable art of Hardware Description Language (HDL) chip design for many years in both European and American companies. He has cleverly captured years of design experience within the pages of this book.

The abundant examples throughout show complete functional designs and not just snippets of code. Doug has spent endless months researching HDL and design topics to ensure that people in the EDA industry were in agreement with his methods. I am certainly an advocate of Doug's HDL guide for EDA veterans and first semester EE freshmen alike. His tips on planning and executing HDL designs (including the modeling caveats) are invaluable. Designers can surely benefit by applying his precepts and principles using the techniques emerged from his design experience. You will probably keep this book close to your desk for many projects to come.

Often, worth is measured by magnitude, however this book not only contains more examples than any other previously published work dealing with HDL driven design, but is more comprehensive than any other book of synthesis recipes whatsoever. A technical work must stand or fall by its accuracy and authority; "HDL Chip Design" stands head-and-shoulders over all other books covering this subject.

The authority of this work rests on almost a lifetime of practical experience, through his career. Its accuracy has been verified through machine-processing of all the examples, and by leading industry experts. As a result "HDL Chip Design" is the very best hands-on book you can own today. It will enable you to survive in the competitive world of HDL chip design, and will be a beacon in your quest for perfect HDL design.

Alex Zamfirescu

IEEE Project 1076.3 (Synthesis Packages) Chariman
IEC TC93 Working Group (HDLs) Convenor

ABOUT THE AUTHOR

Douglas Smith was born in England, and began his career with a four year apprenticeship in a company developing and manufacturing radiation monitoring equipment. He received a B.Sc. in Electrical and Electronic Engineering from Bath University, England, in 1981. He worked at a number of companies in England performing digital design and project management of microprocessor based circuit boards and associated ICs. These IC's included PLD, FPGA, gate array ASICs and standard cell ASIC devices for applications such as ring laser gyro control and frequency hopping radios. He then moved into the EDA industry by becoming applications manager and then product marketing manager for all synthesis products at GenRad Ltd. When GenRad exited from the EDA industry he moved to the USA to Intergraph Electronics, now VeriBest Incorporated, where he is now a member of the technical staff. Doug is currently on the two working groups for VHDL and Verilog, whose charter is to develop public domain synthesis interoperability standards for model portability across multiple synthesis tools.

This book is dedicated to my mum and dad,
who are far away,
but always in my thoughts.

ACKNOWLEDGMENTS

My biggest thanks go to my wife Anne, who apart from looking after two active young children during the day, found time and energy in the evenings to do the drawings and layout the pages of this book.

I thank my daughter Zoe, who at one and a half years, was able to provide some interesting edits to my manuscript. My son, Alexander, at five and a half years, often gave me an excuse to break from writing to play "Power Rangers" or "Cowboys". I must also mention my in-laws, Margaret and Godfrey, and thank them for their interest and encouragement; they now know a new definition for a flip-flop.

I also thank Intergraph Electronics, now VeriBest Incorporated, for allowing me the use of their computers and CAE tools to verify the HDL models in this book.

Special thanks are due to the following four individuals, listed in alphabetical order, for their technical reviews. They are each experts in the field of hardware description languages, and the technology employed by synthesis and simulation tools. I especially appreciate their efforts in taking the time out of their already busy schedules.

J. Bhasker (Bhasker)	Lucent Technologies, Bell Laboratories.
Gabe Moretti	VeriBest Incorporated
Jenjen Tiao	Lucent Technologies, Bell Laboratories.
Alex Zamfirescu	VeriBest Incorporated

Finally, I am very grateful to Charles Montgomery for reviewing the text for grammatical errors, and especially ensuring my English spelling was suitably converted to American.

PREFACE
• • • • • • • • • • • •

This book is intended for practicing design engineers, their managers who need to gain a practical understanding of the issues involved when designing ASICs and FPGAs, and students alike.

The past 10 years has seen a dramatic change in the way digital design is performed. The need to reduce the time to market, the technology advancements and new innovative EDA software tools, have all helped to fuel this dramatic change. In terms of technology, transistors can be manufactured with submicron channel widths, resulting in reduced size (100 times smaller than the thickness of a human hair) and improved switching speed. This has lead to silicon chips containing a million transistors becoming common, and large complex systems being implemented within them. The need to be able to design chips of such size, in a timely manner, has lead to innovative EDA tools being developed with automatic synthesis tools being the major advancement. The introduction of commercial synthesis tools has enabled top down design methodologies to be adopted, starting with an abstract description of a circuit's behavior written in a hardware description language. More recently, the rate of change has slowed and the introduction of standards has enabled EDA tool vendors to develop integrated design tools and with far less risk.

There are two industry standard hardware description languages VHDL and Verilog, thanks to the efforts of the VI (VHDL International) and OVI (open Verilog International). Both the VI and OVI are industry consortiums of design tool vendors, chip vendors, users (designers) and academia. The VI succeeded in establishing VHDL as an IEEE standard (IEEE 1076) first in 1987 and revised it in 1993 (IEEE 1076-1993). The second to become a standard was Verilog. The OVI established Verilog as an IEEE standard in 1995 (IEEE 1364-1995). Although Verilog became an IEEE standard after VHDL, it has been used by digital designers for far longer.

The benefits of adopting a top-down design methodology, adhering to the use of these standards is that, 1) design source files are transportable between different EDA tools and, 2) the design is independent of any particular silicon vendor's manufacturing process technology.

The emphasis of this book is on digital design using such standards.

BOOK OVERVIEW

VHDL and Verilog are covered equally throughout this book. Code examples show VHDL on the left and Verilog on the right because VHDL became a standard first. All language reserved words are shown emboldened. Also, all HDL code related issues in the text apply equally to VHDL and Verilog unless explicitly stated otherwise. Where synthesized circuits are shown they are a result of synthesizing either the VHDL or Verilog version of the associated model.

This book is divided into 12 chapters, a glossary and two appendices.

Chapter 1, "Introduction", defines what ASIC and FPGA devices are, and the criteria for choosing which to use in a given application. Hardware description languages are defined and a comprehensive listing of comparative features between VHDL and Verilog is given. Electronic Design Automation (EDA) tools are discussed with a particular emphasis on synthesis tools.

Chapter 2, "Synthesis Constraint and Optimization Tutorials", shows the effect of different constraints on the synthesized circuit of a particular design. Also, a typical design constraint scenario is posed and a description of how constraints for it are specified, described. For completeness, command line optimization commands are included for the VeriBest Synthesis tools.

Chapter 3, "Language Fundamentals", introduces the fundamentals of the VHDL and Verilog hardware description languages. Code structure is described by first defining the principle of design units and how they link together. The code structure of subsections within a design unit are described all the way down to subfunctions. Assignments are also defined together with the expressions within them. Includes a fully detailed description of the operands and operators that make up an expression.

Chapter 4, "Design/Modeling Recommendations, Issues and Techniques", is one of the most important chapters to the practicing digital design engineer. It provides a list of recommendations, issues and techniques to consider when designing ASICs or FPGAs, from both a design and HDL modeling perspective.

Chapter 5, "Structuring a Design", is devoted to structuring HDL code and hence inferred hardware structure when modeling at the register transfer level. Code constructs are grouped and discussed separately based on their level of granularity.

Chapter 6, "Modeling Combinational Logic Circuits", shows HDL models of commonly used circuit functions that are implemented using combinational logic only. In most cases different ways of modeling the same circuit is shown. Circuit functions covered include: multiplexers, encoders, priority encoders, decoders, comparators and ALUs.

Chapter 7, "Modeling Synchronous Logic Circuits", shows how D-type latches and D-type flip-flops are inferred in HDL models. Also included, are various models of linear-feedback shift-registers and counters.

Chapter 8, "Modeling Finite State Machines", covers in detail the different aspects of modeling finite state machines. Shown are: good and bad coding styles, when resets are needed for fail safe behavior, state machines with Mealy or Moore type outputs, state machines with additional synchronous logic modeled in the code of the state machine, and multiple interactive state machines.

Chapter 9, "Circuit Functions Modeled Combinational or Synchronously", describes how shifters, adders, subtractors, multipliers and dividers may be modeled for a combinational or synchronous logic implementation.

Chapter 10, "Tri-State Buffers", contains various examples of how tri-state buffers are inferred.

Chapter 11, "Writing Test Harnesses", describes the structure of a simulation test harness and all related issues. Detailed examples show how input stimuli may be generated, and how outputs from the model under test may be automatically monitored and tested against reference data.

Chapter 12, "Practical Modeling Examples", contains five larger modeling examples. Each example is posed as a problem and solution. The first shows how an internal tri-state bus is used to reduce circuit area. The second example is of a digital alarm clock. The third example is a three-way round-robin priority encoder used to arbitrate between three microprocessors accessing the same RAM. The fourth example is of a circuit that computes the greatest common divisor of two inputs. It is modeled at the algorithmic level in C, VHDL and Verilog, and again at the RTL level in VHDL and Verilog, and uses common test data files. Test harnesses for the RTL level models are also shown. The fifth example is a model of an error detection and correction circuit that sits between a microprocessor and RAM. Critical data is stored in the RAM along with parity check bits. When data is retrieved single bit errors are detected and corrected, while double bit errors are simply detected and an interrupt generated.

Glossary, contains the definition of over 200 terms.

Appendix A, "VHDL", contains reference information relating to VHDL: reserved words, predefined attributes, listings of packages STANDARD, TEXTIO, STD_LOGIC_1164 and NUMERIC_STD, and reference information relating to VHDL constructs and where they are used.

Appendix B, "Verilog", contains reference information relating to Verilog: reserved words, compiler directives, system tasks and functions, and reference information relating to VHDL constructs and where they are used.

Disclaimer

Every effort has been made to make this book as complete and as accurate as possible. However, there may be mistakes both typographical and in content. Therefore, this text should be used only as a general guide and not the ultimate reference source on the two languages. Please refer to the respective LRMs for syntax accuracy.

The author and publisher shall not be liable for any direct or indirect damages arising from any use, direct or indirect, of the examples provided in this book.

ABBREVIATIONS & ACRONYMS

The list below contains the abbreviations and acronyms used in this book.

ALU	Arithmetic Logic Unit
AQL	Average Quality Level
ASIC	Application-Specific Integrated Circuit
ATPG	Automatic Test Pattern Generation
BIST	Built-In Self-Test
CAD	Computer Aided Design
CAE	Computer Aided Engineering
CDFG	Control-Data Flow-Graph
CMOS	Complementary Metal-Oxide Semiconductor
CPU	Central Processing Unit
DFT	Design-For-Test
DOD	Department of Defence
EDA	Electronic Design Automation
EDAC	Error Detection And Correction
FIFO	First-In First-Out
FPGA	Field Programmable Gate Array
FSM	Finite State Machine
GCD	Greatest Common Divisor
GHDL	GenRad's Hardware Description Language
HDL	Hardware Description Language
I/O	Input/Output
IC	Integrated Circuit
IEEE	IEEE Institute of Electrical and Electronics Engineers
JEDEC	Joint Electronic Device Engineering Council

LFSR	Linear Feedback Shift Register
LRM	Language Reference Manual
LSB	Least Significant Bit
LSI	Large-Scale Integration
LSSD	Level-Sensitive Scan Device
MCM	Multichip Module
MSB	Most Significant Bit
MSI	Medium Scale Integration
NRE	Non-Recurring Engineering
OVI	Open Verilog International
PCB	Printed Circuit Board
PLD	Programmable Logic Design
RAM	Random Access Memory
ROM	Read Only Memory
RTL	Register Transfer Level
SDI	Scan Data In
SDF	Standard Delay Format
SDO	Scan Data Out
TE	Test Enable
VHDL	VHSIC Hardware Description Language
VHSIC	Very High Speed Integrated Circuit
VI	VHDL International
VITAL	VHDL Initiative Toward ASIC Libraries
VLSI	Very-Large-Scale Integration

CONTENTS
•••••••••••••••

Chapter Four: Design/modeling Recommendations, Issues and Techniques

Chapter Five: Structuring a Design

Chapter Six: Modeling Combinational Logic Circuits

Chapter Seven: Modeling Synchronous Logic Circuits

Chapter Eight: Modeling Finite State Machines

EXAMPLES
• • • • • • • • • • • • • •

Chapter Seven: Modeling Sequential Logic Circuits

Chapter Eight: Modeling Finite State Machines

Chapter Nine: Circuit Functions modeled Combinationally or Sequentially

Chapter Ten: Tri-State Buffers

All examples are available on disk, see order form at rear of book for details.

Introduction

Chapter 1 Contents

Introduction

Traditionally, digital design was a manual process of designing and capturing circuits using schematic entry tools. This process has many disadvantages and is rapidly being replaced by new methods.

System designers are always competing to build cost-effective products as fast as possible in a highly competitive environment. In order to achieve this, they are turning to using top-down design methodologies that include using hardware description languages and synthesis, in addition to just the more traditional process of simulation. A product in this instance, is any electronic equipment containing Application-Specific Integrated Circuits (ASICs), or Field-Programmable Gate-Arrays (FPGAs).

In recent years, designers have increasingly adopted top down design methodologies even though it takes them away from logic and transistor level design to abstract programming. The introduction of industry standard hardware description languages and commercially available synthesis tools have helped establish this revolutionary design methodology. The advantages are clear and engineers' design methods must change. Some of the advantages are:

- increased productivity yields shorter development cycles with more product features and reduced time to market,
- reduced Non-Recurring Engineering (NRE) costs,
- design reuse is enabled,
- increased flexibility to design changes,
- faster exploration of alternative architectures
- faster exploration of alternative technology libraries,
- enables use of synthesis to rapidly sweep the design space of area and timing, and to automatically generate testable circuits,
- better and easier design auditing and verification.

This book uses the two industry standard hardware description languages VHDL and Verilog. Both languages are used world wide and have been adopted by the Institute of Electrical and Electronic Engineers (IEEE). The particular language versions used in this book are IEEE 1076 '93 for VHDL and IEEE 1364 for Verilog. All models have been verified using the simulation and synthesis tools developed by VeriBest Incorporated. Where synthesized logic circuits are shown they have been optimized for area unless explicitly specified otherwise.

ASIC and FPGA devices

Standard "off-the-shelf" integrated circuits have a fixed functional operation defined by the chip manufacturer. Contrary to this, both ASIC and FPGAs are types of integrated circuit whose function is not fixed by the manufacturer. The function is defined by the designer for a particular application. An ASIC requires a final manufacturing process to customize its operation while an FPGA does not.

ASICs

An application-specific integrated circuit is a device that is partially manufactured by an ASIC vendor in generic form. This initial manufacturing process is the most complex, time consuming, and expensive part of the total manufacturing process. The result is silicon chips with an array of unconnected transistors.

The final manufacturing process of connecting the transistors together is then completed when a chip designer has a specific design he or she wishes to implement in the ASIC. An ASIC vendor can usually do this in a couple of weeks and is known as the turn-round time. There are two categories of ASIC devices; Gate Arrays and Standard Cells.

Gate Arrays

There are two types of gate array; a channeled gate array and a channel-less gate array. A channeled gate array is manufactured with single or double rows of basic cells across the silicon. A basic cell consists of a number of transistors. The channels between the rows of cells are used for interconnecting the basic cells during the final customization process. A channel-less gate array is manufactured with a "sea" of basic cells across the silicon and there are no dedicated channels for interconnections. Gate arrays contain from a few thousand equivalent gates to hundreds of thousands of equivalent gates. Due to the limited routing space on channeled gate arrays, typically only 70% to 90% of the total number of available gates can be used.

The library of cells provided by a gate array vendor will contain: primitive logic gates, registers, hard-macros and soft-macros. Hard-macros and soft-macros are usually of MSI and LSI complexity, such as multiplexers, comparators and counters. Hard macros are defined by the manufacturer in terms of cell primitives. By comparison, soft-macros are characterized by the designer, for example, by specifying the width a particular counter.

Standard cell

Standard cell devices do not have the concept of a basic cell and no components are prefabricated on the silicon chip. The manufacturer creates custom masks for every stage of the device's process and means silicon is utilized much more efficiently than for gate arrays.

Manufacturers supply hard-macro and soft-macro libraries containing elements of LSI and VLSI complexity, such as controllers, ALUs and microprocessors. Additionally, soft-macro libraries contain RAM functions that cannot be implemented efficiently in gate array devices; ROM functions are more efficiently implemented in cell primitives.

FPGAs

The field-programmable gate array is a device that is completely manufactured, but that remains design independent. Each FPGA vendor manufactures devices to a proprietary architecture. However, the architecture will include a number of programmable logic blocks that are connected to programmable switching matrices. To configure a device for a particular functional operation these switching matrices are programmed to route signals between the individual logic blocks.

The choice of ASIC or FPGA

The nonrecurring engineering (NRE) costs involved with customizing an ASIC is currently somewhere in the region of $20,000 to more than $100,000. However, after this initial outlay the unit cost for production devices might only be about $10. This is much cheaper than the production costs of FPGA devices that are typically $150 to $250 per device. The advantage of FPGAs is that they are quick and easy to program (functionally customize). Also, FPGAs allow printed circuit board CAD layout to begin while the internal FPGA design is still being completed. This procedure allows early hardware and software integration testing. If system testing fails, the design can be modified and another FPGA device programmed immediately at relatively low cost. For these reasons, designs are often targeted to FPGA devices first for system testing and for small production runs. The design is then retargeted to an ASIC for larger scale production.

Design trade-offs must be considered when retargeting FPGAs to ASICs. For example, a long hold time may never appear in an ASIC because of the improved speed of operation.

Top-Down Design Methodology

In an ideal world, a true top-down system level design methodology would mean describing a complete system at an abstract level using a Hardware Description Language (HDL) and the use of automated tools, for example, partitioners and synthesizers. This would drive the abstract level description to implementation on PCBs or MCMs (Multichip Modules) which contain: standard ICs, ASICs, FPGA, PLDs and full-custom ICs. This ideal is not fulfilled, however, EDA tools are constantly being improved in the strive towards this vision. This means designers must constantly take on new rolls and learn new skills. More time is now spent designing HDL models, considering different architectures and considering system test & testability issues. Practically no time is spent designing at the gate level.

Technology advancements over the last six years or so has seen a tenfold increase in the number of gates that an ASIC can contain: 100K gates is now common. This has increased the complexity of standard ICs and ASICs and resulted in the concept, "system on a chip". A top-down design methodology is the only practical option to design such chips.

Any ASIC or FPGA designs in a hardware development project are usually on the critical path of the development schedule. Traditionally, such designs have been produced by entering them as circuit diagrams using a schematic entry tool. In rare cases for reasons of cost, this may still be a viable design method for small devices such as PLDs. Provided the budget is available for simulation and synthesis tools, a top-down design approach using a Hardware Description Language (HDL), is by far the best design philosophy to adopt.

The saying, "a picture paints a thousand words", seems to go against the grain of using HDLs instead of schematics. This is evident in the popularity of graphical front end input tools which output HDL models. However, there are many advantages of adopting a top-down design methodology as summarized in the introduction on page 3.

Imagine using schematics to design a 100k gate ASIC; a small design change could result in major time consuming changes to the schematics. The philosophy of using a hardware description language to develop electronic hardware is similar to that of a software development project using a high-level programming language such as C.

The levels of hierarchical refinement of electronic hardware in a top-down design process, is shown in Figure 1.1. It indicates how synthesis is the key link in this process.

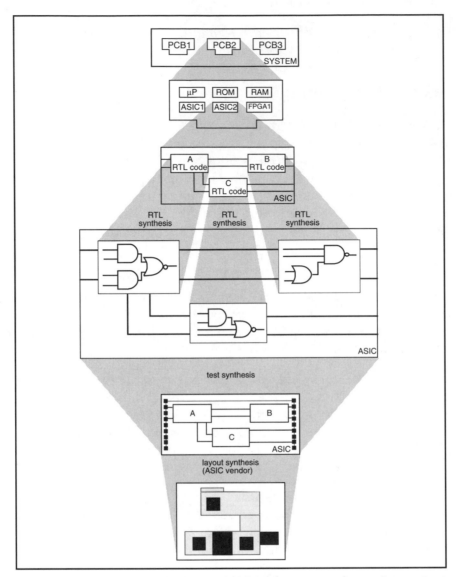

Figure 1.1 Hierarchical refinement of electronic hardware in a top down design environment

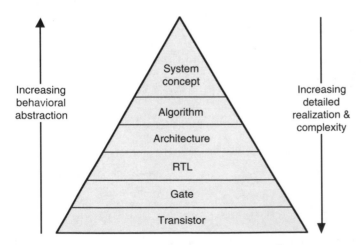

A top-down design methodology takes the HDL model of hardware, written at a high level of behavioral abstraction (system or algorithmic), down through intermediate levels, to a low (gate or transistor) level; Figure 1.2.

Figure 1.2 Behavioral level of abstraction pyramid

The term behavior represents the behavior of intended hardware and is independent of the level of abstraction by which it is modeled. A design represented at the gate level still represents the behavior of hardware intent. As hardware models are translated to progressively lower levels they become more complex and contain more structural detail. The benefit of modeling hardware at higher levels of behavioral abstraction is that designers are not overwhelmed with large amounts of unnecessary detail and the complexity of the design task is reduced.

Hardware structure is ignored when modeling hardware at the two high levels of behavior. However, when modeling hardware at the RTL level it is essential to keep the hardware intent in mind at all times. Figure 1.3 shows how the different behavioral levels of abstraction overlap between the different design domains of pure abstraction, structural decomposition and physical implementation.

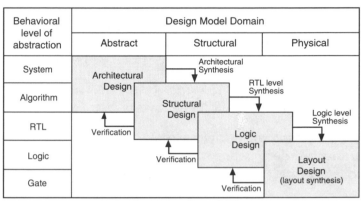

Figure 1.3 Design domain for different levels of design abstraction

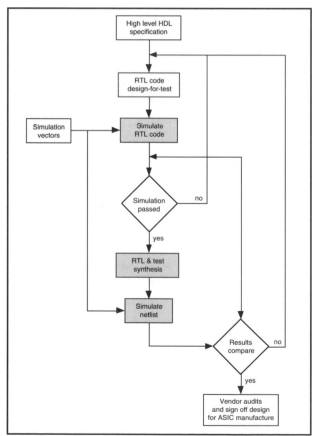

Figure 1.4 Typical ASIC design flow using simulation and RTL level synthesis.

A typical ASIC design flow using simulation and RTL level synthesis is shown in Figure 1.4. The same test vectors are used to verify the RTL and synthesized netlist level models. The netlist level corresponds to the gate level, but may also include larger macro cells, or even bigger mega cells. By comparing the simulation results at each level, netlist level testing can be automated.

Hardware Description Languages (HDLs)

What is an HDL?

A Hardware Description Language (HDL) is a software programming language used to model the intended operation of a piece of hardware. There are two aspects to the description of hardware that an HDL facilitates; true abstract behavior modeling and hardware structure modeling.

Abstract behavior modeling. A hardware description language is declarative in order to facilitate the abstract description of hardware behavior for specification purposes. This behavior is not prejudiced by structural or design aspects of the hardware intent.

Hardware structure modeling. Hardware structure is capable of being modeled in a hardware description language irrespective of the design's behavior.

The behavior of hardware may be modeled and represented at various levels of abstraction during the design process. Higher level models describe the operation of hardware abstractly, while lower level models include more detail, such as inferred hardware structure.

History of VHDL

1980

The USA Department of Defense (DOD) wanted to make circuit design self documenting, follow a common design methodology and be reusable with new technologies. It became clear there was a need for a standard programming language for describing the function and structure of digital circuits for the design of integrated circuits (IC's). The DOD funded a project under the Very High Speed Integrated Circuit (VHSIC) program to create a standard hardware description language. The result was the creation of the VHSIC hardware description language or VHDL as it is now commonly known.

1983

The development of VHDL began under the VHSIC contract with a joint effort by IBM, Texas Instruments and Intermetrics. These companies pooled their experiences of high level languages and top-down design techniques to jointly develop the new language together with associated simulation tools.

VHDL provided government contractors with a standard method of communicating that facilitated top-down design techniques, and addressed the concern of how to upgrade systems when technologies became obsolete.

1987

Two significant things happened. First, the DOD mandated that all digital electronic circuits be described in VHDL, and second, the Institute of Electrical and Electronics Engineers (IEEE) ratified it as IEEE Standard 1076. The success of VHDL was now assured.

The F-22 advanced tactical fighter aircraft was one of the first major government programs to mandate the use of VHDL descriptions for all electronic subsystems in the project. Different subcontractors designed various subsystems, and so the interfaces between them were crucial and tightly coupled. The VHDL code was self-documenting and formed the basis of the top-down strategy. The success of this project helped establish VHDL and top-down design methodology.

Now that VHDL was an industry standard, Electronic Design Automation (EDA) vendors could start developing tools for it with considerably less risk. However, demand was low and the investment needed to develop commercial quality tools was high, so few tools were developed. This initial lack of tools meant VHDL was slow to be adopted commercially.

1993

The VHDL language was revised to IEEE 1076 '93.

1996

Both commercial simulation and synthesis tools became available adhering to IEEE 1076 '93 standard. This enabled designers to start using this version of the standard in a top-down design methodology. A VHDL package for use with synthesis tools become part of the IEEE 1076 standard, specifically it is IEEE 1076.3. This will greatly improve the portability of designs between different synthesis vendor tools. Another part of the standard, IEEE 1076.4 (VITAL), has been completed and sets a new standard for modeling ASIC and FPGA libraries in VHDL. This will make life considerably easier for ASIC vendors, EDA tool vendors and designers.

History of Verilog

1981

A CAE software company called Gateway Design Automation was founded by Prabhu Goel. One of Gateway's first employees was Phil Moorby, who was an original author of GenRad's Hardware Description Language (GHDL) and HILO simulator.

1983

Gateway released the Verilog Hardware Description Language known as "Verilog HDL" or simply "Verilog" together with a Verilog simulator.

1985

The language and simulator were enhanced; the new version of the simulator was called "Verilog-XL".

1983 to 1987

Verilog-XL gained a strong foothold among advanced, high-end designers for the following reasons:
- The behavioral constructs of Verilog could describe both hardware and test stimulus.
- The Verilog-XL simulator was fast, especially at the gate level and could handle designs in excess of 100,000 gates.
- The Verilog-XL simulator was an "interpreter" (interpretive software executes source code directly instead of pre-compiling the source code into intermediate "object" code). The interpretive nature of Verilog-XL gave hardware design engineers something they wanted and needed with an easy way to interactively debug their hardware designs. With Verilog-XL, engineers could do more than just model and simulate, they could also troubleshoot a design the same way they would troubleshoot real hardware on a breadboard.

1987

Verilog-XL was becoming more popular. Design sizes of a single chip began to exceed the realistic capacity of many other simulator products. Gateway began to aggressively pursue ASIC foundry endorsement. Another start-up company, Synopsys, began to use the proprietary Verilog behavioral language as an input to their synthesis product. At the same time, the IEEE released the "VHDL" standard, drawing attention to the possibilities of "top down design" using a behavioral Hardware Description Language and synthesis. All of these factors combined to increase the use and acceptance of Verilog-XL.

December 1989

Cadence bought Gateway.

Early 1990

Cadence split the Verilog Hardware Description Language (HDL) and the Verilog-XL simulator into separate products, and then released the Verilog HDL to the public domain. Cadence did this partly to compete with VHDL, which was a nonproprietary HDL, and mostly because Verilog users wanted to share models and knowledge about Verilog, which was not easy with a proprietary language. At this time the "Open Verilog International" (OVI) was formed to control the language specification. OVI is an industry consortium comprised of both Verilog users and CAE vendors.

1990

Nearly all ASIC foundries supported Verilog and most used Verilog-XL as a "golden" simulator. This is one that a chip vendor will use to sign-off a chip against, and guarantee that a manufactured chip will meet the same timing as that of the simulated model.

1993

Of all designs submitted to ASIC foundries in this year, 85% were designed and submitted using Verilog. (Source EE Times.)

December 1995

The Verilog language was reviewed and adopted by the IEEE as IEEE standard 1364.

VHDL/Verilog compared & contrasted

Each of the following paragraphs in this section compares and contrasts one aspect of the two languages and are listed in alphabetical order.

Capability

Hardware structure can be modeled equally effectively in both VHDL and Verilog. When modeling abstract hardware, the capability of VHDL can sometimes only be achieved in Verilog when using the PLI. The choice of which to use, is therefore, not based solely on technical capability but on:

- personal preferences,
- EDA tool availability,
- commercial, business and marketing issues.

The modeling constructs of VHDL and Verilog cover

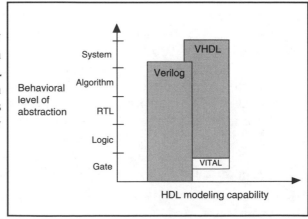

Figure 1.5 HDL modeling capability

a slightly different spectrum across the levels of behavioral abstraction; see Figure 1.5.

Compilation

VHDL. Multiple *design units* (**entity-architecture** pairs), that reside in the same system file, may be separately compiled if so desired. However, it is good design practice to keep each design unit in its own system file.

Verilog. The Verilog language is still rooted in its native interpretative mode. Compilation is a means of speeding up simulation, but has not changed the original nature of the language. As a result care must be taken with both the compilation order of code written in a single file and the compilation order of multiple files. Simulation results can change by simply changing the order of compilation.

Data types

VHDL. A multitude of language or user-defined data types can be used. This may mean dedicated conversion functions are needed to convert objects from one type to another. The choice of which data types to use should be considered wisely, especially enumerated (abstract) data types. This will make models easier to write, clearer to read and avoid unnecessary conversion functions that can clutter the code. VHDL may be preferred because it allows a multitude of language or user defined data types to be used.

Verilog. Compared to VHDL, Verilog data types are very simple, easy to use and very much geared towards modeling hardware structure as opposed to abstract hardware modeling. Unlike VHDL, all data types used in a Verilog model are defined by the Verilog language and not by the user. There are net data types, for example **wire**, and a register data type called **reg**. A model with a signal whose type is one of the net data types has a corresponding electrical wire in the implied modeled circuit. Objects of type **reg** are updated under the control of the procedural flow of constructs that surround them. Verilog may be preferred because the simplicity of its data types.

Design reusability

VHDL. Procedures and functions may be placed in a package so that they are available to any *design unit* that uses them.

Verilog. There is no concept of packages in Verilog. Functions and procedures used within a model <u>must</u> be defined in the **module** statement with which it will be used. To make functions and procedures generally accessible from different **module** statements they must be placed in a separate system file and included using the 'include compiler directive.

Easiest to Learn

Starting with zero knowledge of either language, Verilog is probably the easiest to grasp and understand. This assumes the Verilog compiler directive language for simulation and the PLI language is not included. If these languages are included they can be looked upon as two additional languages that need to be learned.

VHDL may seem less intuitive at first for two primary reasons. First, it is very strongly typed; a feature that makes it robust and powerful for the advanced user after a longer learning phase. Second, there are many ways to model the same circuit, especially those with large hierarchical structures.

Forward and back annotation

A spin-off from Verilog is the Standard Delay Format (SDF). This is a general purpose format used to define the timing delays in a circuit. The format provides a bidirectional link between chip layout tools, and either synthesis or simulation tools in order to provide more accurate timing representations. The SDF format is now an industry standard in its own right.

High level constructs

VHDL. There are more constructs and features for high-level modeling in VHDL than there are in Verilog. Abstract data types can be used along with the following statements:

- package statements for model reuse,
- configuration statements for configuring design structure,
- generate statements for replicating structure,
- generic statements for generic models that can be individually characterized, for example, bit width.

All these language statements are useful in synthesizable models.

Verilog. Except for being able to parameterize models by overloading parameter constants, there is no equivalent to the high-level VHDL modeling statements in Verilog.

Language Extensions

The use of language extensions will make a model nonstandard and most likely not portable across other design tools. However, sometimes they are necessary in order to achieve the desired results.

VHDL. Has an attribute called 'foreign that allows architectures and subprograms to be modeled in another language.

Verilog. The Programming Language Interface (PLI) is an interface mechanism between Verilog models and Verilog software tools. For example, a designer, or more likely, a Verilog tool vendor, can specify user defined tasks or functions in the C programming language, and then call them from the Verilog source description. Use of such tasks or functions make a Verilog model nonstandard and so may not be usable by other Verilog software tools. Their use is not recommended.

Libraries

VHDL. A library is a storage area in the host environment for compiled entities, architectures, packages and configurations. Useful for managing multiple design projects.

Verilog. There is no concept of a library in Verilog. This is due to its origins as an interpretive language.

Low Level Constructs

VHDL. Simple two input logical operators are built into the language, they are: NOT, AND, OR, NAND, NOR, XOR and XNOR. Any timing must be separately specified using the **after** clause. Separate constructs defined in IEEE 1076.4 (VITAL) must be used to define the cell primitives of ASIC and FPGA libraries.

Verilog. The Verilog language was originally developed with gate level modeling in mind, and so has very good constructs for modeling at this level <u>and</u> for modeling the cell primitives of ASIC and FPGA libraries. Examples include User Defined Primitives (UDP), truth tables and the specify block for specifying timing delays across a module.

Managing large designs

VHDL. Configuration, generate and package statements, together with the generic clause, all help manage large design structures.

Verilog. There are no statements in Verilog that help manage large designs.

Operators

The majority of operators are the same between the two languages. Verilog does have very useful unary reduction operators that are not predefined in VHDL. A loop statement can be used in VHDL to perform the same operation as a Verilog unary reduction operator. VHDL has the mod operator that is not found in Verilog.

Parameterizable models

VHDL. A specific bit width model can be instantiated from a generic *n*-bit model using the generic clause. The generic model will not synthesize until it is instantiated and the value of the generic given.

Verilog. A specific width model can be instantiated from a generic *n*-bit model using overloaded parameter values. The generic model must have a default parameter value defined. This means two things. In the absence of an overloaded value being specified, it will still synthesize, but will use the default parameter settings. Also, it does not need to be instantiated with an overloaded parameter value specified, before it will synthesize.

Procedures and tasks

VHDL allows concurrent **procedure** calls; Verilog does not allow concurrent **task** calls.

Readability

This is more a matter of coding style and experience than language feature. VHDL is a concise and verbose language; its roots are based on Ada. Verilog is more like C because its constructs are based approximately 50% on C and 50% on Ada. For this reason a C programmer may prefer Verilog over VHDL. Although a programmer of both C and Ada may find the mix of constructs somewhat confusing at first. Whatever HDL is used, when writing or reading an HDL model to be synthesized, it is important to think about hardware intent.

Structural replication

VHDL. The **generate** statement replicates a number of instances of the same *design unit* or some sub part of a design, and connect it appropriately.

Verilog. There is no equivalent to the **generate** statement in Verilog.

Test harnesses

Designers typically spend about 50% of their time writing synthesizable models and the other 50% writing a test harness to verify the synthesizable models. Test harnesses are not restricted to the synthesizable subset and so are free to use the full potential of the language. VHDL has generic and configuration statements that are useful in test harnesses, that are not found in Verilog.

Verboseness

VHDL. Because VHDL is a strongly typed language, models must be coded precisely with defined and matching data types. This may be considered an advantage or disadvantage. However, it does mean models are often more verbose, and the code often longer, than its Verilog equivalent.

Verilog. Signals representing objects of different bits widths may be assigned to each other. The signal representing the smaller number of bits is automatically padded out to that of the larger number of bits, and is independent of whether it is the assigned signal to or not. Unused bits will be automatically optimized away during the synthesis process. This has the advantage of not needing to model quite so explicitly as in VHDL, but does mean unintended modeling errors will <u>not</u> be identified by an analyzer.

Design Automation Tools

Software tools used to assist in the design of hardware come under one of two categories; Computer Aided Design (CAD) or Computer Aided Engineering (CAE). Tools used to design circuit board related hardware come under the category of computer aided design, while tools used for chip design come under the category of computer aided engineering. However, this distinction is not clear cut, for example, a simulator can be used to simulate both boards and integrated circuits (chips). Only tools needed for chip design are discussed in this book.

Simulation

Simulation is the fundamental and essential part of the design process for any electronic based product; not just ASIC and FPGA devices. For ASIC and FPGA devices, simulation is the process of verifying the functional characteristics of models at any level of behavior, that is, from high levels of abstraction down to low levels. The basic arrangement for simulation is shown in Figure 1.6.

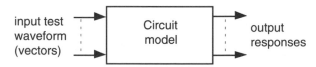

Figure 1.6 Basic simulation arrangement

A simulator, in this context, is a CAE software tool that simulates the behavior of a hardware model. Simulators use the timing defined in an HDL model before synthesis, or the timing from the cells of the target technology library, after synthesis. A simulator may be a basic functional simulator, a detailed dynamic timing analysis simulator, or both. Dynamic timing analysis is used in simulation to evaluate timing delays through the model more accurately than if static timing analysis were used. Static timing analysis is used by synthesis tools during optimization by simply extracting delays from the cells of the technology library. However, static timing analysis has difficulty with:

- multiple clocks and complex clocking schemes,
- asynchronous circuits and interfaces with asynchronous circuits,
- transparent latches,
- identifying and ignoring false paths.

Dynamic timing analysis is more accurate as illustrated in Figure 1.7. From Figure 1.7a), let Y1 be at logic 1 with all other wires at logic 0. If the delay of Buf1 is large and ambiguous relative to that of FF1 and FF2, then a rising edge on the clock produces the timing diagram shown in Figure

1.7b). The term ambiguous in this context, means the delay of Buf1 may have a wide range of values determined by both the static and dynamic characteristics of the circuit. There is an apparent hazard for FF2 because it appears that the edge on signal BufClock may occur either before or after Y1 changes value. However, when the common ambiguity due to Buf1's delay is removed it is clear that the edge on BufClock comes first; therefore, there is no hazard, and Y2 changes cleanly to logic 1 as shown.

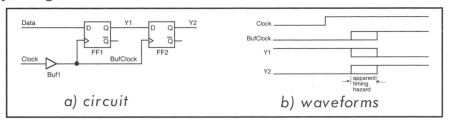

a) circuit   *b) waveforms*

Figure 1.7 Example showing need for dynamic timing analysis

Fault Simulation

Definition. Fault simulation is the simulation of the model of a digital circuit with particular input stimuli (vectors), and with typical manufacturing faults injected into that model. Fault simulation applies equally to integrated circuits (ICs) and printed circuit boards (PCBs).

Fault simulation is necessary for the following reasons:

- to identify areas of a circuit that are not being functionally tested by the functional test vectors, that is, certain internal nodes may not be toggled during functional simulation testing,
- to check the quality of test vectors and their ability to detect potential manufacturing defects,
- to perform board and in-circuit chip testing for both production and repair testing.

Fault simulation is particularly important for ASIC devices. However, it is still important for both anti-fuse programmable FPGAs and static RAM (SRAM) based programmable FPGAs.

The ability of manufacturing test vectors to test a device is called fault coverage and is measured as a percentage of the number of faults detected against the number of faults considered, that is:

$$\text{fault coverage} = \frac{\text{faults detected} \times 100}{\text{faults considered}} \qquad \text{(typically 70\% to 99.9\%)}$$

Another important measurement in detecting defective manufactured parts is the Average Quality Level (AQL) which is a measure of the manufacturing yield. It is a ratio of defective parts shipped and the total number of parts shipped, that is,

$$\text{AQL} = \frac{\text{defective parts shipped}}{\text{total number of parts shipped}} \qquad \text{(typically 0.1\% to 5\%)}$$

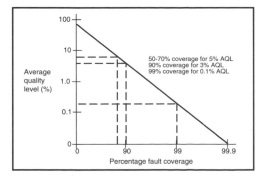

The fault coverage and AQL measurements together determine the potential number of faulty chips that will go undetected. Figure 1.8 shows the relationship between AQL and fault coverage, while Figure 1.9 identifies the percentage of undetected faulty chip. Figure 1.10 provides percentage figures for undetectable fault chips.

Figure 1.8 Log graph of AQL versus fault coverage

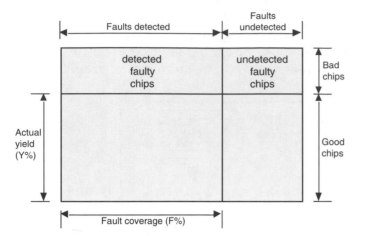

Figure 1.9 Undetectable faulty chips from AQL and fault coverage

Yield

Fault coverage	0	10	20	30	40	50	60	70	80	90	100
0	100	90	80	70	60	50	40	30	20	10	0
10	100	89	78	67	57	47	37	27	18	9	0
20	100	87	76	65	54	44	34	25	16	8	0
30	100	86	73	62	51	41	32	23	14	7	0
40	100	84	70	58	47	37	28	20	13	6	0
50	100	81	66	53	42	33	25	17	11	5	0
60	100	78	61	48	37	28	21	14	9	4	0
70	100	72	54	41	31	23	16	11	6	3	0
80	100	64	44	31	23	16	11	7	4	2	0
81	100	63	43	30	22	15	11	7	4	2	0
82	100	61	41	29	21	15	10	7	4	1	0
83	100	60	40	28	20	14	10	6	4	1	0
84	100	59	39	27	19	13	9	6	3	1	0
85	100	57	37	25	18	13	9	6	3	1	0
86	100	55	35	24	17	12	8	5	3	1	0
87	100	53	34	23	16	11	7	5	3	1	0
88	100	51	32	21	15	10	7	4	2	1	0
89	100	49	30	20	14	9	6	4	2	1	0
90	100	47	28	18	13	9	6	4	2	1	0
91	100	44	26	17	11	8	5	3	2	0	0
92	100	41	24	15	10	7	5	3	1	0	0
93	100	38	21	14	9	6	4	2	1	0	0
94	100	35	19	12	8	5	3	2	1	0	0
95	100	31	16	10	6	4	3	2	1	0	0
96	100	26	13	8	5	3	2	1	0	0	0
97	100	21	10	6	4	2	1	1	0	0	0
98	100	15	7	4	2	1	1	0	0	0	0
99	100	8	3	2	1	0	0	0	0	0	0
100	100	0	0	0	0	0	0	0	0	0	0

Figure 1.10 Percentage figures for undetectable faulty chips

Fault simulation is a very CPU intensive back-end design process and can lead to unexpected delays in getting a product to market. The short life cycle of many products containing ASIC or FPGA devices can mean that the cost of delays dwarf the cost of field repair; even at 5% AQL.

The need to perform fault simulation has become increasingly important for several reasons. One of the main reasons is that early fault detection reduces costs considerably; see Figure 1.11. The vast increase in the number of gates on a chip, the increased gate to pin ratio, and the reduced timing of submicron transistor technology, have all increased the need for fault simulation.

Some of the advantages of using fault simulation are:

- greater confidence that the design is correct,
- only way of verifying the quality of production test vectors,
- gives early warning of any production problems,
- the only way of testing integrated circuits with a high gate to pin ratio,
- greater confidence that the final system will work,
- less failures in the field,
- reduced cost and time in the long run,
- retained company image and reputation,
- easier to repair and replace units.

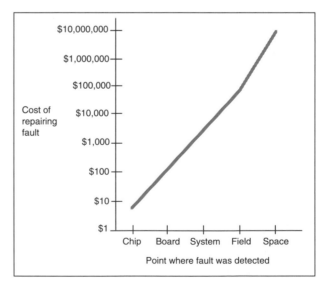

Figure 1.11 Relative cost of not finding faults early

Another advantage for PCB testing is:

- bed of nails not needed for PCB testing.

The industry accepted fault coverage for good yield is 95%. However, a chip designer with test vectors that give a 95% fault coverage cannot determine the percentage of potentially faulty chips that will go undetected. The reason for this is chip vendors do not like to divulge their yield figures. For example, if the fault coverage is 98%, but the manufacturers AQL is 40%, then 2% of the chips will have faults that are not detected.

Fault simulators first simulate the model of a chip without any faults; this is known as the fault free model. Typical manufacturing defects are then injected into the model and the simulation rerun. If the output vectors from the two simulation runs are different then the particular fault is detectable. The process then continues by injecting other faults throughout the model. Because of the vast number of potential faults that need to be modeled, it is easy to see why fault simulation run times are so long.

There are three main algorithms used by fault simulators; they are:

- serial,
- parallel,
- concurrent.

Serial. Serial fault simulation is the simplest. Two copies of the same circuit are stored in memory, a fault is injected into one of them, both circuits are simulated and their output is compared.

Parallel. Parallel fault simulation uses several complete copies of the circuit; one is good and the others have one fault injected into each of them. Each model is simulated concurrently on the same machine or distributed across multiple machines. The parallel algorithm method must continue until every parallel fault is detected whereas the serial algorithm can stop immediately when the fault is detected.

Concurrent. The concurrent algorithm method is the most powerful. It simulates one good and one bad model, with the bad model containing hundreds or thousands of injected faults. At the point a good and bad simulation differ the algorithm copies each fault to a separate machine and simulates them separately. It is faster and requires much less memory than the serial or parallel algorithm method.

Traditionally, fault simulators have simulated defects that cause stuck-at-logic-0 or stuck-at-logic-1 faults. Because of the speed and critical timing of silicon chips manufactured with submicron transistor channel widths, new fault simulators are adding the ability to perform delay fault testing. The risk is that critical timing from time optimized circuits may have longer delays in the manufactured chip than are expected. Both gate delay faults and path delay faults are considered.

Register Transfer Level Synthesis

Definition. Register transfer level synthesis is the process of translating a register transfer level model of hardware, written in a hardware description language at the register transfer level, into an optimized technology specific gate level implementation; see Figure 1.12.

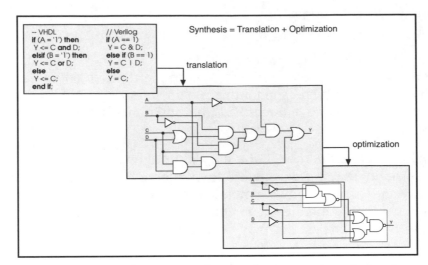

Figure 1.12 Synthesis equals translation and optimization

A register transfer level synthesis software tool automates this part of the ASIC and FPGA design process and forms the central link in a top-down design methodology. Synthesis is by far the quickest, and most effective means of designing and generating circuits. A typical synthesis process flow using a synthesis tool is shown in Figure 1.13. It shows an initial translation to a netlist without optimization. In practice, fundamental high-level optimization is performed, but is transparent to the user. This provides the starting point on the area-time curve for optimization. Figure 1.13 shows a design optimized three times with three different constraint settings to yield three different points on the area-time curve. The typical optimization methodology is to optimize for area first, and then only optimize for timing if any timing constraints are not met. Hierarchical blocks in a large design are normally optimized starting from the lower level blocks in a *bottom-up* process.

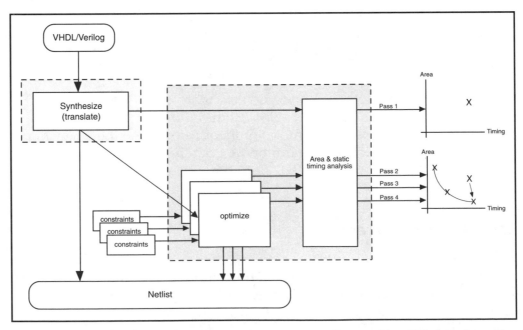

Figure 1.13 Translation and optimization process flow using RTL level synthesis

Synthesis consists of multiple stages of translation and optimization. It takes a design through three main internal levels of intermediate refinement (abstraction); see Figure 1.14.

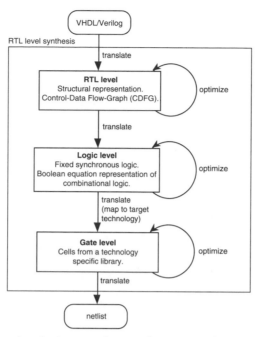

Figure 1.14 RTL synthesis internal translation and optimization processes

Automatic optimization occurs at each of these intermediate levels and is guided by user defined constraints. Constraints provide the goals that the optimization and translation processes try to meet. Current synthesis tools typically allow constraints to be set for minimal area and minimal timing delay. Power and testability constraints may also be available. In the future, layout and packaging constraints may also be available.

Minimal and maximal. The words minimal and maximal are used instead of minimum and maximum because optimization by a synthesis tool is a heuristic process. Optimization uses different algorithms on a trial and error basis to find a circuit implementation that best fits the constraints. A circuit optimized for minimum area will have minimum area based on what the optimizer can find. This may not always be the absolute minimum circuit that could be produced if the design were carefully designed by hand.

There is a correlation between minimal area and minimal power. A circuit that is optimized for minimal area is often the one that consumes minimal power for a given frequency. For this reason, the majority of synthesis tools do not optimize separately for minimal power. It is up to the designer to accurately specify constraints to trade off the two conflicting requirements of minimal area and maximal speed. The circuit version optimized for minimal area will not be the fastest. Similarly, the version of a circuit optimized to operate as fast as possible will not be implemented and have minimal area. However, the spread of possible area and timing implementations of different circuits is unique. It is possible that a circuit version optimized for minimal area also operates the fastest.

The types of optimizations that occur at each translated level of synthesis are now discussed.

RTL level optimization

Code related processing is first performed when a model is synthesized (compiled). Some examples are:

- expansion - subprograms are in-line expanded,
- constant folding - constants are folded together, for example, A + 3 + 2 becomes A + 5,
- loop unrolling - loop statements are unrolled to a series of individual statements,
- dead code removal - any unused (dead) code is discarded,
- bit minimization - for example, VHDL state encoding or assignments of different width in Verilog.

A control-data flow-graph (CDFG) format is often used by synthesis tools for the highest internal representation of a design. A CDFG is a graphical means of representing hardware structure, an example of which is shown in Figure 1.15. Optimization of a CDFG facilitates high level (architectural) synthesis techniques and includes synchronous logic optimization techniques such as: scheduling, resource binding, data path structuring and partitioning.

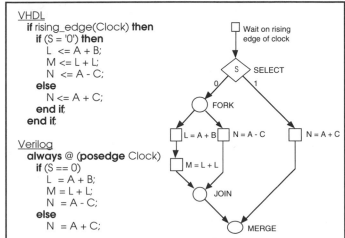

Figure 1.15 Control-data flow-graph representation of high level structure

Logic level optimization

Once synthesis has translated a design to the logic level, all registered elements are fixed and only combinational logic is optimized. Optimization at this level involves restructuring boolean equations according to the rules of boolean logic. Combinational logic is, therefore, optimized on a much finer grain basis than at the RTL level. The types of boolean optimization include: minimization, equation flattening, equation factorization and optimization. The synthesis algorithms used to perform these operations operate on a multiple level (equation) and multiple output basis. The algorithms have multiple dimensions and are much more complex than the manual process of using a two dimensional Karnaugh map to optimize a single equation with a single output. An example of what happens during logic level optimization is shown in Figure 1.16.

Flattening. The conversion of multiple boolean equations into a two level sum-of-products form is called flattening. All intermediate terms are removed.

Factoring. The factorization of boolean equations is the process of adding intermediate terms. This adds implied logic structure which both reduces the size of the implied circuit and reduces large fan-outs. Factoring is a varied design and constraint

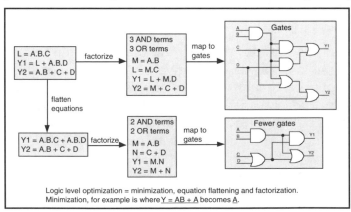

Figure 1.16 Example of the logic level optimization of boolean equations

dependent process. Adding structure adds levels of logic which tends to make a smaller, but slower operating circuit. Note, it is possible a circuit optimized for minimal area also has minimal timing delays.

Gate level optimization

Once synthesis has translated a design to the gate level, area and timing information is extracted from the cells of the targeted technology library for fine grain local optimization of cell primitives. Gate level optimization is a process of looking at a local area of logic containing a few cells and trying to replace them by other cells from the technology library that fit the constraints better. It then looks at another local area with an overlap with the first local area. If the effort level for such an optimization is increased the optimizer will typically look at a slightly larger local area each time. For a flat level ASIC containing 50,000 to 100,000 equivalent gates, it is easy to see how such optimizations can last many hours. An example of what happens during gate level optimization is shown in Figure 1.17.

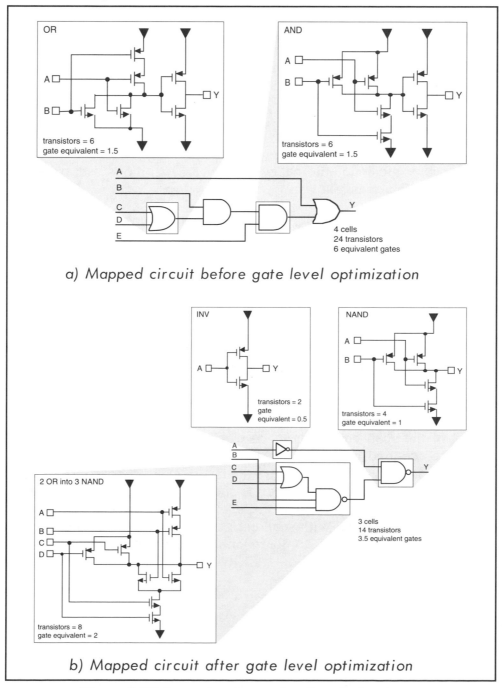

Figure 1.17 Example of gate level optimization

Test Synthesis

Definition. Test synthesis is the modification of a chip design to make both the chip, and the system (PCB) where it will reside, more testable, and the Automatic Test Pattern Generation (ATPG) of test vectors.

The process of modifying a design to make a circuit more testable is called Design For Test (DFT). There are many DFT techniques that can be implemented in both the HDL model before synthesis and circuit after synthesis; test synthesis tools can assist on both accounts.

Traditionally, the issue of how to test manufactured chips has been a back end process. However, due to the number of gates implemented in chips today, it is necessary to consider testability issues up front when designing and writing HDL code. If the up front issue of test is ignored, and a test synthesis tool is not available, then RTL level synthesis may be a fast and efficient means of producing untestable logic.

The use of test synthesis for DFT techniques and ATPG will reduce the time it takes to generate manufacturing test vectors from months to days. Design for test techniques known as "ad-hoc" are typically not supported by synthesis tools, but are a result of careful design practices. Examples include: redundancy removal, avoiding asynchronous logic, avoiding large fan-in and Built-in Self-Test (BIST), etc. DFT features of test synthesis tools are aimed at improving signal controllability and observability of internal circuit nodes. Operations performed by test synthesis after RTL/logic synthesis are as follows:

- full internal scan,
- partial internal scan,
- boundary scan.

For ASICs, these tasks are often performed by the ASIC vendor.

Internal scan

The use of internal scan cells enables ATPG tools to easily generate a near 100% fault coverage on the combinational logic. Internal scan is the replacement of latches and flip-flops by their scan equivalent latch or flip-flop. Each scan cell has a scan data input (SDI), a scan data output (SDO) and a test enable input (TE). Groups of these cells are then connected in chains of equal or similar length. The TE input is used to put the register element in test mode. There are three parts to the test mode. First, on successive clock cycles data is scanned from an input pin of the chip to the input of the scan cell ready to be clocked in on the next rising edge of the clock signal. Second, the scanned in data is clocked into the register element. Third, data on the output of the register is scanned through the scan chain on successive clock cycles to an output pin on the chip. An example of internal scan is shown in Figure 1.18. It shows a synchronous sequential circuit before and after inserting a scan chain. The synchronous circuit would be quite difficult to test without scan cells. With scan cells, access from the pins of the chip to the scan cells reduces the test problem to a combinational logic problem which is easily resolved by FPGA tools.

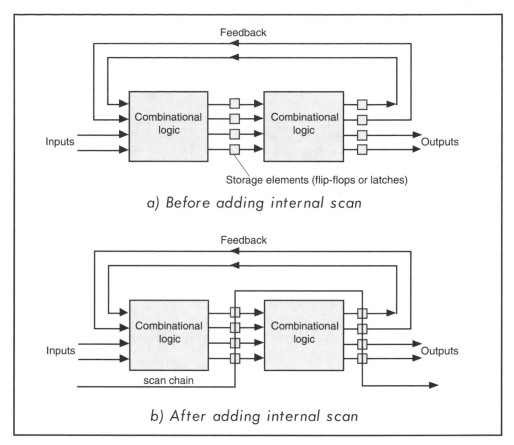

a) Before adding internal scan

b) After adding internal scan

Figure 1.18 Internal scan - automatically implemented by test synthesis

There are three types of scan replacement dependent upon the technology library being used; they are SCAN, MUXED and LSSD (Level-sensitive scan-design); see Figure 1.19.

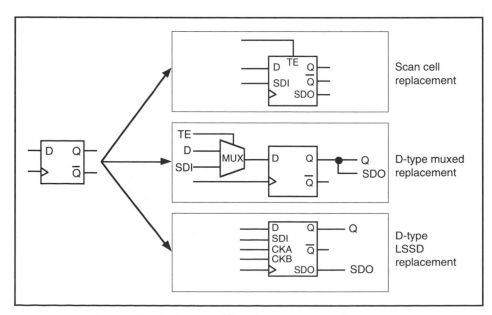

Figure 1.19 D-type flip-flop scan replacements

SCAN. If the technology library contains scan cells, sequential logic cells will be replaced by their scan equivalent. Many ASIC vendors provide SCAN equivalent cells whose timing and area overhead are minimal. The percentage increase in gate count as a result of changing D-type flip-flops with their scan equivalents are shown in Figure 1.20.

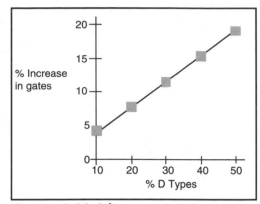

Figure 1.20 Silicon area percentage increase when using scan cells

MUXED. A multiplexer is inserted before the data input to the sequential cell. This may be the only method available if the ASIC library does not contain scan equivalent cells. The disadvantage is the area overhead of using a multiplexer, but may be reduced during optimization with other logic.

LSSD. A sequential logic cell is replaced with an equivalent LSSD cell, which uses two non-overlapping clocks (Clock-A and Clock-B), to drive the scan operation of the circuit. Example LSSD replacements are double-latch, clocked and auxiliary clock.

Full internal scan. Every single register element in a circuit is replaced by its scan equivalent. The disadvantage, which often outweighs the advantage, is that chip area increases significantly.

Partial internal scan. This is the same as full scan except that only certain register elements are replaced by their scan equivalent. In this case a test synthesis tool will perform controllability and observability checks on each node and intelligently decides which registers should be scan type registers. Compared to full scan, silicon area overhead is reduced, but ATPG tools have a harder job generating test vectors with a near 100% fault coverage. Also, more test vectors will be needed.

Boundary scan

The purpose of boundary scan is to make the PCB on which the chip will reside more testable, not to make the chip more testable. A printed circuit board in this context could be any type of board, for example, surface mount, wire bonded, etc. Boundary scan is an IEEE standard (IEEE 1149). All input and output cells of an ASIC are replaced with their scan equivalent cell and connected together to form a single chain around the chip, and controlled by a dedicated controller called a Test Activity Port (TAP) Controller; Figure 1.21. ASIC vendors often have TAP cells in their technology library. Designers can do one of two things. One, instantiate the boundary scan related cells in the HDL code and simulate to

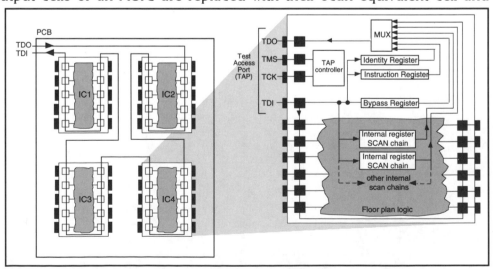

Figure 1.21 Boundary scan - automatically implemented by test synthesis

ensure it does not affect circuit operation. Two, take a low risk chance that it will not affect circuit operation and let the ASIC vendor perform automatic boundary scan insertion.

HDL Support for Synthesis

Certain constructs in a hardware description language are either ignored or are not supported by synthesis tools. The reason for this is that some constructs have no direct hardware correlation or the hardware intent is extremely abstract. For example, timing related constructs are ignored as the timing should come from the cells of the technology specific library. Constructs that are not supported typically include floating point arithmetic operators, loop statements without a globally static range and file manipulation related constructs. There is no standard for which constructs are supported and those that are not supported. As a consequence, the supported subset of constructs may be different for different synthesis tools. A VHDL working group has been set up to formalize an industry standard subset of constructs that should be supported by synthesis tools, with the intention of making designs portable. Effort is ongoing under the OVI to define an industry standard subset of Verilog constructs for synthesis. The main point is that there are differences, but these differences are not the deciding factor on selecting which synthesis tool to use. It is far better to write code that is independent of the synthesis tool being used. All synthesis models in this book are independent of the synthesis tool except where indicated otherwise.

Synthesis Constraint & Optimization Tutorials

Chapter 2 Contents

Introduction

This chapter graphically describes some of the types of constraints used by synthesis and how they affect resulting optimized circuits. Constraints represent desired circuit characteristics, that is, design goals for the optimizer to attempt to achieve. Different constraints cause different optimized circuits to be generated, but with the same functionality. There is no industry standard for how constraints are specified so the format is likely to be different for different synthesis tools. Constraints are typically set through a graphical user interface or via the command line. This chapter includes the command syntax for the VeriBest Synthesis tools.

Constraints fall into one of two categories:

- global,
- circuit specific.

Global default constraints. Once global constraints have been set, they apply equally to all designs by default, that is, without needing to be explicitly defined for each individual design. Example constraints are:

- library process factor,
- operating voltage,
- operating temperature.

Circuit specific constraints. Circuit specific constraints are specific to one particular design. Possible examples are:

1) area
   - maximum area,
2) timing
   - input and output loading,
   - input maximum fan-out constraints,
   - input driving capability,
   - input arrival times,
   - output driving capability constraints,
   - output arrival time constraints,
   - minimum clock frequency.
3) power
   - maximum power
4) testability (test synthesis)
   - replacement scan cell types
   - maximum scan cell length
   - full or partial scan
   - boundary scan

The most common constraints used in RTL level synthesis tools today are area and timing.

Area. An area constraint is a number corresponding to the desired maximum area of a specified design module, and may, or may not, contain hierarchical structure. The area number will have units corresponding to the units defined in the cells of the technology library, for example, equivalent gates, grids or transistors. The units will depend upon the type of ASIC or FPGA.

Timing. Timing constraints tell the synthesis tool when signal values arrive and when they need to arrive at specific points in time. The static timing analyzer in the synthesis tool will extract timing information from the technology library in order to compute actual path delays. This includes the setup and hold times of registered elements and signal delays through combinational logic, given specific global constraints. Signal path delays in the model are computed and compared with desired timing constraints, whereby automatic optimization is performed as necessary in order to improve timing characteristics. Typically, a designer will want to progressively increase timing optimization effort levels in order to progressively trade off area for improved timing, depending on the type of ASIC or FPGA. Note that timing constraints, or any constraints for that matter, should not be more restrictive than are necessary.

Combinational Logic Optimization

A combinational logic circuit conforming to the function table, Table 2.1, is shown optimized with different constraints set. The VHDL and Verilog models are coded using a **case** statement.

A	B	C	D	Y1	Y2
0	0	0	0	1	0
0	0	0	1	1	0
0	0	1	0	1	0
0	0	1	1	1	0
0	1	0	0	1	0
0	1	0	1	1	0
0	1	1	0	1	0
0	1	1	1	1	0
1	0	0	0	1	0
1	0	0	1	0	1
1	0	1	0	0	1
1	0	1	1	1	1
1	1	0	0	1	0
1	1	0	1	1	0
1	1	1	0	1	0
1	1	1	1	1	0

Table 2.1 Function table of combinational logic

HDL of combinational logic function

VHDL	Verilog

`library IEEE;`
`use IEEE.STD_Logic_1164.all, IEEE.Numeric_STD.all;`
 	
`entity COMB_1 is`
`  port ( A, B, C, D:  in   std_logic;`
`         Y1, Y2:      out std_logic);`
`end entity COMB_1;`
 	
`architecture LOGIC of COMB_1 is`
`begin`
`  process (A, B, C, D)`
`    variable ABCD: unsigned(3 downto 0);`
`  begin`
`    ABCD := unsigned'(A & B & C & D);`
`    case ABCD is`
`      when "0000" => Y1 <= '1'; Y2 <= '0';`
`      when "0001" => Y1 <= '1'; Y2 <= '0';`
`      when "0010" => Y1 <= '1'; Y2 <= '0';`
`      when "0011" => Y1 <= '1'; Y2 <= '0';`
`      when "0100" => Y1 <= '1'; Y2 <= '0';`
`      when "0101" => Y1 <= '1'; Y2 <= '0';`
`      when "0110" => Y1 <= '1'; Y2 <= '0';`
`      when "0111" => Y1 <= '1'; Y2 <= '0';`
`      when "1000" => Y1 <= '1'; Y2 <= '0';`
`      when "1001" => Y1 <= '0'; Y2 <= '1';`
`      when "1010" => Y1 <= '0'; Y2 <= '1';`
`      when "1011" => Y1 <= '1'; Y2 <= '1';`
`      when "1100" => Y1 <= '1'; Y2 <= '0';`
`      when "1101" => Y1 <= '1'; Y2 <= '0';`
`      when "1110" => Y1 <= '1'; Y2 <= '0';`
`      when "1111" => Y1 <= '1'; Y2 <= '0';`
`      when others => Y1 <= '0'; Y2 <= '0';`
`    end case;`
`  end process;`
`end architecture LOGIC;`
	`module COMB_1 (A, B, C, D, Y1, Y2);`
	`  input  A, B, C, D;`
	`  output Y1, Y2;`
	`  reg Y1, Y2;`
	
	`  always @(A or B or C or D)`
	`    begin`
	`      case ({A, B, C, D})`
	`        4'b 0000 : begin Y1 = 1; Y2 = 0; end`
	`        4'b 0001 : begin Y1 = 1; Y2 = 0; end`
	`        4'b 0010 : begin Y1 = 1; Y2 = 0; end`
	`        4'b 0011 : begin Y1 = 1; Y2 = 0; end`
	`        4'b 0100 : begin Y1 = 1; Y2 = 0; end`
	`        4'b 0101 : begin Y1 = 1; Y2 = 0; end`
	`        4'b 0110 : begin Y1 = 1; Y2 = 0; end`
	`        4'b 0111 : begin Y1 = 1; Y2 = 0; end`
	`        4'b 1000 : begin Y1 = 1; Y2 = 0; end`
	`        4'b 1001 : begin Y1 = 0; Y2 = 1; end`
	`        4'b 1010 : begin Y1 = 0; Y2 = 1; end`
	`        4'b 1011 : begin Y1 = 1; Y2 = 1; end`
	`        4'b 1100 : begin Y1 = 1; Y2 = 0; end`
	`        4'b 1101 : begin Y1 = 1; Y2 = 0; end`
	`        4'b 1110 : begin Y1 = 1; Y2 = 0; end`
	`        4'b 1111 : begin Y1 = 1; Y2 = 0; end`
	`        default  : begin Y1 = 0; Y2 = 0; end`
	`      endcase`
	`    end`
	`endmodule`

The model is first synthesized (translated) and then optimized four times with four different design constraint configurations set. They are:

- minimal area irrespective of timing delays,
- minimal area, but with low drive inputs,
- maximal speed irrespective of area,
- maximal speed, but with low drive inputs.

The affect of these constraints on the circuit is shown in Figure 2.1.

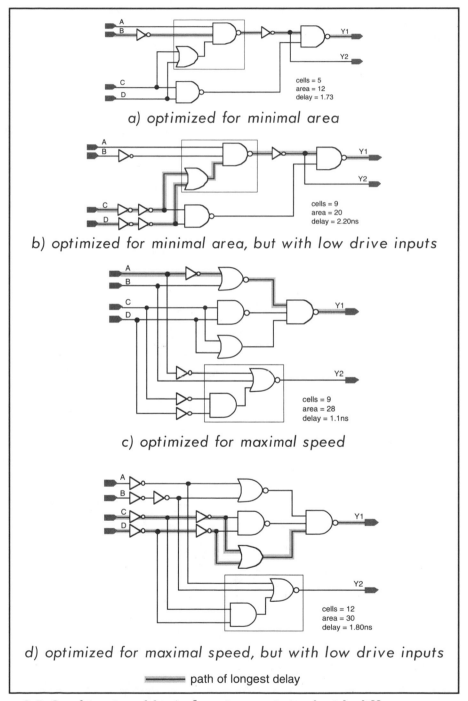

a) optimized for minimal area

b) optimized for minimal area, but with low drive inputs

c) optimized for maximal speed

d) optimized for maximal speed, but with low drive inputs

path of longest delay

Figure 2.1 Combinational logic function optimized with different constraints

A typical design constraint scenario

This tutorial considers a typical design scenario for which constraints must be specified and may represent part of a design or large project which has been partitioned among several designers. The following timing paths are considered and shown graphically in Figure 2.2.

- begin at registers outside the design being optimized,
- begin at registers inside the design being optimized,
- begin outside the design being optimized, but not at registers,
- end at registers outside the design being optimized,
- end at registers inside the design being optimized,
- end outside the design being optimized, but not at registers.

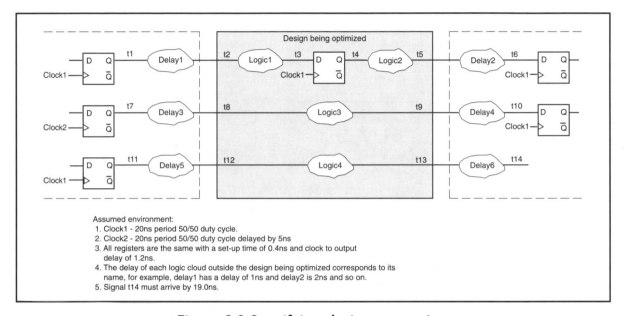

Assumed environment:
1. Clock1 - 20ns period 50/50 duty cycle.
2. Clock2 - 20ns period 50/50 duty cycle delayed by 5ns.
3. All registers are the same with a set-up time of 0.4ns and clock to output delay of 1.2ns.
4. The delay of each logic cloud outside the design being optimized corresponds to its name, for example, delay1 has a delay of 1ns and delay2 is 2ns and so on.
5. Signal t14 must arrive by 19.0ns.

Figure 2.2 Specifying design constraints

Timing constraints represent specific points in time. Therefore, in order to correctly constrain the design the optimizer must be told the times at which signals t2, t8 and t12 arrive, and the times when signals t5, t9 and t13 need to arrive. In this example, signal delays through "logic clouds" Delay1 to Delay6 are fixed, that is, they are outside the designer's control; only the logic in Logic1 to Logic4 is being optimized.

The assumed environment for the design is described in Figure 2.2. Example constraint commands are shown for the Lucent synthesis tools. Vendor specific constraints are an obstacle to portability.

Defining clock waveforms

The first step in correctly constraining this design is to define clock waveforms and associate them with the clock signals of the design. For Lucent the commands are:

```
set waveform name=clockwave definition=(>(u10 d10))
apply waveform name=clockwave signal=Clock1
apply waveform name=clockwave signal=Clock2 delay=5
```

This example does not show two registers with logic between them wholly contained in the design being optimized. These clock constraints are enough to automatically constrain such logic.

Input constraints

Input constraints are usually the easiest to specify; it is the delay outside the circuit being optimized that is being specified. The following constraints specify the point in time that signals t2, t8 and t12 arrive and are shown graphically in Figure 2.3.

1. Constraint for t2

When a signal originates at a register outside the design, the delay should be specified with respect to the clock that controls the register. For signal t3, the delay is calculated as follows:

$$arrival\_time(t2) = delay\_outside\_circuit$$
$$= delay(FF\_clock\_output) + delay(Delay1)$$
$$= 1.2 \text{ ns} + 1.0 \text{ ns}$$
$$= 2.2 \text{ ns}$$

The VeriBest command is:

    set arrival_time data=t2 clock_source=Clock1 edge=R rise=2.2 fall=2.2

This provides the optimizer with enough information to constrain the logic in *logic1*. The clock waveform has already been specified and the optimizer can determine the setup time for the register from the technology library. Thus, the logic in logic1 has the following timing requirement.

$$max\_delay(Logic1) = clock\_period - FF\_setup\_time - external\text{-}delay$$
$$= 20 \text{ ns} - 0.4 \text{ ns} - 2.2 \text{ ns}$$
$$= 17.4 \text{ ns}$$

2. Constraint for t8

The constraint for t8 is specified in the same way as for t2. The delay calculation is:

$$arrival\_time(t8) = delay\_outside\_circuit$$
$$= delay(FF\_clock\_output) + delay(Delay3)$$
$$= 1.2 \text{ ns} + 3.0 \text{ ns}$$
$$= 4.2 \text{ ns}$$

The VeriBest command is:

    set arrival_time data=t8 clock_source=Clock2 edge=R rise=4.2 fall=4.2

Unlike the previous constraint, this does not provide the optimizer with enough information to constrain the internal logic. Additional information is needed to constrain the logic in Logic3; specifically the optimizer must know the time that data must arrive at t9, which has not yet been specified.

3. Constraint for t12

The path to t12 does not originate at a register so the constraint specification becomes very simple. The delay calculation is:

$$arrival\_time(t12) = delay\_outside\_circuit$$
$$= delay(FF\_clock\_output) + delay(Delay5)$$
$$= 1.2 \text{ ns} + 5.0 \text{ ns}$$
$$= 6.2 \text{ ns}$$

The Lucent command is:

    set arrival_time data=t12 rise=6.2 fall=6.2

Like signal t8, this does not provide enough information to constrain Logic4; the optimizer must know the time that data must arrive at signal t13.

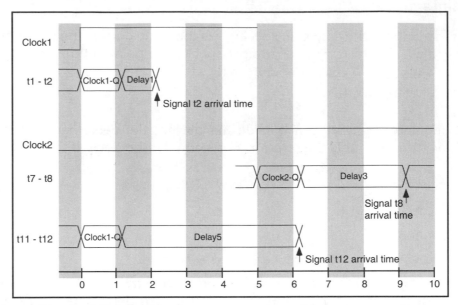

Figure 2.3 Graphical representation of input constraints

Output constraints

Output constraints are slightly more complicated. Constraints specifying the point in time that signals t5, t9 and t13 must arrive are described. Figure 2.4. shows a graphical representation of the combined input and output constraints.

1. Constraint for t5

When a signal is ultimately driving a register outside the design, the same type of calculation must be performed as was performed for Logic1. The constraint value is the clock period minus both the setup time for the external register and the delay through the external combinational logic (Delay2).

```
required_time(t5) = clock_edge(Clock1) - delay(FF_Clock_output) - external_delay
                  = clock_edge(Clock1) - delay(FF_Clock_output) - (delay(Delay2) + FF_setup_time)
                  = 20 ns - 1.2 ns - 2.0 ns - 0.4 ns
                  = 16.4 ns
```

The Lucent command is:

```
set required time_time data=t5 clock_cource= Clock1 edge=R rise=16.4 fall=16.4
```

2. Constraint for t9

To constrain t9, a similar calculation must be performed as was performed for t5:

```
required_time(t9) = clock_edge(Clock1) - external_delay
                  = clock_edge(Clock1) - (delay(Delay4) + delay(FF_setup_time))
                  = 20 ns - 4.0 ns - 0.4 ns
                  = 15.6 ns
```

The Lucent command is:

```
set required time_time data=t9 clock_source= Clock1 edge=R rise=15.6 fall=15.6
```

From this specified required time and the specified arrival time for signal t8, the optimizer will automatically calculate how much time is left for the internal logic in Logic3. Now, because the arrival time for t8 is specified with respect to Clock2, which is not at time 0ns, the arrival time of the clock edge must be added into the equation. This is determined as follows:

max_delay(Logic3) = required_time(t9) - real_arrival_time(t8)
= 15.6 ns - (edge_time(Clock2) + specific_arrival_time(t8))
= 15.6 ns - (5.0 ns + 4.2 ns)
= 15.6 ns - 9.2 ns
= 6.4 ns

3. Constraint for t13

As the path from t13 does not end at the register, the constraint specification becomes very simple. The delay calculation is:

required_time(t13) = required_time(t14) - delay(Delay6)
= 19 ns - 6.0 ns
= 13 ns

The Lucent command is:

```
set required time_time data=t13 rise=13.0 fall=13.0
```

From this specified required time and the specified arrival time for signal t12, the optimizer will automatically calculate how much time is left for the internal logic in Logic4. This is determined as follows:

max_delay(Logic4) = required_time(t13) - arrival_time(t12)
= 13.0 ns - (1.2 ns + 5.0 ns)
= 6.8 ns

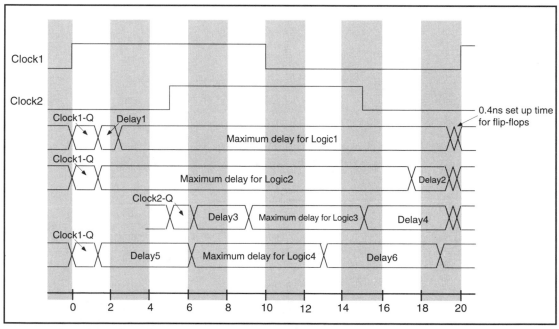

Figure 2.4 Graphical representation of combined input and output constraints

Language
Fundamentals

Chapter 3 Contents

Design Entities

When designing and modeling digital systems in VHDL or Verilog it is necessary to partition the design into natural abstract blocks known as components. Each component is the instantiation of a *design entity*, which is normally modeled in a separate system file for easy management and individual compilation by simulation or synthesis tools, for example. A total system is then modeled using a hierarchy of components known as a *design hierarchy* that has individual subcomponents (subdesign entities) being brought together in a single higher level component (design entity). When the coded models of design entities are to be synthesized, an assumption made throughout this book, the designer should partition the system into suitably sized design entities, that when synthesized will yield up to a maximum of about 5000 equivalent gates. An equivalent gate equates to the size of a two input NAND gate. There is no absolute rule about what is the most optimal sized circuit to synthesize and optimize, but anything from 2000 to 5000 equivalent gates typically gives good optimal results without being too CPU intensive.

Design entities are quite different in VHDL and Verilog.

VHDL design entities

Design entities are constructed in VHDL using five different types of *design units* as depicted in Figure 3.1. The **entity** declaration, **package** declaration and **configuration** declaration are primary design units and are visible within a **library**. A **library** is a storage area of the host environment for compiled design units. The **architecture** and **package body** declarations are secondary design units because they are not visible within a **library**. A *design entity* consists of two design units; an **entity-architecture** pair. An **entity** provides the port information of a particular design entity, while the **architecture** provides the functional body description of a design entity. This design entity can use common design data which is stored in a **package**. The **package** and possible **package body** contain globally available design data, for example, data types and subprograms, that can be made available for use by any other design units as required. A **package** may have a **package body** for the declaration of the subprogram etc. A **package body** has the same name as its corresponding **package**.

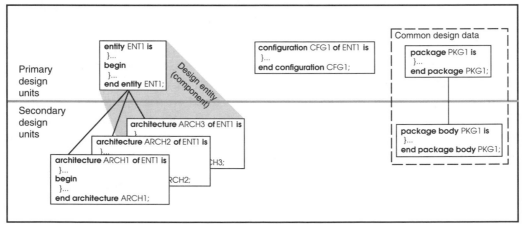

Figure 3.1 VHDL Design Units

The five kinds of VHDL *design units* are:

Entity declaration. An **entity** declaration describes the interface of a design entity through which it communicates with other design entities in the same environment. The interface typically includes all input, output and bidirectional signals defined in the port declaration section plus any model parameterizing parameters defined using generic declarations.

Architecture body. An **architecture** body describes the functional composition of a design. Multiple architecture bodies can describe different architecture versions of the same design entity. In this context different **architecture** versions have matched signal names to a single **entity**. For example there may be two slightly different RTL models of the same circuit, in different **architecture** bodies, or there may be another at the gate level resulting from synthesis.

Configuration declaration. A **configuration** declaration is a primary design unit used to bind **entity** statements to particular **architecture** bodies to form components of a design. A single **configuration** can specify multiple **entity-architecture** bindings throughout a design hierarchy. Configurations allow the late binding of components after multiple **architecture** bodies have been written and compiled. It is possible to have more than one configuration declaration for an **entity**, each of which defines a different set of bindings for components.

Package declaration. A package declaration is a repository for storing commonly used declarations that can be made globally accessible across multiple design units. Example declarations are data types, constants and subprograms. A **package** declaration has an associated **package body** if subprograms (functions and procedures) are declared.

Package body: A package body is always associated with a package declaration of the same name and contains the subprogram bodies of functions and procedures declared in the package declaration.

Verilog design entities

In Verilog, a *design entity* has only one *design unit*; the **module** declaration as depicted in Figure 3.2.

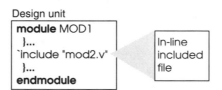

Figure 3.2 Verilog design entity

Module declaration. The **module** declaration is the only design unit (*design entity*) in Verilog. It describes both a design's interface to other designs in the same environment, and its functional composition. All declarations used within a model must be declared locally within the **module**. However, the compiler directive `include, is often used to reference a separate system file. This directive is replaced with the contents of the file it references when compiled by a simulator, synthesizer, or other similar tool. This is very useful for writing generic Verilog code in a separate file that can be referenced from the code in any other Verilog file.

Code Structure

A *design unit* may instantiate other design units, which in turn may instantiate other design units in a hierarchial manner. This hierarchical code structure should mimic inferred hardware structure when hardware structure is being modeled, see Chapter 5.

Coded statements within a design unit fall into one of three categories: declaration, concurrent or sequential. Appendix A includes the syntax of VHDL statements and Appendix B includes the syntax of Verilog statements.

Declaration statements

These statements declare objects for use in concurrent and sequential statements.

VHDL. In VHDL, the component of a sublevel design unit must be declared before it can be instantiated. Similarly subprograms must be declared before they can be used. A subprogram in VHDL is a **procedure** or **function**. A declaration statement is placed before the **begin** clause in an **architecture**, **block**, **process**, **procedure** or **function** statement, see Figure 3.3.

Verilog. In Verilog a design unit, that is, a **module** statement, does not need to be declared; nor do subprograms, that is, a **task** or **function**. There is no dedicated declarative region in a **module**, sequential block, concurrent block, **task** or **function**, see Figure 3.4.

Concurrent statements

These are statements that are executed in parallel, that is, at the same time. They operate independently of all other concurrent statements. When modeling hardware structure they represent independent sections of the circuit being modeled. Each concurrent statement is executed asynchronously with all other concurrent statements.

VHDL. The **block** and **process** are concurrent statements. Signal assignments and **procedure** calls are concurrent provided they do not reside in a **process** statement. Similarly a **function** call is concurrent provided it is called from within the expression of a concurrent signal assignment.

Verilog. The continuous assignment and **always** statement are concurrent. A continuous assignment uses the reserved word **assign** to assign data objects of any of the net data types. A **task** cannot be called concurrently, see Figure 3.5.

Sequential statements

Sequential statements are statements that are executed depending upon the procedural flow of constructs that surround them.

VHDL. Sequential statements reside after the **begin** clause in a **process**; again see Figure 3.3.

Verilog. Sequential statements reside in an **always** statement, that may, or may not, contain sequential **begin-end** procedural blocks. The assigned objects are of type **reg** or **integer**, again see Figure 3.4.

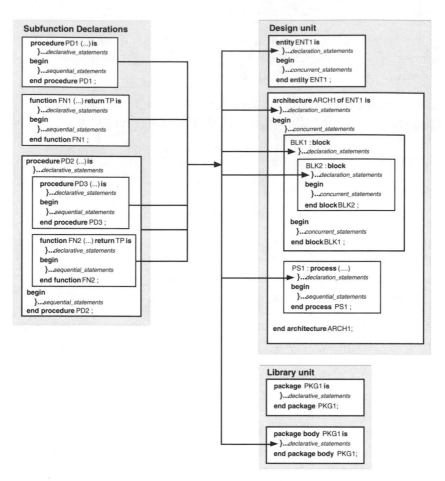

Figure 3.3 VHDL - subprogram declarations in a design or library unit

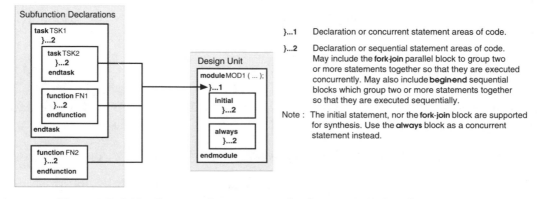

Figure 3.4 Verilog - subprogram declarations in a design unit

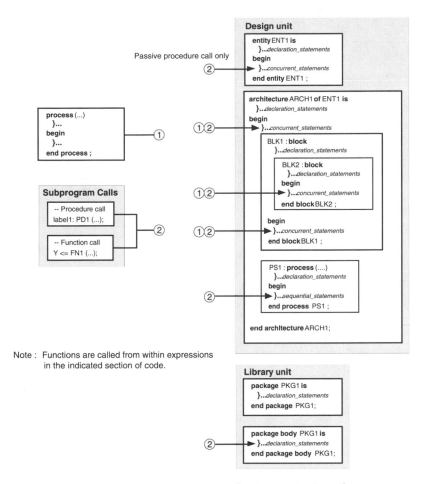

Figure 3.5 VHDL - process statements in a design unit & subprogram calls in a design or library unit

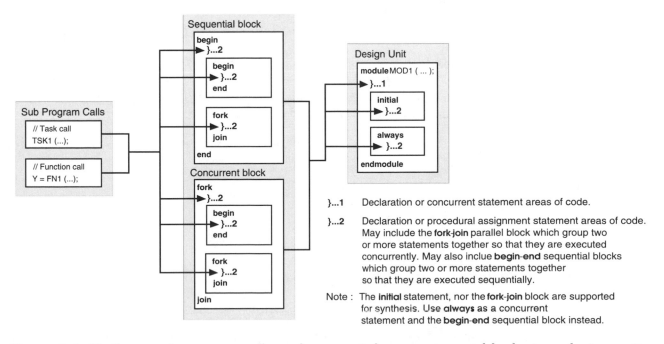

Figure 3.6 Verilog - subprogram calls and sequential or concurrent blocks in a design unit

Data Types and Data Objects

Models in either language pass data from one point to another using data objects. Each data object has a collection of possible values known as a *value set*. A data type defines this value set. The concept of the data type and data object is quite different between the two languages as explained below.

VHDL		Verilog	
Data types	Data Objects (of a data type)	Data types	Data Objects (of the data type)
Scalar types **enumeration** **integer** **physical** ‡ **floating point** ‡ Composite types **array** **record** **access** (pointers) ‡	**constant** **variable** **signal** **file** ‡	01XZ (defined by the language)	signal nets **wire** **tri** wired nets **wand** **triand** ‡ **wor** **trior** ‡ **trireg** ‡ **tri0** ‡ **tri1** ‡ supply nets **supply0** **supply1** **register** **parameter** **integer** **time** ‡ **memory** (array)

‡ These data types and data objects are not supported by synthesis tools.

Figure 3.7 VHDL and Verilog data types and data objects

The data types and data objects that are indicated in Figure 3.7 as not being supported by synthesis tools, or are not needed in a simulation test harness, are not discussed further.

There are 8 kinds of VHDL data types defined by the language. It is not until a VHDL data object of one of these types is declared in a model, using a **type** or **subtype** declaration, that the value set is defined. Therefore, the value set is always defined in a model using a type declaration along with the object kind, **constant**, **variable**, **signal** or **file**.

In Verilog, the language itself defines a single base data type which has the following four value, value set.

0 - represents a logic zero, or false condition
1 - represents a logic one or true condition
X - represents an unknown logic value
Z - represents high-impedance state

Data objects of this type are declared in a model to have a single element, or an array of elements, of this type, for example,

```
wire W1;
wire (31:0) W2;
```

There are more kinds of data objects in Verilog than there are VHDL, and relate closely to the detailed hardware structure being modeled.

Individual VHDL and Verilog data types and objects are described below.

VHDL data types

Enumeration data type. An enumerated data type contains a set of user defined values. Each value may be an identifier, for example, Red, Multiply or character literal, for example, '0', '1', 'U', 'Z'. The syntax of an enumerated type declaration is:

type enum_type_name **is** (enum_value {,enum_value});

where

enum_type_name   is the identifier name of the enumerated data type

enum_value   is an identifier or character literal

example

type Rainbow **is** (Red, Orange, Yellow, Green, Blue, Indigo, Violet);

The order in which enumerated values are declared determines the numerical order of numbers assigned to them by a synthesis tool. The binary numbers assigned to the above example would be:

Red   = 000
Orange = 001
Yellow = 010
Green = 011
Blue   = 100
Indigo = 101
Violet = 110

These assigned numbers enable relational operators to be used on enumerated data types; for example,

if (Red < Orange) **then**

An attribute is often provided by synthesis tools to provide a means of specifying particular enumerated values to the set of identifiers or character literals. For example, the synthesis tools from VeriBest Incorporated defines an attribute called ENUM_TYPE_ENCODING, which can be used to ensure objects of type rainbow use Gray coded assigned values, as follows:

attribute ENUM_TYPE_ENCODING: string;
attribute ENUM_TYPE_ENCODING **of** rainbow: **type is**
    "000 001 011 010 110 111 101 100";

Integer data type. An integer type declaration defines a range of integer numbers. The actual range should always be specified; otherwise, the language default of $(2^{-31} + 1)$ to $(2^{31} - 1)$ is used (IEEE 1076 '93). This is excessive and when synthesized will yield much more logic than is necessary. This leaves the optimizer with the task of optimizing away all the redundant logic.

Syntax: **type** type_name_identifier **is range** integer_range;

where   type_name_identifier   is the identifier name of the data type
         integer_range   is the defined subrange of integers
example
         type CountValue **is range** 0 **to** 15;
         type Twenties **is range** 20 **to** 29;
         type Thirties **is range** 39 **downto** 30;

There is no difference between using **to** or **downto** when declaring an integer range.

Note that when a synthesis tool synthesizes and assigns the necessary number of bits for an integer range it counts from zero. This means the signal of type Thirties synthesizes to six bits (0-

39) and is not normalized to four bits for an integer range of ten (30-39). Therefore, it makes sense to always specify integer ranges beginning from zero.

Composite data type. Composite data types are used to define collections of values (elements) which together constitute an array or record. Individual elements of an array must belong to the same type while record elements may be of a different type.

Composite array data type. Array types are useful for modeling linear structures such as RAMS and ROMS. Elements of an array may be of any type provided all the elements are of the same type. An element is a constituent part of a type, for example, the constrained array type below has 8 (0 to 7) constituent elements. The range of the array is specified with an upper and lower bound integer separated with the word **to** or **downto**. It is possible to specify arrays of arrays to any dimension, however, only one or two dimensions are supported by synthesis tools. Multidimensional arrays of three or more are not needed for modeling physical hardware.

The declaration of an array data type may specify a specific range, in which case it is said to be constrained. It is possible not to specify a range of an array type. This has the advantage of deferring the declaration of its range until a signal or variable of that type is declared.

example   **type** unsigned **is array** (natural **range** <>) **of** std_logic;   -- unconstrained array
                type unsigned **is array** (natural **range** 7 **downto** 0) **of** std_logic;   -- constrained array

Composite record data type. Record types are useful for modeling data packets. A record may contain values which belong to the same or different type. Assignments to individual elements in the record are made using the record identifier name and element name separated by a period (.).

example   **type** FloatPointType **is**
                record
                    Sign: std_logic;
                    Exponent: unsigned(0 **to** 6);
                    Fraction: unsigned(24 **downto** 1);
                end record;

VHDL Data Objects

Constant. A constant holds one specific value of the specified type. Once declared, the value of a constant cannot change.

example   **constant** DataWidth: integer := 24;
                constant Stop: unsigned(1 **downto** 0) := "00";

Variable. A variable holds any single value from the values of the specified type. Often used to hold temporary values within a process and need not relate to a node in the implied circuit.

example   **variable** ThreeBits: unsigned (0 **to** 2);

Signal. A signal holds a <u>list of values</u> which includes its current value and a set of possible future values that are to appear on the signal.

example   **signal** RegB, RegQ: unsigned (A'length - 1 **downto** 0);

File. A file refers to a system file and contains a sequence of values of a specified type. File objects are not supported by synthesis tools, but are very useful in test harnesses. Values are written to, or read from, a file using procedures.

example   **file** VectorFile: text **open** read_mode **is** "./vectorfile.vec";

Verilog data types

The Verilog language defines the only allowable data type. It has the value set {0, 1, X, Z} as described earlier.

Verilog data objects

Net and Register data objects. If a net (**wire, wand, wor**), or register (**reg**) data objects are declared without a range, then by default, they are one bit wide and referred to as a scalar. If a range is declared, it has multiple bits and is known as a vector. A vector may be referenced in its entirety, in part, or each individual bit as desired. Net and register data objects are described below.

> *Net.* The synthesizable net data objects indicated in Figure 3.7, represent and model the physical connection of signals. A net object must always be assigned using a *continuous assignment* statement. An *assignment* in Verilog is the basic mechanism for assigning values to net and register data types. In particular, a continuous assignment statement assigns values to any of the *net* data types and so makes a connection to an actual wire in the inferred circuit.

> **wire**: Models a wire which structurally connects two signals together.
> **wor**: Models a wired OR of several drivers driving the same net. An OR gate will be synthesized.
> **wand**: Models a wired AND of several drivers driving the same net. An AND gate will be synthesized.
> example **wire** Net1;
> **wire** (2:0) Net234;

Register. The register (**reg**) data object holds its value from one *procedural assignment* statement to the next and means it holds its value over simulation delta cycles. A procedural assignment is an assignment for a register data type and does <u>not</u> imply a physical register will be synthesized, although it is used for this purpose. It is used to assign values under trigger conditions such as **if** and **case** statements. A procedural assignment stores a value in a register data type and is held until the next procedural assignment to that register data type.

> example **reg** (3:0) Y1, Y2;

Parameter. A parameter data object defines a constant. Only integer (and not real) parameter constants should be used with synthesis. Like all other data types, their position defines whether they are global to a **module** or local to a particular **always** statement.

> example **parameter** A = 4'b 1011, B = 4'b 1000;
> **parameter** Stop = 0, Slow = 1, Medium = 2, Fast = 3;

Integer. Integer data objects are used to declare general purpose variables for use in loops; they have no direct hardware intent and hold numerical values. No range is specified when an integer object is declared. Integers are signed and produce 2's complement results.

> example **integer** N;

Expressions

An expression comprises of operators and operands, see Figure 3.8, and are covered separately in the following two sections.

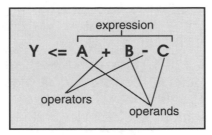

Figure 3.8 Expression consisting of operands and operators

Operands

Data objects form the operands of an expression and it is their value that is used by operators in an expression. There are more kinds of VHDL operands than there are in Verilog. All Verilog and most VHDL operands are supported by synthesis tools, see Figure 3.9.

VHDL Operands
Literals
abstract ‡
string (bit & character)
enumeration
numeric
physical ‡
real ‡
Identifiers
entity
architecture
configuration
constant
signal
variable
subprogram
Index & Slice Names
Function Calls
Record & Record Fields
Aggregates
Qualified Expressions
Type Conversion
Allocators ‡

Verilog Operands
Literals
string (bit & character)
numeric
real
Identifiers
module
parameter
wire
register
macros (text substitutions)
Index & Slice Names
Function Calls

‡ does not make sense to use when modeling for synthesis and so not supported by synthesis tools.

Figure 3.9 VHDL and Verilog Operands

Literal Operands

A literal is a constant-valued operand. Only string, enumeration and numeric literals can be used in synthesizable models and are described below.

String Literals. A string literal is a one dimensional array of characters enclosed in double quotes (" ") for both languages. There are two kinds:

1. Character string literals. These are sequences of characters and are useful when designing simulatable test harnesses around a synthesizable model.
   example   "ABC"
2. Bit string literals (VHDL): These apply to VHDL only and represent binary (B), octal (O) or hexadecimal (X) based numbers. The string is prefixed by a "B", "O" or "X" depending on the base required and may be in upper or lower case as shown below.
   example   B"1010"
              O"57"
              X"9FDE" or x"9FDE"

Enumeration Literals (VHDL). Enumeration literals are the individual values of an enumerated data type. An enumerated literal may be an identifier, a character or a mixture of both. The VHDL language predefines the following enumeration types: BIT, BOOLEAN, CHARACTER and SEVERITY_LEVEL. (see package STANDARD in Appendix A.)

Numeric Literals

VHDL. Numeric literals may be of type integer, real or physical. Only integer numeric literals should be used with synthesis. Integer numeric literals are the values of integer constants. They may be defined in the default base 10 or any other base from 2 to 16. Underscores may separate individual digits without changing the meaning of the numeric literal.

   example   314159
              3_14159
              2#1010_0101#
              8#57#
              16#9FDE#

Verilog. Numeric literals are simple constant numbers that may be specified in binary, octal, decimal or hexadecimal. The specification of its size is optional as Verilog calculates size based on the longest operand value in an expression, and corresponding assigned value in an assignment.

example		
12'b 0011_0101_1100	12-bit sized binary constant number
6'O 57	6-bit number represented in octal
3_14159	default decimal number
16'h 9FDE	16-bit number represented in hexadecimal

Literal operands

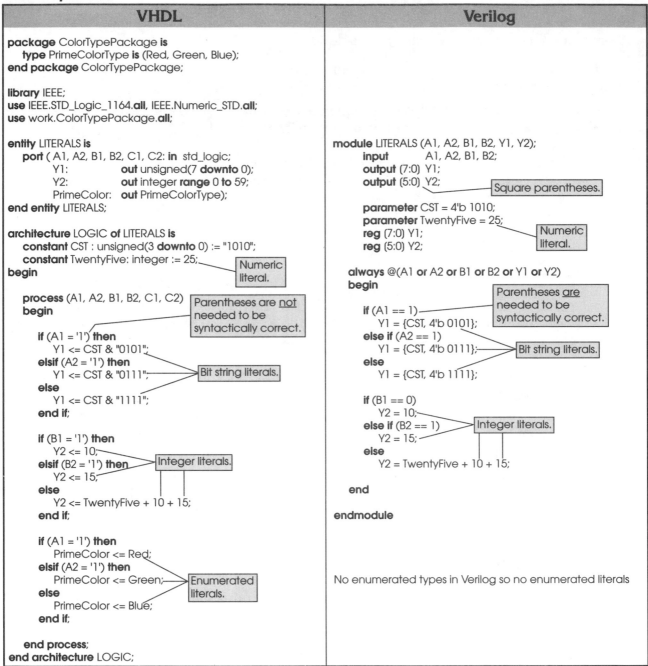

VHDL	Verilog

package ColorTypePackage **is**
    type PrimeColorType **is** (Red, Green, Blue);
end package ColorTypePackage;
 	
library IEEE;
use IEEE.STD_Logic_1164.**all**, IEEE.Numeric_STD.**all**;
use work.ColorTypePackage.**all**;
 	
entity LITERALS **is**
    port (A1, A2, B1, B2, C1, C2: **in** std_logic;
        Y1:   **out** unsigned(7 **downto** 0);
        Y2:   **out** integer **range** 0 **to** 59;
        PrimeColor: **out** PrimeColorType);
end entity LITERALS;
 	
architecture LOGIC **of** LITERALS **is**
    constant CST : unsigned(3 **downto** 0) := "1010";
    constant TwentyFive: integer := 25;   `Numeric literal.`
begin
 	
    process (A1, A2, B1, B2, C1, C2) `Parentheses are not needed to be syntactically correct.`
    begin
 	
        if (A1 = '1') **then**
            Y1 <= CST & "0101";
        elsif (A2 = '1') **then**
            Y1 <= CST & "0111";   `Bit string literals.`
        else
            Y1 <= CST & "1111";
        end if;
 	
        if (B1 = '1') **then**
            Y2 <= 10;
        elsif (B2 = '1') **then** `Integer literals.`
            Y2 <= 15;
        else
            Y2 <= TwentyFive + 10 + 15;
        end if;
 	
        if (A1 = '1') **then**
            PrimeColor <= Red;
        elsif (A2 = '1') **then**
            PrimeColor <= Green; `Enumerated literals.`
        else
            PrimeColor <= Blue;
        end if;
 	
    end process;
end architecture LOGIC;
	module LITERALS (A1, A2, B1, B2, Y1, Y2);
	    input A1, A2, B1, B2;
	    output (7:0) Y1;
	    output (5:0) Y2; `Square parentheses.`
	
	    parameter CST = 4'b 1010;
	    parameter TwentyFive = 25; `Numeric literal.`
	    reg (7:0) Y1;
	    reg (5:0) Y2;
	
	    always @(A1 **or** A2 **or** B1 **or** B2 **or** Y1 **or** Y2)
	    begin
	                        `Parentheses are needed to be syntactically correct.`
	        if (A1 == 1)
	            Y1 = {CST, 4'b 0101};
	        else if (A2 == 1)
	            Y1 = {CST, 4'b 0111}; `Bit string literals.`
	        else
	            Y1 = {CST, 4'b 1111};
	
	        if (B1 == 0)
	            Y2 = 10;
	        else if (B2 == 1) `Integer literals.`
	            Y2 = 15;
	        else
	            Y2 = TwentyFive + 10 + 15;
	
	    end
	
	endmodule
	
	No enumerated types in Verilog so no enumerated literals

Identifier Operands

An identifier is used to give a name to a data object so that it may be easily referenced in an HDL model. They are the most commonly used type of operand. The value of the named object is returned as the operand value.

VHDL identifiers consists of letters, digits and underscores (_). Verilog identifiers have these plus the dollar sign ($).

As VHDL is case insensitive, upper and lower case identifier names are treated as being the same identifier. Verilog is case sensitive, so upper and lower case identifier names are treated as being different identifiers.

Identifier operands

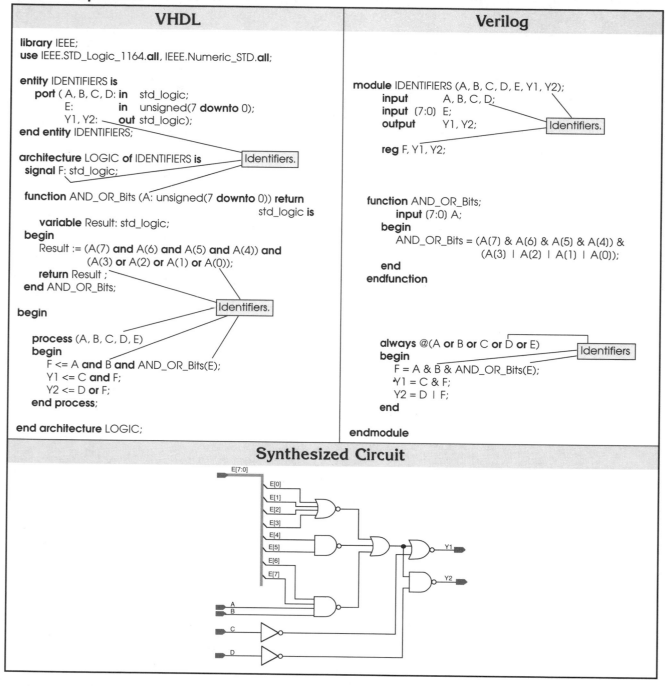

VHDL	Verilog

library IEEE;
use IEEE.STD_Logic_1164.**all**, IEEE.Numeric_STD.**all**;
 	
entity IDENTIFIERS **is**
    port (A, B, C, D: **in**   std_logic;
          E: **in**   unsigned(7 **downto** 0);
          Y1, Y2:   **out** std_logic);
end entity IDENTIFIERS;
 	
architecture LOGIC **of** IDENTIFIERS **is**
   signal F: std_logic;   Identifiers.
 	
   function AND_OR_Bits (A: unsigned(7 **downto** 0)) **return**
                         std_logic **is**
     variable Result: std_logic;
   begin
     Result := (A(7) **and** A(6) **and** A(5) **and** A(4)) **and**
          (A(3) **or** A(2) **or** A(1) **or** A(0));
     return Result ;
   end AND_OR_Bits;
 	
begin
 	
   process (A, B, C, D, E)   Identifiers.
   begin
     F <= A **and** B **and** AND_OR_Bits(E);
     Y1 <= C **and** F;
     Y2 <= D **or** F;
   end process;
 	
end architecture LOGIC;
	module IDENTIFIERS (A, B, C, D, E, Y1, Y2);
	    input A, B, C, D;
	    input (7:0) E;
	    output Y1, Y2; Identifiers.
	
	    reg F, Y1, Y2;
	
	    function AND_OR_Bits;
	       input (7:0) A;
	    begin
	       AND_OR_Bits = (A(7) & A(6) & A(5) & A(4)) &
	                 (A(3) I A(2) I A(1) I A(0));
	    end
	    endfunction
	
	    always @(A **or** B **or** C **or** D **or** E) Identifiers
	    begin
	       F = A & B & AND_OR_Bits(E);
	       Y1 = C & F;
	       Y2 = D I F;
	    end
	
	endmodule

Synthesized Circuit

Aggregate Operands (VHDL)

A VHDL aggregate is a set of one or more elements of an array or record separated by commas and enclosed within parentheses, for example, ('0', '1', A, B). The syntax of an aggregate operand is:

        type_name'((choice =>) expression {, (choice =>), expression})
   where:
        type_name - is any constrained array or record type
        choice   - is optional and used for explicit named association
        expression - is the value of the particular element
   example unsigned'('0', '1', A, B)

Aggregate operands can, therefore, be considered as array or record operands. Synthesis tools typically support both array and record aggregates. An aggregate may also be the target of a signal or variable in an assignment statement.

example   (A, B, C) <= unsigned'("101");

An example of aggregate array operands is shown below using *positional association* (assignment to Y1), named association (assignment to Y2), and where the assigned target is an aggregate. Positional and named association cannot be mixed. The keyword **others** can be used but it must be the last choice in the aggregate.

Aggregate operands

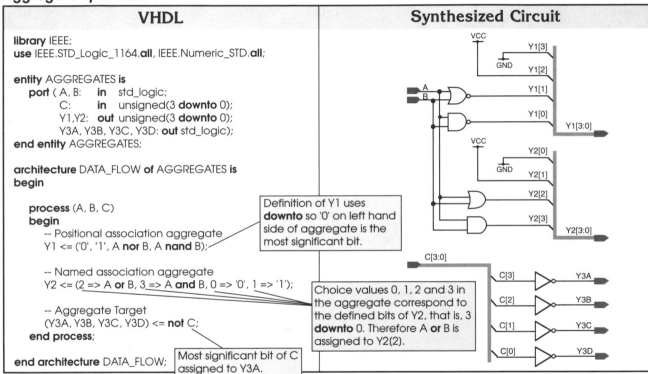

Function Call Operands

Function calls, which must reside in an expression, are operands. The single value returned from a function is the operand value used in the expression.

Function call operands

VHDL	Verilog

library IEEE;
use IEEE.STD_Logic_1164.**all**;
 	
entity FUNCTION_CALLS is
    port (A1, A2, A3, A4, B1, B2: in   std_logic;
            Y1, Y2, Y3:   out std_logic);
end entity FUNCTION_CALLS;
 	
architecture LOGIC of FUNCTION_CALLS is
 	
    function Fn1 (F1, F2, F3, F4: std_logic) return std_logic is
        variable Result: std_logic;
    begin
        Result := (F1 and F2) or (F3 and F4);
        return Result ;
    end function Fn1;   *continued*
	module FUNCTION_CALLS (A1, A2, A3, A4, B1, B2, Y1, Y2);
	    input A1, A2, A3, A4, B1, B2;
	    output Y1, Y2;
	
	    reg Y1, Y2;
	
	function Fn1;
	    input F1, F2, F3, F4;
	begin
	    Fn1 = (F1 & F2)
		(F3 & F4);
		end
		endfunction
		
		                                                    continued

Function call operands

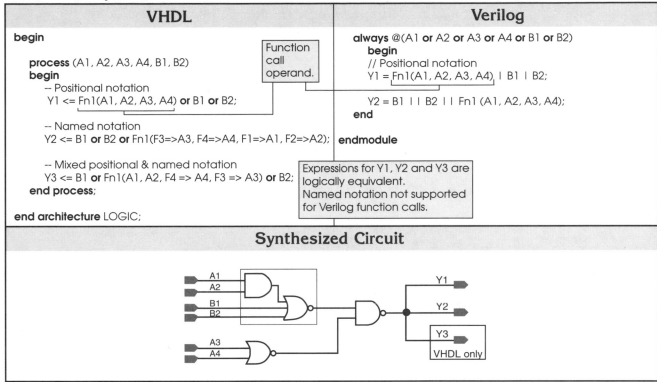

Index and Slice Name Operands

An index named operand specifies a single element of an array. For synthesis the array may be of type constant, variable or signal. A slice named operand is a sequence of elements within an array and is identified in VHDL using **to** or **downto**, and in Verilog using the colon ":".

Index and slice name operands

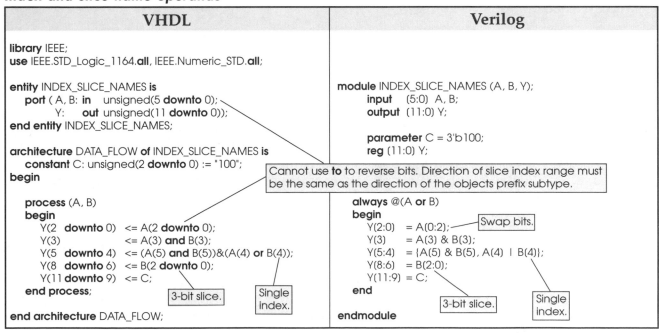

Index and slice name operands

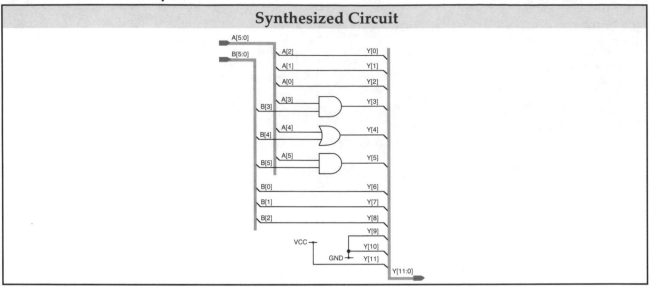

Synthesized Circuit

Qualified Expression Operands (VHDL)

A qualified expression operand is used to explicitly state the **type** or **subtype** of the operand itself. The operand may be a complete expression in its own right or an aggregate. By using qualified operands, any possible ambiguities in an operands type is resolved. This includes the use of an enumerated literal or aggregate, where their type is not known from the context in which they are used.

Syntax of a qualified expression operand:

> type_name ' (expression)
>
> or
>
> type_name ' aggregate

The two models, VHDL 1 and VHDL 2, show examples of qualified expression operands (VHDL 1) and qualified aggregate expressions (VHDL 2).

VHDL 1. Two enumerated data types, PrimeColorType and RainbowType have been declared in the package, ColorsPKG, and are used by two identically named functions, ColorTest, defined in the package body. The model, QUALIFIED_EXPRESSION, has a total of six calls to the two functions. The problem is that, because the enumerated literals of the enumerated data type overlap (Red, Green and Blue), when one of these overlapping literals is used in a function call to ColorTest, there is no way of deducing which of the two functions should be used. Therefore, when enumerated literals Red, Green and Blue are used, they must be qualified as shown. Function calls which pass any of the enumerated literals; Orange, Yellow, Indigo or Violet to the function, do not need to be qualified. Such a function call must use the first ColorTest function which uses the data type RainbowType.

VHDL 2. The package BusTypes defines three unsigned subtypes (Bus4, Bus6 and Bus8) consisting of 4, 6 and 8-bits, respectfully. The model, QUALIFIED_AGGREGATE, infers two adders assuming the synthesis tool's automatic resource sharing option is used. The plus (+) operator, which infers an adder, has left and right operands of 8 and 4-bits each, and is assigned to the 8-bit output Y1. The right hand operand is a 4-bit qualified aggregate. The second plus operator inferring a second adder has 8 and 6-bit inputs respectively and has an 8-bit output Y2. The plus operator's right hand operand is an aggregate and is required to be either 4 or 6-bits wide. Only the two most significant bits of this right hand operand needs to be explicitly defined: all other bits have a default assignment using the **others** clause. The problem is two fold; 1) unless the operand is qualified, it will not be of type unsigned as required by the "+" operator and 2) it would not be of the correct bit width.

Qualified expressions   *Qualified aggregates*

VHDL 1	VHDL 2

```
package ColorsPKG is
    type PrimeColorType is (Red, Green, Blue);
    type RainbowType is
         (Red, Orange, Yellow, Green, Blue, Indigo, Violet);
end package ColorsPKG;

package body ColorsPKG is
    function ColorTest(Color: RainbowType)
            return RainbowType is
    begin
      if (Color = Red) then
         return Violet;
      else
         return Color;
      end if;
    end ColorTest;
    function ColorTest(Color: PrimeColorType)
            return PrimeColorType is
    begin
      if (Color = Red) then
         return Blue;
      else
         return Color;
      end if;
    end ColorTest;
end package body ColorsPKG;

library IEEE;
use IEEE.STD_Logic_1164.all, IEEE.Numeric_STD.all;
use work.ColorsPKG.all;

entity QUALIFIED_EXPRESSION is
    port ( A1, A2: in   std_logic;
          Y1:     out PrimeColorType;
          Y2:     out RainbowType );
end entity QUALIFIED_EXPRESSION;

architecture LOGIC of QUALIFIED_EXPRESSION is
begin
    process (A1, A2)
    begin                    Qualified expression.
      if (A1 = '1') then
         Y1 <= ColorTest(PrimeColorType'(Red));
         Y2 <= ColorTest(Indigo);
      elsif (A2 = '1') then
         Y1 <= ColorTest(PrimeColorType'(Green));
         Y2 <= ColorTest(RainbowType'(Green));
      else
         Y1 <= ColorTest(PrimeColorType'(Blue));
         Y2 <= ColorTest(Yellow);
      end if;
    end process;

end architecture LOGIC;
```

```
library IEEE;
use IEEE.STD_Logic_1164.all, IEEE.Numeric_STD.all;

package BusTypes is
    subtype Bus4 is unsigned(3 downto 0);
    subtype Bus6 is unsigned(5 downto 0);
    subtype Bus8 is unsigned(7 downto 0);
end package BusTypes;

library IEEE;
use IEEE.STD_Logic_1164.all, IEEE.Numeric_STD.all;
use work.BusTypes.all;

entity QUALIFIED_AGGREGATE is
    port (A1, A2, B, C, D, E: in  std_logic;
         Data1, Data2:  in  unsigned(7 downto 0);
         Y1: out Bus4;
         Y2: out Bus6);
end entity QUALIFIED_AGGREGATE;

architecture DATA_FLOW of QUALIFIED_AGGREGATE is
begin
    process (A1, A2, B, C, D, E)   3 element qualified
    begin                          aggregate.
      if (A1 = '1') then
         Y1 <= Data1 + Bus4'(B or C, B and C, others =>not D);
         Y2 <= Data2 + Bus6'(B or C, B and C, others =>not D);
      elsif (A2 = '1') then
         Y1 <= Data1 + Bus4'(B, C, others => D);
         Y2 <= Data2 + Bus6'(B, C, others => D);
      else
         Y1 <= Data1 + Bus4'(others => not E);
         Y2 <= Data2 + Bus6'(others => not E);
      end if;
    end process;

end architecture DATA_FLOW;
```

Type Conversion Operands (VHDL)

Because VHDL is a strongly typed language the need to change an operand's type within an expression is sometimes an unavoidable necessity. Type conversion operands change the type of the returned operand.

The syntax is:
```
          originating operand
                 |
  target_type_name (expression)
  |_____|
         |
  New operand of different type
```

example   **signal** A, B: unsigned (9 **downto** 0);
          std_logic_vector(A(5 **downto** 0) + B(5 **downto** 0))

The type of the originating expression is implicit. The closely related types that may be converted are:

1. *Abstract numeric types of type integer.* Includes floating point numbers and are not supported for synthesis.
2. *Particular kinds of array types.* Array types that have the same dimensionality and where each element is of the same type, can be converted. Array types that have the same dimensionality and where each element is a closely related property of the array types, can be converted.

Such operands usually contain a function call to a type conversion function; this is always the case for models that are to be synthesized. Type conversions that are used in synthesizable models typically do not infer logic.

VHDL 1 (Non-synthesizable). A type conversion can be modeled very efficiently using a look-up table defined in a constant. The problem is, that this constant array is typically <u>not</u> supported by synthesis tools. VHDL 1 has been included for completeness, but is not synthesizable by commercial synthesis tools. The constant To_Prime is used to convert data objects of type RainbowType to type PrimeColorType and vice versa for the constant To_Rainbow. Note that if this particular model were synthesizable To_Rainbow would not infer logic while To_Prime would.

Non-synthesizable conversion functions

```
                   VHDL 1

package ColorTypePackage is
    type PrimeColorType is (Red, Green, Blue);
    type RainbowType    is (Red, Orange, Yellow, Green, Blue,
                            Indigo, Violet);
    type ParrofR is array (PrimeColorType) of RainbowType;
    type RarrofP is array (RainbowType) of PrimeColorType;

    Constant To_Rainbow:
        ParrofR := (Red => Red, Green => Green, Blue => Blue);
    Constant To_Prime:
        RarrofP := (Red => Red, Green => Green, Blue => Blue,
                    Orange => Red, Yellow => Red,
                    Indigo => Blue, Violet => Blue);
end package ColorTypePackage;

library IEEE;
use IEEE.STD_Logic_1164.all, IEEE.Numeric_STD.all;
use work.ColorTypePackage.all;
entity TYPE_CONVERSION_NON_SYNTH is
    port ( Convert: in   std_logic;
           A1:      in   PrimeColorType;
           A2:      in   RainbowType;
           Y1:      out  PrimeColorType;
           Y2:      out  RainbowType);
end entity TYPE_CONVERSION_NON_SYNTH;

architecture LOGIC of TYPE_CONVERSION_NON_SYNTH is
begin
    process (A1, A2)
    begin
        if (Convert = '1') then
            Y1 <= To_Prime(A2);
            Y2 <= To_Rainbow(A1);
        else
            Y1 <= A1;
            Y2 <= A2;
        end if;
    end process;
end architecture LOGIC;
```

VHDL 2. Commonly used type conversion functions are typically placed in packages for global use. Standard packages like the IEEE 1164 package STD_Logic_1164, contains commonly needed conversion functions that can be called at will. The model TYPE_CONVERSION identifies a situation where tri-state buffers are being modeled, but the input values A and B are of type bit and bit_vector. As these bits do not contain a tri-state value, that is Z, it must be converted to a type that does, in this case std_ulogic_vector. It uses function calls to the functions To_stdulogic and To_stdulogicvector which are defined in package STD_Logic_1164.

Use of predefined conversion functions

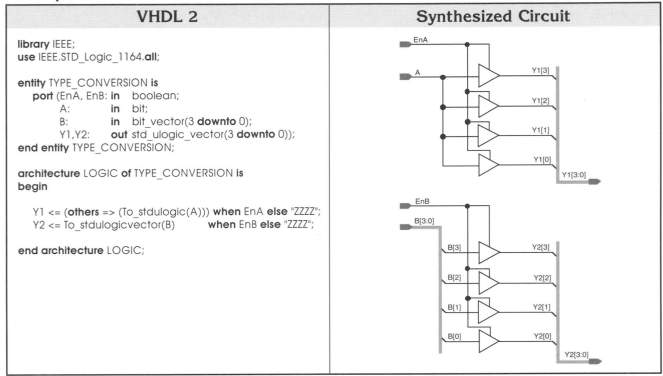

VHDL 2	Synthesized Circuit
| ```
library IEEE;
use IEEE.STD_Logic_1164.all;

entity TYPE_CONVERSION is
  port (EnA, EnB: in    boolean;
        A:          in    bit;
        B:          in    bit_vector(3 downto 0);
        Y1,Y2:    out std_ulogic_vector(3 downto 0));
end entity TYPE_CONVERSION;

architecture LOGIC of TYPE_CONVERSION is
begin

   Y1 <= (others => (To_stdulogic(A))) when EnA else "ZZZZ";
   Y2 <= To_stdulogicvector(B)          when EnB else "ZZZZ";

end architecture LOGIC;
``` | |

Record and Record Element Operands (VHDL)

A record is used to group objects of the same or different type. A record type declaration defines the different types that can be used in a particular record. Each element of a record is referred to as a field. The whole record or a particular element within a record can be used as an operand in an expression, the syntax of which is shown below. The period (.) is used to separate record names and record element names when referencing record elements.

        record_name   (record)
        record_name.field_name   (record field)

The two following two examples demonstrate record and record elements assignments and their use as operands. By defining record types in a separate package, signals using these types can appear in the interface list of **entity** statements.
```

Two examples of record and record element operands

VHDL	VHDL

library IEEE;
use IEEE.STD_Logic_1164.all, IEEE.Numeric_STD.all;
package RecordTypes is
   type R1_Type is record
     I: integer range 7 downto 0;
     J: std_logic;
   end record;
   type R2_Type is record
     I: integer range 0 to 7;
     J: unsigned(1 downto 0);
   end record;
end package RecordTypes;
 	
use work.RecordTypes.all;
 	
entity RECORDS is
   port(A1, A2: in   std_logic;
       B1, B2: in   integer range 0 to 7;
       C: in   R1_Type;
       Y: out R2_Type);
end entity RECORDS;
 	
architecture RTL of RECORDS is
   signal M: R1_Type;
begin
 	
   process (A1, A2, B1, B2, C)
   begin
     M.I <= B1 + B2;
     M.J <= A1 and A2;
     if (C = M) then
       Y.I <= M.I - C.I;
       Y.J <= M.J & C.J;
     else
       Y.I <= 0;
       Y.J <= "00";
     end if;
   end process;
 	
end architecture RTL;
 	
Record element operands. (annotation pointing to Y.I and Y.J lines)
	library IEEE;
	use IEEE.STD_Logic_1164.all, IEEE.Numeric_STD.all;
	package RecordPKG is
	   type FloatPointType is
	     record
	       Sign: std_logic;
	       Exponent: unsigned(6 downto 0);
	       Fraction: unsigned(23 downto 0);
	     end record;
	end package RecordPKG;
	
	library IEEE;
	use IEEE.STD_Logic_1164.all, IEEE.Numeric_STD.all;
	use work.RecordPKG.all;
	
	entity RECORDS_FLOATING_POINT is
	   port (Si: in std_logic;
	       Ex: in unsigned(6 downto 0);
	       Fr: in unsigned(23 downto 0);
	       A, B: in std_logic;
	       F1, F2: in FloatPointType;
	       Y1: out unsigned(31 downto 0);
	       Y2: out std_logic;
	       Y3: out FloatPointType);
	end entity RECORDS_FLOATING_POINT;
	
	architecture RTL of RECORDS_FLOATING_POINT is
	begin
	   process (Si, Ex, Fr)
	     variable F: FloatPointType;
	   begin
	     F.Sign := Si;
	     F.Exponent := Ex;
	     F.Fraction := Fr;
	     Y1 <= F.Sign & F.Exponent & F.Fraction;
	   end process;
	
	   process (A, F1, F2)
	   begin
	     if (F1 = F2) then
	       Y2 <= A;
	       Y3 <= F1;
	     else
	       Y2 <= B;
	       Y3 <= F2;
	     end if;
	   end process;
	end architecture RTL;
	
	Record operands. (annotation pointing to Y3 lines)

Operators

Operators perform an operation on one or more operands within an expression. An expression combines operands with appropriate operators to produce the desired functional expression.

VHDL Operators. There are seven functional groups of VHDL operators, see Table 3.1. Operators within a particular group have the same level of precedence when used within an expression. Starting from the top, each group of operators has precedence over the next.

Verilog Operators. The Verilog operators are shown in Table 3.2. Although not all operators can be used in the same expressional part of code, where they can, they are shown in descending order of precedence. Operators with equal precedence are shown grouped. There are nine functional groups of operators. The group to which each operator belongs is indicated in the third column of the table. The group to which each operator belongs does not govern precedence.

VHDL and Verilog Operators. A comparison of VHDL and Verilog operators is shown in Table 3.3. Operators are categorized into functional groups and are not in precedence order. Where there is no equivalent operator in the other language the entry in the table is left blank.

The models in the remaining sections in this chapter show use of all VHDL and Verilog operators. Like all models in this book they are geared towards being simulated, synthesized and then resimulated using the synthesized gate level netlist.

Overloaded Operators (VHDL)

VHDL operators that operate on single bit values are defined by the VHDL language to operate on objects of type bit only. A data type (signal or variable) of type bit is defined to have one of two values 0 or 1. The only multi-valued data types defined by the VHDL language is of type integer. For this reason, overloaded VHDL operators from the IEEE 1076.3 synthesis package Numeric_STD are used.

Type std_logic is used for single bit data types, which can have one of nine possible values {U, X, 0, 1, Z, W, L, H, -}. Data type, std_logic, is defined in the IEEE library package STD_Logic_1164 along with all the appropriate overloaded language operators.

For multiple bit data types, types unsigned and signed are used and are defined in both IEEE 1076.3 synthesis packages Numeric_bit and Numeric_STD. Types unsigned and signed are defined in Numeric_bit to be a one dimensional array of values of type bit. Types unsigned and signed are defined in Numeric_STD to be a one dimensional array of values of type std_logic. For this reason, only package Numeric_STD is used throughout this book.

VHDL Operator	Operation	Operand Type		Result Type
		Left	Right	
Miscellaneous Operators				
**	exponential	any integer	INTEGER	same as left
		any floating point	INTEGER	same as left
abs	absolute value	any numeric type	any numeric type	same numeric type
Arithmetic (multiplying) Operators				
*	multiplication	any integer	same type	same type
		any floating point	same type	same type
/	division	any integer	same type	same type
		any floating point	same type	same type
mod	modulus	any integer	same type	same type
rem	remainder	any integer	same type	same type
Unary Arithmetic (sign) Operators				
+	identity	any numeric type	any numeric type	same type
-	negation	any numeric type	any numeric type	same type
Adding Operators				
+	addition	any numeric type	same type	same type
-	subtraction	any numeric type	same type	same type
&	concatination	any array type	same array type	same array type
		any array type	the element type	same array type
		the element type	any array type	same array type
		the element type	the element type	any array type
Shift Operators				
sll	logical shift left	One dimensional array of bit or boolean	INTEGER	same as left
srl	logical shift right	One dimensional array of bit or boolean	INTEGER	same as left
sla	arithmetic shift left	One dimensional array of bit or boolean	INTEGER	same as left
sra	arithmetic shift right	One dimensional array of bit or boolean	INTEGER	same as left
rol	logical rotate left	One dimensional array of bit or boolean	INTEGER	same as left
ror	logical rotate right	One dimensional array of bit or boolean	INTEGER	same as left
Relational Operators				
=	equality	any type	any type	BOOLEAN
/=	inequality	any type	any type	BOOLEAN
<	less than	any scalar type or discrete array type	any scalar type or discrete array type	BOOLEAN
<=	less than or equal to	any scalar type or discrete array type	any scalar type or discrete array type	BOOLEAN
>	greater than	any scalar type or discrete array type	any scalar type or discrete array type	BOOLEAN
>=	greater than or equal to	any scalar type or discrete array type	any scalar type or discrete array type	BOOLEAN
Logical Operators				
not	logical NOT	BOOLEAN, BIT or BIT_VECTOR		same as left
and	logical AND	BOOLEAN, BIT or BIT_VECTOR		same as left
or	logical OR	BOOLEAN, BIT or BIT_VECTOR		same as left
nand	logical NAND	BOOLEAN, BIT or BIT_VECTOR		same as left
nor	logical NOR	BOOLEAN, BIT or BIT_VECTOR		same as left
xor	logical XOR	BOOLEAN, BIT or BIT_VECTOR		same as left
xnor	logical XNOR	BOOLEAN, BIT or BIT_VECTOR		same as left

Table 3.1   VHDL Operators

Verilog Operator	Name	Functional Group
( )	bit-select or part-select	
( )	parenthesis	
!	logical negation	Logical
~	negation	Bit-wise
&	reduction AND	Reduction
|	reduction OR	Reduction
~&	reduction NAND	Reduction
~|	reduction NOR	Reduction
^	reduction XOR	Reduction
~^ or ^~	reduction XNOR	Reduction
+	unary (sign) plus	Arithmetic
-	unary (sign) minus	Arithmetic
{ }	concatenation	Concatenation
{{ }}	replication	Replication
*	multiply	Arithmetic
/	divide	Arithmetic
%	modulus	Arithmetic
+	binary plus	Arithmetic
-	binary minus	Arithmetic
<<	shift left	Shift
>>	shift right	Shift
>	greater than	Relational
>=	greater than or equal to	Relational
<	less than	Relational
<=	less than or equal to	Relational
==	logical equality	Equality
!=	logical inequality	Equality
===	case equality	Equality
!==	case inequality	Equality
&	bit-wise AND	Bit-wise
^	bit-wise XOR	Bit-wise
^~ or ~^	bit-wise XNOR	Bit-wise
|	bit-wise OR	Bit-wise
&&	logical AND	Logical
||	logical OR	Logical
?:	conditional	Conditional

Table 3.2   Verilog Operators

Operation	Operator	
	VHDL	**Verilog**
Arithmetic Operators		
exponential	**	
multiplication	*	*
division	/	/
addition	+	+
subtraction	-	-
modulus	mod	%
remainder	rem	
absolute value	abs	
Unary Arithmetic (Sign) Operators		
identity	+	+
negation	-	-
Relational Operators		
less than	<	<
less than or equal to	<=	<=
greater than	>	>
greater than or equal to	>=	>=
Equality Operators		
equality	=	==
inequality	/=	!=
Logical Comparison Operators		
NOT	not	!
AND	and	&&
OR	or	||
Logical Bit-wise Operators		
unary negation NOT	not	~
binary AND	and	&
binary OR	or	|
binary nAND	nand	
binary NOR	nor	
binary XOR	xor	^
binary XNOR	xnor	^~ or ~^
Shift Operators		
logical shift left	sll	<<
logical shift right	srl	>>
arithmetic shift left	sla	
arithmetic shift right	sra	
logical rotate left	rol	
logical rotate right	ror	
Concatenation & Replication Operators		
concatenation	&	{ }
replication		{{ }}
Reduction Operators		
AND		&
OR		|
NAND		~&
NOR		~|
XOR		^
XNOR		^~ or ~^
Conditional Operator		
conditional		? :

Table 3.3 Comparison of VHDL and Verilog Operators

Arithmetic Operators

There are eight VHDL arithmetic operators, but only five of them are found in Verilog; see Table 3.3. The five common operators are shown in the first example, while the second example shows the three remaining VHDL operators.

Arithmetic operators common to both languages

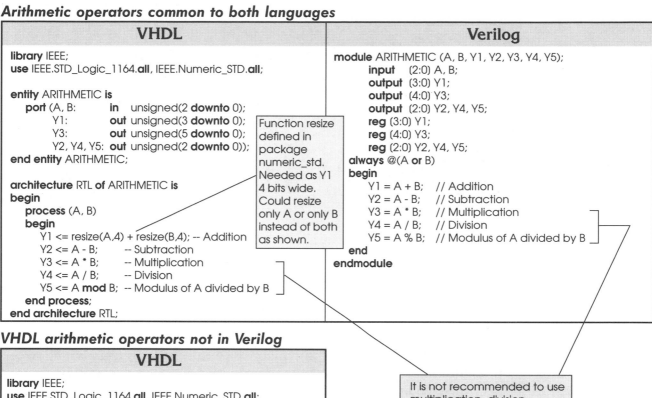

VHDL	Verilog

library IEEE;
use IEEE.STD_Logic_1164.**all**, IEEE.Numeric_STD.**all**;
 	
entity ARITHMETIC **is**
   port (A, B: **in**   unsigned(2 **downto** 0);
         Y1:   **out** unsigned(3 **downto** 0);
         Y3:   **out** unsigned(5 **downto** 0);
         Y2, Y4, Y5: **out** unsigned(2 **downto** 0));
end entity ARITHMETIC;
 	
architecture RTL **of** ARITHMETIC **is**
begin
   process (A, B)
   begin
      Y1 <= resize(A,4) + resize(B,4); -- Addition
      Y2 <= A - B;   -- Subtraction
      Y3 <= A * B;   -- Multiplication
      Y4 <= A / B;   -- Division
      Y5 <= A **mod** B; -- Modulus of A divided by B
   end process;
end architecture RTL;
	module ARITHMETIC (A, B, Y1, Y2, Y3, Y4, Y5);
	      input (2:0) A, B;
	      output (3:0) Y1;
	      output (4:0) Y3;
	      output (2:0) Y2, Y4, Y5;
	      reg (3:0) Y1;
	      reg (4:0) Y3;
	      reg (2:0) Y2, Y4, Y5;
	always @(A **or** B)
	begin
	      Y1 = A + B; // Addition
	      Y2 = A - B; // Subtraction
	      Y3 = A * B; // Multiplication
	      Y4 = A / B; // Division
	      Y5 = A % B; // Modulus of A divided by B
	   end
	endmodule

Function resize defined in package numeric_std. Needed as Y1 4 bits wide. Could resize only A or only B instead of both as shown.

VHDL arithmetic operators not in Verilog

VHDL
library IEEE; use IEEE.STD_Logic_1164.**all**, IEEE.Numeric_STD.**all**; **entity** ARITHMETIC **is**   **port** (A, B: **in**   unsigned(4 **downto** 0);   C: **in**   signed(3 **downto** 0);   Y1, Y2, Y3: **out** unsigned(4 **downto** 0)); **end entity** ARITHMETIC; **architecture** RTL **of** ARITHMETIC **is** **begin**   **process** (A, B)   **begin**   Y1 <= 4 ** 2;   -- 4 to the power of 2.   Y2 <= A **rem** B; -- Remainder of A divided by B   Y3 <= **abs** C;   -- Absolute value of C.   **end process**; **end architecture** RTL;

It is not recommended to use multiplication, division, modulus, to the power of, remainder or absolute value in a model which is to be synthesized. More efficient synthesized circuits usually result when specifying these functions with more structural detail, see Chapter 9.

(A synthesis tool may generate a warning, or more likely an error, when these operators are used with non-constant operands.)

Sign Operators

These operators simply assign a positive (+) or negative (-) sign to a singular operand. Usually no sign operator is defined, in which case the default "+" is assumed.

Sign operators

VHDL	Verilog

library IEEE;
use IEEE.STD_Logic_1164.**all**, IEEE.Numeric_STD.**all**;
 	
entity SIGN **is**
  port (A, B: **in** unsigned(2 **downto** 0);
        Y1, Y2:   **out** unsigned(2 **downto** 0);
        Y3:   **out** unsigned(5 **downto** 0));
end entity SIGN;
architecture RTL **of** SIGN **is**
begin
   process (A, B)
   begin
      Y1 <= A **or** (-B);
      Y2 <= (-A) + (-B);
      Y3 <= A * (-B);
   end process;
end architecture RTL;
 	
"*" is overloaded in Numeric_STD such that the width of Y3 (6 bits) is equal to the width of A (3 bits) plus the width of B (3 bits).
	module SIGN (A, B, Y1, Y2, Y3);
	    input (2:0) A, B;
	    output (2:0) Y1, Y2;
	    output (5:0) Y3;
	    reg (3:0) Y1, Y2, Y3;
	    reg (5:0) Y3;
	  always @(A **or** B)
	  begin
	     Y1 = A | -B;
	     Y2 = - A + -B;
	     Y3 = A * -B;
	  end
	
	endmodule

Relational Operators

Relational operators compare two operands and returns an indication of whether the compared relationship is true or false.

VHDL. The two operands need not be of the same type and the result need not be of type boolean; it depends on the overloading. The comparison of enumeration types is performed according to the positional ordering of each element in the enumeration type declaration. Record or array types compare corresponding elements of each operand.

Verilog. The result of a comparison is either 0 or 1. It is 0 if the comparison is false and 1 if the comparison is true.

Relational operators

VHDL	Verilog

library IEEE;
use IEEE.STD_Logic_1164.**all**, IEEE.Numeric_STD.**all**;
 	
entity RELATIONAL_OPERATORS **is**
  port (A, B: **in**   unsigned(2 **downto** 0);
      Y1, Y2, Y3: **out** boolean;
      Y4:   **out** std_logic);
end entity RELATIONAL_OPERATORS;
architecture LOGIC **of** RELATIONAL_OPERATORS **is**
begin
   process (A, B)
   begin
      Y1 <= A < B;   -- Less than
      Y2 <= A <= B;   -- Less than or equal to
      Y3 <= A > B;   -- Greater than
      if (A >= B) **then** -- Greater than or equal to
        Y4 <= '1' ;
      else
        Y4 <= '0' ;
      end if;
   end process;
end architecture LOGIC;
	module RELATIONAL_OPERATORS (A, B, Y1, Y2, Y3, Y4);
	    input (2:0) A, B;
	    output Y1, Y2, Y3, Y4;
	
	   reg Y1, Y2, Y3, Y4;
	
	    always @(A **or** B)
	     begin
	        Y1 = A < B; // Less than
	        Y2 = A <= B; // Less than or equal to
	        Y3 = A > B; // Greater than
	        If (A >= B); // Greater than or equal to
	          Y4 = 1;
	        else
	          Y4 = 0;
	     end
	  endmodule

Relational operators

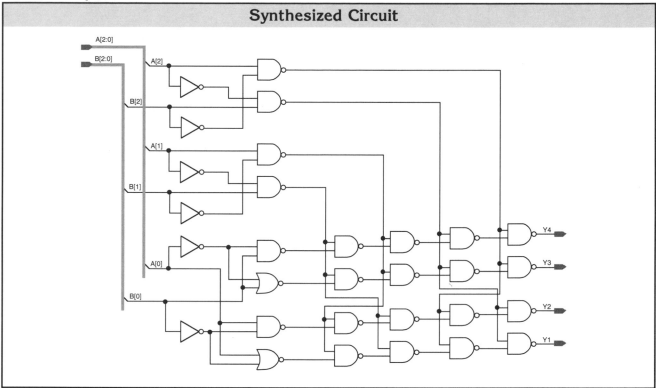

Synthesized Circuit

Equality & Inequality Operators

Equality and inequality operators are used in exactly the same way as relational operators and return a true or false indication in exactly the same way as relational operators, depending on whether any two operands are equivalent or not.

Equality operators

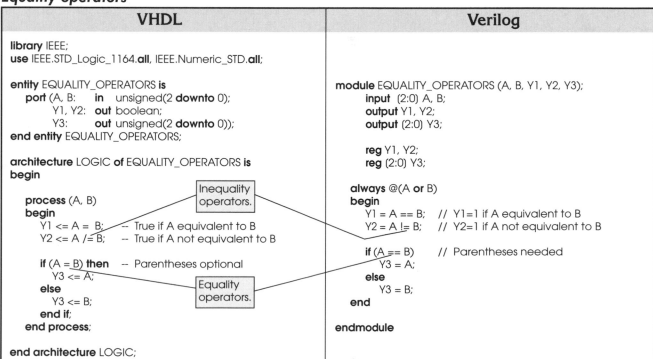

VHDL	Verilog

library IEEE;
use IEEE.STD_Logic_1164.**all**, IEEE.Numeric_STD.**all**;
 	
entity EQUALITY_OPERATORS **is**
    port (A, B: **in**   unsigned(2 **downto** 0);
        Y1, Y2:   **out** boolean;
        Y3:   **out** unsigned(2 **downto** 0));
end entity EQUALITY_OPERATORS;
 	
architecture LOGIC **of** EQUALITY_OPERATORS **is**
begin
 	
    process (A, B)
    begin
        Y1 <= A = B;   -- True if A equivalent to B
        Y2 <= A /= B;   -- True if A not equivalent to B
 	
        if (A = B) **then**   -- Parentheses optional
            Y3 <= A;
        else
            Y3 <= B;
        end if;
    end process;
 	
end architecture LOGIC;
	module EQUALITY_OPERATORS (A, B, Y1, Y2, Y3);
	    input (2:0) A, B;
	    output Y1, Y2;
	    output (2:0) Y3;
	
	    reg Y1, Y2;
	    reg (2:0) Y3;
	
	    always @(A **or** B)
	    begin
	        Y1 = A == B; // Y1=1 if A equivalent to B
	        Y2 = A != B; // Y2=1 if A not equivalent to B
	
	        if (A == B) // Parentheses needed
	            Y3 = A;
	        else
	            Y3 = B;
	    end
	
	endmodule

Inequality operators.

Equality operators.

Equality operators

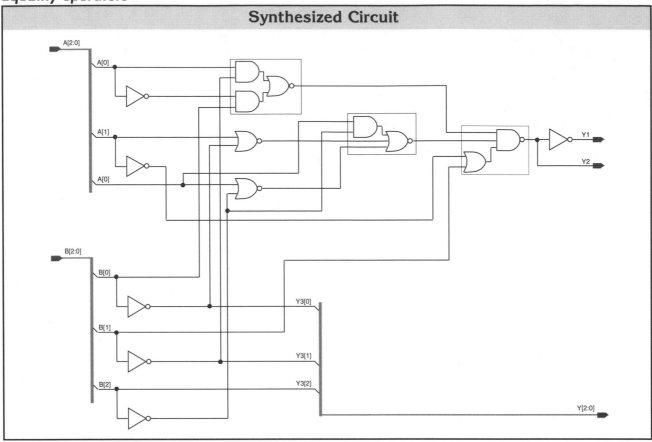

Synthesized Circuit

Logical Comparison Operators

Logical comparison operators are used in conjunction with relational and equality operators as described in the previous two sections. They provide a means to perform multiple comparisons within a single expression.

Logical comparison operators

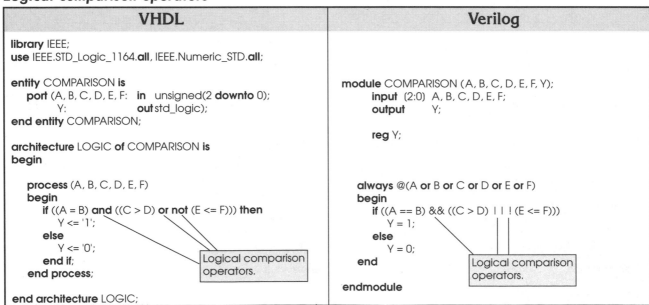

VHDL	Verilog

library IEEE;
use IEEE.STD_Logic_1164.**all**, IEEE.Numeric_STD.**all**;
 	
entity COMPARISON **is**
　　port (A, B, C, D, E, F:　**in**　unsigned(2 **downto** 0);
　　　　Y:　　　　　　　　**out** std_logic);
end entity COMPARISON;
 	
architecture LOGIC **of** COMPARISON **is**
begin
 	
　　process (A, B, C, D, E, F)
　　begin
　　　if ((A = B) **and** ((C > D) **or not** (E <= F))) **then**
　　　　Y <= '1';
　　　else
　　　　Y <= '0';
　　　end if;
　　end process;
 	
end architecture LOGIC;
	module COMPARISON (A, B, C, D, E, F, Y);
	　　input　(2:0)　A, B, C, D, E, F;
	　　output　　　Y;
	
	　　reg Y;
	
	　　always @(A **or** B **or** C **or** D **or** E **or** F)
	　　begin
	　　　if ((A == B) && ((C > D) | | ! (E <= F)))
	　　　　Y = 1;
	　　　else
	　　　　Y = 0;
	　　end
	
	endmodule

Logical comparison operators.

Logical comparison operators

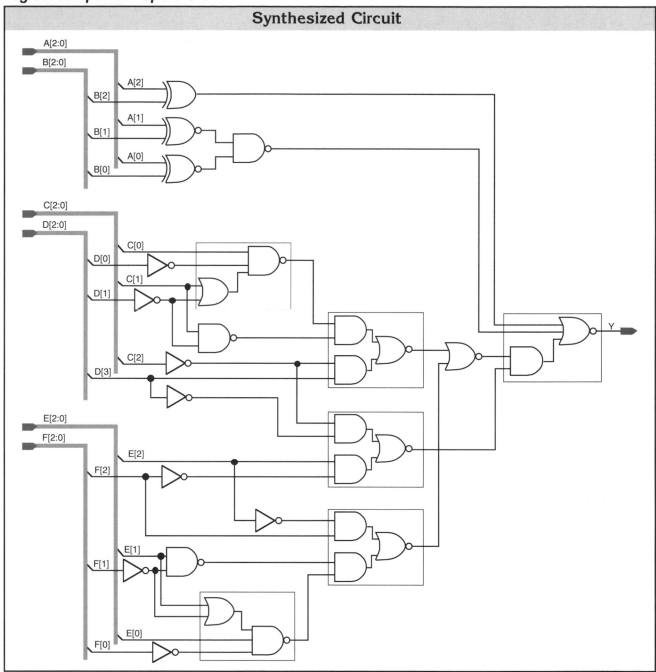

Logical Bit-wise Operators

Logical bit-wise operators take two single or multiple bit operands on either side of the operator and return a single bit result. The only exception is the NOT operator, which negates the single operand that follows. Note that Verilog does not have the equivalent of a NAND or NOR operator, though their function is implemented in the following Verilog model by negating the AND and OR operators so that the VHDL and Verilog models remain identical.

Bit-wise logical operators

VHDL	Verilog

library IEEE;
use IEEE.STD_Logic_1164.**all**, IEEE.Numeric_STD.**all**;
 	
entity BITWISE **is**
   port (A: **in**   unsigned(6 **downto** 0);
        B: **in**   unsigned(5 **downto** 0);
        Y: **out** unsigned(6 **downto** 0));
end entity BITWISE;
 	
architecture LOGIC **of** BITWISE **is**
begin
 	
   process (A, B)
   begin
     Y(0) <= A(0) **and** B(0);   -- Binary AND
     Y(1) <= A(1)   **or** B(1);   -- Binary OR
     Y(2) <= A(2) **nand** B(2);   -- Binary NAND
     Y(3) <= A(3) **nor** B(3);   -- Binary NOR
     Y(4) <= A(4) **xor** B(4);   -- Binary XOR
     Y(5) <= A(5) **xnor** B(5);   -- Binary XNOR
     Y(6) <= **not** A(6);   -- Unary negation
   end process;
 	
end architecture LOGIC;
	module BITWISE (A, B, Y);
	   input (6:0) A;
	   input (5:0) B;
	   output (6:0) Y;
	
	   reg (6:0) Y;
	
	   always @(A **or** B)
	   begin
	     Y(0) = A(0) & B(0); // Binary AND
	     Y(1) = A(1)
		B(1); // Binary OR
		     Y(2) = !(A(2) & B(2)); // Negated AND (No NAND)
		     Y(3) = !(A(3)
			B(3)); // Negated OR (No NOR)
			     Y(4) = A(4) ^ B(4); // Binary XOR
			     Y(5) = A(5) ~^ B(5); // Binary XNOR
			     Y(6) = ! A(6); // Unary negation
			   end
			
			endmodule

Synthesized Circuit

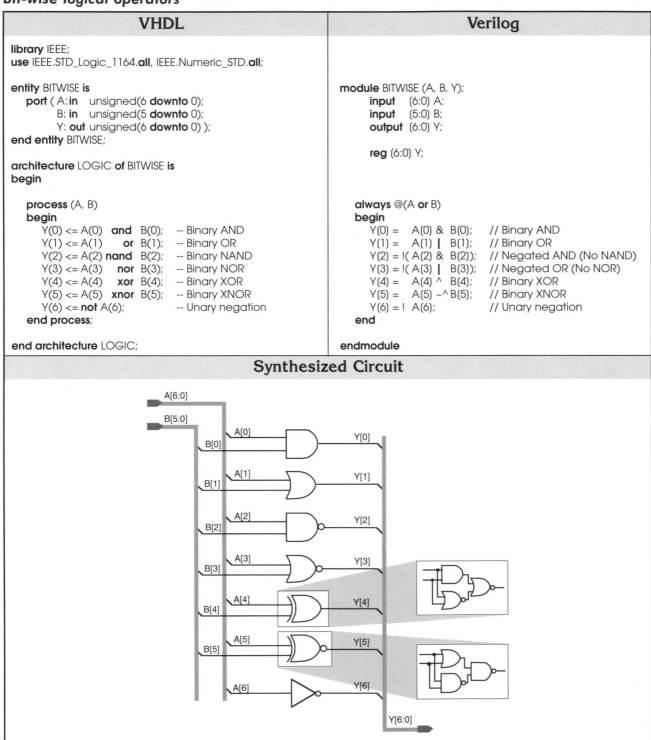

Shift Operators

Shift operators require two operands. The operand before the operator contains data to be shifted and the operand after the operator contains the number of single bit shift operations to be performed.

In this instance, the two models are not identical because the Verilog model does not include the two rotate and two arithmetic shift operators. These operators do not exist in Verilog, however, their function can be implemented with little extra code, see shifters in Chapter 9.

Shift operators

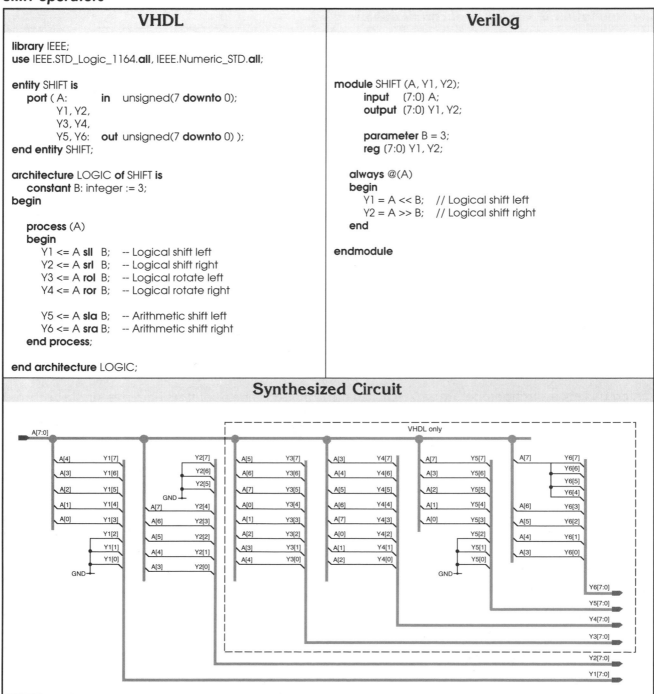

VHDL	Verilog

library IEEE;
use IEEE.STD_Logic_1164.all, IEEE.Numeric_STD.all;
 	
entity SHIFT is
    port (A: in   unsigned(7 downto 0);
        Y1, Y2,
        Y3, Y4,
        Y5, Y6:   out unsigned(7 downto 0));
end entity SHIFT;
 	
architecture LOGIC of SHIFT is
    constant B: integer := 3;
begin
 	
    process (A)
    begin
        Y1 <= A sll B;   -- Logical shift left
        Y2 <= A srl B;   -- Logical shift right
        Y3 <= A rol B;   -- Logical rotate left
        Y4 <= A ror B;   -- Logical rotate right
 	
        Y5 <= A sla B;   -- Arithmetic shift left
        Y6 <= A sra B;   -- Arithmetic shift right
    end process;
 	
end architecture LOGIC;
	module SHIFT (A, Y1, Y2);
	        input (7:0) A;
	        output (7:0) Y1, Y2;
	
	        parameter B = 3;
	        reg (7:0) Y1, Y2;
	
	    always @(A)
	    begin
	        Y1 = A << B; // Logical shift left
	        Y2 = A >> B; // Logical shift right
	    end
	
	endmodule

Synthesized Circuit

Concatenation & Verilog replication Operators

VHDL. The concatenation operator "&" is an infix operator that combines (concatenates) the bits of the single or multiple bit operands either side of the operator. The operands must be one dimensional.

Verilog. The concatenation operator "{ , }" combines (concatenates) the bits of two or more data objects. These objects may be scaler (single bit) or vectored (multiple bit). Multiple concatenations may be performed with a constant prefix and is known as replication. Replication in this way is not supported in VHDL.

Concatenation & Verilog replication operators

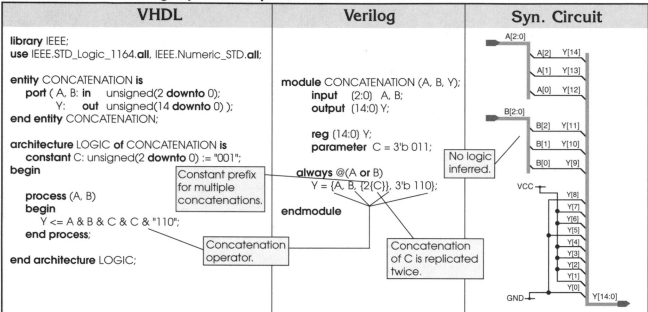

VHDL	Verilog	Syn. Circuit

library IEEE;
use IEEE.STD_Logic_1164.**all**, IEEE.Numeric_STD.**all**;
 	
entity CONCATENATION **is**
  port (A, B: **in**   unsigned(2 **downto** 0);
       Y: **out** unsigned(14 **downto** 0));
end entity CONCATENATION;
 	
architecture LOGIC **of** CONCATENATION **is**
  constant C: unsigned(2 **downto** 0) := "001";
begin
 	
  process (A, B)
  begin
    Y <= A & B & C & C & "110";
  end process;
 	
end architecture LOGIC;
	module CONCATENATION (A, B, Y);
	  input (2:0) A, B;
	  output (14:0) Y;
	
	  reg (14:0) Y;
	  parameter C = 3'b 011;
	
	  always @(A **or** B)
	    Y = {A, B, {2{C}}, 3'b 110};
	
	endmodule	

Reduction Operators (Verilog)

Verilog has six reduction operators, VHDL has none built-in. The operators accept a single vectored (multiple bit) operand, performs the appropriate bit-wise reduction operation on all bits of the operand, and returns a single bit result. For example, the four bits of A are ANDed together to produce Y1. The equivalent of these Verilog operators can be achieved in VHDL by using a **loop** statement as indicated in the model, or by using a function (AND_REDUCE in the VeriBest synthesis tools).

Verilog reduction operators and VHDL coded equivalent

VHDL	Verilog

library IEEE;
use IEEE.STD_Logic_1164.**all**, IEEE.Numeric_STD.**all**;
 	
entity REDUCTION_OPERATORS **is**
  port (A: **in** unsigned(3 **downto** 0);
       Y1, Y2, Y3, Y4, Y5, Y6: **out** std_logic);
end entity REDUCTION_OPERATORS;
 	
architecture LOGIC **of** REDUCTION_OPERATORS **is**
begin
  process (A)
  variable Y1_var, Y2_var, Y3_var, Y4_var,
      Y5_var, Y6_var: std_logic;   *continued*
	module REDUCTION (A, Y1, Y2, Y3, Y4, Y5, Y6);
	  input (3:0) A;
	  output Y1, Y2, Y3, Y4, Y5, Y6;
	
	  reg Y1, Y2, Y3, Y4, Y5, Y6;
	
	  always @(A)
	  begin
	                        continued

Verilog reduction operators and VHDL coded equivalent

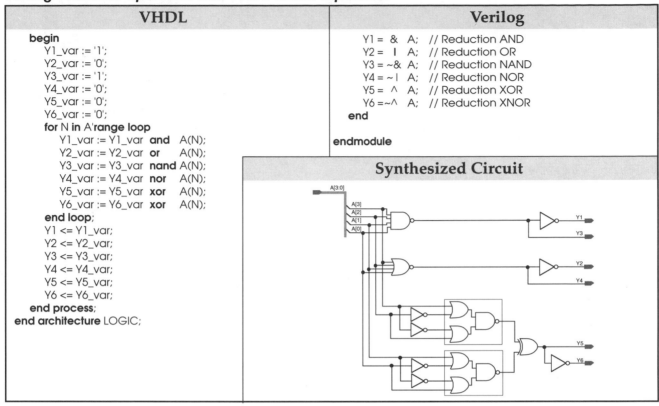

VHDL	Verilog

begin
  Y1_var := '1';
  Y2_var := '0';
  Y3_var := '1';
  Y4_var := '0';
  Y5_var := '0';
  Y6_var := '0';
  for N **in** A'range **loop**
    Y1_var := Y1_var **and** A(N);
    Y2_var := Y2_var **or**   A(N);
    Y3_var := Y3_var **nand** A(N);
    Y4_var := Y4_var **nor** A(N);
    Y5_var := Y5_var **xor** A(N);
    Y6_var := Y6_var **xor** A(N);
  end loop;
  Y1 <= Y1_var;
  Y2 <= Y2_var;
  Y3 <= Y3_var;
  Y4 <= Y4_var;
  Y5 <= Y5_var;
  Y6 <= Y6_var;
  end process;
end architecture LOGIC;
	Y1 = & A; // Reduction AND
	Y2 = I A; // Reduction OR
	Y3 = ~& A; // Reduction NAND
	Y4 = ~I A; // Reduction NOR
	Y5 = ^ A; // Reduction XOR
	Y6 =~^ A; // Reduction XNOR
	end
	
	endmodule

Synthesized Circuit

Conditional Operator (Verilog)

Only Verilog has a conditional operator and consists of the symbols "?" and ":". An expression using the conditional operator evaluates the logical expression before the "?". If the expression is true then the expression before the colon (:) is evaluated and assigned to the output. If the logical expression is false then the expression after the colon is evaluated and assigned to the output. The functionally equivalent VHDL model uses the **if** statement for comparison.

Verilog conditional operator and VHDL coded equivalent

VHDL	Verilog

entity CONDITIONAL **is**
  port (Time: **in**   integer **range** 0 **to** 7;
      Y: **out** integer **range** 0 **to** 7);
end entity CONDITIONAL;
 	
architecture LOGIC **of** CONDITIONAL **is**
begin
  process (Time)
    constant Zero: integer **range** 0 **to** 7 := 0;
    constant TimeOut: integer **range** 0 **to** 7 := 6;
  begin
    if (Time /= TimeOut) **then**
      Y <= Time + 1;
    else
      Y <= Zero;
    end if;
  end process;
end architecture LOGIC;
	module CONDITIONAL (Time, Y);
	  input (2:0) Time;
	  output (2:0) Y;
	
	  reg (2:0) Y;
	  parameter Zero = 3'b 000;
	  parameter TimeOut = 3'b 110;
	
	  always @(Time)
	    Y = (Time != TimeOut) ? Time +1 : Zero;
	
	endmodule
	
	          Two parts to the
	          conditional operator.

Design/modeling Recommendations, Issues and Techniques

Chapter 4 Contents

Introduction

This is an important chapter dealing with design and modeling recommendations, issues and techniques that designers should be aware of, in order to produce good, well structured and efficient models from both a simulation and synthesis view point. They are finite in number and once understood will make modeling more productive and enjoyable.

First, a summary of modeling recommendations is given followed by more detailed issues and techniques.

Design and Modeling Recommendations

1. Design and process recommendations:

- Adopt a top-down design and modeling methodology and bottom-up optimization strategy by hierarchical block.

- Define a design's requirement specification as tightly as practically possible in terms of input, output, associated timing and functionality before writing HDL models. It is very easy to design the "wrong thing right".

- It is good design practice to use global clock and reset signals where possible.

- Consider testability issues early in the total system design process, otherwise synthesis can be a fast and efficient means of producing large amounts of untestable logic. Techniques to consider are boundary scan, internal scan (full or partial) and BIST, for example LFSRs. Full scan is often too expensive in terms of area and possibly timing, therefore a mixture of partial scan and BIST techniques is often the most suitable compromise.

2. Power reduction recommendations:

- Use dynamic power management to:
  a) switch circuits to a low frequency standby mode, when applicable, and wake them up again using interrupts.
  b) disable the clock to inactive parts of a circuit and activate only when needed to process data.
- Use weak drivers on tri-state busses.

3. Design-for-test (DFT) and test issues

- Avoid asynchronous feedback.

- Remove any race conditions.

- Split large counters.

- Use spare pins to aid controllability and observability of internal circuit nodes.

- Make the circuit easy to initialize to a known state.

- Use scan testing where appropriate on register elements that are clocked off the same clock.

- Run fault simulation on areas of the circuit not covered using scan techniques. Examples include gated clocks or possibly an asynchronous interface to a microprocessor.

- Use test vector comparison techniques during simulation to ensure test insertion does not alter the functionality of the design.

- Break the scan chain into several small chains of similar length. Use any spare pins to increase the number of scan chains and reduce their length. This will reduce the number of test vectors and also test cycles on a chip tester. Chip vendors normally base their test costs on the number of clock cycles. Minimizing the length of scan chains will help minimize this cost. If extra pins are not available consider using a pin to put the chip in test mode and multiplex functional input and output pins with test pins to include scan-in and scan-out test functions.

4. Test harness recommendations:

- Use test harnesses only when necessary to verify functional behavior. With experience test harnesses will not be necessary at lower levels of hierarchy.

- Exploit the full richness of constructs in the hardware description language being used.

5. General HDL modeling recommendations

- Before attempting to code a model at the register transfer level, determine a sound architecture and partition accordingly.

- Write HDL code to reflect the architectural partitioning of a design. Partitioning should be sufficiently course grained to allow the synthesis tool sufficient scope to perform efficient logic optimization. A synthesis tool can typically synthesize circuits containing up to 5,000 equivalent gates fairly well. Above 5,000 equivalent gates, the algorithms used by synthesis tools do not always yield such optimal results and can be excessively CPU intensive. More detailed structural partitioning should be achieved using the concurrent statements **process** (VHDL)/**always** (Verilog); this does not mean describing down to the gate level.

- Only include timing in a model when critical at interfacing boundaries. Timing should come from the technology cells mapped to by the synthesis tool.

- While VHDL is a strongly typed language, Verilog is not. This allows the freedom of assigning signals of different width to each other in Verilog. For this reason, be more diligent when using Verilog as Verilog compilers cannot detect unintentional bit width mismatches. If widths do not match in Verilog, either bits are chopped off or extra bits are filled with logic 0s.

- When writing HDL code keep in mind:
    the hardware intent, and
    the synthesis modeling style and its associated restrictions.

- Use subprograms wherever possible to help structure a design making the code shorter and easier to read. A primary advantage of using subprograms is code reuse.

- Make models generic as far as possible for model reuse. This means having parameterizable bit widths.

- Do not repeat identical sections of code in different branches of the same conditional statement; they should be moved out of the conditional expression. Similarly, loop invariant signals should not be contained in a loop. Although this may seem obvious, it is a mistake often made and slows simulation time.

- Be aware that Verilog is case sensitive so identifiers "A" and "a" are different, while VHDL is case insensitive so identifiers "A" and "a" are treated as being the same. Note that, character literals in VHDL, "A" and"a" <u>are</u> different.

- Make use of abstract data types to make models easier to read and maintain. This means using the VHDL enumerated data types and the Verilog `define compiler directives to represent data values. Although Verilog does not allow enumerated data types, use of the `define compiler directive can be very powerful in many different ways, not just for abstract data type values.

- Use meaningful signal names. For active low control signals use <signal_name>_n for a clearer understanding of its functionality and easier debugging, for example, Reset_n would be active when at logic 0.

- Use comments liberally. A header should describe the functionality of the module and each signal declaration should have a comment describing what it does.

6. Ensuring simulation accuracy

- *VHDL & Verilog.* Ensure the sensitivity list of **process** statements (VHDL) and the event list of **always** (Verilog) statements are complete.

7. Improving simulation speed

- *VHDL & Verilog.* Use a **process** (VHDL) or **always** (Verilog) statement in preference to concurrent signal assignments. This reduces the number of signals a simulator must continually monitor for changes and so improves simulation time.

- *VHDL & Verilog.* Design models to minimize the number of signals in the sensitivity list of **process** (VHDL)/**always** (Verilog) statements. Less signals to monitor will improve simulation speed.

- *VHDL & Verilog.* Do not model many small **process** (VHDL)/**always** (Verilog) statements. It takes time to activate and deactivate them. If there are many registers being clocked from the same clock source it is better to put them in one process rather than in separate ones.

- *VHDL.* Do not use the **block** statement in RTL modeling for synthesis. Use a **process** instead. There is no advantage to be gained from using the block statement and is always active during simulation.

- *VHDL.* Convert vectored data types, for example signed and unsigned, to integer data types when convenient to do so.

- *VHDL.* Use variables instead of signals in a **process** wherever possible.

- *VHDL.* Use 'event in preference to 'stable when using objects of type bit; the 'stable attribute looks for a level so is always active during simulation. However, it is better to use the functions, rising_edge and falling_edge, in preference to 'event to detect edge transitions. These functions are defined in the IEEE 1076.3 packages Numeric_Bit and Numeric_STD respectively.

8. Synthesis modeling recommendations

- *VHDL & Verilog.* When modeling purely combinational logic, ensure signals are assigned in every branch of conditional signal assignments.

- *VHDL & Verilog.* For combinational logic from a **case** statement, ensure that either default outputs are assigned immediately before the **case** statement or that the outputs are always assigned regardless of which branch is taken through the **case** statement. This will avoid latches being inferred. The **others** (VHDL) default **case** branch is <u>optional</u> to ensure all branch values are covered. The **default** (Verilog) default **case** branch is <u>essential</u> to ensure all branch values are covered and avoid inferring latches.

- *VHDL & Verilog.* Data objects assigned from within a **for** loop should be assigned a default value immediately before the **for** statement.

- *VHDL.* Use **case** statements in preference to **if** statements containing **else-if** clauses where applicable for efficient synthesized circuits. The **if** statement operates on a priority encoded basis. Unlike VHDL, the Verilog **case** statement is often interpreted by synthesis tools as being priority encoded like the **if** statement.

- *VHDL.* Do not use unbounded integer data types. They default to the maximum range defined by the language which, for IEEE 1076 '93, is 32-bit. This gives the synthesizer more work to do in optimizing away the extra and redundant logic .

- *VHDL.* Standardize on using the IEEE packages STD_Logic_1164 and Numeric_STD as the basic minimum. Use types std_logic for single bit values, and either signed or unsigned for vector array types.

- *VHDL.* Only use 'event for the edge detection of two value object types such as bit and boolean. To use 'event with multi-valued data types, such as std_logic the attribute 'last_value must also be used to detect a true rising edge from logic 0 to 1, and not unknown X to 1 for example. The problem is 'last_value is not supported by synthesis tools.

- *VHDL.* Use parentheses in expressions to provide a finer grain structural control.

- *VHDL.* Use only variable assignments within a **for-loop** statement wherever possible.

- *VHDL.* There is no need to use the **wait** statement to infer flip-flops. The **if** statement can do all that the **wait** statement does and has the added advantage of allowing purely combinational logic and separate sequential logic to be modeled in the same process.

- *Verilog.* Do not attempt to model synchronous logic in a **task**. A **task** can only be called from within a procedural block, which for synthesis means a sequential **begin-end** block. A **begin-end** block can only reside inside an **always** statement which must contain a **posedge** or **negedge** construct in the sensitivity list, in order to model synchronous logic. Because synthesis tools do not support nested edge-triggered constructs, a **task** cannot be used to model synchronous logic.

9. Joint simulation and synthesis modeling recommendations:

- *VHDL & Verilog.* Keep loop invariant assignments outside **for** loop statements, otherwise, models will take longer to simulate and will synthesize unneeded repeated blocks of logic which must then be optimized away by the optimizer.

Simulation Compilation Issues

This section contains simulation compilation issues related only to VHDL because it is a strongly typed language and there are many more issues to discuss. Verilog types are very straight forward and even allow objects of different bit width to be assigned to each other; again, diligence is needed because a Verilog compiler will not detect objects having a different bit width than intended.

1. Output and buffer port modes (VHDL)

Problem. A model containing ports of mode (direction) **out** can only be written to (assigned) within the model itself, they cannot be read as shown by signal Sum in the model below.

```
library IEEE;
use IEEE.STD_LOGIC_1164.all; IEEE.NUMERIC_STD.all;

entity ACCUMULATOR is
    port (Clock, Reset, Enable: in  std_logic;
          Data: in   unsigned(2 downto 0);
          Sum:  out unsigned(5 downto 0));    -- Sum is of type out
end entity ACCUMULATOR;
architecture RTL of ACCUMULATOR is
begin
    process (Clock)
    begin
      if rising_edge(Clock) then
        if (Reset = '1') then
           Sum <= (others <= '0');
        elsif (Enable = '1') then
           Sum <= Sum + ("000" & Data);  -- Error (Sum being read, i.e. on right hand side of expression)
        else
           Sum <= Sum + 1;               -- Error (Sum being read, i.e. on right hand side of expression)
        end if;
      end if;
    end process;
end architecture RTL;
```

Solution. Port signals could be defined to be of mode **buffer**. However, this would lead to problems when used hierarchically as signals of mode **buffer** may only be connected to other port signals of mode **buffer** in a component instantiation. This would mean objects of mode **buffer** would have to be replicated throughout the design hierarchy. This would cause problems at higher levels of hierarchy as local **buffer** ports will need to be connected to ports of mode **out**.

Port signals of type **inout** could be defined, however, this would also lead to problems and confusion throughout the design hierarchy due to their resolution.

The preferred solution is to declare and use an intermediate variable because its value can be read, and then assign their variable directly to a port of mode **out**.

```
process (Clock)
    variable Sum_v: unsigned(5 downto 0);        -- intermediate variable declaration
begin
    if rising_edge(Clock) then
        if (Reset = '1') then
            Sum_v <= (others <= '0');
        elsif (Enable = '1') then
            Sum_v := Sum_v + ("000" & Data);     -- intermediate variable assignment
        else
            Sum_v := Sum_v + 1;                  -- intermediate variable assignment
        end if;
    end if;
    Sum <= Sum_v;
end process;
```

2. Width qualification of unconstrained arrays (VHDL)

Problem. Sometimes the resulting type from an expression cannot be determined from the context from which it is used. Examples are:

- when individual bits are concatenated together to form a **case** statement's choice value.
  ```
  case (A & B & C) is   -- Error, will not analyze
  ```

  The reason this does not analyze is that (A & B & C) is an unconstrained array and the VHDL language states that all arrays must be constrained.

- when literal values are used in overloaded subprogram calls in such a way that it is not clear which subprogram should be used.
  ```
  function FN1 (A: in bit; out integer);
  function FN1 (A: in std_logic; out integer);
  Y <= FN1('1', N);   -- Error, will not analyze
  ```

  The literal ('1') is a value of both type bit and std_logic and so both functions match the parameter profile.

Solution. Qualify an expression with its desired type as shown below, that is, preceed with the type name and a single quote character. Qualification is also useful for type checking and does not imply any type conversion.

```
subtype unsigned_3bit is unsigned(0 to 2);      -- must use "to" and not "downto"
case unsigned_3bit'(A & B & C) is               -- case choice value is qualified
Y <= FN1(unsigned'(1), N);                      -- bit literal is qualified for the function call
```

Notice the type declaration has an increasing range (0 **to** 2) and not a decreasing range (2**downto** 0). This is necessary as a compiler will read a qualified expression from left to right; the use of **downto** will result in an analysis error.

3. Operators to the left of the assignment operator

Problem. Operators cannot be used on the left side of an assignment.

```
ShiftRegA & ShiftRegB <= shift_left((ShiftRegA & ShiftRegB), 1);
```

Solution. Declare an extra variable that will hold the desired expression from the left hand side of the assignment and assign it to this extra variable.

```
variable ShiftRegAB: unsigned(A'left + B'left - 1 downto 0);
ShiftRegA     <= ShiftRegAB(A'left + B'left - 1 downto B'left);
ShiftRegB     <= ShiftRegAB(B'left - 1 downto 0);
ShiftRegAB    <= shift_left(ShiftRegAB, 1);
```

4. Unconstrained subprogram parameters in reusable models (VHDL)

Problem. It is good practice to model subprograms for reuse using unconstrained parameters. However, if a subprogram uses the **others** clause as an aggregate assigned to an object, that is, of an unconstrained array type, compilation will cause an analysis error.

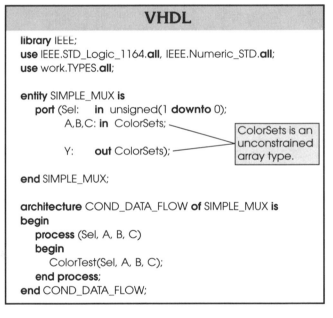

VHDL
| ```
library IEEE;
use IEEE.STD_Logic_1164.all, IEEE.Numeric_STD.all;
package TYPES is
    type RainbowType is (Red, Orange, Yellow, Green, Blue,
                         Indigo, Violet);
    type ColorSets is array (natural range <>) of RainbowType;
    procedure ColorTest (Sel:    in:    unsigned(1 downto 0);
                         A,B,C:  in:    ColorSets;
                         Y:      out    ColorSets);
end package;
package body TYPES is
    procedure ColorTest (Sel:    in:    unsigned(1 downto 0);
                         A,B,C:  in:    ColorSets;
                         Y:      out    ColorSets) is
    begin
        case (Sel) is
            when "00"  => Y <= A;
            when "01"  => Y <= B;
            when "10"  => Y <= C;
            when "11"  => Y <= (others => Red)
                                              [Aggregates not constrained.]

            when others => Y <= (others => Violet)

        end case;
    end procedure ColorTest;
end package body TYPES;
``` |

VHDL
| ```
library IEEE;
use IEEE.STD_Logic_1164.all, IEEE.Numeric_STD.all;
use work.TYPES.all;

entity SIMPLE_MUX is
    port (Sel:    in  unsigned(1 downto 0);
          A,B,C: in  ColorSets;

          Y:      out ColorSets);        [ColorSets is an
                                          unconstrained
                                          array type.]
end SIMPLE_MUX;

architecture COND_DATA_FLOW of SIMPLE_MUX is
begin
    process (Sel, A, B, C)
    begin
        ColorTest(Sel, A, B, C);
    end process;
end COND_DATA_FLOW;
``` |

Solution. Declare a fixed range subtype wherever the subprogram is used (called). It must always have the same name, but will have a different range as desired for its particular use. Use this subtype to qualify the range of the unqualified aggregate in the body of the subprogram itself. Code segments overleaf replace those of the models above.

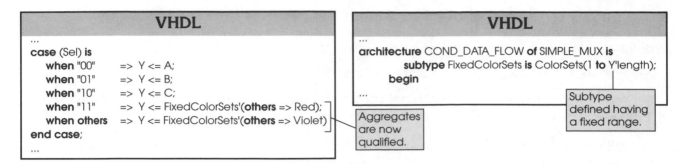

```
VHDL
...
case (Sel) is
    when "00"      => Y <= A;
    when "01"      => Y <= B;
    when "10"      => Y <= C;
    when "11"      => Y <= FixedColorSets'(others => Red);
    when others    => Y <= FixedColorSets'(others => Violet)
end case;
...
```

Aggregates are now qualified.

```
VHDL
...
architecture COND_DATA_FLOW of SIMPLE_MUX is
            subtype FixedColorSets is ColorSets(1 to Y'length);
        begin
...
```

Subtype defined having a fixed range.

5. Invisible subprograms from separate packages (VHDL)

Problem. If two or more subprograms having the same name and parameter type profile are declared in separate packages, they cannot both be given the same scope. In such a case, a compiler would not know which subprogram to use from a subprogram call. The effect of this is that the subprogram name is not directly visible making it appear not to exist.

```
use work.ASIC_cells.all;
use work.FPGA_cells.all;
...
    Y1 <= AND3_OR2(A,B);  -- analysis error (AND3_OR2 defined in both packages)
...
```

Solution. Use a selected name.

```
Y1 <= work.FPGA_cells.AND3_OR2(A,B);
```

6. Subprogram overloading using type integer and subtype natural (VHDL)

Problem. Multiple subprogram declarations which have similar parameter type profiles, that differ only by an integer and natural data type, will not analyze when compiled. This is because type natural is a subtype of type integer and means subprograms are indistinguishable.

```
function to_stdlogicvector(A: integer) return std_logic_vector;
function to_stdlogicvector(A: natural) return std_logic_vector;
```

Solution. Use different named functions to make them distinct.

```
function to_stdlogicvector_int(A: integer) return std_logic_vector;
function to_stdlogicvector_nat(A: natural) return std_logic_vector;
```

7. Concatenation in the expression of a subprogram's formal list (VHDL)

Problem. The concatenation operator (&) can be used in the expression for the inputs of a subprogram call's parameter list. However, it cannot be used for output and bidirectional parameters.

```
-- subprogram declaration
procedure ALU1(A,B: unsigned(31 downto 0);
                Y: unsigned(31 downto 0));
...
-- illegal procedure call
ALU1(DataBus1_16bit & DataBus2_16bit,
    DataBus3_16bit & DataBus4_16bit,
    ResultBus1_16bit & ResultBus2_16bit);  -- error (output concatenation)
```

Solution. Perform the concatenation inside the body of the procedure.

Simulation Run Time Issues

This section covers modeling issues affecting simulation results only. A separate section covers modeling issues affecting both simulation and synthesis results.

1. Full sensitivity/event list (VHDL & Verilog)

A *sensitivity list* is a list of signals in a VHDL **process** statement that a simulator monitors for changes. If a change occurs, in one or more of these signals, then the **process** will be executed. Similarly an *event list* is a list of signals in a Verilog **always** statement that a simulator monitors for changes. If the **process** or **always** statement infers only flip-flop(s) with associated combinational logic on their input or output there is no need to include all input signals in the sensitivity/event list. Only the clock signal and any asynchronous reset is needed. On the other hand, if only combinational logic is being modeled then <u>all</u> input signals to the **process**/**always** statement <u>must</u> be included in the sensitivity/event list.

Problem. A signal is inadvertently omitted from the sensitivity list. This will not affect the synthesized circuit at all, but may yield unexpected and misleading simulation results. The reason for this is that the **process** or **always** statement will not always be triggered into being executed, so assignments within the **process** or **always** statement will not be updated. In the code below D is missing from the sensitivity/event list.

```
VHDL:
    process (Sel, A, B, C)
    begin
        if (Sel = '1') then
            Y <= (A and B) or (C and D);
        end if;
    end process;
```

```
Verilog:
    always @(Sel or A or B or C)
    begin
        if (Sel)
            Y = A + B;
        else
            Y = C + D;
    end
```

Solution. Ensure all signals are included in the sensitivity list when modeling combinational logic.

```
VHDL:
    process (Sel, A, B, C, D)
```

```
Verilog:
    always @(Sel or A or B or C or D)
```

2. Reversing a vectored array direction (VHDL & Verilog)

Problem. If an object is declared in one direction and assigned in the opposite direction the bits will be reversed and connected accordingly. This will not give simulation or synthesis compilation errors, but simulation results may be different than expected and lead to unnecessary confusion.

```
VHDL:
    entity REVERSE_RANGE is
        port (A,B: in unsigned(7 downto 0);
    end entity REVERSE_RANGE;

    architecture LOGIC of REVERSE_RANGE is
    begin
        Y <= A and B;  -- Y(0) is A(7) ANDed with B(7)
    end LOGIC;
```

```
Verilog:
    module REVERSE_RANGE (A, B, Y);
        input    (7:0) A, B;
        output  (0:7) Y;
        reg (0:7) Y;



        assign Y = A & B;  // Y(0) is A(7) ANDed with B(7)
    endmodule
```

Solution. Standardize on using vector arrays defined with a descending range and finishing at bit 0 wherever possible. This will avoid the possibility of trying to access bits of an array that do not exist. Also, objects and slices of objects can be assigned with ease.

3. True leading edge detection - wait and if (VHDL)

Problem. The edge detection of a data object whose type has more than two values must detect the current <u>and</u> previous value in order to detect a true '0' to '1' transition and not, for example, an 'X' to '1'. If this is not the case, the model will not simulate correctly. In the code below a transition from any of the other 8 values of std_logic to '1' would be considered a rising edge.

```
-- Enable is of type std_logic {U, X, 0, 1, Z, W, L, H, -}
process (Enable, A, B, C, D)
begin
    wait until (Clock = '1');        -- wait causes the execution of the whole process to halt.
    if (Enable = '1') then           -- Its execution is resumed when the wait expression becomes true.
        Y <= (A and B) or (C and D);
    end if;
end process;

-- Clock is of type std_logic {U, X, 0, 1, Z, W, L, H, -}
process (Clock)
begin
    if (Clock'event and Clock = '1') then
        Y <= (A and B) or (C and D);
    end if;
end process;
```

Solution. The model should contain an additional check to ensure that the clock signal really did transition from '0' to '1' and not from some other value to '1', for example, 'X' to '1'.

```
wait until (Clock = '1' and Clock'last_value = '0');
```

```
if (Clock'event and Clock = '1' and Clock'last_value = '0') then
```

Note that this solves a simulation problem, but the attribute 'last_value is not supported for synthesis. For this reason, functions rising_edge or falling_edge should be used from the IEEE 1076.3 synthesis package Numeric_STD, as is the case throughout this book.

4. Order dependency of concurrent statements

Problem. The order of concurrent statements in VHDL or Verilog never affects how a synthesizer synthesizes a circuit. However, it can effect simulation results as demonstrated by the following two **process** statements in VHDL and two **always** statements in Verilog. This problem rarely arises in VHDL due to the concept of simulation delta delays which are intended to make the order in which all current statements are executed irrelevant. However, order dependency of **process** statements can be an issue when using shared variables as shown. The problem for both the VHDL and Verilog model is that when a rising edge occurs on Clock (VHDL shared variable or Verilog register type), Y1 is assigned a value in the first concurrent statement CONCURRENT_1, but is also used in the second, CONCURRENT_2. If CONCURRENT_1 is executed first by a simulator, then the simulation results will <u>not</u> match that of the synthesized circuit. If CONCURRENT_2 is executed first then they <u>will</u> match that of the synthesized circuit. However, there is no guarantee in which order the concurrent statements will be executed by a simulator, as is the intent. This is a more common problem in Verilog as there is no concept of simulation delta delays.

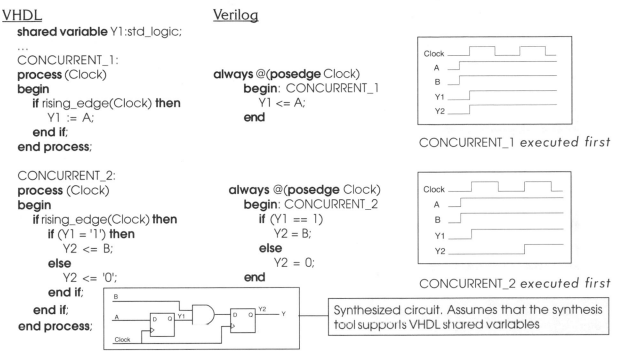

<u>VHDL</u>

```
shared variable Y1:std_logic;
...
CONCURRENT_1:
process (Clock)
begin
    if rising_edge(Clock) then
        Y1 := A;
    end if;
end process;

CONCURRENT_2:
process (Clock)
begin
    if rising_edge(Clock) then
        if (Y1 = '1') then
            Y2 <= B;
        else
            Y2 <= '0';
        end if;
    end if;
end process;
```

<u>Verilog</u>

```
always @(posedge Clock)
    begin: CONCURRENT_1
        Y1 <= A;
    end


always @(posedge Clock)
    begin: CONCURRENT_2
        if (Y1 == 1)
            Y2 = B;
        else
            Y2 = 0;
    end
```

CONCURRENT_1 *executed first*

CONCURRENT_2 *executed first*

Synthesized circuit. Assumes that the synthesis tool supports VHDL shared variables

Solution. <u>VHDL</u>: Do not use shared variables in models that are to be synthesized. The problem model above would work fine if Y1 was changed from a shared variable to a signal. The **process** statements may be more conveniently combined as shown below, although this is not necessary provide Y1 is a signal. <u>Verilog</u>: The **always** statements must be combined as shown so that the sequential order in which Y1 and Y2 are assigned is controlled during simulation. The synthesized circuit is the same.

<u>VHDL</u>

```
ALL_IN_ONE:
process (Clock)
begin
    if rising_edge(Clock) then
        if (Y1 = '1') then
            Y2 <= B;
        else
            Y2 <= '0';
        end if;
        Y1 <= A;
    end if;
end process;
```

<u>Verilog</u>

```
always @(posedge Clock)
    begin: ALL_IN_ONE
        if (Y1 == 1)
            Y2 <= B;
        else
            Y2 <= 0;
        Y1 <= A;
    end
```

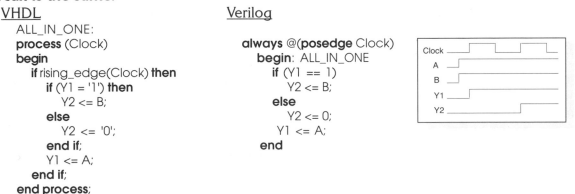

Synthesis Compilation Issues

1. Non-static data objects and non-static loops (VHDL & Verilog)

All multiple bit data objects must have a statically determinable number of bits at synthesis compile time. (Data objects are VHDL signals or variables, or Verilog variables.) Also, all **for** loop statements must also have a statically determinable range at synthesis compile time. If either of these conditions are not statically determinable, a synthesis tool does not know how much logic to synthesize and an appropriate error message will be returned. This is not a problem for simulation. Example 4.1 shows a non-statically determinable slice, while Example 4.2 shows a non-statically determinable loop.

Example 4.1. Non-Static Slice

The slice of signal A and constant AllOnes, that is R **downto** 0, is variable at compile time because R may be any integer value between 0 and 15.

Non-static slice - not synthesizable

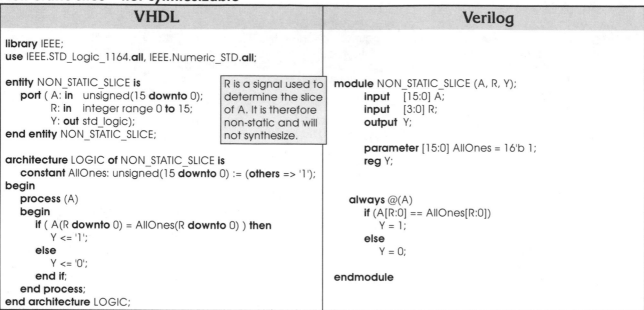

VHDL	Verilog

library IEEE;
use IEEE.STD_Logic_1164.**all**, IEEE.Numeric_STD.**all**;
 	
entity NON_STATIC_SLICE **is**
   port (A: **in** unsigned(15 **downto** 0);
        R: **in** integer range 0 **to** 15;
        Y: **out** std_logic);
end entity NON_STATIC_SLICE;
 	
architecture LOGIC of NON_STATIC_SLICE **is**
   constant AllOnes: unsigned(15 **downto** 0) := (**others** => '1');
begin
   process (A)
   begin
      if (A(R **downto** 0) = AllOnes(R **downto** 0)) **then**
        Y <= '1';
      else
        Y <= '0';
      end if;
   end process;
end architecture LOGIC;
 	
[annotation: R is a signal used to determine the slice of A. It is therefore non-static and will not synthesize.]
	module NON_STATIC_SLICE (A, R, Y);
	   input [15:0] A;
	   input [3:0] R;
	   output Y;
	
	   parameter [15:0] AllOnes = 16'b 1;
	   reg Y;
	
	   always @(A)
	      if (A[R:0] == AllOnes[R:0])
	        Y = 1;
	      else
	        Y = 0;
	
	endmodule

Example 4.2. Non-Static Loop

Input R is of type integer ranged between 0 and 7. The value of R is used as a **loop** variable which determines the number of bits of inputs A and B should be ANDed together. As R is not determinable at compile time, a synthesis tool cannot determine how many corresponding bits of A and B to logically AND together.

Non-static slice - not synthesizable

VHDL	Verilog

library IEEE;
use IEEE.STD_Logic_1164.**all**, IEEE.Numeric_STD.**all**;
 	
entity NON_STATIC_LOOP **is**
   port (A, B:**in** unsigned(7 **downto** 0);
        R: **in** integer **range** 0 **to** 7;
        Y: **out** unsigned(7 **downto** 0));
end entity NON_STATIC_LOOP;
 	
architecture LOGIC of NON_STATIC_LOOP **is**
begin
   process (A)
      variable R_Var: integer **range** 0 **to** 7;
   begin
      Y <= (**others** => '0');
      R_Var := R;
      for N in 0 **to** R_Var **loop**
        Y(N) <= A(N) **and** B(N);
      end loop;
   end process;
end architecture LOGIC;
 	
[annotation: R_Var is non-static.]
	module NON_STATIC_LOOP (A, B, R, Y);
	   input [7:0] A, B;
	   input [2:0] R;
	   output [7:0] Y;
	
	   reg [7:0] Y;
	   integer N;
	
	   always @(A)
	      begin
	        Y = 8'b 0;
	        for (N = 0; N < R; N = N + 1)
	           Y[N] = A[N] & B[N];
	      end
	
	endmodule
	
	[annotation: R is non-static.]

Joint Simulation and Synthesis Issues

This section covers issues affecting both simulation and synthesis results.

1. When to use others (VHDL) and default (Verilog)

It is important to know when and how to use the **others** clause (VHDL) and **default** clause (Verilog); they can affect simulation results and synthesized circuits greatly. They define a default branch condition in multi-way branch statements which for VHDL means a **case** statement or selected signal assignment, and for Verilog just a **case** statement. When to use these clauses in the two languages is similar, but there are subtle differences and are described separately below.

There are many examples throughout this book showing use of the **others** and **default** clauses; the description below references specific examples.

a) Others clause in a VHDL case statement.

The VHDL Language Reference Manual (LRM), states that a **case** statement must have each value of the base type of the expression represented once, and only once, in the set of choices, and that no other value is allowed. This means, if a designer does not want to explicitly define every choice value, then it is necessary to always use a "**when others** => ..." type statement. If modeling combinational logic, and do not want to explicitly specify every **case** branch condition, use for example:

    when others => Y <= "000000";   (See Example 6.9 - binary decoder)

Or use the following statement with assigned "don't care" output values, provided the **case** expression is of a type that includes a "don't care" value, for example, signed or unsigned. This has the advantage of minimizing inferred combinational logic.

    when others => Y <= "XXX"; -- X = don't care   (See Example 6.6 - binary encoder)

If it is necessary to automatically infer latches from a **case** statement, and hold the last output value defined in one of the explicitly defined choice values, the **null** default branch condition could be used, for example,

    when others => Y <= **null**;   (See Examples 7.5 and 7.6)

The **null** construct means "do nothing", Y is not updated and a latch is inferred provided all choice values have not been explicitly defined in the **case** statement. Note that by using a **case** statement and not an **if** statement to infer a latch or latches, the latch enable signal is implied by the model and does not explicitly exist in the model. This is not recommended.

If a **case** statement resides in a synchronous part of code inferring flip-flops, either of the above three branch conditions can be used; the assigned output from a **case** statement will be held regardless.

b) Others clause in a VHDL selected signal assignment

The VHDL selected signal assignment is very similar to the **case** statement; in fact the LRM states that a selected signal assignment must have an exact equivalent **case** statement. This means, all the above conditions for using the **others** clause in a **case** statement apply equally to a selected signal assignment. A selected signal assignment is a concurrent statement residing outside a process, while the **case** statement is a sequential statement that must reside inside a **process** statement. The examples referenced above for **case** statements also have equivalent models using selected signal assignments.

<u>c) The **default** clause in a Verilog **case** statement</u>

The Verilog **case** statement uses the **default** clause to define a default branch for a choice **case** expression, much like the **others** clause does in VHDL. The difference in Verilog is that all case choice values do not need to have a branch defined in order to be Verilog LRM compliant. However, when modeling combinational logic, and all **case** expression choice values have already been explicitly defined, it is still necessary to use a **default** clause to define a branch, which assigns an output value, to avoid inferring a latch. There is one exception to this, and that is if an output signal assignment is included immediately before the **case** statement, see Example 8.2 FSM2_GOOD1. For example, by defining the output to be at logic 0 before the **case** statement, there is no need to assign it in all the other branches when the required output is to be at logic 0.

For Verilog LRM compliance a **case** statement need not have a branch for each choice value. However, a good coding standard should be used and do the same as in VHDL, that is, define a branch for each **case** expression value once, and only once, either explicitly, or implicitly using the **default** clause.

Example **default** clauses corresponding to the VHDL **others** clause above, are shown below.

Define a default output value, for example

   default: Y = 6'b 0;   (See Example 6.9 - binary decoder)

Define a don't care default output value, and minimize inferred combinational logic, for example

   default: Y = 3'b X;   (See Example 6.6 - binary encoder)

The **null** clause in VHDL is the same as the semi colon (;) in Verilog. The following **default** statement, therefore, says "do nothing - output not assigned" for the default choice value, and can be used to infer latches.

   default: ;   (See Examples 7.5 and 7.6)

2. Signal and Variable Assignments (VHDL)

There are four kinds of data objects in VHDL; signal, variable, constant and file. Only signals, variables and constants are relevant for synthesis. Signals may be considered synthesized directly in hardware, that is, they have hardware intent and are always associated with one or more drivers; each driver holds the signal's projected waveform of values. Variables and constants provide containers for values used in the computation of signal values.

The important points to remember about variables and signals are:

1) variables are updated immediately, that is, before any delta delay in which the assignment is executed. There is no concept of delta delays for variables.
2) signal assignments cause an event to be scheduled in a future cycle. This cycle could be the second, third, fourth etc. delta delay in the same simulation time unit or at some scheduled simulation time in the future.

Signal assignments can explicitly specify a zero delay, or, as is normally the case, a delay is not specified, for example,

```
Y <= A after 0 ns;
Y <= A;  -- (0 ns assumed by default)
```

The signal driver does not update the signal value until at least one delta delay after the assignment was evaluated by the simulator within the current simulation time step. If a signal assignment contains a delay value of more than zero, for example,

```
Y <= A after 2 ns;
```

then the event is scheduled to occur at the appropriate time step in the future.

The delta delay and signal updating during simulation (VHDL)

During simulation, the scheduling and assigning of signals at each simulation cycle, a delay period known as a simulation *delta*. When a signal's predicted value matures the driver holding that value becomes the active value. This activity will cause the following to occur in order.

1. All driver contributions to a signal are resolved to a single value. This identifies what drives that particular signal if there is more than one driver. Signals and ports will be updated immediately with new values or will retain their old value.
2. The effect of changed signal values are propagated from the port signals down through the circuit network.
3. Signal events for which a **process** is sensitive will cause the **process** to be triggered into being executed. This means signals and variables within a **process** may also be updated and is dependent upon the path taken through the sequential statements within the **process**.

Example 4.3 shows scheduled signal assignments during simulation. Example 4.4 shows both signal assignments scheduled during simulation. Example 4.5 shows the effect of modeling combinational and synchronous logic using signals and variables.

Note: The number of deltas needed to compute the new signal's current value might be different in the pre and post synthesis models, especially when resources like adders and multiplexers are shared. Sometimes statements that are executed in one delta in the RTL model have to be executed in two different deltas when simulating the synthesized gate level model.

Signals & variables in loops (VHDL)

Both signal and variable assignments are acceptable within a VHDL loop. However, it is better to use only variable assignments because; 1) simulation will be faster and 2) the resulting synthesized circuit is more easily predicted, see Example 4.6.

Example 4.3. Signal assignments and delta delay iterations (VHDL)

The coded order of successive signal assignments does not matter whether they are: 1) concurrent or 2) sequential assignments within a **process** in the branch of an **if** or **case** statement. All signal assignments will be scheduled and updated as necessary. Note, this assumes the process sensitivity is complete. Figure 4.1 shows that three delta delay cycles are needed for all signals to become stable. There are two assignments, that is, two drivers to the signal Y2. This means the synthesis tool must be guided as to how to synthesize the desired wired logic. For example, it could be implemented as a wired tri-state, wired AND or wired OR. The synthesized circuit shows a wired OR.

Signal assignments requiring 3 simulation delta delay iterators

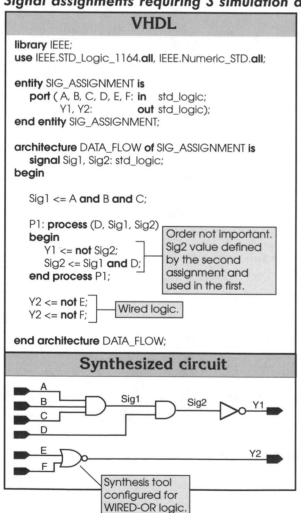

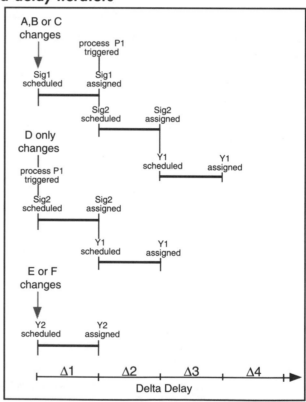

Figure 4.1 Three simulation delta iterations needed for all signals to become stable

Example 4.4 Variable assignments and delta delay iterations (VHDL)

In this example variable assignments are included within a **process**. The first assignment is an assignment to variable Var1, while the third assignment is the second variable assignment to Var2 and uses Var1 in its expression. For synthesis, it would not matter if the assignments to Var1 and Var2 were swapped over, that is,

Var2 := Var1 **and** D; ⎤ *Variable assignments*
Y1 <= **not** Var2; ⎥ *swapped over*
Var1 := A **and** B **and** C; ⎦

as there is no conflict and the synthesis tool is able to correctly interpret their values in the computation of signal Y1. However, this is not recommended as it <u>does</u> matter for simulation. A simulator will assign values to both variables in the sequential order in which they appear in the code prior to any simulator delta delay. There is no concept of a delta cycle for variables. This means Var1 is old when used in the equation for the assignment of Y1. The postiion of the signal assignment to signal Y1 can appear anywhere in the model because it will be scheduled to be updated in the first delta cycle of the simulator, that is, after the variables have been assigned values.

The ordering effect of variables is shown again by the two successive variable assignments to the same variable Var3. This time the order is important for simulation and synthesis. The second variable assignment overrides the first and provides the computed value that is assigned to the signal Y2. The synthesized circuit therefore leaves input E unconnected.

Variable and signal assignments

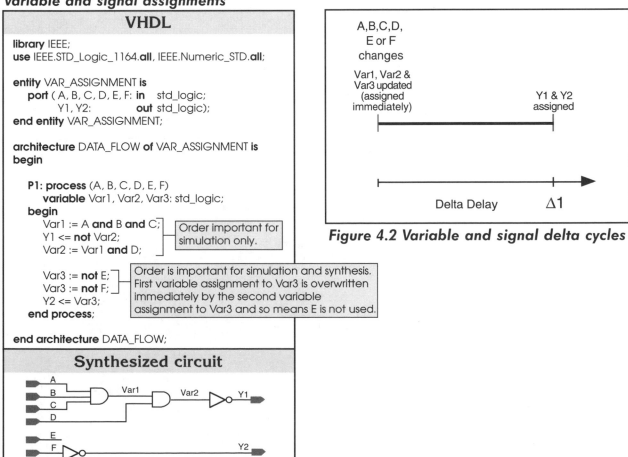

Figure 4.2 Variable and signal delta cycles

Example 4.5 Signal and variable assignments (VHDL)

Four process statements show the effect of modeling combinational and synchronous logic using signals and variables. The model is similar to Example 4.7 showing Verilog blocking and non-blocking procedural assignments. Assignments to a variable always occur instantaneously, that is, they cannot be scheduled to occur at some simulation time in the future. However, a variable does holds its value over simulation time steps. A variable assignment containing an **after** clause will yield syntax errors. The four processes included in this example are:

1. VARIABLE_COMB   - Combinational logic using a variable.
2. SIGNAL_COMB   - Combinational logic using only signals.
3. VARIABLE_SYNCH - Synchronous logic using a variable.
4. SIGNAL_SYNCH   - Synchronous logic using only signals.

Signal and varaiable assignments

Notice one flip-flop is synthesized from the single signal assignment in the third process (VARIABLE_SYNCH), while two flip-flops are synthesized from the two signal assignments in the fourth process (SIGNAL_SYNCH). Signals M2 and M4 are local to their respective processes to reduce simulation time.

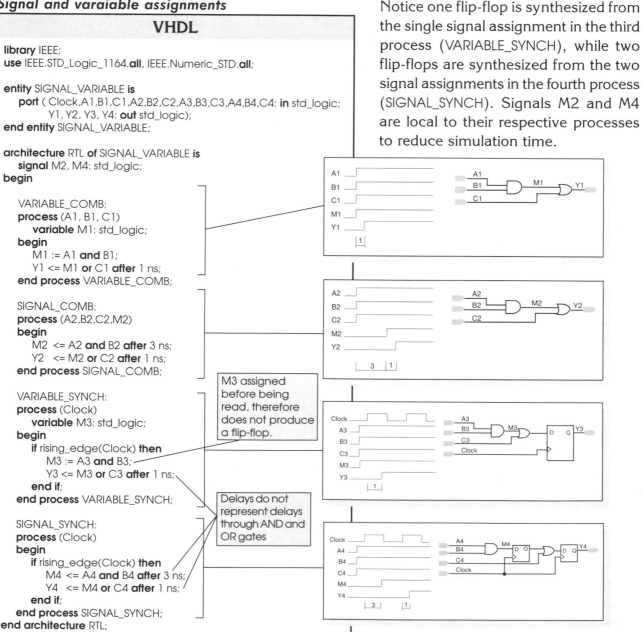

```
                         VHDL

library IEEE;
use IEEE.STD_Logic_1164.all, IEEE.Numeric_STD.all;

entity SIGNAL_VARIABLE is
    port ( Clock,A1,B1,C1,A2,B2,C2,A3,B3,C3,A4,B4,C4: in std_logic;
           Y1, Y2, Y3, Y4: out std_logic);
end entity SIGNAL_VARIABLE;

architecture RTL of SIGNAL_VARIABLE is
    signal M2, M4: std_logic;
begin

    VARIABLE_COMB:
    process (A1, B1, C1)
        variable M1: std_logic;
    begin
        M1 := A1 and B1;
        Y1 <= M1 or C1 after 1 ns;
    end process VARIABLE_COMB;

    SIGNAL_COMB:
    process (A2,B2,C2,M2)
    begin
        M2 <= A2 and B2 after 3 ns;
        Y2 <= M2 or C2 after 1 ns;
    end process SIGNAL_COMB;

    VARIABLE_SYNCH:
    process (Clock)
        variable M3: std_logic;
    begin
        if rising_edge(Clock) then
            M3 := A3 and B3;
            Y3 <= M3 or C3 after 1 ns;
        end if;
    end process VARIABLE_SYNCH;

    SIGNAL_SYNCH:
    process (Clock)
    begin
        if rising_edge(Clock) then
            M4 <= A4 and B4 after 3 ns;
            Y4 <= M4 or C4 after 1 ns;
        end if;
    end process SIGNAL_SYNCH;
end architecture RTL;
```

M3 assigned before being read, therefore does not produce a flip-flop.

Delays do not represent delays through AND and OR gates

Example 4.6 Signal and variable assignments in a for loop (VHDL)

This example demonstrates the effect of using **signal** or **variable** assignments in a **for** loop when modeling synchronous logic. The intended model is of a simple shift register feeding a separate buffering output register, but this is not always the case.

First process statement (VARIABLE_FOR)

The first **process** uses a **for loop** containing a variable assignment to shift the bits of the intended shift register, PipeA. An important note to remember is that under an edge triggered section of code, a variable infers one or more flip-flops if the variable is read (in this example the right hand side of an expression) before it is assigned, and that a signal assignment will always infer one or more flip-flops. Depending upon whether the loop is ascending or descending they unroll as follows.

PipeA(1) := PipeA(0);	— Variable PipeA(0) read before assigned - flip-flop inferred.	
	— Variable PipeA(1) assigned before read - no flip-flop inferred.	Ascending
PipeA(2) := PipeA(1);	— Variable PipeA(2) assigned before read - no flip-flop inferred.	
PipeA(3) := PipeA(2);	— Variable PipeA(3) assigned and not read - no flip-flop inferred.	
PipeA(0) := Data;		
YA <= PipeA;	— signal assignment - 4 flip-flops inferred.	

	PipeA(3) := PipeA(2);	— Variable PipeA(2) read before assigned - flip-flop inferred.
		— Variable PipeA(3) assigned before read - no flip-flop inferred.
Descending	PipeA(2) := PipeA(1);	— Variable PipeA(1) read before assigned - flip-flop inferred.
	PipeA(1) := PipeA(0);	— Variable PipeA(0) read before assigned - flip-flop inferred.
	PipeA(0) := Data;	
	YA := Pipea(0);	— signal assignment - 4 flip-flops inferred.

Signals and variables in a for loop

```
                    VHDL

library IEEE;
use IEEE.STD_Logic_1164.all, IEEE.Numeric_STD.all;

entity SIGNAL_VARIABLE_FORLOOP is
    port ( Clock, Data:  in   std_logic;
           YA, YB:       out unsigned(3 downto 0));
end entity SIGNAL_VARIABLE_FORLOOP;

architecture RTL of SIGNAL_VARIABLE_FORLOOP is
    signal PipeB: unsigned(3 downto 0);
begin
    VARIABLE_FOR:
    process (Clock)
        variable PipeA: unsigned(3 downto 0);
    begin
        if rising_edge(Clock) then
            -- for N in 1 to 3 loop    -- ascending range
            for N in 3 downto 1 loop   -- descending range
                PipeA(N) := PipeA(N - 1);
            end loop;
            PipeA(0) := Data;
            YA <= PipeA;
        end if;
    end process;

    SIGNAL_FOR:
    process (Clock)
    begin
        if rising_edge(Clock) then
            for N in 3 downto 1 loop
                PipeB(N) <= PipeB(N - 1);
            end loop;
            PipeB(0) <= Data;
            YB <= PipeB;
        end if;
    end process;
end architecture RTL;
```

Second **process** statement (SIGNAL_FOR)

In this statement the **for**-loop uses signal assignments that when unrolled are executed concurrently after a positive edge clock. This means a descending range (3 **downto** 1) or an ascending range (1 **to** 3) makes no difference, a shift register is inferred as intended, followed by the buffer register.

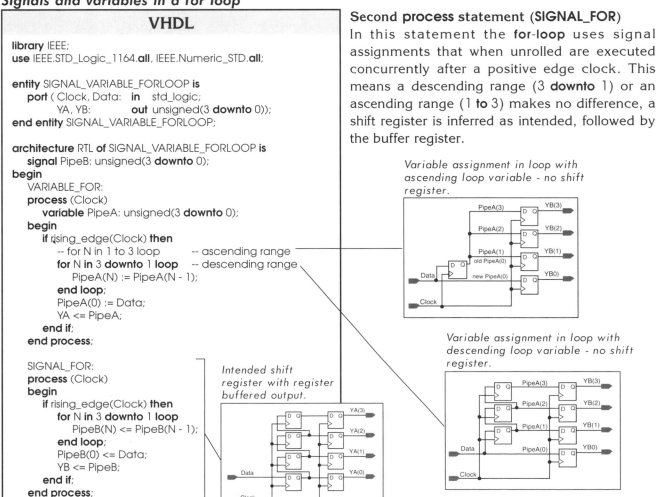

Variable assignment in loop with ascending loop variable - no shift register.

Variable assignment in loop with descending loop variable - no shift register.

Intended shift register with register buffered output.

3. Blocking and non-blocking procedural assignments (Verilog)

There are two types of procedural assignment in Verilog, blocking and non-blocking. Depending on which are used in a sequential procedural block, that is, between reserved words **begin** and **end**, simulation and synthesis results may be different. This is demonstrated in Example 4.7.

Blocking procedural Assignments

A blocking procedural assignment must be executed before the procedural flow can pass to the subsequent statement. This means that any timing delay associated with such statements is related to the time at which the previous statements in the particular procedural block are executed. Successive blocking procedural assignments in an edge triggered **always** statement do <u>not</u> infer successive stages of synchronous logic (flip-flops); they act like a VHDL variable.

Non-Blocking procedural Assignments

A non-blocking procedural assignment is scheduled to occur without blocking the procedural flow to subsequent statements. This means the timing in an assignment is relative to the absolute time at which the procedural block was triggered into being executed. As synthesis tools ignore all timing from the model, and non-blocking signal assignments are scheduled to occur at the same time, successive assignments in an edge triggered **always** statement <u>will</u> each infer synchronous logic (flip-flops).

Example 4.7 Blocking and non-blocking procedural assignments (Verilog)

The model in this example contains blocking and non-blocking procedural assignments with timing in sequential procedural blocks. Each block belongs to an **always** statement and infers either combinational logic, or combinational and sequential logic. The simulated waveform and synthesized circuit is shown for each of the four sequential **always** blocks. Timing delays for the two edge triggered **always** statements are unrealistic for the circuit being modeled, but serve to demonstrate blocking and non-blocking assignments with delays.

Blocking and non-blocking signal assignments

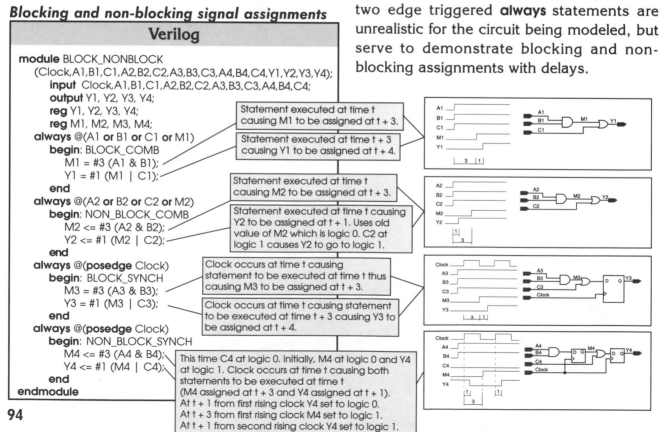

```
module BLOCK_NONBLOCK
   (Clock,A1,B1,C1,A2,B2,C2,A3,B3,C3,A4,B4,C4,Y1,Y2,Y3,Y4);
   input  Clock,A1,B1,C1,A2,B2,C2,A3,B3,C3,A4,B4,C4;
   output Y1, Y2, Y3, Y4;
   reg Y1, Y2, Y3, Y4;
   reg M1, M2, M3, M4;
   always @(A1 or B1 or C1 or M1)
      begin: BLOCK_COMB
         M1 = #3 (A1 & B1);
         Y1 = #1 (M1 | C1);
      end
   always @(A2 or B2 or C2 or M2)
      begin: NON_BLOCK_COMB
         M2 <= #3 (A2 & B2);
         Y2 <= #1 (M2 | C2);
      end
   always @(posedge Clock)
      begin: BLOCK_SYNCH
         M3 = #3 (A3 & B3);
         Y3 = #1 (M3 | C3);
      end
   always @(posedge Clock)
      begin: NON_BLOCK_SYNCH
         M4 <= #3 (A4 & B4);
         Y4 <= #1 (M4 | C4);
      end
endmodule
```

Statement executed at time t causing M1 to be assigned at t + 3.

Statement executed at time t + 3 causing Y1 to be assigned at t + 4.

Statement executed at time t causing M2 to be assigned at t + 3.

Statement executed at time t causing Y2 to be assigned at t + 1. Uses old value of M2 which is logic 0. C2 at logic 1 causes Y2 to go to logic 1.

Clock occurs at time t causing statement to be executed at time t thus causing M3 to be assigned at t + 3.

Clock occurs at time t causing statement to be executed at time t + 3 causing Y3 to be assigned at t + 4.

This time C4 at logic 0. Initially, M4 at logic 0 and Y4 at logic 1. Clock occurs at time t causing both statements to be executed at time t (M4 assigned at t + 3 and Y4 assigned at t + 1). At t + 1 from first rising clock Y4 set to logic 0. At t + 3 from first rising clock M4 set to logic 1. At t + 1 from second rising clock Y4 set to logic 1.

Example 4.8 Blocking and non-blocking assignments in a for loop (Verilog)

This example reveals the effect of using blocking and non-blocking procedural assignments in an edge triggered **always** statement containing a **for** loop. The intended model is of a simple shift register feeding a separate buffering output register (without using ">>" and "<<" operators), but this is not always the case.

First **always** statement (BLOCKING_FOR)

The first **always** statement uses a **for** loop containing a blocking procedural assignment to shift the bits of the intended shift register, PipeA. An important note to remember is that under an edge triggered **always** statement, a blocking procedural assignment infers one or more flip-flops if the variable is read (in this example the right hand side of an expression) before it is assigned, and that a nonblocking procedural assignment will always infer one or more flip-flops. Depending upon whether the loop is ascending or descending they unroll as follows.

PipeA(1) := PipeA(0);	— Blocking assignment PipeA(0) read before assigned - 1 flip-flop inferred.	
	— Blocking assignment PipeA(1) assigned before read - no flip-flop inferred.	Ascending
PipeA(2) := PipeA(1);	— Blocking assignment PipeA(2) assigned before read - no flip-flop inferred.	
PipeA(3) := PipeA(2);	— Blocking assignment PipeA(3) assigned and not read - no flip-flop inferred.	
PipeA(0) := Data;		
YA <= PipeA;	— Nonblocking assignment - 4 flip-flops inferred.	

	PipeA(3) := PipeA(2);	— Blocking assignment PipeA(2) read before assigned - 1 flip-flop inferred.
		— Blocking assignment PipeA(3) assigned before read - no flip-flop inferred.
Descending	PipeA(2) := PipeA(1);	— Blocking assignment PipeA(1) read before assigned - 1 flip-flop inferred.
	PipeA(1) := PipeA(0);	— Blocking assignment PipeA(0) read before assigned - 1 flip-flop inferred.
	PipeA(0) := Data;	
	YA := Pipea(0);	— Nonblocking assignment - 4 flip-flops inferred.

Second **always** statement (NON_BLOCKING_FOR)

The **for** loop in the second sequential **always** block uses non-blocking procedural assignments that, when unrolled, are executed concurrently after a positive edge clock. This means it makes no difference whether the loop range is descending (N = 3; N >= 1; N = N - 1) or ascending (N = 1; N <= 3; N = N + 1), a shift register is inferred as intended, followed by the buffer register.

Blocking and non-blocking statement in a for loop

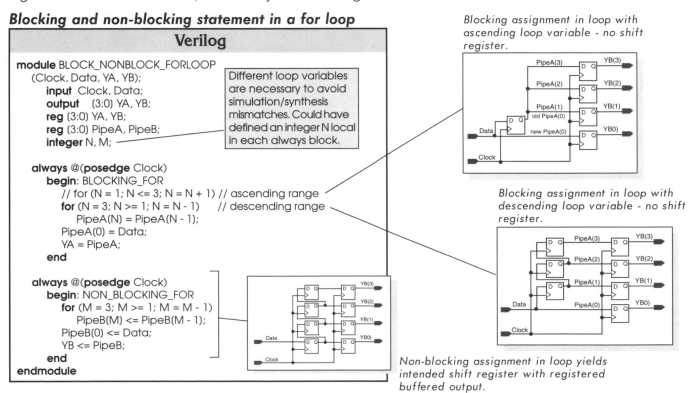

```
module BLOCK_NONBLOCK_FORLOOP
    (Clock, Data, YA, YB);
    input  Clock, Data;
    output    (3:0) YA, YB;
    reg (3:0) YA, YB;
    reg (3:0) PipeA, PipeB;
    integer N, M;

    always @(posedge Clock)
        begin: BLOCKING_FOR
        // for (N = 1; N <= 3; N = N + 1) // ascending range
        for (N = 3; N >= 1; N = N - 1)      // descending range
            PipeA(N) = PipeA(N - 1);
        PipeA(0) = Data;
        YA = PipeA;
        end

    always @(posedge Clock)
        begin: NON_BLOCKING_FOR
        for (M = 3; M >= 1; M = M - 1)
            PipeB(M) <= PipeB(M - 1);
        PipeB(0) <= Data;
        YB <= PipeB;
        end
endmodule
```

Different loop variables are necessary to avoid simulation/synthesis mismatches. Could have defined an integer N local in each always block.

Blocking assignment in loop with ascending loop variable - no shift register.

Blocking assignment in loop with descending loop variable - no shift register.

Non-blocking assignment in loop yields intended shift register with registered buffered output.

4. "Don't Care" inputs to a case statement (VHDL & Verilog)

Both VHDL and Verilog support "don't care" input values to a **case** statement when specifying branch conditions.

VHDL

The data type std_logic has a value, '-' to represent "don't care" conditions. However, the values of std_logic (U, X, 0, 1, Z, W, L, H and -) are just an enumeration. This means simulators and synthesizers treat '-' as a logic value and not a true "don't care" in terms of logic reduction. The following attempt of modeling a leading '1' priority encoder demonstrates this effect.

```
case A is                        -- A is of type unsigned.
    when "1---"  => Y <= 3;      -- "Don't Care" inputs do not typically yield
    when "01--"  => Y <= 2;      -- an efficiently synthesized circuit.
    when "001-"  => Y <= 1;
    when others  => Y <= 0;
end case;
```

The circuit must be modeled differently to synthesize a priority encoder circuit. The **case** statement above, is shown remodeled in three different ways below. The first method uses an **if** statement. It is the better method as the code is straight forward and does not produce excessive amounts of initial synthesized logic that must then be optimized away by the optimizer. The second method works fine, but an optimizer will typically have more redundant logic to remove. This problem becomes more acute for larger bit width inputs. The third method tests each bit in turn, just like the first **if** statement, but maintains a **case** statement mentality by nesting multiple **case** statements. Nesting **case** statements in this way is clumsy and not recommended.

```
-- A is of type unsigned
if (A(3) = '1') then
    Y <= 3;
elsif (A(3 downto 2) = "01") then
    Y <= 2;
elsif (A(3 downto 1) = "001") then
    Y <= 1;
else
    Y <= 0;
end if;
```

```
-- A is of type integer
case A is
    when 8 to 16  => Y <= 3;
    when 4 to 7   => Y <= 2;
    when 2 to 3   => Y <= 1;
    when others   => Y <= 0;
end case;
```

```
-- A is of type unsigned
case A(3) is
    when '1' => Y <= 3;
    when '0' =>
        case A(2) is
            when '1' => Y <= 2;
            when '0' =>
                case A(1) is
                    when '1'   => Y <= 1;
                    when others => Y <= 0;
                end case;
            when others => Y <= 0;
        end case;
    when others => Y <= 0;
end case;
```

Verilog

There are three types of Verilog case statement; **case**, **casex** and **casez** . The **case** statement does not allow case branch conditions to be specified that contain "don't care" values. The other two case statements, **casex** and **casez**, are intended to be used with "don't care" input branch values specified, and must be represented in either binary or hexadecimal format. The difference between **casex** and **casez** is that **casex** allows "X", "?" or "Z" to represent a "don't care" input value, while **casez** allows just "?" or "Z" to be used. For this reason there is no need to ever use **casez**. Do not use "Z" with **casex** or **casez** as it can easily be confused with a high impedance value.

```
casex (A)
    // X, ? or Z = don't care input
    4'b 1XXX : Y = 3;
    4'b 01XX : Y = 2;
    4'b 001X : Y = 1;
    default :  Y = 0;
endcase
```

```
casez (A)
    // ? or Z = don't care input
    4'b 1??? : Y = 3;
    4'b 01?? : Y = 2;
    4'b 001? : Y = 1;
    default :   Y = 0;
endcase
```

Don't cares in the case expression or case item expression are ignored for the comparison.

5. "Don't care" output values from a case statement (VHDL & Verilog)

By using "don't care" output values wisely, synthesis tools are typically able to make the decision as to whether they should be a logic 0 or logic 1 in order to minimize logic.

Example 4.9 Effect of "don't care" output values

Two **case** statements are modeled in this example. The first assigns values to Y1 and does not use a "don't care" default condition, but has a default of logic 0 value assigned. The second **case** statement assigns values to Y2 and is functionally the same as the first, but this time the Verilog model does use a "don't care" default condition. The Karnaugh maps, Figure 4.3, indicates the benefit exploited by a synthesis tool when "don't care" conditions are used.

The VHDL version of the model uses the std_logic data type which has a "don't care" value (-). However this is a "don't care" in terms of a simulation logic value and not a "don't care" in terms of logic reduction. The VHDL input to synthesis tools typically do not support "don't care" values as good as Verilog input. Only the Verilog model in this example uses a logic reduction "don't care".

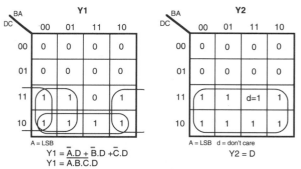

$Y1 = \overline{A}.D + \overline{B}.D + \overline{C}.D$
$Y1 = \overline{A.B.C.D}$

$Y2 = D$

Figure 4.3 Effect of "don't care" output values

Case statement with or without a "don't care" output

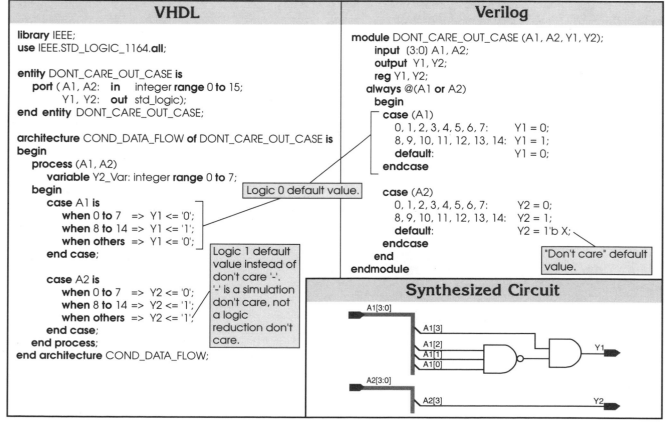

VHDL	Verilog

library IEEE;
use IEEE.STD_LOGIC_1164.**all**;
 	
entity DONT_CARE_OUT_CASE **is**
   port (A1, A2: **in**   integer **range** 0 **to** 15;
         Y1, Y2: **out** std_logic);
end entity DONT_CARE_OUT_CASE;
 	
architecture COND_DATA_FLOW **of** DONT_CARE_OUT_CASE **is**
begin
   process (A1, A2)
      variable Y2_Var: integer **range** 0 **to** 7;
   begin
      case A1 **is**
         when 0 **to** 7 => Y1 <= '0';
         when 8 **to** 14 => Y1 <= '1';
         when others => Y1 <= '0';
      end case;
 	
      case A2 **is**
         when 0 **to** 7 => Y2 <= '0';
         when 8 **to** 14 => Y2 <= '1';
         when others => Y2 <= '1';
      end case;
   end process;
end architecture COND_DATA_FLOW;
	module DONT_CARE_OUT_CASE (A1, A2, Y1, Y2);
	   input (3:0) A1, A2;
	   output Y1, Y2;
	   reg Y1, Y2;
	   always @(A1 **or** A2)
	   begin
	      case (A1)
	         0, 1, 2, 3, 4, 5, 6, 7: Y1 = 0;
	         8, 9, 10, 11, 12, 13, 14: Y1 = 1;
	         default: Y1 = 0;
	      endcase
	
	      case (A2)
	         0, 1, 2, 3, 4, 5, 6, 7: Y2 = 0;
	         8, 9, 10, 11, 12, 13, 14: Y2 = 1;
	         default: Y2 = 1'b X;
	      endcase
	   end
	endmodule

Logic 0 default value.

Logic 1 default value instead of don't care '-'. '-' is a simulation don't care, not a logic reduction don't care.

"Don't care" default value.

Synthesized Circuit

6. Comparing Vector Array Types of Different Width (VHDL)

The expression in an **if** statement compares the values of multiple pairs of data objects. Each comparison returns a boolean TRUE or FALSE depending upon whether the comparison is true or not. The types being compared need not be of the same type. As a 7-bit unsigned data type object is not the same as an 8-bit unsigned data type object, their comparison always returns a FALSE condition as defined by the VHDL LRM, see the following example.

Example 4.10 Comparing vectors of different width return a boolean FALSE

The **if** expression contains the comparison (S1 = S2). Signal S1 is a four bit value while S2 is a three bit value and so a boolean FALSE is always returned. Similarly the comparison (S5 = "11") is comparing a value with a two bit value and also always returns a boolean FALSE. Signals S3 and S4 are the same so the comparison (S3 = S4) is fine, but because it is being ANDed with the result of (S5 = "11"), which is always FALSE, the returned value from ((S3 = S4) **and** (S5 = "11")) will always be FALSE. Therefore, the complete **if** expression, that is, ((S1 = S2) **or** ((S3 = S4) **and** (S5 = "11"))), will always be FALSE and means the synthesized circuit will contain no logic and B will be permanently connected to Y.

Multiple compares in an if statement

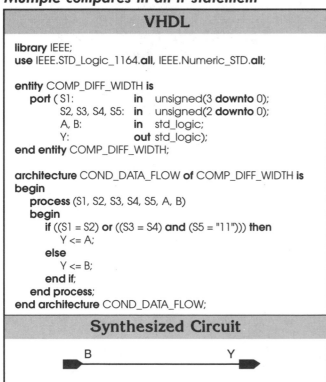

```
                          VHDL
library IEEE;
use IEEE.STD_Logic_1164.all, IEEE.Numeric_STD.all;

entity COMP_DIFF_WIDTH is
    port ( S1:              in   unsigned(3 downto 0);
           S2, S3, S4, S5:  in   unsigned(2 downto 0);
           A, B:            in   std_logic;
           Y:               out  std_logic);
end entity COMP_DIFF_WIDTH;

architecture COND_DATA_FLOW of COMP_DIFF_WIDTH is
begin
    process (S1, S2, S3, S4, S5, A, B)
    begin
       if ((S1 = S2) or ((S3 = S4) and (S5 = "11"))) then
          Y <= A;
       else
          Y <= B;
       end if;
    end process;
end architecture COND_DATA_FLOW;
```

Synthesized Circuit

B ————————————→ Y

General Modeling Issues

1. Using Attributes (VHDL)

All attributes predefined by the VHDL language are listed in Appendix A. Not all attributes make sense or are needed for models that are to be synthesized; attributes typically supported by synthesis tools are shown in Table 4.1. Attributes not supported by synthesis tools either relate to timing or are not necessary to model the physical structure of logic. There is no concept of attributes in Verilog.

The syntax when using a VHDL attribute is

        object'attribute

User-defined constant attributes are allowed in VHDL, but are not supported by synthesis tools.

Examples 4.11, 4.12 and 4.13 show models using type, array and signal related attributes respectively, that are typically supported by synthesis tools.

Attribute	Kind	Prefix	Returned result type	Returned result
<u>Type related</u>				
T'base	type	any type or subtype	base type of T	
T'left	value	any scalar type or subtype T	same type as T	left bound of T
T'right	value	any scalar type or subtype T	same type as T	right bound of T
T'high	value	any scalar type or subtype T	same type as T	upper bound of T
T'low	value	any scalar type or subtype T	same type as T	lower bound of T
<u>Array related</u>				
A'range[(N)]	range	any array object A	type of the Nth index of A	range A'left(N) to A'right(N) if A ascending or A'left(N) downto A'right(N) if A is descending.
A'reverse_ range[(N)]	range	any array object A	type of the Nth index of A	range A'right(N) downto A'left(N) if A ascending for the Nth index. A'right(N) downto A'left(N) if A is descending.
A'length[(N)]	range	any array object A	universal integer	number of values in the Nth index range of N.
<u>Signal related</u>				
S'stable	signal	any signal S	boolean	TRUE when event not occured, otherwise FALSE
S'event	function	any signal S	boolean	TRUE when an event has occured, otherwise FALSE

Table 4.1. VHDL Predefined attributes generally supported by synthesis tools

Example 4.11 Type related VHDL attributes - 'base, 'left, 'right, 'high and 'low

The first **process** uses predefined VHDL attributes 'left, 'right, 'high and 'low . Attribute 'left returns the left bound of signals A or B while attribute 'right returns the right bound of signals A or B. Attributes 'high and 'low return the upper and lower bounds of signals A or B regardless of whether their range is declared using **to** or **downto**.

The second **process** uses the 'base attribute. One enumerated data type, RainbowType, and two enumerated subtypes of RainbowType, that is, LowMidRangeColorType and MidRangeColorType are defined in a separate package. The two subtypes are of the base type RainbowType. The range for the **for** loop uses type MidRangeColorType, however, because the 'base attribute is used the actual range is of the base type RainbowType, that is, Red to Violet.

Use of type related attributes

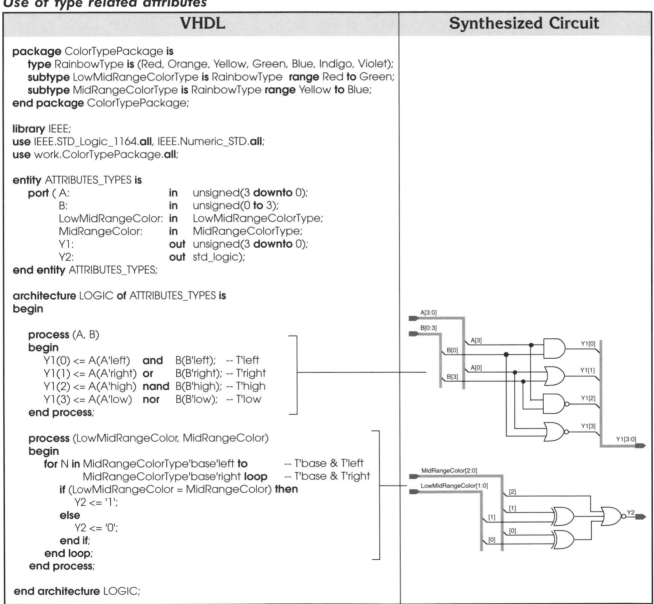

VHDL	Synthesized Circuit
| ```
package ColorTypePackage is
    type RainbowType is (Red, Orange, Yellow, Green, Blue, Indigo, Violet);
    subtype LowMidRangeColorType is RainbowType range Red to Green;
    subtype MidRangeColorType is RainbowType range Yellow to Blue;
end package ColorTypePackage;

library IEEE;
use IEEE.STD_Logic_1164.all, IEEE.Numeric_STD.all;
use work.ColorTypePackage.all;

entity ATTRIBUTES_TYPES is
    port ( A:                 in   unsigned(3 downto 0);
           B:                 in   unsigned(0 to 3);
           LowMidRangeColor:  in   LowMidRangeColorType;
           MidRangeColor:     in   MidRangeColorType;
           Y1:                out  unsigned(3 downto 0);
           Y2:                out  std_logic);
end entity ATTRIBUTES_TYPES;

architecture LOGIC of ATTRIBUTES_TYPES is
begin

    process (A, B)
    begin
        Y1(0) <= A(A'left)   and   B(B'left);  -- T'left
        Y1(1) <= A(A'right)  or    B(B'right); -- T'right
        Y1(2) <= A(A'high)   nand  B(B'high);  -- T'high
        Y1(3) <= A(A'low)    nor   B(B'low);   -- T'low
    end process;

    process (LowMidRangeColor, MidRangeColor)
    begin
        for N in MidRangeColorType'base'left to          -- T'base & T'left
                 MidRangeColorType'base'right loop        -- T'base & T'right
            if (LowMidRangeColor = MidRangeColor) then
                Y2 <= '1';
            else
                Y2 <= '0';
            end if;
        end loop;
    end process;

end architecture LOGIC;
``` | |
```

Example 4.12 Array related VHDL attributes - 'range, 'reverse_range and 'length

This model uses two generics Width1 and Width2 which make it generic for different bit width bus signals. This particular model is configurable in that it will synthesize to one of two different types of circuit depending upon whether the value of Width1 and Width2 are the same or not. The 'length attribute is used to determine if the value of Width1 and Width2 are the same, that is signals A and B are of the same width. If they are the same, then the model will synthesize to a circuit that counts the number bits of A and B that are of the same value. The 'range attribute is used to provide the loop variables in the **for** loop; the result is output on signal Y. The first synthesized circuit shows the case when Width1 = Width2 = 6.

If Width1 and Width2 do not have the same value, a completely different circuit is synthesized; in this case a priority encoder. It uses the 'reverse_range attribute in a **for** loop so that it starts from the most significant bit and counts down. By doing this the **exit** statement is used to exit the loop when the first most significant bit having a value of logic 1 is found. The advantage of modeling in this way is a slightly improved simulation speed. The synthesized circuit shows the case when Width1 = 6 and Width2 = 7, that is, a 6-3 priority encoder.

Use of array related attributes

```vhdl
VHDL

library IEEE;
use IEEE.STD_Logic_1164.all, IEEE.Numeric_STD.all;

entity ATTRIBUTES_ARRAY is
    generic (Width1, Width2: natural);
    port ( A:    in    unsigned(Width1 - 1 downto 0);
           B:    in    unsigned(Width2 - 1 downto 0);
           Valid: out  std_logic;
           Y:     out  unsigned(3 downto 0));
end entity ATTRIBUTES_ARRAY;

architecture LOGIC of ATTRIBUTES_ARRAY is
begin
    process (A, B)
        variable Y_var: unsigned(3 downto 0);
    begin
        -- Number of equivalent bits in A and B
        if (A'length = B'length) then    -- A'length
            Valid <=1;
            Y_var := "0000";
            for N in A'range loop        -- A'range          ── See Circuit A.
                if (A(N) = B(N)) then
                    Y_var := Y_var + 1;
                else
                    Y_var := Y_var;
                end if;
            end loop;
        else
            -- priority encode of A
            Valid <= '0';
            Y_var := "XXXX";
            for N in A'reverse_range loop  -- A'reverse_range
                if (A(N) = '1') then
                    Y_var := to_unsigned(N,4);       ── See Circuit B.
                    Valid <= '1';
                    exit;
                end if;
            end loop;
        end if;
        Y <= Y_var;
    end process;
end architecture LOGIC;
```

Use of array related attributes

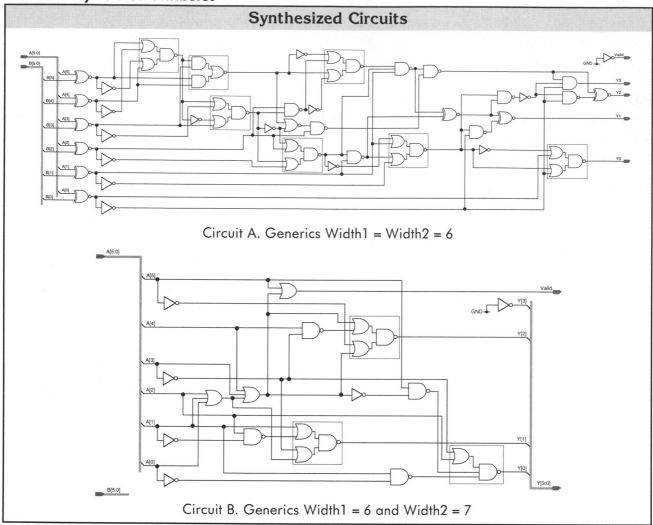

Synthesized Circuits

Circuit A. Generics Width1 = Width2 = 6

Circuit B. Generics Width1 = 6 and Width2 = 7

Example 4.13 Signal related VHDL attributes - 'stable and 'event

Attribute 'stable. The S'stable(T) attribute returns a boolean true when signal S has not had an event for time T. Time T is ignored for synthesis. Although the 'stable attribute is usually supported by synthesis tools as shown in this example, there is no advantage in using it and will slow simulation time so its use is not recommended.

Attribute 'event. The S'event attribute returns a boolean true if an event has occurred in the current simulation time. The model shows the detection of a rising edge by detecting the occurrence of an event, and that its new value is a logic 1. Notice that the clock signals are of type bit which has two possible values 0 or 1 and so a rising edge is correctly detected, that is, an event has occurred and the new value is at logic 1. However, if the clock was of type std_logic, it is not enough to detect the occurrence of an event and that the new value is a logic 1. Type std_logic has nine possible values {U, X, 0, 1, Z, W, L, H, -} and the signal could be changing from any one of the other eight state values to logic 1. The model would still synthesize correctly, but may not simulate correctly. For this reason, functions rising_edge and falling_ edge from the IEEE 1164 package STD_Logic_1164, should be used, as is the case in most examples in this book.

Use of signal related attributes

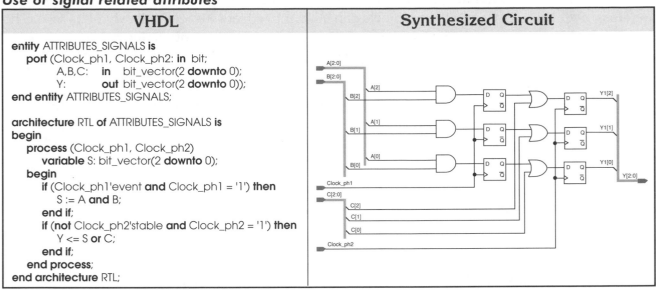

VHDL	Synthesized Circuit
| ```
entity ATTRIBUTES_SIGNALS is
    port (Clock_ph1, Clock_ph2: in  bit;
        A,B,C:    in    bit_vector(2 downto 0);
        Y:        out  bit_vector(2 downto 0));
end entity ATTRIBUTES_SIGNALS;

architecture RTL of ATTRIBUTES_SIGNALS is
begin
    process (Clock_ph1, Clock_ph2)
        variable S: bit_vector(2 downto 0);
    begin
        if (Clock_ph1'event and Clock_ph1 = '1') then
            S := A and B;
        end if;
        if (not Clock_ph2'stable and Clock_ph2 = '1') then
            Y <= S or C;
        end if;
    end process;
end architecture RTL;
``` | |

2. Using Packages (VHDL)

Packages in VHDL provide a means of storing precompiled and verified design code for use by other design units as discussed in Chapter 3. Type and subprogram declarations are typical of the generic code placed in packages, so that they can be made available on an as needed basis, across multiple designs and multiple projects. Using already proven and precompiled subprograms provides a powerful means of enabling designers to build hardware models quicker, more efficiently and at a higher level of abstraction. A model containing subprogram calls to subprograms in such a package has the following advantages:

- the design time is shortened,
- the model's structure is improved,
- the coded model is often shorter and easier to read,
- the model is easier to debug.

Packages are made accessible to particular models with the **library** and **use** clauses; see Examples 4.14 and 4.15. The **library** clause will make a particular library visible and the **use** clause will make a particular package within a library visible.

A package consists of two distinct parts; the **package** declaration and the **package body** declaration. These two parts are known as primary and secondary library units, respectively; see Figure 4.4. The syntax for the **package** and **package body** is shown in Appendix A and indicates the kind of declarations that are allowed. Typical declarations supported by synthesis tools are also shown in Figure 4.4.

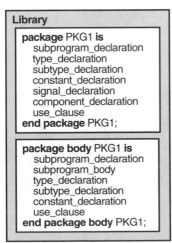

```
Library
    package PKG1 is
        subprogram_declaration
        type_declaration
        subtype_declaration
        constant_declaration
        signal_declaration
        component_declaration
        use_clause
    end package PKG1;

    package body PKG1 is
        subprogram_declaration
        subprogram_body
        type_declaration
        subtype_declaration
        constant_declaration
        use_clause
    end package body PKG1;
```

*Figure 4.4
Typical package declarations supported by synthesis tools*

VHDL design models are usually compiled into the default working library called work. However, packages may be compiled into this work library or a completely new library defined by the user. Typically, all common design data that relates specifically to one project might
```

be compiled into the default library called work. Common design data that is intended to be generally available across multiple projects can be compiled into a specific library of its own. The standard VHDL packages defined by the IEEE will be precompiled into a library called "IEEE" by the EDA tool vendor. The two IEEE packages used throughout this book are STD_Logic_1164 and Numeric_STD.

A **package body** is optional and is always associated with a **package** of the same name. It is needed for the declaration of the bodies of subprograms and the value of any deferred constants. The **package body** may be hidden from the users of a **package** with only their interfaces being made visible in the **package**.

Example 4.14 Data types defined in a package

The **package** DATA_TYPES, defines only **types** and **subtypes** and so a corresponding **package body** is not needed. If this package was compiled into the default library called work, then the following **use** clause before the **entity** statement would make all the types visible inside the particular design unit.

        use work.data_types.**all**;

Notice the package declaration uses the name DATA_TYPES in capitals, while the **use** clause uses data_types in lower case. This does not matter as VHDL is case insensitive. If the package was compiled into a library called Project1, then the **library** clause is also needed, that is,

        library Project1;
        use Project1.data_types.**all**;

The VHDL reserved word **all** means make all declarations in the package visible. This is the norm, however, it could be replaced with the name of a particular declaration if required, for example,

        use Project1.data_types.MyLogic;

In this case only the type MyLogic would be visible.

Various types defined in a package

```
                    VHDL
library IEEE;
use IEEE.STD_Logic_1164.all, IEEE.Numeric_STD.all;

package DATA_TYPES is

    type MyLogic is ('1', '0', Unknown, TirState);

    type PrimeColor is (Red, Green, Blue);
    type Rainbow is (Red, Orange, Yellow, Green, Blue, Indigo, Violet);
    subtype MidRangeColor is Rainbow range Yellow to Blue;
    subtype HexLetters is character range 'A' to 'F';
    type MicroCode_Ops is (StoreA, StoreB, Load, IncAccA, IncAccB,
                           ShiftLeft, ShiftRight);

    type R1 is record
        I: integer range 0 to 7;
        J: unsigned(1 downto 0);
    end record;

    type FloatPointType is
        record
            Sign: std_logic;
            Exponent: unsigned(0 to 6);
            Fraction: unsigned(24 downto 1);
        end record;

end package DATA_TYPES;
```

3. Operator and subprogram overloading (VHDL)

Operator and subprogram overloading is one of the most useful features in VHDL. They allow either language operators or user defined subprograms to operate on operands of different data types.

Operator overloading. Operators are overloaded by defining a function whose name is the same as the operator itself. Because the operator and function name are the same, the function name must be enclosed within double quotes to distinguish it from the actual VHDL operator. Calls to overloaded operators can use either the standard infix operator notation with operands either side of the operator, or a function call notation by enclosing the operator in double quotes followed by the operand list in brackets. Example 4.15. shows the "+" operator overloaded and calls to it using both these methods.

Subprogram overloading. Multiple functions and procedures (subprograms) of the same name can be defined, but have inputs and outputs that have different data types. A subprogram call will use the correct subprogram based on, 1) a match of its declared name and, 2) a match of the base types of the objects used in the subprogram call, to the base type of the declared parameters in the subprogram declaration. Example 4.17. shows two functions and two procedures all with the same name defined in a package, and a model that calls each of them.

Example 4.15 Overloaded "+" operator

The plus (+) operator is overloaded, that is, a function called "+" is declared with its name enclosed in double quotes ("+") to distinguish it from the operator itself. The function is declared in a package, as is normally the case, so that it is globally accessible from any design unit wishing to make a call to it. The function is defined to accept two record type operands and return an operand of the same record type. The record contains two fields of different type. The first field is a 16 value integer type having values from 0 to 15, while the second is a 4-bit array of type unsigned. The operation of the overloaded "+" function is to add the two integer fields from the two operands and add the two unsigned values from the two operands.

The model OVERLOADED_OPERATOR_CALLS contains four plus operators as described below.

> *First "+" operator.* Has operands of type integer so uses the standard "+" infix operator defined by the VHDL language.

> *Second "+" operator.* Has operands of type unsigned and uses the overloaded "+" infix operator function defined in the IEEE 1076.3 synthesis package, Numeric_STD.

> *Third "+" operator.* Has operands of type int_unsi, as defined in the package shown, and uses the overloaded "+" infix operator function defined in this package.

> *Fourth "+" operator.* Calls the same overloaded "+" operator as the third "+" operator; the difference being that it uses the more unusual function call notation and so is known as a prefix operator.

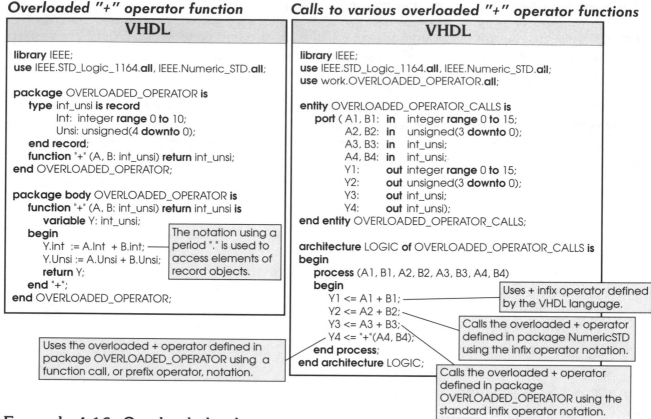

Overloaded "+" operator function

VHDL

```
library IEEE;
use IEEE.STD_Logic_1164.all, IEEE.Numeric_STD.all;

package OVERLOADED_OPERATOR is
    type int_unsi is record
        Int:  integer range 0 to 10;
        Unsi: unsigned(4 downto 0);
    end record;
    function "+" (A, B: int_unsi) return int_unsi;
end OVERLOADED_OPERATOR;

package body OVERLOADED_OPERATOR is
    function "+" (A, B: int_unsi) return int_unsi is
        variable Y: int_unsi;
    begin
        Y.int  := A.Int  + B.int;
        Y.Unsi := A.Unsi + B.Unsi;
        return Y;
    end "+";
end OVERLOADED_OPERATOR;
```

> The notation using a period "." is used to access elements of record objects.

> Uses the overloaded + operator defined in package OVERLOADED_OPERATOR using a function call, or prefix operator, notation.

Calls to various overloaded "+" operator functions

VHDL

```
library IEEE;
use IEEE.STD_Logic_1164.all, IEEE.Numeric_STD.all;
use work.OVERLOADED_OPERATOR.all;

entity OVERLOADED_OPERATOR_CALLS is
    port ( A1, B1:  in   integer range 0 to 15;
           A2, B2:  in   unsigned(3 downto 0);
           A3, B3:  in   int_unsi;
           A4, B4:  in   int_unsi;
           Y1:      out  integer range 0 to 15;
           Y2:      out  unsigned(3 downto 0);
           Y3:      out  int_unsi;
           Y4:      out  int_unsi);
end entity OVERLOADED_OPERATOR_CALLS;

architecture LOGIC of OVERLOADED_OPERATOR_CALLS is
begin
    process (A1, B1, A2, B2, A3, B3, A4, B4)
    begin
        Y1 <= A1 + B1;
        Y2 <= A2 + B2;
        Y3 <= A3 + B3;
        Y4 <= "+"(A4, B4);
    end process;
end architecture LOGIC;
```

> Uses + infix operator defined by the VHDL language.

> Calls the overloaded + operator defined in package NumericSTD using the infix operator notation.

> Calls the overloaded + operator defined in package OVERLOADED_OPERATOR using the standard infix operator notation.

Example 4.16 Overloaded subprogram

This example demonstrates the use of overloaded subprograms. There are two packages. The first, COLOR_TYPES, defines four enumerated data types and does not need a package body. A second package, OVERLOADED_SUBPROGS, contains four subprograms all with the same name MixColor and are hence overloaded. Two of the subprograms are procedures while the other two are functions. The package declaration declares the four subprograms while the package body contains their corresponding functional bodies. Each subprogram performs the same logical operation, that is, they mix colors. There is a **procedure** and **function** for mixing the three primary light colors and there is another **procedure** and **function** that mixes the three primary pigment colors as indicated by Figure 4.5.

When a subprogram call is made to MixColor the correct body is called by virtue of it being either a procedure or function call and by virtue of matching the data types supplied.

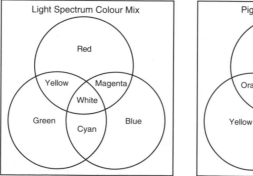
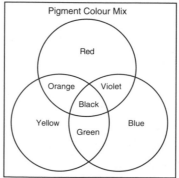

Figure 4.5 Light spectrum and pigment color mix

Two VHDL packages declaring overloaded subprograms

VHDL

```vhdl
package COLOR_TYPES is
    type SpectrumPrimeColor is (Red, Green, Blue);
    type SpectrumSecColor   is (Yellow, Magenta, Cyan);
    type PigmentPrimeColor  is (Red, Yellow, Blue);
    type PigmentSecColor    is (Orange, Violet, Green);
end package COLOR_TYPES;
```

> Red and Blue are overloaded enumerated literals.

```vhdl
use work.COLOR_TYPES.all;
package OVERLOADED_SUBPROGS is
    procedure MixColor (signal C1,C2: in  SpectrumPrimeColor;
                        signal Mix:   out SpectrumSecColor);
    procedure MixColor (signal C1,C2: in  PigmentPrimeColor;
                        signal Mix:   out PigmentSecColor);
    function MixColor (C1, C2: SpectrumPrimeColor)
                return SpectrumSecColor;
    function MixColor (C1, C2: PigmentPrimeColor)
                return PigmentSecColor;
end OVERLOADED_SUBPROGS;


package body OVERLOADED_SUBPROGS is

    procedure MixColor
        (signal C1, C2: in  SpectrumPrimeColor;
         signal Mix: out SpectrumSecColor) is
    begin
        if    (C1=Red and C2=Green) then  Mix <= Yellow;
        elsif (C1=Red and C2=Blue) then   Mix <= Magenta;
        else                              Mix <= Cyan;
                -- (C1=Green and C2=Blue)
        end if;
    end MixColor;


    function MixColor (C1, C2: SpectrumPrimeColor)
                        return SpectrumSecColor is
        variable Mix: SpectrumSecColor;
    begin
        if    (C1=Red and C2=Green) then  Mix := Yellow;
        elsif (C1=Red and C2=Blue) then Mix := Magenta;
        else      Mix := Cyan; -- (C1=Green and C2=Blue)
        end if;
        return Mix;
    end function MixColor;


    procedure MixColor
        (signal C1, C2: in  PigmentPrimeColor;
            signal Mix:   out PigmentSecColor) is
    begin
        if    (C1=Red and C2=Yellow) then   Mix <= Orange;
        elsif (C1=Red and C2=Blue) then Mix <= Violet;
        else      Mix <= Green; -- (C1=Yellow and C2=Blue)
        end if;
    end procedure MixColor;


    function MixColor (C1, C2: PigmentPrimeColor) return
PigmentSecColor is
        variable Mix: PigmentSecColor;
    begin
        if    (C1=Red and C2=Yellow) then   Mix := Orange;
        elsif (C1=Red and C2=Blue) then Mix := Violet;
        else      Mix := Green; -- (C1=Yellow and C2=Blue)
        end if;
        return Mix;
    end function MixColor;
end package body OVERLOADED_SUBPROGS;
```

Concurrent and sequential procedure and function calls

VHDL

```vhdl
library IEEE;
use IEEE.STD_Logic_1164.all;
use work.COLOR_TYPES.all;
use work.OVERLOADED_SUBPROGS.all;

entity CALL_OVERLOADED_SUBPROGS is
    port ( Clock, En:  in  std_logic;
           A1,B1:  in  SpectrumPrimeColor;
           A2,B2:  in  SpectrumPrimeColor;
           A3,B3:  in  PigmentPrimeColor;
           A4,B4:  in  PigmentPrimeColor;
           Y1,Y2:  out SpectrumSecColor;
           Y3,Y4:  out PigmentSecColor);
end entity CALL_OVERLOADED_SUBPROGS;

architecture LOGIC of CALL_OVERLOADED_SUBPROGS is
begin

    MixColor(A1, B1, Y1);
    Y2 <= MixColor(A2, B2);

    process (Clock, En, A4, B4)
    begin
        if rising_edge (Clock) then
            MixColor(A3, B3, Y3);
        end if;
        if (En = '1') then
            Y4 <= MixColor(A4, B4);
        end if;
    end process;
end architecture LOGIC;
```

> Four subprograms calls to different subprograms of the same name.

> Concurrent procedure call.

> Concurrent function call.

> Sequential procedure call.

> Sequential function call.

Synthesized Circuit

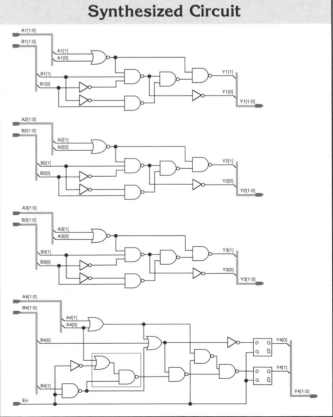

4. Deferred constants (VHDL)

A constant declaration normally declares the constant's identifier name and its associated constant value, for example,

> **constant** WidthBusA: integer := 16;   -- constant declaration

On the other hand, a deferred constant declaration declares the constant's identifier name, but not its value, for example,

> **constant** WidthBusA: integer; -- deferred constant declaration

Deferred constants are used when a constant value may need to be changed such that only a **package body** need be re-compiled. If a constant is not deferred, then not only would the package need to be recompiled, but all models dependant upon the constant would also need to be recompiled.

A deferred constant can only be declared inside a **package** and its declaration is completed with an associated full constant declaration that associates its value declared in the corresponding **package body**; see Example 4.17.

Example 4.17 Using a deferred constant (VHDL)

A deferred constant is used to define the number of most significant bits of a multiple bit bus that should be ANDed together in the function called AND_MSBs.

Deferred constant declared in a package   *Two function calls*

VHDL

library IEEE;
use IEEE.STD_Logic_1164.**all**, IEEE.Numeric_STD.**all**;
 	
package DEF_CONST_PKG **is** ⟶ Constant declaration.
    constant Width: integer := 8;
    constant NO_MSBs: integer; ⟶ Deferred constant declaration.
    function AND_MSBs (A: unsigned(Width - 1 **downto** 0))
                          return std_logic;
end package DEF_CONST_PKG;
 	
package body DEF_CONST_PKG **is**
 	
    constant NO_MSBs: integer := 3; ⟶ Value of deferred constant specified.
 	
    function AND_MSBs (A: unsigned(Width - 1 **downto** 0))
                          return std_logic **is**
        variable V: std_logic;
    begin
        V := '1';
        for N **in** 7 **downto** 8 - NO_MSBs **loop**
            V := V **and** A(N);
        end loop;
        return V;
    end AND_MSBs;
 	
end package body DEF_CONST_PKG;

VHDL

library IEEE;
use IEEE.STD_Logic_1164.**all**, IEEE.Numeric_STD.**all**;
 	
use work.DEF_CONST_PKG.**all**;
 	
entity DEF_CONST_CALL **is**
    port (A1, A2: **in**   unsigned(7 **downto** 0);
        Y1, Y2: **out** std_logic);
end entity DEF_CONST_CALL;
 	
architecture LOGIC **of** DEF_CONST_CALL **is**
begin
 	
    process (A1, A2)
    begin
        Y1 <= AND_MSBs(A1);
        Y2 <= AND_MSBs(A2);
    end process;
 	
end architecture LOGIC;

Synthesized Circuit

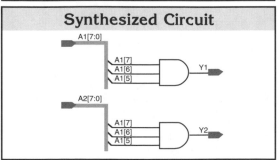

5. Translation Functions - Extension and Truncation (VHDL)

Extension and truncation functions in a package

```
                          VHDL
library IEEE;
use IEEE.STD_LOGIC_1164.all, IEEE.Numeric_STD.all;

package SIGNED_EXT_TRUNC is
    function Ext      (A: unsigned; Size: integer) return unsigned;
    function Trunc  (A: unsigned; Size: integer) return unsigned;
end package SIGNED_EXT_TRUNC;

package body SIGNED_EXT_TRUNC is

    --$ synthesis_compile_off
    constant ExtSize:      string := "Can't extened to a smaller width bus!";
    constant TruncSize:  string := "Can't truncate to a larger width bus!";
    --$ synthesis_compile_on

    procedure Message (MESS: String; SEV: Severity_Level) is
    begin
        assert false report MESS severity SEV;
    end procedure Message;

    function Ext (A: unsigned; Size: integer) return unsigned is
        variable Extended: unsigned(Size - 1 downto 0);
    begin
        --$ synthesis_compile_off
        if A'length > Size then
            Message(ExtSize, Error);
            return (A);
        end if;
        --$ synthesis_compile_on

        Extended(A'length - 1 downto 0) := A;
        for N in Size-1 downto A'length loop
            Extended(N) := A(A'left);
        end loop;
        return (Extended);
    end function Ext;

    function Trunc (A: unsigned; Size: integer) return unsigned is
        variable Truncated_downto: unsigned (A'low+Size-1 downto A'low);
        variable Truncated_to:      unsigned (A'low to A'low+Size-1);
    begin
        --$ synthesis_compile_off
        if A'length < Size then
            Message(TruncSize, Error);
            return (A);
        end if;
        --$ synthesis_compile_on

        for N in A'low to A'low + Size - 1 loop
            Truncated_downto(N):= A(N + A'length - Size);
            Truncated_to(N)        := A(N + A'length - Size);
        end loop;

        if (A'left > A'right) then
            return Truncated_downto;
        else
            return Truncated_to;
        end if;
    end function Trunc;

end package body SIGNED_EXT_TRUNC;
```

Packages are often used to store precompiled conversion functions, which when called, convert data objects from one data type to another. Alternatively such functions may simply manipulate bits of the same type. These functions do not imply logic to be synthesized; they simply manipulate the various bits of the particular data type.

Example 4.18 Translation Functions

This example shows a package containing two functions; one for sign extension of the most significant bit and one for truncation of the least significant bit(s). They use the data type unsigned as defined by the IEEE 1076.3 package Numeric_STD. The **library** and **use** clause makes the two packages Std_Logic_1164 and Numeric_STD visible to the package Signed_Ext_Trunc.

When the Ext and Trunc functions are called they require 1) the vector to be extended or truncated and 2) an integer indicating the size of the returned vector.

Both functions contain a check that extension is not attempting to extend to a smaller bit width or that truncation is not attempting to truncate to a larger bit width. If this is the case, an appropriate error message is displayed. This checking mechanism uses an assertion statement in the **procedure** named Message which may be called from either function. The subprogram Message, must be a **procedure** and not a **function** as there is no return value, it is purely passive.

Assertion statements are not supported by synthesis tools, so comment directives are used to tell the synthesis compiler to ignore these constructs. In this example, the compiler directives --$ synthesis_compile_off and --$ synthesis_compile_on are used corresponding to the synthesis tools from VeriBest Incorporated. All code between these complier directives are ignored by the synthesis compiler.

Extension and truncation function calls

```
                          VHDL
library IEEE
use IEEE.STD_LOGIC_1164.all, IEEE.Numeric_Std.all;
use work.SIGNED_EXT_TRUNC.all;

entity SIGNED_EXT_TRUNC_CALL is
    port ( A, B:        in    unsigned(15 downto 8);
           C, D:        in    unsigned(8 to 15);
           Y_A_EXT:    out  unsigned(17 downto 8);
           Y_B_TRC:    out  unsigned(13 downto 8);
           Y_C_EXT:    out  unsigned(8 to 17);
           Y_D_TRC:    out  unsigned(8 to 13));
end entity SIGNED_EXTENSION_TRUNCATION;

architecture DATA_FLOW of SIGNED_EXT_TRUNC_CALL is
begin
    Y_A_EXT <= Ext(A, 10);
    Y_B_TRC <= Trunc(B, 6);
    Y_C_EXT <= Ext(C, 10);
    Y_D_TRC <= Trunc(D, 6);
end architecture DATA_FLOW;
```

6. Resource Sharing

During synthesis, a process called resource allocation, assigns each operator to a piece of hardware. If this process assigns two or more operators to a single piece of combinational logic hardware they are known to be shared and the process is called resource sharing. Operators that can typically be automatically shared by a synthesis tool are:

"+", "-", "*" and "\"   (VHDL)
"+", "-", "*" and "/"   (Verilog)

Because multiply and divide operators are not synthesized efficiently using RTL synthesis tools only the "+" and "-" operators are best suited to being shared. A synthesis tool will make the decision as to whether a resource may be shared based upon certain criteria. The criteria for sharing is typically:

1. Operators must reside in the same **process** (VHDL)/**always** (Verilog) statement.
2. Operators must reside in different branches of the same conditional assignment statement.

When a synthesis tool performs resource sharing, it will typically add multiplexers to the inputs and outputs of shared hardware resources as needed to channel data into, and out of, the common resource. A synthesis tool will usually provide an option to switch automatic resource sharing on or off.

Example 4.19 Automatic resource sharing.

First **process/always** *statement.* Explicitly infers a shared adder using an **if** statement.

Second **process/always** *statement.* Implied shared adder through synthesis using an **if** statement.

Third **process/always** *statement.* Implied shared adder/subtracter circuit from synthesis using a **case** statement.

HDL explicit and synthesis implied resource sharing

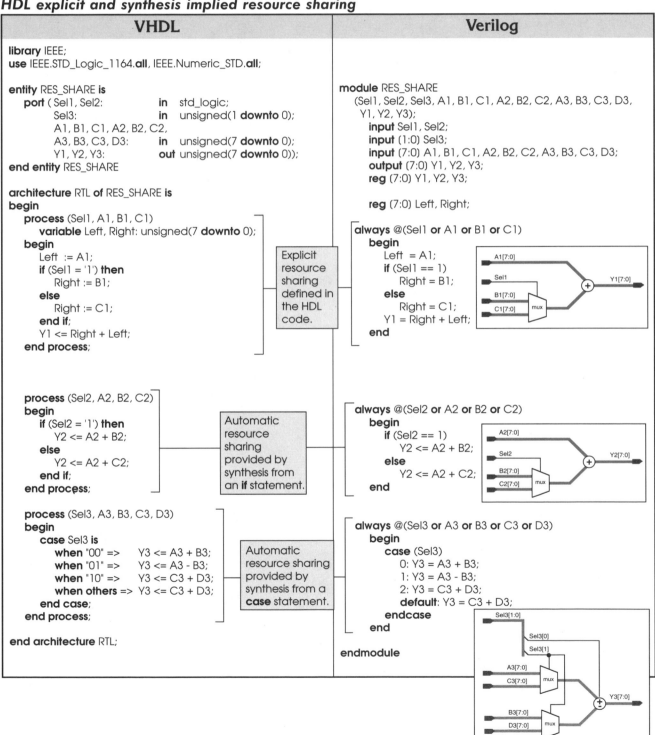

VHDL	Verilog

library IEEE;
use IEEE.STD_Logic_1164.**all**, IEEE.Numeric_STD.**all**;
 	
entity RES_SHARE **is**
  port (Sel1, Sel2:   **in** std_logic;
      Sel3:   **in** unsigned(1 **downto** 0);
      A1, B1, C1, A2, B2, C2,
      A3, B3, C3, D3:   **in** unsigned(7 **downto** 0);
      Y1, Y2, Y3:   **out** unsigned(7 **downto** 0));
end entity RES_SHARE
 	
architecture RTL **of** RES_SHARE **is**
begin
  process (Sel1, A1, B1, C1)
    variable Left, Right: unsigned(7 **downto** 0);
  begin
    Left := A1;
    if (Sel1 = '1') **then**
      Right := B1;
    else
      Right := C1;
    end if;
    Y1 <= Right + Left;
  end process;
	module RES_SHARE
	  (Sel1, Sel2, Sel3, A1, B1, C1, A2, B2, C2, A3, B3, C3, D3,
	  Y1, Y2, Y3);
	  input Sel1, Sel2;
	  input (1:0) Sel3;
	  input (7:0) A1, B1, C1, A2, B2, C2, A3, B3, C3, D3;
	  output (7:0) Y1, Y2, Y3;
	  reg (7:0) Y1, Y2, Y3;
	
	  reg (7:0) Left, Right;
	
	  always @(Sel1 **or** A1 **or** B1 **or** C1)
	    begin
	      Left = A1;
	      if (Sel1 == 1)
	        Right = B1;
	      else
	        Right = C1;
	      Y1 = Right + Left;
	    end

process (Sel2, A2, B2, C2)
begin
  if (Sel2 = '1') **then**
    Y2 <= A2 + B2;
  else
    Y2 <= A2 + C2;
  end if;
end process;
	always @(Sel2 **or** A2 **or** B2 **or** C2)
	  begin
	    if (Sel2 == 1)
	      Y2 <= A2 + B2;
	    else
	      Y2 <= A2 + C2;
	  end

process (Sel3, A3, B3, C3, D3)
begin
  case Sel3 **is**
    when "00" =>   Y3 <= A3 + B3;
    when "01" =>   Y3 <= A3 - B3;
    when "10" =>   Y3 <= C3 + D3;
    when others => Y3 <= C3 + D3;
  end case;
end process;
 	
end architecture RTL;
	always @(Sel3 **or** A3 **or** B3 **or** C3 **or** D3)
	  begin
	    case (Sel3)
	      0: Y3 = A3 + B3;
	      1: Y3 = A3 - B3;
	      2: Y3 = C3 + D3;
	      default: Y3 = C3 + D3;
	    endcase
	  end
	
	endmodule

Explicit resource sharing defined in the HDL code.

Automatic resource sharing provided by synthesis from an **if** statement.

Automatic resource sharing provided by synthesis from a **case** statement.

Structuring a Design

Chapter 5 Contents

Structuring a Design

This chapter describes the motivation for building good structure into a model's design and how it is achieved.

The motivation for good model structure is modularity and clarity; the benefits of which are:

- models are less cluttered and easier to read,
- previously designed and verified submodels can be used (called) repeatedly within a design,
- previously designed and verified models can be quickly and easily incorporated into new designs,
- a well partitioned design, having structure corresponding to its functional operation, and breaks the total design and verification task into smaller, more manageable pieces.

The constructs used to build structure into HDL models are listed in Table 5.1 with reference to their granularity.

structural granularity	structural modeling unit	HDL construct	
		VHDL	Verilog
coarse grain	entity/architecture pairing	configuration *	
coarse grain	primary design unit	entity/architecture	module
coarse/medium grain	replication of concurrent statements	for/if-generate	
coarse/medium grain	grouping of concurrent statements	block	
medium grain	grouping of sequential statements	process	always
fine grain	subprogram	procedure	task
fine grain	subprogram	function	function

* Ignored by synthesis tools, but can be used to configure the structure of synthesizable models for simulation.

Table 5.1 Constructs used to build structure into HDL models

The following sections describe these constructs and include examples. Appendices A and B show the syntax of VHDL and Verilog constructs, respectively.

Coarse Grain

Configurations (VHDL)

A configuration is a separate *design unit* (see Figure 3.1) that allows different **architecture** and **component** bindings to be specified after a model has been analyzed and compiled, by a simulator for example. There are two types; the *configuration declaration* and the *configuration specification*.

Configuration declarations

The standard VHDL design entity consists of an **entity** and **architecture** pair. The **entity** defines input and output signals, while the **architecture** defines its functional operation. An **entity-architecture** pair normally resides in the same system file, however, an **entity** does not need to be locked into being associated with one particular **architecture**. An **entity** can be configured, using a *configuration declaration*, to be bound to any one of a number of different **architecture** bodies for simulation purposes. Different **architecture** bodies may have different modeled structures or may be the gate level implication resulting from synthesis.

In summary a configuration declaration defines a **configuration** for a particular **entity** in order too:

- bind the **entity** to a particular **architecture** body,
- bind components, used in the specified **architecture**, to a particular **entity** (a component is an **entity-architecture** pair),
- bind components statements, used in the specified **architecture**, to a particular **configuration** statement.

Configuration specifications

In contrast to the configuration declaration, a *configuration specification* can be used to enable a component to be associated with any one of a set of **entity** statements. The component declaration may have its name and the names, types, and number of ports and generics different from those of its entities. This is achieved with a configuration specification.

In summary, a configuration specification can be used to specify the binding of component instances to a particular **entity-architecture** pair.

Example 5.1 Structural configuration for simulation using a configuration

Two similar models have the same **entity** name, ADDSUB_STRUCT, and each reside in their own system file. They are different in the way parentheses are used in the assignment of signal Y and are identified by having a different **architecture** name; LOGIC_STRUCT1 or LOGIC_STRUCT2. The configuration declaration used to decide which model version to use during simulation is also shown and resides in a separate system file. Once the two models have been compiled only the configuration declaration need be changed and recompiled in order to change which architecture to simulate. The configuration declaration shown is enabled for LOGIC_STRUCT2.

Configuration of one of two architectures

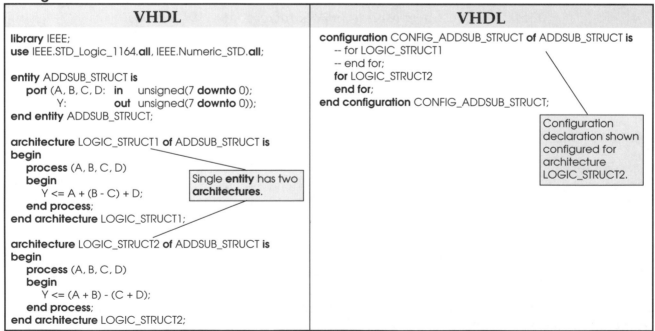

VHDL	VHDL

library IEEE;
use IEEE.STD_Logic_1164.**all**, IEEE.Numeric_STD.**all**;
 	
entity ADDSUB_STRUCT **is**
    port (A, B, C, D: **in**   unsigned(7 **downto** 0);
         Y: **out** unsigned(7 **downto** 0));
end entity ADDSUB_STRUCT;
 	
architecture LOGIC_STRUCT1 **of** ADDSUB_STRUCT **is**
begin
    process (A, B, C, D)
    begin
        Y <= A + (B - C) + D;
    end process;
end architecture LOGIC_STRUCT1;
 	
architecture LOGIC_STRUCT2 **of** ADDSUB_STRUCT **is**
begin
    process (A, B, C, D)
    begin
        Y <= (A + B) - (C + D);
    end process;
end architecture LOGIC_STRUCT2;
	configuration CONFIG_ADDSUB_STRUCT **of** ADDSUB_STRUCT **is**
	    -- for LOGIC_STRUCT1
	    -- end for;
	    for LOGIC_STRUCT2
	    end for;
	end configuration CONFIG_ADDSUB_STRUCT;

Single **entity** has two **architectures**.

Configuration declaration shown configured for architecture LOGIC_STRUCT2.

Entity-architecture (VHDL) / module (Verilog)

A *design entity* is the VHDL **entity-architecture** pair or Verilog **module**, both of which provide coarse grain control over a design's hierarchical structure. A design entity can instantiate lower level design entities in which case they are known as a component, which in turn, can instantiate lower level components to provide a course grain multiple level hierarchical structure.

When a VHDL **architecture** instantiates a lower-level **entity**, it must be declared in the declarative part of the **architecture** before it can be instantiated in the statement part. This is not the case in Verilog; it just needs to be instantiated, see Example 5.2.

Signals passing to and from sublevel components may be defined in the instantiating statement using positional or named notation, or additionally for VHDL, a mixture of both. Positional notation means that signals in the upper level component are connected to signals in the lower level component, corresponding to their relative position in the instantiating statement. Named notation means each signal in the upper level is explicitly defined as being connected to a specific signal in the lower level, and therefore, their relative order in the instantiation statement is not important. The mixed positional and named notation supported by VHDL allows signals to be listed using positional notation until the first named notation signal. After the first named notation signal, all other signals must also use named notation. Note, a signal can represent; a single bit, multiple bits, or selected bits from a multiple bit bus. There is no real advantage of using a mixed notation and is less readable.

Example 5.2 shows multiple levels of hierarchy using both positional and named notation. It also shows mixed notation in the VHDL model. Example 5.3 shows a bus whose bits are split and connected to different sublevel design units.

Example 5.2 Coarse grain structuring - multi-level components

The coarse grain structuring of a design in this example has three levels of hierarchy. It uses the **entity-architecture** (VHDL) and **module** (Verilog) to model the hierarchical structure indicated in Figure 5.1. The top level instantiates two middle level components which in turn instantiates the lower level components. The lowest level in this example contains only the model of a single two input logic gate for demonstration purposes, but would typically contain large sections of a larger design, which could be synthesizing circuits from 2000 to 5000 equivalent gates.

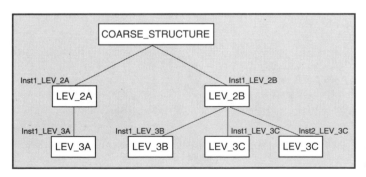

Figure 5.1 Coarse grain hierarchical structure

Three hierarchical levels of coarse grain structuring

VHDL	Verilog
| ```
library IEEE;
use IEEE.STD_Logic_1164.all;
entity COARSE_STRUCTURE is
    port ( A1, A2, A3, A4, B1, B2, B3, B4: in   std_logic;
           Y1, Y2, Y3, Y4:                 out std_logic);
end entity COARSE_STRUCTURE;

architecture STRUCT of COARSE_STRUCTURE is
    component LEV_2A
        port (A1, B1: in std_logic; Y1: out std_logic);
    end component;
    component LEV_2B
        port (A2, A3, A4, B2, B3, B4: in std_logic;
              Y2, Y3, Y4: out std_logic);
    end component;
begin
    Inst1_LEV_2A: LEV_2A  port map (A1, B1, Y1);
    Inst1_LEV_2B: LEV_2B  port map (A2,A3,A4,B2,B3,B4,Y2,Y3,Y4);
end architecture STRUCT;
``` | ```
module COARSE_STRUCTURE
    (A1, A2, A3, A4, B1, B2, B3, B4, Y1, Y2, Y3, Y4);
    input   A1, A2, A3, A4, B1, B2, B3, B4;
    output Y1, Y2, Y3, Y4;

    LEV_2A Inst1_LEV_2A (A1, B1, Y1);
    LEV_2B Inst1_LEV_2B (A2,A3,A4,B2,B3,B4,Y2,Y3,Y4);
endmodule
``` |
| ```
library IEEE;
use IEEE.STD_Logic_1164.all;
entity LEV_2A is
    port (A1, B1: in std_logic; Y1: out std_logic);
end entity LEV_2A;

architecture STRUCT of LEV_2A is
    component LEV_3A
        port (A, B: in std_logic; Y: out std_logic);
    end component;
begin
    Inst1_LEV_3A: LEV_3A  port map (A1, B1, Y1);
end architecture STRUCT;
``` | ```
module LEV_2A (A1, B1, Y1);
    input  A1,B1;
    output Y1;

    LEV_3A Inst1_LEV_3A (A1, B1, Y1);
endmodule
``` |

Positional notation.

VHDL	Verilog
| ```
library IEEE;
use IEEE.STD_Logic_1164.all;
entity LEV_2B is
    port (A2,A3,A4,B2,B3,B4: in std_logic; Y2,Y3,Y4: out std_logic);
end entity LEV_2B;

architecture STRUCT of LEV_2B is
    component LEV_3B
        port (A, B: in std_logic;  Y: out std_logic);
    end component;
    component LEV_3C
        port (A, B: in std_logic;  Y: out std_logic);
    end component;
begin
    Inst1_LEV_3B: LEV_3B   port map (A => A2, B => B2, Y => Y2);
    Inst1_LEV_3C: LEV_3C   port map (Y => Y3, A => A3, B => B3);
    Inst2_LEV_3C: LEV_3C   port map (A => A4, B => B4, Y => Y4);
end architecture STRUCT;
``` | ```
module LEV_2B (A2, A3, A4, B2, B3, B4, Y2, Y3, Y4);
    input   A2, A3, A4, B2, B3, B4;
    output Y2,Y3,Y4;

    LEV_3B  Inst1_LEV_3B (.A(A2), .B(B2), .Y(Y2));
    LEV_3C  Inst1_LEV_3C (.Y(Y3),.. A(A3), .B(B3)),
            Inst2_LEV_3C (.A(A4), .B(B4), .Y(Y4));
endmodule
``` |

Named notation. / Named notation.

VHDL	Verilog
| ```
library IEEE;
use IEEE.STD_Logic_1164.all, IEEE.Numeric_STD.all;
entity LEV_3A is
    port (A, B: in std_logic; Y: out std_logic);
end entity LEV_3A;

architecture STRUCT of LEV_3A is
begin
    Y <= (A nand B);
end architecture STRUCT;
``` | ```
module LEV_3A (A, B, Y);
    input  A, B;
    output Y;

    assign Y = ! (A & B);
endmodule
``` |

continued   *continued*

Three hierarchical levels of coarse grain structuring

VHDL	Verilog

library IEEE;
use IEEE.STD_Logic_1164.**all**;
entity LEV_3B **is**
    port (A, B: **in** std_logic; Y: **out** std_logic);
end entity LEV_3B;
 	
architecture STRUCT **of** LEV_3B **is**
begin
    Y <= (A **nor** B);
end architecture STRUCT;
	module LEV_3B (A, B, Y);
	    input A, B;
	    output Y;
	
	    assign Y = ! (A | B);
	endmodule

library IEEE;
use IEEE.STD_Logic_1164.**all**;
entity LEV_3C **is**
    port (A, B: **in** std_logic; Y: **out** std_logic);
end entity LEV_3C;
 	
architecture STRUCT **of** LEV_3C **is**
begin
    Y <= (A **xor** B);
end architecture STRUCT;
	module LEV_3C (A, B, Y);
	    input A, B;
	    output Y;
	
	    assign Y = (A ^ B);
	endmodule

Synthesized circuit showing model structure

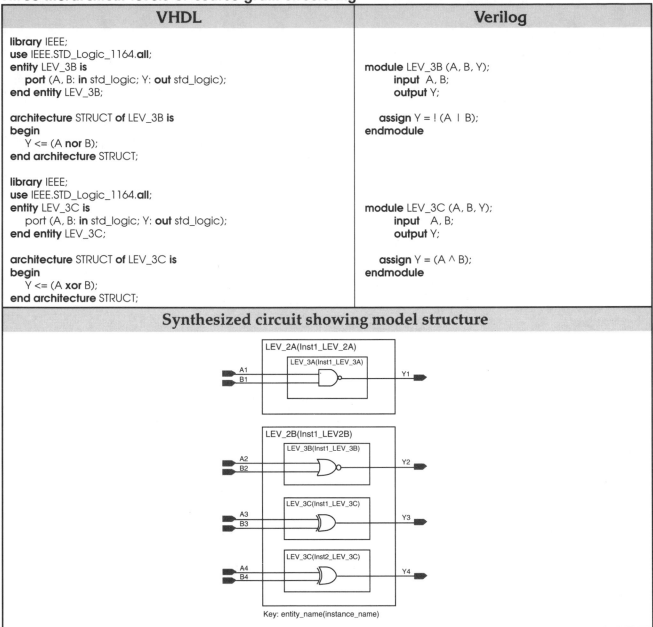

Key: entity_name(instance_name)

Example 5.3 Coarse grain structuring - components connected via split busses

The model COARSE_STR_SPLIT_BUS instantiates three separate ALU models; ALU1, ALU2 and ALU3. The model, ALU, is included for completeness.

The input bus signals Control, A and B are each split into three and connected to the three ALUs. The output signals from the ALUs are then combined into one output bus Y. The instantiation of ALU1 uses positional notation to link signals between the two levels of hierarchy. The instantiation of ALU2 uses named notation; each signal connection is specified in random order. The instantiation of ALU3 also uses named notation with signal connections specified in the same order as for ALU1.

Entity/module instantiations corrected via split busses

VHDL	Verilog

library IEEE;
use IEEE.STD_Logic_1164.**all**, IEEE.Numeric_STD.**all**;
entity ALU **is**
    port (Operator: **in** unsigned(2 **downto** 0);
         Operand1, Operand2: **in** unsigned(7 **downto** 0);
         Result: **out** unsigned(7 **downto** 0));
end entity ALU;
 	
architecture COMB **of** ALU **is**
begin
   process (Operator, Operand1, Operand2)
   begin
      case (Operator) **is**
         when "000" => Result <= (**others** => '0');
         when "001" => Result <= Operand1 **and** Operand2;
         when "010" => Result <= Operand1 **or** Operand2;
         when "011" => Result <= Operand1 **xor** Operand2;
         when "100" => Result <= shift_right(Operand1, 1);
         when "101" => Result <= shift_right(Operand2, 1);
         when "110" => Result <= shift_left(Operand1, 1);
         when "111" => Result <= shift_left(Operand2, 1);
         when **others** => Result <= (**others** => '0');
      end case;
   end process;
end architecture COMB;
	module ALU (Operator, Operand1, Operand2, Result);
	    input (2:0) Operator;
	    input (7:0) Operand1, Operand2;
	    output (7:0) Result;
	    reg (7:0) Result;
	
	    always @(Operator **or** Operand1 **or** Operand2)
	      case (Operator)
	        0: Result = 8'b 0;
	        1: Result = Operand1 + Operand2;
	        2: Result = Operand1 - Operand2;
	        3: Result = Operand1 ∧ Operand2;
	        4: Result = Operand1 >> 1;
	        5: Result = Operand2 >> 1;
	        6: Result = Operand1 << 1;
	        7: Result = Operand2 << 1;
	        default: Result = 8'b 0;
	      endcase
	endmodule

library IEEE;
use IEEE.STD_Logic_1164.**all**, IEEE.Numeric_STD.**all**;
entity COARSE_STR_SPLIT_BUS **is**
    port (Control: **in**   unsigned(8 **downto** 0);
        A, B: **in**   unsigned(23 **downto** 0);
        Y: **out** unsigned(23 **downto** 0));
end entity COARSE_STR_SPLIT_BUS;
 	
architecture STRUCT **of** COARSE_STR_SPLIT_BUS **is**
   component ALU
        port (Operator: **in** unsigned(2 **downto** 0);
             Operand1, Operand2: **in** unsigned(7 **downto** 0);
             Result: **out** unsigned(7 **downto** 0));
   end component;
begin
   ALU1: ALU **port map** (Control(2 **downto** 0), A(7 **downto** 0),
               B(7 **downto** 0), Y(7 **downto** 0));
   ALU2: ALU **port map** (Operand2 => A(15 **downto** 8),
           Operator => Control(5 **downto** 3),
           Result   => Y(15 **downto** 8),
           Operand1 => B(15 **downto** 8));
   ALU3: ALU **port map** (operator => Control(8 **downto** 6),
           Operand1 => A(23 **downto** 16),
           Operand2 => B(23 **downto** 16),
           Result   => Y(23 **downto** 16));
end architecture STRUCT;
	module COARSE_STR_SPLIT_BUS (Control, A, B, Y);
	    input (8:0) Control;
	    input (23:0) A, B;
	    output (23:0) Y;
	
	   ALU ALU1(Control(2:0), A(7:0), B(7:0), Y(7:0));
	
	   ALU ALU2(.Operand2(A(15:8)), .Operator(Control(5:3)),
	            .Result(Y(15:8)), .Operand1(B(15:8)));
	
	   ALU ALU3(.Operator(Control(8:6)), .Operand1(A(23:16)),
	            .Operand2(B(23:16)), .Result(Y(23:16)));
	
	endmodule

Entity/module instantiations corrected via split busses

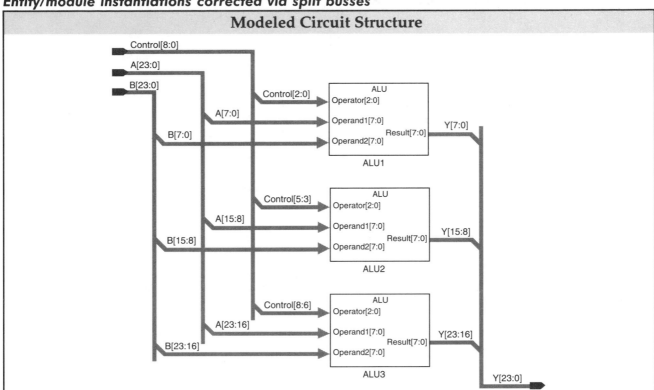

Coarse/Medium Grain

For/if-generate (VHDL)

Coarse/medium grain structural replication is achieved in VHDL using **generate** statements, which replicate the enclosed concurrent statements; there is no Verilog equivalent. The two VHDL **generate** schemes are:

    for-generate   - replicates the enclosed concurrent statements a given number of times
    if-generate   - conditionally replicates the enclosed concurrent statements

Example 5.4 Coarse/medium grain structural replication - for/if-generate (VHDL)

The VHDL model uses both the **for-generate** and **if-generate** statements to provide coarse/medium grain structuring. The first **for-generate** statement, GEN_1, generates three instances of ALU2 in exactly the same way as in Example 5.3. As ALU1 is instantiated repetitively, the **generate** statement is better suited and requires less code than the three individual instantiations in Example 5.3.

The **for-generate** statement, GEN_2, contains two nested **if-generate** statements. The first **if-generate** statement, GEN_3, instantiates two instances of ALU1, while the second, GEN_4, instantiates another three instances of ALU2. This can be seen in the modeled circuit structure after the HDL models.

Structural replication for/if-generate (VHDL)

<table>
<tr><td colspan="2" align="center">VHDL</td></tr>
<tr><td valign="top">

```vhdl
library IEEE;
use IEEE.STD_Logic_1164.all, IEEE.Numeric_STD.all;

entity ALU1 is
    port ( Operator:   in  unsigned(1 downto 0);
           Operand1, Operand2: in unsigned(7 downto 0);
           Result:     out unsigned(7 downto 0));
end entity ALU1;

architecture COMB of ALU1 is
begin
    process (Operator, Operand1, Operand2)
    begin
        case (Operator) is
            when "00" => Result <= (others => '0');
            when "01" => Result <= Operand1 and Operand2;
            when "10" => Result <= Operand1 or Operand2;
            when "11" => Result <= Operand1 xor Operand2;
            when others => Result <= (others => '0');
        end case;
    end process;
end architecture COMB;
```

```vhdl
library IEEE;
use IEEE.STD_Logic_1164.all, IEEE.Numeric_STD.all;

entity ALU2 is
    port ( Operator:  in  unsigned(2 downto 0);
           Operand1, Operand2: in unsigned(7 downto 0);
           Result:    out unsigned(7 downto 0));
end entity ALU2;

architecture COMB of ALU2 is
begin
    process (Operator, Operand1, Operand2)
    begin
        case (Operator) is
            when "000" => Result <= (others => '0');
            when "001" => Result <= Operand1 and Operand2;
            when "010" => Result <= Operand1 or Operand2;
            when "011" => Result <= Operand1 xor Operand2;
            when "100" => Result <= shift_right(Operand1, 1);
            when "101" => Result <= shift_right(Operand2, 1);
            when "110" => Result <= shift_left(Operand1, 1);
            when "111" => Result <= shift_left(Operand2, 1);
            when others => Result <= (others => '0');
        end case;
    end process;
end architecture COMB;
```

</td><td valign="top">

```vhdl
library IEEE;
use IEEE.STD_Logic_1164.all, IEEE.Numeric_STD.all;
entity COARSE_MED_GENERATE is
    port (Ctl_AB: in   unsigned(8 downto 0);
          A, B:   in   unsigned(23 downto 0);
          Y1:     out  unsigned(23 downto 0);
          Ctl_CD: in   unsigned(12 downto 0);
          C, D:   in   unsigned(39 downto 0);
          Y2:     out  unsigned(39 downto 0));
end entity COARSE_MED_GENERATE;

architecture STRUCT of COARSE_MED_GENERATE is
    component ALU1
        port (Operator:            in  unsigned(1 downto 0);
              Operand1, Operand2:in unsigned(7 downto 0);
              Result:             out unsigned(7 downto 0));
    end component;
    component ALU2
        port (Operator:            in  unsigned(2 downto 0);
              Operand1, Operand2:in unsigned(7 downto 0);
              Result:             out unsigned(7 downto 0));
    end component;
begin
    -- Generates 3 instances of ALU2.
    GEN1: for N in 0 to 2 generate
            ALU2_X3: ALU2
                port map (Ctl_AB(2 + N * 3 downto N * 3),
                          A(7 + N * 8 downto N * 8),
                          B(7 + N * 8 downto N * 8),
                          Y1(7 + N * 8 downto N * 8));
          end generate;
    -- Generates 2 instances of ALU1 and 3 instances of ALU2.
    GEN2: for N in 0 to 4 generate
    GEN3:   if N <= 1 generate
                TWO_ALU1S: ALU1
                    port map (Ctl_CD(1 + N * 2 downto N * 2),
                              C(7 + N * 8 downto N * 8),
                              D(7 + N * 8 downto N * 8),
                              Y2(7 + N * 8 downto N * 8));
            end generate;
    GEN4:   if N >= 2 generate
                THREE_ALU2S: ALU2
                    port map (Ctl_CD(N * 3 downto  N * 3 - 2),
                              C(7 + N * 8 downto N * 8),
                              D(7 + N * 8 downto N * 8),
                              Y2(7 + N * 8 downto N * 8));
            end generate;
          end generate;

end architecture STRUCT;
```

</td></tr>
</table>

Structural replication for/if-generate (VHDL)

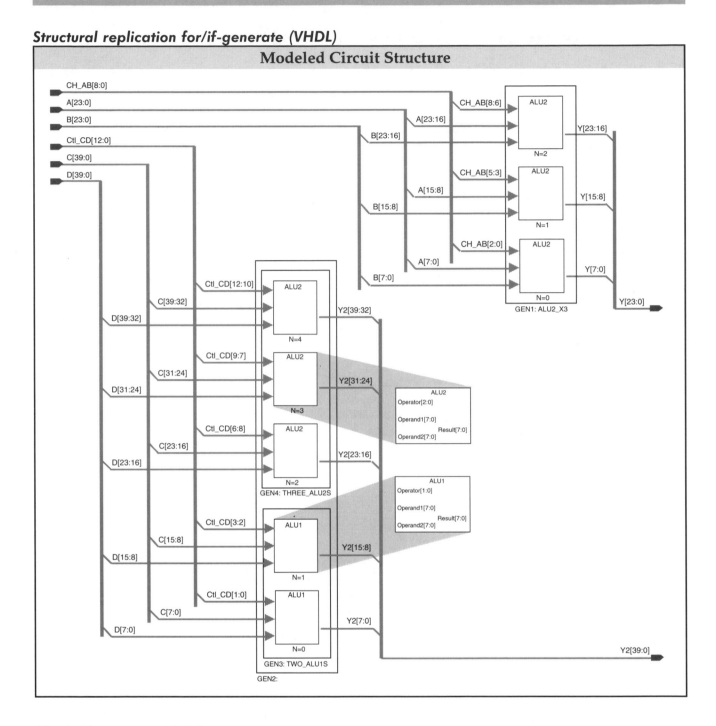

Block Statement (VHDL)

Coarse/medium grain structuring can also be achieved in VHDL with the concurrent **block** statement. The **block** statement, contains zero or more concurrent statements, and can be nested; see Example 5.5. Typically, RTL synthesizable models rarely use the **block** statement as there is no advantage in doing so; there is no sensitivity list and the concurrent statements are treated in exactly the same way as if they are not in a **block** statement. The **process** statement is far more commonly used. There is no Verilog equivalent.

Example 5.5 Coarse/medium grain structuring using blocks (VHDL)

The VHDL model has two blocks; BLK1 and BLK2.

>   BLK1. Uses identical **generate** statements as those used in Example 5.4 to instantiate the same number of ALU components. The ALUs are the same as those in Example 5.4.
>   BLK2. Groups two **process** statements (PRC1 and PRC2) together and defines a 24-bit bus signal, Bus12. Bus12 is local to BLK2 and global to the two processes.

Structuring a design using VHDL blocks

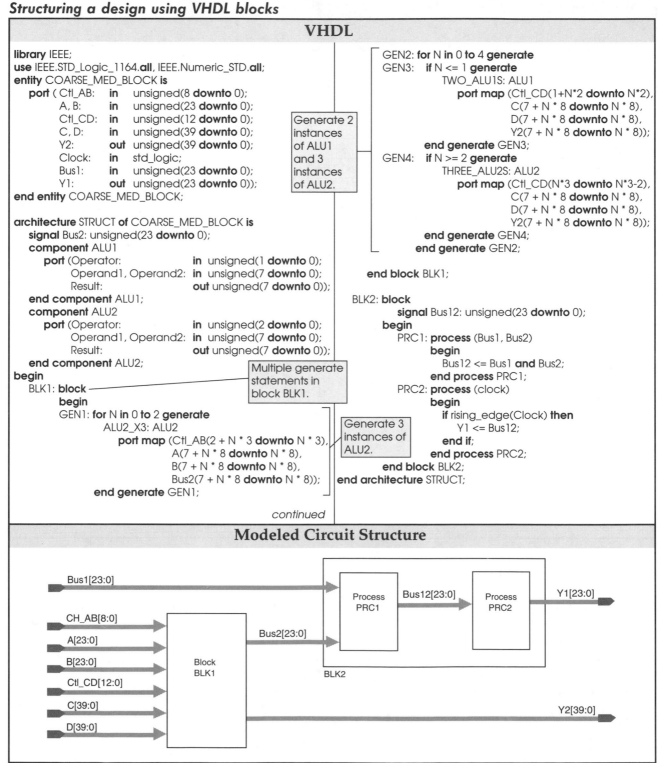

VHDL

```
library IEEE;
use IEEE.STD_Logic_1164.all, IEEE.Numeric_STD.all;
entity COARSE_MED_BLOCK is
    port ( Ctl_AB:    in    unsigned(8 downto 0);
           A, B:      in    unsigned(23 downto 0);
           Ctl_CD:    in    unsigned(12 downto 0);
           C, D:      in    unsigned(39 downto 0);
           Y2:        out   unsigned(39 downto 0);
           Clock:     in    std_logic;
           Bus1:      in    unsigned(23 downto 0);
           Y1:        out   unsigned(23 downto 0));
end entity COARSE_MED_BLOCK;

architecture STRUCT of COARSE_MED_BLOCK is
    signal Bus2: unsigned(23 downto 0);
    component ALU1
        port (Operator:            in unsigned(1 downto 0);
              Operand1, Operand2:  in unsigned(7 downto 0);
              Result:              out unsigned(7 downto 0));
    end component ALU1;
    component ALU2
        port (Operator:            in unsigned(2 downto 0);
              Operand1, Operand2:  in unsigned(7 downto 0);
              Result:              out unsigned(7 downto 0));
    end component ALU2;
begin
    BLK1: block
        begin
        GEN1: for N in 0 to 2 generate
            ALU2_X3: ALU2
                port map (Ctl_AB(2 + N * 3 downto N * 3),
                          A(7 + N * 8 downto N * 8),
                          B(7 + N * 8 downto N * 8),
                          Bus2(7 + N * 8 downto N * 8));
            end generate GEN1;
```

Generate 2 instances of ALU1 and 3 instances of ALU2.

Multiple generate statements in block BLK1.

```
        GEN2: for N in 0 to 4 generate
        GEN3:    if N <= 1 generate
                     TWO_ALU1S: ALU1
                         port map (Ctl_CD(1+N*2 downto N*2),
                                   C(7 + N * 8 downto N * 8),
                                   D(7 + N * 8 downto N * 8),
                                   Y2(7 + N * 8 downto N * 8));
                 end generate GEN3;
        GEN4:    if N >= 2 generate
                     THREE_ALU2S: ALU2
                         port map (Ctl_CD(N*3 downto N*3-2),
                                   C(7 + N * 8 downto N * 8),
                                   D(7 + N * 8 downto N * 8),
                                   Y2(7 + N * 8 downto N * 8));
                 end generate GEN4;
             end generate GEN2;

    end block BLK1;

    BLK2: block
             signal Bus12: unsigned(23 downto 0);
         begin
             PRC1: process (Bus1, Bus2)
                 begin
                     Bus12 <= Bus1 and Bus2;
                 end process PRC1;
             PRC2: process (clock)
                 begin
                     if rising_edge(Clock) then
                         Y1 <= Bus12;
                     end if;
                 end process PRC2;
         end block BLK2;
end architecture STRUCT;
```

Generate 3 instances of ALU2.

continued

Modeled Circuit Structure

Bus1[23:0]

CH_AB[8:0]

A[23:0]

B[23:0]

Ctl_CD[12:0]

C[39:0]

D[39:0]

Block BLK1

Bus2[23:0]

Process PRC1

Bus12[23:0]

Process PRC2

Y1[23:0]

BLK2

Y2[39:0]

Medium Grain

The VHDL **process** and Verilog **always** statements are used repeatedly in RTL synthesizable models. They provide medium grain structural control of a design. They are concurrent and activated when specified signals change value. In VHDL the list of signals which can activate the execution of a **process** statement is called a *sensitivity list*. In Verilog, the list of signals which can activate the execution of an **always** statement is called an *event list*. This activation is critical when simulating RTL models but does not affect the synthesized circuit.

VHDL **process** *statement.* This statement is activated in one of two ways depending upon whether it contains a **wait** statement or not. If it does not contain a **wait** statement, it is activated by the changing values of the signal or signals contained in the sensitivity list. If it does contain a **wait** statement, the **process** waits until the expression in the **wait** statement becomes true in which case a sensitivity list should not be used. For RTL synthesizable models, the **wait** should be the first and only **wait** statement in a process. The expression in a **wait** statement can wait for, 1) a particular signal's state to occur or, 2) the detection of a rising or falling edge to occur.

Verilog **always** *statement.* This statement is only activated when signals in the event list change value. The event list almost always contains signals separated by a logical OR (||) operator. The logical AND (&&) operator is allowed, but should not be used in models that are to be synthesized as simulation mismatches may occur between RTL and netlist level models. The reason for this is that the **always** statement will only be triggered into being executed when both signals either side of the logical AND operator (&&) change at the <u>same</u> time. The **always** statement will not be executed when only one signal changes. When modeling sequential logic, the clock and possible asynchronous reset in the event list, must always be preceded with either of the reserved words **posedge** or **negedge**.

Both **process** *(VHDL) and* **always** *(Verilog).* When modeling purely combinational logic, sensitivity list or event list must contain all input signals to the **process** or **always** statement. If they do not, the model will still synthesize correctly, but RTL and netlist level simulation mismatches may occur.

Examples using the **process** and **always** statements are shown extensively throughout this book. Chapter 7 shows VHDL examples using the **wait** statement.

Fine Grain

Fine grain structural control is achieved with the use of subprograms. These are the VHDL **procedure** and **function**, and Verilog **task** and **function**. They provide fine grain structural control of a design. The **procedure** and **task** are similar, as are the two **function**s in VHDL and Verilog. The use of subprograms make models far easier to design, read and verify.

VHDL subprogram bodies are defined in either; the declaration region of an **architecture**, or within a **package body**. If the subprogram body is defined in a **package body**, its port list header must also be declared in the corresponding **package**. It is good design practice to always define subprograms in a **package body** so that they are then accessible to be used by any of the five types of design unit; see Chapter 3. It also means the calling models are less cluttered. Verilog does not have an equivalent to VHDL packages; subprograms are typically placed in a separate system file and included within a model using the `include compiler directive. Table 5.2 compares the **procedure/task** with the **function**.

procedure (VHDL)/task (Verilog)	function (VHDL and Verilog)
can contain timing so may or may not execute in zero simulation time*	must not contain timing - executes in zero simulation time
can enable other procedures/tasks and functions	can enable other functions a VHDL function <u>can</u> enable procedures a Verilog function <u>cannot</u> enable tasks
	must have at least one input value
returns zero or more values	returns a single value
enabled from concurrent or sequential statements	enabled from an expression's operand
	return value is substituted for the expression's operand

* Although the Verilog task may contain timing, timing is not supported by synthesis tools.

Note 1. In VHDL formal actual parameter associations in subprogram calls could be either positional, named or mixed positional and named. Verilog supports only positional notation for subprogram calls.

Note 2. Different VHDL subprograms may have the same name provided the input and output data types are different. Only one signal or variable need have a different data type in order to make it unique. When the subprogram is called, it will use whichever one has input and output data types that exactly matches those of the signals in the calling statement. The technique is known as subprogram overloading.

Table 5.2 Comparison of subprograms - Procedure/Task and functions

Procedure/Task

The **procedure** (VHDL) and **task** (Verilog) are ideal for partitioning models containing large amounts of code. A **procedure** may be called concurrently or sequentially, that is, from outside or inside a **process**. A task may only be called from within an **always** statement. The **procedure** is similar to the **process** in that it can always be rewritten as an equivalent **process**. The same is true for the **task** and a sequential **always** block.

VHDL or Verilog RTL synthesis tools typically do not allow more than one statement to be used in a sequential section of code that causes a wait on particular signal conditions. For VHDL, this means no more than one **wait** statement in a **process**. For Verilog, it means **always** statements cannot be nested. As a **task** can only be called from within an **always** statement or sequential **always** block, a **task** <u>cannot </u>be used to infer sequential logic, unlike the **procedure**.

In summary, when a model is to be synthesized:
1. synchronous logic may only be modeled in a **procedure** using the **if** statement, and not a **wait** statement,
2. synchronous logic may <u>not</u> be modeled in a **task**. Only combinational logic can be modeled which means a **task** can always be remodeled as a **function**.

Example 5.6 shows a **procedure** modeling synchronous logic and how the equivalent **task** is modeled differently because it cannot model synchronous logic.

Example 5.6 Fine grain structuring - Procedure/task

Linear feedback shift registers are modeled using subprograms.

VHDL. A generic *n*-bit **procedure** contains the full LFSR model and is called three times. The first call is concurrent and uses positional signal association. The second call is sequential and uses named association. The third is also sequential and uses a mixed positional and named association.

Verilog. A **task** representing the combinational feedback logic for an 8-bit LFSR are declared. Notice the names of the **task** and **function** are different; they may not have the same name. No task can model synchronous logic if it is to be synthesized. Therefore, in this example, only the exclusive OR feedback logic is modeled in the task. This means a synthesizable task can always be remodeled using an equivalent function. The equivalent function is shown. There are two calls to the **task** while the third call, calls the **function**.

Procedure and task calls

VHDL	Verilog

library IEEE;
use IEEE.STD_Logic_1164.**all**, IEEE.Numeric_STD.**all**;
 	
entity PROCEDURE_CALLS **is**
   port (Clock, Reset1, Reset2, Reset3: **in** std_logic;
       Y1, Y2, Y3: **out** unsigned(7 **downto** 0));
end PROCEDURE_CALLS;
 	
architecture RTL **of** PROCEDURE_CALLS **is**
 	
   procedure LFSR8 (**signal** Clk, Rst: **in** std_logic;
             signal Y: **out** unsigned(7 **downto** 0)) **is**
    constant Taps: unsigned(7 **downto** 0) :=
          (1 | 2 | 3 | 7 => '1', **others** => '0');
    variable Y_var: unsigned(7 **downto** 0);
  begin
    if (Rst = '0') **then**
      Y_var := (**others** => '0');
    elsif rising_edge (Clk) **then**
      for N **in** 7 **downto** 1 **loop**
        if (Taps(N - 1) = '1') **then**
          Y_var(N) := Y_var(N - 1) **xor** Y_var(7);
        else
          Y_var(N) := Y_var(N - 1);
        end if;
      end loop;
      Y_var(0) := Y_var(7);
      Y <= Y_var;
    end if;
  end LFSR8;
 	
begin
 	
  LFSR8(Clock, Reset1, Y1);   ← Concurrent procedure call.
 	
  P1: **process** (Clock, Reset2, Reset3)
  begin
 	
    LFSR8(Y => Y2, Clk => Clock, Rst => Reset2);
              ← Sequential procedure calls.
    LFSR8(Clock, Y => Y3, Rst => Reset3);
 	
  end process;
 	
end RTL;
	module TASK_CALLS (Clock,Reset1,Reset2,Reset3,Y1,Y2,Y3);
	   input Clock, Reset1, Reset2, Reset3;
	   output (7:0) Y1, Y2, Y3; **reg** (7:0) Y1, Y2, Y3;
	   task LFSR_TAPS8_TASK; ⎤
	      input (7:0) A; **output** (7:0) Y;
	      parameter (7:0) Taps = 8'b 10001110;
	      parameter Width = 8;
	      integer N;
	    begin
	      for (N = Width - 1; N >= 1; N = N - 1)
	        if (Taps(N - 1) == 1)
	          Y(N) = A(N - 1) ^ A(Width - 1);
	        else
	          Y(N) = A(N - 1);
	      Y(0) = A(Width - 1);
	    end
	   endtask
	   function (7:0) LFSR_TAPS8_FN; ⎦ ← Task and equivalent function.
	      input (7:0) Reg8;
	      parameter (7:0) Taps = 8'b 10001110;
	      parameter Width = 8;
	      integer N;
	    begin
	      for (N = Width - 1; N >= 1; N = N - 1)
	        if (Taps(N-1) == 1)
	          LFSR_TAPS8_FN(N) = Reg8(N-1) ^ Reg8(Width-1);
	        else
	          LFSR_TAPS8_FN(N) = Reg8(N - 1);
	      LFSR_TAPS8_FN(0) = Reg8(Width - 1);
	    end
	   endfunction
	   always @(**negedge** Reset1 **or posedge** Clock)
	    if (! Reset1)
	      Y1 = 0;
	    else
	      LFSR_TAPS8_TASK(Y1, Y1); ⎤
	   always @(**negedge** Reset2 **or posedge** Clock) ⎟ ← Task calls.
	    if (! Reset2)
	      Y2 = 0;
	    else
	      LFSR_TAPS8_TASK(Y2, Y2); ⎦
	   always @(**negedge** Reset3 **or posedge** Clock)
	    if (! Reset3)
	      Y3 = 0;
	    else
	      Y3 = LFSR_TAPS8_FN(Y3); ← Function call.
	endmodule

Procedure and task calls

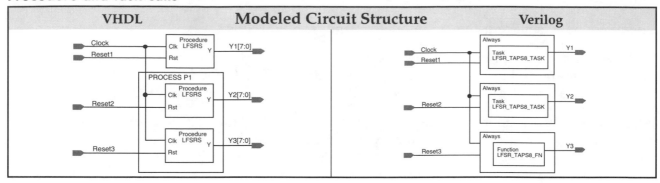

Function

The **function** in both VHDL and Verilog, provides the finest structural control of all. They are called as the operand from within an expression. The single returned value from a function, replaces the function call itself within the expression from which it is called.

Example 5.7 shows a **function** defined and called within the same model. Example 5.8 shows subprograms declared in a separate system file; the VHDL model has overloaded subprograms declared in a **package** and defined in a **package body**, while its Verilog equivalent shows a single **task** and **function** defined in a separate system and referenced using the `include compiler directive.

Example 5.7 Fine grain structuring - function

The model in this example contains the definition of a **function** and three separate calls to it. The VHDL model uses; named, positional, and mixed named and positional notation to associate signals in the model's body to signals in the function. Note again, Verilog does not support named notation for subprogram calls.

Function calls

VHDL	Verilog

library IEEE;
use IEEE.STD_Logic_1164.all;
 	
entity FUNCTION_CALLS is
  port (S1, S2, A1, B1, C1, D1, A2, B2, C2, D2,
     A3, B3, C3, D3: in std_logic;
     Y1, Y2, Y3: out std_logic);
end entity FUNCTION_CALLS;
 	
architecture LOGIC of FUNCTION_CALLS is
  function Fn1 (F1, F2, F3, F4: std_logic) return std_logic is
    variable Result: std_logic;
  begin
    Result := (F1 xor F2) or (F3 xnor F4);
    return Result ;
  end Fn1;
 	
       ┌─────────────────────┐
       │ Positional notation. │
       └─────────────────────┘
begin
  Y1 <= Fn1(A1, B1, C1, D1) or S1 or S2;
 	
  process (S1, S2, A1, B1, C1, D1, A2, B2, C2, D2)
  begin   ┌──────────────────┐
            │ Named notation. │
            └──────────────────┘
    Y2 <= S1 or S2 or Fn1(F3=>C2, F4=>D2, F1=>A2, F2=>B2);
    Y3 <= S1 or Fn1(A3, B3, F4 => D3, F3 => C3) or S2;
  end process;
     ┌───────────────────────────────────┐
     │ Mixed positional & named notation. │
     └───────────────────────────────────┘
end architecture LOGIC;
	module FUNCTION_CALLS
	  (S1,S2, A1,B12,C1,D1,Y1, A2,B2,C2,D2,Y2, A3,B3,C3,D3,Y3);
	
	  input S1,S2, A1,B1,C1,D1, A2,B2,C2,D2, A3,B3,C3,D3;
	  output Y1, Y2, Y3;
	  reg Y2, Y3;
	
	  function Fn1;
	    input F1, F2, F3, F4;
	    begin
	      Fn1 = ((F1 ^ F2) & ! (F3 ^ F4));
	    end
	  endfunction
	┌──┐
	│ Only positional notation allowed in Verilog subprograms calls. │
	└──┘
	  assign Y1 = Fn1(A1, B1, C1, D1) | S1 | S2;
	
	  always @(S1 or S2 or A2 or B2 or C2 or D2 or A3 or B3 or
	        C3 or D3)
	  begin
	    Y2 = S1 | Fn1(A2, B2, C2, D2) | S2;
	
	    Y3 = S1 | S2 | Fn1(A3, B3, C3, D3);
	  end
	endmodule

Function calls

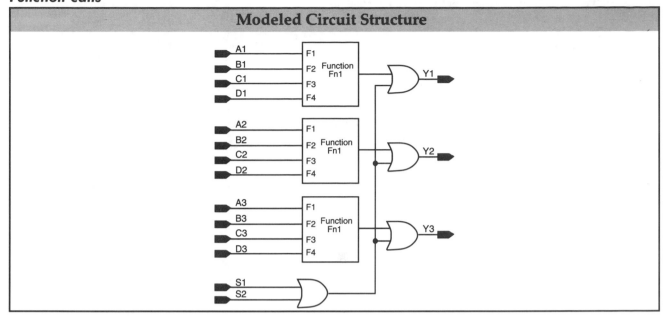

Example 5.8 Fine grain structuring - separate subprograms

This example uses the preferred method of defining subprograms in a separate system file. The subprograms provide the color resulting from mixing any two of three paints together.

VHDL. Uses two packages. The first, COLOR_TYPES, defines the data types used by the subprograms in the second package. The second package, SUBPROGS, has a **package** and **package body**. The subprograms are declared in the **package** declaration and their functional bodies are specified in the **package body**. There are two procedures and two functions all of which have the same name. Although in this case, the two procedures and two functions perform the exact same operation, they are different in that they use different enumerated data types, as defined in the first **package** COLOR_TYPES. Both the two procedure names and two function names are also said to be overloaded.

Verilog. Uses a single `include complier directive which has the effect of being replaced with the contents of the file it references. Subprograms cannot be overloaded so there is only one **task** and one **function**. Enumerated data types are also not allowed, so the **task** and **function** use Color1, Color2, and Color3 instead of Red, Green and Blue.

Sub programs defined in a separate system file

VHDL	Verilog
package COLOR_TYPES **is** **type** PigmentColorPrime **is** (Red, Yellow, Blue); **type** PigmentColorSec **is** (Orange, Violet, Green); **end package** COLOR_TYPES; **use** work.COLOR_TYPES.**all**; **package** SUBPROGS **is** **procedure** MixColor (**signal** C1, C2: **in** PigmentColorPrime; **signal** Mix: **out** PigmentColorSec); **function** MixColor (C1, C2: PigmentPrimeColor) **return** PigmentSecColor; **end package** SUBPROGS; *continued*	// filename "define_colors.v" `**define** Color1 2'b 00 `**define** Color2 2'b 01 `**define** Color3 2'b 10 `**define** MixColor1 2'b 00 `**define** MixColor2 2'b 01 `**define** MixColor3 2'b 10 Separate text substitution definition file "define_colors.v"

Sub programs defined in a separate system file

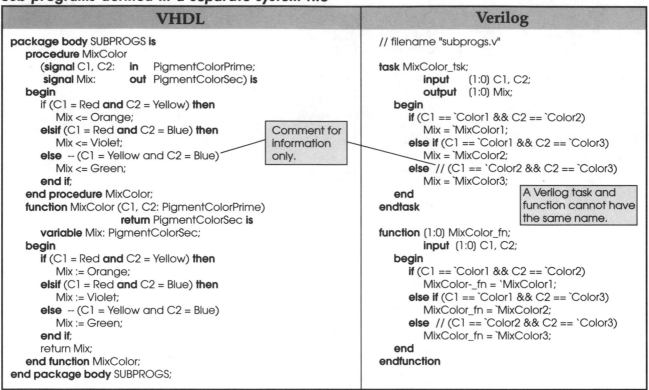

VHDL	Verilog
| ```
package body SUBPROGS is
  procedure MixColor
    (signal C1, C2:   in    PigmentColorPrime;
     signal Mix:          out PigmentColorSec) is
  begin
    if (C1 = Red and C2 = Yellow) then
      Mix <= Orange;
    elsif (C1 = Red and C2 = Blue) then
      Mix <= Violet;
    else  -- (C1 = Yellow and C2 = Blue)
      Mix <= Green;
    end if;
  end procedure MixColor;
  function MixColor (C1, C2: PigmentColorPrime)
                  return PigmentColorSec is
    variable Mix: PigmentColorSec;
  begin
    if (C1 = Red and C2 = Yellow) then
      Mix := Orange;
    elsif (C1 = Red and C2 = Blue) then
      Mix := Violet;
    else  -- (C1 = Yellow and C2 = Blue)
      Mix := Green;
    end if;
    return Mix;
  end function MixColor;
end package body SUBPROGS;
``` | ```
// filename "subprogs.v"

task MixColor_tsk;
         input    (1:0) C1, C2;
         output   (1:0) Mix;
  begin
    if (C1 == `Color1 && C2 == `Color2)
      Mix = `MixColor1;
    else if (C1 == `Color1 && C2 == `Color3)
      Mix = `MixColor2;
    else // (C1 == `Color2 && C2 == `Color3)
      Mix = `MixColor3;
  end
endtask

function (1:0) MixColor_fn;
         input (1:0) C1, C2;
  begin
    if (C1 == `Color1 && C2 == `Color2)
      MixColor-_fn = `MixColor1;
    else if (C1 == `Color1 && C2 == `Color3)
      MixColor_fn = `MixColor2;
    else // (C1 == `Color2 && C2 == `Color3)
      MixColor_fn = `MixColor3;
  end
endfunction
``` |

> Comment for information only.

> A Verilog task and function cannot have the same name.

Calls to generic sub programs defined in a separate system file

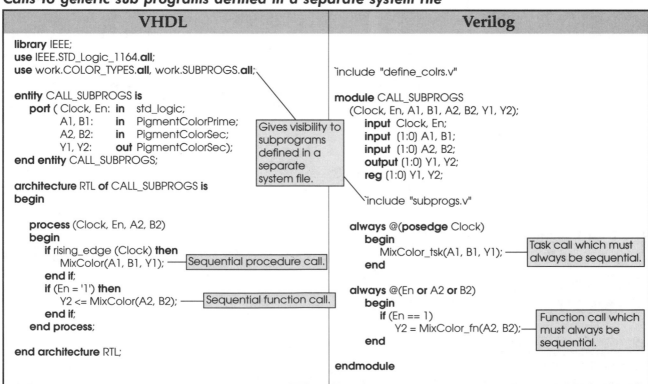

VHDL	Verilog
| ```
library IEEE;
use IEEE.STD_Logic_1164.all;
use work.COLOR_TYPES.all, work.SUBPROGS.all;

entity CALL_SUBPROGS is
  port ( Clock, En: in    std_logic;
         A1, B1:    in    PigmentColorPrime;
         A2, B2:    in    PigmentColorSec;
         Y1, Y2:    out   PigmentColorSec);
end entity CALL_SUBPROGS;

architecture RTL of CALL_SUBPROGS is
begin

  process (Clock, En, A2, B2)
  begin
    if rising_edge (Clock) then
      MixColor(A1, B1, Y1);
    end if;
    if (En = '1') then
      Y2 <= MixColor(A2, B2);
    end if;
  end process;

end architecture RTL;
``` | ```
`include "define_colrs.v"

module CALL_SUBPROGS
  (Clock, En, A1, B1, A2, B2, Y1, Y2);
    input  Clock, En;
    input  (1:0) A1, B1;
    input  (1:0) A2, B2;
    output (1:0) Y1, Y2;
    reg    (1:0) Y1, Y2;

`include "subprogs.v"

  always @(posedge Clock)
    begin
      MixColor_tsk(A1, B1, Y1);
    end

  always @(En or A2 or B2)
    begin
      if (En == 1)
        Y2 = MixColor_fn(A2, B2);
    end

endmodule
``` |

> Gives visibility to subprograms defined in a separate system file.

> Sequential procedure call.

> Sequential function call.

> Task call which must always be sequential.

> Function call which must always be sequential.

Modeling Combinational Logic Circuits

Chapter 6 Contents

Modeling Combinational Logic

This chapter demonstrates the different ways in which purely combinational logic may be modeled. It does not include tri-state logic which is covered separately in Chapter 10. The types of combinational logic circuit commonly used in digital design and covered in this chapter are listed in Table 6.1.

logical/arithmetic equations
logical structure control
multiplexers
encoders
priority encoders
decoders
comparators
ALUs

Table 6.1 Functional types of combinational logic circuit

These more standard functional types of circuit are used in both control path and datapath structures. Typically each circuit type can be modeled in different ways using **if**, **case**, and **for** statements etc. Additionally for VHDL only, the concurrent selected and conditional signal assignments can also be used. The selected signal assignment is synonymous with the **if** statement and the conditional signal assignment is synonymous with the **case** statement, but reside outside a **process**. This means they are always active and so may increase the time it takes to simulate a model when compared to using a **process** with a sensitivity list. Also, the VHDL **for-loop** may include one or more **next** or **exit** statements. The **next** statement causes a jump to the next loop iteration, while the **exit** statement causes an exit from the **for-loop** altogether. There is no equivalent to the **next** or **exit** statements in Verilog. The VHDL **while-loop** statement, and the Verilog **forever** and **while-loop** statements, are not often used to model combinational logic; their loop range must have a static value at synthesis compile time so that a predetermined amount of logic can be synthesized. They are not supported by the synthesis tools from VeriBest Incorporated.

Note, that when modeling combinational logic, the sensitivity list of a **process** statement (VHDL) or the event list of an **always** statement (Verilog), must contain <u>all</u> inputs used in the particular statement. If it does not, the model will still synthesize correctly, but may not simulate correctly. This is because **process/always** statements are concurrent and will not be triggered into being executed when the omitted signals change, and means the output signals will not be updated.

Because the examples in this chapter are relatively small for demonstration purposes, VHDL models use mostly signal assignments and relatively few variable assignments. VHDL models with more code in a **process**, typically use more variable assignments. Variables and constants are used in the computation of signal values, see Chapter 4. A number of VHDL model versions in this chapter use **for-loop** statements. It is better to use only variable assignments, and not signal assignments in **for-loop** statements. This is not mandatory as identical circuits will be synthesized, but it will simulate faster for reasons given in Chapter 4.

The logic synthesized from the majority of the models in this chapter have little or no inherent logical structure. This means area, timing and power characteristics are often considerably improved when the synthesized circuit is optimized. Logic optimization breaks down the logical structure of a circuit and creates a new one in the process of attempting to improve any area, timing or power requirements that have been specified.

The following sections describe each of the circuit functions listed in Table 6.1. Shifters, multipliers and dividers can also be modeled using synchronous logic and are included in Chapter 9.

Logical/Arithmetic Equations

Both logical and arithmetic equations may be modeled using the logical and arithmetic operators in the expressions of continuous data flow assignments, see Example 6.1.

Example 6.1 Equations modeled using continuous assignments

Logical and arithmetic equations are modeled using continuous data flow assignments, incorporating both logical and arithmetic operators. Both concurrent (outside **process**/**always**) and sequential (inside **process**/**always**) assignments are shown.

VHDL signals S1 and S2 and variables V1 and V2, have identical names in the Verilog model for comparison, but are all variables of type **reg** in the Verilog model. The Verilog variables V1 and V2 are not local to the sequential block as the variables are in the VHDL model. Although Verilog supports locally defined data types of type **reg**, this is not generally supported by synthesis tools. The VHDL output Y1 is defined from a concurrent continuous assignment and so the Verilog equivalent must be of type **wire**. The data type of Y1 could have been explicitly defined as a **wire**, for example, "**wire** Y1;", however, this is not necessary as type **wire** is implied by default as defined by the Verilog language.

Mathememematical equations modeled using continous assignments

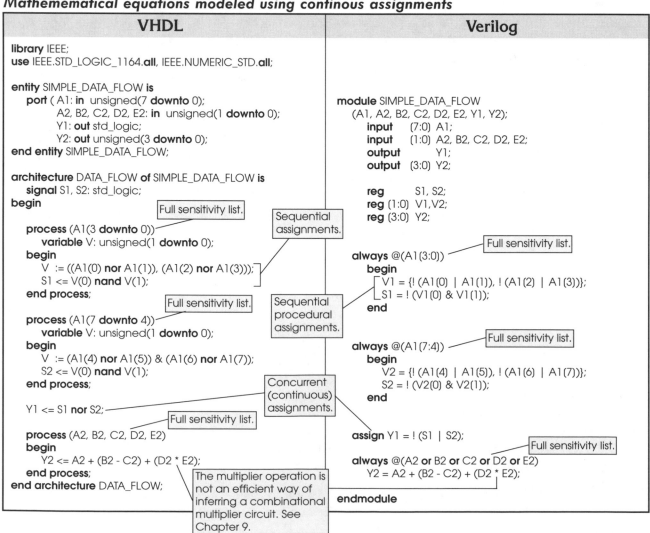

VHDL	Verilog
`library IEEE;` `use IEEE.STD_LOGIC_1164.all, IEEE.NUMERIC_STD.all;` `entity SIMPLE_DATA_FLOW is` `    port ( A1: in  unsigned(7 downto 0);` `           A2, B2, C2, D2, E2: in  unsigned(1 downto 0);` `           Y1: out std_logic;` `           Y2: out unsigned(3 downto 0);` `end entity SIMPLE_DATA_FLOW;` `architecture DATA_FLOW of SIMPLE_DATA_FLOW is` `    signal S1, S2: std_logic;` `begin` `    process (A1(3 downto 0))` *Full sensitivity list.* `        variable V: unsigned(1 downto 0);` `    begin` `        V := ((A1(0) nor A1(1)), (A1(2) nor A1(3)));` `        S1 <= V(0) nand V(1);` `    end process;` `    process (A1(7 downto 4))` *Full sensitivity list.* `        variable V: unsigned(1 downto 0);` `    begin` `        V := (A1(4) nor A1(5)) & (A1(6) nor A1(7));` `        S2 <= V(0) nand V(1);` `    end process;` `    Y1 <= S1 nor S2;` `    process (A2, B2, C2, D2, E2)` *Full sensitivity list.* `    begin` `        Y2 <= A2 + (B2 - C2) + (D2 * E2);` `    end process;` `end architecture DATA_FLOW;`	`module SIMPLE_DATA_FLOW` `    (A1, A2, B2, C2, D2, E2, Y1, Y2);` `        input     (7:0) A1;` `        input     (1:0) A2, B2, C2, D2, E2;` `        output          Y1;` `        output    (3:0) Y2;` `    reg       S1, S2;` `    reg (1:0) V1,V2;` `    reg (3:0) Y2;` `    always @(A1(3:0))` *Full sensitivity list.* `        begin` ` V1 = {! (A1(0)	A1(1)), ! (A1(2)	A1(3))};` ` S1 = ! (V1(0) & V1(1));` ` end`  ` always @(A1(7:4))`   *Full sensitivity list.* ` begin` ` V2 = {! (A1(4)	A1(5)), ! (A1(6)	A1(7))};` ` S2 = ! (V2(0) & V2(1));` ` end`  ` assign Y1 = ! (S1 | S2);`   *Full sensitivity list.*  ` always @(A2 or B2 or C2 or D2 or E2)` ` Y2 = A2 + (B2 - C2) + (D2 * E2);`  `endmodule`

Annotations: *Sequential assignments.* *Sequential procedural assignments.* *Concurrent (continuous) assignments.* *The multiplier operation is not an efficient way of inferring a combinational multiplier circuit. See Chapter 9.*

Logical Structure Control

Parentheses can be used for course grain control of synthesized logic structure. Logic optimization can still be used to break down all, or most, of a circuit's logic structure and restructure it in the process of attempting to meet specific constraints. However, the use of parentheses in the model's expressions can make the optimizer's job far easier and less cpu intensive, but more importantly, the optimizer may not be able to achieve such good results that careful choice of parentheses can bring, see Example 6.2.

Example 6.2 Parentheses used to control logical structure

Parentheses are used to control the structure of inferred adders. The model contains two assignments, each implying the synthesis of three adders. The first assignment to Y1 does not use parentheses and so defaults to a left to right priority; this results in a worst case timing delay which passes through three adders. The second assignment to Y2 does use parentheses for a more course grain structural control and infers a circuit structure whose longest timing delay this time passes through only two adders instead of three.

Parentheses used to control logical structure

VHDL	Verilog

library IEEE;
use IEEE.STD_STDLOGIC_1164.**all**; IEEE.NUMERIC_STD.**all**;
 	
entity COMB_LOGIC_STRUCT **is**
    port (A1,B1,C1,D1,A2,B2,C2,D2: **in** unsigned(8 **downto** 0);
        Y1, Y2: **out** unsigned(8 **downto** 0));
end entity COMB_LOGIC_STRUCT;
 	
architecture LOGIC **of** COMB_LOGIC_STRUCT **is**
begin
 	
    process (A1, B1, C1, D1, A2, B2, C2, D2)
    begin
 	
        Y1 <= A1 + B1 + C1 + D1;
 	
        Y2 <= (A2 + B2) + (C2 + D2);
 	
    end process;
 	
end architecture LOGIC;
	module COMB_LOGIC_STRUCT
	    (A1, B1, C1, D1, A2, B2, C2, D2, Y1, Y2);
	        input (8:0) A1, B1, C1, D1, A2, B2, C2, D2;
	        output (8:0) Y1, Y2;
	
	    reg (8:0) Y1, Y2;
	
	    always @(A1 **or** B1 **or** C1 **or** D1 **or** A2 **or** B2 **or** C2 **or** D2)
	        begin
	
	        Y1 = A1 + B1 + C1 + D1;
	
	        Y2 = (A2 + B2) + (C2 + D2);
	
	    end
	
	endmodule

Synthesized Circuit Structure

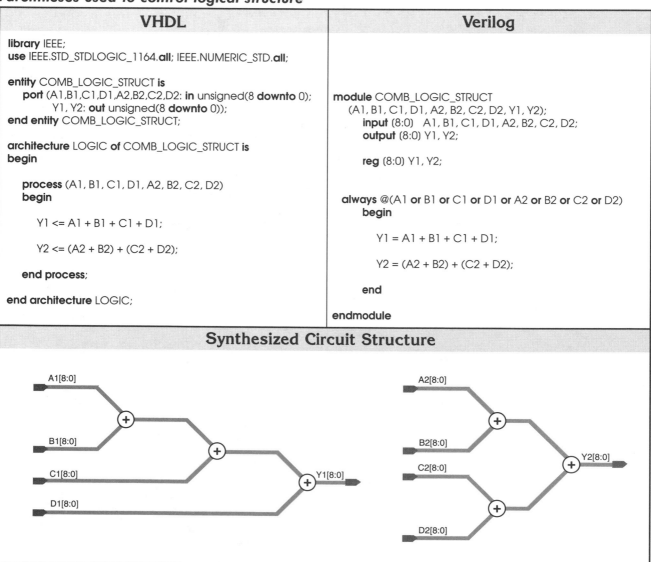

Multiplexers

A multiplexer selectively passes the value of one, of two or more input signals, to the output. One or more control signals control which input signal's value is passed to the output, see Figure 6.1. Each input signal, and the output signal, may represent single bit or multiple bit busses. The select inputs are normally binary encoded such that n select inputs can select from one of up to 2^n inputs.

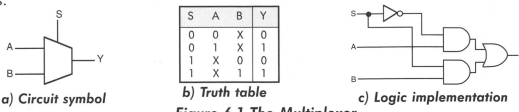

S	A	B	Y
0	0	X	0
0	1	X	1
1	X	0	0
1	X	1	1

a) Circuit symbol   *b) Truth table*   *c) Logic implementation*

Figure 6.1 The Multiplexer

RTL level synthesis tools are not particularly good at identifying multiplexer type functions and mapping them directly onto multiplexer macro cells in a given technology library. If this is desired a multiplexer macro cell should be explicitly instantiated in the HDL model. However, a multiplexer circuit is often better implemented in cell primitives as they can be optimized with their surrounding logic and often produce a more optimal overall circuit implementation. Example 6.3 shows three ways of modeling a 2-1 multiplexer. Example 6.4 shows a 4-1 multiplexer modeled in several different ways and Example 6.5 shows a 2-bit wide 8-1 multiplexer.

Example 6.3 One-bit wide 2-1 multiplexer

The model of the one-bit wide 2-1 multiplexer described above is shown modeled using the **if** statement in its most simplest form. Multiplexer output Y1 is derived concurrently via a selected signal assignment in VHDL and a conditional continuous assignment in Verilog. The second and third multiplexer outputs, Y2 and Y3, are derived from an **if** statement. The first **if** statement defines a default output value for Y2 in an assignment immediately before the **if** statement, while the second **if** statement uses the more normal method of using an **else** clause.

One bit wide 2-1 multiplexer

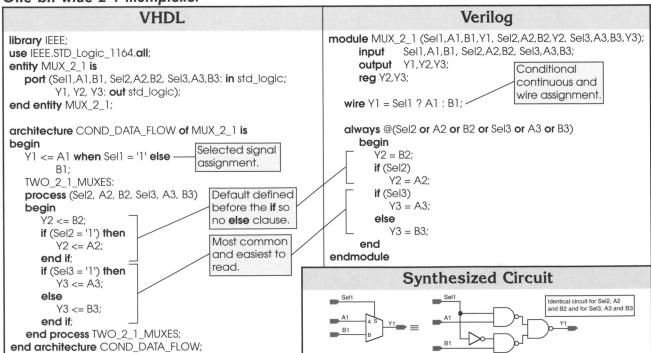

Example 6.4 Modeling styles of a 4-1 multiplexer

Five ways of modeling a 4-1 multiplexer in VHDL, and three ways of modeling it in Verilog are indicated. They are:

1. one **if** statement with multiple **elsif/else if** clauses,
2. a conditional signal assignment (VHDL),
3. nested **if** statements,
4. **case** statement,
5. uses a selected signal assignment (VHDL).

All models synthesize to the same circuit as shown.

There is no incorrect modeling method, however using the **case** statement requires less code and is easier to read when compared with the **if** statement. This becomes more distinct with increasing inputs per output; see also Example 6.5. The two VHDL only models, 2 and 5, use concurrent signal assignments so reside outside a process. This means they are always active and so will usually take longer to simulate.

Different ways of modeling a 4-1 multiplexer

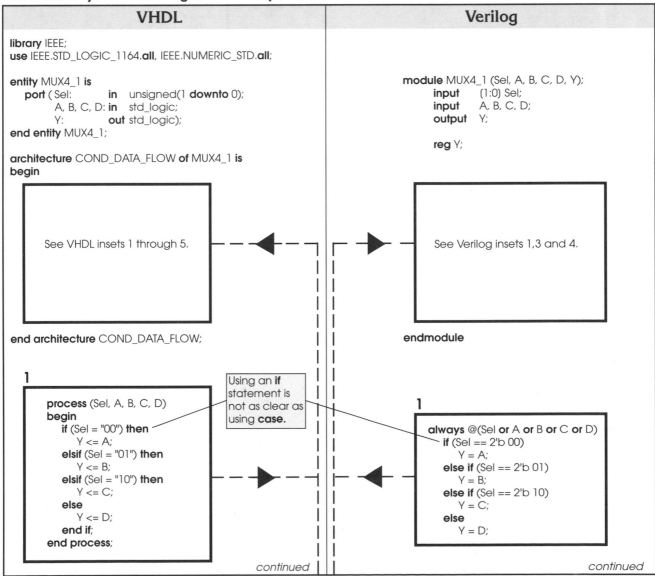

VHDL	Verilog
| ```
library IEEE;
use IEEE.STD_LOGIC_1164.all, IEEE.NUMERIC_STD.all;

entity MUX4_1 is
    port ( Sel:        in   unsigned(1 downto 0);
           A, B, C, D: in   std_logic;
           Y:               out std_logic);
end entity MUX4_1;

architecture COND_DATA_FLOW of MUX4_1 is
begin


    See VHDL insets 1 through 5.


end architecture COND_DATA_FLOW;
``` | ```
module MUX4_1 (Sel, A, B, C, D, Y);
    input    (1:0) Sel;
    input    A, B, C, D;
    output   Y;

    reg Y;



    See Verilog insets 1,3 and 4.


endmodule
``` |

1

```
process (Sel, A, B, C, D)
begin
    if (Sel = "00") then
        Y <= A;
    elsif (Sel = "01") then
        Y <= B;
    elsif (Sel = "10") then
        Y <= C;
    else
        Y <= D;
    end if;
end process;
```

Using an **if** statement is not as clear as using **case**.

1

```
always @(Sel or A or B or C or D)
    if (Sel == 2'b 00)
        Y = A;
    else if (Sel == 2'b 01)
        Y = B;
    else if (Sel == 2'b 10)
        Y = C;
    else
        Y = D;
```

continued   *continued*

Different ways of modeling a 4-1 multiplexer

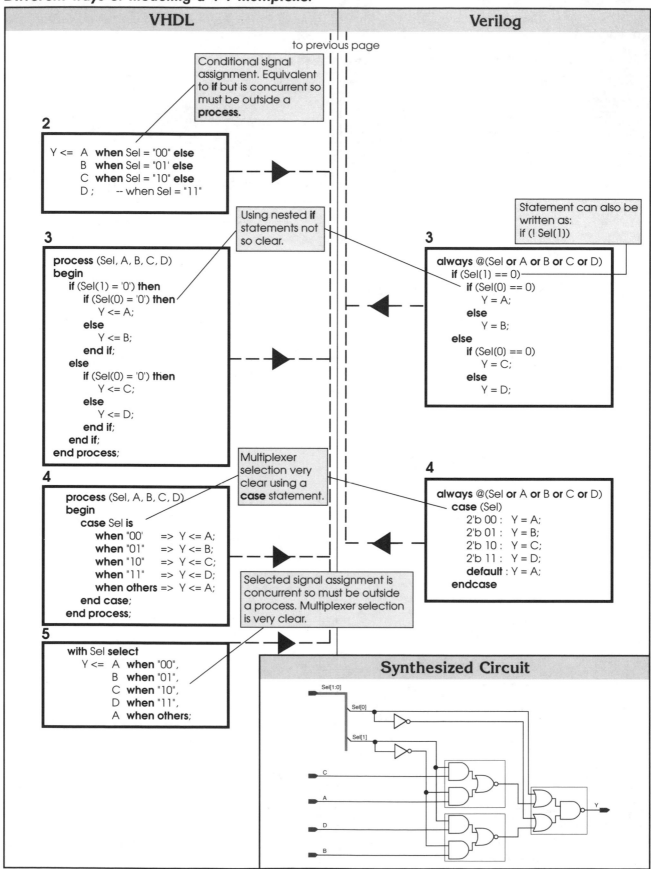

VHDL	Verilog

to previous page

Conditional signal assignment. Equivalent to **if** but is concurrent so must be outside a **process.**

2
```
Y <=  A  when Sel = "00" else
      B  when Sel = "01' else
      C  when Sel = "10" else
      D ;     -- when Sel = "11"
```

Using nested **if** statements not so clear.

3
```
process (Sel, A, B, C, D)
begin
   if (Sel(1) = '0') then
      if (Sel(0) = '0') then
         Y <= A;
      else
         Y <= B;
      end if;
   else
      if (Sel(0) = '0') then
         Y <= C;
      else
         Y <= D;
      end if;
   end if;
end process;
```

Statement can also be written as:
if (! Sel(1))

3
```
always @(Sel or A or B or C or D)
   if (Sel(1) == 0)
      if (Sel(0) == 0)
         Y = A;
      else
         Y = B;
   else
      if (Sel(0) == 0)
         Y = C;
      else
         Y = D;
```

Multiplexer selection very clear using a **case** statement.

4
```
process (Sel, A, B, C, D)
begin
   case Sel is
      when "00'  => Y <= A;
      when "01"  => Y <= B;
      when "10"  => Y <= C;
      when "11"  => Y <= D;
      when others => Y <= A;
   end case;
end process;
```

4
```
always @(Sel or A or B or C or D)
   case (Sel)
      2'b 00 :  Y = A;
      2'b 01 :  Y = B;
      2'b 10 :  Y = C;
      2'b 11 :  Y = D;
      default : Y = A;
   endcase
```

Selected signal assignment is concurrent so must be outside a process. Multiplexer selection is very clear.

5
```
with Sel select
   Y <=  A  when "00",
         B  when "01",
         C  when "10",
         D  when "11",
         A  when others;
```

Synthesized Circuit

Example 6.5 Two-bit wide 8-1 multiplexer using case

A 2-bit wide 8-1 multiplexer is modeled to the truth table in Table 6.1. Models use the **case** statement, and additionally for VHDL only, selected signal assignment. The **if** statement becomes cumbersome for the wider inputs. It is different from the previous example in that a VHDL integer data type is used for the select input Sel, and the Verilog **case** selector values are specified in integer form, that is, 4 instead of 3'b 0100.

Sel	A7	A6	A5	A4	A3	A2	A1	A0	Y
000	XX	XX	XX	XX	XX	XX	XX	DD	DD
001	XX	XX	XX	XX	XX	XX	DD	XX	DD
010	XX	XX	XX	XX	XX	DD	XX	XX	DD
011	XX	XX	XX	XX	DD	XX	XX	XX	DD
100	XX	XX	XX	DD	XX	XX	XX	XX	DD
101	XX	XX	DD	XX	XX	XX	XX	XX	DD
110	XX	DD	XX	XX	XX	XX	XX	XX	DD
111	DD	XX	XX	XX	XX	XX	XX	XX	DD

XX = two bit don't care   DD = two bit data

Table 6.1 Truth table for a two bit wide 8-1 multiplexer

Two bit wide 8-1 multiplexer

VHDL	Verilog
| ```
library IEEE;
use IEEE.STD_LOGIC_1164.all, IEEE.NUMERIC_STD.all;
entity MUX2X8_1_CASE is
    port ( Sel: in  integer range 0 to 7;
           A0,A1,A2,A3,A4,A5,A6,A7: in  unsigned(1 downto 0);
           Y: out unsigned(1 downto 0));
end entity MUX2X8_1_CASE;
architecture COND_DATA_FLOW of MUX2X8_1_CASE is
begin
    process (Sel, A0, A1, A2, A3, A4, A5, A6, A7)
    begin
        case Sel is
            when 0  => Y <= A0;
            when 1  => Y <= A1;
            when 2  => Y <= A2;
            when 3  => Y <= A3;
            when 4  => Y <= A4;
            when 5  => Y <= A5;
            when 6  => Y <= A6;
            when 7  => Y <= A7;
        end case;
    end process;

end architecture COND_DATA_FLOW;
``` | ```
module MUX2X8_1_CASE
    (Sel, A0, A1, A2, A3, A4, A5, A6, A7, Y);
    input    (2:0) Sel;
    input    (1:0) A0, A1, A2, A3, A4, A5, A6, A7;
    output   (1:0) Y;

    reg (1:0) Y;

    always @(Sel or A0 or A1 or A2 or
             A3 or A4 or A5 or A6 or A7)
    case (Sel)
        0 : Y = A0;
        1 : Y = A1;
        2 : Y = A2;
        3 : Y = A3;
        4 : Y = A4;
        5 : Y = A5;
        6 : Y = A6;
        7 : Y = A7;
        default : Y = A0;
    endcase

endmodule
``` |

VHDL
| ```
library IEEE;
use IEEE.STD_LOGIC_1164.all, IEEE.NUMERIC_STD.all;
entity MUX2X8_1_SSA is
    port ( Sel: in  integer range 0 to 7;
           A0,A1,A2,A3,A4,A5,A6,A7: in  unsigned(1 downto 0);
           Y: out unsigned(1 downto 0));
end entity MUX2X8_1_SSA;
architecture COND_DATA_FLOW of MUX2X8_1_SSA is
begin
    with Sel select
        Y <= A0 when 0,
             A1 when 1,
             A2 when 2,
             A3 when 3,
             A4 when 4,
             A5 when 5,
             A6 when 6,
             A7 when 7;

end architecture COND_DATA_FLOW;
``` |
```

Two-bit wide 8-1 multiplexer

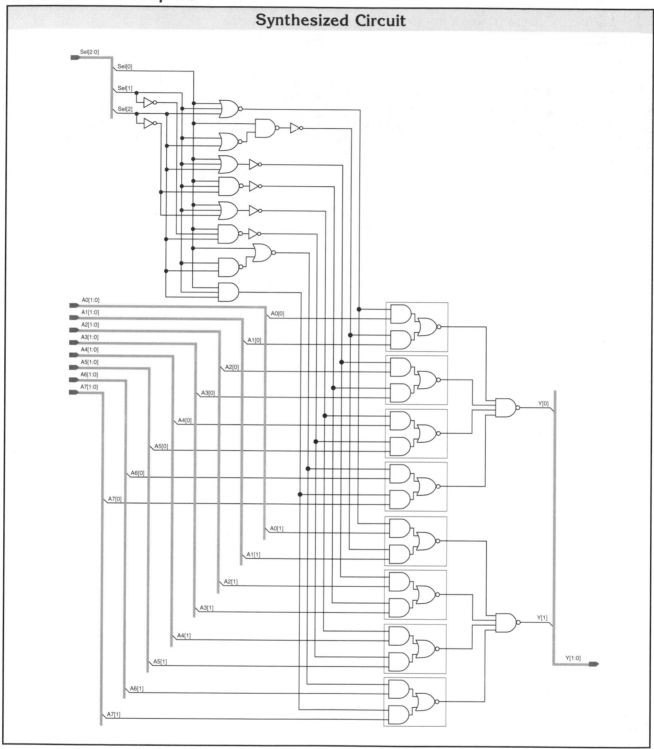

Encoders

Discrete quantities of digital information, data, are often represented in a coded form; binary being the most popular. Encoders are used to encode discrete data into a coded form and decoders are used to convert it back into its original undecoded form. An encoder that has 2^n (or less) input lines encodes input data to provide n encoded output lines. The truth table for an 8-3 binary encoder (8 inputs and 3 outputs) is shown in Table 6.2. It is assumed that only one input has a value of 1 at any given time, otherwise the output has some undefined value and the circuit is meaningless.

inputs								outputs		
A7	A6	A5	A4	A3	A2	A1	A0	Y2	Y1	Y0
0	0	0	0	0	0	0	1	0	0	0
0	0	0	0	0	0	1	0	0	0	1
0	0	0	0	0	1	0	0	0	1	0
0	0	0	0	1	0	0	0	0	1	1
0	0	0	1	0	0	0	0	1	0	0
0	0	1	0	0	0	0	0	1	0	1
0	1	0	0	0	0	0	0	1	1	0
1	0	0	0	0	0	0	0	1	1	1

Table 6.2 Truth table for an 8-3 binary encoder

The truth table can be modeled using the **if**, **case** or **for** statements.

Models using a **case** statement are clearer than those using an **if** statement. The **for** loop is better for modeling a larger or more generic *m-n* bit encoder. All models of such a circuit must use a default "don't care" value to minimize the synthesized circuit as only 8 of the 256 (2^8) input conditions need to be specified. The synthesis tool, if capable, replaces "don't care" values with logic 0 or 1 values as necessary in order to minimize the circuit's logic. This means VHDL integer data type cannot be used for the case selector in a **case** statement. However, whatever data type is used, for example, unsigned, it can always be converted from an integer data type before the **case** statement and back again after, although this can be cumbersome.

Example 6.6 shows models of the 8-3 binary encoder described above, using either the **if**, **case** or **for** statement.

Example 6.6 An 8-3 binary encoder

An 8-3 encoder is modeled according to the truth table of Table 6.2 using the **if**, **case** or **for** statement, and additionally for VHDL, conditional and selected signal assignments.

All models use a default assigned output value to avoid having to explicitly define all $2^8 - 8 = 248$ input conditions that should not occur under normal operating conditions. The default assignment is a "don't care" value to minimize synthesized logic. If all 248 input conditions that are not explicitly defined default to binary 000, more logic would be synthesized than is necessary.

8-3 encoder modeled from the truth table

VHDL	Verilog

library IEEE;
use IEEE.STD_LOGIC_1164.**all**, IEEE.NUMERIC_STD.**all**;
entity ENCODE_8_3_IF_ELSE **is**
   port (A: **in**   unsigned(7 **downto** 0);
         Y: **out** unsigned(2 **downto** 0));
end entity ENCODE_8_3_IF_ELSE;
 	
architecture COND_DATA_FLOW **of** ENCODE_8_3_IF_ELSE **is**
begin
   process (A)
   begin
     if (A = "00000001") **then** Y <= "000";
     elsif (A = "00000010") **then** Y <= "001";
     elsif (A = "00000100") **then** Y <= "010";
     elsif (A = "00001000") **then** Y <= "011";
     elsif (A = "00010000") **then** Y <= "100";
     elsif (A = "00100000") **then** Y <= "101";
     elsif (A = "01000000") **then** Y <= "110";
     elsif (A = "10000000") **then** Y <= "111";
     else Y <= "XXX";
     end if;
   end process;
end architecture COND_DATA_FLOW;
	module ENCODER_8_3_IF_ELSE (A, Y);
	   input (7:0) A;
	   output (2:0) Y;
	
	   reg (2:0) Y;
	
	  always @(A)
	    begin
	     if (A == 8'b 00000001) Y = 0;
	     else if (A == 8'b 00000010) Y = 1;
	     else if (A == 8'b 00000100) Y = 2;
	     else if (A == 8'b 00001000) Y = 3;
	     else if (A == 8'b 00010000) Y = 4;
	     else if (A == 8'b 00100000) Y = 5;
	     else if (A == 8'b 01000000) Y = 6;
	     else if (A == 8'b 10000000) Y = 7;
	     else Y = 3'b X;
	    end
	
	endmodule

VHDL

library IEEE;
use IEEE.STD_LOGIC_1164.**all**, IEEE.NUMERIC_STD.**all**;
entity ENCODE_8_3_CSA **is**
   port (A: **in**   unsigned(7 **downto** 0);
         Y: **out** unsigned(2 **downto** 0));
end entity ENCODE_8_3_CSA;
 	
architecture LOGIC **of** ENCODE_8_3_CSA **is**
begin
  Y <= "000" **when** A = "00000001" **else**
        "001" **when** A = "00000010" **else**
        "010" **when** A = "00000100" **else**
        "011" **when** A = "00001000" **else**
        "100" **when** A = "00010000" **else**
        "101" **when** A = "00100000" **else**
        "110" **when** A = "01000000" **else**
        "111" **when** A = "10000000" **else**
        "XXX";
end architecture LOGIC;

Conditional signal assignment which is the concurrent equivalent of **if** statement.

8-3 encoder modeled from the truth table (continued)

VHDL	Verilog

library IEEE;
use IEEE.STD_LOGIC_1164.**all**, IEEE.NUMERIC_STD.**all**;
 	
entity ENCODE_8_3_CASE **is**
    port (A: **in**   unsigned(7 **downto** 0);
          Y: **out** unsigned(2 **downto** 0));
end entity ENCODE_8_3_CASE;
 	
architecture LOGIC **of** ENCODE_8_3_CASE **is**
begin
    process (A)
    begin
       case A **is**
          when "00000001" => Y <= "000";
          when "00000010" => Y <= "001";
          when "00000100" => Y <= "010";
          when "00001000" => Y <= "011";
          when "00010000" => Y <= "100";
          when "00100000" => Y <= "101";
          when "01000000" => Y <= "110";
          when "10000000" => Y <= "111";
          when others   => Y <= "XXX";
       end case;
    end process;
end architecture LOGIC;
	module ENCODE_8_3_CASE (A, Y);
	    input (7:0) A;
	    output (2:0) Y;
	    reg (2:0) Y;
	
	    always @(A)
	       begin
	          casex (A)
	             8'b 00000001 : Y = 0;
	             8'b 00000010 : Y = 1;
	             8'b 00000100 : Y = 2;
	             8'b 00001000 : Y = 3;
	             8'b 00010000 : Y = 4;
	             8'b 00100000 : Y = 5;
	             8'b 01000000 : Y = 6;
	             8'b 10000000 : Y = 7;
	             default : Y = 3'b X;
	          endcase
	       end
	
	endmodule

> **case** statement is very clear.

VHDL

library IEEE;
use IEEE.STD_LOGIC_1164.**all**, IEEE.NUMERIC_STD.**all**;
 	
entity ENCODE_8_3_SSA **is**
    port (A: **in**   unsigned(7 **downto** 0);
          Y: **out** unsigned(2 **downto** 0));
end entity ENCODE_8_3_SSA;
 	
architecture LOGIC **of** ENCODE_8_3_SSA **is**
begin
    with A **select**
       Y <= "000" **when** "00000001",
              "001" **when** "00000010",
              "010" **when** "00000100",
              "011" **when** "00001000",
              "100" **when** "00010000",
              "101" **when** "00100000",
              "110" **when** "01000000",
              "111" **when** "10000000",
              "XXX" **when others**;
end architecture LOGIC;

> Selected signal assignment is also very clear. It is the concurrent equivalent of **case** statement.

8-3 encoder modeled from the truth table (continued)

VHDL	Verilog

```vhdl
library IEEE;
use IEEE.STD_LOGIC_1164.all, IEEE.NUMERIC_STD.all;

entity ENCODE_8_3_FOR is
    port ( A: in   unsigned(7 downto 0);
           Y: out unsigned(2 downto 0));
end entity ENCODE_8_3_FOR;

architecture LOGIC of ENCODE_8_3_FOR is
begin

    process (A)
        variable N: integer range 0 to 7;
        variable Test: unsigned(7 downto 0);
    begin
        Test := "00000001";
        Y <= "XXX";
        for N in 0 to 7 loop
            if (A = Test) then
                Y <= To_unsigned(N, 3);
                exit;
            end if;
            Test := shift_left(Test, 1);
        end loop;
    end process;
end architecture LOGIC;
```

Integer range specified to avoid 32 bit logic being synthesized.

for loop statement. Code stays condensed when bit width increase.

loop integer converted to type unsigned for output.

```verilog
module ENCODE_8_3_FOR (A, Y);
    input   (7:0) A;
    output  (2:0) Y;
    reg (2:0) Y;

    reg (7:0) Test;
    integer N;

    always @(A)
        begin
            Test = 8'b 00000001;
            Y = 3'b X;
            for (N = 0; N < 8; N = N + 1)
                begin
                    if (A == Test)
                        Y = N;
                    Test = Test << 1;
                end
        end

endmodule
```

Synthesized Circuit

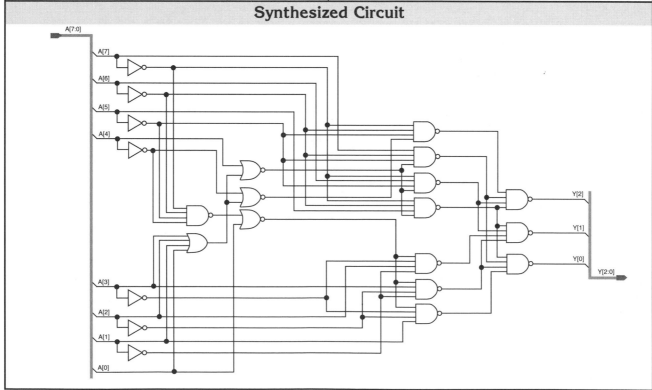

Priority Encoders

The operation of the priority encoder is such that if two or more single bit inputs are at a logic 1, then the input with the highest priority will take precedence, and its particular coded value will be output. Models of an 8-3 binary priority encoder are included in Example 6.7.

Example 6.7 An 8-3 binary priority encoder

An 8-3 priority encoder is modeled in several different ways to the truth table shown in Table 6.3. The most significant bit, A7, has the highest priority. The output signal Valid indicates that at least one input bit is at logic 1 and signifies the 3-bit output Y is valid.

Different models use **if**, **case** and **for** statements. They all use "don't care" default value for the 3-bit output Y for the condition when all 8 inputs are at logic 0. This gives the synthesis tool the potential to reduce the logic, although it makes little or no difference in this particular model.

Using **if** *statements.* The first model uses an **if** statement to test each bit in turn starting from the highest priority bit, A7.

inputs								outputs			
A7	A6	A5	A4	A3	A2	A1	A0	Y2	Y1	Y0	Valid
0	0	0	0	0	0	0	0	X	X	X	0
0	0	0	0	0	0	0	1	0	0	0	1
0	0	0	0	0	0	1	X	0	0	1	1
0	0	0	0	0	1	X	X	0	1	0	1
0	0	0	0	1	X	X	X	0	1	1	1
0	0	0	1	X	X	X	X	1	0	0	1
0	0	1	X	X	X	X	X	1	0	1	1
0	1	X	X	X	X	X	X	1	1	0	1
1	X	X	X	X	X	X	X	1	1	1	1

X = don't care

Table 6.3 Truth table of an 8-3 binary priority encoder

Using **case/casex** *statements.* The second model uses a VHDL **case** statement and Verilog **casex** statement. The Verilog **casex** statement is ideally suited for this model as it allows "don't care" input conditions to be used. The VHDL **case** statement is <u>not</u> suitable at all, and the only practical way of using it is to convert signal A from an unsigned to integer data type and specify the appropriate range or each choice value. This type of model will typically cause a synthesis tool to generate large amounts of redundant logic which must then be optimized away by the optimizer. In this particular sized model the optimizer is able to produce identical circuits. However, this may not be the case for larger priority encoders due to the heuristic nature of logic optimizers.

Using conditional signal assignments (VHDL). If the priority encoder was modeled using VHDL conditional signal assignments, two assignments would be needed; one for each output, Valid and Y. Each assignment would be similar in that they would separately select each value of the input A. The synthesized circuit would also be the same, but there would be code duplication for the input selection. This results in more code that is less comprehensible. It is not recommended, and not shown in this example.

Using **for** *loop statements.* The third model uses the **for** loop and tests each bit in turn. The advantage is that the code does not get progressively larger as input and output bit widths increase. Default output values are defined before the **for** statement. There are two VHDL versions; the first checks each bit in turn starting from the least LSB, the second checks each bit in turn starting from the MSB and exits the loop when it has found the first bit having a logic 1 value.

Different ways of modeling an 8-3 priority encoder

VHDL	Verilog

```
library IEEE;
use IEEE.STD_LOGIC_1164.all, IEEE.NUMERIC_STD.all;

entity PRI_EN8_3 is
    port ( A:     in   unsigned(7 downto 0);
          Valid: out std_logic;
          Y:      out unsigned(2 downto 0));
end entity PRI_EN8_3;

architecture COND_DATA_FLOW of PRI_EN8_3 is
begin
```

```
module PRI_EN8_3 (A, Valid, Y);
    input  (7:0) A;
    output Valid;
    output (2:0) Y;

    integer N;
    reg Valid;
    reg (2:0) Y;
```

> Only needed for the model version using the **for** loop.

[See VHDL insets 1 through 4.] ◄ ¦ ► [See Verilog insets 1 through 3.]

```
end architecture COND_DATA_FLOW;
```

```
endmodule
```

1

```
process (A)
begin
    Valid <= '1';
    if (A(7) = '1') then    Y <= "111";
    elsif (A(6) = '1') then Y <= "110";
    elsif (A(5) = '1') then Y <= "101";
    elsif (A(4) = '1') then Y <= "100";
    elsif (A(3) = '1') then Y <= "011";
    elsif (A(2) = '1') then Y <= "010";
    elsif (A(1) = '1') then Y <= "001";
    elsif (A(0) = '1') then Y <= "000";
    else
        Valid <= '0';
        Y <= "XXX";
    end if;
end process;
```

1

```
always @(A)
    begin
        Valid = 1;
        if (A(7))      Y = 7;
        else if (A(6)) Y = 6;
        else if (A(5)) Y = 5;
        else if (A(4)) Y = 4;
        else if (A(3)) Y = 3;
        else if (A(2)) Y = 2;
        else if (A(1)) Y = 1;
        else if (A(0)) Y = 0;
        else
            begin
                Valid = 0;
                Y = 3'b X;
            end
    end
```

> "Don't care" inputs to a VHDL **case** statement, e.g., X--, are not true "don't care" values in terms of logic reduction, see Chapter 4. Therefore, this model version uses an integer range but, its operation is unclear. Also, it produces more initial redundant synthesized logic that must be optimized away by the optimizer.

2

```
process (A)
    variable A_int: integer range 0 to 255;
begin
    A_int := to_integer(A);
    Valid <= '1';
    case (A) is
        when 128 to 255  => Y <= "111";
        when 64 to 128   => Y <= "110";
        when 32 to 63    => Y <= "101";
        when 16 to 31    => Y <= "100";
        when 8 to 15     => Y <= "011";
        when 4 to 7      => Y <= "010";
        when 2 to 3      => Y <= "001";
        when 1           => Y <= "000";
        when others      => Valid <= '0';
                            Y <= "XXX";
    end case;
end process;
```

2

```
always @(A)
    begin
        Valid = 1;
        casex (A)
            8'b 1XXXXXXX : Y = 7;
            8'b 01XXXXXX : Y = 6;
            8'b 001XXXXX : Y = 5;
            8'b 0001XXXX : Y = 4;
            8'b 00001XXX : Y = 3;
            8'b 000001XX : Y = 2;
            8'b 0000001X : Y = 1;
            8'b 00000001 : Y = 0;
            default :        begin
                                Valid = 0;
                                Y = 3'b X;
                            end
        endcase
    end
```

continued ¦¦ *continued*

Different ways of modeling an 8-3 priority encoder

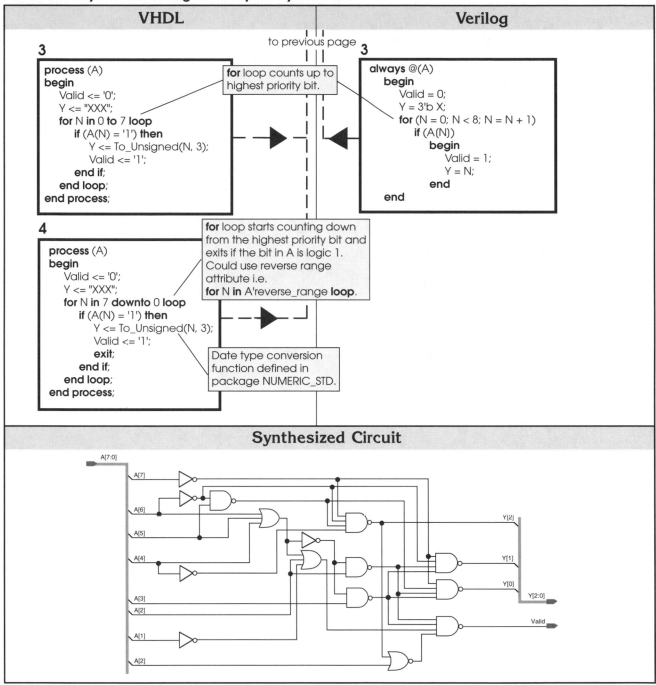

VHDL	Verilog

3

```
process (A)
begin
    Valid <= '0';
    Y <= "XXX";
    for N in 0 to 7 loop
        if (A(N) = '1') then
            Y <= To_Unsigned(N, 3);
            Valid <= '1';
        end if;
    end loop;
end process;
```

for loop counts up to highest priority bit.

to previous page

3

```
always @(A)
    begin
        Valid = 0;
        Y = 3'b X;
        for (N = 0; N < 8; N = N + 1)
            if (A(N))
                begin
                    Valid = 1;
                    Y = N;
                end
    end
```

4

```
process (A)
begin
    Valid <= '0';
    Y <= "XXX";
    for N in 7 downto 0 loop
        if (A(N) = '1') then
            Y <= To_Unsigned(N, 3);
            Valid <= '1';
            exit;
        end if;
    end loop;
end process;
```

for loop starts counting down from the highest priority bit and exits if the bit in A is logic 1. Could use reverse range attribute i.e.
for N **in** A'reverse_range **loop**.

Date type conversion function defined in package NUMERIC_STD.

Synthesized Circuit

Decoders

Decoders are used to decode data that has been previously encoded using a binary, or possibly other, type of coded format. An n-bit code can represent up to 2^n distinct bits of coded information, so a decoder with n inputs can decode up to 2^n outputs. Various models of a 3-8 binary decoder are included in Example 6.8, while various models of a 3-6 binary decoder having a separate enable input are included in Example 6.9.

Example 6.8 A 3-8 binary decoder

The models of a 3-8 binary decoder in this example conform to the truth table in Table 6.4.

Different model versions use **if**, **case** and **for** statements along with VHDL conditional and selected signal assignments. All $2^3 = 8$ possible input values of this 3-8 decoder are decoded to a unique output. This means the automatic priority encoding employed by **if** and Verilog **case** statements do not affect the circuit and "don't care" output values are not needed. Like most other examples in this chapter there is no right or wrong modeling technique. The **case** statement is commonly used because

inputs			outputs							
A2	A1	A0	Y7	Y6	Y5	Y4	Y3	Y2	Y1	Y0
0	0	0	0	0	0	0	0	0	0	1
0	0	1	0	0	0	0	0	0	1	0
0	1	0	0	0	0	0	0	1	0	0
0	1	1	0	0	0	0	1	0	0	0
1	0	0	0	0	0	1	0	0	0	0
1	0	1	0	0	1	0	0	0	0	0
1	1	0	0	1	0	0	0	0	0	0
1	1	1	1	0	0	0	0	0	0	0

Table 6.4 Truth table for a 3-8 line binary decoder

of its clarity, and the fact it is not a continuous assignment and so may simulate faster. As input and output bit widths increase, it is more code efficient to use the **for** loop statement. Again, all models synthesize to the same circuit.

Different ways of modeling a 3-8 decoder

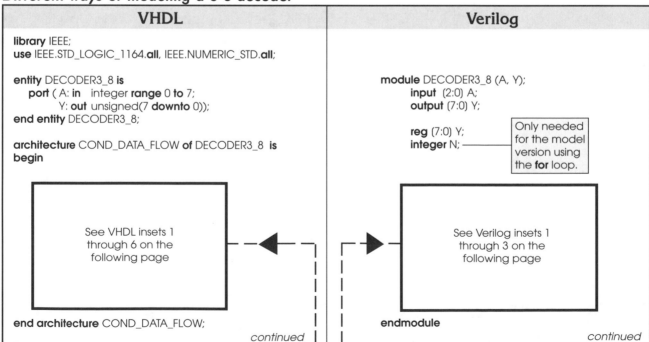

Different ways of modeling an 3-8 decoder

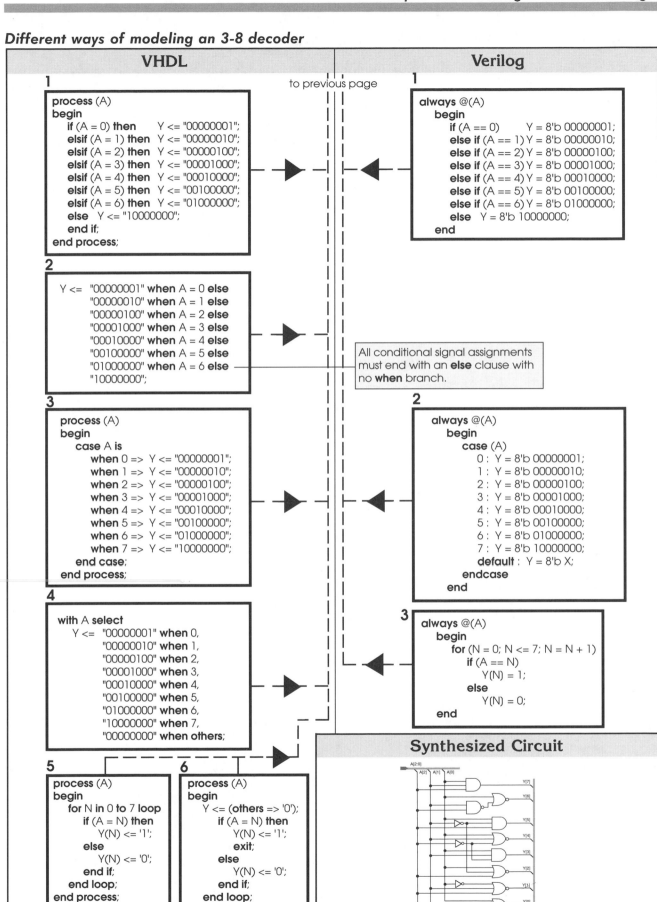

Example 6.9 A 3-6 binary decoder with enable

The two model versions of a 3-6 binary decoder are included in this example and conform to the truth table; Table 6.5. Because of the similarities of this example to Example 6.8, only the versions using a **case** statement are covered. This example is different because it has a separate input enable signal and there are two unused binary values for the 3-bit input A. When the enable is inactive (En = 0), or A has an unused value, the 6-bit output must be at logic 0. Like the previous example, "don't care" default assigned values cannot be used.

En	A2	A1	A0	Y5	Y4	Y3	Y2	Y1	Y0
inputs				outputs					
0	X	X	X	0	0	0	0	0	0
1	0	0	0	0	0	0	0	0	1
1	0	0	1	0	0	0	0	1	0
1	0	1	0	0	0	0	1	0	0
1	0	1	1	0	0	1	0	0	0
1	1	0	0	0	1	0	0	0	0
1	1	0	1	1	0	0	0	0	0
1	1	1	0	0	0	0	0	0	0
1	1	1	1	0	0	0	0	0	0

X=don't care

Table 6.5 Truth table for a 3-6 line binary decoder with enable

The first model version below also uses an **if** statement to check the enable input En, separately from the enclosed **case** statement. The second version on the following page has the enable input En, concatenated with the encoded input A and the combined signal used in the **case** statement. Both are correct and synthesize to the same circuit as shown.

3-6 decoder with separate if branch which tests the enable input

VHDL	Verilog

<pre>library IEEE;
use IEEE.STD_LOGIC_1164.all, IEEE.NUMERIC_STD.all;
 	
entity DECODER3_6_CASE1 is
    port (En: in std_logic;
           A: in   integer range 0 to 7;
           Y: out unsigned(5 downto 0));
end entity DECODER3_6_CASE1;
 	
architecture COND_DATA_FLOW of DECODER3_6_CASE1 is
begin
    process (A)
    begin
      if (En = '0') then
        Y <= "000000";
      else
        case A is
          when 0 => Y <= "000001";
          when 1 => Y <= "000010";
          when 2 => Y <= "000100";
          when 3 => Y <= "001000";
          when 4 => Y <= "010000";
          when 5 => Y <= "100000";
          when others => Y <= "000000";
        end case;
      end if;
    end process;
end architecture COND_DATA_FLOW;</pre>
	<pre>module DECODER3_6_CASE1 (A, En, Y);
	    input En;
	    input [2:0] A;
	    output [5:0] Y;
	
	    reg [5:0] Y;
	
	    always @(En or A)
	      begin
	        if (! En)
	          Y = 6'b 0;
	        else
	          case (A)
	            0 : Y = 6'b 000001;
	            1 : Y = 6'b 000010;
	            2 : Y = 6'b 000100;
	            3 : Y = 6'b 001000;
	            4 : Y = 6'b 010000;
	            5 : Y = 6'b 100000;
	            default : Y = 6'b 0;
	          endcase
	      end
	
	endmodule</pre>

3-6 decoder with concanentated enable/encoded input for case selector

VHDL	Verilog

library IEEE;
use IEEE.STD_LOGIC_1164.**all**, IEEE.NUMERIC_STD.**all**;
 	
entity DECODER3_6_CASE2 **is**
  port (En: **in** std_logic;
         A: **in** unsigned(2 **downto** 0);
         Y: **out** unsigned(5 **downto** 0));
end entity DECODER3_6_CASE2;
 	
architecture COND_DATA_FLOW **of** DECODER3_6_CASE2 **is**
begin
  process (En, A)
    variable En_concat_A: unsigned(3 **downto** 0);
  begin
    En_concat_A := En & A;
    case En_concat_A **is**
      when "1000" => Y <= "000001";
      when "1001" => Y <= "000010";
      when "1010" => Y <= "000100";
      when "1011" => Y <= "001000";
      when "1100" => Y <= "010000";
      when "1101" => Y <= "100000";
      when others => Y <= "000000";
    end case;
  end process;
end architecture COND_DATA_FLOW;
	module DECODER3_6_CASE2 (A, En, Y);
	  input En;
	  input (2:0) A;
	  output (5:0) Y;
	
	  reg (5:0) Y;
	
	  always @(En **or** A)
	    begin
	      case ({En, A})
	      4'b 1000 : Y = 6'b 000001;
	      4'b 1001 : Y = 6'b 000010;
	      4'b 1010 : Y = 6'b 000100;
	      4'b 1011 : Y = 6'b 001000;
	      4'b 1100 : Y = 6'b 010000;
	      4'b 1101 : Y = 6'b 100000;
	      default : Y = 6'b 0;
	    endcase
	  end
	
	endmodule

Separate concatenation expression. Not allowed in **case** expression like Verilog.

Concatenation in **case** expression.

Synthesized Circuit

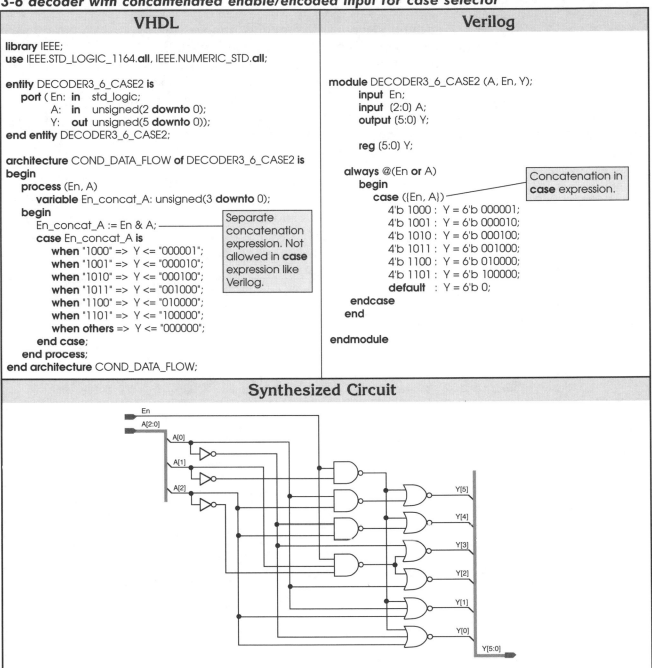

Example 6.10 Four bit address decoder

This example is of a four bit address decoder. It provides enable signals for segments of memory, the address map of which, is shown in Figure 6.3. The decoder's inputs could be the upper four bits of a larger address bus in which case the decoded outputs would enable larger segments of memory. Seven enable outputs are provided; one for each memory segment. The address map is divided into quarters, and the second quarter is further subdivided into four. There are four outputs from the second quarter corresponding to four consecutive binary input values.

Figure 6.3
Address map

The first model version uses a **for** loop enclosing an **if** statement while the second model uses a **case** statement. As a general rule, it is better to use the **for** loop and **if** statements when a large number of consecutively decoded outputs are required. This is because a **case** statement requires a separate choice branch for each decoded output.

Four bit address decoder using "if" in a "for" loop

VHDL	Verilog

<pre>library IEEE;
use IEEE.STD_LOGIC_1164.all, IEEE.NUMERIC_STD.all;
entity ADD_DEC_IF is
    port (Address: in integer range 0 to 15;
           AddDec_0to3,AddDec_8to11,
           AddDec_12to15: out std_logic;
           AddDec_4to7: out unsigned(3 downto 0));
end entity ADD_DEC_IF;
architecture COND_DATA_FLOW of ADD_DEC_IF is
begin
    process (Address)
    begin
        -- First quarter
        if (Address >= 0 and Address <= 3) then
            AddDec_0to3 <= '1';
        else
            AddDec_0to3 <= '0';
        end if;
 	
        -- Third quarter
        if (Address >= 8 and Address <= 11) then
            AddDec_8to11 <= '1';
        else
            AddDec_8to11 <= '0';
        end if;
 	
        -- Fourth quarter
        if (Address >= 12 and Address <= 15) then
            AddDec_12to15 <= '1';
        else
            AddDec_12to15 <= '0';
        end if;
 	
        -- Second quarter
        for N in AddDec_4to7'range loop
            if (Address = N + 4) then
                AddDec_4to7(N) <= '1';
            else
                AddDec_4to7(N) <= '0';
            end if;
        end loop;
    end process;
 	
end architecture COND_DATA_FLOW;</pre>
	<pre>module ADD_DEC_IF
	    (Address, AddDec_0to3, AddDec_4to7,
	    AddDec_8to11, AddDec_12to15);
	        input (3:0) Address;
	        output AddDec_0to3, AddDec_8to11,
	                      AddDec_12to15;
	        output (3:0) AddDec_4to7;
	        integer N;
	        reg AddDec_0to3, AddDec_8to11,
	                      AddDec_12to15;
	        reg (3:0) AddDec_4to7;
	    always @(Address)
	    begin
	        // First quarter
	        if (Address >= 0 && Address <= 3)
	            AddDec_0to3 = 1;
	        else
	            AddDec_0to3 = 0;
	
	        // Third quarter
	        if (Address >= 8 && Address <= 11)
	            AddDec_8to11 = 1;
	        else
	            AddDec_8to11 = 0;
	
	        // Fourth quarter
	        if (Address >= 12 && Address <= 15)
	            AddDec_12to15 = 1;
	        else
	            AddDec_12to15 = 0;
	
	        // Second quarter
	        for (N = 0; N <= 3; N = N + 1)
	            if (Address == N + 4)
	                AddDec_4to7(N) = 1;
	            else
	                AddDec_4to7(N) = 0;
	    end
	
	endmodule</pre>

Four bit address decoder using "case"

VHDL	Verilog

library IEEE;
use IEEE.STD_LOGIC_1164.**all**, IEEE.NUMERIC_STD.**all**;
 	
entity ADD_DEC_CASE **is**
   port (Address: **in** integer **range** 0 **to** 15;
        AddDec_0to3, AddDec_8to11,
        AddDec_12to15: **out** std_logic;
        AddDec_4to7:   **out** unsigned(3 **downto** 0));
end entity ADD_DEC_CASE;
 	
architecture COND_DATA_FLOW **of** ADD_DEC_CASE **is**
begin
 	
   process (Address)
   begin
     AddDec_0to3   <= '0';
     AddDec_4to7   <= (**others** => '0');
     AddDec_8to11 <= '0';
     AddDec_12to15 <= '0';
 	
     case Address **is**
     -- First quarter
     when 0 **to** 3 =>
       AddDec_0to3 <= '1';
 	
     -- Second quarter
     when 4 => AddDec_4to7(0) <= '1';
     when 5 => AddDec_4to7(1) <= '1';
     when 6 => AddDec_4to7(2) <= '1';
     when 7 => AddDec_4to7(3) <= '1';
 	
     -- Third quarter
     when 8 **to** 11 =>
       AddDec_8to11 <= '1';
 	
     -- Fourth quarter
     when 12 **to** 15 =>
       AddDec_12to15 <= '1';
   end case;
   end process;
 	
end architecture COND_DATA_FLOW;
	module ADD_DEC_CASE
	  (Address, AddDec_0to3, AddDec_4to7, AddDec_8to11,
	  AddDec_12to15);
	   input (3:0) Address;
	   output AddDec_0to3, AddDec_8to11,
	               AddDec_12to15;
	   output (3:0) AddDec_4to7;
	
	   reg AddDec_0to3, AddDec_8to11, AddDec_12to15;
	   reg (3:0) AddDec_4to7;
	
	  always @(Address)
	   begin
	     AddDec_0to3 = 0;
	     AddDec_4to7 = 0;
	     AddDec_8to11 = 0;
	     AddDec_12to15 = 0;
	
	     case (Address)
	     // First quarter
	     0, 1, 2, 3:
	       AddDec_0to3 = 1;
	
	     // Second quarter
	     4: AddDec_4to7(0) = 1;
	     5: AddDec_4to7(1) = 1;
	     6: AddDec_4to7(2) = 1;
	     7: AddDec_4to7(3) = 1;
	
	     // Third quarter
	     8, 9, 10, 11:
	       AddDec_8to11 = 1;
	
	     // Fourth quarter
	     12, 13, 14, 15:
	       AddDec_12to15 = 1;
	    endcase
	   end
	endmodule

Synthesized Circuit

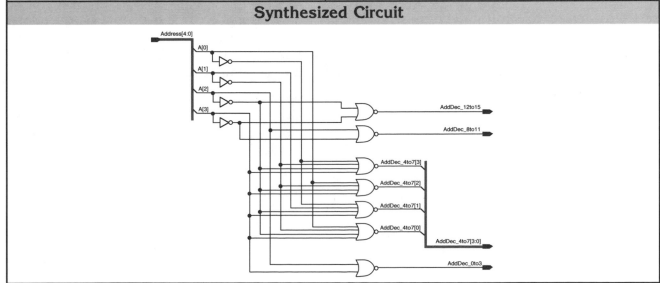

Example 6.11 Generic N to M bit binary decoder

A generic n-bit input, m-bit output binary decoder is illustrated and incorporates a separate enable input. Like Example 6.9, all outputs will be at logic 0 if the decoder is not enabled, that is, En = 0, or it is enabled, but n has a value that is not used in the decoder. This generic decoder is called twice for the inference of a 2-4 and a 3-6 decoder.

The four models in this example are:

VHDL 1   - a generic VHDL decoder using an **entity**,
Verilog 1 - a generic Verilog decoder using a **module**,
VHDL 2   - a generic VHDL decoder using a function in a package,
Verilog 2 - non-generic Verilog using a decoder function Verilog 2.

There are two parts to each of the four models. The first part of VHDL 1 and Verilog 1 show the decoder model while the second part shows two separate instantiations of it. The first part of VHDL 2 and Verilog 2 show the decoder modeled in a function and the second part shows two function calls to it.

VHDL 1. Modeled using an **entity** statement and separately instantiated. The number of decoded input and output lines, needed for any given instance, are specified using a generic clause which specifies a value for SizeIn and SizeOut.

Verilog 1. Modeled using a **module** statement and instantiated from a separate module. Uses overloaded parameters for both input and output bit widths. These parameters have values defined for them in the generic decoder (SizeIn = 3 and SizeOut = 8), and overridden when instantiated from the instantiation in another **module**.

VHDL 2. Uses a generic function defined in a package. This is a more practical and easier method to use when compared with using a VHDL **entity** as described above. The function is called from an expression, either concurrently (outside a process) or sequentially (inside a process), by supplying;

• the enable input of type std_logic,
• the encoded input of type unsigned,
• the desired number of encoded inputs of type integer,
• the desired number of decoded outputs of type integer.

Verilog 2. The Verilog language does not support the overriding of parameters in a function call. Instead of being able to model a generic decoder, a predefined number of n-m bit decoders must be specified so that the appropriate decoder may be called when needed. In this version, two functions have been declared for 2-4 and 3-6 decoders. These decoders have been placed in a separate file and included in the calling **module** using the compiler directive `include.

Generic decoder (entity/module)

VHDL 1	Verilog 1
| ```vhdl
library IEEE;
use IEEE.STD_LOGIC_1164.all, IEEE.NUMERIC_STD.all;

entity GENERIC_DECODER_ENTITY is
   generic (SizeIn: integer := 2; SizeOut: integer := 4);
   port ( En: in  std_logic;
          A: in   unsigned(SizeIn - 1 downto 0);
          Y: out unsigned(SizeOut - 1 downto 0));
end entity GENERIC_DECODER_ENTITY;

architecture DATA_FLOW of GENERIC_DECODER_ENTITY is
begin

   process (En, A)
   begin
     if (En = '0') then
        Y <= (others => '0');
     else
        for N in 0 to SizeOut - 1 loop
           if (to_integer(A) = N) then
              Y(N) <= '1';
           else
              Y(N) <= '0';
           end if;
        end loop;
     end if;
   end process;

end architecture DATA_FLOW;
``` | Some synthesis tools demand generics are given default values.<br><br>```verilog
module GENERIC_DECODER_MODULE (En, A, Y);
        parameter SizeIn  = 3,
                  SizeOut = 8;
     input    En;
     input    (SizeIn - 1:0)  A;
     output   (SizeOut - 1:0) Y;
     reg (SizeOut - 1:0) Y;

     integer N;

     always @(En or A)
        begin
          if (! En)
             Y = 0;
          else
             if (A > SizeOut - 1)
                for (N = 0; N <= SizeOut - 1; N = N + 1)
                   Y(N) = 1'b X;
             else
                for (N = 0; N <= SizeOut - 1; N = N + 1)
                   if (A == N)
                      Y(N) = 1;
                   else
                      Y(N) = 0;
        end

endmodule
``` |

Two instantiations of the generic decoder

VHDL 1	Verilog 1
| ```vhdl
library IEEE;
use IEEE.STD_LOGIC_1164.all, IEEE.NUMERIC_STD.all;

entity GENERIC_DECODER_ENTITY_CALL is
   port ( EnA, EnB:  in  std_logic;
          AddA:     in  unsigned(1 downto 0);
          AddB:     in  unsigned(2 downto 0);
          DecAddA:  out unsigned(3 downto 0);
          DecAddB:  out unsigned(5 downto 0));
end entity GENERIC_DECODER_ENTITY_CALL;

architecture STRUCT of GENERIC_DECODER_ENTITY_CALL is
   component GENERIC_DECODER_ENTITY
      generic (SizeIn, SizeOut: integer);
      port ( En: in  std_logic;
             A: in   unsigned(SizeIn - 1 downto 0);
             Y: out unsigned(SizeOut - 1 downto 0));
   end component;
begin

   Decoder2_4: GENERIC_DECODER_ENTITY
             generic map (2, 4)
             port map (EnA, AddA, DecAddA);

   Decoder3_6: GENERIC_DECODER_ENTITY
             generic map (3, 6)
             port map (EnB, AddB, DecAddB);

end architecture STRUCT;
``` | ```verilog
module GENERIC_DECODER_MODULE_CALL
     (EnA, EnB, AddA, AddB, DecAddA, DecAddB);
     input          EnA, EnB;
     input    (1:0) AddA;
     input    (2:0) AddB;
     output   (3:0) DecAddA;
     output   (5:0) DecAddB;

   GENERIC_DECODER_MODULE
        #(2, 4) Decoder2_4(EnA, AddA, DecAddA);

   GENERIC_DECODER_MODULE
        #(3, 6) Decoder3_6(EnB, AddB, DecAddB);

endmodule
```<br><br>Two instantiations, 2-4 and 3-6, of the generic decoder. |

VHDL generic decoder (function) - Verilog specific decoders (functions)

VHDL 2	Verilog 2
| ```
library IEEE;
use IEEE.STD_LOGIC_1164.all, IEEE.NUMERIC_STD.all;

package GENERIC_DECODER_FN_PKG is
   function Decoder (En:  std_logic;
                     A:   unsigned;
                     SizeIn, SizeOut: integer) return unsigned;
end package GENERIC_DECODER_FN_PKG;

package body GENERIC_DECODER_FN_PKG is
   function Decoder (En:  std_logic;
                     A:   unsigned;
                     SizeIn, SizeOut: integer) return unsigned is
      variable Y: unsigned(SizeOut - 1 downto 0);
   begin
      if (En = '0' or A > SizeIn - 1) then
         Y := (others => '0');
      else
         for N in 0 to SizeOut - 1 loop
             if (to_integer(A) = N) then
                Y(N) := '1';
             else
                Y(N) := '0';
             end if;
         end loop;
      end if;
      return Y;
   end function Decoder;
end package body GENERIC_DECODER_FN_PKG;
``` | ```
// ——————————————————————
// This file must be called "decoder_fns.v".
// ——————————————————————
function (3:0) Decode2_4;
      input En;
      input (1:0) A;
      integer N;
   begin
      if (!En)
         Decode2_4 = 4'b 0;
      else
         for (N = 0; N < 4; N = N + 1)
             if (A == N)
                Decode2_4(N) = 1;
             else
                Decode2_4(N) = 0;
   end
endfunction

function (5:0) Decode3_6;
      input En;
      input (2:0) A;
      integer N;
   begin
      if (!En)
         Decode3_6 = 6'b 0;
      else
         for (N = 0; N < 6; N = N + 1)
             if (A == N)
                Decode3_6(N) = 1;
             else
                Decode3_6(N) = 0;
   end
endfunction
``` |

Generic decoder function defined in a package.

Two specific decoder functions.

Two decoder function calls

VHDL 2	Verilog 2
| ```
library IEEE;
use IEEE.STD_LOGIC_1164.all, IEEE.NUMERIC_STD.all;

use work.GENERIC_DECODER_FN_PKG.all;

entity GENERIC_DECODER_CALL_FN is
   port ( EnA, EnB:   in   std_logic;
          AddA:       in   unsigned(1 downto 0);
          AddB:       in   unsigned(2 downto 0);
          DecAddA:    out  unsigned(3 downto 0);
          DecAddB:    out  unsigned(5 downto 0));
end entity GENERIC_DECODER_CALL_FN;

architecture DATA_FLOW of GENERIC_DECODER_CALL_FN is
begin

   process (EnA, AddA, EnB, AddB)
   begin
      DecAddA <= Decoder(EnA, AddA, 2, 4);
      DecAddB <= Decoder(EnB, AddB, 3, 6);
   end process;

end architecture DATA_FLOW;
``` | ```
module DECODER_FN_CALLS
   (EnA, EnB, AddA, AddB, DecAddA, DecAddB);
      input     EnA, EnB;
      input     (1:0) AddA;
      input     (2:0) AddB;
      output    (3:0) DecAddA;
      output    (5:0) DecAddB;

      reg (3:0) DecAddA;
      reg (5:0) DecAddB;

      `include "decoder_fns.v"

   always @(EnA or EnB or AddA or AddB)
      begin
         DecAddA = Decode2_4(EnA, AddA);
         DecAddB = Decode3_6(EnB, AddB);
      end

endmodule
``` |

Two function calls to the generic decoder.

Function calls to 2_4 and 3_6 decoders.

Comparators

A comparator compares two or more inputs using one, or a number of different comparisons. When the given relationship(s) is true, an output signal is given (logic 0 or logic 1). Comparators are only modeled using the **if** statement with an **else** clause and no **else-if** clauses. A VHDL conditional signal assignment or Verilog conditional continuous assignment could also be used, but is less common as a sensitivity list (VHDL) or event list (Verilog) cannot be specified to improve simulation time. Any two data objects are compared using equality and relational operators in the expression part of the **if** statement. Only two data objects can be compared at once, that is, statements like "**if** (A = B = C)" cannot be used. However, logical operators can be used to logically test the result of multiple comparisons, for example, **if** ((A = B) **and** (A = C)). These equality, relational and logical operators are listed in Table 6.6.

Example 6.12 shows a 6-bit two input equality comparator. Example 6.13 shows how multiple comparisons are used.

Operators	VHDL	Verilog
Equality & Relational	=	==
	!=	!=
	<	<
	<=	<=
	>	>
	>=	>=
Logical	not	!
	and	&&
	or	| |

Table 6.6 Equality, relational and logical operators

Example 6.12 Simple Comparator

Identical equality comparators are shown coded in three different ways. The single bit output is at logic 1 when the two 6-bit input busses are the same, otherwise it is at logic 0.

Three ways to infer a 6-bit equality comparator

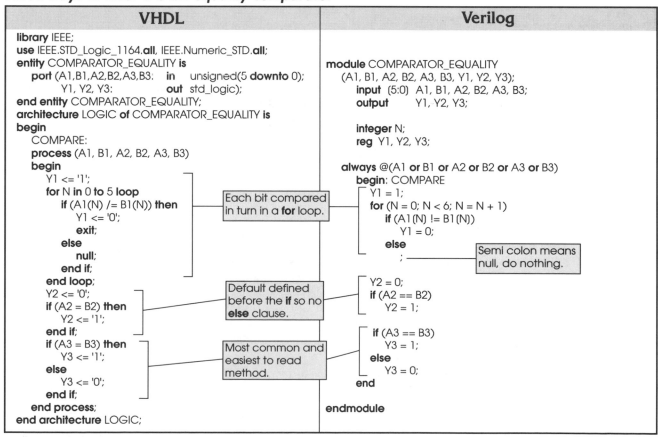

```vhdl
library IEEE;
use IEEE.STD_Logic_1164.all, IEEE.Numeric_STD.all;
entity COMPARATOR_EQUALITY is
    port (A1,B1,A2,B2,A3,B3:   in    unsigned(5 downto 0);
          Y1, Y2, Y3:      out std_logic);
end entity COMPARATOR_EQUALITY;
architecture LOGIC of COMPARATOR_EQUALITY is
begin
    COMPARE:
    process (A1, B1, A2, B2, A3, B3)
    begin
        Y1 <= '1';
        for N in 0 to 5 loop
            if (A1(N) /= B1(N)) then      -- Each bit compared in turn in a for loop.
                Y1 <= '0';
                exit;
            else
                null;
            end if;
        end loop;
        Y2 <= '0';                         -- Default defined before the if so no else clause.
        if (A2 = B2) then
            Y2 <= '1';
        end if;
        if (A3 = B3) then                  -- Most common and easiest to read method.
            Y3 <= '1';
        else
            Y3 <= '0';
        end if;
    end process;
end architecture LOGIC;
```

```verilog
module COMPARATOR_EQUALITY
    (A1, B1, A2, B2, A3, B3, Y1, Y2, Y3);
        input  (5:0)  A1, B1, A2, B2, A3, B3;
        output       Y1, Y2, Y3;

        integer N;
        reg Y1, Y2, Y3;

    always @(A1 or B1 or A2 or B2 or A3 or B3)
        begin: COMPARE
            Y1 = 1;
            for (N = 0; N < 6; N = N + 1)
                if (A1(N) != B1(N))
                    Y1 = 0;
                else
                    ;               // Semi colon means null, do nothing.
            Y2 = 0;
            if (A2 == B2)
                Y2 = 1;

            if (A3 == B3)
                Y3 = 1;
            else
                Y3 = 0;
        end
endmodule
```

Three ways to infer a 6-bit equality comparator

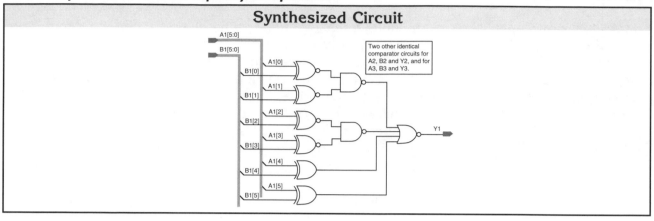

Example 6.13 Multiple Comparison Comparator

Extra parentheses enclosing "C /= D **or** E >= F" means that either one of these conditions and "A = B" must be true for the output to be at logic 1.

Comparator using multiple comparisons

VHDL	Verilog

library IEEE;
use IEEE.STD_LOGIC_1164.**all**, IEEE.NUMERIC_STD.**all**;
entity COMPARATOR_MULT_COMP **is**
  port (A, B, C, D, E, F: **in** unsigned(2 **downto** 0);
      Y: **out** std_logic);
end entity COMPARATOR_MULT_COMP;
 architecture LOGIC **of** COMPARATOR_MULT_COMP **is**
begin
  process (A, B, C, D, E, F)
  begin
    if (A = B **and** (C /= D **or** E >= F)) **then**
      Y <= '1';
    else
      Y <= '0';
    end if;
  end process;
end architecture LOGIC;
	module COMPARATOR_MULT_COMP (A, B, C, D, E, F, Y);
	    input [2:0] A, B, C, D, E, F;
	    output Y;
	
	    reg Y;
	
	    always @(A **or** B **or** C **or** D **or** E **or** F)
	    if (A == B && (C != D || E >= F))
	      Y = 1;
	    else
	      Y = 0;
	
	endmodule

Synthesized Circuit

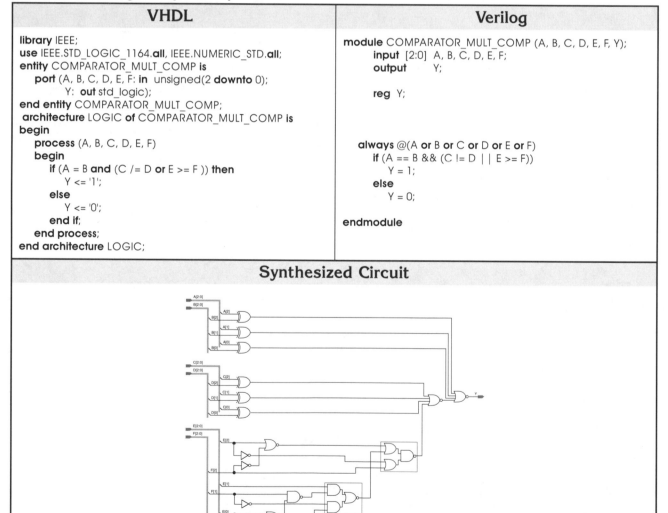

ALU

An arithmetic logic unit (ALU) is the center core of a central processing unit (CPU). It consists of purely combinational logic circuit and performs a set of arithmetic and logic micro operations on two input busses. It has n encoded inputs for selecting which operation to perform. The select lines are decoded within the ALU to provide up to 2^n different operations. The ALU in Example 6.14 is capable of performing 14 different micro operations.

Example 6.14 An arithmetic logic unit

An Arithmetic Logic Unit (ALU) is modeled to the function table of Table 6.7.

S4	S3	S2	S1	S0	Cin	Operation	Function	Implementation block
0	0	0	0	0	0	Y <= A	Transfer A	Arithmetic Unit
0	0	0	0	0	1	Y <= A + 1	Increment A	Arithmetic Unit
0	0	0	0	1	0	Y <= A + B	Addition	Arithmetic Unit
0	0	0	0	1	1	Y <= A + B + 1	Add with carry	Arithmetic Unit
0	0	0	1	0	0	Y <= A + Bbar	A plus 1's complement of B	Arithmetic Unit
0	0	0	1	0	1	Y <= A + Bbar + 1	Subtraction	Arithmetic Unit
0	0	0	1	1	0	Y <= A - 1	Decrement A	Arithmetic Unit
0	0	0	1	1	1	Y <= A	Transfer A	Arithmetic Unit
0	0	1	0	0	0	Y <= A and B	AND	Logic Unit
0	0	1	0	1	0	Y <= A or B	OR	Logic Unit
0	0	1	1	0	0	Y <= A xor B	XOR	Logic Unit
0	0	1	1	1	0	Y <= Abar	Complement A	Logic Unit
0	0	0	0	0	0	Y <= A	Transfer A	Shifter Unit
0	1	0	0	0	0	Y <= shl A	Shift left A	Shifter Unit
1	0	0	0	0	0	Y <= shr A	Shift right A	Shifter Unit
1	1	0	0	0	0	Y <= 0	Transfer 0's	Shifter Unit

Table 6.7 ALU Function table

This whole function table could be modeled using a single **case** statement, however, its synthesized structure would be poor. Instead, the ALU has been modeled with a separate arithmetic unit, logic unit and shifter, as indicated by the modeled circuit structure. By separating the arithmetic and logic units in this way, and multiplexing their outputs to the shifter, better pre-optimized timing will result. It is very likely, that even after optimization, the shortest timing delay through the ALU will be longer if the arithmetic and logic units were combined into one process.

The arithmetic unit modeled using a single **case** statement. The reason it can be modeled in this way is because the synthesis tools from VeriBest Incorporated, synthesizes expressions like A + B + 1 to a single adder with the carry in set to logic 1. If a synthesis tool is being used that does not support this, it is necessary to remodel it in a way that avoids multiple adders being synthesized. Provided the synthesis tools resource sharing option is turned on, the synthesized logic of the arithmetic unit will consist of just one adder for <u>all</u> add and subtract operations.

Arithmetic logic unit

VHDL	Verilog
library IEEE; **use** IEEE.STD_LOGIC_1164.**all**, IEEE.NUMERIC_STD.**all**; **entity** ALU **is** **port** (Sel: **in** unsigned(4 **downto** 0); CarryIn: **in** std_logic; A, B: **in** unsigned(7 **downto** 0); Y: **out** unsigned(7 **downto** 0)); **end entity** ALU; *continued*	**module** ALU (Sel, CarryIn, A, B, Y); **input** (4:0) Sel; **input** CarryIn; **input** (7:0) A, B; **output** (7:0) Y; **reg** (7:0) Y; *continued*

Arithmetic logic unit

VHDL	Verilog

```vhdl
architecture COND_DATA_FLOW of ALU is
begin
   ALU_AND_SHIFT:
   process (Sel, A, B, CarryIn)
      variable Sel0_1_CarryIn: unsigned(2 downto 0);
      variable LogicUnit, ArithUnit,
            ALU_NoShift: unsigned(7 downto 0);
   begin
      ------------------
      -- Logic Unit
      ------------------
      LOGIC_UNIT: case Sel(1 downto 0) is
         when "00"    =>  LogicUnit := A and B;
         when "01"    =>  LogicUnit := A or B;
         when "10"    =>  LogicUnit := A xor B;
         when "11"    =>  LogicUnit := not A;
         when others  =>  LogicUnit := (others => 'X');
      end case LOGIC_UNIT;
      --------------------------
      -- Arithmetic Unit
      --------------------------
      Sel0_1_CarryIn := Sel(1 downto 0) & CarryIn;
      ARITH_UNIT: case Sel0_1_CarryIn is
         when "000"   =>  ArithUnit := A;
         when "001"   =>  ArithUnit := A + 1;
         when "010"   =>  ArithUnit := A + B;
         when "011"   =>  ArithUnit := A + B + 1;
         when "100"   =>  ArithUnit := A + not B;
         when "101"   =>  ArithUnit := A - B;
         when "110"   =>  ArithUnit := A - 1;
         when "111"   =>  ArithUnit := A;
         when others  =>  ArithUnit := (others => 'X');
      end case ARITH_UNIT;
      ---------------------------------------------------
      -- Multiplex between Logic & Arithmetic Units
      ---------------------------------------------------
      LA_MUX: if (Sel(2) = '1') then
         ALU_NoShift := LogicUnit;
      else
         ALU_NoShift := ArithUnit;
      end if LA_MUX;
      ----------------------------
      -- Shift operations
      ----------------------------
      SHIFT: case Sel(4 downto 3) is
         when "00"    =>  Y <= ALU_NoShift;
         when "01"    =>  Y <= Shift_left(ALU_NoShift, 1);
         when "10"    =>  Y <= Shift_right(ALU_NoShift, 1);
         when "11"    =>  Y <= (others => '0');
         when others  =>  Y <= (others => 'X');
      end case SHIFT;
   end process ALU_AND_SHIFT;
end architecture COND_DATA_FLOW;
```

```verilog
   reg (7:0) LogicUnit, ArithUnit,
         ALU_NoShift;

   always @(Sel or A or B or CarryIn)
      begin: ALU_PROC



      //----------------
      // Logic Unit
      //----------------
      case (Sel(1:0))
         2'b 00  :  LogicUnit = A & B;
         2'b 01  :  LogicUnit = A | B;
         2'b 10  :  LogicUnit = A ^ B;
         2'b 11  :  LogicUnit = ! A;
         default :  LogicUnit = 8'b X;
      endcase
      //----------------------
      // Arithmetic Unit
      //----------------------
      case ({Sel(1:0), CarryIn})
         3'b 000  :  ArithUnit = A;
         3'b 001  :  ArithUnit = A + 1;
         3'b 010  :  ArithUnit = A + B;
         3'b 011  :  ArithUnit = A + B + 1;
         3'b 100  :  ArithUnit = A + ! B;
         3'b 101  :  ArithUnit = A - B;
         3'b 110  :  ArithUnit = A - 1;
         3'b 111  :  ArithUnit = A;
         default  :  ArithUnit = 8'b X;
      endcase
      //------------------------------------------------------
      // Multiplex between Logic & Arithmetic Units
      //------------------------------------------------------
      if (Sel(2))
         ALU_NoShift = LogicUnit;
      else
         ALU_NoShift = ArithUnit;

      //------------------------
      // Shift operations
      //------------------------
      case (Sel(4:3))
      2'b 00  :  Y = ALU_NoShift;
      2'b 01  :  Y = ALU_NoShift << 1;
      2'b 10  :  Y = ALU_NoShift >> 1;
      2'b 11  :  Y = 8'b 0;
      default :  Y = 8'b X;
      endcase
   end

endmodule
```

> Separate VHDL concatenation. Cannot be incorporated in case expression like Verilog.

Modeled Circuit Structure

Modeling Synchronous Logic Circuits

Chapter 7 Contents

Introduction

This chapter describes the models of circuit functions that are implemented using synchronous logic. The two basic types of synchronous element, cell primitives in an ASIC or FPGA library), that are, 1) found in an ASIC or FPGA library of cells, and 2) mapped to by synthesis tools are:

- the D-type flow-through latch, and
- the D-type flip-flop.

About a third of ASIC vendor libraries contain JK and toggle type flip-flops but they are not generally mapped to by commercial RTL synthesis tools. The sections in this chapter cover: latches, flip-flops, linear feedback shift registers (LFSRs) and counters. The section on counters also includes clock dividers.

Modeling synchronous logic is fairly straightforward provided that one adheres to the modeling style recommended by the particular synthesis tool being used. The modeling styles shown in this chapter, and throughout this book, are typical of most, if not all, commercial RTL level synthesis tools.

Modeling Latch Circuits

A latch is a level sensitive memory cell that is transparent to signals passing from the D input to Q output when enabled, and holds the value of D on Q at the time when it becomes disabled; see Figure 7.1.

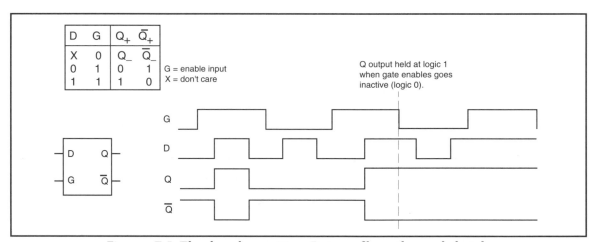

Figure 7.1 The level sensitive D-type flow-through latch

There are typically many latch variants in an ASIC or FPGA technology library. They may have active high or low enable signals, and optional active high or low preset and clear signals. The advantages of using latches over flip-flops is that if successive latches are enabled with phased enable signals, *cycle stealing* is possible which can yield faster operating circuits. Figure 7.2 shows the configuration of two and three phase latch enabling.

Cycle stealing occurs when combinational logic is moved from one clock phase to another in order to equalize latch-to-latch signal delays throughout a latch based design having multiple latch-to-latch stages. In a two phase system, combinational logic is moved to an adjacent latch-to-latch stage. In a three phase system, combinational logic is moved to one of the two closest stages, forwards or backwards. Synthesis tools may have the ability to automatically perform cycle stealing during optimization. The synthesis tools from VeriBest Incorporated has this capability.

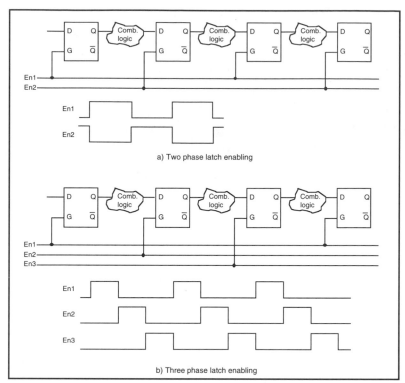

Figure 7.2 Two and three phase latch enabling

The main disadvantage of using latches, instead of flip-flops, is that timing analysis of synthesized circuits can be very complex making it difficult to verify correct operation under all conditions; temperature, voltage and chip manufacturing process variations.

No latch in target technology library. There are FPGA libraries that do not contain latches. If using such a library, do not model latches in the HDL code. If latches are modeled, the synthesis tool will probably give a warning and may even try to decompose the function of a latch into combinational logic gates with asynchronous feedback in an attempt to find a mapping of equivalent functionality. This would almost certainly lead to race conditions. A latch based circuit can usually be remodeled using flip-flops instead of latches and still have the same required functional operation. The advice here is to be fully aware of the hardware intent when writing structural HDL code.

How latches are inferred

A latch is synthesized from an HDL model when a signal needs to hold its value over time. In VHDL **if**, **case** or **wait** statements, or conditional or selected signal assignments, can be used. In Verilog **if** and **case** statements can be used. Verilog does have a **wait** statement specifically for modeling the function of a latch, but it is not supported by synthesis tools, so should not be used. As a general rule, it is better not to use a **case** statement to infer latches as there is no way of explicitly specifying the enable signal; Example 7.5 shows what happens if you do. If it is desirable to use a **case** statement, it should be modeled within an **if** statement or the VHDL **wait** statement, as these allow the enable signal to be specified explicitly.

Chapter 6 showed how combinational logic is inferred when a signal is defined in all possible branches of a conditional expression, that is, **if** , **case**, etc. Conversely, if one or more branches of a conditional expression does not define a value for a particular output signal, and no default output value is defined before the conditional statement, then a latch is automatically inferred. A latch is inferred if a path through the code exists such that a particular signal is not updated (assigned) a new value.

Unintentional latch inference from **case** statements

VHDL. A VHDL **case** statement must always have a branch for <u>every</u> case choice value for VHDL LRM compliance and often means an **others** clause must be used. This does not mean each branch must assign a particular output value, although it usually does. If a particular output is assigned a value in every branch then a latch will not be inferred. The output must be assigned a value in <u>all</u> branches, otherwise latches are inferred.

Verilog. In Verilog, a branch for every case choice value is <u>not</u> needed for Verilog LRM compliance and so the **default** clause is always optional. However, if the **default** clause is omitted a latch will always be inferred, even if the **case** statement already has an output signal explicitly assigned in what is thought to be all branches covering all case choice values. The reason for this is that although all case conditions may be thought of as being covered, every possible combination of the four value, value set {X, 0, 1, Z}, is almost always not covered for all **case** choice values.

Six latch related examples follow and are summarized below.

Example 7.1. Simple latch model that shows the effect of VHDL signal versus variable assignments and Verilog blocking versus non-blocking procedural assignments.

Example 7.2. Various latch models with preset and clear inputs.

Example 7.3. Multiple gated enables signals feeding the enable input of a latch.

Example 7.4. Nested **if** statements where one branch does not assign a particular output value resulting in the inference of a latch.

Example 7.5. Inadvertent inference of a latch due to a **case** statement not having an output assignment for every **case** choice value.

Example 7.6. Similar to Example 7.5, but uses nested **case** statements. All **case** choice values do not contain an output assignment in the inner most **case** statement and so latches are inferred for the 4-bit output.

Example 7.1 Simple and multiple latch inference using if statements

First **if** *statement.* Signal Y1 has no **else** clause and shows the model of a latch in its most simplest form.

Second **if** *statement.* Contains two assignments to two single bit signals. Signal M2 is assigned a value in the first assignment statement and is used in the second. Now, because M2 is of type signal in the VHDL model, and the assignment is non-blocking (<=) in the Verilog model, two separate latches are inferred with combinational logic between them as shown.

Third **if** *statement.* Identical to second **if** statement except M3 is now a variable instead of a signal in the VHDL model, and the non-blocking signal assignment is now a blocking signal assignment (=) in the Verilog model. The synthesized circuit consists of just one latch as shown by the synthesized circuit. Only one latch is inferred because the VHDL signal assignment and Verilog blocking procedural assignment for Y3 uses the new value of M3 computed in the assignment of M3 immediately before the assignment of Y3.

Simple latch inference

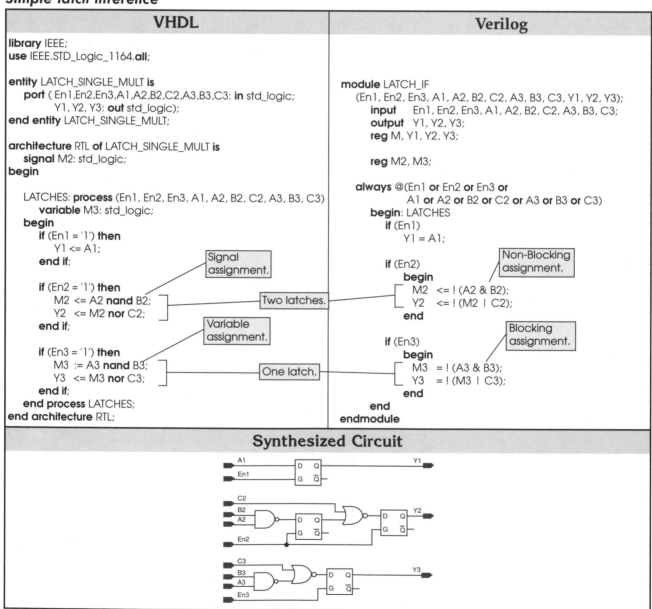

VHDL	Verilog
| ```
library IEEE;
use IEEE.STD_Logic_1164.all;

entity LATCH_SINGLE_MULT is
   port ( En1,En2,En3,A1,A2,B2,C2,A3,B3,C3: in std_logic;
          Y1, Y2, Y3: out std_logic);
end entity LATCH_SINGLE_MULT;

architecture RTL of LATCH_SINGLE_MULT is
   signal M2: std_logic;
begin

   LATCHES: process (En1, En2, En3, A1, A2, B2, C2, A3, B3, C3)
      variable M3: std_logic;
   begin
      if (En1 = '1') then
         Y1 <= A1;
      end if;

      if (En2 = '1') then
         M2 <= A2 nand B2;
         Y2  <= M2 nor C2;
      end if;

      if (En3 = '1') then
         M3  := A3 nand B3;
         Y3  <= M3 nor C3;
      end if;
   end process LATCHES;
end architecture RTL;
``` | ```
module LATCH_IF
   (En1, En2, En3, A1, A2, B2, C2, A3, B3, C3, Y1, Y2, Y3);
   input   En1, En2, En3, A1, A2, B2, C2, A3, B3, C3;
   output  Y1, Y2, Y3;
   reg M, Y1, Y2, Y3;

   reg M2, M3;

   always @(En1 or En2 or En3 or
             A1 or A2 or B2 or C2 or A3 or B3 or C3)
   begin: LATCHES
      if (En1)
         Y1 = A1;

      if (En2)
         begin
            M2  <= ! (A2 & B2);
            Y2  <= ! (M2 | C2);
         end

      if (En3)
         begin
            M3  = ! (A3 & B3);
            Y3  = ! (M3 | C3);
         end
   end
endmodule
``` |

Signal assignment.

Two latches.

Variable assignment.

One latch.

Non-Blocking assignment.

Blocking assignment.

Synthesized Circuit

Example 7.2 Modeling latches with preset and clear inputs

Latches with preset and clear input signals are modeled. Preset and clear inputs to a latch are always asynchronous with the enable.

Latches with preset and clear

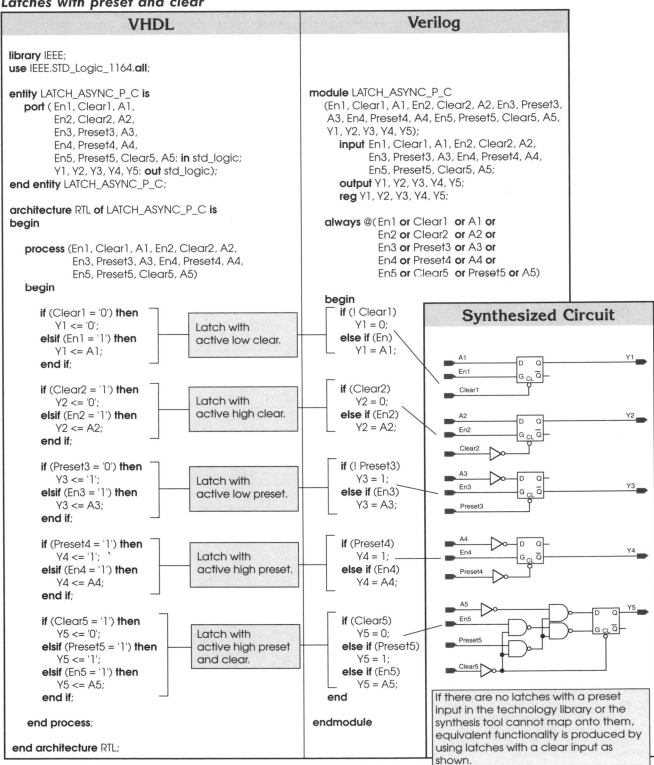

VHDL	Verilog

```
library IEEE;
use IEEE.STD_Logic_1164.all;

entity LATCH_ASYNC_P_C is
    port ( En1, Clear1, A1,
            En2, Clear2, A2,
            En3, Preset3, A3,
            En4, Preset4, A4,
            En5, Preset5, Clear5, A5: in std_logic;
            Y1, Y2, Y3, Y4, Y5: out std_logic);
end entity LATCH_ASYNC_P_C;

architecture RTL of LATCH_ASYNC_P_C is
begin

    process (En1, Clear1, A1, En2, Clear2, A2,
            En3, Preset3, A3, En4, Preset4, A4,
            En5, Preset5, Clear5, A5)
    begin

        if (Clear1 = '0') then
            Y1 <= '0';
        elsif (En1 = '1') then
            Y1 <= A1;
        end if;

        if (Clear2 = '1') then
            Y2 <= '0';
        elsif (En2 = '1') then
            Y2 <= A2;
        end if;

        if (Preset3 = '0') then
            Y3 <= '1';
        elsif (En3 = '1') then
            Y3 <= A3;
        end if;

        if (Preset4 = '1') then
            Y4 <= '1'; `
        elsif (En4 = '1') then
            Y4 <= A4;
        end if;

        if (Clear5 = '1') then
            Y5 <= '0';
        elsif (Preset5 = '1') then
            Y5 <= '1';
        elsif (En5 = '1') then
            Y5 <= A5;
        end if;

    end process;

end architecture RTL;
```

Latch with active low clear.

Latch with active high clear.

Latch with active low preset.

Latch with active high preset.

Latch with active high preset and clear.

```
module LATCH_ASYNC_P_C
    (En1, Clear1, A1, En2, Clear2, A2, En3, Preset3,
    A3, En4, Preset4, A4, En5, Preset5, Clear5, A5,
    Y1, Y2, Y3, Y4, Y5);
    input En1, Clear1, A1, En2, Clear2, A2,
            En3, Preset3, A3, En4, Preset4, A4,
            En5, Preset5, Clear5, A5;
    output Y1, Y2, Y3, Y4, Y5;
    reg Y1, Y2, Y3, Y4, Y5;

    always @( En1 or Clear1  or A1 or
            En2 or Clear2  or A2 or
            En3 or Preset3 or A3 or
            En4 or Preset4 or A4 or
            En5 or Clear5  or Preset5 or A5)

    begin
        if (! Clear1)
            Y1 = 0;
        else if (En)
            Y1 = A1;

        if (Clear2)
            Y2 = 0;
        else if (En2)
            Y2 = A2;

        if (! Preset3)
            Y3 = 1;
        else if (En3)
            Y3 = A3;

        if (Preset4)
            Y4 = 1;
        else if (En4)
            Y4 = A4;

        if (Clear5)
            Y5 = 0;
        else if (Preset5)
            Y5 = 1;
        else if (En5)
            Y5 = A5;
    end

endmodule
```

Synthesized Circuit

If there are no latches with a preset input in the technology library or the synthesis tool cannot map onto them, equivalent functionality is produced by using latches with a clear input as shown.

Example 7.3 Multiple gated enable latch

Provided an **if** statement is not in an edge triggered section of code, it does not matter how many **elsif** (VHDL) or **else if** (Verilog) clauses there are. If there is no **else** clause and there is no default output assignment before the **if** clause, latches will always be inferred.

Multiple enable latch

VHDL	Verilog

library IEEE;
use IEEE.STD_Logic_1164.**all**;
 	
entity LATCH_IF_ELSEIF **is**
   port (En1, En2, En3, A1, A2, A3: **in** std_logic;
       Y: **out** std_logic);
end entity LATCH_IF_ELSEIF;
 	
architecture RTL **of** LATCH_IF_ELSEIF **is**
begin
   process (En1, En2, En3, A1, A2, A3)
   begin
      if (En1 = '1') **then**
         Y <= A1;
      elsif (En2 = '1') **then**
         Y <= A2;
      elsif (En3 = '1') **then**
         Y <= A3;
      end if;
   end process;
 	
end architecture RTL;
	module LATCH_IF_ELSEIF (En1, En2, En3, A1, A2, A3, Y);
	   input En1, En2, En3, A1, A2, A3;
	   output Y;
	
	   reg Y;
	
	   always @(En1 **or** En2 **or** En3 **or** A1 **or** A2 **or** A3)
	      if (En1 == 1)
	         Y = A1;
	      else if (En2 == 1)
	         Y = A2;
	      else if (En3 == 1)
	         Y = A3;
	
	endmodule

Synthesized Circuit	

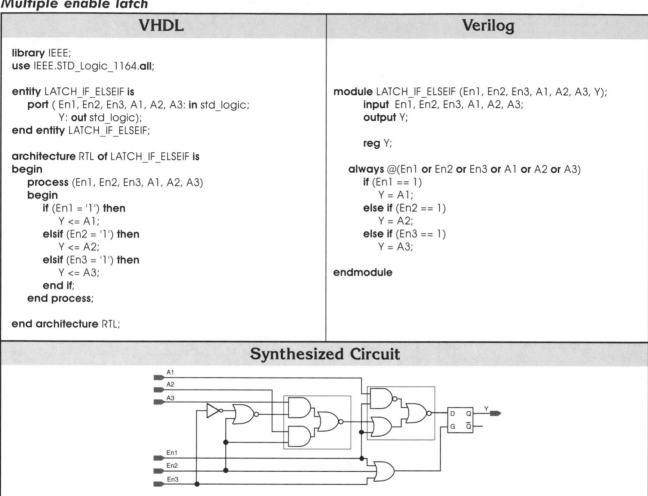

Example 7.4 Latch inference from nested if statements

The single bit output Y2 is only defined in 3 of the 4 possible branches of the nested **if** statements so a single latch is inferred.

Nested if statements inferring a latch

VHDL	Verilog
library IEEE; **use** IEEE.STD_Logic_1164.**all**, IEEE.Numeric_STD.**all**; **entity** LATCH_NESTED_IF **is** **port** (Sel: **in** std_logic; A: **in** unsigned(4 **downto** 0); Y1: **out** unsigned(4 **downto** 0); Y2: **out** std_logic); **end entity** LATCH_NESTED_IF; **architecture** COND_DATA_FLOW **of** LATCH_NESTED_IF **is** **begin** <div align="right">continued</div>	**module** LATCH_NESTED_IF (Sel, A, Y1, Y2); **input** Sel; **input** [4:0] A; **output** [4:0] Y1; **output** Y2; **reg** [4:0] Y1; **reg** Y2; <div align="right">continued</div>

Nested if statements inferring a latch

VHDL	Verilog

process (Sel, A)
begin
  if Sel = '0' then
    if A >= 12 then
      Y1 <= (others => '0');
      Y2 <= 0;
    else
      Y1 <= A + 1;
      Y2 <= 1;
    end if;
  else
    if A >= 24 then
      Y1 <= (others => '0');
    else
      Y1 <= A + 2;
      Y2 <= 1;
    end if;
  end if;
end process;
end architecture COND_DATA_FLOW;
	always @(Sel or A)
	  if (! Sel)
	    if (A >= 12)
	      begin
	        Y1 = 0;
	        Y2 = 0;
	      end
	    else
	      begin
	        Y1 = A + 1;
	        Y2 = 1;
	      end
	  else
	    if (A >= 24)
	      Y1 = 0;
	    else
	      begin
	        Y1 = A + 2;
	        Y2 = 1;
	      end
	endmodule

Synthesized Circuit

Example 7.5 Inadvertent latch inference from a case statement

This model shows a bad way of inferring a latch whether deliberate or not. The **case** statement is of the 16 valued input A. The output Y, is defined for all the choice values, however, because the output is not defined in the **others** clause (VHDL) or **default** clause (Verilog), a latched output is inferred.

Output Y will never have a value of 3 because **case** choice values 7 and 12 are also included in the case branch that assigns Y to 2.

Latch inference from case - not recommended

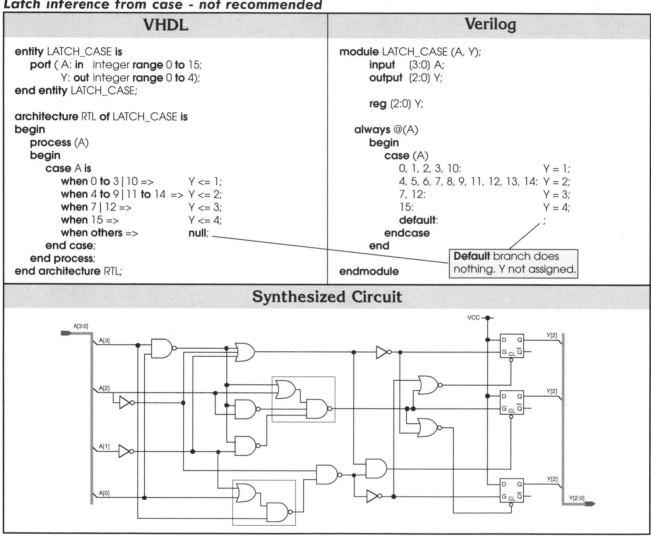

VHDL	Verilog

entity LATCH_CASE **is**
    port (A: **in**   integer **range** 0 **to** 15;
          Y: **out** integer **range** 0 **to** 4);
end entity LATCH_CASE;
 	
architecture RTL **of** LATCH_CASE **is**
begin
    process (A)
    begin
       case A **is**
          when 0 **to** 3 | 10 =>   Y <= 1;
          when 4 **to** 9 | 11 **to** 14 => Y <= 2;
          when 7 | 12 =>   Y <= 3;
          when 15 =>   Y <= 4;
          when others =>   null;
       end case;
    end process;
end architecture RTL;
	module LATCH_CASE (A, Y);
	    input (3:0) A;
	    output (2:0) Y;
	
	    reg (2:0) Y;
	
	    always @(A)
	    begin
	       case (A)
	          0, 1, 2, 3, 10: Y = 1;
	          4, 5, 6, 7, 8, 9, 11, 12, 13, 14: Y = 2;
	          7, 12: Y = 3;
	          15: Y = 4;
	          default:
	       endcase
	    end
	
	endmodule
	
	Default branch does nothing. Y not assigned.

Synthesized Circuit

Example 7.6 Latch inference from nested case statements

All conditions of A are covered in the outer **case**, but are not for Number in the inner **case**; output Y is therefore latched.

VHDL. The inner most **case** statement contains a **when others** branch for LRM compliance, but contains a **null** statement to infer latches for the 4-bit output Y.

Verilog. The inner most **case** statement contains a **default** clause, but contains a null, ";", statement to infer latches for the 4-bit output Y.

Latch inference from nested case statements

VHDL	Verilog
package Types is type PrimeColor is (Red, Green, Blue); end Types; library IEEE; use IEEE.STD_Logic_1164.all, IEEE.Numeric_STD.all; use work.Types.all; entity LATCH_NESTED_CASE is port (ScreenColor: in PrimeColor; Number: in unsigned(1 downto 0); A: in unsigned(3 downto 0); Y: out unsigned(3 downto 0); end entity LATCH_NESTED_CASE; architecture RTL of LATCH_NESTED_CASE is begin process (ScreenColor, Number, A) variable Y_var: unsigned(3 downto 0); begin case ScreenColor is when Red => Y_Var := A + 1; when Green => Y_Var := A + 2; when Blue => case Number is when "00" => Y_Var := A; when "01" => Y_Var := A + 1; when "10" => Y_Var := A + 2; when others null; end case; when others => Y_Var <= A + 1; end case; Y <= Y_var; end process; end architecture RTL;	\`define Red     2'b 00 \`define Green 2'b 01 \`define Blue   2'b 10    module LATCH_NESTED_CASE (ScreenColor, Number, A, Y);     input    (1:0) ScreenColor, Number;     input    (3:0) A;     output  (3:0) Y;      reg (3:0) Y;    always @(ScreenColor or Number or A)     begin       case (ScreenColor)         \`Red: Y = A + 1; \`Green: Y = A + 2;         \`Blue: case (Number) 2'b 00: Y = A; 2'b 01: Y = A + 1; 2'b 10: Y = A + 2; default: ; endcase default: Y = A + 1; endcase end endmodule

The D-Type Flip-Flop

The D-type flip-flop is an edge-triggered memory device (cell primitive) that transfers a signal's value on its D input, to its Q output, when an active edge transition occurs on its clock input. The output value is held until the next active clock edge. The Q-bar output signal is always the inverse of the Q output signal, see Figure 7.3. A bank of flip-flops clocked from a common clock signal is often referred to as a register.

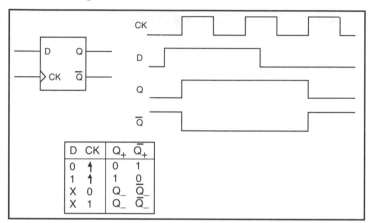

Figure 7.3 The edge triggered D-type flip-flop

Like the latch, there are usually many variants of the flip-flop in an ASIC or FPGA technology library. A flip-flop may have a rising or falling edge triggered clock. It may, or may not, have preset and clear inputs which may be active high or low, and which may be synchronous or asynchronous with the clock.

A circuit, whose sequential elements consist only of D-type flip-flops, can be designed and verified quicker and easier than if latches were used. For this reason, flip-flops are usually preferred over latches. Latches with phased enable signals are used to reduce circuit timing when timing becomes a critical issue.

Flip-Flops are inferred differently in VHDL and Verilog and are described separately.

VHDL flip-flop inference

Flip-flops are inferred in VHDL using **wait** or **if** statements within a process. The difference from latch inferencing is that instead of detecting the occurrence of a signal's level, a signal's edge is now detected. Example edge detecting expressions are:

```
Clock'event and Clock = '1'        -- rising edge detection using 'event attribute
Clock'event and Clock = '0'        -- falling edge detection using 'event attribute
not Clock'stable and Clock = '1'   -- rising edge detection using 'stable
not Clock'stable and Clock = '0'   -- falling edge detection using 'stable
rising_edge(Clock)                 -- rising edge detection using a function call
falling_edge(Clock)                -- falling edge detection using a function call
```

Example use of these edge expressions in **wait** or **if** statements are as follow:

```
Wait until (Clock'event and Clock = '1');
if (Clock'event and Clock = '0') then
wait until rising_edge(Clock);
if falling_edge(Clock) then
```

The above edge detection methods use either VHDL attributes, for example 'event, or function calls, for example rising_edge or falling_edge. The functions rising_edge and falling_edge also use these VHDL attributes. Use of function calls simplifies a model slightly and is preferred, especially if using multi-valued data types, like for example std_logic, that has nine possible values, {U, X, 0, 1, Z, W, L, H, -}. The reason function calls are preferred is that in order to detect a rising edge (logic 0 to 1 transition) for a signal of type std_logic, it is necessary to ensure transitions like X to 1 are <u>not</u> detected.

example,

Clock is of type std_logic.

-- Attribute 'event detects X to 0 and X to 1 transitions which may not be a transition at all
if (Clock'event **and** Clock = '0') **then** -- Detects X to 1 transitions

-- Attribute 'event detects only 0 to 1 transitions
if (Clock'event **and** Clock'last_value = '0' **and** Clock = '1') **then**

-- Detects only logic 0 to logic 1 transitions and has simplified code
if rising_edge(Clock) **then**

Models that are to be simulated and synthesized, an assumption made throughout this book, should use multi-valued data types, and so from the above description, it is better to use function calls. Almost all edge detections throughout this book use function calls, mostly rising_edge, except for the examples in this section showing the use of attributes. Functions rising_edge and falling_edge are defined in the IEEE 1164 package STD_Logic_1164 for clock signals of type std_logic and in the IEEE 1076.3 synthesis package NUMERIC_BIT for clocks of type bit.

Wait *versus* **if**. The **wait** and **if** statements can be used for level detection to infer latches and edge detection to infer flip-flops. The **wait** statement delays the execution of the whole process until its expression becomes true. This means <u>all</u> other signal assignments in the process will infer one or more flip-flops depending on a signal's bit width. Synthesis tools only allow one **wait** statement in a process and it should be the first statement within the process. Because the **if** statement does not stop the execution of the whole **process** it does not prohibit separate purely combinational logic from also being modeled in the same **process**. For this reason the **if** statement is normally preferred over the **wait** statement.

Examples 7.7 and 7.8 use both **wait** and **if** statements, though for the reason just stated, all other examples in this book use **if** statements.

Verilog flip-flop inference

Flip-flops are only inferred using edge triggered **always** statements and so this is similar to using the **wait** statement in VHDL. The Verilog **always** statement is edge-triggered by including either a **posedge** or **negedge** clause in the event list. Combinational logic may be modeled on the inputs to the flip-flops, but independent combinational logic may not be modeled in the same **always** statement. Purely combinational logic must be modeled in a separate **always** statement. For this reason, certain VHDL models may need to be modeled differently in Verilog. Example 7.10 in the LFSR section shows one such case where two **always** statements in Verilog equate to one **process** statement in VHDL.

Example sequential **always** statements:

```
always @(posedge Clock)
always @(negedge Clock)
always @(posedge Clock or posedge Reset)
always @(posedge Clock or negedge Reset)
always @(negedge Clock or posedge Reset)
always @(negedge Clock or negedge Reset)
```

If an asynchronously reset flip-flop is being modeled a second **posedge** or **negedge** clause is needed in the event list of the **always** statement. Also, most synthesis tools require that the reset must be used in an **if** statement directly following the **always** statement, or after the **begin** if it is in a sequential **begin**-**end** block.

example

```
// Active low asynchronous reset
always @(posedge Clock or negedge Reset)
    begin
        if (! Reset)
            ...
            ...
        end
```

Example 7.8 shows VHDL **if** and **wait** statements and Verilog synchronous **always** statements used to model flip-flops with a positive or negative edge triggered clock.

Example 7.9 shows the inference of numerous flip-flop variants having active high (logic 1) or low (logic 0) synchronous and asynchronous set, reset and enable inputs.

Example 7.7 Flip-flops (+ve/-ve clocked) - VHDL attributes and function calls

This is the only example that uses VHDL attributes, for example, 'event, for signal edge detection. The normal function call edge detection is also included for comparison. The model infers flip-flops with a positive or negative edge triggered clock. If the target technology does not contain negative edge triggered flip-flops a positive edge triggered flip-flop will be inferred and the clock signal will be inverted through a separately inferred inverter.

VHDL. Both **if** and **wait** statements use the 'event attribute and rising_edge and falling_edge function calls. Outputs Y1, Y2, Y3 and Y4 are derived using the 'event attribute while outputs Y5, Y6, Y7 and Y8 are derived using function calls. Modeled are four different ways of modeling a positive edge-triggered flip-flop (Y1, Y3, Y5 and Y7), and four different ways of modeling a negative edge-triggered flip-flop (Y2, Y4, Y6 and Y8).

Verilog. There is only one way to model either a positive edge-triggered flip-flop or negative edge triggered flip-flop as indicated below.

+ve and -ve clocked flip-flops - VHDL model uses attributes and function calls

VHDL	Verilog

library IEEE;
use IEEE.STD_Logic_1164.**all**, IEEE.Numeric_STD.**all**;
 	
entity FF_POS_NEG_CLK **is**
    port (Clock: **in**   std_logic;
        A1, A2, A3, A4: **in**   bit;
        A5, A6, A7, A8: **in**   std_logic;
        Y1, Y2, Y3, Y4: **out** bit;
        Y5, Y6, Y7, Y8: **out** std_logic);
end entity FF_POS_NEG_CLK;
 	
architecture RTL **of** FF_POS_NEG_CLK **is**
begin
  P1: **process** (Clock)
  begin
    if (Clock 'event **and** Clock = '1') **then**
      Y1 <= A1;
    end if;
    if (Clock 'event **and** Clock = '0') **then**   *continued*
	module FF_POS_NEG_CLK (Clock, A1, A2, Y1, Y2);
	    input Clock;
	    input A1, A2;
	    output Y1, Y2;
	
	    reg Y1, Y2;
	
	    always @(**posedge** Clock)
	      Y1 = A1;
	
	    always @(**negedge** Clock)
	      Y2 = A2;
	
	endmodule

+ve and -ve clocked flip-flops - VHDL model uses attributes and function calls

VHDL	Synthesized Circuit

<pre>   Y2 <= A2;
    end if;
end process P1;
 	
P2: process
begin
    wait until (Clock 'event and Clock = '1');
        Y3 <= A3;
end process P2;
 	
P3: process
begin
    wait until (Clock 'event and Clock = '0');
        Y4 <= A4;
end process P3;
 	
P4: process (Clock)
begin
    if rising_edge(Clock) then
        Y5 <= A5;
    end if;
 	
    if falling_edge(Clock) then
        Y6 <= A6;
    end if;
end process P4;
 	
P5: process
begin
    wait until rising_edge(Clock);
        Y7 <= A7;
end process P5;
 	
P6: process
begin
    wait until falling_edge(Clock);
        Y8 <= A8;
end process P6;
 	
end architecture RTL;</pre>
	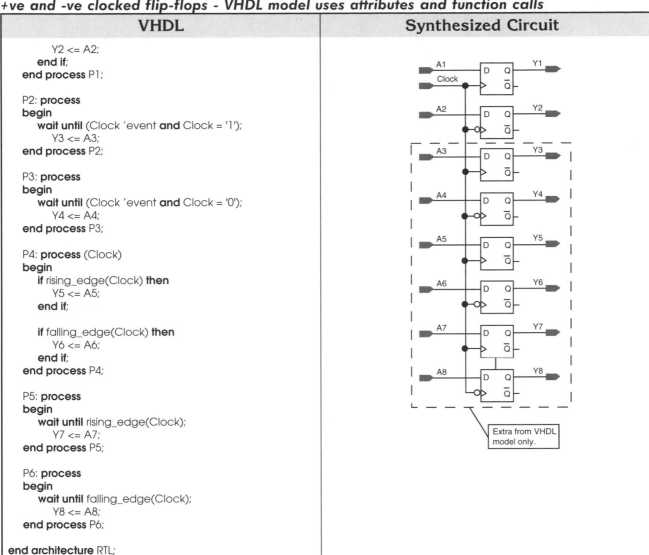

Example 7.8 Various flip-flop models

Different flip-flops with enable inputs, and asynchronous and synchronous resets are modeled. The coding style conforms to that described earlier in this section. An ASIC library, or more probably an FPGA library, may not have all the flip-flop types modeled in this example. This means extra logic gates are inferred with a flip-flop that is in the library to ensure the synthesized circuit maintains correct functionality.

Various filip-flop inferences

VHDL	Verilog

library IEEE;
use IEEE.STD_Logic_1164.**all**, IEEE.Numeric_STD.**all**;
 	
entity FLIP_FLOPS **is**
    port (Clock,
            SynReset1, SynReset2,
            AsynReset1, AsynReset2,
            Enable1, Enable2,
            Data1, Data2:   **in**   std_logic;   *continued*
	module FLIP_FLOPS (Clock,
	        SynReset1, SynReset2, AsynReset1, AsynReset2, Enable1,
	        Enable2, Data1, Data2, Y1, Y2, Y3, Y4, Y5, Y6, Y7, Y8, Y9);
	        input Clock,
	            SynReset1, SynReset2,
	            AsynReset1, AsynReset2, *continued*

175

Various filip-flop inferences

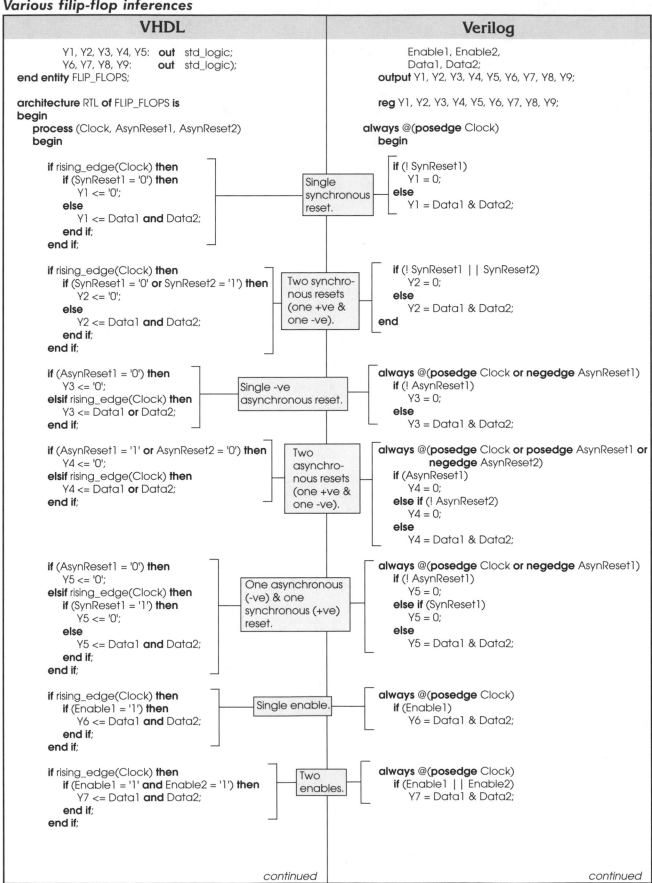

VHDL	Verilog

Y1, Y2, Y3, Y4, Y5: **out** std_logic;
Y6, Y7, Y8, Y9: **out** std_logic);
end entity FLIP_FLOPS;
 	
architecture RTL **of** FLIP_FLOPS **is**
begin
  process (Clock, AsynReset1, AsynReset2)
  begin
	Enable1, Enable2,
	Data1, Data2;
	output Y1, Y2, Y3, Y4, Y5, Y6, Y7, Y8, Y9;
	
	reg Y1, Y2, Y3, Y4, Y5, Y6, Y7, Y8, Y9;
	
	always @(**posedge** Clock)
	  begin

```
      if rising_edge(Clock) then                              if (! SynReset1)
          if (SynReset1 = '0') then         Single               Y1 = 0;
              Y1 <= '0';                    synchronous       else
          else                              reset.               Y1 = Data1 & Data2;
              Y1 <= Data1 and Data2;
          end if;
      end if;
```

```
      if rising_edge(Clock) then                              if (! SynReset1 || SynReset2)
          if (SynReset1 = '0' or SynReset2 = '1') then  Two synchro-    Y2 = 0;
              Y2 <= '0';                    nous resets       else
          else                              (one +ve &           Y2 = Data1 & Data2;
              Y2 <= Data1 and Data2;        one -ve).         end
          end if;
      end if;
```

```
      if (AsynReset1 = '0') then                              always @(posedge Clock or negedge AsynReset1)
          Y3 <= '0';                        Single -ve           if (! AsynReset1)
      elsif rising_edge(Clock) then         asynchronous            Y3 = 0;
          Y3 <= Data1 or Data2;             reset.            else
      end if;                                                    Y3 = Data1 & Data2;
```

```
      if (AsynReset1 = '1' or AsynReset2 = '0') then         always @(posedge Clock or posedge AsynReset1 or
          Y4 <= '0';                        Two                           negedge AsynReset2)
      elsif rising_edge(Clock) then         asynchro-         if (AsynReset1)
          Y4 <= Data1 or Data2;             nous resets           Y4 = 0;
      end if;                               (one +ve &        else if (! AsynReset2)
                                            one -ve).             Y4 = 0;
                                                              else
                                                                 Y4 = Data1 & Data2;
```

```
      if (AsynReset1 = '0') then                              always @(posedge Clock or negedge AsynReset1)
          Y5 <= '0';                        One asynchronous     if (! AsynReset1)
      elsif rising_edge(Clock) then         (-ve) & one             Y5 = 0;
          if (SynReset1 = '1') then         synchronous (+ve) else if (SynReset1)
              Y5 <= '0';                    reset.                  Y5 = 0;
          else                                                else
              Y5 <= Data1 and Data2;                             Y5 = Data1 & Data2;
          end if;
      end if;
```

```
      if rising_edge(Clock) then                              always @(posedge Clock)
          if (Enable1 = '1') then           Single enable.       if (Enable1)
              Y6 <= Data1 and Data2;                              Y6 = Data1 & Data2;
          end if;
      end if;
```

```
      if rising_edge(Clock) then                              always @(posedge Clock)
          if (Enable1 = '1' and Enable2 = '1') then  Two          if (Enable1 || Enable2)
              Y7 <= Data1 and Data2;        enables.              Y7 = Data1 & Data2;
          end if;
      end if;
```

continued

continued

Various filip-flop inferences

VHDL	Verilog
| ```
if rising_edge(Clock) then
    if (SynReset1 = '1') then
        Y8 <= '0';
    elsif (Enable1 = '1' and Enable2 = '1') then
        Y8 <= Data1 and Data2;
        Y8 <= Y8;
end if;
``` | ```
always @(posedge Clock)
    if (SynReset1)
        Y8 = 0;
    else if (Enable1)
        Y8 = Data1 & Data2;
``` |

Synchro-nous reset and enable.

VHDL	Verilog
| ```
if (AsynReset1 = '1') then
    Y9 <= '0';
elsif rising_edge(Clock) then
    if (SynReset1 = '1') then
        Y9 <= '0';
    elsif (Enable1 = '1' and Enable2 = '1') then
        Y9 <= Data1 and Data2;
    end if;
end if;
``` | ```
always @(posedge Clock or posedge AsynReset1)
    if (AsynReset1)
        Y9 = 0;
    else if (SynReset1)
        Y9 = 0;
    else if (Enable1 || Enable2)
        Y9 = Data1 & Data2;
``` |

One asynchronous reset (+ve), one synchronous reset (+ve) and two enables.

```
    end process;
end architecture RTL;
```

```
endmodule
```

Synthesized Circuit

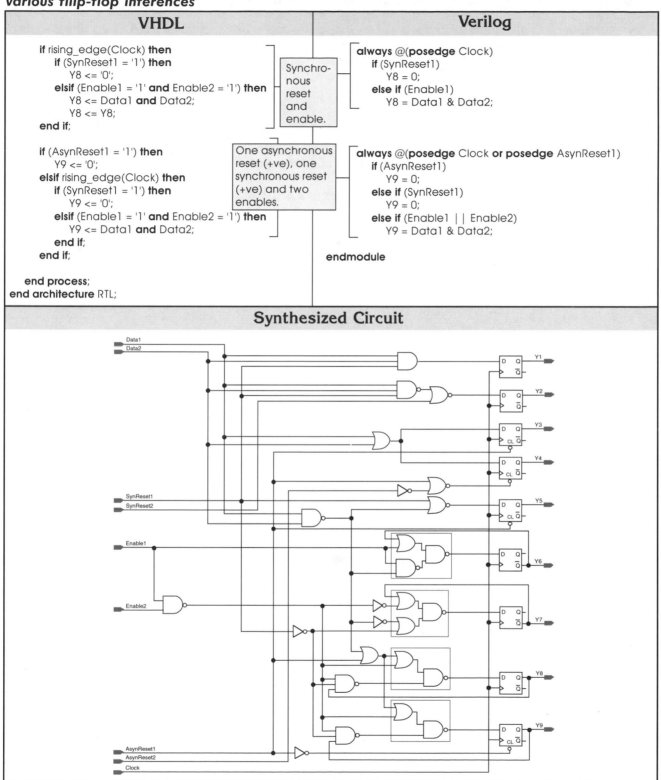

Example 7.9 Combinational logic between two flip-flops

This example is similar to Example 7.1, but infers flip-flops instead of latches. Two flip-flops are modeled with combinational logic on the input to the first flip-flop and between them both. This is achieved with a single **process** (VHDL)/**always** (Verilog) statement.

VHDL. Signal assignments in an edge triggered section of code infer one or more flip-flops. In this example signals M and Y both infer a single flip-flop. Because signal M is used in the expression for the assignment to Y, the output from one flip-flop feeds the input to the other. As data object N is a variable, it does not infer a flip-flop. The new computed value of N in the second assignment is used in computing the value of Y in the third assignment.

Verilog. The explicit assignment to N must appear in a separate, non-edge sensitive, **always** block to avoid inferring a third flip-flop. Also, the assignment to M uses a non-blocking signal assignment so that the NAND of A and B appears on the input to the first flip-flop. If a blocking signal assignment were used the NAND of A and B would feed the input to the NOR gate and the first flip-flop would be redundant.

Combinational logic between two flip-flops

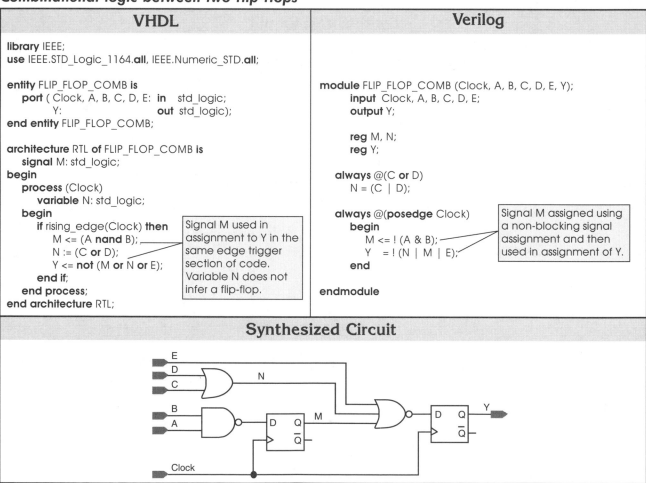

VHDL	Verilog

library IEEE;
use IEEE.STD_Logic_1164.**all**, IEEE.Numeric_STD.**all**;
 	
entity FLIP_FLOP_COMB **is**
   port (Clock, A, B, C, D, E: **in** std_logic;
     Y: **out** std_logic);
end entity FLIP_FLOP_COMB;
 	
architecture RTL **of** FLIP_FLOP_COMB **is**
   signal M: std_logic;
begin
   process (Clock)
     variable N: std_logic;
     begin
       if rising_edge(Clock) **then**
         M <= (A **nand** B);
         N := (C **or** D);
         Y <= **not** (M **or** N **or** E);
       end if;
   end process;
end architecture RTL;
	module FLIP_FLOP_COMB (Clock, A, B, C, D, E, Y);
	   input Clock, A, B, C, D, E;
	   output Y;
	
	   reg M, N;
	   reg Y;
	
	   always @(C **or** D)
	     N = (C | D);
	
	   always @(**posedge** Clock)
	     begin
	       M <= ! (A & B);
	       Y = ! (N | M | E);
	     end
	
	endmodule

VHDL annotation: Signal M used in assignment to Y in the same edge trigger section of code. Variable N does not infer a flip-flop.

Verilog annotation: Signal M assigned using a non-blocking signal assignment and then used in assignment of Y.

Synthesized Circuit

Linear Feedback Shift Registers

A Linear Feedback Shift Register (LFSR) is a sequential shift register with combinational feedback logic around it that causes it to pseudo-randomly cycle through a sequence of binary values. Linear feedback shift registers have a multitude of uses in digital system design. A design modeled using LFSRs often has both speed and area advantages over a functionally equivalent design that does not use LFSRs; unfortunately, these advantages are often overlooked by designers. Typical applications include: counters, Built-in Self Test (BIST), pseudo-random number generation, data encryption and decryption, data integrity checksums, and data compression techniques.

Feedback around an LFSR's shift register comes from a selection of points (taps) in the register chain and constitutes either XORing or XNORing these taps to provide tap(s) back into the register. Register bits that do not need an input tap, operate as a standard shift register. It is this feedback that causes the register to loop through repetitive sequences of pseudo-random values. The choice of taps determines how many values there are in a given sequence before the sequence is repeated. Certain tap settings yield maximal length sequences of $(2^n - 1)$. If the application requires all 2^n values to be included in the sequence, the circuit can be modified slightly, see below. If $(2^n - 1)$ or less is sufficient, the LFSR must be prohibited from randomly powering-up and becoming permanently stuck with the prohibited value on the register output; see below.

The structural design aspects to consider when modeling LFSRs follow.

XOR or XNOR feedback gates

The feedback path may consist of either all XOR gates or all XNOR gates. They are interchangeable, and given particular tap settings, an LFSR will sequence through the same number of values in a loop before the loop repeats itself; the only difference is that the sequence will be different. Figure 7.4 has LFSR configurations using XOR gates, but XNOR gates could equally be used.

One-to-many or many-to-one feedback structure

Both one-to-many or many-to-one feedback structures using XOR or XNOR gates can be implemented and use the same number of logic gates, Figure 7.4. A one-to-many structure will always have a shorter worst case clock-to-clock path delay as it only passes through a single two input XOR (XNOR) gate, instead of a tree of XOR (or XNOR) gates in the case of the many-to-one structure. For this reason, Example 7.10 uses only a one-to-many structure.

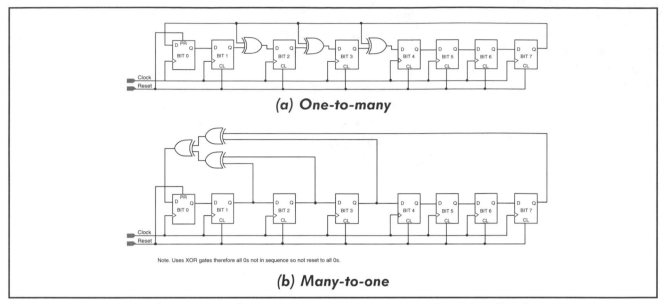

(a) One-to-many

(b) Many-to-one

Note. Uses XOR gates therefore all 0s not in sequence so not reset to all 0s.

Figure 7.4 8-bit LFSR with a one-to-many or many-to-one feedback structure

What taps to use

The choice of which taps to use determines how many values are included in a sequence of pseudo-random values before the sequence is repeated. For example, a 3-bit LFSR with taps at register bits [1,2] will cause it to enter a loop comprising only two values: the actual values of which is dependent upon the initial value. By comparison, taps at bits [0,2] is said to give a sequence of *maximal length* ($2^n - 1$). It will sequence through every possible value, excluding the value where all 3-bits are at logic 0, before returning to its initial value.

For any given width LFSR there are many tap combinations that give *maximal length* sequences. For example, a 10-bit LFSR has two 2-tap combinations that result in a *maximal length* sequence ([2,9] and [6,9]), along with twenty 4-tap combinations, twenty-eight 6-tap combinations, and ten 8-tap combinations. Again, the sequence of binary values will vary depending on which tap selection is used.

Table 7.1 shows a minimum number of taps that yield maximal length sequences for LFSRs ranging from 2 to 32 bits.

Table 7.1 Taps for maximal length LFSRs with 2 to 32 bits

Number of bits	Length of Loop	Taps
2	3	[0,1]
3	7	[0,2]
4	15	[0,3]
5	31	[1,4]
6	63	[0,5]
7	127	[0,6]
8	255	[1,2,3,7]
9	511	[3,8]
10	1023	[2,9]
11	2047	[1,10]
12	4095	[0,3,5,11]
13	8191	[0,2,3,12]
14	16383	[0,2,4,13]
15	32767	[0,14]
16	65535	[1,2,4,15]
17	131071	[2,16]
18	262143	[6,17]
19	524287	[0,1,4,18]
20	1,048,575	[2,19]
21	2,097,151	[1,20]
21	4,194,303	0,21]
23	8,388,607	[4,22]
24	16,777,215	[0,2,3,23]
25	33,554,431	[2,24]
26	67,108,863	[0,1,5,25]
27	134,217,727	[0,1,4,26]
28	268,435,455	[2,27]
29	536,870,911	[1,28]
30	1,073,741,823	[0,3,5,29]
31	2,147,483,647	[2,30]
32	4,294,967,295	[1,5,6,31]

Extracted from the book "Bebop to the Boolean Boogie" ISBN 1-878707-22-1 by permission of HighText Publications Inc.

Avoid becoming stuck in the prohibited state

Using XOR gates, the LFSR will not sequence through the binary value where all bits are at logic 0. Should it find itself with all bits at logic 0, it will continue to shift all 0s indefinitely. Therefore, the LFSR should be prohibited from randomly initializing to all logic 0s during power-up. Similarly, an XNOR based LFSR will not sequence through the binary value where all bits are at logic 1 and so should be prohibited from randomly initializing to all 1's during power-up.

This can be overcome by:

- using a reset to either preset or clear the individual register flip-flops to a known good value. In this case, the value is "hard wired" and cannot be changed,
- provide a means of loading an initial seed value into the register; either parallel or serial,
- model extra circuitry that allows all 2^n values to be included in the sequence (see following section).

Ensuring a sequence of all 2^n values

Provided taps for a *maximal length* sequence is used, the LFSR configurations described so far will sequence through (2^n - 1) binary values. A sequence of (2^n - 1) values may not be a problem in many applications, but for ATPG applications, or if modeling a 4-bit 16 value counter, for example, all 2^n values are needed in the sequence. The feedback path can be modified with extra circuitry to ensure that all 2^n binary values are included in the sequence. Figure 7.5 shows the two 8-bit XOR based LFSRs of Figure 7.4 modified for a sequence of 2^n values. The principle behind this is now described.

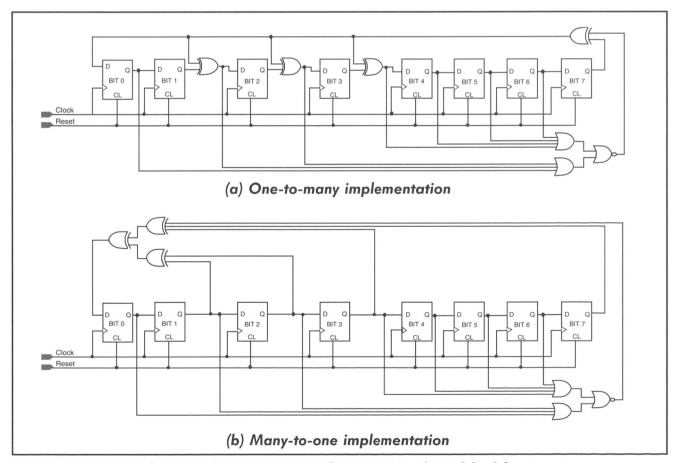

(a) One-to-many implementation

(b) Many-to-one implementation

Figure 7.5 8-bit LFSR (many-to-one and one-to-many) modified for 2^n sequences

Principle behind a 2^n looping sequence. Notice from Table 7.1 the taps for maximal length sequences always include the most significant bit plus a group of taps from the least significant end of the register. The most significant bit tap, when XORed (XNORed), inverts the smaller looping sequence caused by the taps at the least significant end. Knowing that the all 0s value does not occur naturally in the sequence when using XOR feedback gates, when all bits, except the most significant bit, are at logic 0, the most significant bit must be at logic 1. This condition is detected and the most significant bit is then inverted to a logic 0 so that the feedback signal is forced to logic 0 and all logic 0 values are forced onto the register. This inversion is achieved by XORing the NOR of all bits, bar the most significant bit, with the rest of the XOR gates in the feedback path. When all bits have been set at logic 0, the inversion sets the feedback back to logic 1 and the sequence continues.

Constructing generic n-bit LFSR models

Generic *n*-bit LFSRs can be modeled and referenced as needed. The best way of achieving this, is to define a generic model. In VHDL an **entity** can use generics, while in Verilog overloaded **parameter** values can be used; see Example 7.11. Another way would be to define a generic VHDL **procedure** in a separate **package**. Verilog does not support parameterizable subprograms. The disadvantage of using a VHDL **procedure**, is that the feedback logic would need to be modeled using a signal (not a variable), which must be capable of being read and because signals cannot be defined in a procedure the output must be of type **inout** or **buffer**. This would lead to confusion and complications when used.

Example 7.10 contains the model of the one-to-many 8-bit LFSR modified for a 2^n looping sequence shown in Figure 7.5 (a). Example 7.11 has a model of a generic *n*-bit LFSR. The next section on counters contains Example 7.13 which uses a 4-bit one-to-many non-modified LFSR to model a 13 count counter.

Example 7.10 One-to-many 8-bit LFSR modified for 2^n sequence values

An 8-bit LFSR is modeled for a one-to-many XOR feedback structure, Figure 7.5(a), and has been modified for a 2^n looping sequence.

The VHDL version has a single **process** containing variable assignments. The Verilog version cannot be modeled in a similar way using a single edge triggered **always** statement because the VHDL variables would become Verilog procedural assignments and infer extra flip-flops. Therefore, as is often the case when using Verilog, it is better to model sequential logic in one **always** statement and combinational logic in a separate **always** statement. This Verilog model is a classic example of when this is necessary.

The LFSR taps have been defined in a **constant** (VHDL)/**parameter** (Verilog), and is called Taps. The NOR of all LFSR bits minus the most significant bit, that is, Y(6:0) generates the extra circuitry needed for all 2^n sequence values. This is achieved in VHDL using a **for** loop, while in Verilog the NOR reduction operator (~|) is used, and produces Bits0_6_Zero. By XORing Bits0_6_Zero, with the most significant bit of the LFSR, LFSRS_Reg(7), the feedback signal Feedback is generated. A loop is then used to perform the shifting operation which either; 1) shifts each bit to the next most significant bit, or 2) shifts each bit to the next most significant bit XORed with Feedback if it is a tap bit.

VHDL. Uses variable LFSR_Reg to calculate and hold the next value of the shift register. This variable is then assigned to the output signal Y after each clock edge. The assignments to this variable could have been modeled to be direct to signal Y, negating the need for LFSR_Reg, but this would mean the output port for Y would need to be of type **buffer** instead of type **out**, which may, or may not, be a problem. As a general rule in VHDL, it is better to only use variable assignments within **for** loop statements as discussed in Chapter 4.

Verilog. As already stated in this example, sequential and combinational logic has been modeled in separate **always** statements. The first **always** statement infers just the register part of the LFSR and its output signal is called LFSR_Reg. The second **always** statement infers the combinational feedback logic and outputs the next register value as a signal called Next_LFSR_Reg. Output Y is assigned in a separate continuous assignment statement to avoid the output needing to be of type **inout**, as would be the case if the output was to come direct from the signal LFSR_Reg. This makes the model clearer and avoids the need to use type **inout** which could be mistaken for a bidirectional signal. There is no inherent problem if output Y was to be of type **inout** as it would be in VHDL.

One-to-many 8-bit LFSR that sequences through all 2^n binary values

VHDL	Verilog

`library IEEE;`
`use IEEE.STD_Logic_1164.all, IEEE.Numeric_STD.all`
 	
`entity LFSR_8BIT is`
`    port ( Clock, Reset: in  std_logic;`
`          Y;  out unsigned(7 downto 0));`
`end entity LFSR_8BIT;`
 	
`architecture RTL of LFSR_8BIT is`
`    constant Taps: unsigned(7 downto 0) :=`
`               (1 | 2 | 3 | 7 => '1', others => '0');`
`begin`
`    process (Reset, Clock)`
`        variable LFSR_Reg: unsigned(7 downto 0);`
`        variable Bits0_6_Zero, Feedback: std_logic;`
`    begin`
`        if (Reset = '0') then`
`            LFSR_Reg:= (others => '0');`
`        elsif rising_edge(Clock) then`
`            Bits0_6_Zero := '0';`
`            for N in 0 to 6 loop`
`                Bits0_6_Zero := Bits0_6_Zero nor LFSR_Reg(N);`
`            end loop;`
`            Feedback := LFSR_Reg(7) xor Bits0_6_Zero;`
`            for N in 7 downto 1 loop`
`                if (Taps(N - 1) = '1') then`
`                    LFSR_Reg(N) := LFSR_Reg(N-1) xor Feedback;`
`                else`
`                    LFSR_Reg(N) := LFSR_Reg(N - 1);`
`                end if;`
`            end loop;`
`            LFSR_Reg(0) := Feedback;`
`        end if;`
`        Y <= LFSR_Reg;`
`    end process;`
`end architecture RTL;`
	`module LFSR_8BIT (Clock, Reset, Y);`
	`    input  Clock, Reset;`
	`    output (7:0) Y;`
	
	`    integer N (1:7);`
	`    parameter Taps = 8'b 10001110;`
	`    reg Bits0_6_Zero, Feedback;`
	`    reg (7:0) LFSR_Reg, Next_LFSR_Reg;`
	
	`    always @(negedge Reset or posedge Clock)`
	`        begin: LFSR_Reg`
	`            if (! Reset)`
	`                LFSR_Reg = 8'b 0;`
	`            else`
	`                LFSR_Reg = Next_LFSR_Reg;`
	`        end`
	
	`    always @(LFSR_Reg)`
	`        begin : LFSR_Feedback`
	`            Bits0_6_Zero = ~| LFSR_Reg(6:0);`
	`            Feedback = LFSR_Reg(7) ^ Bits0_6_Zero;`
	`            for (N = 7; N >= 1; N = N - 1)`
	`                if (Taps(N - 1) == 1)`
	`                    Next_LFSR_Reg(N) = LFSR_Reg(N - 1) ^ Feedback;`
	`                else`
	`                    Next_LFSR_Reg(N) = LFSR_Reg(N - 1);`
	`            Next_LFSR_Reg(0) = Feedback;`
	`        end`
	
	`    assign Y = LFSR_Reg;`
	
	`endmodule`
	
	[annotation pointing to the always blocks:] Cannot be modeled in one synchronous **always** block otherwise signals Bits0_6_Zero and Next_LFSR_Reg would also infer flip-flops.

Synthesized Circuit	
(see Figure 7.5a)	

Example 7.11 Generic n-bit LFSR

A generic *n*-bit LFSR is modeled where *n* is any value from 2 to 32. The generic LFSR is modeled in an **entity** (VHDL)/**module** (Verilog). The width of a specific LFSR is specified when the **entity** or **module** is instantiated. Like any parameterizable model, the VHDL model uses a **generic** while the Verilog model uses an overloaded **parameter** value to define the width of any given LFSR instantiation. A separate model is shown that calls the generic model twice for the instantiation of a 5 and 8-bit LFSR. The modeled LFSR structure is identical to that used for the 8-bit LFSR shown in Example 7.10, that is, a one-to-many XOR feedback modified for a 2^n looping sequence.

Feedback tap settings for all LFSRs ranging from 2 to 32-bits, see Table 7.1, are modeled in a two dimensional array and referenced as needed. This is achieved differently in VHDL and Verilog as described below.

VHDL taps. A two dimensional array type, TapsArrayType, is defined to have 31 elements, numbered 2 to 32, that are each 32-bits wide. Each 32-bit value is of type unsigned because this is the type used in the model and saves the need to use a conversion function call. A constant array of type TapsArrayType, that is, TapsArray, defines the individual taps needed for each LFSR. Tap settings for each LFSR are assigned to each 32-bit element of the array using an aggregate for code efficiency and easier reading. The aggregate consists of two elements separated by a comma. The first element defines all the tap bits to be at logic 1 by listing the appropriate taps separated by the logical OR choice separator "|". All other non tap bits are defined to be at logic 0 in the second element, using the **others** clause and includes all 32 bits whether the constant is for a 2 or 32-bit LFSR.

The value of the generic, Width, is of type integer and specifies the required size of the instantiated LFSR. This value is used to assign the appropriate taps from the constant array to the signal Taps.

Verilog taps. A memory array, TapsArray, is defined to hold the tap constants. In a non-synthesizable model tap constants would typically be assigned in an **initial** statement. However, as **initial** statements are not supported by synthesis tools the tap constants have been assigned in a sequential **always** block and is triggered into running when a reset signal occurs on Reset. The memory array, TapsArray, is not synthesized to gates because:

- 30 of the 31 constants are not used and are not connected to anything so will be removed during the initial stages of synthesis,
- the constant array element that is used for a particular width LFSR will be optimized during synthesis, such that an array of logic gates is not formed with inputs connected to logic 0 or logic 1 as implied by the tap settings.

Verilog does not have an equivalent to VHDL aggregates. This means the Verilog **default** clause cannot be used to define tap values in the same way as the VHDL **others** clause did in the VHDL model. Although each element of the constant memory array is 32-bits only those bits needed for a particular width LFSR is specified. The underscore character (_) is used to split the constant tap value setting into groups of 8-bits for easier reading.

Generic n-bit LFSR using one-to-many feedback

VHDL	Verilog
| ```vhdl
library IEEE;
use IEEE.STD_Logic_1164.all, IEEE.Numeric_STD.all;

entity LFSR_GENERIC_MOD is
   generic (Width: integer);
   port ( Clock, Reset: std_logic;
          Y: out unsigned(Width - 1 downto 0));
end entity LFSR_GENERIC_MOD;

architecture RTL of LFSR_GENERIC_MOD is
   type TapsArrayType is array (2 to 32) of
                         unsigned(31 downto 0);
   constant TapsArray: TapsArrayType :=
      (2  => (0|1          => '1', others => '0'),
       3  => (0|2          => '1', others => '0'),
       4  => (0|3          => '1', others => '0'),
       5  => (1|4          => '1', others => '0'),
       6  => (0|5          => '1', others => '0'),
       7  => (0|6          => '1', others => '0'),
       8  => (1|2|3|7      => '1', others => '0'),
       9  => (3|8          => '1', others => '0'),
       10 => (2|9          => '1', others => '0'),
       11 => (1|10         => '1', others => '0'),
       12 => (0|3|5|11     => '1', others => '0'),
       13 => (0|2|3|12     => '1', others => '0'),
       14 => (0|2|4|13     => '1', others => '0'),
       15 => (0|14         => '1', others => '0'),
       16 => (1|2|4|15     => '1', others => '0'),
       17 => (2|16         => '1', others => '0'),
       18 => (6|17         => '1', others => '0'),
       19 => (0|1|4|18     => '1', others => '0'),
       20 => (2|19         => '1', others => '0'),
       21 => (1|20         => '1', others => '0'),
       22 => (0|21         => '1', others => '0'),
       23 => (4|22         => '1', others => '0'),
       24 => (0|2|3|23     => '1', others => '0'),
       25 => (2|24         => '1', others => '0'),
       26 => (0|1|5|25     => '1', others => '0'),
       27 => (0|1|4|26     => '1', others => '0'),
       28 => (2|27         => '1', others => '0'),
       29 => (1|28         => '1', others => '0'),
       30 => (0|3|5|29     => '1', others => '0'),
       31 => (2|30         => '1', others => '0'),
       32 => (1|5|6|31     => '1', others => '0'));
   signal Taps: unsigned(Width - 1 downto 0);
begin

   LFSR: process (Reset, Clock)
      variable LFSR_Reg: unsigned(Width - 1 downto 0);
      variable Bits0_Nminus1_Zero, Feedback: std_logic;
   begin

      Taps <= TapsArray(Width)(Width - 1 downto 0);

      if (Reset = '0') then
         LFSR_Reg := (others => '0');
      elsif rising_edge(Clock) then
         Bits0_Nminus1_Zero := '0';
         for N in 0 to Width-1 loop
            Bits0_Nminus1_Zero := Bits0_Nminus1_Zero nor
                                  LFSR_Reg(N);
         end loop;
         Feedback := LFSR_Reg(Width - 1) xor
                     Bits0_Nminus1_Zero;
``` | ```verilog
module LFSR_GENERIC_MOD (Clock, Reset, Y);
   parameter Width = 8;
   input  Clock, Reset;
   output (Width - 1:0) Y;

   reg (31:0) TapsArray (2:32);
   wire (Width - 1:0) Taps;
   integer N;
   reg Bits0_Nminus1_Zero, Feedback;
   reg (Width - 1:0) LFSR_Reg, Next_LFSR_Reg;

   always @(Reset)
      begin
         TapsArray(2)  = 2'b  11;
         TapsArray(3)  = 3'b  101;
         TapsArray(4)  = 4'b  1001;
         TapsArray(5)  = 5'b  10010;
         TapsArray(6)  = 6'b  100001;
         TapsArray(7)  = 7'b  1000001;
         TapsArray(8)  = 8'b  10001110;
         TapsArray(9)  = 9'b  10000100_0;
         TapsArray(10) = 10'b 10000001_00;
         TapsArray(11) = 11'b 10000000_010;
         TapsArray(12) = 12'b 10000010_1001;
         TapsArray(13) = 13'b 10000000_01101;
         TapsArray(14) = 14'b 10000000_010101;
         TapsArray(15) = 15'b 10000000_0000001;
         TapsArray(16) = 16'b 10000000_00010110;
         TapsArray(17) = 17'b 10000000_00000010_0;
         TapsArray(18) = 18'b 10000000_00010000_00;
         TapsArray(19) = 19'b 10000000_00000010_011;
         TapsArray(20) = 20'b 10000000_00000000_0100;
         TapsArray(21) = 21'b 10000000_00000000_00010;
         TapsArray(22) = 22'b 10000000_00000000_000001;
         TapsArray(23) = 23'b 10000000_00000000_0010000;
         TapsArray(24) = 24'b 10000000_00000000_00001101;
         TapsArray(25) = 25'b 10000000_00000000_00000010_0;
         TapsArray(26) = 26'b 10000000_00000000_00001000_11;
         TapsArray(27) = 27'b 10000000_00000000_00000010_011;
         TapsArray(28) = 28'b 10000000_00000000_00000000_0100;
         TapsArray(29) = 29'b 10000000_00000000_00000000_00010;
         TapsArray(30) = 30'b 10000000_00000000_00000000_101001;
         TapsArray(31) = 31'b 10000000_00000000_00000000_0000100;
         TapsArray(32) = 32'b 10000000_00000000_00000000_01100010;
      end
   assign Taps(Width - 1:0) = TapsArray(Width);

   always @(negedge Reset or posedge Clock)
      begin: LFSR_Register
         if (! Reset)
            LFSR_Reg = 0;
         else
            LFSR_Reg = Next_LFSR_Reg;
      end

   always @(LFSR_Reg)
      begin: LFSR_Feedback
         Bits0_Nminus1_Zero = ~| LFSR_Reg(Width - 2:0);
         Feedback = LFSR_Reg(Width-1) ^ Bits0_Nminus1_Zero;
         for (N = Width - 1; N >= 1; N = N -1)
            if (Taps(N - 1) == 1)
               Next_LFSR_Reg(N) = LFSR_Reg(N - 1) ^ Feedback;
            else
               Next_LFSR_Reg(N) = LFSR_Reg(N - 1);
         Next_LFSR_Reg(0) = Feedback;
      end

   assign Y = LFSR_Reg;
endmodule
``` |

> The "|" symbol is used to separate a list of index values, for which all elements have the same value.

> No multiple dimensions in Verilog so each memory element defining tap constants must be explicitly defined. Not in an **initial** statement as not supported by synthesis.

continued

185

Generic n-bit LFSR using one-to-many feedback

VHDL	Verilog

<pre>   for N in 1 to Width-1 loop
                if (Taps(N - 1) = '1') then
                    LFSR_Reg(N) := LFSR_Reg(N - 1) xor Feedback;
                else
                    LFSR_Reg(N) := LFSR_Reg(N - 1);
                end if;
            end loop;
            LFSR_Reg(0) := Feedback;
        end if;
        Y <= LFSR_Reg;
    end process;
 	
end architecture RTL;</pre>	

Instantiation of a 5-bit and 8-bit generic LFSR

VHDL	Verilog

<pre>library IEEE;
use IEEE.STD_Logic_1164.all, IEEE.Numeric_STD.all;
 	
entity LFSR_5AND8_MOD is
    port (Clock, Reset: in std_logic;
           Y1: out unsigned(4 downto 0);
           Y2: out unsigned(7 downto 0));
end entity LFSR_5AND8_MOD;
 	
architecture STRUCTURAL of LFSR_5AND8_MOD is
    component LFSR_GENERIC_MOD
        generic (Width: integer);
        port (Clock, Reset: in std_logic;
               Y: out unsigned(Width - 1 downto 0));
    end component LFSR_GENERIC_MOD;
begin
 	
    LFSR_5: LFSR_GENERIC_MOD
        generic map (5)
        port map (Clock, Reset, Y1);
    LFSR_8: LFSR_GENERIC_MOD
        generic map (8)
        port map (Clock, Reset, Y2);
 	
end architecture STRUCTURAL;</pre>
	<pre>module LFSR_8AND5_MOD (Clock, Reset, Y1, Y2);
	    input Clock, Reset;
	    output (4:0) Y1;
	    output (7:0) Y2;
	
	    LFSR_GENERIC_MOD #(5) LFSR_5(Clock, Reset, Y1);
	    LFSR_GENERIC_MOD #(8) LFSR_8(Clock, Reset, Y2);
	
	endmodule</pre>

Counters

A register that goes through a predetermined sequence of binary values (states), upon the application of input pulses on one or more inputs, is called a counter. Counters count the number of occurrences of an event, that is, input pulses, that occur either randomly or at uniform intervals of time. Counters are used extensively in digital design for all kinds of applications. Apart from general purpose counting, counters can be used as clock dividers and for generating timing control signals.

Deciding on a counter's structure and modeling

There are many ways in which a counter can be implemented depending upon the design requirements. Some options follow depending upon whether a synchronous or asynchronous counter is needed.

1. Synchronous counters

All flip-flops in a synchronous counter receive the same clock pulse and so change state simultaneously, that is, synchronously. Synchronous counters are easier to design and verify, and are less layout dependent than their asynchronous equivalent. Three options for a synchronous counter are:

a). *Simplest and most common*. A synchronous incrementing or decrementing binary counter is modeled by adding or subtracting a constant 1 using the "+" or "-" arithmetic operators in assignments residing in a section of code inferring synchronous logic. The inferred logic for the adder or subtractor can be controlled during synthesis to have a ripple-carry or carry-look-ahead structure. See Example 7.13.

b). *Model detailed structure*. Like adder or subtractor circuits, synchronous counters can be modeled to have a specific detailed structure, see structural adders in Chapter 9. The adder or subtractor circuit is simply placed in a section of code that infers synchronous logic. Most applications do not require counters to be modeled at this level of detail.

c). *Use an LFSR*. LFSRs can be used to model synchronous counters. The design is slightly more complex because the counting sequence is pseudo-random, but the much reduced feedback logic yields a smaller and faster operating circuit than would be produced from an equivalent binary counter. This is especially true for counters which count to a large number of events and require a larger width count register. Such a counter should be first simulated without an end count so that it counts continuously, and enables the pseudo-random sequence to be derived. See Example 7.14.

2. Asynchronous counters

Sometimes called ripple counters because flip-flop transitions ripple through from one flip-flop to the next in sequence until all flip-flops reach a new stable value (state). Each single flip-flop stage divides the frequency of its input signal by two. Asynchronous counters can be significantly smaller, especially for clock dividers dividing by a factor of 2^n where n is any positive integer of 4 and above. Depending upon the application an extra resynchronizing flip-flop may be needed on the output stage. In order to count to any value that is not a factor of 2^n, extra feedback logic is needed to detect an end count value and reset the counter back to the start count value. In this case, a resynchronizing flip-flop is essential to generate a clean, glitch free, asynchronous reset. See Examples 7.15 and 7.16.

Example 7.12 5-bit up-by-one down-by-two counter

This 5-bit counter counts up-by-one when Up is a logic 1 and down-by-two when Down is a logic 1. For all other conditions of Up and Down the counter will hold its value. The synchronous reset (Reset) overrides the Up and Down signals and sets the counter to zero.

A **case** statement of the concatenation of Up and Down makes the model easy to read. Automatic resource sharing means the "+" and "-" operators will synthesize to a single adder/subtractor circuit. The synthesis tools from VeriBest Incorporated will implement a carry-look-ahead type circuit by default.

VHDL. The "+" and "-" operators make a function call to the overloaded "+" and "-" functions defined in the IEEE 1076.3 VHDL package Numeric_STD. This allows an object of type unsigned to be added to an object of type integer.

Up-by-one down-by-two counter

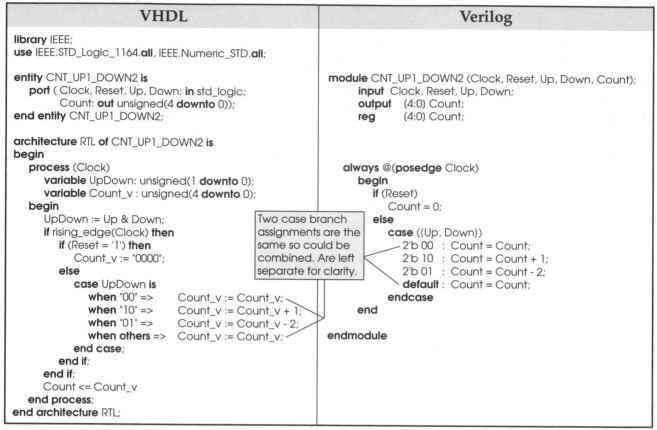

VHDL	Verilog

library IEEE;
use IEEE.STD_Logic_1164.**all**, IEEE.Numeric_STD.**all**;
 	
entity CNT_UP1_DOWN2 **is**
  port (Clock, Reset, Up, Down: **in** std_logic;
        Count: **out** unsigned(4 **downto** 0));
end entity CNT_UP1_DOWN2;
 	
architecture RTL **of** CNT_UP1_DOWN2 **is**
begin
  process (Clock)
    variable UpDown: unsigned(1 **downto** 0);
    variable Count_v : unsigned(4 **downto** 0);
  begin
    UpDown := Up & Down;
    if rising_edge(Clock) **then**
      if (Reset = '1') **then**
        Count_v := "0000";
      else
        case UpDown **is**
          when "00" =>   Count_v := Count_v;
          when "10" =>   Count_v := Count_v + 1;
          when "01" =>   Count_v := Count_v - 2;
          when others => Count_v := Count_v;
        end case;
      end if;
    end if;
    Count <= Count_v
  end process;
end architecture RTL;
	module CNT_UP1_DOWN2 (Clock, Reset, Up, Down, Count);
	  input Clock, Reset, Up, Down;
	  output (4:0) Count;
	  reg (4:0) Count;
	
	  always @(**posedge** Clock)
	  begin
	    if (Reset)
	      Count = 0;
	    else
	    case ({Up, Down})
	      2'b 00 : Count = Count;
	      2'b 10 : Count = Count + 1;
	      2'b 01 : Count = Count - 2;
	      default : Count = Count;
	    endcase
	  end
	endmodule

> Two case branch assignments are the same so could be combined. Are left separate for clarity.

Example 7.13 Divide by 13 clock divider using an LFSR counter

A 4-bit LFSR is used to model this divide by 13 clock dividing counter. The output goes high for one clock cycle every 13th input clock. The LFSR uses XNOR feedback gates in a one-to-many configuration and does not have the extra logic needed for a 2^n looping sequence. This means the binary value 1111 will not occur in the looping sequence and so the asynchronous reset is used to guard against random power-up to binary 1111.

This model was initially simulated with the indicated lines commented out. This enabled the counter to continually cycle through all 15 values in order to determine the actual pseudo-random sequence, see Figure 7.6. Now the sequence is known, the commented out lines are put back in, and the start count and end count values can be chosen and modeled for the desired counter. In this model, StartCount = A_{hex} and EndCount = 0 for a divide by 13 counter.

LFSR sequence	8	1	A	5	2	C	9	3	E	D	B	7	6	4	0
"StartCount" divide by number	15	14	13	12	11	10	9								

For divide by 13: StartCount = A_{HEX} EndCount = 0
Use a 3-bit LFSR if dividing by 8 or less

Figure 7.6 Pseudo-random sequence of modeled 4-bit LFSR

Divide by 13 LFSR clock dividing counter

VHDL	Verilog

<pre>library IEEE;
use IEEE.STD_Logic_1164.all, IEEE.Numeric_STD.all;
 	
entity CNT_LFSR_DIV13 is
   port (Clock, Reset: in   std_logic;
          Y: out std_logic);
end entity CNT_LFSR_DIV13;
 	
architecture RTL of CNT_LFSR_DIV13 is
   constant Taps: unsigned(3 downto 0) := "1001";
   constant StartCount: unsigned(3 downto 0) := "1010";
   constant EndCount: unsigned(3 downto 0) := "0000";
begin
   process (Reset, Clock)
      variable Count: unsigned(3 downto 0);
   begin
      if (Reset = '0') then
         Count := StartCount;
         Y <= '0';
      elsif rising_edge(Clock) then
         if (Count = EndCount) then
            Count := StartCount;
            Y <= '1';
         else
            for N in 1 to 3 loop
               if (Taps(N) = '1') then
                  Count(N) := Count(N - 1) xor Count(3);
               else
                  Count(N) := Count(N - 1);
               end if;
            end loop;
            Count(0) := Count(3);
            Y <= '0';
         end if;
      end if;
   end process;
end architecture RTL;</pre>
	<pre>module CNT_LFSR_DIV13 (Clock, Reset, Y);
	   input Clock, Reset;
	   output Y;
	   reg Y;
	   integer N;
	   parameter Taps = 4'b 1001,
	             StartCount = 4'b 1010,
	             EndCount = 4'b 0000;
	   reg (3:0) Count;
	
	   always @(negedge Reset or posedge Clock)
	      begin
	         if (! Reset)
	            begin
	               Count = StartCount;
	               Y = 0;
	            end
	         else
	            if (Count == EndCount)
	               begin
	                  Count = StartCount;
	                  Y = 1;
	               end
	            else
	               begin
	                  for (N = 1; N <= 3; N = N + 1)
	                     if (Taps(N))
	                        Count(N) = Count(N - 1) ~^ Count(3);
	                     else
	                        Count(N) = Count(N - 1);
	                  Count(0) = Count(3);
	                  Y = 0;
	               end
	      end
	
	endmodule</pre>

Lines which may be "commented out" to determine the count sequence. Prefixed with "--" (VHDL) or "//" (Verilog).

Simulated Waveforms

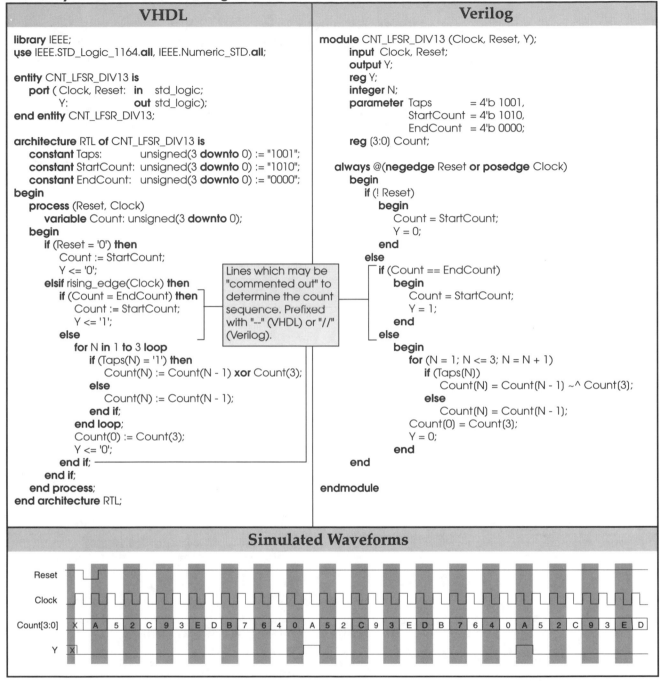

189

Example 7.14 Divide by 16 clock divider using an asynchronous (ripple) counter

This asynchronous ripple counter divides an input clock by 16. It has four ripple stages each consisting of a D-type flip-flop whose output is connected back to its D input such that each stage divides its particular input clock by two. Circuits like this are often seen with the Qbar output fed back to the D input. As seen by the synthesized circuit, the Q output is fed back to the D input through an inverter. This is deliberate to minimize the potential of violating flip-flop set-up times. The four stages provide an overall divide by 16 of the input clock. A fifth flip-flop synchronizes the asynchronous divided by 16 clock DIV16, back to the source clock Clock.

Divide by 16 ripple counter

VHDL	Verilog

library IEEE;
use IEEE.STD_Logic_1164.**all**;
 	
entity CNT_ASYNC_CLK_DIV16 **is**
   port (Clock, Reset: **in** std_logic;
       Y: **out** std_logic);
end entity CNT_ASYNC_CLK_DIV16;
 	
architecture RTL **of** CNT_ASYNC_CLK_DIV16 **is**
   signal Div2, Div4, Div8, Div16: std_logic;
begin
   process (Clock, Reset, Div2, Div4, Div8)
   begin
      if (Reset = '0') **then**
         Div2 <= '0';
      elsif rising_edge(Clock) **then**
         Div2 <= **not** Div2;
      end if;
      if (Reset = '0') **then**
         Div4 <= '0';
      elsif rising_edge(Div2) **then**
         Div4 <= **not** Div4;
      end if;
      if (Reset = '0') **then**
         Div8 <= '0';
      elsif rising_edge(Div4) **then**
         Div8 <= **not** Div8;
      end if;
      if (Reset = '0') **then**
         Div16 <= '0';
      elsif rising_edge(Div8) **then**
         Div16 <= **not** Div16;
      end if;
      -- Resynchronise back to Clock
      if (Reset = '0') **then**
         Y <= '0';
      elsif rising_edge(Clock) **then**
         Y <= Div16;
      end if;
   end process;
end architecture RTL;
 	
For long ripple counters use the for-generate and if-generate scheme to replicate single ripple stage instantiations, see pages 121-123.
	module CNT_ASYNC_CLK_DIV16 (Clock, Reset, Y);
	   input Clock, Reset;
	   output Y;
	
	   reg Div2, Div4, Div8, Div16, Y;
	
	For long ripple counters use the multiple component instantiations of a single ripple stage.
	
	   always @(**posedge** Clock **or negedge** Reset)
	      if (! Reset)
	         Div2 = 0;
	      else
	         Div2 = ! Div2;
	
	   always @(**posedge** Div2 **or negedge** Reset)
	      if (! Reset)
	         Div4 = 0;
	      else
	         Div4 = ! Div4;
	   always @(**posedge** Div4 **or negedge** Reset)
	      if (! Reset)
	         Div8 = 0;
	      else
	         Div8 = ! Div8;
	   always @(**posedge** Div8 **or negedge** Reset)
	      if (! Reset)
	         Div16 = 0;
	      else
	         Div16 = ! Div16;
	
	   // Resynchronize back to Clock
	   always @(**posedge** Clock **or negedge** Reset)
	      if (! Reset)
	         Y = 0;
	      else
	         Y = Div16;
	
	endmodule

Synthesized Circuit

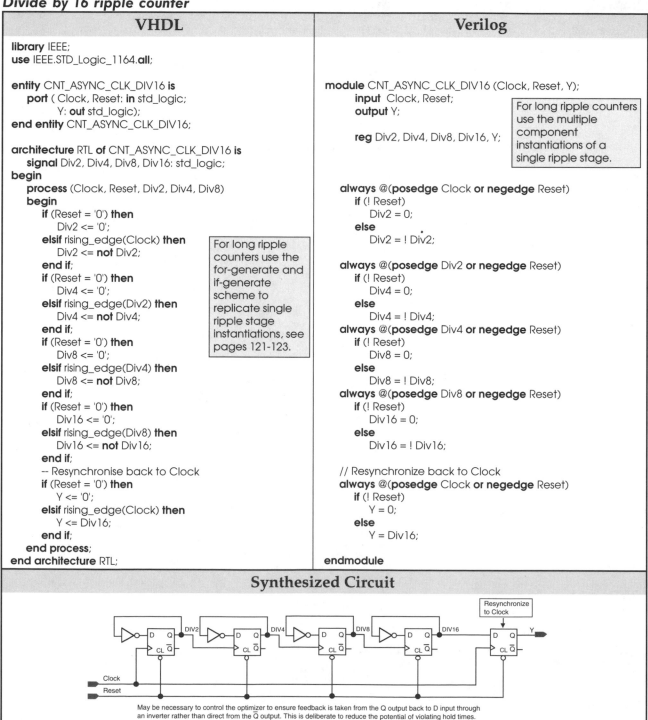

May be necessary to control the optimizer to ensure feedback is taken from the Q output back to D input through an inverter rather than direct from the Q̄ output. This is deliberate to reduce the potential of violating hold times.

Example 7.15 Divide by 13 clock divider using an asynchronous (ripple) counter

This asynchronous ripple counter counts every 13 input clock cycles and sets the output to a logic 1 for one clock cycle. Like Example 7.14, the counter has four, divide by two, ripple stages. However, unlike Example 7.14, the link between each chain is between the Q output via an inferring buffer (instead of the Q output) and D input of the next stage. This causes the counter to count up instead of down. There is no difference in the logic synthesized, but it does make determining the taps for the particular terminal count easier.

Detection of the thirteenth clock pulse and resynchronization is achieved with a fifth flip-flop. It detects when the Qbar outputs from the ripple stages have a value of 13 - 2 = 11 (1011 binary). The reason a count of 11, and not 13, is detected in this particular model, is that two clock cycles are lost; one during the reset and the other because the ripple flip-flop Qbar outputs are reset to logic 1 and then clocked to a logic 0 after the first clock cycle.

The simulated waveforms show the counting process. Notice the asynchronous reset CntRst is at logic 1 for only half a clock cycle when the terminal count is reached. This enables the counter to start counting again on the clock cycle immediately following a reset.

Divide by 13 ripple counter

VHDL	Verilog

library IEEE;
use IEEE.STD_Logic_1164.all;
 	
entity CNT_ASYNC_CLK_DIV13 is
   port (Clock, Reset: in std_logic;
        Y: out std_logic);
end entity CNT_ASYNC_CLK_DIV13;
 	
architecture RTL of CNT_ASYNC_CLK_DIV13 is
   signal   Div2, Div2_b, Div4, Div4_b, Div8, Div8_b,
            Div16, Div16_b, CntRst: std_logic;
begin
   process (Clock, Reset, CntRst)
      variable Y_var: std_logic;
   begin
      if (Reset = '0' or CntRst = '1') then
         Div2 <= '0';
      elsif rising_edge(Clock) then
         Div2 <= not Div2;
      end if;
 	
      Div2_b <= not Div2;
 	
      if (Reset = '0' or CntRst = '1') then
         Div4 <= '0';
      elsif rising_edge(Div2) then
         Div4 <= not Div4;
      end if;
 	
      Div4_b <= not Div4;
 	
      if (Reset = '0' or CntRst = '1') then
         Div8 <= '0';
      elsif rising_edge(Div4) then
	module CNT_ASYNC_CLK_DIV13 (Clock, Reset, Y);
	   input Clock, Reset;
	   output Y;
	
	   reg Div2, Div4, Div8, Div16, Y;
	   wire Div2_b, Div4_b, Div8_b, Div16_b, CntRst;
	
	   always @(posedge Clock or negedge Reset or
	              posedge CntRst)
	      if (! Reset)
	         Div2 = 0;
	      else if (CntRst)
	         Div2 = 0;
	      else
	         Div2 = ! Div2;
	
	   assign Div2_b = ! Div2;
	
	   always @(posedge Div2 or negedge Reset or
	              posedge CntRst)
	      if (! Reset)
	         Div4 = 0;
	      else if (CntRst)
	         Div4 = 0;
	      else
	         Div4 = ! Div4;
	
	   assign Div4_b = ! Div4;
	
	   always @(posedge Div4 or negedge Reset or
	              posedge CntRst)
	      if (! Reset)
	         Div8 = 0;
	      else if (CntRst)

continued	*continued*

Divide by 13 ripple counter

VHDL	Verilog

<pre>   Div8 <= **not** Div8;
    end if;
 	
    Div8_b <= **not** Div8;
 	
    if (Reset = '0' **or** CntRst = '1') **then**
        Div16 <= '0';
    elsif rising_edge(Div8) **then**
        Div16 <= **not** Div16;
    end if;
 	
    Div16_b <= **not** Div16;
 	
    -- Resynchronize back to Clock
 	
    if (Reset = '0') **then**
        Y_var := '0';
    elsif rising_edge(Clock) **then**
        Y_var <= Div16_b **and not** Div8_b **and**
            Div4_b **and** Div2_b;
    end if;
 	
    -- Async reset when terminal count reached
    CntRst := Y_var **and** Clock;
    Y <= Y_var;
 	
    end process;
end architecture RTL;</pre>
	<pre> Div8 = 0;
	    else
	        Div8 = ! Div8;
	
	assign Div8_b = ! Div8;
	
	always @(posedge Div8 **or negedge** Reset **or**
	                    posedge CntRst)
	    if (! Reset)
	        Div16 = 0;
	    else if (CntRst)
	        Div16 = 0;
	    else
	        Div16 = ! Div16;
	
	assign Div16_b = ! Div16;
	
	// Resynchronize back to Clock
	always @(posedge Clock **or negedge** Reset)
	    if (!Reset)
	        Y = 0;
	    else
	        Y = Div16_b & ! Div8_b & Div4_b & Div2_b;
	
	// Async reset when terminal count reached
	assign CntRst = Y & Clock;
	
	endmodule</pre>

Simulated Waveforms

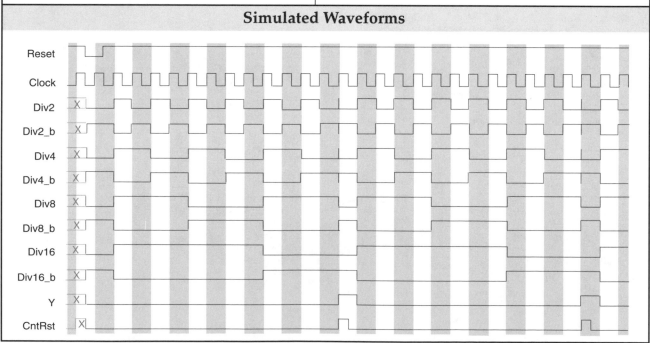

Modeling Finite State Machines

Chapter 8 Contents

Introduction

Designers of digital circuits are invariably faced with needing to design circuits that perform specific sequences of operations, for example, controllers used to control the operation of other circuits. Finite State Machines (FSMs) have proven to be a very efficient means of modeling sequencer circuits. By modeling FSMs in a hardware description language for use with synthesis tools, designers can concentrate on modeling the desired sequences of operations without being overly concerned with circuit implementation; this is left to the synthesis tool. FSMs are an important part of hardware design and hence HDL hardware modeling.

A designer should consider the different aspects of an FSM before attempting to write a model. A well written model is essential for a functionally correct circuit that meets requirements in the most optimal manner. A badly written model may not meet either criteria. For this reason, it is important to fully understand FSMs and to be familiar with the different HDL modeling issues.

The Finite State Machine

A FSM is any circuit specifically designed to sequence through specific patterns of states in a predetermined sequential manner, and which conforms to the structure shown in Figure 8.1. A state is represented by the binary value held on the current state register. The FSM structure consists of three parts and may, or may not, be reflected in the structure of the HDL code that is used to model it.

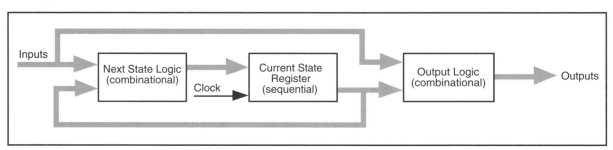

Figure 8.1 Simple structure of a finite state machine

1. *Current State Register.* Register of *n*-bit flip-flops used to hold the current state of the FSM. Its value represents the current stage in the particular sequence of operations being performed. When operating, it is clocked from a free running clock source.

2. *Next State Logic.* Combinational logic used to generate the next stage (state) in the sequence. The next state output is a function of the state machine's inputs and its current state.

3. *Output Logic.* Combinational logic is used to generate required output signals. Outputs are a function of the state register output and possibly state machine inputs.

The State Table and State Diagram

A state diagram is a graphical representation of a state machine's sequential operation and are often supported as a direct input to commercial synthesis tools from which synthesized circuits and HDL simulation models are generated. Whether to use a state diagram or HDL entry method is often a choice for the designer, provided the tools are available. Sometimes a company will dictate a particular design methodology, in which case, the choice has already been made.

Figure 8.2 shows two state diagram representations of the same five state, state machine; the

Inputs		Current state		Next state		Outputs	
A	Hold					Y_Me	Y_Mo
0	X	000	(ST0)	000	(ST0)	1	0
1	X	000	(ST0)	001	(ST1)	0	0
0	X	001	(ST1)	000	(ST0)	0	1
1	X	001	(ST1)	010	(ST2)	1	1
X	X	010	(ST2)	011	(ST3)	0	0
X	1	011	(ST3)	011	(ST3)	1	1
0	0	011	(ST3)	000	(ST0)	1	1
1	0	011	(ST3)	100	(ST4)	0	1
X	X	100	(ST4)	000	(ST0)	0	1

X = don't care condition

Table 8.1 State table for state diagrams of Figure 8.2

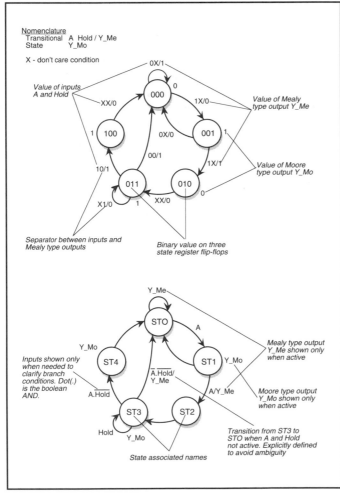

Figure 8.2 Two equivalent state diagrams

equivalent state table is indicated in Table 8.1. The description of the two state diagrams of Figure 8.2 now follows.

Circles represent states and lines with arrows represent transitions between states which occur after every clock cycle. The clock signal is implied, but not shown on a state diagram, nor in a state table.

The binary number representing the value on the state register flip-flops (first state diagram), or its associated state name (second state diagram) is contained inside the circle. The input signal conditions that dictate state transitions are indicated next to the appropriate line and before any slash (/). A slash is used to separate input and output signals. The two inputs, A and Hold, are shown before the slash. Values shown after the slash, if any, indicate output signal values that are a function of both the inputs and current state register. These are called Mealy type outputs described later. The value of any output signals that are a function of the current state register only, are shown next to the circle representing the appropriate state. These are called Moore type outputs also described later. The major difference in the second state diagram, is that input and output signals are shown only when they are active, otherwise they are left off to aid functional comprehension and avoid cluttering the diagram. Example 8.8 shows the HDL models of this particular state diagram.

FSM Design and Modeling Issues

State machine design and modeling issues to consider are:

1. HDL coding style,
2. Resets and fail safe behavior,
3. State encoding,
4. Mealy or Moore type outputs,
5. Sequential next state or output logic,
6. Interactive state machines.

The structure of a state machine can take one of three forms, Figure 8.3, and consists of a combinational "Next State Logic" block, a sequential "Current State Register" block, and an optional combinational "Output Logic" block. Output logic is not needed if the outputs only come direct from the state register flip-flops. The current state is stored in flip-flops; latches would cause state oscillations when transparent. The next state and output logic blocks may contain additional sequential logic, inferred from within the body of the model, but is not considered part of the state machine. A state machine can only be in one state at any given time, and each active transition of the clock causes it to change from its current state to the next as defined by the next state logic.

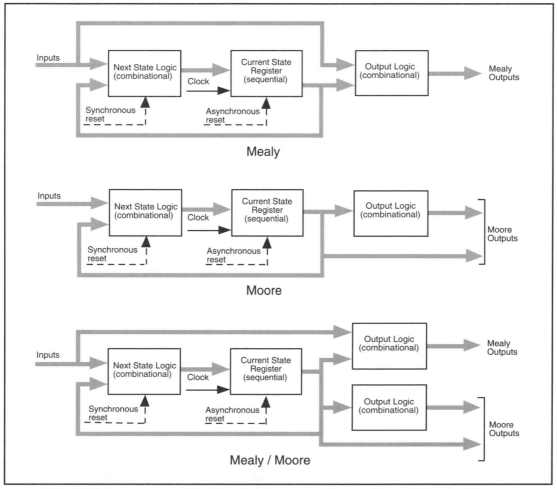

Figure 8.3 FSM Structures with Mealy, Moore and combined Mealy/Moore outputs

A state machine with n state flip-flops has 2^n possible binary numbers that can be used to represent states. Often, not all 2^n numbers are needed, so the unused ones should be designed not to occur during normal operation. A state machine with five states, for example, requires a minimum of three flip-flops in which case there are ($2^3 - 5 = 3$) unused binary numbers.

1. HDL coding style

There are different ways of modeling the same state machine, on the other hand, a small code change can cause a model to behave differently than expected. Designers should be aware of the different modeling styles supported by the synthesis tool being used, and should consider modeling state machines to be tool independent; this applies to modeling any type of circuit. The HDL code may be structured into three separate parts representing the three parts of a state machine, see Figure 8.3. Alternatively, different combinations of blocks can be combined in the model. Either way, the coding style is independent of the state machine being designed.

The next state logic is best modeled using the **case** statement, though the VHDL next state logic could be modeled using a selected signal assignment, but means the FSM cannot be modeled in one process. The **others** clause (VHDL) and **default** clause (Verilog) used in a **case** statement, avoids having to explicitly define all 2^n values that are not part of the state machine.

Examples 8.1 and 8.2, show bad and good modeling styles for three and four state FSMs respectively. Models in example 8.2 demonstrate how the three parts of a state machine may be combined, or separated in a model, and how to ensure portability between synthesis tools. Example 8.3 shows a state machine modeled with either the inputs or the current state, as the primary branch directive.

2. Resets and fail safe behavior

Depending on the application, a reset signal may not be available, there may only be a synchronous or asynchronous reset, or there may be both. To guarantee fail safe behavior, one of two things must be done, depending on the type of reset:

- <u>Use an asynchronous reset.</u> This ensures the state machine is always initialized to a known valid state, before the first active clock transition and normal operation commences. This has the advantage of not needing to decode any unused current state values, and so minimizes the next state logic.

- <u>With no reset or a synchronous reset.</u> In the absence of an asynchronous reset there is no way of predicting the initial value of the state register flip-flops when implemented in an IC and "powered up". It could power up and become permanently stuck in an uncoded state. All 2^n binary values must, therefore, be decoded in the next state logic, whether they form part of the state machine or not. There is generally only a small area overhead in the next state logic, and is partially offset by using smaller flip-flops that do not have an asynchronous reset input.

Take for example, a ten state state machine modeled using Johnson State encoding. The state register consists of 5 flip-flops and there are ($2^5 - 10$) unused states. The area optimized result of the next state logic is 11% bigger if a synchronous reset is used rather than an asynchronous one. This is partially offset by the asynchronously reset state register flip-flops, being slightly larger than synchronously reset flip-flops. The overall result is a 3% increase in area when an asynchronous reset is changed to a synchronous one.

In VHDL an asynchronous reset can only be modeled using the **if** statement, while a synchronous reset can be modeled using either a **wait** or **if** statement; the disadvantage of using the **wait** statement is that the whole process is synchronous so other **if** statements cannot be used to model purely combinational logic. In Verilog only the **if** statement can be used, and if asynchronous, must be included in the event list of the **always** statement with the **posedge** or **negedge** clause.

Example 8.4 shows a state machine with combined current and next state logic modeled with; an asynchronous reset, a synchronous reset, and with no reset. It also shows the minimal effect it has on the implied next state logic.

If the current and next state logic are modeled separately, an asynchronous reset must be included in the sequential current state logic while a synchronous reset may be included with either the current or next state logic. Clearly by always including a reset in the current state logic it is easy to change it from an asynchronous to synchronous reset or vice versa if needed. There are many examples of such resets in this chapter.

3. State encoding

The way in which binary numbers are assigned to states, is called the state encoding. The different state encoding formats commonly used are:

- sequential,
- gray,
- Johnson,
- one-hot,
- define your own,
- defined by synthesis.

These formats are shown in Table 8.2 for 16 states and their descriptions follows.

Example 8.6 shows a state machine for a Blackjack card game controller using all state encoding formats, and includes a synthesis defined format. The example also shows the effect state encoding has on the synthesized circuit of this particular model.

No.	Sequential	Gray	Johnson	One-Hot
0	0000	0000	00000000	0000000000000001
1	0001	0001	00000001	0000000000000010
2	0010	0011	00000011	0000000000000100
3	0011	0010	00000111	0000000000001000
4	0100	0110	00001111	0000000000010000
5	0101	0111	00011111	0000000000100000
6	0110	0101	00111111	0000000001000000
7	0111	0100	01111111	0000000010000000
8	1000	1100	11111111	0000000100000000
9	1001	1101	11111110	0000001000000000
10	1010	1111	11111100	0000010000000000
11	1011	1110	11111000	0000100000000000
12	1100	1010	11110000	0001000000000000
13	1101	1011	11100000	0010000000000000
14	1110	1001	11000000	0100000000000000
15	1111	1000	10000000	1000000000000000

Table 8.2 Standard State Machine Encoding Formats

State Encoding Formats

Sequential. Each state is simply assigned increasing binary numbers.

Gray and Johnson. Each state in both Gray and Johnson state encoding is assigned successive binary numbers where only one bit changes from one number to the next. A primary motive for using such coding, is to reduce the possibility of state transition errors caused by asynchronous inputs changing during flip-flop setup times.

All 2^n binary numbers can be used in Gray Code state encoding. However, because of the pattern of 1's and 0's in Johnson state encoding, more flip-flops are required, and there are always unused binary numbers. This means that an asynchronous reset is preferred, otherwise the next state logic must decode all 2^n binary numbers, and result in a larger circuit. Example 8.5 shows a state machine for a platform position controller using both Gray and Johnson state encoding.

One-hot. In one-hot state encoding, each state is assigned its own flip-flop, so n states requires n flip-flops and only one flip-flop is in its true state at any one time. The increased number of flip-flops usually results in a larger circuit.

Define your own. Each state is assigned a binary number according to a particular design requirement.

Defined by Synthesis. These formats are chosen by the synthesis tool to minimize next state logic. Clearly the actual assignments are design dependent. It is necessary to consult the appropriate synthesis manual to find out how this can be achieved. The synthesis tools provided by VeriBest Incorporated allow a panel entry of FSM parameters from which it will choose optimal state encoding for minimal next state logic using one of three different algorithms. It also provides an HDL (VHDL or Verilog) model for simulation purposes.

4. Mealy or Moore type outputs

The structures of a Mealy, a Moore, and a combined Mealy/Moore state machines are shown in Figure 8.3. A Mealy state machine has outputs that are a function of the current state, and primary inputs. A Moore state machine has outputs that are a function of the current state only, and so includes outputs direct from the state register. If outputs come direct from the state register only, there is no output logic. A combined Mealy/Moore state machine has both types of output. The choice between modeling Mealy or Moore type outputs are clearly design dependent.

Example 8.7 shows the same state machine modeled with a Mealy or Moore type output, while Example 8.8 show models of the example state diagram, Figure 8.2, which has one Mealy and one Moore type output.

5. Sequential next state or output logic

Both the next state and output logic in a state machine, consists of combinational logic only. However, depending upon the application, you may want to model additional sequential logic in either of these blocks, and which may be imbedded within the code of a state machine model. Note that by not defining next state or output signals in all branches of a state machine's **case** statement, it is easy to inadvertently model unwanted latches.

Sequential Next State Logic. Sequential next state logic controls state branching from previously set signals. Such signals could be set when the state machine was in another state, passed through a particular sequence of states, or because of some accumulated value resulting from looping around successive sequences of states. These next state control signals could also provide state machine outputs. Example 8.8 shows such a model which encompasses a single controlling flip-flop in the next state logic.

Sequential Output Logic. Sequential output logic, registers the fact that a certain state or sequence of states has occurred. Example 8.9 shows a typical application of this, where an accumulator is incremented every time the state machine passes through a particular state.

6. Interactive state machines

If a state machine's current state or output signals are used to influence the operation of other state machines, they are known to be interactive. Interaction between state machines may be unidirectional or bidirectional.

Unidirectional. State machines may be hierarchically structured, in which case, they are useful in breaking down large complicated control path structures into more manageable pieces. Figure 8.4 shows the structure of two state machines where FSM1 has unidirectional control over FSM2, and means the next state of FSM2 is dependent upon its own inputs and current state, plus the state of FSM1. Example 8.10 shows three different state machine configurations of a control path model, used to control the same data path. The controller is modeled in three separate ways; (1) a master FSM controlling three sub hierarchial FSMs, (2) three FSMs with series control from one to the next, and (3) using a single FSM.

Bidirectional. State machines having bidirectional control over each other are useful for modeling circuits requiring handshaking mechanisms. Figure 8.5 shows the structure of three interactive state machines where each state machine

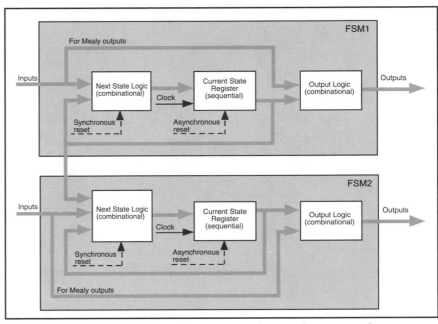

Figure 8.4 Structure of two FSMs with uni-directional interaction

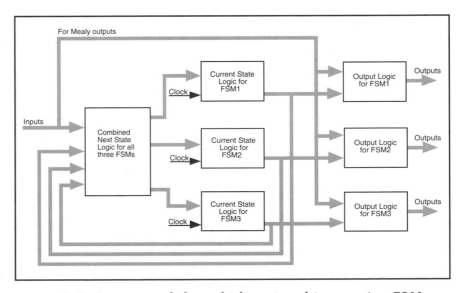

Figure 8.5 Structure of three bidirectional interactive FSMs.

has bidirectional control over the other two. Example 8.11 shows two bidirectionally interactive state machines; each has four states representing the angular position of two interlocking mechanical rotors.

Example 8.1 A Bad and good coded models of a three state FSM (FSM1)

Bad and good models of a three state FSM are modeled to the state diagrams, Figure 8.6. The two VHDL models use a single state variable of an enumerated type, and means the synthesis tool will automatically assign sequential binary numbers to the states. The two Verilog models use one of three **parameter** values for the states, and so the state numbers are defined in the model itself.

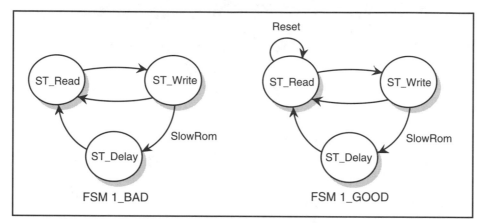

Figure 8.6 FSM1 State Diagram

Bad Model

The first model, FSM1_BAD, is incorrect for the reasons listed below. Notice, that in this particular example the state type, and its declaration, are local to the VHDL **process** and Verilog **always** block.

1. The state machine has three states requiring two flip-flops, but two flip-flop have four possible binary values, so one is unused. There is no reset and there is no next state value defined for the unused state. This means the physical state machine could be implemented such that it has the potential of "powering up" and becoming stuck in this unused state.

2. The current state, next state and output logic, are all defined in the same VHDL **process** and Verilog **always** block. Because the VHDL **process** contains a **wait** statement, the Read and Write output assignments infer two extra flip-flops. Likewise, because the Verilog **always** block is triggered off the positive edge of the clock, the Read and Write output assignments also infer an extra flip-flop.

3. The variable definition for State in the VHDL version has an initial value of ST_Read. This is fine for simulation, but is ignored by synthesis tools. Variables or signals should not be initialized in this way if the model is to be synthesized; it does not represent the initial state of the physical hardware. Procedural assignments in Verilog are only initialized through **initial** blocks, which are not supported by synthesis tools, and so this problem should not occur.

FSM1 Modeled incorrectly (FSM1_BAD)

VHDL	Verilog
| ```
library IEEE;
use IEEE.STD_Logic_1164.all;

entity FSM1_BAD is
    port ( Clock:       in   std_logic;
           SlowRAM:     in   std_logic;
           Read, Write: out  std_logic);
end entity FSM1_BAD;

architecture RTL of FSM1_BAD is
begin

    SEQ_AND_COMB: process
        type StateType is (ST_Read, ST_Write, ST_Delay);
        variable State: StateType := ST_Read;
    begin
        wait until rising_edge(Clock);
        case State is
            when ST_Read =>
                Read  <= '1';
                Write <= '0';
                State := ST_Write;
            when ST_Write =>
                Read  <= '0';
                Write <= '1';
                if (SlowRAM = '1') then
                    State := ST_Delay;
                else
                    State := ST_Read;
                end if;
            when ST_Delay =>
                Read  <= '0';
                Write <= '0';
                State := ST_Read;
        end case;
    end process SEQ_AND_COMB;

end architecture RTL;
``` | ```
module FSM1_BAD (Clock, SlowRAM, Read,Write);
    input   Clock, SlowRAM;
    output  Read, Write;

    reg Read,Write;

    always @(posedge Clock)
        begin: SEQ_AND_COMB
            parameter ST_Read = 0, ST_Write = 1, ST_Delay = 2;
            integer State;
            case (State)
                ST_Read :
                    begin
                        Read  = 1;
                        Write = 0;
                        State = ST_Write;
                    end
                ST_Write :
                    begin
                        Read  = 0;
                        Write = 1;
                        if (SlowRAM == 1)
                            State = ST_Delay;
                        else
                            State = ST_Read;
                    end
                ST_Delay :
                    begin
                        Read  = 0;
                        Write = 0;
                        State = ST_Read;
                    end
            endcase
        end

endmodule
``` |

*No **others** clause. Does not effect synthesized circuit but means it is not LRM compliant.*

*Because there is no **default** and therefore no new value for Read and Write, the two extra outputs flip-flops will also have feedback logic around them.*

Good Model

The second model, FSM1_GOOD, shows the corrected version. The sequential current state logic has been separated from the combined combinational next state and output logic. The VHDL version still uses a **wait** statement, though as a general rule it is often better to use the **if** statement. The VHDL **if** statement can model all synchronous and asynchronous logic needs, and has the added advantage of allowing sequential and combinational logic to be mixed within the same process.

FSM1 Modeled correctly (FSM1_GOOD)

VHDL	Verilog

```vhdl
library IEEE;
use IEEE.STD_Logic_1164.all;

entity FSM1_GOOD is
    port ( Clock, Reset:  in   std_logic;
           SlowRAM:       in   std_logic;
           Read, Write:   out std_logic);
end entity FSM1_GOOD;

architecture RTL of FSM1_GOOD is
    type StateType is (ST_Read, ST_Write, ST_Delay);
    signal CurrentState, NextState: StateType;
begin

    SEQ: process
    begin
        wait until rising_edge(Clock);
        if (Reset = '1') then
            CurrentState <= ST_Read;
        else
            CurrentState <= NextState;
        end if;
    end process SEQ;

    COMB: process (CurrentState, SlowRAM)
    begin
        case CurrentState is
            when ST_Read =>
                Read  <= '1';
                Write <= '0';
                NextState <= ST_Write;
            when ST_Write =>
                Read  <= '0';
                Write <= '1';
                if (SlowRAM = '1') then
                    NextState <= ST_Delay;
                else
                    NextState <= ST_Read;
                end if;
            when ST_Delay =>
                Read  <= '0';
                Write <= '0';
                NextState <= ST_Read;
        end case;
    end process COMB;
end architecture RTL;
```

No sensitivity list as **process** contains a **wait**.

when others not needed; all 3 conditions of type StateType have a case branch explicitly defined.

```verilog
module FSM1_GOOD (Clock, Reset, SlowRAM, Read, Write);
    input  Clock, Reset, SlowRAM;
    output Read, Write;

    reg Read,Write;

    parameter (1:0) ST_Read = 0, ST_Write = 1, ST_Delay = 2;
    reg       (1:0) CurrentState, NextState;

    always @(posedge Clock)
        begin: SEQ
            if (Reset)
                CurrentState = ST_Read;
            else
                CurrentState = NextState;
        end

    always @(CurrentState or SlowRAM)
        begin: COMB
            case (CurrentState)
                ST_Read :
                    begin
                        Read  = 1;
                        Write = 0;
                        NextState = ST_Write;
                    end
                ST_Write :
                    begin
                        Read  = 0;
                        Write = 1;
                        if (SlowRAM)
                            NextState = ST_Delay;
                        else
                            NextState = ST_Read;
                    end
                ST_Delay :
                    begin
                        Read  = 0;
                        Write = 0;
                        NextState = ST_Read;
                    end
                default :
                    begin
                        Read = 0;
                        Write = 0;
                        NextState = ST_Read;
                    end
            endcase
        end
endmodule
```

Needed to avoid outputs being separatly latched.

Needed to avoid next state logic being latched.

Synthesized Circuit

Example 8.2 One bad and four good models of an FSM

One bad and four good models of the state machine, Figure 8.7. are shown in this example. It has four states and uses an asynchronous reset. As in the previous example, the VHDL models use an enumerated data type for the state variable, while the Verilog models use parameter values.

The first model, FSM2_BAD, is incorrect for similar reasons to the bad model in Example 8.1, that is, flip-flops are synthesized in the output logic. The outputs in the VHDL model are this time assigned under the statement "**if** rising_edge(Clock)".

The good models (FSM2_GOOD1 to FSM2_GOOD4) show different combinations in which the current state, next state and output logic may be combined or separated within a model. The design is modeled as follows:

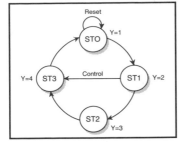

Figure 8.7 FSM2 State Diagram

FSM2_GOOD1	Separate CS, NS and OL
FSM2_GOOD2	Combined CS and NS. Separate OL
FSM2_GOOD3	Combined NS and OL. Separate CS
FSM2_GOOD4	Combined CS, NS and OL (VHDL only)

where: CS = Current State, NS = Next State, OL = Output Logic

FSM2 modeled incorrectly (FSM2_BAD)

VHDL	Verilog
<pre>library IEEE;
use IEEE.STD_Logic_1164.all;
entity FSM2_BAD is
  port (Clock, Reset: in std_logic;
         Control: in std_logic;
         Y: out integer range 1 to 4);
end entity FSM2_BAD;

architecture RTL of FSM2_BAD is
begin
  ALL_IN_1: process (Clock, Reset)
    type StateType is (ST0, ST1, ST2, ST3);
    variable STATE: StateType := ST0;
  begin
    if (Reset = '1') then
        Y <= 1;
        STATE := ST0;
    elsif rising_edge(Clock) then
        case (STATE) is
          when ST0 => Y <= 1;
                       STATE := ST1;
          when ST1 => Y <= 2;
                       if (Control = '1') then
                           STATE := ST2;
                       else
                           STATE := ST3;
                       end if;
          when ST2 => Y <= 3;
                       STATE := ST3;
          when ST3 => Y <= 4;
                       STATE := ST0;
        end case;
    end if;
  end process ALL_IN_1;
end architecture RTL;</pre> | <pre>module FSM2_BAD (Clock, Reset, Control, Y);
  input Clock, Reset, Control;
  output (2:0) Y; // enable range 1 to 4
  reg (2:0) Y;

  always @ (posedge Clock or posedge Reset)
    begin: ALL_IN_1
      parameter (1:0) ST0 = 0, ST1 = 1, ST2 = 2, ST3 = 3;
      integer (1:0) STATE;
      if (Reset) begin
          Y = 1;
          STATE = ST0;
      end
      else
        case (STATE)
          ST0: begin Y = 1;
                      STATE = ST1;
          end
          ST1: begin Y = 2;
                      if (Control)
                          STATE = ST2;
                      else
                          STATE = ST3;
          end
          ST2: begin Y = 3;
                      STATE = ST3;
          end
          ST3: begin Y = 4;
                      STATE = ST0;
          end
        endcase
    end
endmodule</pre> |

Range of 4 values, but starts at 1 (not 0). Synthesis starts from 0 so 3 flip flops inferred.

Output Y assigned under synchronous clock'event... statement so three extra latches inferred.

Output Y assigned under synchronous **always** block so three extra latches inferred.

Separate current state, next state and output logic (FSM2_GOOD1)

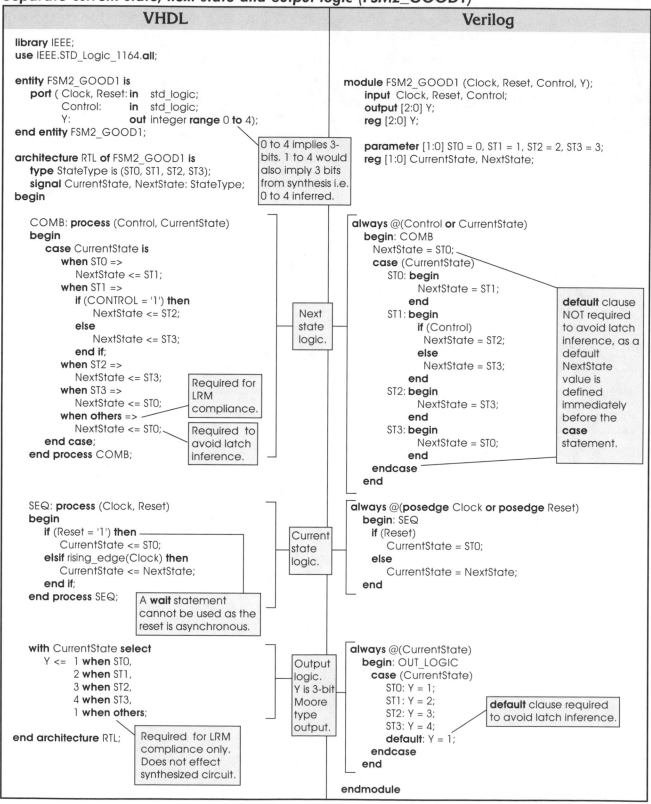

VHDL	Verilog

```vhdl
library IEEE;
use IEEE.STD_Logic_1164.all;

entity FSM2_GOOD1 is
    port ( Clock, Reset: in    std_logic;
           Control:      in    std_logic;
           Y:                  out integer range 0 to 4);
end entity FSM2_GOOD1;

architecture RTL of FSM2_GOOD1 is
    type StateType is (ST0, ST1, ST2, ST3);
    signal CurrentState, NextState: StateType;
begin

    COMB: process (Control, CurrentState)
    begin
        case CurrentState is
            when ST0 =>
                NextState <= ST1;
            when ST1 =>
                if (CONTROL = '1') then
                    NextState <= ST2;
                else
                    NextState <= ST3;
                end if;
            when ST2 =>
                NextState <= ST3;
            when ST3 =>
                NextState <= ST0;
            when others =>
                NextState <= ST0;
        end case;
    end process COMB;

    SEQ: process (Clock, Reset)
    begin
        if (Reset = '1') then
            CurrentState <= ST0;
        elsif rising_edge(Clock) then
            CurrentState <= NextState;
        end if;
    end process SEQ;

    with CurrentState select
        Y <=  1 when ST0,
              2 when ST1,
              3 when ST2,
              4 when ST3,
              1 when others;

end architecture RTL;
```

```verilog
module FSM2_GOOD1 (Clock, Reset, Control, Y);
    input  Clock, Reset, Control;
    output [2:0] Y;
    reg [2:0] Y;

    parameter [1:0] ST0 = 0, ST1 = 1, ST2 = 2, ST3 = 3;
    reg [1:0] CurrentState, NextState;

    always @(Control or CurrentState)
        begin: COMB
            NextState = ST0;
            case (CurrentState)
                ST0: begin
                        NextState = ST1;
                     end
                ST1: begin
                        if (Control)
                            NextState = ST2;
                        else
                            NextState = ST3;
                     end
                ST2: begin
                        NextState = ST3;
                     end
                ST3: begin
                        NextState = ST0;
                     end
            endcase
        end

    always @(posedge Clock or posedge Reset)
        begin: SEQ
            if (Reset)
                CurrentState = ST0;
            else
                CurrentState = NextState;
        end

    always @(CurrentState)
        begin: OUT_LOGIC
            case (CurrentState)
                ST0: Y = 1;
                ST1: Y = 2;
                ST2: Y = 3;
                ST3: Y = 4;
                default: Y = 1;
            endcase
        end

endmodule
```

Annotations:

- 0 to 4 implies 3-bits. 1 to 4 would also imply 3 bits from synthesis i.e. 0 to 4 inferred.
- Next state logic.
- Required for LRM compliance.
- Required to avoid latch inference.
- Current state logic.
- A **wait** statement cannot be used as the reset is asynchronous.
- Output logic. Y is 3-bit Moore type output.
- Required for LRM compliance only. Does not effect synthesized circuit.
- **default** clause NOT required to avoid latch inference, as a default NextState value is defined immediately before the **case** statement.
- **default** clause required to avoid latch inference.

Combined current state and next state logic, separate output logic (FSM2_GOOD2)

VHDL	Verilog

```vhdl
library IEEE;
use IEEE.STD_Logic_1164.all;

entity FSM2_GOOD2 is
    port ( Clock, Reset:  in    std_logic;
           Control:       in    std_logic;
           Y:                    out integer range 0 to 4);
end entity FSM2_GOOD2;

architecture RTL of FSM2_GOOD2 is
    type StateType is (ST0, ST1, ST2, ST3);
    signal STATE: StateType;
begin

    NEXT_CURR: process (Clock, Reset)
    begin
      if (Reset = '1') then
         STATE <= ST0;
      elsif rising_edge(Clock) then
         case (STATE) is
            when ST0 =>
               STATE <= ST1;
            when ST1 =>
               if (Control = '1') then
                  STATE <= ST2;
               else
                  STATE <= ST3;
               end if;
            when ST2 =>
               STATE <= ST3;
            when ST3 =>
               STATE <= ST0;
            when others =>
               null;
         end case;
      end if;
    end process NEXT_CURR;

    with STATE select
       Y <=  1 when ST0,
             2 when ST1,
             3 when ST2,
             4 when ST3,
             1 when others;

end architecture RTL;
```

```verilog
module FSM2_GOOD2 (Clock, Reset, Control, Y);
    input  Clock, Reset, Control;
    output (2:0) Y;

    reg (2:0) Y;
    parameter (1:0) ST0 = 0, ST1 = 1, ST2 = 2, ST3 = 3;
    reg (1:0) STATE;

    always @(posedge Clock or posedge Reset)
       begin: NEXT_CURR
          if (Reset)
             STATE = ST0;
          else
             case (STATE)
                ST0: STATE = ST1;
                ST1: if (Control)
                        STATE = ST2;
                     else
                        STATE = ST3;
                ST2: STATE = ST3;
                ST3: STATE = ST0;
             endcase
       end

    always @(STATE)
       begin: OUT_LOGIC
          case (STATE)
             ST0: Y = 1;
             ST1: Y = 2;
             ST2: Y = 3;
             ST3: Y = 4;
             default: Y = 1;
          endcase
       end
endmodule
```

Current state and next state logic.

Concurrent selected signal assignment used instead of another process.

3-bit Moore type output Y.

Output logic.

default not required for LRM compliance, and not needed here as the assignments are in an edge triggered **always** statement, which infers flip-flops anyway.

default required, even though all conditions covered. This is because **case** is in a combinational **always** block and avoids inferring latches.

Synthesized Circuit

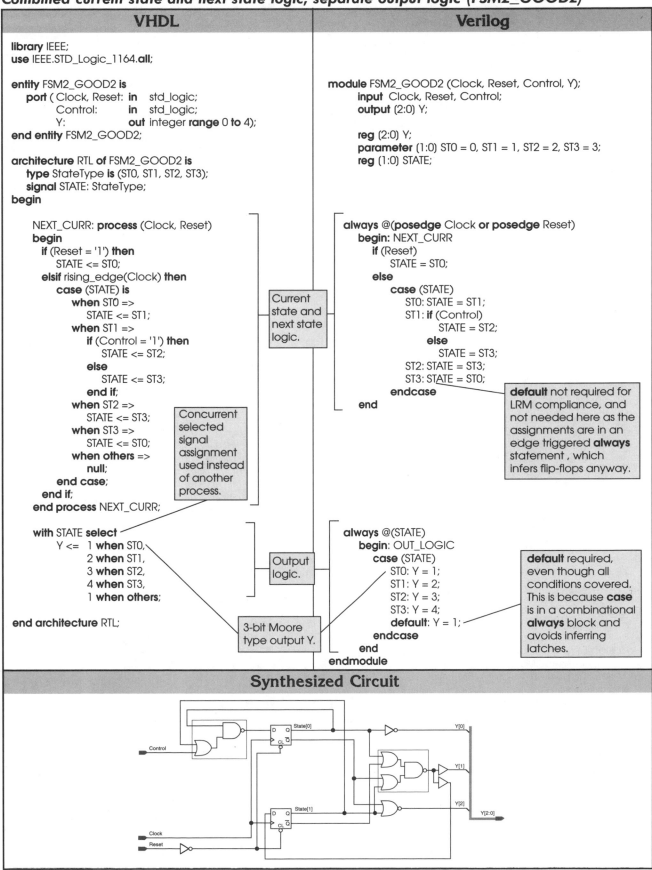

Combined next state and output logic, separate current state logic (FSM2_GOOD3)

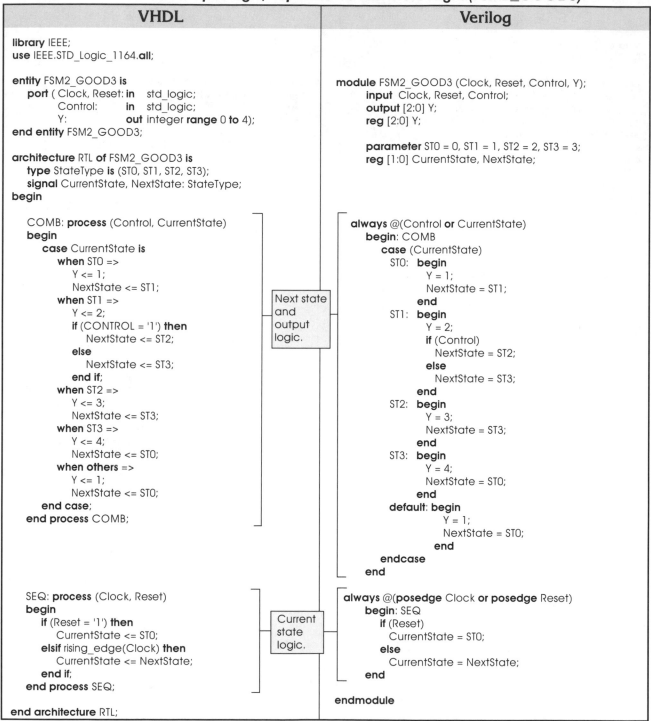

VHDL	Verilog

```vhdl
library IEEE;
use IEEE.STD_Logic_1164.all;

entity FSM2_GOOD3 is
    port ( Clock, Reset: in    std_logic;
           Control:      in    std_logic;
           Y:                  out integer range 0 to 4);
end entity FSM2_GOOD3;

architecture RTL of FSM2_GOOD3 is
    type StateType is (ST0, ST1, ST2, ST3);
    signal CurrentState, NextState: StateType;
begin

    COMB: process (Control, CurrentState)
    begin
        case CurrentState is
            when ST0 =>
                Y <= 1;
                NextState <= ST1;
            when ST1 =>
                Y <= 2;
                if (CONTROL = '1') then
                    NextState <= ST2;
                else
                    NextState <= ST3;
                end if;
            when ST2 =>
                Y <= 3;
                NextState <= ST3;
            when ST3 =>
                Y <= 4;
                NextState <= ST0;
            when others =>
                Y <= 1;
                NextState <= ST0;
        end case;
    end process COMB;


    SEQ: process (Clock, Reset)
    begin
        if (Reset = '1') then
            CurrentState <= ST0;
        elsif rising_edge(Clock) then
            CurrentState <= NextState;
        end if;
    end process SEQ;

end architecture RTL;
```

Next state and output logic.

Current state logic.

```verilog
module FSM2_GOOD3 (Clock, Reset, Control, Y);
    input  Clock, Reset, Control;
    output [2:0] Y;
    reg [2:0] Y;

    parameter ST0 = 0, ST1 = 1, ST2 = 2, ST3 = 3;
    reg [1:0] CurrentState, NextState;

    always @(Control or CurrentState)
        begin: COMB
            case (CurrentState)
                ST0:  begin
                        Y = 1;
                        NextState = ST1;
                    end
                ST1:  begin
                        Y = 2;
                        if (Control)
                            NextState = ST2;
                        else
                            NextState = ST3;
                    end
                ST2:  begin
                        Y = 3;
                        NextState = ST3;
                    end
                ST3:  begin
                        Y = 4;
                        NextState = ST0;
                    end
                default: begin
                            Y = 1;
                            NextState = ST0;
                        end
            endcase
        end

    always @(posedge Clock or posedge Reset)
        begin: SEQ
            if (Reset)
                CurrentState = ST0;
            else
                CurrentState = NextState;
        end

endmodule
```

Combined current state, next state and output logic (FSM2_GOOD4)

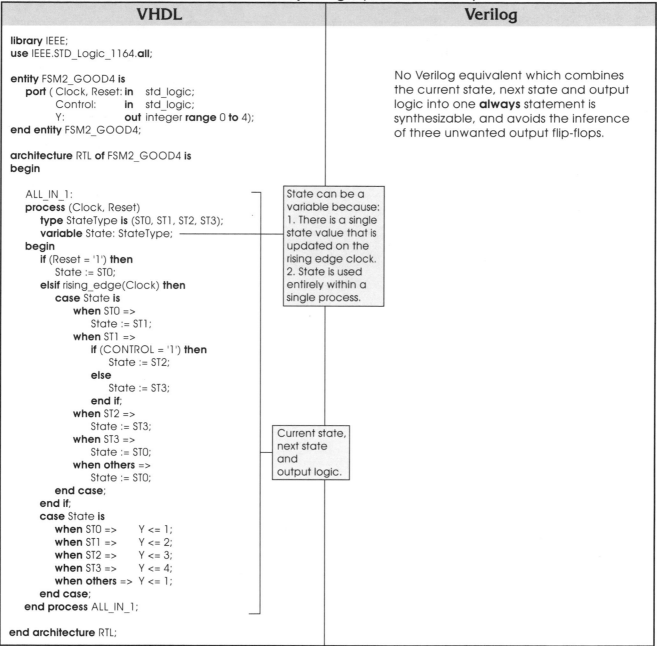

VHDL	Verilog
| ```
library IEEE;
use IEEE.STD_Logic_1164.all;

entity FSM2_GOOD4 is
    port ( Clock, Reset: in   std_logic;
           Control:      in   std_logic;
           Y:                 out integer range 0 to 4);
end entity FSM2_GOOD4;

architecture RTL of FSM2_GOOD4 is
begin

    ALL_IN_1:
    process (Clock, Reset)
        type StateType is (ST0, ST1, ST2, ST3);
        variable State: StateType;
    begin
        if (Reset = '1') then
            State := ST0;
        elsif rising_edge(Clock) then
            case State is
                when ST0 =>
                    State := ST1;
                when ST1 =>
                    if (CONTROL = '1') then
                        State := ST2;
                    else
                        State := ST3;
                    end if;
                when ST2 =>
                    State := ST3;
                when ST3 =>
                    State := ST0;
                when others =>
                    State := ST0;
            end case;
        end if;
        case State is
            when ST0 =>    Y <= 1;
            when ST1 =>    Y <= 2;
            when ST2 =>    Y <= 3;
            when ST3 =>    Y <= 4;
            when others => Y <= 1;
        end case;
    end process ALL_IN_1;

end architecture RTL;
``` | No Verilog equivalent which combines the current state, next state and output logic into one **always** statement is synthesizable, and avoids the inference of three unwanted output flip-flops. |

State can be a variable because:
1. There is a single state value that is updated on the rising edge clock.
2. State is used entirely within a single process.

Current state, next state and output logic.
```

Example 8.3 FSM with inputs or state value as the primary branch directive

The state machine corresponding to the state machine in Figure 8.8, is modeled in two different ways. The state diagram represents a car speed controller.

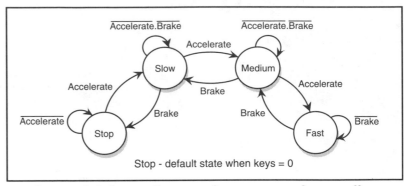

Figure 8.8 State diagram for car speed controller

The first model versions use the Brake and Accelerate inputs in a two way **if** branch directive, and then, using a **case** statement in both branches, assigns the new state value. For this particular state machine the increasing and decreasing speeds can be clearly seen by the two **case** statements. The second model versions on the following page show the more usual method of using the state value as the primary branch directive.

Input primary branch directives

VHDL	Verilog
| ```
library IEEE;
use IEEE.STD_Logic_1164.all, IEEE.Numeric_STD.all;
entity FSM_CAR_SPEED_CNTL_1 is
    port ( Clock, Keys, Brake, Accelerate: in std_logic;
           Speed: out unsigned(1 downto 0));
end entity FSM_CAR_SPEED_CNTL_1;
architecture RTL of FSM_CAR_SPEED_CNTL_1 is
    constant Stop:     unsigned(1 downto 0) := "00";
    constant Slow:     unsigned(1 downto 0) := "01";
    constant Medium:   unsigned(1 downto 0) := "10";
    constant Fast:     unsigned(1 downto 0) := "11";
begin
    FSM1: process (Clock, Keys)
        variable Speed_v: unsigned(1 downto 0);
    begin
        if (Keys = '0') then
            Speed_v := Stop;
        elsif rising_edge(Clock) then
            if (Accelerate = '1') then
                case (Speed_v) is
                    when Stop =>      Speed_v := Slow;
                    when Slow =>      Speed_v := Medium;
                    when Medium =>    Speed_v := Fast;
                    when Fast =>      Speed_v := Fast;
                    when others =>    Speed_v := Stop;
                end case;
            elsif (Brake = '1') then
                case (Speed_v) is
                    when Stop =>      Speed_v := Stop;
                    when Slow =>      Speed_v := Stop;
                    when Medium =>    Speed_v := Slow;
                    when Fast =>      Speed_v := Medium;
                    when others =>    Speed_v := Stop;
                end case;
            else
                Speed_v := Speed_v;
            end if;
        end if;
        Speed <= Speed_v;
    end process FSM1;
end architecture RTL;
``` | ```
module FSM_CAR_SPEED_CNTL_1
    (Clock, Keys, Brake, Accelerate, Speed);
    input  Clock, Keys, Brake, Accelerate;
    output [1:0] Speed;
    reg [1:0] Speed;

    parameter Stop    = 2'b 00,
              Slow    = 2'b 01,
              Medium  = 2'b 10,
              Fast    = 2'b 11;

    always @(posedge Clock or negedge keys)
    begin: FSM1
        if (! Keys)
            Speed = Stop;
        else if (Accelerate)
            case (Speed)
                Stop:     Speed = Slow;
                Slow:     Speed = Medium;
                Medium:   Speed = Fast;
                Fast:     Speed = Fast;
            endcase
        else if (Brake)
            case (Speed)
                Stop:     Speed = Stop;
                Slow:     Speed = Stop;
                Medium:   Speed = Slow;
                Fast:     Speed = Medium;
            endcase
        else
            Speed = Speed;
    end

endmodule
``` |

Annotations: Asynchronous reset to state stop. Accelerate/Brake are primary branch directives.

State value primary branch directives

VHDL	Verilog
| ```
library IEEE;
use IEEE.STD_Logic_1164.all, IEEE.Numeric_STD.all;

entity FSM_CAR_SPEED_CNTL_2 is
    port ( Clock, Keys, Brake, Accelerate: in std_logic;
            Speed: out unsigned(1 downto 0));
end entity FSM_CAR_SPEED_CNTL_2;

architecture RTL of FSM_CAR_SPEED_CNTL_2 is
    constant Stop:      unsigned(1 downto 0) := "00";
    constant Slow:      unsigned(1 downto 0) := "01";
    constant Medium:    unsigned(1 downto 0) := "10";
    constant Fast:      unsigned(1 downto 0) := "11";
    signal NextSpeed:   unsigned(1 downto 0);
    signal Speed_s:     unsigned(1 downto 0);
begin

    FSM2_COMB: process (Brake, Accelerate, Speed_s,
                        NextSpeed)
    begin
        case (Speed_s) is
            when Stop =>
                if (Accelerate = '1') then
                    NextSpeed <= Slow;
                else
                    NextSpeed <= Stop;
                end if;
            when Slow =>
                if (Brake = '1') then
                    NextSpeed <= Stop;
                elsif (Accelerate = '1') then
                    NextSpeed <= Medium;
                else
                    NextSpeed <= Slow;
                end if;
            when Medium =>
                if (Brake = '1') then
                    NextSpeed <= Slow;
                elsif (Accelerate = '1') then
                    NextSpeed <= Fast;
                else
                    NextSpeed <= Medium;
                end if;
            when Fast =>
                if (Brake = '1') then
                    NextSpeed <= Medium;
                else
                    NextSpeed <= Fast;
                end if;
            when others =>
                NextSpeed <= Stop;
        end case;
    end process FSM2_COMB;

    FSM2_SEQ: process (Clock, Keys)
    begin
        if (Keys = '0') then
            Speed_s <= Stop;
        elsif rising_edge(Clock) then
            Speed_s <= NextSpeed;
        end if;
        Speed <= Speed_s;
    end process FSM2_SEQ;
end architecture RTL;
``` | ```
module FSM_CAR_SPEED_CNTL_2
    (Clock, Keys, Brake, Accelerate, Speed);
    input  Clock, Keys, Brake, Accelerate;
    output (1:0) Speed;
    reg (1:0) Speed, NewSpeed;

    parameter Stop     = 2'b 00,
              Slow     = 2'b 01,
              Medium   = 2'b 10,
              Fast     = 2'b 11;

    always @(Brake or Accelerate or Speed)
        begin: FSM2_COMB
        case (Speed)
            Stop:
                if (Accelerate)
                    NewSpeed = Slow;
                else
                    NewSpeed = Stop;

            Slow:
                if (Brake)
                    NewSpeed = Stop;
                else if (Accelerate)
                    NewSpeed = Medium;
                else
                    NewSpeed = Slow;

            Medium:
                if (Brake)
                    NewSpeed = Slow;
                else if (Accelerate)
                    NewSpeed = Fast;
                else
                    NewSpeed = Medium;

            Fast:
                if (Brake)
                    NewSpeed = Medium;
                else
                    NewSpeed = Fast;
            default:
                NewSpeed = Stop;
        endcase
    end

    always @(posedge Clock or negedge Keys)
        begin: FSM2_SEQ
        if (! Keys)
            Speed = Stop;
        else
            Speed = NewSpeed;
    end

endmodule
``` |

The state "Speed" is the primary branch directive.

"Speed_s" is an internal signal so that port signal "Speed" may maintain the mode **out**.

Asynchronous reset to state stop.

Example 8.4 FSM reset configurations

In order to demonstrate the different ways in which resets may be modeled for a finite state machine, only the **process**/**always** statements are included. The sections of code are of the state machine used in Example 8.8, and whose state diagram was indicated in Figure 8.2. The first two sections of code are for an asynchronous reset and the last three on the following page are for a synchronous reset.

Two ways of implementing the same asynchronous reset for the FSM

VHDL	Verilog
| ```
FSM1: process (Clock, A, Hold)
begin
   case CurrentState is
      when ST0 =>
         Y_Mo <= '0';
         if (A = '1') then
            Y_Me <= '1';
            NextState <= ST0;
         else
            Y_Me <= '0';
            NextState <= ST1;
         end if;
         ...
   end case;

   if (Reset = '0') then        [Asynchronous reset.]
      CurrentState <= ST0;
   elsif rising_edge(Clock) then
      CurrentState <= NextState;
   end if;
end process FSM1;
``` | ```
always @(A or Hold)
   begin: FSM1_COMB
      case (CurrentState)
         ST0 :  begin   Y_Mo = 0;
                   if (A) begin
                      Y_Me = 1;
                      NextState = ST0;
                   end
                else   begin
                      Y_Me = 0;
                      NextState = ST1;
                   end
                end
         ...
      endcase
   end
always @(posedge Clock or posedge Reset)
   begin: FSM1_SEQ
      if (! Reset)
         CurrentState = ST0;
      else
         CurrentState = NextState;
   end
``` |
| ```
FSM2: process (Clock, A, Hold)
   variable State: StateType;
begin
   if (Reset = '0') then     [Asynchronous reset.]
      State := ST0;
   elsif rising_edge(Clock) then
      case State is
         when ST0 =>
            if (A = '1') then
               State := ST0;
            else
               State := ST1;
            end if;
            ...
      end case;
   end if;

   case State is
      when ST0 =>
         Y_Mo <= '0';
         if (A = '1') then
            Y_Me <= '1';
         else
            Y_Me <= '0';
         end if;
         ...
   end case;
end process FSM2;
``` | ```
always @(posedge Clock or negedge Reset)
   begin: FSM2_CS_NS
      if (! Reset)
         State = ST0;
      else
         case (State)
            ST0 :  if (A)
                      State = ST0;
                   else
                      State = ST1;
            ...
         endcase
   end
always @(A or Hold or State)
   begin: FSM2_OL
      case (State)
         ST0 :  begin
                   Y_Mo = 0;
                   if (A)
                      Y_Me = 1;
                   else
                      Y_Me = 0;
                end
         ...
      endcase
   end
``` |

Three ways of implementing the same synchronous reset for the FSM

VHDL	Verilog

```
FSM3_NS_OL: process (Clock, A, Hold)
begin
    case CurrentState is
        when ST0 =>    Y_Mo <= '0';
                       if (A = '1') then
                           Y_Me <= '1';
                           NextState <= ST0;
                       else
                           ...
    end case;
end process FSM3_NS_OL;
FSM3_CS: process (Clock)
begin
    if rising_edge(Clock) then                    ┌─ Synchronous reset. ─┐
        if (Reset = '0') then CurrentState <= ST0;
        else CurrentState <= NextState;
        end if;
    end if;
end process FSM3_CS;
```

```
always @(A or Hold or CurrentState)
    begin: FSM3_NS_OL
        case (CurrentState)
            ST0 :  begin    Y_Mo = 0;
                            if (A) begin
                                Y_Me = 1;
                                NextState = ST0;
                            end
                        else  begin
                                Y_Me = 0;
                                NextState = ST1;
                            end
                   end
            ...
        endcase
    end
always @(posedge Clock)
    begin: FSM3_CS
        if (! Reset)   CurrentState = ST0;
        else           CurrentState = NextState;
    end
```

```
FSM4_NS_OL: process (Clock, A, Hold)
begin
    if (Reset = '0') then NextState <= ST0;
    else
        case CurrentState is
            when ST0 =>    Y_Mo <= '0';
                           if (A = '1') then
                               Y_Me <= '1';
                               NextState <= ST0;
                           else
                               ...
        end case;
    end if;
end process FSM4_NS_OL;
FSM4_CS: process (Clock)
begin
    if rising_edge(Clock) then
        CurrentState <= NextState;
    end if;
end process FSM4_CS;
```

┌─ Synchronous reset.
│ Reset defined with
│ combinational logic. ─┐

```
always @(A or Hold or CurrentState)
    begin: FSM4_NS_OL
        if (! Reset) NextState = ST0;
        else
            case (CurrentState)
                ST0 :  begin    Y_Mo = 0;
                                if (A) begin
                                    Y_Me = 1;
                                    NextState = ST0;
                                end
                            else  begin
                                    Y_Me = 0;
                                    NextState = ST1;
                                end
                       end
                ...
            endcase
    end
always @(posedge Clock)
    begin: FSM4_CS   CurrentState = NextState;
    end
```

```
FSM5: process (Clock, A, Hold)
begin
    if rising_edge(Clock) then State <= ST0;
    elsif (Reset = '0') then             ┌─ Synchronous reset. ─┐
        case State is
            when ST0 =>    if (A = '1') then
                               State <= ST0;
                           else
                               State <= ST1;
                           end if;
            ...
        end case;
    end if;
    case State is
        when ST0 =>    Y_Mo <= '0';
                       if (A = '1') then
                           Y_Me <= '1';
                       else
                           Y_Me <= '0';
                       end if;
        ...
    end case;
end process FSM5;
```

```
always @(posedge Clock)
    begin: FSM5_NS_OL
        if (! Reset) NextState = ST0;
        else
            case (CurrentState)
                ST0 :  if (A) NextState = ST0;
                           else  NextState = ST1;
                ...
            endcase
    end
always @(A or Hold or State)
    begin: FSM5_OL
        case (State)
            ST0 :  begin    Y_Mo = 0;
                            if (A)
                                Y_Me = 1;
                            else
                                Y_Me = 0;
                   end
            ...
        endcase
    end
```

Example 8.5 Angular position FSM using Gray and Johnson state encoding

The state diagram for the state machine in this example, Figure 8.9, shows eight states. The states are encoded using either Gray or Johnson state encoding and represent the desired angular position of a rotor in 45 degree increments. State transitions occur from its current state to an adjacent state, representing a 45 degree shift of the rotor in either a clockwise or counterclockwise direction.

Because external forces can move the rotor from its desired position, the input PhysicalPosition may change, and is asynchronous to the clock. For this reason, Gray or Johnson state encoding is ideal because, if the asynchronous input changes during the setup time of the state register flip-flops, it will not cause a meta stable state, and so there is no risk of the state machine transitioning to an erroneous state. With other state encoding formats there is a small, but finite risk that a rotor movement through 180 degrees could be requested in one clock cycle. The state encoding is achieved differently in the VHDL and Verilog models, and are described separately below. There is no output logic, as the state value itself represents the angular position.

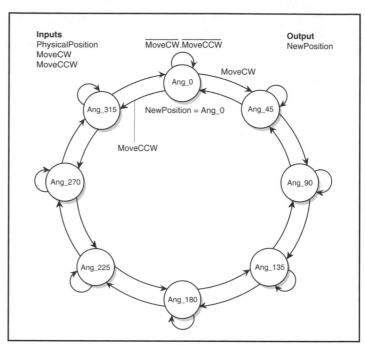

Figure 8.9 Angular Position FSM

VHDL Model. There are two ways to specify state encoding.

1. Use a signal of an enumerated type for which a single synthesis specific attribute is applied. This is a convenient way to specify the state encoding, but because the attribute's name is specific to the synthesis tool, it may need to be changed for portability to other tools. The first package ENUM_STATE_ENCODE_TYPES defines two identical enumerated state encoding types, one for Gray and Johnson encoding. Different attributes are then applied to these types that specify the specific state encoding, which is three bits wide for Gray and four bits wide for Johnson. The attribute is called ENUM_TYPE_ENCODING in the VeriBest synthesis tools, but may be different for other synthesis tools.

2. Use constants to represent the individual state values; these are assigned to a signal representing the particular state, and is directly portable to other synthesis tools. The model shows two packages for the two encoding methods. The **entity-architecture** of the state machine is the same for the two state encoding methods, except for the **use** clause, which references the appropriate package. The second package shows the unsigned type definition for the Gray and Johnson state value, and the individual state constants. The state machine is modeled using a single process similar to the last model in Example 8.2 (FSM2_GOOD4). The input PhysicalPosition and output NewPosition, are either of type GRAY_POS_EcodeStates or JOHNSON_POS_EncodeStates depending on the state encoding method, and is the only change needed.

Verilog Model. Uses **parameter** constants to declare state values in one of two separate system files. The state machine model uses the `include compiler directive to select the desired file for the required state encoding. Alternatively, `define compiler directives could have been used to allow the simple text substitution of state names for the binary state encoded values. Again, these could have been placed in separate system files and included in the model with `include compiler directives.

State encoding definitions for angular position FSM

VHDL	Verilog
| ```
library IEEE;
use IEEE.STD_Logic_1164.all, IEEE.Numeric_STD.all;
package CONST_GRAY_STATE_ENCODE_TYPES is
   constant Ang_0:    unsigned(3 downto 0) := "0010";
   constant Ang_45:   unsigned(3 downto 0) := "0110";
   constant Ang_90:   unsigned(3 downto 0) := "0111';
   constant Ang_135: unsigned(3 downto 0) := "0101";
   constant Ang_180: unsigned(3 downto 0) := "0100';
   constant Ang_225: unsigned(3 downto 0) := "1100";
   constant Ang_270: unsigned(3 downto 0) := "1101";
   constant Ang_315: unsigned(3 downto 0) := "1111";
end package CONST_GRAY_STATE_ENCODE_TYPES;

library IEEE;
use IEEE.STD_Logic_1164.all, IEEE.Numeric_STD.all;
package CONST_JOHN_STATE_ENCODE_TYPES is
   constant Ang_0:    unsigned(3 downto 0) := "0000";
   constant Ang_45:   unsigned(3 downto 0) := "0001";
   constant Ang_90:   unsigned(3 downto 0) := "0011";
   constant Ang_135: unsigned(3 downto 0) := "0111";
   constant Ang_180: unsigned(3 downto 0) := "1111";
   constant Ang_225: unsigned(3 downto 0) := "1110";
   constant Ang_270: unsigned(3 downto 0) := "1100";
   constant Ang_315: unsigned(3 downto 0) := "1000";
end package  CONST_JOHN_STATE_ENCODE_TYPES;
``` | ```
// File name = fsm_ang_pos_gray_params.v

// Specify state bit width
parameter StateWidth = 3;

// Gray State Definitions
parameter Ang_0   = 3'b 000,
          Ang_45  = 3'b 001,
          Ang_90  = 3'b 011,
          Ang_135 = 3'b 010,
          Ang_180 = 3'b 110,
          Ang_225 = 3'b 111,
          Ang_270 = 3'b 101,
          Ang_315 = 3'b 100;
``` |

VHDL	Verilog
| ```
package ENUM_STATE_ENCODE_TYPES is
   attribute ENUM_TYPE_ENCODING: string;

   type GRAY_POS_EncodeStates is
      (Ang_0, Ang_45, Ang_90, Ang_135, Ang_180, Ang_225,
       Ang_270, Ang_315);
   attribute ENUM_TYPE_ENCODING of
   GRAY_POS_EncodeStates:type is
   "0000 0001 0011 0010 0110 0111 0101 0100";

   type JOHNSON_POS_EncodeStates is
      (Ang_0, Ang_45, Ang_90, Ang_135, Ang_180, Ang_225,
       Ang_270, Ang_315);
   attribute ENUM_TYPE_ENCODING of
   JOHNSON_POS_EncodeStates: type is
   "0000 0001 0011 0111 1111 1110 1100 1000";
end package STATE_ENCODE_TYPES;
``` | ```
// File name = fsm_ang_pos_john_params.v

// Specify state bit width
parameter StateWidth = 4;

// Johnson State Definitions
parameter Ang_0   = 4'b 0000,
          Ang_45  = 4'b 0001,
          Ang_90  = 4'b 0011,
          Ang_135 = 4'b 0111,
          Ang_180 = 4'b 1111,
          Ang_225 = 4'b 1110,
          Ang_270 = 4'b 1100,
          Ang_315 = 4'b 1000;
``` |

Angular position FSM

VHDL	Verilog

VHDL

```vhdl
library IEEE;
use IEEE.STD_Logic_1164.all, IEEE.Numeric_STD.all;

use work.CONST_GRAY_STATE_ENCODE_TYPES.all;
-- use work.CONST_JOHN_STATE_ENCODE_TYPES.all;
-- use work.ENUM_STATE_ENCODE_TYPES.all;
```

One construct selects state encoding.

```vhdl
entity FSM_ANG_POS is
   port ( Clock, Reset: in  std_logic;
          PhysicalPosition:    in  unsigned(3 downto 0);
          --PhysicalPosition:  in  GRAY_POS_EncodeStates;
          --PhysicalPosition:  in  JOHN_POS_EncodeStates;
          MoveCW, MoveCCW: in std_logic;
          NewPosition: out unsigned(3 downto 0));
          --NewPosition: out GRAY_POS_EncodeStates);
          --NewPosition: out JOHN_POS_EncodeStates);
end entity FSM_ANG_POS;

architecture RTL of FSM_ANG_POS is
   signal CurrentState, NextState: unsigned(3 downto 0);
   --signal CurrentState, NextState: GRAY_POS_EncodeStates;
   --signal CurrentState, NextState:JOHN_POS_EncodeStates;
begin

   COMBINATIONAL: process (PhysicalPosition, MoveCW,
                    MoveCCW, CurrentState)
   begin
      case CurrentState is
         when Ang_0 =>
            if (MoveCW = '1') then
               NextState <= Ang_45;
            elsif (MoveCCW = '1') then
               NextState <= Ang_315;
            else
               NextState <= Ang_0;
            end if;
         when Ang_45 =>
            if (MoveCW = '1') then
               NextState <= Ang_90;
            elsif (MoveCCW = '1') then
               NextState <= Ang_0;
            else
               NextState <= Ang_45;
            end if;
         when Ang_90 =>
            if (MoveClockwise = '1') then
               NextState <= Ang_135;
            elsif (MoveCCW = '1') then
               NextState <= Ang_45;
            else
               NextState <= Ang_90;
            end if;
         when Ang_135 =>
            if (MoveCW = '1') then
               NextState <= Ang_180;
            elsif (MoveCCW = '1') then
               NextState <= Ang_90;
            else
               NextState <= Ang_135;
            end if;
         when Ang_180 =>
            if (MoveCW = '1') then
               NextState <= Ang_225;
```

State values representing angular position of rotor.

continued

Verilog

```verilog
module FSM_ANG_POS
   (Clock,Reset, PhysicalPosition, MoveCW, MoveCCW,
   NewPosition);
      input  Clock, Reset;
      input  (2:0) PhysicalPosition;
      input  MoveCW, MoveCCW;
      output (2:0) NewPosition;


   // Select one of the following for state encoding
   `include "fsm_ang_gray_params.v"
   // `include "fsm_ang_john_params.v"

   reg (StateWidth - 1:0) CurrentState, NextState;

   always @( PhysicalPosition or MoveCW or
                 MoveCCW or CurrentState)
      begin: COMBINATIONAL
         case (CurrentState)
            Ang_0 :
               if (MoveCW == 1)
                  NextState = Ang_45;
               else if (MoveCCW == 1)
                  NextState = Ang_315;
               else
                  NextState = Ang_0;

            Ang_45 :
               if (MoveCW == 1)
                  NextState = Ang_90;
               else if (MoveCCW == 1)
                  NextState = Ang_0;
               else
                  NextState = Ang_45;

            Ang_90 :
               if (MoveCW == 1)
                  NextState = Ang_135;
               else if (MoveCCW == 1)
                  NextState = Ang_45;
               else
                  NextState = Ang_90;

            Ang_135 :
               if (MoveCW == 1)
                  NextState = Ang_180;
               else if (MoveCCW == 1)
                  NextState = Ang_90;
               else
                  NextState = Ang_135;

            Ang_180 :
               if (MoveCW == 1)
                  NextState = Ang_225;
               else if (MoveCCW == 1)
                  NextState = Ang_135;
```

continued

Angular position FSM

VHDL	Verilog
``` NextState <= Ang_225; elsif (MoveCCW = '1') then NextState <= Ang_135; else NextState <= Ang_180; end if; when Ang_225 => if (MoveCW = '1') then NextState <= Ang_270; elsif (MoveCCW = '1') then NextState <= Ang_180; else NextState <= Ang_225; end if; when Ang_270 => if (MoveCW = '1') then NextState <= Ang_315; elsif (MoveCCW = '1') then NextState <= Ang_225; else NextState <= Ang_270; end if; when Ang_315 => if (MoveCW = '1') then NextState <= Ang_0; elsif (MoveCCW = '1') then NextState <= Ang_270; else NextState <= Ang_315; end if; when others => NextState <= PhysicalPosition end case; end process COMBINATIONAL; SEQUENTIAL: process (Clock, Reset, PhysicalPosition) begin if (Reset = '0') then CurrentState <= PhysicalPosition; elsif rising_edge(Clock) then CurrentState <= NextState; end if; end process; NewPosition <= CurrentState; end architecture RTL; ```	``` else NextState = Ang_180; Ang_225 : if (MoveCW == 1) NextState = Ang_270; else if (MoveCCW == 1) NextState = Ang_180; else NextState = Ang_225; Ang_270 : if (MoveCW == 1) NextState = Ang_315; else if (MoveCCW == 1) NextState = Ang_225; else NextState = Ang_270; Ang_315 : if (MoveCW == 1) NextState = Ang_0; else if (MoveCCW == 1) NextState = Ang_270; else NextState = Ang_315; default : NextState = PhysicalPosition; endcase end always @(posedge Clock or negedge Reset) begin: SEQUENTIAL if (! Reset) CurrentState = PhysicalPosition; else CurrentState = NextState; end assign NewPosition = CurrentState; endmodule ```

> Necessary when using states defined using constants to ensure all case values are covered and ensure only combinational logic. Must not be used when using states defined using enumerated types as all enumerated types are already covered in case choice values.

> Needed to avoid **always** statement inferring latches.

> CurrentState assigned to the output "NewPosition".

Example 8.6 FSM state encoding formats - Blackjack Game Machine

The model of a state machine with selectable state encoding is shown. The effect state encoding has on this particular state machine's area and timing is also shown. The different state encoding used are: sequential, Gray, Johnson, one-hot and three types of Nova. The first four are shown defined in the HDL models, while the three types of Nova state encoding are chosen by the VeriBest synthesis tool and requires the state machine be entered in a graphical, non VHDL or Verilog, format. This has been done and the results included in Figure 8.10.

The model is of a Blackjack card game machine; see inset for description. The model includes a state machine controller for which the different state encoding formats apply, plus data path accumulators. The accumulators are not affected by the state encoding, but are included in this model for completeness. They hold the accumulated card value and the number of aces counted as having a value of 11.

The state machine has 16 states as seen by the state diagram, Figure 8.11.

When an HDL model is synthesized, the VeriBest synthesis tools create a separate design database file for each **process** (VHDL) and **always** block (Verilog), which can be independently optimized and analyzed. Because of this, and the need to analyze

> **Blackjack**
> Blackjack is the most popular of the card games played at the tables in casinos. It is played with a standard deck of 52 cards. The four suits; spades, hearts, diamonds and clubs have no significance and are ignored. The value of the cards is important. The Jack, Queen and King all have a value of 10. The ace is the most powerful card having a value of 1 or 11 depending upon what the player chooses.
>
> Blackjack is also known as pontoon or "21" because 21 is the highest rated total card value a player can hold. Blackjack is the name given to the strongest hand consisting of an ace and a 10 valued card.
>
> The object of the game is to beat the dealer. The dealer has no object other than to follow the rules of the casino, which is to stand (hold) on hands of 17 or more, and to draw another card on hands of 16 or less.
>
> A player looses if his or her total card value is less than the dealer's total, or, he or she has over 21 and so has bust. If a player wants to improve his hand he can ask the dealer for another card. This is called drawing or hitting. If satisfied with the total card value he can stand (hold).

the effect state encoding has on the state machine's next state, current state and output logic, they have all been modeled in separate **process** (VHDL)/ **always** (Verilog) statements. The designed architecture of the Blackjack machine, Figure 8.12, represents the structure of the **process** (VHDL) and **always** (Verilog) statements in the HDL models.

This same design is remodeled in Example 8.10 with various blocks combined, and has the sequential logic buried within the FSM, resulting in reduced code.

Defining the state encoding

There are four statements in each model (VHDL and Verilog), that relate to the state encoding. One of the statements is enabled to set the desired state encoding, while the other three must be "commented out". The phrase "commenting out" means turning a particular line of code into a comment by prefixing it with "--" (VHDL) or "//" (Verilog). The models shown have sequential state encoding enabled.

> *VHDL state encoding.* State encoding is specified in the VHDL model, by defining the two signals CurrentState and NextState, to be one of four types defined in the VHDL package STATE_ENCODE_TYPES. This package first defines an attribute called ENUM_TYPE_ENCODING to be of type string. This attribute is known to the VeriBest synthesis tools, and is used specifically to define a string representing the enumerated encoding of enumerated data types. Most

synthesis tools allow an attribute to be used in this way, although its name, ENUM_TYPE_ENCODING, may be different. Four identical enumerated data types are declared in the package, each having 16 possible values representing the state of the state machine. Each type has the attribute, ENUM_TYPE_ENCODING, attributed to it, and contains a binary string representing the particular state encoding.

Verilog state encoding. The state encoding is defined in the Verilog model by selecting one of four statements similar to the VHDL version. Each statement uses the `include compiler directive to reference a system file and has the effect of replacing the `include statement with the contents of the file it references. Each statement references a different file depending upon the desired state encoding. Each file defines the bit width of the CurrentState and NextState signals, which changes depending on which state encoding is used. Each file also defines the 16 parameter values which represent the binary value of each state.

The simulated waveforms are shown in Figure 8.13.

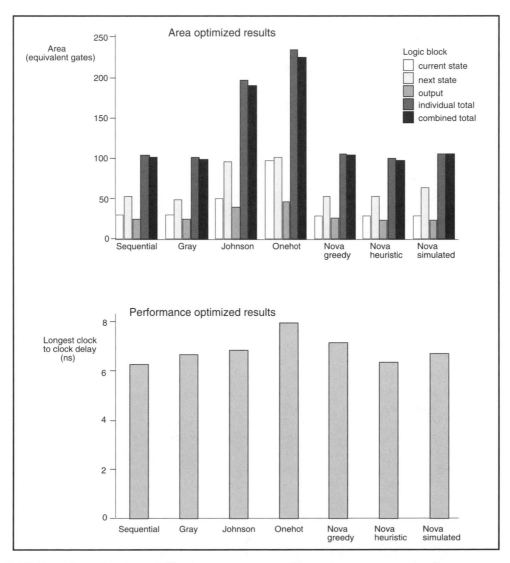

Figure 8.10 Results of using different state encodings for one particular state machine

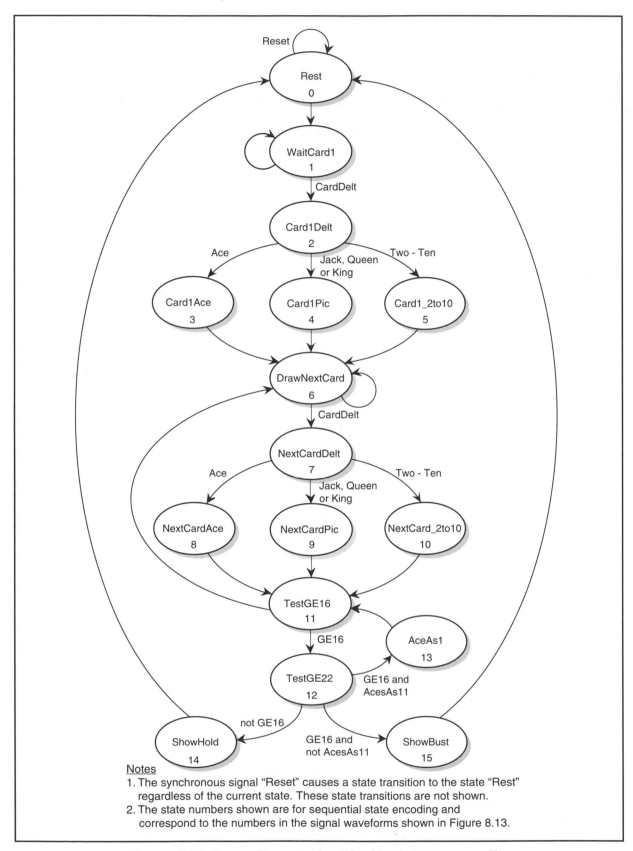

Figure 8.11 State diagram for Blackjack FSM controller

Notes
1. The synchronous signal "Reset" causes a state transition to the state "Rest" regardless of the current state. These state transitions are not shown.
2. The state numbers shown are for sequential state encoding and correspond to the numbers in the signal waveforms shown in Figure 8.13.

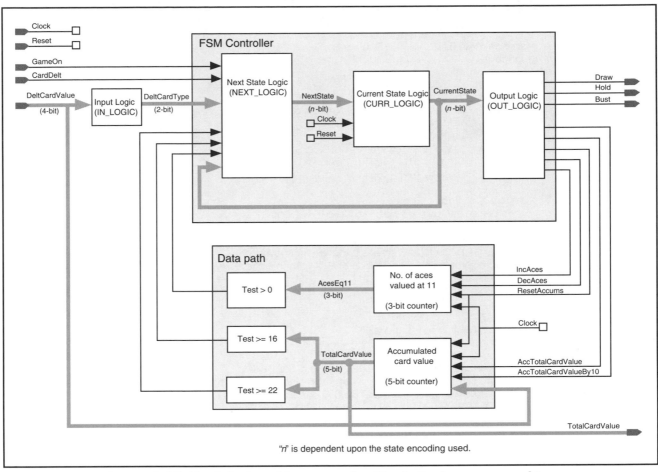

Figure 8.12 Modeled architecture of a Black Jack game machine

VHDL package defining four enumerated state encoding data types

```
                              VHDL

package STATE_ENCODE_TYPES is
   attribute ENUM_TYPE_ENCODING: string;

   type SEQ_EncodeStates is
       ( Rest, WaitCard1, Card1delt, Card1Ace, Card1Pic,
         Card1_2to10, DrawNextCard, NextCardDelt,
         NextCardAce, NextCardPic, NextCard_2to10,
         TestGE16, TestGE22, AceAs1, ShowHold, ShowBust);
   attribute ENUM_TYPE_ENCODING of SEQ_EncodeStates: type is
       "0000 0001 0010 0011 0100 0101 0110 0111" &
       "1000 1001 1010 1011 1100 1101 1110 1111";

   type GRAY_EncodeStates is
       ( Rest, WaitCard1, Card1delt, Card1Ace, Card1Pic,
         Card1_2to10, DrawNextCard, NextCardDelt,
         NextCardAce, NextCardPic, NextCard_2to10,
         TestGE16, TestGE22, AceAs1, ShowHold, ShowBust);
   attribute ENUM_TYPE_ENCODING of GRAY_EncodeStates: type is
       "0000 0001 0011 0010 0110 0111 0101 0100" &
       "1100 1101 1111 1110 1010 1011 1001 1000";

   type JOHN_EncodeStates is
       ( Rest, WaitCard1, Card1delt, Card1Ace, Card1Pic,
         Card1_2to10, DrawNextCard, NextCardDelt,
         NextCardAce, NextCardPic, NextCard_2to10,
         TestGE16, TestGE22, AceAs1, ShowHold, ShowBust);
   attribute ENUM_TYPE_ENCODING of JOHN_EncodeStates: type is
       "00000000 00000001 00000011 00000111" &
       "00001111 00011111 00111111 01111111" &
       "11111111 11111110 11111100 11111000" &
       "11110000 11100000 11000000 10000000 ";

   type ONEHOT_EncodeStates is
       ( Rest, WaitCard1, Card1delt, Card1Ace, Card1Pic,
         Card1_2to10, DrawNextCard, NextCardDelt,
         NextCardAce, NextCardPic, NextCard_2to10,
         TestGE16, TestGE22, AceAs1, ShowHold, ShowBust);
   attribute ENUM_TYPE_ENCODING of ONEHOT_EncodeStates: type is
       "0000000000000001 0000000000000010" &
       "0000000000000100 0000000000001000" &
       "0000000000010000 0000000000100000" &
       "0000000001000000 0000000010000000" &
       "0000000100000000 0000001000000000" &
       "0000010000000000 0000100000000000" &
       "0001000000000000 0010000000000000" &
       "0100000000000000 1000000000000000";

end package STATE_ENCODE_TYPES;
```

Four Verilog `include *files defining state parameter values and their width*

sequential state encoding

```
                    Verilog

// File name = state_encoding_seq.v

// Specify state bit width
parameter StateWidth = 4;

// State Definitions
parameter Rest          = 4'b 0000,
          WaitCard1     = 4'b 0001,
          Card1Delt     = 4'b 0010,
          Card1Ace      = 4'b 0011,
          Card1Pic      = 4'b 0100,
          Card1_2to10   = 4'b 0101,
          DrawNextCard  = 4'b 0110,
          NextCardDelt  = 4'b 0111,
          NextCardAce   = 4'b 1000,
          NextCardPic   = 4'b 1001,
          NextCard_2to10 = 4'b 1010,
          TestGE16      = 4'b 1011,
          TestGE22      = 4'b 1100,
          AceAs1        = 4'b 1101,
          ShowHold      = 4'b 1110,
          ShowBust      = 4'b 1111;
```

Johnson state encoding

```
                    Verilog

// File name = state_encoding_john.v

// specify state bit width
parameter StateWidth = 8;

// State Definitions
parameter Rest          = 8'b 00000000,
          WaitCard1     = 8'b 00000001,
          Card1Delt     = 8'b 00000011,
          Card1Ace      = 8'b 00000111,
          Card1Pic      = 8'b 00001111,
          Card1_2to10   = 8'b 00011111,
          DrawNextCard  = 8'b 00111111,
          NextCardDelt  = 8'b 01111111,
          NextCardAce   = 8'b 11111111,
          NextCardPic   = 8'b 11111110,
          NextCard_2to10 = 8'b 11111100,
          TestGE16      = 8'b 11111000,
          TestGE22      = 8'b 11110000,
          AceAs1        = 8'b 11100000,
          ShowHold      = 8'b 11000000,
          ShowBust      = 8'b 10000000;
```

Gray state encoding

```
                    Verilog

// File name = state_encoding_gray.v

// Specify state bit width
parameter StateWidth = 4;

// State Definitions
parameter Rest          = 4'b 0000,
          WaitCard1     = 4'b 0001,
          Card1Delt     = 4'b 0011,
          Card1Ace      = 4'b 0010,
          Card1Pic      = 4'b 0110,
          Card1_2to10   = 4'b 0111,
          DrawNextCard  = 4'b 0101,
          NextCardDelt  = 4'b 0100,
          NextCardAce   = 4'b 1100,
          NextCardPic   = 4'b 1101,
          NextCard_2to10 = 4'b 1111,
          TestGE16      = 4'b 1110,
          TestGE22      = 4'b 1010,
          AceAs1        = 4'b 1011,
          ShowHold      = 4'b 1001,
          ShowBust      = 4'b 1000;
```

one-hot state encoding

```
                    Verilog

// File name = state_encoding_onehot.v

// Specify state bit width
parameter StateWidth = 16;

// State Definitions
parameter Rest          = 16'b 0000000000000001,
          WaitCard1     = 16'b 0000000000000010,
          Card1Delt     = 16'b 0000000000000100,
          Card1Ace      = 16'b 0000000000001000,
          Card1Pic      = 16'b 0000000000010000,
          Card1_2to10   = 16'b 0000000000100000,
          DrawNextCard  = 16'b 0000000001000000,
          NextCardDelt  = 16'b 0000000010000000,
          NextCardAce   = 16'b 0000000100000000,
          NextCardPic   = 16'b 0000001000000000,
          NextCard_2to10 = 16'b 0000010000000000,
          TestGE16      = 16'b 0000100000000000,
          TestGE22      = 16'b 0001000000000000,
          AceAs1        = 16'b 0010000000000000,
          ShowHold      = 16'b 0100000000000000,
          ShowBust      = 16'b 1000000000000000;
```

FSM with selectable state encoding - Blackjack game machine

VHDL	Verilog
| ```
library IEEE;
use IEEE.STD_Logic_1164.all, IEEE.Numeric_STD.all;
use work.STATE_ENCODE_TYPES.all;
entity FSM_STATE_ENCODING is
    port (Clock, Reset:          in    std_logic;
          GameOn, CardDelt:      in    std_logic;
          DeltCardValue:         in    unsigned(3 downto 0);
          TotalCardValue:        out   unsigned(4 downto 0);
          Draw, Hold, Bust:      out   std_logic);
end entity FSM_STATE_ENCODING;

architecture RTL of FSM_STATE_ENCODING is
    -- DeltCardValue
    constant Ace:      integer := 1;
    constant Two:      integer := 2;
    constant Three:    integer := 3;
    constant Four:     integer := 4;
    constant Five:     integer := 5;
    constant Six:      integer := 6;
    constant Seven:    integer := 7;
    constant Eight:    integer := 8;
    constant Nine:     integer := 9;
    constant Ten:      integer := 10;
    constant Jack:     integer := 11;
    constant Queen:    integer := 12;
    constant King:     integer := 13;

    -- DeltCardType
    type TypeDeltCardType is (CardTypeAce,
                              CardTypeNo2to10,
                              CardTypePic);

    -- State encoding defined by one of the following
    signal CurrentState,   NextState: SEQ_EncodeStates;
    -- signal CurrentState,   NextState: GRAY_EncodeStates;
    -- signal CurrentState,   NextState: JOHN_EncodeStates;
    -- signal CurrentState,   NextState: ONEHOT_EncodeStates;

    signal AcesAs11, GE16, GE22: std_logic;
    signal AcesEq11: integer range 0 to 4;
    signal DeltCardType: TypeDeltCardType;
    signal ResetAccums, IncAces, DecAces: std_logic;
    signal AccTotalCardValue, AccTotalCardValueBy10 :
                                           std_logic;

begin
    -----------------------------------------
    -- Input logic for card type
    -----------------------------------------
    IN_LOGIC: process (DeltCardValue)
    begin
      case (to_integer(DeltCardValue)) is
        when Ace =>
          DeltCardType <= CardTypeAce;
        when Jack | Queen | King =>
          DeltCardType <= CardTypeAce;
        when others =>
          DeltCardType <= CardTypeNo2to10;
      end case;
    end process IN_LOGIC;

    ---------------------------------
    -- FSM Next state logic
    ---------------------------------
    NEXT_LOGIC: process (Reset, CurrentState, GameOn,
                    CardDelt, DeltCardType, GE16,
                    GE22, AcesAs11,)        continued
``` | ```
module FSM_STATE_ENCODING
  (Clock, Reset, GameOn, CardDelt, DeltCardValue,
   TotalCardValue, Draw, Hold, Bust);
    input  Clock, Reset;
    input  GameOn, CardDelt;
    input  (3:0) DeltCardValue;
    output (4:0) TotalCardValue;
    output Draw, Hold, Bust;
    reg    (4:0) TotalCardValue;
    reg    Draw, Hold, Bust;

    // DeltCardValue
    parameter   Ace     = 1,
                Two     = 2,
                Three   = 3,
                Four    = 4,
                Five    = 5,
                Six     = 6,
                Seven   = 7,
                Eight   = 8,
                Nine    = 9,
                Ten     = 10,
                Jack    = 11,
                Queen   = 12,
                King    = 13;

    // DeltCardType
    parameter   CardTypeAce     = 0,
                CardTypeNo2to10 = 1,
                CardTypePic     = 2;

    // State encoding defined by one of the following
    `include "state_encoding_seq.v"
    //`include "state_encoding_gray.v"
    //`include "state_encoding_john.v"
    //`include "state_encoding_onehot.v"

    reg (StateWidth - 1:0) CurrentState, NextState;
    reg AcesAs11, GE16, GE22;
    reg (2:0) AcesEq11;
    reg (1:0) DeltCardType;
    reg ResetAccums, IncAces, DecAces;
    reg AccTotalCardValue, AccTotalCardValueBy10;

    //-----------------------------------------
    // Input logic for card type
    //-----------------------------------------
    always @(DeltCardValue)
      begin: IN_LOGIC
        case (DeltCardValue)
          Ace:              DeltCardType = CardTypeAce;
          Jack,Queen,King:  DeltCardType = CardTypePic;
          default:          DeltCardType = CardTypeNo2to10;
        endcase
      end

    //---------------------------------
    // FSM Next state logic
    //---------------------------------
    always @( Reset or CurrentState or GameOn or
              CardDelt or DeltCardType or GE16 or
              GE22 or AcesAs11 )        continued
``` |

FSM with selectable state encoding - Blackjack Game Machine

VHDL	Verilog
| ```
begin
  if (Reset = '1') then
    NextState <= Rest;
  else
    case (CurrentState) is
      when Rest =>
        if (GameOn = '1') then
          NextState <= WaitCard1;
        else
          NextState <= Rest;
        end if;
      when WaitCard1 =>
        if (CardDelt = '1') then
          NextState <= Card1Delt;
        else
          NextState <= WaitCard1;
        end if;
      when Card1Delt =>
        if (DeltCardType = CardTypeAce) then
          NextState <= Card1Ace;
        elsif (DeltCardType = CardTypePic) then
          NextState <= Card1Pic;
        else
          NextState <= Card1_2to10;
        end if;
      when Card1Ace =>
        NextState <= DrawNextCard;
      when Card1Pic =>
        NextState <= DrawNextCard;
      when Card1_2to10 =>
        NextState <= DrawNextCard;
      when DrawNextCard =>
        if (CardDelt = '1') then
          NextState <= NextCardDelt;
        else
          NextState <= DrawNextCard;
        end if;
      when NextCardDelt =>
        if (DeltCardType = CardTypeAce) then
          NextState <= NextCardAce;
        elsif (DeltCardType = CardTypePic) then
          NextState <= NextCardPic;
        else
          NextState <= NextCard_2to10;
        end if;
      when NextCardAce =>
        NextState <= TestGE16;
      when NextCardPic =>
        NextState <= TestGE16;
      when NextCard_2to10 =>
        NextState <= TestGE16;
      when TestGE16 =>
        if (GE16 = '1') then
          NextState <= TestGE22;
        else
          NextState <= DrawNextCard;
        end if;
      when TestGE22 =>
        if (GE22 = '1') then
          if (AcesAs11 = '0') then
            NextState <= ShowBust;
          else
            NextState <= AceAs1;
          end if;
        else
``` | ```
begin: NEXT_LOGIC
  if (Reset == 1)
    NextState = Rest;
  else
    case (CurrentState)
      Rest:
        if (GameOn == 1)
          NextState = WaitCard1;
        else
          NextState = Rest;

      WaitCard1:
        if (CardDelt == 1)
          NextState = Card1Delt;
        else
          NextState = WaitCard1;

      Card1Delt:
        if (DeltCardType == CardTypeAce)
          NextState = Card1Ace;
        else if (DeltCardType == CardTypePic)
          NextState = Card1Pic;
        else
          NextState = Card1_2to10;

      Card1Ace:
        NextState = DrawNextCard;
      Card1Pic:
        NextState = DrawNextCard;
      Card1_2to10:
        NextState = DrawNextCard;
      DrawNextCard:
        if (CardDelt == 1)
          NextState = NextCardDelt;
        else
          NextState = DrawNextCard;

      NextCardDelt:
        if (DeltCardType == CardTypeAce)
          NextState = NextCardAce;
        else if (DeltCardType == CardTypePic)
          NextState = NextCardPic;
        else
          NextState = NextCard_2to10;

      NextCardAce:
        NextState = TestGE16;
      NextCardPic:
        NextState = TestGE16;
      NextCard_2to10:
        NextState = TestGE16;
      TestGE16:
        if (GE16 == 1)
          NextState = TestGE22;
        else
          NextState = DrawNextCard;
      TestGE22:
        if (GE22 == 1)
          if (AcesAs11 == 0)
            NextState = ShowBust;
          else
            NextState = AceAs1;
        else
          NextState = ShowHold;
``` |
| continued | continued |

FSM with selectable state encoding - Blackjack Game Machine

VHDL	Verilog

```vhdl
                NextState <= ShowHold;
            end if;
        when AceAs1 =>
            NextState <= TestGE16;
        when ShowHold =>
            NextState <= Rest;
        when ShowBust =>
            NextState <= Rest;
        when others =>
            NextState <= Rest;
        end case;
    end if;
end process NEXT_LOGIC;


--------------------------------------
-- FSM Current state logic
--------------------------------------
CURR_LOGIC: process (Clock)
begin
    if rising_edge(Clock) then
        CurrentState <= NextState;
    end if;
end process CURR_LOGIC;


----------------------------------------------------
-- FSM Output logic (Controls data path)
----------------------------------------------------
OUT_LOGIC: process (CurrentState)
begin
    ResetAccums <= '0';
    IncAces    <= '0';
    DecAces    <= '0';
    AccTotalCardValueBy10 <= '0';
    AccTotalCardValue <= '0';
    Hold   <= '0';
    Bust   <= '0';
    Draw   <= '0';
    case (CurrentState) is
        when Rest =>
            ResetAccums <= '1';
        when Card1Ace =>
            IncAces <= '1';
        when Card1Pic =>
            AccTotalCardValueBy10 <= '1';
        when Card1_2to10 =>
            AccTotalCardValue <= '1';
        when DrawNextCard =>
            Draw <= '1';
        when NextCardAce =>
            IncAces <= '1';
        when NextCardPic =>
            AccTotalCardValueBy10 <= '1';
        when NextCard_2to10 =>
            AccTotalCardValue <= '1';
        when AceAs1 =>
            DecAces <= '1';
        when ShowHold =>
            Hold <= '1';
        when ShowBust =>
            Bust <= '1';
        when others =>
            null;
    end case;
end process OUT_LOGIC;
```

```verilog
        AceAs1:
            NextState = TestGE16;
        ShowHold:
            NextState = Rest;
        ShowBust:
            NextState = Rest;
        default:
            NextState = Rest;
    endcase
end


//-----------------------------------
// FSM Current state logic
//-----------------------------------
always @(posedge Clock)
    begin: CURR_LOGIC
        CurrentState = NextState;
    end


//----------------------------------------------------
// FSM Output logic (Controls data path)
//----------------------------------------------------
always @(CurrentState)
  begin: OUT_LOGIC
    ResetAccums = 0;
    IncAces   = 0;
    DecAces   = 0;
    AccTotalCardValueBy10 = 0;
    AccTotalCardValue = 0;
    Hold    = 0;
    Bust    = 0;
    Draw    = 0;
    case (CurrentState)
      Rest:
        ResetAccums = 1;
      Card1Ace:
        IncAces = 1;
      Card1Pic:
        AccTotalCardValueBy10 = 1;
      Card1_2to10:
        AccTotalCardValue = 1;
      DrawNextCard:
        Draw = 1;
      NextCardAce:
        IncAces = 1;
      NextCardPic:
        AccTotalCardValueBy10 = 1;
      NextCard_2to10:
        AccTotalCardValue = 1;
      AceAs1:
        DecAces = 1;
      ShowHold:
        Hold = 1;
      ShowBust:
        Bust = 1;
      default:
        ;
    endcase
end
```

> Default output values defined before **case** so not needed here.

continued

continued

FSM with selectable state encoding - Blackjack Game Machine

VHDL	Verilog
| ```
------------------
-- Data path
------------------
DATA_PATH: process (Clock, AcesEq11)
   variable TotalCardValue_v: unsigned( 4 downto 0);
begin

   ------------------------------------
   -- No. of aces counted as 11
   ------------------------------------
   if rising_edge(Clock) then
      if (ResetAccums = '1') then
         AcesEq11 <= 0;
      elsif (IncAces = '1') then
         AcesEq11 <= AcesEq11 + 1;
      elsif (DecAces = '1') then
         AcesEq11 <= AcesEq11 - 1;
      end if;
   end if;



   --------------------------------------
   -- Accummulated card value
   --------------------------------------
   if rising_edge(Clock) then
      if (ResetAccums = '1') then
         TotalCardValue_v := "00000";
      elsif (AccTotalCardValueBy10 = '1') then
         TotalCardValue_v := TotalCardValue_v + 10;
      elsif (IncAces = '1') then
         TotalCardValue_v := TotalCardValue_v + 11;
      elsif (AccTotalCardValue = '1') then
         TotalCardValue_v := TotalCardValue_v +
                                    DeltCardValue;
      elsif (DecAces = '1') then
         TotalCardValue_v := TotalCardValue_v + 10;
      end if;
      TotalCardValue <= TotalCardValue_v;
   end if;




   --------------------------------------
   -- Aces counted as 11 status
   --------------------------------------
   if (AcesEq11 > 0) then
      AcesAs11 <= '1';
   else
      AcesAs11 <= '0';
   end if;


   -------------------------------------
   -- Greater than 22 status
   -------------------------------------
   if (TotalCardValue_v >= 22) then
      GE22 <= '1';
   else
      GE22 <= '0';
   end if;
``` | ```
// ------------------------------------------
// Data path (accumulators)
// ------------------------------------------

always @(posedge Clock)
   begin: ACCMULATORS

   //------------------------------------------
   // No. of aces counted as 11
   //------------------------------------------
   if (ResetAccums == 1)
      AcesEq11 = 0;
   else if (IncAces == 1)
      AcesEq11 = AcesEq11 + 1;
   else if (DecAces == 1)
      AcesEq11 = AcesEq11 - 1;




   // ------------------------------------------
   // Accumulated Card Value
   // ------------------------------------------
   if (ResetAccums == 1)
      TotalCardValue = 0;
   else if (AccTotalCardValueBy10 == 1)
      TotalCardValue = TotalCardValue + 10;
   else if (IncAces == 1)
      TotalCardValue = TotalCardValue + 11;
   else if (AccTotalCardValue == 1)
      TotalCardValue = TotalCardValue +
                              DeltCardValue;
   else if (DecAces == 1)
      TotalCardValue = TotalCardValue - 10;
   end



// --------------------------------------------------
// Data path (status of accumulators)
// --------------------------------------------------
always @(AcesEq11 or TotalCardValue)
   begin: ACC_STATUS

   //------------------------------------------
   // Aces counted as 11 status
   //------------------------------------------
   if (AcesEq11 > 0)
      AcesAs11 = 1;
   else
      AcesAs11 = 0;


   //------------------------------------------
   // Greater than 22 status
   //------------------------------------------
   if (TotalCardValue >= 22)
      GE22 = 1;
   else
      GE22 = 0;
``` |

> Variable used to increase simulation speed.

> **else** clauses not needed as in edge triggered section of code.

continued   *continued*

FSM with selectable state encoding - Blackjack Game Machine

VHDL	Verilog

`-----------------------------------`
`-- Greater than 15 status`
`-----------------------------------`
if (TotalCardValue_v >= 16) **then**
   GE16 <= '1';
else
   GE16 <= '0';
end if;
 	
end process DATA_PATH;
 	
end architecture RTL;
	`//-----------------------------------`
	`// Greater  than 15 status`
	`//-----------------------------------`
	
	   if (TotalCardValue >= 16)
	     GE16 = 1;
	   else
	     GE16 = 0;
	   end
	
	endmodule

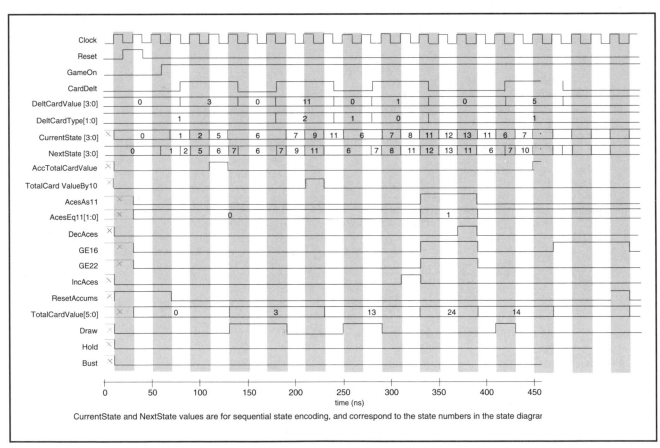

Figure 8.13 Signal waveforms for the state encoding FSM - Blackjack Machine

Example 8.7 FSMs with a Mealy or Moore Output

The two state machines in this example differ in that, one has a Mealy type output, and the other a Moore. The state diagrams, Figure 8.14, and the HDL code, shows how the output (NewColor) is a function of the inputs (Red, Green and Blue) in the Mealy example.

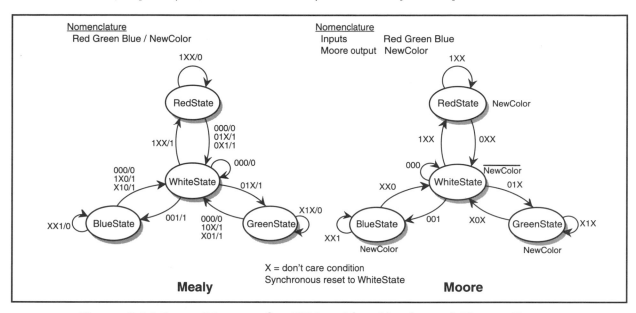

Figure 8.14 State Diagram for FSMs with a Mealy and Moore Output

FSM modeled with "NewColor" as a Mealy type output

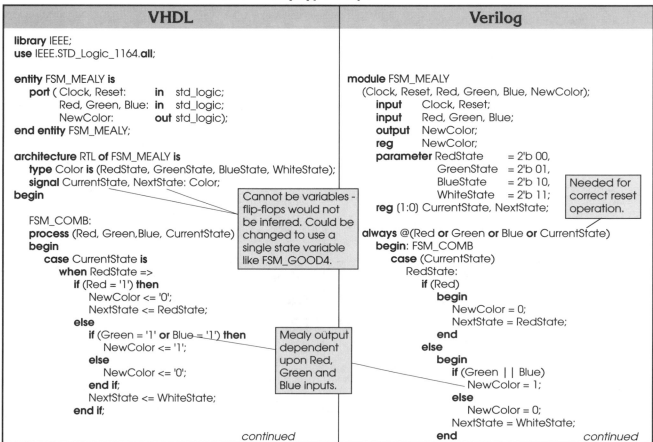

VHDL	Verilog

library IEEE;
use IEEE.STD_Logic_1164.all;
 	
entity FSM_MEALY is
   port (Clock, Reset: in std_logic;
         Red, Green, Blue: in std_logic;
         NewColor: out std_logic);
end entity FSM_MEALY;
 	
architecture RTL of FSM_MEALY is
   type Color is (RedState, GreenState, BlueState, WhiteState);
   signal CurrentState, NextState: Color;
begin
 	
   FSM_COMB:
   process (Red, Green, Blue, CurrentState)
   begin
      case CurrentState is
        when RedState =>
        if (Red = '1') then
          NewColor <= '0';
          NextState <= RedState;
        else
          if (Green = '1' or Blue = '1') then
            NewColor <= '1';
          else
            NewColor <= '0';
          end if;
          NextState <= WhiteState;
        end if;
 	
continued
	module FSM_MEALY
	   (Clock, Reset, Red, Green, Blue, NewColor);
	      input Clock, Reset;
	      input Red, Green, Blue;
	      output NewColor;
	      reg NewColor;
	      parameter RedState = 2'b 00,
	               GreenState = 2'b 01,
	               BlueState = 2'b 10,
	               WhiteState = 2'b 11;
	      reg (1:0) CurrentState, NextState;
	
	   always @(Red or Green or Blue or CurrentState)
	      begin: FSM_COMB
	        case (CurrentState)
	          RedState:
	          if (Red)
	          begin
	            NewColor = 0;
	            NextState = RedState;
	          end
	          else
	          begin
	            if (Green || Blue)
	              NewColor = 1;
	            else
	              NewColor = 0;
	            NextState = WhiteState;
	          end
	
	continued

Callout notes (VHDL): Cannot be variables - flip-flops would not be inferred. Could be changed to use a single state variable like FSM_GOOD4.

Callout notes: Mealy output dependent upon Red, Green and Blue inputs.

Callout notes (Verilog): Needed for correct reset operation.

FSM modeled with "NewColor" as a Mealy type output

VHDL	Verilog

<pre>   when GreenState =>
        if (Green = '1') then
            NewColor <= '0';
            NextState <= GreenState;
        else
          if (Red = '1' or Blue = '1') then
              NewColor <= '1';
          else
              NewColor <= '0';
          end if;
          NextState <= WhiteState;
        end if;
 	
    when BlueState =>
        if (Blue = '1') then
            NewColor <= '0';
            NextState <= BlueState;
        else
          if (Red = '1' or Green = '1') then
              NewColor <= '1';
          else
              NewColor <= '0';
          end if;
          NextState <= WhiteState;
        end if;
 	
    when WhiteState =>
        if (Red = '1') then
            NewColor <= '1';
            NextState <= RedState;
        elsif (Green = '1') then
            NewColor <= '1';
            NextState <= GreenState;
        elsif (Blue = '1') then
            NewColor <= '1';
            NextState <= BlueState;
        else
            NewColor <= '0';
            NextState <= WhiteState;
        end if;
    when others =>
        NewColor <= '0';
        NextState <= WhiteState;
    end case;
end process FSM_COMB;</pre>
	<pre> GreenState :
	        if (Green)
	          begin
	              NewColor = 0;
	              NextState = GreenState;
	          end
	        else
	          begin
	            if (Red || Blue)
	                NewColor = 1;
	            else
	                NewColor = 0;
	            NextState = WhiteState;
	          end
	    BlueState :
	        if (Blue)
	          begin
	              NewColor = 0;
	              NextState = BlueState;
	          end
	        else
	          begin
	            if (Red || Green)
	                NewColor = 1;
	            else
	                NewColor = 0;
	            NextState = WhiteState;
	          end
	    WhiteState :
	        if (Red)
	          begin
	              NewColor = 1;
	              NextState = RedState;
	          end
	        else if (Green)
	          begin
	              NewColor = 1;
	              NextState = GreenState;
	          end
	        else if (Blue)
	          begin
	              NewColor = 1;
	              NextState = BlueState;
	          end
	        else
	          begin
	              NewColor = 0;
	              NextState = WhiteState;
	          end
	        default :
	            NextState = WhiteState;
	    endcase
	end</pre>

<pre>FSM_SEQ: process (clock, reset)
begin
    if (Reset = '0') then
        CurrentState <= WhiteState;
    elsif rising_edge(Clock) then
        CurrentState <= NextState;
    end if;
end process FSM_SEQ;
 	
end architecture RTL;</pre>
	<pre>always @(posedge Clock or negedge Reset)
	    begin: FSM_SEQ
	        if (! Reset)
	            CurrentState = WhiteState;
	        else
	            CurrentState = NextState;
	    end
	
	endmodule</pre>

Sequential section with asynchronous reset.

FSM modeled with "NewColor" as a Moore type output

VHDL	Verilog

library IEEE;
use IEEE.STD_Logic_1164.**all**;
 	
entity FSM_MOORE **is**
    port (Clock, Reset: **in**   std_logic;
          Red, Green, Blue: **in**   std_logic;
          NewColor: **out** std_logic);
end entity FSM_MOORE;
 	
architecture RTL **of** FSM_MOORE **is**
    type Color **is** (RedState, GreenState, BlueState, WhiteState);
    signal CurrentState, NextState: Color;
begin
 	
    FSM_COMB: **process** (Red, Green, Blue, CurrentState)
    begin
        case CurrentState **is**
          when RedState =>
            NewColor <= '1';
            if (Red = '1') **then**
               NextState <= RedState;
            else
               NextState <= WhiteState;
            end if;
          when GreenState =>
            NewColor <= '1';
            if (Green = '1') **then**
               NextState <= GreenState;
            else
               NextState <= WhiteState;
            end if;
          when BlueState =>
            NewColor <= '1';
            if (Blue = '1') **then**
               NextState <= BlueState;
            else
               NextState <= WhiteState;
            end if;
          when WhiteState =>
            NewColor <= '0';
            if (Red = '1') **then**
               NextState <= RedState;
            elsif (Green = '1') **then**
               NextState <= GreenState;
            elsif (Blue = '1') **then**
               NextState <= BlueState;
            else
               NextState <= WhiteState;
            end if;
          when others =>
            NewColor <= '0';
            NextState <= WhiteState;
        end case;
    end process FSM_COMB:
 	
    FSM_SEQ: **process** (Clock, Reset)
    begin
        if (Reset = '0') **then**
          CurrentState <= WhiteState;
        elsif rising_edge(Clock) **then**
          CurrentState <= NextState;
        end if;
    end process FSM_SEQ;
 	
end architecture RTL;
	module FSM_MOORE
	    (Clock, Reset, Red, Green, Blue, NewColor);
	        input Clock, Reset, Red, Green, Blue;
	        output NewColor;
	        reg NewColor;
	
	        parameter RedState = 2'b 00,
	                     GreenState = 2'b 01
	                     BlueState = 2'b 10,
	                     WhiteState = 2'b 11;
	        reg (1:0) CurrentState, NextState;
	
	    always @(Red **or** Green **or** Blue **or** CurrentState)
	        begin: FSM_COMB
	          case (CurrentState)
	            RedState :
	               NewColor = 1;
	               if (Red)
	                  NextState = RedState;
	               else
	                  NextState = WhiteState;
	            GreenState :
	               NewColor = 1;
	               if (Green)
	                  NextState = GreenState;
	               else
	                  NextState = WhiteState;
	
	            BlueState :
	               NewColor = 1;
	               if (Blue)
	                  NextState = BlueState;
	               else
	                  NextState = WhiteState;
	
	            WhiteState :
	               NewColor = 0;
	               if (Red)
	                  NextState = RedState;
	               else if (Green)
	                  NextState = GreenState;
	               else if (Blue)
	                  NextState = BlueState;
	               else
	                  NextState = WhiteState;
	            default :
	              NextState = WhiteState;
	          endcase
	        end
	
	    always @(**posedge** Clock **or** **negedge** Reset)
	        begin: FSM_SEQ
	          if (! Reset)
	            CurrentState = WhiteState;
	          else
	            CurrentState = NextState;
	        end
	
	endmodule

Callout boxes:
- Current and next state must not be a variable; flip-flops would not be inferred since a variable is updated in zero delta time.
- Moore output independent of Red, Green and Blue.
- Sequential section with asynchronous reset.

Example 8.8 FSM with a Mealy and a Moore Output

These models are of the example state diagram described at the beginning of this chapter, see Figure 8.1. The model has a Mealy and a Moore type output (Y_Me and Y_Mo). The Moore type output is clearly seen to be dependent upon the state value only, while the Mealy type output is dependent upon the state value and inputs A and Hold. Because the Mealy output is dependent upon inputs, it is modeled in a section of code that infers combinational logic block, as must all Mealy type outputs.

FSM with a Mealy and a Moore Output

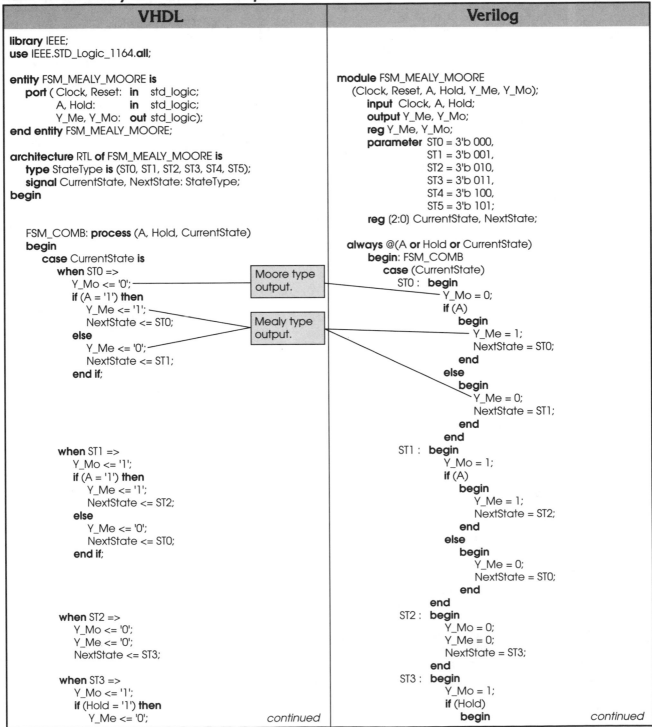

VHDL	Verilog
| ```
library IEEE;
use IEEE.STD_Logic_1164.all;

entity FSM_MEALY_MOORE is
    port ( Clock, Reset:  in    std_logic;
           A, Hold:       in    std_logic;
           Y_Me, Y_Mo:    out std_logic);
end entity FSM_MEALY_MOORE;

architecture RTL of FSM_MEALY_MOORE is
    type StateType is (ST0, ST1, ST2, ST3, ST4, ST5);
    signal CurrentState, NextState: StateType;
begin


    FSM_COMB: process (A, Hold, CurrentState)
    begin
        case CurrentState is
            when ST0 =>
                Y_Mo <= '0';
                if (A = '1') then
                    Y_Me <= '1';
                    NextState <= ST0;
                else
                    Y_Me <= '0';
                    NextState <= ST1;
                end if;




            when ST1 =>
                Y_Mo <= '1';
                if (A = '1') then
                    Y_Me <= '1';
                    NextState <= ST2;
                else
                    Y_Me <= '0';
                    NextState <= ST0;
                end if;



            when ST2 =>
                Y_Mo <= '0';
                Y_Me <= '0';
                NextState <= ST3;

            when ST3 =>
                Y_Mo <= '1';
                if (Hold = '1') then
                    Y_Me <= '0';
``` | ```
module FSM_MEALY_MOORE
    (Clock, Reset, A, Hold, Y_Me, Y_Mo);
        input  Clock, A, Hold;
        output Y_Me, Y_Mo;
        reg Y_Me, Y_Mo;
        parameter ST0 = 3'b 000,
                  ST1 = 3'b 001,
                  ST2 = 3'b 010,
                  ST3 = 3'b 011,
                  ST4 = 3'b 100,
                  ST5 = 3'b 101;
        reg (2:0) CurrentState, NextState;

    always @(A or Hold or CurrentState)
        begin: FSM_COMB
            case (CurrentState)
                ST0 : begin
                          Y_Mo = 0;
                          if (A)
                              begin
                                  Y_Me = 1;
                                  NextState = ST0;
                              end
                          else
                              begin
                                  Y_Me = 0;
                                  NextState = ST1;
                              end
                      end
                ST1 : begin
                          Y_Mo = 1;
                          if (A)
                              begin
                                  Y_Me = 1;
                                  NextState = ST2;
                              end
                          else
                              begin
                                  Y_Me = 0;
                                  NextState = ST0;
                              end
                      end
                ST2 : begin
                          Y_Mo = 0;
                          Y_Me = 0;
                          NextState = ST3;
                      end
                ST3 : begin
                          Y_Mo = 1;
                          if (Hold)
                              begin
``` |

Moore type output.

Mealy type output.

continued   *continued*

FSM with a Mealy and a Moore Output

VHDL	Verilog
| ```
                    NextState <= ST3;
            else
                Y_Me <= '1';
                if (A = '1') then
                    NextState <= ST4;
                else
                    NextState <= ST0;
                end if;
            end if;



            when ST4 =>
                Y_Mo <= '1';
                Y_Me <= '0';
                NextState <= ST3;

            when others =>
                Y_Mo <= '0';
                Y_Me <= '1';
                NextState <= ST0;
        end case;
    end process FSM_COMB;


    FSM_SEQ: process (Clock)
        if rising_edge(Clock) then
            if (Reset = '0') then
                CurrentState <= ST0;
            else
                CurrentState <= NextState;
            end if;
        end if;
    end process FSM_SEQ;

end architecture RTL;
``` | ```
                    Y_Me = 0;
                    NextState = ST3;
                end
            else
                begin
                    Y_Me = 1;
                    if (A)
                        NextState = ST4;
                    else
                        NextState = ST0;
                end
            end
        ST4 :   begin
                    Y_Mo = 1;
                    Y_Me = 0;
                    NextState = ST3;
                end
        default : begin
                    Y_Mo = 0;
                    Y_Me = 1;
                    NextState = ST0;
                end
        endcase
    end

    always @(posedge Clock)
        begin: FSM_SEQ
            if (! Reset)
                CurrentState = ST0;
            else
                CurrentState = NextState;
        end

endmodule
``` |

Sequential section with synchronous reset.

Example 8.9 FSM with sequential next state logic

The state machine in this example models an extra flip-flop in the next state logic. The state diagram, Figure 8.15, indicates the model's functional operation. The modeled architecture is shown after the HDL code.

As the state machine passes around the loop of five states, the three inputs A, B and C, cause the state machine to branch to states ThreeA, ThreeB, ThreeC, respectively, on a priority encoded basis. The synchronous reset is guaranteed to be high for at least five clock cycles, thus ensuring the state machine in state One. After a reset, the output Y1 is high for one clock cycle every five clock cycles while A remains high, likewise for input C and corresponding output Y3. However, when B goes high, its corresponding output Y2 goes high only once. The reason for this is, when the state machine is in state ThreeB, the signal BeenInState3B is set to a logic 1 from an additional flip-flop in the next state logic, and which is used to inhibit the state machine from entering state ThreeB again, until after a reset occurs.

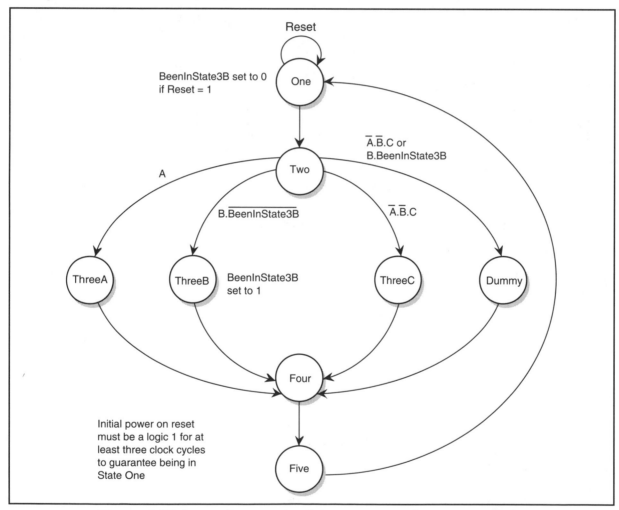

Figure 8.15 State diagram implying sequential next state logic

FSM with sequential next state logic

VHDL	Verilog
| ```
library IEEE;
use IEEE.STD_Logic_1164.all;

entity FSM_SEQ_NEXT is
    port ( Clock, Reset:  in    std_logic;
           A, B, C:       in    std_logic;
           Y1, Y2, Y3:    out   std_logic);
end entity FSM_SEQ_NEXT;

architecture RTL of FSM_SEQ_NEXT is
    type StateType is (One, Two, ThreeA, ThreeB, ThreeC,
                       Dummy, Four, Five);
    signal CurrentState: StateType;
    signal BeenInState3B: std_logic;

begin

    FSM_1: process (Clock)
    begin
        if rising_edge(Clock) then
            case (CurrentState) is
                when One =>
                    if (Reset = '1') then
                        BeenInState3B <= '0';
                        CurrentState <= One;
                    else
                        CurrentState <= Two;
                    end if;


                when Two =>
                    if (A = '1') then
                        CurrentState <= ThreeA;
                    elsif (B = '1') then
                        if (BeenInState3B = '1') then
                            CurrentState <= Dummy;
                        else
                            CurrentState <= ThreeB;
                        end if;
                    elsif (C = '1') then
                        CurrentState <= ThreeC;
                    else
                        CurrentState <= Dummy;
                    end if;
                when ThreeA =>
                    CurrentState <= Four;

                when ThreeB =>
                    BeenInState3B <= '1';
                    CurrentState <= Four;


                when ThreeC =>
                    CurrentState <= Four;
                when Dummy =>
                    CurrentState <= Four;
                when Four =>
                    CurrentState <= Five;
                when Five =>
                    CurrentState <= One;
                when others =>
                    CurrentState <= One;
            end case;
        end if;
``` | ```
module FSM_SEQ_NEXT (Clock, Reset, A, B, C, Y1, Y2, Y3);
    input     Clock, Reset;
    input     A, B, C;
    output    Y1, Y2, Y3;
    reg       Y1, Y2, Y3;
    parameter One    = 3'b 000,
              Two    = 3'b 001,
              ThreeA = 3'b 010,
              ThreeB = 3'b 011,
              ThreeC = 3'b 100,
              Dummy  = 3'b 101,
              Four   = 3'b 110,
              Five   = 3'b 111;
    reg [2:0] CurrentState;
    reg       BeenInState3B;

    always @(posedge Clock)
        begin: CURR_NEXT_LOGIC
            case (CurrentState)
                One :
                    if (Reset)
                        begin
                            BeenInState3B = 0;
                            CurrentState = One;
                        end
                    else
                        CurrentState = Two;
                Two :
                    if (A)
                        CurrentState = ThreeA;
                    else if (B == 1)
                        if (BeenInState3B)
                            CurrentState = Dummy;
                        else
                            CurrentState = ThreeB;
                    else if (C == 1)
                        CurrentState = ThreeC;
                    else
                        CurrentState = Dummy;

                ThreeA :
                    CurrentState = Four;
                ThreeB :
                    begin
                        BeenInState3B = 1;
                        CurrentState = Four;
                    end


                ThreeC :
                    CurrentState = Four;
                Dummy :
                    CurrentState = Four;
                Four :
                    CurrentState = Five;
                Five :
                    CurrentState = One;
            endcase
        end
``` |

Callout 1 (between columns): Synchronous reset must be at logic 1 for 3 clock cycles to guarantee the state machine is in state "One".

Callout 2 (between columns): "BeenInState3B" set to logic 0 when in state "One" and "Reset" is at logic 1.

Callout 3 (between columns): "BeenInState3B" set to logic 1 when the state machine is in "StateThreeB".

continued   continued

FSM with sequential next state logic

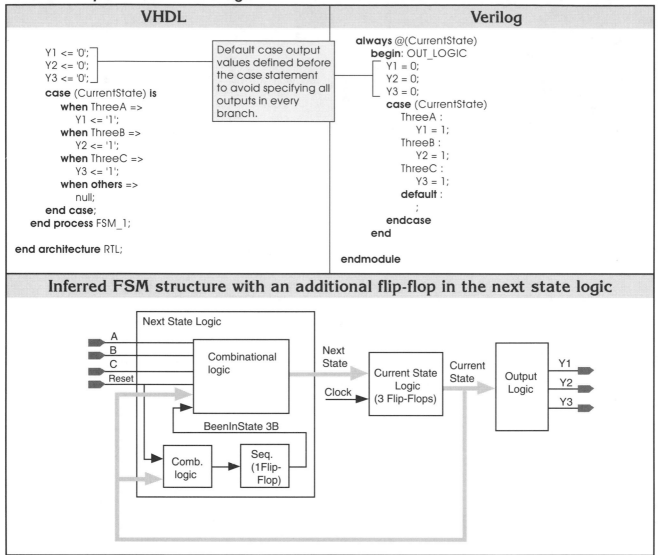

VHDL	Verilog

```
      Y1 <= '0';
      Y2 <= '0';
      Y3 <= '0';
      case (CurrentState) is
         when ThreeA =>
            Y1 <= '1';
         when ThreeB =>
            Y2 <= '1';
         when ThreeC =>
            Y3 <= '1';
         when others =>
            null;
      end case;
   end process FSM_1;

end architecture RTL;
```

Default case output values defined before the case statement to avoid specifying all outputs in every branch.

```
always @(CurrentState)
   begin: OUT_LOGIC
      Y1 = 0;
      Y2 = 0;
      Y3 = 0;
      case (CurrentState)
         ThreeA :
            Y1 = 1;
         ThreeB :
            Y2 = 1;
         ThreeC :
            Y3 = 1;
         default :
            ;
      endcase
   end

endmodule
```

Inferred FSM structure with an additional flip-flop in the next state logic

Example 8.10 FSM with sequential output logic

A state machine with an embedded counter is modeled to the state diagram; Figure 8.16. The counter forms part of the state machine's output logic as shown by the inferred structure.

After a reset, the state machine starts in state One, and the counter in the output logic is set to zero. After the reset, the state machine cycles around a loop of four states. There are two branches for the second stage of the loop, and are represented by the two states, TwoCount and TwoNoCount. When the input EnableCount is high, state TwoCount is used in the loop, otherwise TwoNoCount is used. Therefore, while EnableCount is high the counter is incremented every four clock cycles. The counter's output is output from the model, together with an indication of whether it is greater than, or equal to 25.

Notice this structure causes the counters to be incremented one clock cycle after the state machine has been in State TwoCount. In order to cause the counter to increment at the same time the state machine enters state TwoCount, the next state signal should be passed into the output logic, instead of the current state signal as modeled in this example.

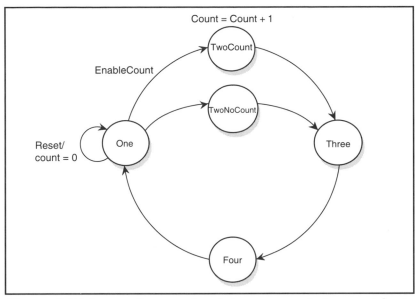

Figure 8.16 State diagram implying sequential output logic

FSM with sequential output logic

VHDL	Verilog

library IEEE;
use IEEE.STD_Logic_1164.**all**, IEEE.Numeric_STD.**all**;
 	
entity FSM_SEQ_OUT **is**
   port (Clock, Reset: **in**   std_logic;
        EnableCount: **in**   std_logic;
        CountGE25:   **out** std_logic;
        Count: **out** unsigned (4 **downto** 0);
end entity FSM_SEQ_OUT;
 	
architecture RTL **of** FSM_SEQ_OUT **is**
   type StateType **is** (One, TwoCount, TwoNoCount, Three,
                  Four);
   signal CurrentState: StateType;
begin
 	
   FSM_ACC: **process** (Clock)
      variable Count_v: unsigned(4 **downto** 0);
   begin
      if rising_edge(Clock) **then**
         case CurrentState **is**
            when One =>
               if (Reset = '1') **then**
                  Count_v := (**others** => '0');
                  CurrentState <= One;
               elsif (EnableCount = '1') **then**
                  CurrentState <= TwoCount;
               else
                  CurrentState <= TwoNoCount;
               end if;
 	
            when TwoCount =>
               Count_v := Count_v + 1;
               CurrentState <= Three;
	module FSM_SEQ_OUT
	   (Clock, Reset, EnableCount, CountGE25, Count);
	   input Clock, Reset, EnableCount;
	   output CountGE25;
	   output [4:0] Count;
	   reg CountGE25;
	   reg [4:0] Count;
	   parameter One = 3'b 000,
	               TwoCount = 3'b 001,
	               TwoNoCount = 3'b 010,
	               Three = 3'b 011,
	               Four = 3'b 110;
	   reg [2:0] CurrentState;
	
	   always @(**posedge** Clock)
	      begin: FSM_ACC
	         case (CurrentState)
	
	         One :
	           if (Reset)
	             begin
	                Count = 0;
	                CurrentState = One;
	             end
	           else if (EnableCount)
	             CurrentState = TwoCount;
	           else
	             CurrentState = TwoNoCount;
	        TwoCount :
	         begin
	           Count = Count + 1;
	           CurrentState = Three;
	         end

continued	continued

Counter embedded in FSM model.

FSM with sequential output logic

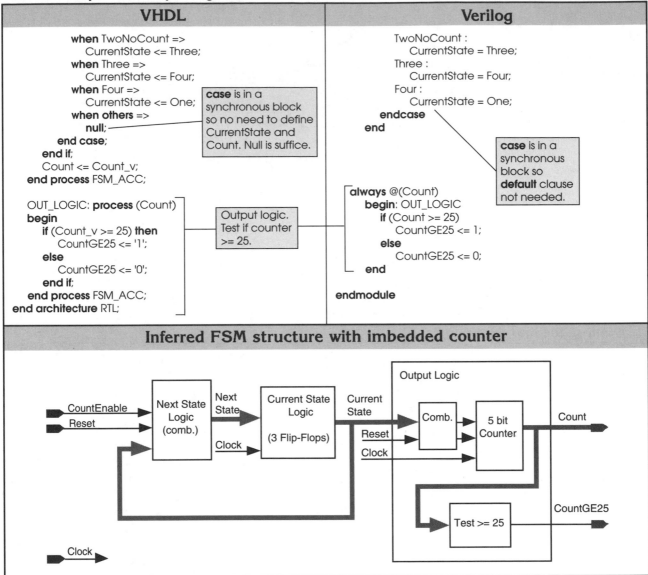

VHDL	Verilog
<pre>   when TwoNoCount =>
            CurrentState <= Three;
        when Three =>
            CurrentState <= Four;
        when Four =>
            CurrentState <= One;
        when others =>
            null;
        end case;
    end if;
    Count <= Count_v;
end process FSM_ACC;

OUT_LOGIC: process (Count)
begin
    if (Count_v >= 25) then
        CountGE25 <= '1';
    else
        CountGE25 <= '0';
    end if;
end process FSM_ACC;
end architecture RTL;</pre> | <pre>   TwoNoCount :
            CurrentState = Three;
        Three :
            CurrentState = Four;
        Four :
            CurrentState = One;
        endcase
    end

    always @(Count)
        begin: OUT_LOGIC
            if (Count >= 25)
                CountGE25 <= 1;
            else
                CountGE25 <= 0;
        end

endmodule</pre> |

case is in a synchronous block so no need to define CurrentState and Count. Null is suffice.

case is in a synchronous block so **default** clause not needed.

Output logic. Test if counter >= 25.

Inferred FSM structure with imbedded counter

Example 8.11 FSM with sequential next and output state logic - Blackjack

The models in this example are functionally the same, imply the same architecture and synthesize to the same circuit as those in Example 8.6. The state diagram is therefore the same, Figure 8.11, and the implied architecture is also the same, Figure 8.12. Example 8.6 was specifically designed with separate input, next state, current state, output logic and data path logic to show the effect of different state encoding. This example combines all these blocks into one **process** (VHDL) and **always** block (Verilog) reducing the code considerably. There is no right or wrong coding method for any model except that it should be easy to comprehend, that is, do not trade off comprehension for the shortest and most efficient use of the code. Example 8.6 and this one demonstrates these two extremes.

Sequential state encoding is used and, unlike Example 8.6, is defined within the model. There is no reference to any next state signals, but these exist by implication; signals CurrentState and NextState from Example 8.6 have been replaced with the signal State. The reduced number of signals can be seen by the reduced number of signals in the simulated waveforms, Figure 8.17.

Blackjack Game Machine with condensed code

VHDL	Verilog

```vhdl
library IEEE;
use IEEE.STD_Logic_1164.all, IEEE.Numeric_STD.all;

entity FSM_SEQ_NEXT_OUT is
    port ( Clock, Reset:        in   std_logic;
           GameOn, CardDelt:    in   std_logic;
           DeltCardValue:       in   unsigned(3 downto 0);
           TotalCardValue_out:  out  unsigned(4 downto 0);
           Draw, Hold, Bust:    out  std_logic);
end entity FSM_SEQ_NEXT_OUT;


architecture RTL of FSM_SEQ_NEXT_OUT is
    constant Ace:    integer := 1;
    constant Two:    integer := 2;
    constant Three:  integer := 3;
    constant Four:   integer := 4;
    constant Five:   integer := 5;
    constant Six:    integer := 6;
    constant Seven:  integer := 7;
    constant Eight:  integer := 8;
    constant Nine:   integer := 9;
    constant Ten:    integer := 10;
    constant Jack:   integer := 11;
    constant Queen:  integer := 12;
    constant King:   integer := 13;

    -- Sequential state encoding
    type SeqStateType is
        (Rest, WaitCard1, Card1Delt, Card1Ace, Card1Pic,
        Card1_2to10, DrawNextCard, NextCardDelt,
        NextCardAce, NextCardPic, NextCard_2to10,
        TestGE15, TestGE22, AceAs1, ShowHold, ShowBust);
    attribute ENUM_TYPE_ENCODING: string;
    attribute ENUM_TYPE_ENCODING of SeqStateType: type is
        "0000 0001 0010 0011 0100 0101 0110 0111 " &
        "1000 1001 1010 1011 1100 1101 1110 1111";




    signal State: SeqStateType;
    signal AcesEq11: integer range 0 to 4;
    signal TotalCardValue: integer range 0 to 31;

begin
    -------------------------------------------
    -- FSM with additional counters
    -- integrated within the model.
    -------------------------------------------
    CURR_SEQ_NEXT_OUT: process (Clock)
    begin
        if rising_edge(Clock) then
            if (Reset = '1') then
                State <= Rest;
            else
                case (State) is
                    when Rest =>
```

```verilog
module FSM_SEQ_NEXT_OUT
    (Clock, Reset, GameOn, CardDelt, DeltCardValue,
    TotalCardValue, Draw, Hold, Bust);
    input   Clock, Reset, GameOn, CardDelt;
    input   [3:0] DeltCardValue;
    output  [4:0] TotalCardValue;
    output  Draw, Hold, Bust;
    reg [4:0] TotalCardValue;
    reg Draw, Hold, Bust;

    // DeltCardValue
    parameter Ace     = 1,
              Two     = 2,
              Three   = 3,
              Four    = 4,
              Five    = 5,
              Six     = 6,
              Seven   = 7,
              Eight   = 8,
              Nine    = 9,
              Ten     = 10,
              Jack    = 11,
              Queen   = 12,
              King    = 13;

    // Sequential state encoding
    parameter Rest            = 0,
              WaitCard1       = 1,
              Card1Delt       = 2,
              Card1Ace        = 3,
              Card1Pic        = 4,
              Card1_2to10     = 5,
              DrawNextCard    = 6,
              NextCardDelt    = 7,
              NextCardAce     = 8,
              NextCardPic     = 9,
              NextCard_2to10  = 10,
              TestGE15        = 11,
              TestGE22        = 12,
              AceAs1          = 13,
              ShowHold        = 14,
              ShowBust        = 15;

    reg [3:0] State;
    reg [2:0] AcesEq11;


    //-----------------------------------------
    // FSM with additional counters
    // integrated within the model.
    //-----------------------------------------
    always @(posedge Clock)
        begin: CURR_SEQ_NEXT_OUT
            if (Reset)
                State = Rest;
            else
                case (State)

                    Rest:
                        begin
```

continued | continued

Blackjack Game Machine with condensed code

Datapath integral to the FSM
(see Figure 8.12)

VHDL	Verilog
| ```
TotalCardValue <= 0;
AcesEq11 <= 0;
if (GameOn = '1') then
    State <= WaitCard1;
else
    State <= Rest;
end if;

when WaitCard1 =>
 if (CardDelt = '1') then
    State <= Card1Delt;
else
    State <= WaitCard1;
end if;
when Card1Delt =>
 if (DeltCardValue = Ace) then
    State <= Card1Ace;
 elsif (DeltCardValue = Jack or
        DeltCardValue = Queen or
        DeltCardValue = King) then
    State <= Card1Pic;
else
    State <= Card1_2to10;
end if;
when Card1Ace =>
    AcesEq11 <= AcesEq11 + 1;
    TotalCardValue <= TotalCardValue + 11;
    State <= DrawNextCard;


when Card1Pic =>
    TotalCardValue <= TotalCardValue + 10;
    State <= DrawNextCard;


when Card1_2to10 =>
    TotalCardValue <= TotalCardValue +
                      to_integer(DeltCardValue);
    State <= DrawNextCard;


when DrawNextCard =>
 if (CardDelt = '1') then
    State <= NextCardDelt;
else
    State <= DrawNextCard;
end if;
when NextCardDelt =>
 if (DeltCardValue = Ace) then
    State <= NextCardAce;
 elsif ( DeltCardValue = Jack or
         DeltCardValue = Queen or
         DeltCardValue = King) then
    State <= NextCardPic;
else
    State <= NextCard_2to10;
end if;
when NextCardAce =>
    AcesEq11 <= AcesEq11 + 1;
    TotalCardValue <= TotalCardValue + 11;
    State <= TestGE15;
``` | ```
TotalCardValue = 0;
AcesEq11 = 0;
if (GameOn)
    State = WaitCard1;
else
    State = Rest;
end

WaitCard1:
 if (CardDelt)
    State = Card1Delt;
else
    State = WaitCard1;

Card1Delt:
 if (DeltCardValue == Ace)
    State = Card1Ace;
 else if (DeltCardValue == Jack ||
          DeltCardValue == Queen ||
          DeltCardValue == King)
    State = Card1Pic;
else
    State = Card1_2to10;

Card1Ace:
 begin
    AcesEq11 = AcesEq11 + 1;
    TotalCardValue = TotalCardValue + 11;
    State = DrawNextCard;
 end
Card1Pic:
 begin
    TotalCardValue = TotalCardValue + 10;
    State = DrawNextCard;
 end
Card1_2to10:
 begin
    TotalCardValue =  TotalCardValue +
                      DeltCardValue;
    State = DrawNextCard;
 end
DrawNextCard:
 if (CardDelt)
    State = NextCardDelt;
else
    State = DrawNextCard;

NextCardDelt:
 if (DeltCardValue == Ace)
    State = NextCardAce;
 else if (DeltCardValue == Jack ||
          DeltCardValue == Queen ||
          DeltCardValue == King)
    State = NextCardPic;
else
    State = NextCard_2to10;

NextCardAce:
 begin
    AcesEq11 = AcesEq11 + 1;
    TotalCardValue = TotalCardValue + 11;
    State = TestGE15;
 end
``` |
| *continued* | *continued* |

Blackjack Game Machine with condensed code

Datapath integral to the FSM
(see Figure 8.12)

VHDL	Verilog
| ```
when NextCardPic =>
  TotalCardValue <= TotalCardValue + 10;
  State <= TestGE15;


when NextCard_2to10 =>
  TotalCardValue <= TotalCardValue +
              to_integer(DeltCardValue);
  State <= TestGE15;


when TestGE15 =>
  if (TotalCardValue >= 15) then
    State <= TestGE22;
  else
    State <= DrawNextCard;
  end if;
when TestGE22 =>
  if (TotalCardValue >= 22) then
    if (AcesEq11 = 0) then
      State <= ShowBust;
    else
      State <= AceAs1;
    end if;
  else
    State <= ShowHold;
  end if;
when AceAs1 =>
  AcesEq11 <= AcesEq11 - 1;
  TotalCardValue <= TotalCardValue - 10;
  State <= TestGE15;


when ShowHold =>
  State <= Rest;
when ShowBust =>
  Bust <= '1';
  State <= Rest;
when others =>
  State <= Rest;
    end case;
  end if;
end if;
TotalCardValue_out <= to_unsigned(TotalCardValue, 5);

Draw <= '0';
Hold <= '0';
Bust <= '0';
case (State) is
  when DrawNextCard =>
    Draw <= '1';
  when ShowHold =>
    Hold <= '1';
  when ShowBust =>
    Bust <= '1';
  when others =>
    Draw <= '0';
    Hold <= '0';
    Bust  <= '0';
end case;

end process CURR_SEQ_NEXT_OUT;

end architecture RTL;
``` | ```
NextCardPic:
  begin
    TotalCardValue = TotalCardValue + 10;
    State = TestGE15;
  end
NextCard_2to10:
  begin
    TotalCardValue = TotalCardValue +
                DeltCardValue;
    State = TestGE15;
  end
TestGE15:
  if (TotalCardValue >= 15)
    State = TestGE22;
  else
    State = DrawNextCard;

TestGE22:
  if (TotalCardValue >= 22)
    if (AcesEq11 == 0)
      State = ShowBust;
    else
      State = AceAs1;
  else
    State = ShowHold;


AceAs1:
  begin
    AcesEq11 = AcesEq11 - 1;
    TotalCardValue = TotalCardValue - 10;
    State = TestGE15;
  end
ShowHold:
  State = Rest;
ShowBust:
  State = Rest;

default:
  State = Rest;
    endcase
  end
end


always @(State)
  begin: OUT_LOGIC
    Draw  = 0;
    Hold  = 0;
    Bust  = 0;
    case (State)
      DrawNextCard: Draw = 1;
      ShowHold:     Hold  = 1;
      ShowBust:     Bust  = 1;
      default:  begin
              Draw  = 0;
              Hold  = 0;
              Bust  = 0;
            end
    endcase
  end

endmodule
``` |

Default value for outputs defined at beginning of **process/always.**

Assignments to the three outputs Draw, Hold and Bust are separate from the current/next state code to avoid inferring three unecessary flip-flops.

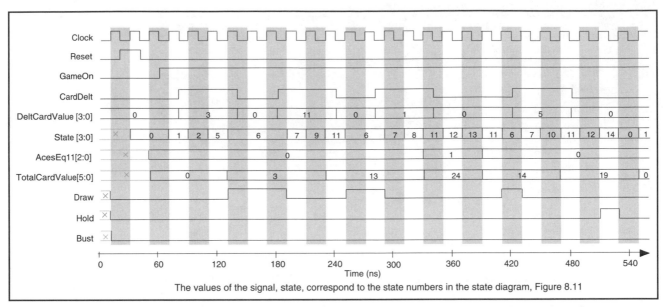

Figure 8.17 Signal waveforms for Blackjack Machine with condensed code

Example 8.12 Unidirectional interactive FSMs

Three differently modeled state machine control paths are used to control the same data path; see Figure 8.18. Control Path 1 is modeled using a master state machine, which controls three slave state machines. Control Path 2 uses three state machines, with a series chain of control between them. Control Path 3 is modeled using a single state machine. All three control paths are functionally equivalent.

Data path

The data path structure, Figure 8.19, and the HDL models are included in this example. The data path does not perform any particular function, but is long enough to demonstrate the different FSM configurations used for its control. The data path accepts sequences of either three or four, 4-bit values on the input, and processes them through the datapath, to provide sequences of either two or three, 9-bit values on the output. The data path is controlled by the control path to perform the following equations. The input data is A, B, C, and D, the output data is Y1, Y2 and Y3.

> Sequence of four inputs (ThreeOnly = 0)
> > Y1 = A.B + A.C
> > Y2 = A.D + B.C
> > Y3 = B.D + C.D
> Sequence of three inputs (ThreeOnly = 1)
> > Y1 = A.B + A.C
> > Y4 = B.C

The sequential flow of data passing through the data path is indicated by the signal waveforms; Figure 8.23. Because six multiplications are needed when four 4-bit input data is used, and there is only one multiplier, the fastest throughput of consecutive data is every six clock cycles. When only three 4-bit input data is used, only three multiplications are needed, and so consecutive sequences of input data are possible.

Control paths

The structural configuration of the three control paths are illustrated in Figure 8.18. Each control path provides the same control signals to the data path.

The description of the three control paths follow; their state diagrams are illustrated in Figures 8.20, 8.21 and 8.22.

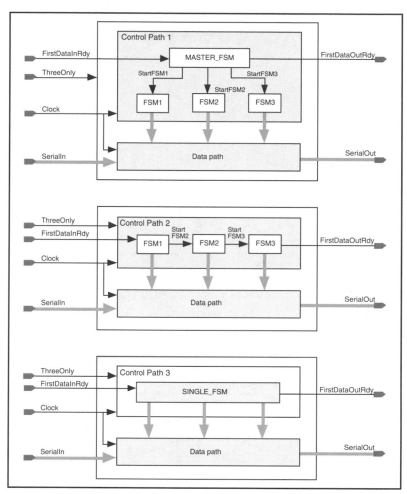

Figure 8.18 Three FSM control path configurations

Control Path 1. The master state machine FSM_MASTER, outputs a single control signal to each of the three slave state machines StartFSM1, StartFSM2 and StartFSM3. These signals trigger the appropriate slave state machine FSM1, FSM2 or FSM3, into cycling through its particular sequence of events. State machine, FSM1, is dedicated to providing four enable signals used to clock the serial input data into the appropriate holding register. State machine, FSM2, provides select signals used to select which of the two held inputs to multiply together, and also provides the enable signals used to clock the multiplied result into the appropriate state register. State machine, FSM3, simply provides the select lines used to select which result to output.

No. bits	Signal names	Comment
1	En_A En_B En_C En_D	Enables serial input data to be clocked into the appropriate 4-bit holding register.
2	Mux1_Sel Mux2_Sel	Selects which of A B C or D to multiply together.
1	En_AB En_AC En_AD En_BC En_BD En_CD	Enables the multiplied result to be clocked into the appropriate 8-bit register.
2	Mux3_Sel	Selects in turn, which of the four 9-bit results to output.

Control Path 2. The three state machines FSM1, FSM2 and FSM3 generate the same data path control signals as those in Control Path 1. The difference is that FSM1 also outputs the control signal StartFSM2 to FSM2, and FSM2 outputs the control signal StartFSM3 to FSM3.

Control Path 3. Modeled using a single state machine. The two main loops in the state diagram, Figure 8.22, indicate the condition when either three or four input words are used.

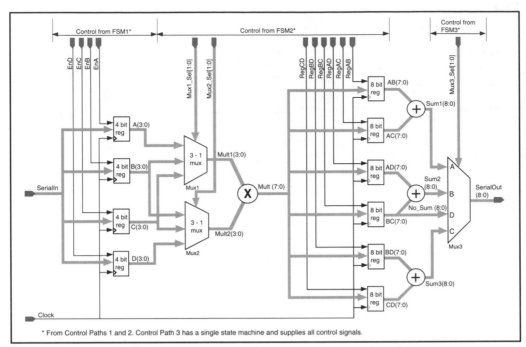

Figure 8.19 Data Path controlled from Control Path 1, 2 or 3

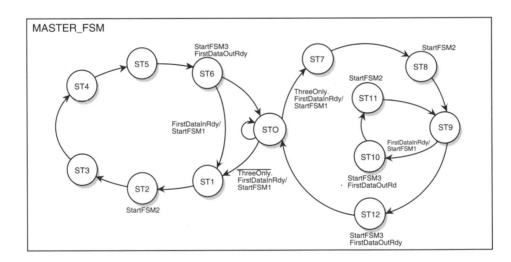

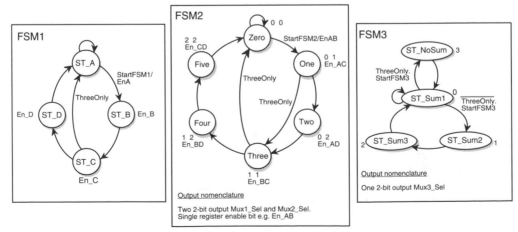

Figure 8.20 State diagrams for Control Path 1

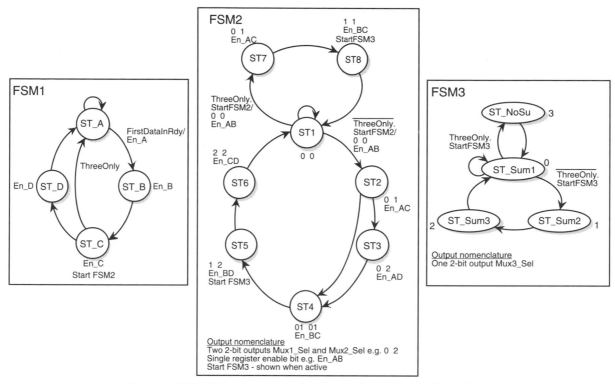

Figure 8.21 Three state diagrams for Control Path 2

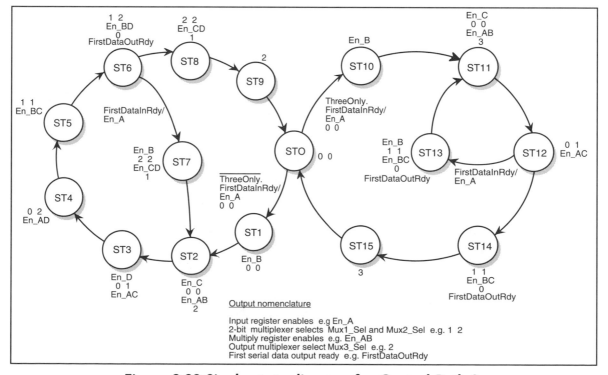

Figure 8.22 Single state diagram for Control Path 3

HDL Models - Data Path

The data path models have been split into three stages; STAGE1, STAGE2, and STAGE3. Each stage is controlled by the corresponding state machine, FSM1, FSM2 and FSM3, in control paths 1 and 2. The VHDL concurrent signal assignments and Verilog continuous assignments for signals Sum1, Sum2, Sum3 and NoSum, are not controlled by the controller, and are positioned between stages two and three. These assignments are not absolutely necessary as they could have been combined into STAGE3. For example, the assignment

        Sum1 <= AB + AC;

could be removed, and Sum1 replaced with AB + AC in the **case** statement of STAGE3. Explicit assignments to Sum1, Sum2, Sum3 and NoSum have been used so that they exist as data objects in the models, which can be monitored during simulation. It also makes comprehending the functional operation slightly easier.

Datapath

VHDL	Verilog

`library IEEE;`
`use IEEE.STD_Logic_1164.`**`all`**`, IEEE.Numeric_STD.`**`all`**`;`
 	
`entity HIER_FSMS_DATAPATH is`
`    port ( Clock:                    in   std_logic;`
`        En_A,En_B,En_C,En_D:  in   std_logic;`
`        Mux1_Sel, Mux2_Sel:     in   integer range 0 to 2;`
`        En_AB, En_AC, En_AD,`
`        En_BC, En_BD, En_CD:  in   std_logic;`
`        Mux3_Sel:                 in   integer range 0 to 3;`
`        SerialIn:                   in   unsigned(3 downto 0);`
`        SerialOut:                 out unsigned(8 downto 0);`
`end entity HIER_FSMS_DATAPATH;`
 	
`architecture RTL of HIER_FSMS_DATAPATH is`
`    signal A, B, C, D:            integer range 0 to 15;`
`    signal Mult1, Mult2:         integer range 0 to 15;`
`    signal Mult:                   integer range 0 to 255;`
`    signal AB, AC, AD, BC, BD, CD: integer range 0 to 255;`
`    signal Sum1,Sum2,Sum3,NoSum:integer range 0 to 511;`
`begin`
	`module HIERFSMS_DATAPATH`
	`    ( Clock, En_A, En_B, En_C, En_D,`
	`    Mux1_Sel, Mux2_Sel,`
	`    En_AB, En_AC, En_AD, En_BC, En_BD, En_CD,`
	`    Mux3_Sel, SerialIn, SerialOut);`
	
	`    input           Clock;`
	`    input           En_A, En_B, En_C, En_D;`
	`    input    (1:0)  Mux1_Sel, Mux2_Sel;`
	`    input           En_AB,En_AC,En_AD,En_BC,En_BD,En_CD;`
	`    input    (1:0)  Mux3_Sel;`
	`    input    (3:0)  SerialIn;`
	`    output   (8:0)  SerialOut;`
	`    reg      (8:0)  SerialOut;`
	
	`    reg  (3:0) A, B, C, D;`
	`    reg  (3:0) Mult1, Mult2;`
	`    reg  (7:0) Mult;`
	`    reg  (7:0) AB, AC, AD, BC, BD, CD;`
	`    wire (8:0) Sum1, Sum2, Sum3, NoSum;`

`-------------------------------------------------`
`-- Datapath stage 1 controlled by FSM1`
`-------------------------------------------------`
`STAGE1: process (Clock)`
`begin`
`    if rising_edge(Clock) then`
`        if (En_A = '1') then`
`            A <= SerialIn;`
`        end if;`
`        if (En_B = '1') then`
`            B <= SerialIn;`
`        end if;`
`        if (En_C = '1') then`
`            C <= SerialIn;`
`        end if;`
`        if (En_D = '1') then`
`            D <= SerialIn;`
`        end if;`
`    end if;`
`end process STAGE1;`
	`//-----------------------------------------------`
	`// Datapath stage 1 controlled by FSM1`
	`//-----------------------------------------------`
	`always @(posedge Clock)`
	`    begin: STAGE1`
	`        if (En_A)`
	`            A = SerialIn;`
	`        if (En_B )`
	`            B = SerialIn;`
	`        if (En_C )`
	`            C = SerialIn;`
	`        if (En_D )`
	`            D = SerialIn;`
	`    end`

continued	*continued*

Datapath

VHDL	Verilog

``
-- 	
-- Datapath stage 2 controlled by FSM2
-- 	
STAGE2: process (A, B, C, D, Mux1_Sel, Mux2_Sel, Clock)
begin
   case (Mux1_Sel) is
      when 0 =>   Mult1 <= A;
      when 1 =>   Mult1 <= B;
      when 2 =>   Mult1 <= C;
      when others =>   Mult1 <= A;
   end case;
   case (Mux2_Sel) is
      when 0 =>   Mult2 <= B;
      when 1 =>   Mult2 <= C;
      when 2 =>   Mult2 <= D;
      when others =>   Mult2 <= B;
   end case;
   Mult <= Mult1 * Mult2;
   if rising_edge(Clock) then
      if (En_AB = '1') then
         AB <= Mult;
      end if;
      if (En_AC = '1') then
         AC <= Mult;
      end if;
      if (En_AD = '1') then
         AD <= Mult;
      end if;
      if (En_BC = '1') then
         BC <= Mult;
      end if;
      if (En_BD = '1') then
         BD <= Mult;
      end if;
      if (En_CD = '1') then
         CD <= Mult;
      end if;
   end if;
end process STAGE2;
 	
-- 	
-- Generate sum values (Not FSM controlled)
-- 	
Sum1   <= resize(AB, 9) + resize(AC, 9);
Sum2   <= resize(AD, 9) + resize(BC, 9);
Sum3   <= resize(BD, 9) + resize(CD, 9);
NoSum <= resize(BC, 9);
 	
-- 	
-- Datapath stage 3 controlled by FSM3
-- 	
STAGE3: process (Sum1, Sum2, Sum3, NoSum, Mux3_Sel)
begin
   case (Mux3_Sel) is
      when 0 =>   SerialOut <= Sum1;
      when 1 =>   SerialOut <= Sum2;
      when 2 =>   SerialOut <= Sum3;
      when 3 =>   SerialOut <= NoSum;
      when others =>   SerialOut <= Sum1;
   end case;
end process STAGE3;
 	
end architecture RTL;
``
	``
	//---------------------------------------
	// Datapath stage 2 controlled by FSM2
	//---------------------------------------
	always @(A or B or C or D or Mux1_Sel or Mux2_Sel)
	   begin: STAGE2_A
	      case (Mux1_Sel)
	         2'b 00 : Mult1 = A;
	         2'b 01 : Mult1 = B;
	         2'b 10 : Mult1 = C;
	         default : Mult1 = A;
	      endcase
	      case (Mux2_Sel)
	         2'b 00 : Mult2 = B;
	         2'b 01 : Mult2 = C;
	         2'b 10 : Mult2 = D;
	         default : Mult2 = B;
	      endcase
	      Mult = Mult1 * Mult2;
	   end
	
	always @(posedge Clock)
	   begin: STAGE2_B
	      if (En_AB)
	         AB = Mult;
	      if (En_AC)
	         AC = Mult;
	      if (En_AD)
	         AD = Mult;
	      if (En_BC)
	         BC = Mult;
	      if (En_BD)
	         BD = Mult;
	      if (En_CD)
	         CD = Mult;
	   end
	
	// --------------------------------------
	// Generate sum values (Not FSM controlled)
	// --------------------------------------
	assign Sum1 = AB + AC;
	assign Sum2 = AD + BC;
	assign Sum3 = BD + CD;
	assign NoSum = BC;
	
	// --------------------------------------
	// Datapath stage 3 controlled by FSM3
	// --------------------------------------
	always @(Sum1 or Sum2 or Sum3 or NoSum or Mux3_Sel)
	   begin: STAGE3
	      case (Mux3_Sel)
	         2'b 00 : SerialOut = Sum1;
	         2'b 01 : SerialOut = Sum2;
	         2'b 10 : SerialOut = Sum3;
	         2'b 11 : SerialOut = NoSum;
	         default : SerialOut = Sum1;
	      endcase
	   end
	
	endmodule
	``

HDL Models - Control Paths

The following description references numbers in the code of Control Path 1, but applies equally to Control Paths 2 and 3.

① The VHDL state encoding is defined as starting from ST0 and not ST1. This is because the synthesis tool automatically assigns sequential states starting from 0, and so when simulated, ST1 has a value of 1 and not 0. However, if for example the state type for FSM2 was

type StateTypeFSM2 **is** (One,Two,Three,Four,Five,Six);

the state encoding would still be

000, 001, 010, 011, 100, 101, 110.

This is fine, but when simulated, the signal values of CurrStateFSM2 and NextStateFSM2 are at logic 0 when in state One, and 1 when in state Two etc. This introduces unnecessary confusion.

② Defining a default logic 0 for the four outputs before the **case** statement avoids having to explicitly define their value in every branch of the **case** statement including the **others** (VHDL) and **default** (Verilog) branches. Either way this is necessary to avoid inferring latches in this combinational part of the state machine. The next state signal, NextStateMasterFSM, does not need a default value assigned to it before the **case** statement, as it is always assigned a new value in every branch of the **case** statement.

③ As default output values are defined before the **case** statement, they do not need to be repeated in the **others** and **default** clauses. However, as a default next state value is not defined before the **case** statement, it is needed in the **others**/**default** clauses to avoid inferring unwanted latches.

Control Path 1 - Master FSM controlling three other FSMs

VHDL	Verilog

VHDL:

```vhdl
library IEEE;
use IEEE.STD_Logic_1164.all, IEEE.Numeric_STD.all;

entity HIERFSMS_CNTLPATH1 is
    port ( Clock, Reset, ThreeOnly, FirstDataInRdy: in std_logic;
           En_A, En_B, En_C, En_D:  out std_logic;
           Mux1_Sel, Mux2_Sel:  out integer range 0 to 2;
           En_AB, En_AC, En_AD,
           En_BC, En_BD, En_CD: out std_logic;
           Mux3_Sel:  out integer range 0 to 3;
           FirstDataOutRdy:  out std_logic);
end entity HIERFSMS_CNTLPATH1;




architecture RTL of HIERFSMS_CNTLPATH1 is
    type  StateTypeMasterFSM is (ST0, ST1, ST2, ST3, ST4,
                                 ST5, ST6, ST7, ST8, ST9,       (1)
                                 ST10, ST11, ST12);

    type  StateTypeFSM1 is (ST_A, ST_B, ST_C, ST_D);
    type  StateTypeFSM2 is (One, Two, Three, Four, Five, Six);  (1)
    type  StateTypeFSM3 is (ST_Sum1, ST_Sum2,
                            ST_Sum3, ST_NoSum);

    signal CurrStateMasterFSM,
           NextStateMasterFSM: StateTypeMasterFSM;
    signal StartFSM1, StartFSM2, StartFSM3: std_ulogic;
    signal CurrStateFSM1, NextStateFSM1: StateTypeFSM1;
    signal CurrStateFSM2, NextStateFSM2: StateTypeFSM2;
    signal CurrStateFSM3, NextStateFSM3: StateTypeFSM3;
begin


    --------------------
    -- MASTER FSM
    --------------------
    MASTER_FSM_COMB:
    process (FirstInDataRdy, ThreeOnly, CurrStateMasterFSM)
    begin
        StartFSM1 <= '0';
        StartFSM2 <= '0';                          (2)
        StartFSM3 <= '0';
        FirstDataOutRdy <= '0';
        case (CurrStateMasterFSM) is
            when ST0  => if (FirstDataInRdy = '1') then
                            StartFSM1 <= '1';
                            if (ThreeOnly = '1') then
                                NextStateMasterFSM <= ST7;
                            else
                                NextStateMasterFSM <= ST1;
                            end if;
                         else
                            NextStateMasterFSM <= ST0;
                         end if;
            when ST1  => NextStateMasterFSM <= ST2;
            when ST2  => StartFSM2 <= '1';
                         NextStateMasterFSM <= ST3;

            when ST3  => NextStateMasterFSM <= ST4;
```

continued

Verilog:

```verilog
module HIERFSMS_CNTLPATH1
( Clock, Reset, ThreeOnly, FirstDataInRdy,
  En_A, En_B, En_C, En_D,
  Mux1_Sel, Mux2_Sel,
  En_AB, En_AC, En_AD, En_BC, En_BD, En_CD,
  Mux3_Sel, FirstDataOutRdy);

    input     Clock, Reset, ThreeOnly, FirstDataInRdy;
    output    En_A, En_B, En_C, En_D;
    output [1:0] Mux1_Sel, Mux2_Sel;
    output    En_AB,En_AC,En_AD,En_BC,En_BD,En_CD;
    output [1:0] Mux3_Sel;
    output    FirstDataOutRdy;
    reg       En_A, En_B, En_C, En_D;
    reg [1:0] Mux1_Sel, Mux2_Sel;
    reg       En_AB,En_AC,En_AD,En_BC,En_BD,En_CD;
    reg [1:0] Mux3_Sel;
    reg       FirstDataOutRdy;

    // MASTER FSM state parameter values
    parameter ST0=0,    ST1=1,    ST2=2,    S3=3, ST4=4,
              ST5=5,    ST6=6,    ST7=7,    S8=8, ST9=9,   (1)
              ST10=10, ST11=11, ST12=12;
    parameter ST_A=0, ST_B=1, ST_C=2, ST_D=3; // FSM1
    parameter Zero=0,   One=1,   Two=2,   // FSM2       (1)
              Three=3, Four=4,   Five=5;
    parameter ST_Sum1=0, ST_Sum2=1,   // FSM3
              ST_Sum3=2,   ST_NoSum=3;



    reg [3:0] CurrStateMasterFSM, NextStateMasterFSM;
    reg       StartFSM1, StartFSM2, StartFSM3;
    reg [1:0] CurrStateFSM1, NextStateFSM1;
    reg [2:0] CurrStateFSM2, NextStateFSM2;
    reg [1:0] CurrStateFSM3, NextStateFSM3;



    // -----------------
    // MASTER FSM
    // -----------------
    always @(FirstDataInRdy or ThreeOnly or
             CurrStateMasterFSM)
    begin: MASTER_FSM_COMB
        StartFSM1 = 0;
        StartFSM2 = 0;                          (2)
        StartFSM3 = 0;
        FirstDataOutRdy = 0;
        case (CurrStateMasterFSM)
            ST0  :  if (FirstDataInRdy)
                        begin
                            StartFSM1 = 1;
                            if (ThreeOnly)
                                NextStateMasterFSM = ST7;
                            else
                                NextStateMasterFSM = ST1;
                        end
                    else
                        NextStateMasterFSM = ST0;
            ST1  : NextStateMasterFSM = ST2;
            ST2  : begin
                       StartFSM2 = 1;
                       NextStateMasterFSM = ST3;
                   end
            ST3  : NextStateMasterFSM = ST4;
```

continued

Control Path 1 - Master FSM controlling three other FSMs

VHDL	Verilog
<pre>   when ST4 => NextStateMasterFSM <= ST5;
    when ST5 => NextStateMasterFSM <= ST6;
    when ST6 => StartFSM3 <= '1';
               FirstDataOutRdy <= '1';
               if (FirstDataInRdy = '1') then
                   StartFSM1 <= '1';
                   NextStateMasterFSM <= ST1;
               else
                   NextStateMasterFSM <= ST0;
               end if;

    when ST7 => NextStateMasterFSM <= ST8;
    when ST8 => StartFSM2 <= '1';
               NextStateMasterFSM <= ST9;

    when ST9 => if (FirstDataInRdy = '1') then
                   StartFSM1 <= '1';
                   NextStateMasterFSM <= ST10;
               else
                   NextStateMasterFSM <= ST12;
               end if;

    when ST10 => StartFSM3 <= '1';
                FirstDataOutRdy <= '1';
                NextStateMasterFSM <= ST11;

    when ST11 => StartFSM2 <= '1';
                NextStateMasterFSM <= ST9;

    when ST12 => StartFSM3 <= '1';
                FirstDataOutRdy <= '1';
                NextStateMasterFSM <= ST13;

    when others =>NextStateMasterFSM <= ST0; (3)
  end case;
end process MASTER_FSM_COMB;

MASTER_FSM_SEQ:
process (Clock)
begin
  if rising_edge(Clock) then
    if (Reset = '1') then
        CurrStateMasterFSM <= ST0;
    else
        CurrStateMasterFSM <= NextStateMasterFSM;
    end if;
  end if;
end process MASTER_FSM_SEQ;

-- FSM1

FSM1_COMB:
process (StartFSM1, ThreeOnly, CurrStateFSM1)
begin
    En_A <= '0';
</pre> | <pre> ST4 : NextStateMasterFSM = ST5;
  ST5 : NextStateMasterFSM = ST6;
  ST6 : begin
             StartFSM3 = 1;
             FirstDataOutRdy = 1;
             if (FirstInDataRdy)
                 begin
                   StartFSM1 = 1;
                   NextStateMasterFSM = ST1;
                 end
             else
                   NextStateMasterFSM = ST0;
         end
  ST7 : NextStateMasterFSM = ST8;
  ST8 : begin
             StartFSM2 = 1;
             NextStateMasterFSM = ST9;
         end
  ST9 : begin
             if (FirstDataInRdy)
                 begin
                   StartFSM1 = 1;
                   NextStateMasterFSM = ST10;
                 end
             else
                   NextStateMasterFSM = ST12;
         end
  ST10 : begin
             StartFSM3 = 1;
             FirstDataOutRdy = 1;
             NextStateMasterFSM = ST11;
         end
  ST11 : begin
             StartFSM2 = 1;
             NextStateMasterFSM = ST9;
         end
  ST12 : begin
             StartFSM3 = 1;
             FirstDataOutRdy = 1;
             NextStateMasterFSM = ST0;
         end
  default : NextStateMasterFSM = ST0; (3)
  endcase
end

always @(posedge Clock)
  begin: MASTER_FSM_SEQ
    if (Reset)
        CurrStateMasterFSM = ST0;
    else
        CurrStateMasterFSM = NextStateMasterFSM;
  end

//----------
// FSM1
//----------
always @(StartFSM1 or ThreeOnly or CurrStateFSM1)
  begin: FSM1_COMB
    En_A = 0;
    En_B = 0;
</pre> |
| *continued* | *continued* |

Control Path 1 - Master FSM controlling three other FSMs

VHDL	Verilog

<pre>En_B <= '0';
En_C <= '0';
En_D <= '0';
case (CurrStateFSM1) is
   when ST_A => if (StartFSM1 = '1') then
                   NextStateFSM1 <= ST_B;
                   En_A <= '1';
               else
                   NextStateFSM1 <= ST_A;
               end if;
 	
   when ST_B => NextStateFSM1 <= ST_C;
                 En_B <= '1';
 	
   when ST_C => if (ThreeOnly = '1') then
                   NextStateFSM1 <= ST_A;
                else
                   NextStateFSM1 <= ST_D;
                end if;
                En_C <= '1';
 	
   when ST_D => NextStateFSM1 <= ST_A;
                En_D <= '1';
 	
   when others => NextStateFSM1 <= ST_A;
   end case;
end process FSM1_COMB;
 	
FSM1_SEQ:
process (Clock)
begin
   if rising_edge(Clock) then
      if (Reset ='1') then
         CurrStateFSM1 <= ST_A;
      else
         CurrStateFSM1 <= NextStateFSM1;
      end if;
   end if;
end process FSM1_SEQ;
 	
------------ 	
-- FSM2
------------ 	
FSM2_COMB:
process (StartFSM2, ThreeOnly, CurrStateFSM2)
begin
   Mux1_Sel <= 0;
   Mux2_Sel <= 0;
   En_AB   <= '0';
   En_AC   <= '0';
   En_AD   <= '0';
   En_BC   <= '0';
   En_BD   <= '0';
   En_CD   <= '0';
   case (CurrStateFSM2) is
      when Zero => if (StartFSM2 = '1') then
                       En_AB <= '1';
                       NextStateFSM2 <= One;
                    else
                       NextStateFSM2 <= Zero;
                    end if;
                    Mux1_Sel <= 0;
                    Mux2_Sel <= 0;</pre>
	<pre>En_C = 0;
	En_D = 0;
	case (CurrStateFSM1)
	   ST_A : if (StartFSM1)
	             begin
	                En_A = 1;
	                NextStateFSM1 = ST_B;
	             end
	          else
	             NextStateFSM1 = ST_A;
	   ST_B : begin
	             En_B = 1;
	             NextStateFSM1 = ST_C;
	          end
	   ST_C : begin
	             En_C = 1;
	             if (ThreeOnly)
	                NextStateFSM1 = ST_A;
	             else
	                NextStateFSM1 = ST_D;
	          end
	   ST_D : begin
	             En_D = 1;
	             NextStateFSM1 = ST_A;
	          end
	   default : NextStateFSM1 = ST_A;
	   endcase
	end
	
	always @(posedge Clock)
	   begin: FSM1_SEQ
	      if (Reset)
	         CurrStateFSM1 = ST_A;
	      else
	         CurrStateFSM1 = NextStateFSM1;
	   end
	
	//---------
	// FSM2
	//---------
	always @(StartFSM2 or ThreeOnly or CurrStateFSM2)
	   begin: FSM2_COMB
	      Mux1_Sel = 0;
	      Mux2_Sel = 0;
	      En_AB = 0;
	      En_AC = 0;
	      En_AD = 0;
	      En_BC = 0;
	      En_BD = 0;
	      En_CD = 0;
	
	      case (CurrStateFSM2)
	         Zero : begin
	                    Mux1_Sel = 0;
	                    Mux2_Sel = 0;
	                    if (StartFSM2)
	                       begin
	                          NextStateFSM2 = One;
	                          En_AB = 1;
	                       end</pre>

continued

continued

251

Control Path 1 - Master FSM controlling three other FSMs

VHDL	Verilog

```vhdl
        when One  => Mux1_Sel <= 0;
                     Mux2_Sel <= 1;
                     En_AC <= '1';
                     if (ThreeOnly = '1') then
                         NextStateFSM2 <= Three;
                     else
                         NextStateFSM2 <= Two;
                     end if;

        when Two  => Mux1_Sel <= 0;
                     Mux2_Sel <= 2;
                     En_AD <= '1';
                     NextStateFSM2 <= Three;


        when Three =>Mux1_Sel <= 1;
                     Mux2_Sel <= 1;
                     En_BC <= '1';
                     if (ThreeOnly = '1') then
                         NextStateFSM2 <= Zero;
                     else
                         NextStateFSM2 <= Four;
                     end if;

        when Four => Mux1_Sel <= 1;
                     Mux2_Sel <= 2;
                     En_BD <= '1';
                     NextStateFSM2 <= Five;


        when Five =>  Mux1_Sel <= 2;
                     Mux2_Sel <= 2;
                     En_CD <= '1';
                     NextStateFSM2 <= Zero;


        when others => NextStateFSM2 <= Zero;
      end case;
end process FSM2_COMB;

FSM2_SEQ:
process (Clock)
begin
    if rising_edge(Clock) then
        if (Reset = '1') then
            CurrStateFSM2 <= Zero;
        else
            CurrStateFSM2 <= NextStateFSM2;
        end if;
    end if;
end process FSM2_SEQ;
```

```verilog
            else
                NextStateFSM2 = Zero;
        end
     One  : begin
            Mux1_Sel = 0;
            Mux2_Sel = 1;
            En_AC = 1;
            if (ThreeOnly)
                NextStateFSM2 = Three;
            else
                NextStateFSM2 = Two;
        end
     Two :  begin
            Mux1_Sel = 0;
            Mux2_Sel = 2;
            En_AD = 1;
            NextStateFSM2 = Three;
        end
     Three: begin
            Mux1_Sel = 1;
            Mux2_Sel = 1;
            En_BC = 1;
            if (ThreeOnly)
                NextStateFSM2 = Zero;
            else
                NextStateFSM2 = Four;
        end
     Four : begin
            Mux1_Sel = 1;
            Mux2_Sel = 2;
            En_BD = 1;
            NextStateFSM2 = Five;
        end
     Five : begin
            Mux1_Sel = 2;
            Mux2_Sel = 2;
            En_CD = 1;
            NextStateFSM2 = Zero;
        end
     default : NextStateFSM2 = Zero;
  endcase
end


always @(posedge Clock)
  begin: FSM2_SEQ
    if (Reset)
        CurrStateFSM2 = Zero;
    else
        CurrStateFSM2 = NextStateFSM2;
  end
```

continued   continued

Control Path 1 - Master FSM controlling three other FSMs

VHDL	Verilog
| ```
-----------
-- FSM3
-----------
FSM3_COMB:
process (StartFSM3, ThreeOnly, CurrStateFSM3)
begin
    Mux3_Sel <= 0;
    case (CurrStateFSM3) is
        when ST_Sum1  =>   Mux3_Sel <= 0;
                           if (StartFSM3 = '1') then
                               if (ThreeOnly = '1') then
                                   NextStateFSM3 <= ST_NoSum;
                               else
                                   NextStateFSM3 <= ST_Sum2;
                               end if;
                           else
                               NextStateFSM3 <= ST_Sum1;
                           end if;

        when ST_Sum2  =>   Mux3_Sel <= 1;
                           NextStateFSM3 <= ST_Sum3;


        when ST_Sum3  =>   Mux3_Sel <= 2;
                           NextStateFSM3 <= ST_Sum1;


        when ST_NoSum =>  Mux3_Sel <= 3;
                           NextStateFSM3 <= ST_Sum1;
        when others   =>   NextStateFSM3 <= ST_Sum1;
    end case;
end process FSM3_COMB;




FSM3_SEQ:
process (Clock)
begin
    if rising_edge(Clock) then
        if (Reset = '1') then
            CurrStateFSM3 <= ST_Sum1;
        else
            CurrStateFSM3 <= NextStateFSM3;
        end if;
    end if;
end process FSM3_SEQ;

end architecture RTL;
``` | ```
//--------
// FSM3
//--------
always @(StartFSM3 or ThreeOnly or CurrStateFSM3)
    begin: FSM3_COMB
    Mux3_Sel = 0;

    case (CurrStateFSM3)
        ST_Sum1  :  begin
                        Mux3_Sel = 0;
                        if (StartFSM3)
                            if (ThreeOnly)
                                NextStateFSM3 = ST_NoSum;
                            else
                                NextStateFSM3 = ST_Sum2;
                            else
                                NextStateFSM3 = ST_Sum1;
                    end

        ST_Sum2  :  begin
                        Mux3_Sel = 1;
                        NextStateFSM3 = ST_Sum3;
                    end
        ST_Sum3  :  begin
                        Mux3_Sel = 2;
                        NextStateFSM3 = ST_Sum1;
                    end
        ST_NoSum : begin
                        Mux3_Sel = 3;
                        NextStateFSM3 = ST_Sum1;
                    end
        default  :    NextStateFSM3 = ST_Sum1;
    endcase
    end


always @(posedge Clock)
    begin: FSM3_SEQ
    if (Reset)
        CurrStateFSM3 = ST_Sum1;
    else
        CurrStateFSM3 = NextStateFSM3;
    end

endmodule
``` |

Control Path 2 - Three serial interactive FSMs

VHDL	Verilog

<pre>library IEEE;
use IEEE.STD_Logic_1164.all, IEEE.Numeric_STD.all;
 	
entity HIERFSMS_CNTLPATH2 is
   port (Clock, Reset, ThreeOnly,
         FirstDataInRdy: in std_logic;
         En_A, En_B, En_C, En_D: out std_logic;
         Mux1_Sel, Mux2_Sel: out integer range 0 to 2;
         En_AB, En_AC, En_AD,
         En_BC, En_BD, En_CD: out std_logic;
         Mux3_Sel: out integer range 0 to 3;
         FirstDataOutRdy: out std_logic);
end entity HIERFSMS_CNTLPATH2;
 	
architecture RTL of HIERFSMS_CNTLPATH2 is
   type StateTypeFSM1 is (ST_A, ST_B, ST_C, ST_D);
   type StateTypeFSM2 is (ST1, ST2, ST3, ST4,
                       ST5, ST6, ST7, ST8);
   type StateTypeFSM3 is (ST_Sum1, ST_Sum2,
                       ST_Sum3, ST_NoSum);
   signal CurrStateFSM1, NextStateFSM1: StateTypeFSM1;
   signal CurrStateFSM2, NextStateFSM2: StateTypeFSM2;
   signal CurrStateFSM3, NextStateFSM3: StateTypeFSM3;
   signal StartFSM2, StartFSM3: std_logic;
begin
 	
   ----------- 	
   -- FSM1
   ----------- 	
   FSM1_COMB:
   process (FirstDataInRdy, ThreeOnly, CurrStateFSM1)
   begin
      En_A <= '0';
      En_B <= '0';
      En_C <= '0';
      En_D <= '0';
      StartFSM2 <= '0';
      case (CurrStateFSM1) is
         when ST_A => if (FirstDataInRdy = '1') then
                          En_A <= '1';
                          NextStateFSM1 <= ST_B;
                       else
                          NextStateFSM1 <= ST_A;
                       end if;
 	
         when ST_B => En_B <= '1';
                       NextStateFSM1 <= ST_C;
 	
         when ST_C => En_C <= '1';
                       StartFSM2 <= '1';
                       if (ThreeOnly = '1') then
                          NextStateFSM1 <= ST_A;
                       else
                          NextStateFSM1 <= ST_D;
                       end if;
 	
         when ST_D => En_D <= '1';
                       NextStateFSM1 <= ST_A;</pre>
	<pre>module HIERFSMS_CNTLPATH2
	   (Clock, Reset, ThreeOnly, FirstDataInRdy,
	    En_A, En_B, En_C, En_D,
	    Mux1_Sel, Mux2_Sel,
	    En_AB, En_AC, En_AD, En_BC, En_BD, En_CD,
	    Mux3_Sel, FirstDataOutRdy);
	
	   input Clock, Reset, ThreeOnly, FirstDataInRdy;
	   output En_A, En_B, En_C, En_D;
	   output [1:0] Mux1_Sel, Mux2_Sel;
	   output En_AB,En_AC,En_AD,En_BC,En_BD,En_CD;
	   output [1:0] Mux3_Sel;
	   output FirstDataOutRdy;
	   reg En_A, En_B, En_C, En_D;
	   reg [1:0] Mux1_Sel, Mux2_Sel;
	   reg En_AB,En_AC,En_AD,En_BC,En_BD,En_CD;
	   reg [1:0] Mux3_Sel;
	   reg FirstDataOutRdy;
	   parameter ST_A = 0, ST_B = 1, ST_C = 2, ST_D = 3;
	   parameter ST0 = 0, ST1 = 1, ST2 = 2, ST3 = 3, ST4 = 4,
	             ST5 = 5, ST6 = 6, ST7 = 7 , ST8 = 8;
	   parameter ST_Sum1 = 0, ST_Sum2 = 1,
	             ST_Sum3 = 2, ST_NoSum = 3;
	   reg [1:0] CurrStateFSM1, NextStateFSM1;
	   reg [3:0] CurrStateFSM2, NextStateFSM2;
	   reg [1:0] CurrStateFSM3, NextStateFSM3;
	   reg StartFSM2, StartFSM3;
	
	   //--------
	   // FSM1
	   //--------
	   always @(FirstDataInRdy or ThreeOnly or CurrStateFSM1)
	     begin: FSM1_COMB
	      En_A = 0;
	      En_B = 0;
	      En_C = 0;
	      En_D = 0;
	      StartFSM2 = 0;
	
	      case (CurrStateFSM1)
	        ST_A : if (FirstDataInRdy == 1)
	                  begin
	                     En_A = 1;
	                     NextStateFSM1 = ST_B;
	                  end
	               else
	                  NextStateFSM1 = ST_A;
	        ST_B : begin
	                  En_B = 1;
	                  NextStateFSM1 = ST_C;
	               end
	        ST_C : begin
	                  En_C = 1;
	                  StartFSM2 = 1;
	                  if (ThreeOnly == 1)
	                     NextStateFSM1 = ST_A;
	                  else
	                     NextStateFSM1 = ST_D;
	               end
	        ST_D : begin
	                  En_D = 1;
	                  NextStateFSM1 = ST_A;
	               end</pre>

<div align="right">continued</div>	<div align="right">continued</div>

Control Path 2 - Three serial interactive FSMs

VHDL	Verilog
``	```

```
            when others => NextStateFSM1 <= ST_A;
        end case;
    end process FSM1_COMB;

    FSM1_SEQ:
    process (Clock)
    begin
        if rising_edge(Clock) then
            if (Reset = '1') then
                CurrStateFSM1 <= ST_A;
            else
                CurrStateFSM1 <= NextStateFSM1;
            end if;
        end if;
    end process FSM1_SEQ;


    ------------
    -- FSM2
    ------------
    FSM2_COMB:
    process (ThreeOnly, StartFSM2, CurrStateFSM2)
    begin
        Mux1_Sel <= 0;
        Mux2_Sel <= 0;
        En_AB   <= '0';
        En_AC   <= '0';
        En_AD   <= '0';
        En_BC   <= '0';
        En_BD   <= '0';
        En_CD   <= '0';
        StartFSM3 <= '0';
        case (CurrStateFSM2) is
            when ST1 =>  Mux1_Sel <= 0;
                         Mux2_Sel <= 0;
                         if (StartFSM2 = '1') then
                             En_AB <= '1';
                             if (ThreeOnly = '1') then
                                 NextStateFSM2 <= ST7;
                             else
                                 NextStateFSM2 <= ST2;
                             end if;
                         else
                             NextStateFSM2 <= ST1;
                         end if;

            when ST2 =>  Mux1_Sel <= 0;
                         Mux2_Sel <= 1;
                         En_AC <= '1';
                         NextStateFSM2 <= ST3;

            when ST3 =>  Mux1_Sel <= 0;
                         Mux2_Sel <= 2;
                         En_AD <= '1';
                         NextStateFSM2 <= ST4;

            when ST4 =>  Mux1_Sel <= 1;
                         Mux2_Sel <= 1;
                         En_BC <= '1';
                         NextStateFSM2 <= ST5;
```

```
            default : NextStateFSM1 = ST_A;
        endcase
    end


    always @(posedge Clock)
    begin: FSM1_SEQ
        if (Reset)
            CurrStateFSM1 = ST_A;
        else
            CurrStateFSM1 = NextStateFSM1;
    end




    //--------
    // FSM2
    //---------
    always @(ThreeOnly or StartFSM2 or CurrStateFSM2)
    begin: FSM2_COMB
        Mux1_Sel = 0;
        Mux2_Sel = 0;
        En_AB = 0;
        En_AC = 0;
        En_AD = 0;
        En_BC = 0;
        En_BD = 0;
        En_CD = 0;
        StartFSM3 = 0;
        case (CurrStateFSM2)
            ST1 :  begin
                       Mux1_Sel = 0;
                       Mux2_Sel = 0;
                       if (StartFSM2 == 1)
                           begin
                               En_AB = 1;
                               if (ThreeOnly == 1)
                                   NextStateFSM2 = ST7;
                               else
                                   NextStateFSM2 = ST2;
                           end
                       else
                           NextStateFSM2 = ST1;
                   end
            ST2 :  begin
                       Mux1_Sel = 0;
                       Mux2_Sel = 1;
                       En_AC = 1;
                       NextStateFSM2 = ST3;
                   end
            ST3 :  begin
                       Mux1_Sel = 0;
                       Mux2_Sel = 2;
                       En_AD = 1;
                       NextStateFSM2 = ST4;
                   end
            ST4 :  begin
                       Mux1_Sel = 1;
                       Mux2_Sel = 1;
                       En_BC = 1;
                       NextStateFSM2 = ST5;
                   end
```

| *continued* | *continued* |

255

Control Path 2 - Three serial interactive FSMs

VHDL	Verilog
<pre>   when ST5 =>   Mux1_Sel <= 1;
                        Mux2_Sel <= 2;
                        En_BD <= '1';
                        StartFSM3 <= '1';
                        NextStateFSM2 <= ST6;

          when ST6 =>   Mux1_Sel <= 2;
                        Mux2_Sel <= 2;
                        En_CD <= '1';
                        NextStateFSM2 <= ST1;

          when ST7 =>   Mux1_Sel <= 0;
                        Mux2_Sel <= 1;
                        En_AC <= '1';
                        NextStateFSM2 <= ST8;

          when ST8 =>   Mux1_Sel <= 1;
                        Mux2_Sel <= 1;
                        En_BC <= '1';
                        StartFSM3 <= '1';
                        NextStateFSM2 <= ST1;

        when others => NextStateFSM2 <= ST1;
      end case;
    end process FSM2_COMB;

FSM2_SEQ:
process (Clock)
begin
    if rising_edge(Clock) then
        if (Reset = '1') then
            CurrStateFSM2 <= NextStateFSM2;
        else
            CurrStateFSM2 <= NextStateFSM2;
        end if;
    end if;
end process FSM2_SEQ;

-- FSM3

FSM3_COMB:
process (StartFSM3, ThreeOnly, CurrStateFSM3)
begin
    Mux3_Sel <= 0;
    FirstDataOutRdy <= '0';
    case (CurrStateFSM3) is
        when ST_Sum1 =>
            Mux3_Sel <= 0;
            if (StartFSM3 = '1') then
                FirstDataOutRdy <= '1';
                if (ThreeOnly = '1') then
                    NextStateFSM3 <= ST_NoSum;
                else
                    NextStateFSM3 <= ST_Sum2;
                end if;
            else</pre> | <pre>   ST5 : begin
                StartFSM3 = 1;
                Mux1_Sel = 1;
                Mux2_Sel = 2;
                En_BD = 1;
                NextStateFSM2 = ST6;
           end
    ST6 : begin
                Mux1_Sel = 2;
                Mux2_Sel = 2;
                En_CD = 1;
                NextStateFSM2 = ST1;
           end
    ST7 : begin
                Mux1_Sel = 0;
                Mux2_Sel = 1;
                En_AC = 1;
                NextStateFSM2 = ST8;
           end
    ST8 : begin
                StartFSM3 = 1;
                Mux1_Sel = 1;
                Mux2_Sel = 1;
                En_BC = 1;
                NextStateFSM2 = ST1;
           end
    default : NextStateFSM2 = ST1;
  endcase
end

always @(posedge Clock)
  begin: FSM2_SEQ
    if (Reset)
        CurrStateFSM2 = ST1;
    else
        CurrStateFSM2 = NextStateFSM2;
  end

//---------
// FSM3
//---------
always @(StartFSM3 or ThreeOnly or CurrStateFSM3)
  begin: FSM3_COMB
    Mux3_Sel = 0;
    FirstDataOutRdy = 0;

    case (CurrStateFSM3)
    ST_Sum1: begin
                Mux3_Sel = 0;
                if (StartFSM3 == 1)
                    begin
                        FirstDataOutRdy = 1;
                        if (ThreeOnly == 1)
                            NextStateFSM3 = ST_NoSum;
                        else
                            NextStateFSM3 = ST_Sum2;
                    end
                else</pre> |
| continued | continued |

Control Path 2 - Three serial interactive FSMs

VHDL	Verilog
| ```
            NextStateFSM3 <= ST_Sum1;
        end if;
    when ST_Sum2 =>
        Mux3_Sel <= 1;
        NextStateFSM3 <= ST_Sum3;

    when ST_Sum3 =>
        Mux3_Sel <= 2;
        NextStateFSM3 <= ST_Sum1;

    when ST_NoSum =>
        Mux3_Sel <= 3;
        NextStateFSM3 <= ST_Sum1;

    when others =>
        NextStateFSM3 <= ST_Sum1;
    end case;
end process FSM3_COMB;


FSM3_SEQ:
process (Clock)
begin
    if rising_edge(Clock) then
        if (Reset = '1') then
            CurrStateFSM3 <= NextStateFSM3;
        else
            CurrStateFSM3 <= NextStateFSM3;
        end if;
    end if;
end process FSM3_SEQ;


end architecture RTL;
``` | ```
                NextStateFSM3 = ST_Sum1;
            end
ST_Sum2:    begin
                Mux3_Sel = 1;
                NextStateFSM3 = ST_Sum3;
            end
ST_Sum3:    begin
                Mux3_Sel = 2;
                NextStateFSM3 = ST_Sum1;
            end
ST_NoSum : begin
                Mux3_Sel = 3;
                NextStateFSM3 = ST_Sum1;
            end
    default:    NextStateFSM3 = ST_Sum1;
    endcase
end


always @(posedge Clock)
    begin: FSM3_SEQ
        if (Reset)
            CurrStateFSM3 = ST_Sum1;
        else
            CurrStateFSM3 = NextStateFSM3;
    end

endmodule
``` |

Control Path 3 - Single FSM

VHDL	Verilog

library IEEE;
use IEEE.STD_Logic_1164.**all**, IEEE.Numeric_STD.**all**;
 	
entity HIERFSMS_CNTLPATH3 **is**
  port (Clock, Reset, ThreeOnly,
      FirstDataInRdy: **in** std_logic;
      En_A, En_B, En_C, En_D: **out** std_logic;
      Mux1_Sel, Mux2_Sel: **out** integer **range** 0 **to** 2;
      En_AB, En_AC, En_AD,
      En_BC, En_BD, En_CD: **out** std_logic;
      Mux3_Sel: **out** integer **range** 0 **to** 3;
      FirstDataOutRdy: **out** std_logic);
end entity HIERFSMS_CNTLPATH3;
 	
architecture RTL **of** HIERFSMS_CNTLPATH3 **is**
  type StateTypeFSM **is** (ST0, ST1, ST2, ST3, ST4, ST5, ST6,
                ST7, ST8, ST9, ST10, ST11, ST12,
                ST13, ST14, ST15);
  signal CurrStateFSM, NextStateFSM: StateTypeFSM;
begin
 	
  ------------------ 	
  -- Single FSM
  ------------------ 	
  FSM_COMB:
  process (FirstDataInRdy, ThreeOnly, CurrStateFSM)
  begin
    En_A <= '0';
    En_B <= '0';
    En_C <= '0';
    En_D <= '0';
    Mux1_Sel <= 0;
    Mux2_Sel <= 0;
    En_AB   <= '0';
    En_AC <= '0';
    En_AD <= '0';
    En_BC <= '0';
    En_BD <= '0';
    En_CD <= '0';
    Mux3_Sel <= 0;
    FirstDataOutRdy <= '0';
    case (CurrStateFSM) **is**
      when ST0 =>
        if (FirstDataInRdy = '1') **then**
          En_A <= '1';
          if (ThreeOnly = '1') **then**
            NextStateFSM <= ST10;
          else
            NextStateFSM <= ST1;
          end if;
        else
          NextStateFSM <= ST0;
        end if;
 	
      when ST1 =>
        En_B <= '1';
        NextStateFSM <= ST2;
 	
      when ST2 =>
        En_C <= '1';
        Mux1_Sel <= 0;
	module HIERFSMS_CNTLPATH3
	  (Clock, Reset, ThreeOnly, FirstDataInRdy,
	  En_A, En_B, En_C, En_D,
	  Mux1_Sel, Mux2_Sel,
	  En_AB, En_AC, En_AD, En_BC, En_BD, En_CD,
	  Mux3_Sel, FirstDataOutRdy);
	
	  input Clock, Reset, ThreeOnly, FirstDataInRdy;
	  output En_A, En_B, En_C, En_D;
	  output [1:0] Mux1_Sel, Mux2_Sel;
	  output En_AB,En_AC,En_AD,En_BC,En_BD,En_CD;
	  output [1:0] Mux3_Sel;
	  output FirstDataOutRdy;
	  reg En_A, En_B, En_C, En_D;
	  reg [1:0] Mux1_Sel, Mux2_Sel;
	  reg En_AB,En_AC,En_AD,En_BC,En_BD,En_CD;
	  reg [1:0] Mux3_Sel;
	  reg FirstDataOutRdy;
	  parameter ST0=0, ST1=1, ST2=2, ST3=3,
	              ST4=4, ST5=5, ST6=6, ST7=7,
	              ST8=8, ST9=9, ST10=10,ST11=11,
	              ST12=12, ST13=13,ST14=14,ST15=15;
	  reg [3:0] CurrStateFSM, NextStateFSM;
	
	  //----------------
	  // Single FSM
	  //----------------
	  always @(FirstDataInRdy **or** ThreeOnly **or** CurrStateFSM)
	    begin: FSM_COMB
	    En_A = 0;
	    En_B = 0;
	    En_C = 0;
	    En_D = 0;
	    Mux1_Sel = 0;
	    Mux2_Sel = 0;
	    En_AB = 0;
	    En_AC = 0;
	    En_AD = 0;
	    En_BC = 0;
	    En_BD = 0;
	    En_CD = 0;
	    Mux3_Sel = 0;
	    FirstDataOutRdy = 0;
	
	    case (CurrStateFSM)
	      ST0 : **begin**
	            if (FirstDataInRdy == 1)
	              begin
	                En_A = 1;
	                if (ThreeOnly == 1)
	                  NextStateFSM = ST10;
	                else
	                  NextStateFSM = ST1;
	              end
	            else
	              NextStateFSM = ST0;
	          end
	      ST1 : **begin**
	          En_B = 1;
	          NextStateFSM = ST2;
	        end
	      ST2 : **begin**
	          En_C = 1;
	          Mux1_Sel = 0;

continued	continued

Control Path 3 - Single FSM

VHDL	Verilog
| ```
        Mux2_Sel <= 0;
        En_AB <= '1';
        Mux3_Sel <= 2;
        NextStateFSM <= ST3;

    when ST3 =>
        En_D <= '1';
        Mux1_Sel <= 0;
        Mux2_Sel <= 1;
        En_AC <= '1';
        NextStateFSM <= ST4;

    when ST4 =>
        Mux1_Sel <= 0;
        Mux2_Sel <= 2;
        En_AD <= '1';
        NextStateFSM <= ST5;

    when ST5 =>
        Mux1_Sel <= 1;
        Mux2_Sel <= 1;
        En_BC <= '1';
        NextStateFSM <= ST6;

    when ST6 =>
        Mux1_Sel <= 1;
        Mux2_Sel <= 2;
        En_BD <= '1';
        Mux3_Sel <= 0;
        FirstDataOutRdy <= '1';
        if (FirstDataInRdy = '1') then
            En_A <= '1';
            NextStateFSM <= ST7;
        else
            NextStateFSM <= ST8;
        end if;

    when ST7 =>
        En_B <= '1';
        Mux1_Sel <= 2;
        Mux2_Sel <= 2;
        En_CD <= '1';
        Mux3_Sel <= 1;
        NextStateFSM <= ST2;

    when ST8 =>
        Mux1_Sel <= 2;
        Mux2_Sel <= 2;
        En_CD <= '1';
        Mux3_Sel <= 1;
        NextStateFSM <= ST9;

    when ST9 =>
        Mux3_Sel <= 2;
        NextStateFSM <= ST0;

    when ST10 =>
        En_B <= '1';
        NextStateFSM <= ST11;

    when ST11 =>
        En_C <= '1';
        Mux1_Sel <= 0;
        Mux2_Sel <= 0;
``` | ```
        Mux2_Sel = 0;
        En_AB = 1;
        Mux3_Sel = 2;
        NextStateFSM = ST3;
    end
ST3 :  begin
        En_D = 1;
        Mux1_Sel = 0;
        Mux2_Sel = 1;
        En_AC = 1;
        NextStateFSM = ST4;
    end
ST4 :  begin
        Mux1_Sel = 0;
        Mux2_Sel = 2;
        En_AD = 1;
        NextStateFSM = ST5;
    end
ST5 :  begin
        Mux1_Sel = 1;
        Mux2_Sel = 1;
        En_BC = 1;
        NextStateFSM = ST6;
    end
ST6 :  begin
        Mux1_Sel = 1;
        Mux2_Sel = 2;
        En_BD = 1;
        Mux3_Sel = 0;
        FirstDataOutRdy = 1;
        if (FirstDataInRdy == 1)
            begin
                En_A = 1;
                NextStateFSM = ST7;
        else
            NextStateFSM = ST8;
    end
ST7 :  begin
        En_B = 1;
        Mux1_Sel = 2;
        Mux2_Sel = 2;
        En_CD = 1;
        Mux3_Sel = 1;
        NextStateFSM = ST2;
    end
ST8 :  begin
        Mux1_Sel = 2;
        Mux2_Sel = 2;
        En_CD = 1;
        Mux3_Sel = 1;
        NextStateFSM = ST9;
    end
ST9 :  begin
        Mux3_Sel = 2;
        NextStateFSM = ST0;
    end
ST10 : begin
        En_B = 1;
        NextStateFSM = ST11;
    end
ST11 : begin
        En_C = 1;
        Mux1_Sel = 0;
        Mux2_Sel = 0;
``` |
| continued | continued |

Control Path3 - Single FSM

VHDL	Verilog

<pre>   En_AB <= '1';
              Mux3_Sel <= 3;
              NextStateFSM <= ST12;
 	
          when ST12 =>
              Mux1_Sel <= 0;
              Mux2_Sel <= 1;
              En_AC <= '1';
              if (FirstDataInRdy = '1') then
                  En_A <= '1';
                  NextStateFSM <= ST13;
              else
                  NextStateFSM <= ST14;
              end if;
 	
          when ST13 =>
              En_B <= '1';
              Mux1_Sel <= 1;
              Mux2_Sel <= 1;
              En_BC <= '1';
              Mux3_Sel <= 0;
              FirstDataOutRdy <= '1';
              NextStateFSM <= ST11;
 	
          when ST14 =>
              En_B <= '1';
              Mux1_Sel <= 1;
              Mux2_Sel <= 1;
              En_BC <= '1';
              Mux3_Sel <= 0;
              FirstDataOutRdy <= '1';
              NextStateFSM <= ST15;
 	
          when ST15 =>
              Mux3_Sel <= 3;
              NextStateFSM <= ST0;
 	
          when others =>
              NextStateFSM <= ST0;
      end case;
  end process FSM_COMB;
 	
  FSM_SEQ:
  process (Clock)
  begin
      if rising_edge(Clock) then
          if (Reset = '1') then
              CurrStateFSM <= NextStateFSM;
          else
              CurrStateFSM <= NextStateFSM;
          end if;
      end if;
  end process FSM_SEQ;
end architecture RTL;</pre>
	<pre> En_AB = 1;
	              Mux3_Sel = 3;
	              NextStateFSM = ST12;
	            end
	      ST12 : begin
	              Mux1_Sel = 0;
	              Mux2_Sel = 1;
	              En_AC = 1;
	              if (FirstDataInRdy == 1)
	                begin
	                  En_A = 1;
	                  NextStateFSM = ST13;
	                end
	              else
	                  NextStateFSM = ST14;
	            end
	      ST13 : begin
	              En_B = 1;
	              Mux1_Sel = 1;
	              Mux2_Sel = 1;
	              En_BC = 1;
	              Mux3_Sel = 0;
	              FirstDataOutRdy = 1;
	              NextStateFSM = ST11;
	            end
	      ST14 : begin
	              En_B = 1;
	              Mux1_Sel = 1;
	              Mux2_Sel = 1;
	              En_BC = 1;
	              Mux3_Sel = 0;
	              FirstDataOutRdy = 1;
	              NextStateFSM = ST15;
	            end
	      ST15 : begin
	              Mux3_Sel = 3;
	              FirstDataOutRdy = 1;
	              NextStateFSM = ST0;
	            end
	      default : NextStateFSM = ST0;
	    endcase
	  end
	
	  always @(posedge Clock)
	    begin: FSM_SEQ
	      if (Reset)
	          CurrStateFSM = NextStateFSM;
	      else
	          CurrStateFSM = NextStateFSM;
	    end
	
	endmodule</pre>

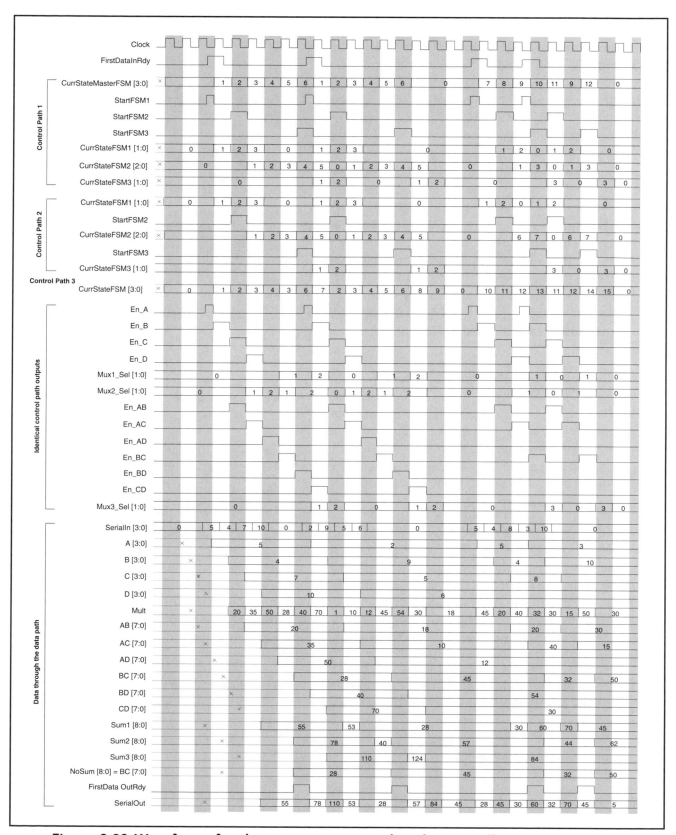

Figure 8.23 Waveforms for three separate control paths controlling one data path

Example 8.13 Two interactive FSMs controlling two rotors

Two bidirectionally interactive state machines are used to control two mechanical interlocking rotors, which rotate in 90 degree increments in a clockwise or counter clockwise rotation, see Figure 8.24. Each rotor may reside in any one of four physical positions angled at 0, 90, 180 or 270 degrees. The mechanical interlocking arrangement between the two rotors prohibits them from being positioned at the same angle. Each rotor is controlled by its own state machine. State machine FSM1 controls the position or rotor R1, while state machine FSM2 controls the position of the rotor R2. The two state diagrams for the two state machine controllers are shown in Figure 8.25a). Each state machine has four states (Ang0, Ang90, Ang180 and Ang270) corresponding to the four positions of each rotor. The state transition equations for the four state transitions indicated in Figure 8.25a) are shown in Figure 8.25b).

Signals CW_R1 and CCW_R1 control the clockwise and counter clockwise movements of rotor R1, while signals CW_R2 and CCW_R2 control the clockwise and counter clockwise movements of rotor R2. A

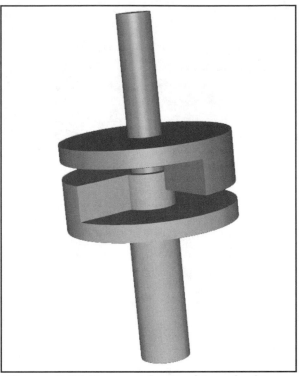

Figure 8.24 Two mechanical interlocking rotors

rotor cannot be requested to move in both directions at the same time, that is, both CW_R1 and CCW_R1 are at logic 1. Also, the movement requests for each rotor are independent of each other, that is, CW_R1 and CCW_R1 are independent of CW_R2 and CCW_R2.

State machine interaction comes from having to ensure the two rotors are never requested to move to the same position. At any one time, one of the rotors is the primary drive while the other is the secondary drive or slave. The primary drive always follows its clockwise and counter clockwise control signals, while secondary drive only follows its clockwise and counter clockwise control signals, provided the primary drive rotor is not in the way. The signal DriveR1_R2b indicates which rotor is the drive at any particular time. As a consequence of the interlocking mechanism, and the requirement for the state machines not to try and drive the two rotors into the same position, the two state machines, FSM1 and FSM2, interact in two ways indicated by the following two scenarios.

1. If rotor R1 is the drive and CW_R1 is at logic 1, then the state machine FSM1 will cycle round its four states in a clockwise rotation causing rotor R1 to rotate clockwise. Now if rotor R2 is not being driven, that is, CW_R2 and CCW_R2 are at logic 0, or it is wanting to move counter clockwise, that is, CCW_R2 is at logic 1, then when rotor R1 sees that R2 is in the way, R1 will override R2's control signals, and R2 will be pushed round in a clockwise direction one position ahead of R1.

2. If rotor R1 is the drive and both CW_R1 and CCW_R1 are at logic 0, then FSM1 stays in the same state, and R1 is stationary. In this case, movement requests for R2 by signals CW_R2 and CCW_R2 will only be granted by the state machine FSM2, provided it is in the bounds of the three positions not occupied by FSM1 (R1). If R2 does want to move to the position occupied by R1, it will hold its current position.

HDL models

The two state machines, FSM1 and FSM2 residing in their own **process** (VHDL)/**always** (Verilog) statement. The interaction between them is communicated via the state machine's current state signals (NewPosR1 and NewPosR2), and is bidirectional by virtue of both state machine's next state signals being a function of both state machine's current state. Placing the two state machines in their own **process/always** statement, is the most natural partitioning for this design, however, if there is other related or unrelated code included in the model, the two state machines may be better placed in the same **process/always** statement. In this case, the communication between the two VHDL state machines could be via variables instead of signals, and so would simulate faster.

Both the VHDL and Verilog versions of this design use a **case** statement to model the next state logic for the state machine when it is the drive. The interactive next state logic modeled for the condition when the other state machine is the drive, is coded differently between the VHDL and Verilog versions. The reason for this is, the Verilog example is able to make use of the **casex** construct which allows "don't care" input choice values. The VHDL language does not allow this, so it is better to use the in built priority encoding provided by the **if** statement.

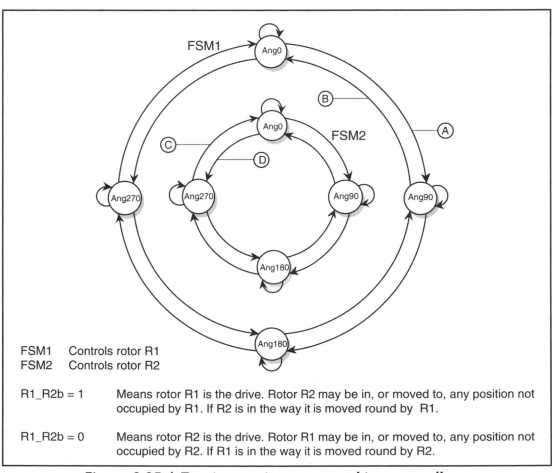

FSM1   Controls rotor R1
FSM2   Controls rotor R2

R1_R2b = 1   Means rotor R1 is the drive. Rotor R2 may be in, or moved to, any position not occupied by R1. If R2 is in the way it is moved round by R1.

R1_R2b = 0   Means rotor R2 is the drive. Rotor R1 may be in, or moved to, any position not occupied by R2. If R1 is in the way it is moved round by R2.

Figure 8.25a) Two interactive state machine controllers

(A) (DriveR1_R2b.CW_R1) or

R1 is the drive.

($\overline{\text{DriveR1\_R2b}}$.CW_R2.PosR2=Ang270) or

R2 is the drive and pushes R1 clockwise.

(($\overline{\text{DriveR1\_R2b}}$.CW_R1)($\overline{\text{CCW\_R2}}$.PosR2=Ang90)

R2 is the drive but is not impeding R1 from independently moving clockwise.

(CW_R1.$\overline{\text{CW\_R2}}$.CCW_R2.PosR2=Ang90)

($\overline{\text{CCW\_R1}}$.$\overline{\text{CW\_R2}}$.$\overline{\text{CCW\_R2}}$.PosR2=Ang270))

(B) (DriveR1_R2b.CCW_R1) or

R1 is the drive.

($\overline{\text{DriveR1\_R2b}}$.CCW_R2.PosR2=Ang180) or

R2 is the drive and pushes R1 counter clockwise.

(($\overline{\text{DriveR1\_R2b}}$.CCW_R1)($\overline{\text{CW\_R2}}$.PosR2=Ang0)

R2 is the drive but is not impeding R1 from independently moving counter clockwise.

(CW_R1.$\overline{\text{CW\_R2}}$.CCW_R2.PosR2=Ang180)

($\overline{\text{CCW\_R1}}$.$\overline{\text{CW\_R2}}$.$\overline{\text{CCW\_R2}}$.PosR2=Ang0))

(C) ($\overline{\text{DriveR1\_R2b}}$.CW_R2) or

R2 is the drive.

($\overline{\text{DriveR1\_R2b}}$.CW_R1.PosR1=Ang180) or

R1 is the drive and pushes R2 clockwise.

((DriveR1_R2b.CW_R2)($\overline{\text{CCW\_R1}}$.PosR1=Ang0)

R1 is the drive but is not impeding R2 from independently moving clockwise.

(CW_R2.$\overline{\text{CW\_R1}}$.$\overline{\text{CCW\_R1}}$.PosR1=Ang0)

($\overline{\text{CCW\_R2}}$.CW_R1.$\overline{\text{CCW\_R1}}$.PosR1=Ang180))

(D) ($\overline{\text{DriveR1\_R2b}}$.CCW_R2) or

R2 is the drive.

(DriveR1_R2b.CCW_R1.PosR1=Ang90) or

R1 is the drive and pushes R2 counter clockwise.

((DriveR1_R2b.CCW_R2)($\overline{\text{CW\_R1}}$.PosR1=Ang270)

R1 is the drive but is not impeding R2 from independently moving counter clockwise.

(CW_R2.$\overline{\text{CW\_R1}}$.$\overline{\text{CCW\_R1}}$.PosR1=Ang90)

($\overline{\text{CCW\_R2}}$.CW_R1.$\overline{\text{CCW\_R1}}$.PosR1=Ang270))

Figure 8.25b) State transition equations for the state diagrams, Figure 8.25a)

Two bidirectionally interactive state machines

VHDL	Verilog

```vhdl
library IEEE;
use IEEE.STD_Logic_1164.all, IEEE.Numeric_STD.all;

entity FSMS_BIDIR_INTERACTIVE is
  port (Clock, Reset:       in  std_logic;
        DriveR1_R2b:        in  std_logic;
        PosR1:              in  unsigned(1 downto 0);
        PosR2:              in  unsigned(1 downto 0);
        CW_R1, CCW_R1:      in  std_logic;
        CW_R2, CCW_R2:      in  std_logic;
        NewPosR1_out:       out unsigned(1 downto 0);
        NewPosR2_out:       out unsigned(1 downto 0));
end entity FSMS_BIDIR_INTERACTIVE;

architecture RTL of FSMS_BIDIR_INTERACTIVE is
  constant Ang0:    unsigned(1 downto 0) := "00";
  constant Ang90:   unsigned(1 downto 0) := "01";
  constant Ang180:  unsigned(1 downto 0) := "10";
  constant Ang270:  unsigned(1 downto 0) := "11";
begin

  FSM_ROTOR1: process (Clock)
    variable CW_CCW_R1: unsigned(1 downto 0);
  begin
    CW_CCW_R1 := CW_R1 & CCW_R1;
    if rising_edge(Clock) then
      if (Reset = '1') then
        NewPosR1 <= PosR1;
      else
        case (NewPosR1) is
          when Ang0 =>
            if (DriveR1_R2b = '1') then
              case (CW_CCW_R1) is
                when "10" =>    NewPosR1 <= Ang90;
                when "01" =>    NewPosR1 <= Ang270;
                when others =>  NewPosR1 <= Ang0;
              end case;
            else
              if (CW_R2 = '1' and PosR2 = Ang270) then
                NewPosR1 <= Ang90;
              elsif (CCW_R2='1' and PosR2=Ang90) then
                NewPosR1 <= Ang270;
              elsif (CW_R1 = '1' and CW_R2 = '0' and
                     CCW_R2='0' and PosR2=Ang90) then
                NewPosR1 <= Ang0;
              elsif (CCW_R1 = '1' and CW_R2 = '0' and
                     CCW_R2='0' and PosR2=Ang270) then
                NewPosR1 <= Ang0;
              elsif (CW_R1 = '1') then
                NewPosR1 <= Ang90;
              elsif (CCW_R1 = '1') then
                NewPosR1 <= Ang270;
              end if;
            end if;
          when Ang90 =>
            if (DriveR1_R2b = '1') then
              case (CW_CCW_R1) is
                when "10" =>    NewPosR1 <= Ang180;
                when "01" =>    NewPosR1 <= Ang0;
                when others =>  NewPosR1 <= Ang90;
              end case;
            else
              if (CW_R2 = '1' and PosR2 = Ang0) then
                NewPosR1 <= Ang180;
```

continued

```verilog
`define AnyAng 2'b XX

module FSMS_BIDIR_INTERACTIVE
  ( Clock, Reset, DriveR1_R2b, PosR1, PosR2, CW_R1,
    CCW_R1, CW_R2, CCW_R2, NewPosR1, NewPosR2);

  input Clock, Reset, DriveR1_R2b;
  input (1:0)   PosR1, PosR2;
  input CW_R1, CCW_R1, CW_R2, CCW_R2;
  output (1:0)  NewPosR1, NewPosR2;
  reg (1:0)     NewPosR1, NewPosR2;
  parameter  Ang0    = 2'b 00,
             Ang90   = 2'b 01,
             Ang180  = 2'b 10,
             Ang270  = 2'b 11;

  always @(posedge Clock)
    begin: FSM_ROTOR1

      if (Reset)
        NewPosR1 = PosR1;
      else
        casex (NewPosR1)
          Ang0 :
            if (DriveR1_R2b)
              case ({CW_R1, CCW_R1})
                2'b 10: NewPosR1 = Ang90;
                2'b 01: NewPosR1 = Ang270;
              endcase
            else
              casex ({CW_R1,CCW_R1,CW_R2,CCW_R2,PosR2})
                {4'b XX10, Ang270}:  NewPosR1 = Ang90;
                {4'b XX01, Ang90}:   NewPosR1 = Ang270;
                {4'b 1000, Ang90}:   NewPosR1 = Ang0;
                {4'b 0100, Ang270}:  NewPosR1 = Ang0;
                {4'b 10XX, `AnyAng}: NewPosR1 = Ang90;
                {4'b 01XX, `AnyAng}: NewPosR1 = Ang270;
              endcase

          Ang90 :
            if (DriveR1_R2b)
              case ({CW_R1, CCW_R1})
                2'b 10: NewPosR1 = Ang180;
                2'b 01: NewPosR1 = Ang0;
              endcase
            else
              casex ({CW_R1,CCW_R1,CW_R2,CCW_R2,PosR2})
                {4'b XX10, Ang0}:    NewPosR1 = Ang180;
                {4'b XX01, Ang180}:  NewPosR1 = Ang0;
```

> Notice **casex** values overlap. Consider using an RTL synthesis specific parallel case directive to avoid generating priority encoded logic.

continued

State values for both FSMs.

Two bidirectionally interactive state machines

VHDL	Verilog
| ```
        elsif (CCW_R2='1' and PosR2=Ang180) then
          NewPosR1 <= Ang0;
        elsif (CW_R1 = '1' and CW_R2 = '0' and
            CCW_R2='0' and PosR2=Ang180) then
          NewPosR1 <= Ang90;
        elsif (CCW_R1 = '1' and CW_R2 = '0' and
            CCW_R2='0' and PosR2=Ang0) then
          NewPosR1 <= Ang90;
        elsif (CW_R1 = '1') then
          NewPosR1 <= Ang180;
        elsif (CCW_R1 = '1') then
          NewPosR1 <= Ang0;
        end if;
      end if;
    when Ang180 =>
      if (DriveR1_R2b = '1') then
        case (CW_CCW_R1) is
          when "10" => NewPosR1 <= Ang270;
          when "01" => NewPosR1 <= Ang90;
          when others => NewPosR1 <= Ang180;
        end case;
      else
        if (CW_R2 = '1' and PosR2 = Ang90) then
          NewPosR1 <= Ang270;
        elsif (CCW_R2='1' and PosR2=Ang270) then
          NewPosR1 <= Ang90;
        elsif (CW_R1 = '1' and CW_R2 = '0' and
            CCW_R2='0' and PosR2=Ang270) then
          NewPosR1 <= Ang180;
        elsif (CCW_R1 = '1' and CW_R2 = '0' and
            CCW_R2='0' and PosR2=Ang90) then
          NewPosR1 <= Ang180;
        elsif (CW_R1 = '1') then
          NewPosR1 <= Ang270;
        elsif (CCW_R1 = '1') then
          NewPosR1 <= Ang90;
        end if;
      end if;
    when Ang270 =>
      if (DriveR1_R2b = '1') then
        case (CW_CCW_R1) is
          when "10" => NewPosR1 <= Ang0;
          when "01" => NewPosR1 <= Ang180;
          when others => NewPosR1 <= Ang270;
        end case;
      else
        if (CW_R2='1' and PosR2=Ang180) then
          NewPosR1 <= Ang0;
        elsif (CCW_R2='1' and PosR2=Ang0) then
          NewPosR1 <= Ang180;
        elsif (CW_R1 = '1' and CW_R2 = '0' and
            CCW_R2 = '0' and PosR2 = Ang0) then
          NewPosR1 <= Ang270;
        elsif (CCW_R1 = '1' and CW_R2 = '0' and
            CCW_R2='0' and PosR2=Ang180) then
          NewPosR1 <= Ang270;
        elsif (CW_R1 = '1') then
          NewPosR1 <= Ang0;
        elsif (CCW_R1 = '1') then
          NewPosR1 <= Ang180;
        end if;
      end if;
    when others => null;
  end case;
``` | ```
    {4'b 1000,  Ang180}:   NewPosR1 = Ang90;
    {4'b 0100,  Ang0}:     NewPosR1 = Ang90;
    {4'b 10XX, `AnyAng}:  NewPosR1 = Ang180;
    {4'b 01XX, `AnyAng}:  NewPosR1 = Ang0;
  endcase




Ang180 :
  if (DriveR1_R2b)
    case ({CW_R1, CCW_R1})
    2'b 10: NewPosR1 = Ang270;
    2'b 01: NewPosR1 = Ang90;
    endcase
  else
    casex ({CW_R1, CCW_R1, CW_R2, CCW_R2, PosR2})
    {4'b XX10, Ang90}:    NewPosR1 = Ang270;
    {4'b XX01, Ang270}:   NewPosR1 = Ang90;
    {4'b 1000, Ang270}:   NewPosR1 = Ang180;
    {4'b 0100, Ang90}:    NewPosR1 = Ang180;
    {4'b 10XX, `AnyAng}: NewPosR1 = Ang270;
    {4'b 01XX, `AnyAng}: NewPosR1 = Ang90;
    endcase







Ang270 :
  if (DriveR1_R2b)
    case ({CW_R1, CCW_R1})
    2'b 10: NewPosR1 = Ang0;
    2'b 01: NewPosR1 = Ang180;
    endcase
  else
    casex ({CW_R1, CCW_R1, CW_R2, CCW_R2, PosR2})
    {4'b XX10, Ang180}:    NewPosR1 = Ang0;
    {4'b XX01, Ang0}:      NewPosR1 = Ang180;
    {4'b 1000, Ang0}:      NewPosR1 = Ang270;
    {4'b 0100, Ang180}:    NewPosR1 = Ang270;
    {4'b 10XX, `AnyAng}:  NewPosR1 = Ang0;
    {4'b 01XX, `AnyAng}:  NewPosR1 = Ang180;
    endcase
  endcase
end
``` |
| continued | continued |

Two bidirectionally interactive state machines

VHDL	Verilog
<pre> end if; end if; NewPosR1_out <= NewPosR1; end process FSM_ROTOR1; FSM_ROTOR2: process (Clock) variable CW_CCW_R2: unsigned(1 downto 0); begin CW_CCW_R2 := CW_R2 & CCW_R2; if rising_edge(Clock) then if (Reset = '1') then NewPosR2 <= PosR2; else case (NewPosR2) is when Ang0 => if (DriveR1_R2b = '0') then case (CW_CCW_R2) is when "10" => NewPosR2 <= Ang90; when "01" => NewPosR2 <= Ang270; when others => NewPosR2 <= Ang0; end case; else if (CW_R1 = '1' and PosR1 = Ang270) then NewPosR2 <= Ang90; elsif (CCW_R1='1' and PosR1=Ang90) then NewPosR2 <= Ang270; elsif (CW_R2 = '1' and CW_R1 = '0' and CCW_R1='0' and PosR1=Ang90) then NewPosR2 <= Ang0; elsif (CCW_R2 = '1' and CW_R1 = '0' and CCW_R1='0' and PosR1=Ang270) then NewPosR2 <= Ang0; elsif (CW_R2 = '1') then NewPosR2 <= Ang90; elsif (CCW_R2 = '1') then NewPosR2 <= Ang270; end if; end if; when Ang90 => if (DriveR1_R2b = '0') then case (CW_CCW_R2) is when "10" => NewPosR2 <= Ang180; when "01" => NewPosR2 <= Ang0; when others => NewPosR2 <= Ang90; end case; else if (CW_R1 = '1' and PosR1 = Ang0) then NewPosR2 <= Ang180; elsif (CCW_R1='1' and PosR1=Ang180) then NewPosR2 <= Ang0; elsif (CW_R2 = '1' and CW_R1 = '0' and CCW_R1='0' and PosR1=Ang180) then NewPosR2 <= Ang90; elsif (CCW_R2 = '1' and CW_R1 = '0' and CCW_R1='0' and PosR1=Ang0) then NewPosR2 <= Ang90; elsif (CW_R2 = '1') then NewPosR2 <= Ang180; elsif (CCW_R2 = '1') then NewPosR2 <= Ang0; end if; end if; when Ang180 => if (DriveR1_R2b = '0') then</pre>	<pre>always @(posedge Clock) begin: FSM_ROTOR2 if (Reset) NewPosR2 = PosR2; else casex (NewPosR2) Ang0 : if (! DriveR1_R2b) case ({CW_R2, CCW_R2}) 2'b 10: NewPosR2 = Ang90; 2'b 01: NewPosR2 = Ang270; endcase else casex ({CW_R1,CCW_R1,CW_R2,CCW_R2,PosR1}) {4'b 10XX, Ang270}: NewPosR2 = Ang90; {4'b 01XX, Ang90}: NewPosR2 = Ang270; {4'b 0010, Ang90}: NewPosR2 = Ang0; {4'b 0001, Ang270}: NewPosR2 = Ang0; {4'b XX10, `AnyAng}:  NewPosR2 = Ang90;           {4'b XX01, `AnyAng}: NewPosR2 = Ang270; endcase Ang90 : if (! DriveR1_R2b) case ({CW_R2, CCW_R2}) 2'b 10: NewPosR2 = Ang180; 2'b 01: NewPosR2 = Ang0; endcase else casex ({CW_R1,CCW_R1,CW_R2,CCW_R2,PosR1}) {4'b 10XX, Ang0}: NewPosR2 = Ang180; {4'b 01XX, Ang180}: NewPosR2 = Ang0; {4'b 0010, Ang180}: NewPosR2 = Ang90; {4'b 0001, Ang0}: NewPosR2 = Ang90; {4'b XX10, `AnyAng}:  NewPosR2 = Ang180;           {4'b XX01, `AnyAng}: NewPosR2 = Ang0; endcase Ang180 : if (! DriveR1_R2b)</pre>
continued	continued

Two bidirectionally interactive state machines

VHDL	Verilog
<pre>   case (CW_CCW_R2) is
                when "10" =>   NewPosR2 <= Ang270;
                when "01" =>   NewPosR2 <= Ang90;
                when others => NewPosR2 <= Ang180;
            end case;
            else
                if (CW_R1 = '1' and PosR1 = Ang90) then
                    NewPosR2 <= Ang270;
                elsif (CCW_R1='1' and PosR1=Ang270) then
                    NewPosR2 <= Ang90;
                elsif (CW_R2 = '1' and CW_R1 = '0' and
                        CCW_R1 = '0' and PosR1 = Ang270) then
                    NewPosR2 <= Ang180;
                elsif (CCW_R2 = '1' and CW_R1 = '0' and
                        CCW_R1 = '0' and PosR1 = Ang90) then
                    NewPosR2 <= Ang180;
                elsif (CW_R2 = '1') then
                    NewPosR2 <= Ang270;
                elsif (CCW_R2 = '1') then
                    NewPosR2 <= Ang90;
                end if;
            end if;
        when Ang270 =>
            if (DriveR1_R2b = '0') then
                case (CW_CCW_R2) is
                when "10" =>   NewPosR2 <= Ang0;
                when "01" =>   NewPosR2 <= Ang180;
                when others => NewPosR2 <= Ang270;
            end case;
            else
                if (CW_R1 = '1' and PosR1 = Ang180) then
                    NewPosR2 <= Ang0;
                elsif (CCW_R1 = '1' and PosR1 = Ang0) then
                    NewPosR2 <= Ang180;
                elsif (CW_R2 = '1' and CW_R1 = '0' and
                        CCW_R1 = '0' and PosR1 = Ang0) then
                    NewPosR2 <= Ang270;
                elsif (CCW_R2 = '1' and CW_R1 = '0' and
                        CCW_R1 = '0' and PosR1 = Ang180) then
                    NewPosR2 <= Ang270;
                elsif (CW_R2 = '1') then
                    NewPosR2 <= Ang0;
                elsif (CCW_R2 = '1') then
                    NewPosR2 <= Ang180;
                end if;
            end if;
        when others => null;
        end case;
    end if;
  end if;
  NewPosR2_out <= NewPosR2;
 end process FSM_ROTOR2;

end architecture RTL;</pre> | <pre>   case ({CW_R2, CCW_R2})
        2'b 10: NewPosR2 = Ang270;
        2'b 01: NewPosR2 = Ang90;
        endcase
    else
    casex ({CW_R1,CCW_R1,CW_R2,CCW_R2,PosR1})
    {4'b 10XX, Ang90}:   NewPosR2 = Ang270;
    {4'b 01XX, Ang270}:   NewPosR2 = Ang90;
    {4'b 0010, Ang270}:   NewPosR2 = Ang180;
    {4'b 0001, Ang90}:   NewPosR2 = Ang180;
    {4'b XX10, `AnyAng}: NewPosR2 = Ang270;
    {4'b XX01, `AnyAng}: NewPosR2 = Ang90;
    endcase

   Ang270 :
     if (! DriveR1_R2b)
       case ({CW_R2, CCW_R2})
       2'b 10: NewPosR2 = Ang0;
       2'b 01: NewPosR2 = Ang180;
       endcase
     else
       casex ({CW_R1,CCW_R1,CW_R2,CCW_R2,PosR1})
       {4'b 10XX, Ang180}:   NewPosR2 = Ang0;
       {4'b 01XX, Ang0}:   NewPosR2 = Ang180;
       {4'b 0010, Ang0}:   NewPosR2 = Ang270;
       {4'b 0001, Ang180}:   NewPosR2 = Ang270;
       {4'b XX10, `AnyAng}:   NewPosR2 = Ang0;
       {4'b XX01, `AnyAng}:   NewPosR2 = Ang180;
       endcase
    endcase
   end

endmodule</pre> |

Two bidirectionally interactive state machines

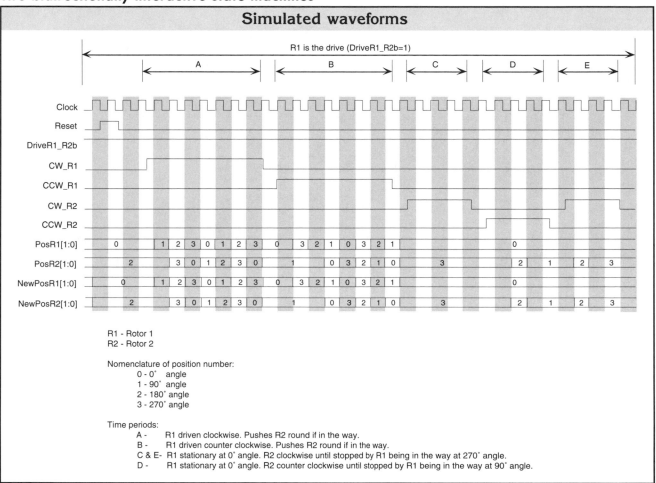

R1 - Rotor 1
R2 - Rotor 2

Nomenclature of position number:
    0 - 0˚ angle
    1 - 90˚ angle
    2 - 180˚ angle
    3 - 270˚ angle

Time periods:
    A -   R1 driven clockwise. Pushes R2 round if in the way.
    B -   R1 driven counter clockwise. Pushes R2 round if in the way.
    C & E- R1 stationary at 0˚ angle. R2 clockwise until stopped by R1 being in the way at 270˚ angle.
    D -   R1 stationary at 0˚ angle. R2 counter clockwise until stopped by R1 being in the way at 90˚ angle.

269

Circuit Functions modeled Combinationally or Synchronously

Chapter 9 Contents

Shifters

Shift operations may be implemented using: 1) purely combinational logic for a combinational shifter or 2) sequential logic, possibly with combinational logic as well, for a synchronous shifter. Combinational logic shifters operate faster than their synchronous counterparts and can perform <u>any</u> shift operation in a single operation. A sequential shift requires two clock cycles; one to load data into a register and another to shift the data within the register. More clock cycles are needed if a shift of more than one bit position is required. Combinational logic shifters do not require any clock cycles, no matter how many shifts are required. The logic for the combinational shifter can be combined with other combinational logic and all operate within a single clock cycle. A typical application of a combinational logic shifter is for the output stage of an ALU.

Combinational Shifters

A combinational shifter circuit can be constructed using multiplexers as shown in Figure 9.1. It shows the structure of a 4-bit wide shifter, the function table of which is shown in Table 9.1.

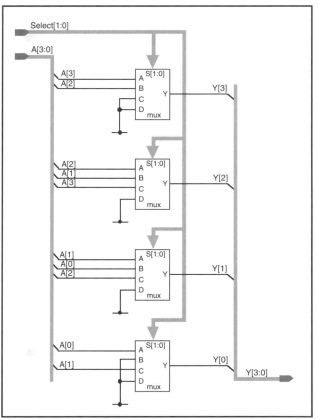

Sel1	Sel0	Operation	Function
0	0	Y <- A	no shift
0	1	Y <- shl A	shift left
1	0	Y <- shr A	shift right
1	1	Y <- 0	zero outputs

Table 9.1 Function table for a combinational shifter

Shifters can be modeled using **if** or **case** statements just like most other circuit functions. It is often better to use the **case** statement as models are slightly easier to read and maintain. For this reason, Examples 9.1, 9.2 and 9.3, only use **case** statements.

Example 9.1 shows a 6-bit shifter similar to the 4-bit shifter described above. Example 9.2 is similar, but includes extra serial shifted input and output data signals. Example 9.3 shows a 6-bit barrel shifter that can shift input data by any number of bit positions defined by the binary value on the select inputs.

Figure 9.1 Structure of a 4-bit combinational shifter

Example 9.1 Combinational logic shifter

A 6-bit wide combinational logic shifter is modeled to the function table; Table 9.2. The implied structure is shown graphically in Figure 9.2, using 4-1 multiplexers for convenience. A synthesized circuit will never use 4-1 multiplexers from the cell library as there would be too much redundant logic. The synthesized circuit will be constructed from cell primitives, as most other types of circuit. A possible implementation from a synthesis tool is indicated on the following page.

Sel	Operation	Function
0	Y <- A	no shift
1	Y <- shl A	shift left
2	Y <- shr A	shift right
3	Y <- 0	zero outputs

Table 9.2 Function table for the shifter

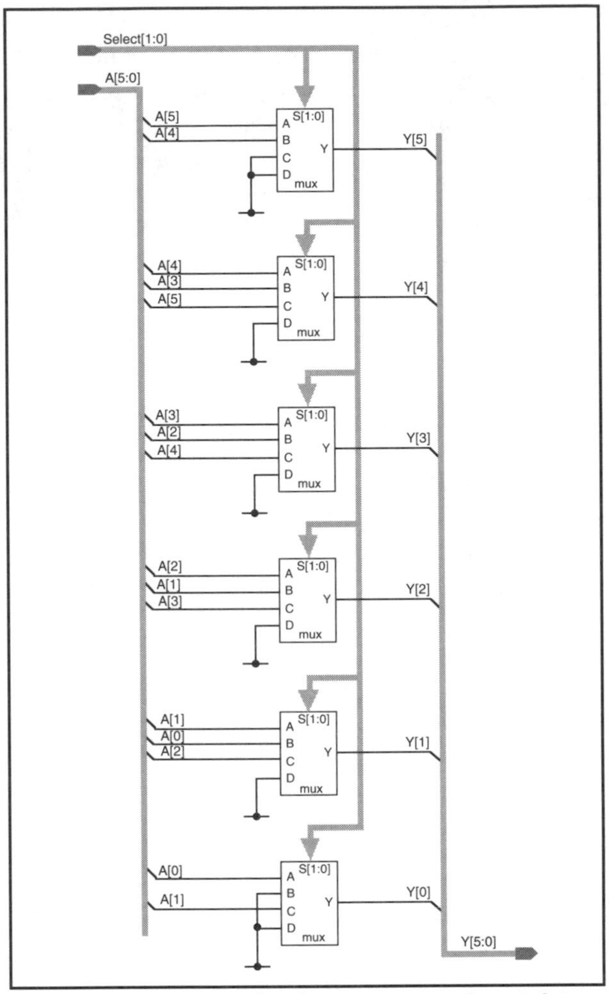

Figure 9.2 Implied structure of a 6-bit combinational shifter

6-bit wide combinational logic shifter

```
                    VHDL

library IEEE;
use IEEE.STD_LOGIC_1164.all; IEEE.Numeric_STD.all;

entity SHIFTER is
    port ( Sel: in   integer range 0 to 3;
           A:  in   unsigned(5 downto 0);
           Y:  out  unsigned(5 downto 0));
end entity SHIFTER;

architecture COND_DATA_FLOW of SHIFTER is
begin

    COMB_SHIFT:
    process (Sel, A)           [Functions defined in IEEE
    begin                       1076.3 package Numeric.STD.]
        case (Sel) is
            when 0 => Y <= A;
            when 1 => Y <= Shift_left (A, 1);
            when 2 => Y <= Shift_right (A, 1);
            when others => Y <= (others =>'0');
        end case;
    end process;

end architecture COND_DATA_FLOW;
```

```
                Verilog

module SHIFTER (Sel, A, Y);
    input  [1:0] Sel;
    input  [5:0] A;
    output [5:0] Y;

    reg [5:0] Y;

    always @(Sel or A)
        begin: COMB_SHIFT
        case (Sel)
            0 : Y = A;
            1 : Y = A << 1;
            2 : Y = A >> 1;
            default : Y = 6'b 0;
        endcase
    end

endmodule
```

6-bit wide combinational logic shifter

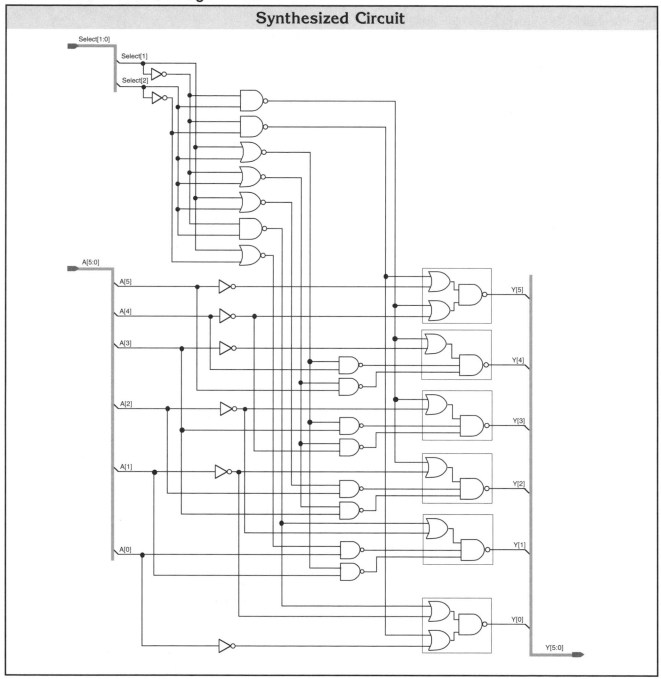

Example 9.2 Combinational logic shifter with shift in and out signals

A 6-bit wide combinational logic shifter is modeled to the function table; Table 9.3. The model is similar to Example 9.1, but signals ShiftLeftIn and ShiftRightIn are used as serial inputs for the shift left and shift right operations, respectively. Similarly, signals ShiftLeftOut and ShiftRightOut correspond to the shifted output data from the shift left and shift right operations, respectively.

The 6-bit input data to be shifted is assigned to the inner six bits of an 8-bit data type. This leaves a bit either side that can hold the shift left and right overflows which are then assigned to the ShiftLeftOut and ShiftRightOut signals, respectively. The inner six bits of the 8-bit data type is then assigned to the output Y.

Sel	Operation	Function
0	Y <- A ShiftLeftOut <- 0 ShiftRightOut <- 0	no shift
1	Y <- shl A ShiftLeftOut <- A[5] ShiftRightOut <- 0	shift left
2	Y <- shr A ShiftLeftOut <- 0 ShiftRightOut <- A[0]	shift right
3	Y <- 0 ShiftLeftOut <- 0 ShiftRightOut <- 0	zero outputs

Table 9.3 Function table for shifter with shift in and out signals

6-bit wide conbinational logic shifter with shift in and shift out

VHDL	Verilog
| ```
library IEEE;
use IEEE.STD_LOGIC_1164.all; IEEE.Numeric_STD.all;

entity SHIFTER_SHIFTINOUT is
    port ( Sel:           in integer range 0 to 3;
        ShiftLeftIn,
        ShiftRightIn:  in std_logic;
        A:             in unsigned(5 downto 0);
        ShiftLeftOut,
        ShiftRightOut: out std_logic;
        Y:             out unsigned(5 downto 0));
end entity SHIFTER_SHIFTINOUT;

architecture COND_DATA_FLOW of SHIFTER_SHIFTINOUT is
begin

    COMB_SHIFT:
    process (Sel, A, ShiftLeftIn, ShiftRightIn)
        variable; A_Wide, Y_Wide: unsigned(7 downto 0);
    begin
        A_Wide := ShiftLeftIn & A & ShiftRightIn;
        case (Sel) is
            when 0 => Y_Wide := A_Wide;
            when 1 => Y_Wide := shift_left(A_wide,1);
            when 2 => Y_Wide := shift_right(A_wide,1);
            when 3 => Y_Wide := (others =>'0');
            when others => Y_Wide := (others =>'0');
        end case;
        ShiftLeftOut <= Y_Wide(0);
        Y <= Y_Wide(6 downto 1);
        ShiftRightOut <= Y_Wide(7);
    end process COMB_SHIFT;

end architecture COND_DATA_FLOW;
``` | ```
module SHIFTER_SHIFTINOUT
    (Sel, ShiftLeftIn, ShiftRightIn, A,
    ShiftLeftOut, ShiftRightOut, Y);
    input    (1:0) Sel;
    input    ShiftLeftIn, ShiftRightIn;
    input    (5:0) A;
    output   ShiftLeftOut, ShiftRightOut;
    output   (5:0) Y;

    reg ShiftLeftOut, ShiftRightOut;
    reg (5:0) Y;

    reg (7:0) A_Wide, Y_Wide;

always @(Sel or A or ShiftLeftIn or ShiftRightIn)
    begin: COMB_SHIFT
        A_Wide = {ShiftLeftIn, A, ShiftRightIn};
        case (Sel)
            0 : Y_Wide = A_Wide;
            1 : Y_Wide = A_Wide << 1;
            2 : Y_Wide = A_Wide >> 1;
            3 : Y_Wide = 8'b0;
            default : Y = A_Wide;
        endcase
        ShiftLeftOut = Y_Wide(0);
        Y = Y_Wide(6:0);
        ShiftRightOut = Y_Wide(7);
    end

endmodule
``` |

Example 9.3 Combinational barrel shifter

A 6-bit wide combinational logic barrel shifter is modeled to the function table; Table 9.4. The value of the Rotate, specifies how many rotation operations are to be performed. The 6-bit input may be functionally rotated from 0 to 5 positions.

Only one model version using a **case** statement is included, it is easier to code and comprehend than if the **if** statement was used. Also, a model using the **if** statement would be very similar to the models in Examples 9.1 and 9.2. A **for** loop cannot be used to model this barrel shifter as the signal, Rotate, would need to be used to determine the loop range. This is not allowed by synthesis tools as a loop's range <u>must</u> be statically computable at compile time in order do synthesize a finite amount of logic.

Sel	Operation	Function
0	Y <- A	no shift
1	Y <- A rol 1	rotate once
2	Y <- A rol 2	rotate twice
3	Y <- A rol 3	rotate three times
4	Y <- A rol 4	rotate four times
5	Y <- A rol 5	rotate five times

Table 9.4 Function table for 6-bit wide barrel shifter

Verilog

```verilog
// File name: rotate_left.v
function (5:0) rotate_left;
    input (5:0) A;
    input (2:0) NumberShifts;

    reg (5:0) Shifting;
    integer N;

  begin
    Shifting = A;
    for (N = 1; N <= NumberShifts; N = N + 1)
      begin
        Shifting = {Shifting(4:0), Shifting(5)};
      end
    rotate_left = Shifting;;
  end

endfunction
```

Rotate operation not available in Verilog so must be defined in a separate function for a specific bit width.

VHDL

```vhdl
library IEEE;
use IEEE.STD_LOGIC_1164.all; IEEE.Numeric_STD.all;

entity SHIFTER_BARREL is
    port ( Rotate:  in   integer range 0 to 5;
           A:       in   unsigned(5 downto 0);
           Y:       out  unsigned(5 downto 0));
end entity SHIFTER_BARREL;

architecture COND_DATA_FLOW of SHIFTER_BARREL is
begin

    COMB_BARREL_SHIFT:
    process (Rotate, A)
    begin
        case (Rotate) is
            when 0 => Y <= A;
            when 1 => Y <= rotate_left(A, 1);
            when 2 => Y <= rotate_left(A, 2);
            when 3 => Y <= rotate_left(A, 3);
            when 4 => Y <= rotate_left(A, 4);
            when 5 => Y <= rotate_left(A, 5);
            when others => Y <= (others =>'0');
        end case;
    end process COMB_BARREL_SHIFT;

end architecture COND_DATA_FLOW;
```

Rotate left operator.

Number of times being rotated and must be constant at synthesis compile time.

Verilog

```verilog
module SHIFTER_BARREL (Rotate, A, Y);
    input (2:0) Rotate;
    input (5:0) A;
    output (5:0) Y;

    reg (5:0) Y;

    `include "rotate_left.v"

    always @(Rotate or A)
        begin: COMB_BARREL_SHIFT
            case (Rotate)
                0 : Y = A;
                1 : Y = rotate_left(A, 1);
                2 : Y = rotate_left(A, 2);
                3 : Y = rotate_left(A, 3);
                4 : Y = rotate_left(A, 4);
                5 : Y = rotate_left(A, 5);
                default : Y = 6'b X;
            endcase
        end

endmodule
```

Function call.

Number of times being rotated.

Synchronous Shifters - Shift Registers

Synchronous shifters, commonly known as shift registers, are inferred in the same way as standard registers, but with a shifted version of the registered output fed back to its input. Alternatively, they can be thought of as being modeled as a combinational shifter, but in an edge triggered section of code; see Example 9.4.

Example 9.4 Shift registers

Two 5-bit loadable shift registers are shown. The first shift register, ShiftReg1, shifts the register bits one bit to the left (up one towards the most significant bit) and uses only **if** statements. The second shift register, ShiftReg2, can shift the register one bit to the left or right depending upon the value of the two bit select line Sel2. A **case** statement selects which shift, if any, to perform. The synthesized circuit only includes an implementation of the first shift register, ShiftReg1.

Two 5-bit loadable shift registers, one shift left and one shift left and right

VHDL	Verilog

library IEEE;
use IEEE.STD_Logic_1164.**all**, IEEE.Numeric_STD.**all**;
entity SHIFT_REG **is**
  port (Clock, Reset: **in** std_logic;
     Load1, SL1, Load2: **in** std_logic;
     Sel2:   **in** unsigned(1 **downto** 0);
     Data1, Data2:   **in** unsigned(4 **downto** 0);
     ShiftReg1, ShiftReg2:**out** unsigned(4 **downto** 0));
end entity SHIFT_REG;
architecture COND_DATA_FLOW **of** SHIFT_REG **is**
begin
  SYNCH_SHIFTERS:
  process (Clock)
    variable ShiftReg1_v, ShiftReg2_v: unsigned(4 **downto** 0);
  begin
    if rising_edge(Clock) **then**
      if (Reset = '1') **then**
        ShiftReg1_v := (**others** => '0');
      elsif (Load1 = '1') **then**
        ShiftReg1_v := Data1;
      elsif (SL1 = '1') **then**
        ShiftReg1_v := shift_left(ShiftReg1_v,1);
      else
        ShiftReg1_v := ShiftReg1_v;
      end if;
    end if;
    ShiftReg1 <= ShiftReg1_v;
 	
    if rising_edge(Clock) **then**
      if (Reset = '1') **then**
        ShiftReg2_v := (**others** => '0');
      elsif (Load2 = '1') **then**
        ShiftReg2_v := Data2;
      else
        case Sel2 **is**
          when "00" => ShiftReg2_v := ShiftReg2_v;
          when "01" => ShiftReg2_v := Shift_left(ShiftReg2_v, 1);
          when "10" => ShiftReg2_v := Shift_right(ShiftReg2_v, 1);
          when others => ShiftReg2_v := ShiftReg2_v;
        end case;
      end if;
    end if;
    ShiftReg2 <= ShiftReg2_v;
  end process SYNCH_SHIFTERS;
end architecture COND_DATA_FLOW;
	module SHIFT_REG
	  (Clock, Reset, Load1, SL1, Load2, Sel2, Data1,
	  Data2, ShiftReg1, ShiftReg2);
	  input Clock, Reset;
	  input Load1, SL1, Load2;
	  input [1:0] Sel2;
	  input [4:0] Data1, Data2;
	  output [4:0] ShiftReg1, ShiftReg2;
	  reg [4:0] ShiftReg1, ShiftReg2;
	
	  always @(posedge Clock)
	    begin: SYNCH_SHIFTERS
	      if (Reset)
	        ShiftReg1 = 0;
	      else if (Load1)
	        ShiftReg1 = Data1;
	      else if (SL1)
	        ShiftReg1 = ShiftReg1 << 1;
	      else
	        ShiftReg1 = ShiftReg1;
	
	      if (Reset)
	        ShiftReg2 = 0;
	      else if (Load2)
	        ShiftReg2 = Data2;
	      else
	        case (Sel2)
	          2'b 00 : ShiftReg2 = ShiftReg2;
	          2'b 01 : ShiftReg2 = ShiftReg2 << 1;
	          2'b 10 : ShiftReg2 = ShiftReg2 >> 1;
	          default : ShiftReg2 = ShiftReg2;
	        endcase
	    end
	
	endmodule

Loadable shift left register (see synthesized circuit).

Loadable left or right shift register (synthesized circuit not shown).

5-bit loadable shift left register only

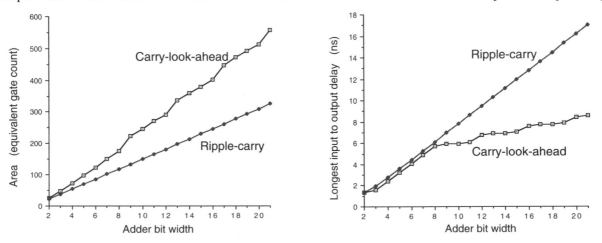

Synthesized Circuit

Adders and Subtractors

Digital circuits that perform addition and subtraction operations can be realized in parallel using purely combinational logic, or serially, in a synchronous manner, using combinational and sequential logic. Most are realized in parallel because they operate considerably faster, and although the circuit will be bigger, it is often not prohibitively excessive.

Combinational adders and subtractors

Adder and subtractor circuits can be modeled in different ways for different circuit implementations. Subtractors are implemented in the same way as adders, but with the 2's complement of one of the inputs, that is,

A - B is the same as A + the 2's complement of B.
(The 2's complement is the 1's complement plus 1; the 1's complement is each bit inverted.)

The simplest modeling method is to use the "+" and "-" arithmetic operators, they work equally well for both signed and unsigned numbers. In VHDL, the "+" and "-" operators are overloaded with different data types in order to facilitate the use of signed and unsigned numbers, that is, multiple functions named "+" and "-" are defined in the two IEEE 1076.3 synthesis packages.

Figure 9.3 Typical area/delay relationship of carry-look-ahead and ripple-carry adders

Typically, particular comment directives can be used in a model to guide a synthesis tool as to how an adder or subtractor should be structured. This allows adder/subtractor circuits to be synthesized with carry-look-ahead or ripple-carry structures, or a mixture of both, see Example

9.5. There is no standard for such comment directives and so may differ between synthesis tools. Carry-look-ahead circuits are faster, but larger than ripple-carry circuits, see Figure 9.3.

If each "+" and "-" operator in a model is synthesized to a separate adder or subtractor circuit, the chip area required to implement them could be needlessly excessive. When synthesis tools bind an operator like "+" or "-" to a particular circuit, called *resource binding*, the synthesis tool can choose to bind multiple operators to the same circuit. This is called *resource sharing*, see Chapter 4.

If the standard carry-look-ahead or ripple-carry implementation does not meet specific area, timing or power requirements one of two things can be done.

1. Use the logic optimizer to remove logical structure (flatten) and then restructure (factorize) to a circuit that better meets the requirements. Flattening and factorizing represents what happens to the boolean equations representing the function of adders or subtractors, as described in Chapter 1. When boolean equations are completely flattened, each output is represented in terms of only inputs; there are no intermediate terms. When equations are factorized, intermediate common terms, known as factors, are introduced producing multiple, but smaller equations.

2. Write a more detailed model describing the specific structure of a circuit that better meets the requirements. Example 9.6 shows how gate primitives, single bit half adders and single bit full adders are constructed to model a circuit that adds or subtracts a 2-bit value, to or from a 6-bit value. These single bit adders could be the direct instantiation of cells from a particular ASIC or FPGA technology library, and which will already have an efficient layout model.

Optimization Strategies. These are not discussed in any depth, however, a designer typically wants to optimize for the smallest possible area, and then, if the circuit does not meet specific timing requirements, reoptimize for timing until it does. Timing driven optimization reduces circuit timing, but its effect on the area is somewhat unknown because it is very much design dependent. Circuit area generally increases with reduced timing, however, it is possible that a circuit optimized for the minimal area also has the shortest timing delay paths through the circuit.

Sequential adders and subtractors

Serial addition and subtraction is performed synchronously using sequential logic, one bit at a time and using a single full adder. For this reason, it can be the preferred method if either, or both, inputs are already in a serial form, or the output is required in a serial form, see Example 9.7.

Example 9.5 Comment directives for Carry-Look-Ahead and Ripple-Carry adders and subtractors

Adder and subtractor circuits are modeled using of the "+" and "-" arithmetic operators. Synthesis specific comment directives plus other related constructs are also included and are specific to a particular synthesis tool. These directives tell the synthesis tool how the circuit should be structured, that is, carry-look-ahead or ripple-carry. Directives in the first **process** tell the synthesis tool to construct carry-look-ahead structures, while directives in the second **process** requests ripple-carry structures to be synthesized. The third process has a normal (non directive) comment which defaults to a carry-look-ahead structure in the case of this particular synthesis tool.

Synthesis comment directed carry-look-ahead/ripple-carry add/subtract

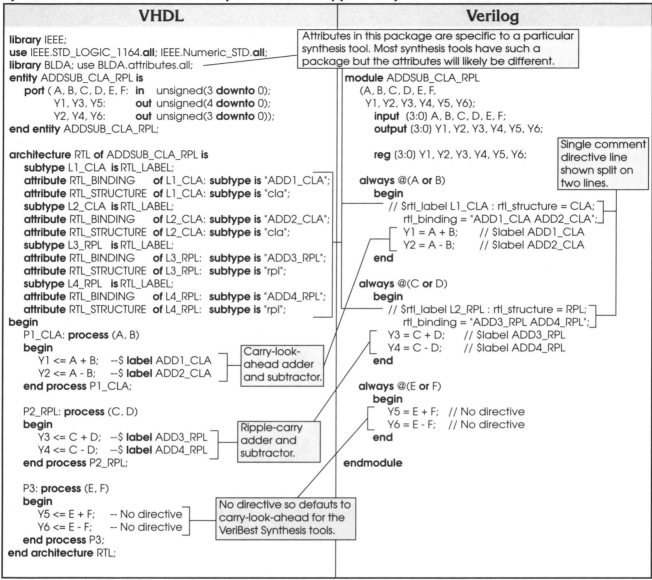

VHDL	Verilog

```
library IEEE;
use IEEE.STD_LOGIC_1164.all; IEEE.Numeric_STD.all;
library BLDA; use BLDA.attributes.all;
entity ADDSUB_CLA_RPL is
    port ( A, B, C, D, E, F: in    unsigned(3 downto 0);
            Y1, Y3, Y5:      out unsigned(4 downto 0);
            Y2, Y4, Y6:      out unsigned(3 downto 0));
end entity ADDSUB_CLA_RPL;

architecture RTL of ADDSUB_CLA_RPL is
    subtype L1_CLA is RTL_LABEL;
    attribute RTL_BINDING    of L1_CLA: subtype is "ADD1_CLA";
    attribute RTL_STRUCTURE of L1_CLA: subtype is "cla";
    subtype L2_CLA is RTL_LABEL;
    attribute RTL_BINDING    of L2_CLA: subtype is "ADD2_CLA";
    attribute RTL_STRUCTURE of L2_CLA: subtype is "cla";
    subtype L3_RPL is RTL_LABEL;
    attribute RTL_BINDING    of L3_RPL: subtype is "ADD3_RPL";
    attribute RTL_STRUCTURE of L3_RPL: subtype is "rpl";
    subtype L4_RPL is RTL_LABEL;
    attribute RTL_BINDING    of L4_RPL: subtype is "ADD4_RPL";
    attribute RTL_STRUCTURE of L4_RPL: subtype is "rpl";
begin
    P1_CLA: process (A, B)
    begin
        Y1 <= A + B;   --$ label ADD1_CLA
        Y2 <= A - B;   --$ label ADD2_CLA
    end process P1_CLA;

    P2_RPL: process (C, D)
    begin
        Y3 <= C + D;   --$ label ADD3_RPL
        Y4 <= C - D;   --$ label ADD4_RPL
    end process P2_RPL;

    P3: process (E, F)
    begin
        Y5 <= E + F;   -- No directive
        Y6 <= E - F;   -- No directive
    end process P3;
end architecture RTL;
```

```
module ADDSUB_CLA_RPL
    (A, B, C, D, E, F,
    Y1, Y2, Y3, Y4, Y5, Y6);
        input  (3:0) A, B, C, D, E, F;
        output (3:0) Y1, Y2, Y3, Y4, Y5, Y6;

        reg (3:0) Y1, Y2, Y3, Y4, Y5, Y6;

    always @(A or B)
        begin
            // $rtl_label L1_CLA : rtl_structure = CLA;
                rtl_binding = "ADD1_CLA ADD2_CLA";
            Y1 = A + B;    // $label ADD1_CLA
            Y2 = A - B;    // $label ADD2_CLA
        end

    always @(C or D)
        begin
            // $rtl_label L2_RPL : rtl_structure = RPL;
                rtl_binding = "ADD3_RPL ADD4_RPL";
            Y3 = C + D;    // $label ADD3_RPL
            Y4 = C - D;    // $label ADD4_RPL
        end

    always @(E or F)
        begin
            Y5 = E + F;  // No directive
            Y6 = E - F;  // No directive
        end

endmodule
```

Annotations:
- Attributes in this package are specific to a particular synthesis tool. Most synthesis tools have such a package but the attributes will likely be different.
- Single comment directive line shown split on two lines.
- Carry-look-ahead adder and subtractor.
- Ripple-carry adder and subtractor.
- No directive so defauts to carry-look-ahead for the VeriBest Synthesis tools.

Example 9.6 Combined adder and subtractor with detailed structure

The detailed logical structure of a circuit that either adds or subtracts a 2-bit value, to or from, a 6-bit value is modeled to the structure shown in Figure 9.4.

A single bit half adder is modeled using a single XOR logical operator and a single AND logical operator. Two of these half adders and the OR logical operator are used to model a single bit full adder. The adder/subtractor circuit, SIXBIT_ADDSUB2BIT, is then modeled by instantiating six of these full adders with a ripple carry chain from one full adder to the next. As input B, the addend, is only two bits wide, only two XOR functions are needed in order to create the 1's complement; they are XORed with the two least significant bits of input A, the augend. The 2's complement needed for subtraction, is created by connecting Sub_AddBar (logic 1 for subtraction) to the carry in of the first, least significant bit, full adder. It is worth considering at this point, the ASIC or FPGA technology library being used. It is likely single bit half and full adders already exist in the technology specific library of cells. If so, simply change the names of the full adders in SIXBIT_ADDSUB2BIT to match the cell name in the library.

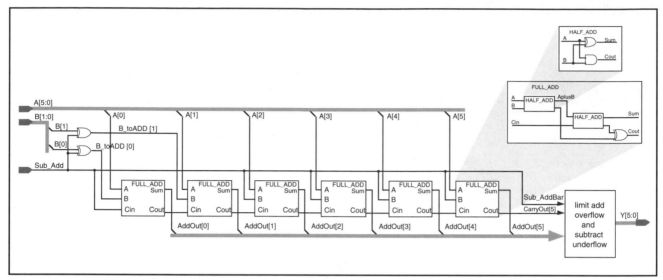

Figure 9.4 Detailed logical structure of a specific adder/subtractor

Extra logic is modeled to force the output to binary 111111 if an addition causes an overflow, and to binary 000000 if a subtraction causes an underflow. An overflow has occurred when adding, that is, Sub_AddBar = 0, and the carry out from the most significant bit full adder, that is, Carry_Out[5], is at logic 1. An underflow has occurred when subtracting, that is, Sub_AddBar = 1, and Carry_Out[5] = 0.

The model has been designed so that only minimal changes are necessary in order to remodel it for different bit widths. VHDL constants and Verilog parameters specify the bus width of inputs A and B which are then referenced in the body of the model. The VHDL model uses **generate** statements to instantiate the single bit adders in such a way that only the constants WidthA and WidthB, need to be changed in order to change the input and output bit widths. Verilog has no equivalent to the **generate** statement and so, in addition to changing the parameters WidthA and WidthB, the number of single bit full adders instantiated must also be changed to match the width of input A. The width of B is either the same or smaller than the width of A.

Single bit half adder

VHDL	Verilog

library IEEE;
use IEEE.STD_Logic_1164.**all**;
 	
entity HALF_ADD **is**
   port (A, B: **in** std_logic; Sum, Cout: **out** std_logic);
end entity HALF_ADD;
 	
architecture LOGIC **of** HALF_ADD **is**
begin
   Sum <= A **xor** B;
   Cout <= A **and** B;
end architecture LOGIC;
	module HALF_ADD (A, B,Sum, Cout);
	   input A, B;
	   output Sum, Cout;
	
	   assign Sum = A ^ B;
	   assign Cout = A & B;
	endmodule

Single bit full adder

VHDL	Verilog
library IEEE; use IEEE.STD_Logic_1164.**all**, IEEE.Numeric_STD.**all**;	Package not needed in this example, but left in for consistency.

entity FULL_ADD **is**
    port (A, B, Cin: **in** std_logic; Sum, Cout: **out** std_logic);
end entity FULL_ADD;
 	
architecture LOGIC **of** FULL_ADD **is**
    component HALF_ADD
      port (A, B: **in** std_logic; Sum, Cout: **out** std_logic);
    end component;
    signal AplusB, CoutHA1, CoutHA2: std_logic;
begin
    HA1: HALF_ADD **port map** (A => A, B => B, Sum => AplusB,
                      Cout => CoutHA1);
    HA2: HALF_ADD **port map** (A => AplusB, B => Cin,
                    Sum => Sum, Cout => CoutHA2);
    Cout <= CoutHA1 **or** CoutHA2;
end architecture LOGIC;
	module FULL_ADD (A, B, Cin, Sum, Cout);
	    input A, B, Cin;
	    output Sum, Cout;
	
	    wire AplusB, CoutHA1, CoutHA2;
	
	    HALF_ADD HA1(.A(A), .B(B),
	                  .Sum(AplusB), .Cout(CoutHA1));
	    HALF_ADD HA2(.A(AplusB), .B(Cin),
	                  .Sum(Sum), .Cout(CoutHA2));
	    assign Cout = CoutHA1 | CoutHA2;
	endmodule

Six bit add or subtract a two bit

VHDL	Verilog

library IEEE;
use IEEE.STD_LOGIC_1164.**all**; IEEE.STD_Numeric_STD.**all**;
 	
entity SIXBIT_ADDSUB2BIT **is**
    port (Sub_AddBar: **in** std_logic;
        A: **in**   unsigned(5 **downto** 0);
        B: **in**   unsigned(1 **downto** 0);
        Y: **out** unsigned(5 **downto** 0));
end entity SIXBIT_ADDSUB2BIT;
 	
architecture LOGIC **of** SIXBIT_ADDSUB2BIT **is**
    constant WidthA: integer := 6;
    constant WidthB: integer := 2;
    component FULL_ADD
      port (A, B, Cin: **in** std_logic; Sum, Cout: **out** std_logic);
    end component;
    signal B_toADD: unsigned(WidthB-1 **downto** 0);
    signal CarryOut: unsigned(WidthA-1 **downto** 0);
    signal AddOut: unsigned(WidthA-1 **downto** 0);
begin
    INV_B_FOR_SUB: **process** (Sub_AddBar,B)
      variable B_toADD_Var: unsigned(1 **downto** 0);
    begin
      for N in 0 **to** WidthB-1 **loop**
        B_toADD_Var(N) := Sub_AddBar **xor** B(N);
      end loop;
      B_toADD <= B_toADD_Var;
    end process INV_B_FOR_SUB;
 	
ADDERS: **block**
    begin
      G1_ALL_FA: **for** M **in** 0 **to** WidthA - 1 **generate**
        G2: **if** (M = 0) **generate**
          FA_0: FULL_ADD **port map**
            (A => A(M), B => B_toADD(M),
            Cin => Sub_AddBar, Sum => AddOut(M),
            Cout => CarryOut(M));
        end generate G2;
        G3: **if** (M>0 **and** M<WidthB) **generate**
          FA_1toB: FULL_ADD **port map**
            (A = > A(M), B => B_toADD(M),   *continued*
	module SIXBIT_ADDSUB2BIT (Sub_AddBar, A, B, Y);
	    parameter WidthA = 6;
	    parameter WidthB = 2;
	    input Sub_AddBar;
	    input (WidthA-1:0) A;
	    input (WidthB-1:0) B;
	    output (WidthA-1:0) Y;
	
	    integer N;
	    reg (WidthA-1:0) B_toADD;
	    wire (WidthA-1:0) CarryOut;
	    wire (WidthA-1:0) AddOut;
	    reg (WidthA-1:0) Y;
	
	    //INV_B_FOR_SUB:
	      always @(Sub_AddBar **or** B)
	        for (N = 0; N < WidthB; N = N + 1)
	          B_toADD(N) = Sub_AddBar ^ B(N);
	
	    //ADDERS:
	      FULL_ADD FA1_BIT0
	        (.A(A(0)), .B(B_toADD(0)), .Cin(Sub_AddBar),
	        .Sum(AddOut(0)), .Cout(CarryOut(0)));
	
	      FULL_ADD FA2_BIT1
	        (.A(A(1)), .B(B_toADD(1)), .Cin(CarryOut(0)),
	        .Sum(AddOut(1)), .Cout(CarryOut(1)));
	
	      FULL_ADD FA1_BIT2
	        (.A(A(2)), .B(CarryOut(1)), .Cin(Sub_AddBar),
	                                  continued

Full adder instantiations.

Six bit add or subtract a two bit

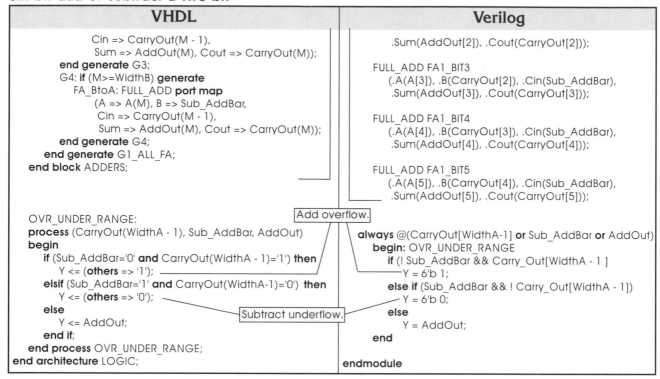

VHDL	Verilog
| ```
            Cin => CarryOut(M - 1),
            Sum => AddOut(M), Cout => CarryOut(M));
      end generate G3;
      G4: if (M>=WidthB) generate
        FA_BtoA: FULL_ADD port map
           (A => A(M), B => Sub_AddBar,
            Cin => CarryOut(M - 1),
            Sum => AddOut(M), Cout => CarryOut(M));
      end generate G4;
   end generate G1_ALL_FA;
 end block ADDERS;


 OVR_UNDER_RANGE:
 process (CarryOut(WidthA - 1), Sub_AddBar, AddOut)
 begin
     if (Sub_AddBar='0' and CarryOut(WidthA - 1)='1') then
        Y <= (others => '1');
     elsif (Sub_AddBar='1' and CarryOut(WidthA-1)='0') then
        Y <= (others => '0');
     else
        Y <= AddOut;
     end if;
 end process OVR_UNDER_RANGE;
end architecture LOGIC;
``` | ```
        .Sum(AddOut[2]), .Cout(CarryOut[2]));

   FULL_ADD FA1_BIT3
        (.A(A[3]), .B(CarryOut[2]), .Cin(Sub_AddBar),
         .Sum(AddOut[3]), .Cout(CarryOut[3]));

   FULL_ADD FA1_BIT4
        (.A(A[4]), .B(CarryOut[3]), .Cin(Sub_AddBar),
         .Sum(AddOut[4]), .Cout(CarryOut[4]));

   FULL_ADD FA1_BIT5
        (.A(A[5]), .B(CarryOut[4]), .Cin(Sub_AddBar),
         .Sum(AddOut[5]), .Cout(CarryOut[5]));


   always @(CarryOut[WidthA-1] or Sub_AddBar or AddOut)
     begin: OVR_UNDER_RANGE
        if (! Sub_AddBar && Carry_Out[WidthA - 1 ]
            Y = 6'b 1;
        else if (Sub_AddBar && ! Carry_Out[WidthA - 1])
            Y = 6'b 0;
        else
            Y = AddOut;
     end
 endmodule
``` |

Add overflow. / *Subtract underflow.*

Example 9.7 Serial adder/subtractor

A serial sequential adder or subtracter circuit is modeled to the structure shown in Figure 9.5. It subtracts if register A is parallel loaded with a 2's complement number and so, unlike Example 9.6, the exclusive OR of the adders addend needed for subtraction is not needed.

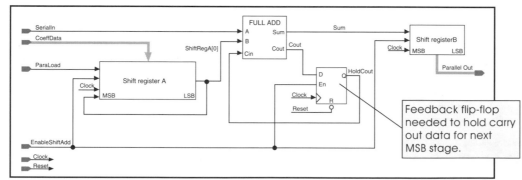

Figure 9.5 Structure of serial sequential adder/subtractor

The circuit being modeled assumes a serial input, possibly coming from a communications channel feeding directly onto the chip. This input assumes the adder's augend. The adders addend is a coefficient that is parallel loaded into shift register A in preparation for being adder to, or subtracted from, the augend. Register A, therefore, contains a programmable coefficient that can be used to normalize any inherent offset in the serial input data. The serial input must be received LSB first, and in this case consists of sequences of 8-bit data. Sequential addition is performed one bit at a time, LSB first, using a single bit full adder and the result is shifted into Register B. The carry output from each addition is needed for the carry input of the next, more significant bit addition, and so is delayed one clock cycle through the feedback flip-flop. This feedback flip-flop has a reset to ensure a logic 0 for the first single bit addition; Registers A and B do not need a reset. The summed result resides in Register B and can be parallel read by the controlling system.

Serial adder/subtractor

VHDL	Verilog

```vhdl
library IEEE;
use IEEE.STD_Logic_1164.all; IEEE.Numeric_STD.all;

entity ADD_SEQ is
   port ( Clock, Reset: in   std_logic;
          ParaLoad, SerialIn, EnableShiftAdd: in std_logic;
          CoeffData:   in   unsigned(7 downto 0);
          ParallelOut:  out unsigned(7 downto 0));
end entity ADD_SEQ;

architecture RTL of ADD_SEQ is
   component FULL_ADD
      port (A, B, Cin: in std_logic; Sum, Cout: out std_logic);
   end component;
   signal ShiftRegA, ShiftRegB: unsigned(7 downto 0);
   signal Sum, Cout, HoldCout: std_logic;
begin
   REG_AB: process (Clock)
   begin
      if rising_edge(Clock) then

         -------------------------
         -- Shift register A
         -------------------------

         if (ParaLoad = '1') then
            ShiftRegA <= CoeffData;
         elsif (EnableShiftAdd = '1') then
            ShiftRegA <= rotate_right(ShiftRegA, 1);
         end if;



         -------------------------
         -- Shift register B
         -------------------------

         if (EnableShiftAdd = '1') then
             ShiftRegB <= rotate_right(ShiftRegB, 1);
         end if;
      end if;
   end process REG_AB;
   ParallelOut <= ShiftRegB;

   ------------------------------------
   -- Single bit full adder
   ------------------------------------

   FA1: FULL_ADD port map
      (A => ShiftRegA(0), B => ShiftRegB(0),
       Cin => HoldCout, Sum => Sum, Cout => Cout);


   ---------------------------------------------
   -- Hold carry out for next add
   ---------------------------------------------

   HOLD_COUT: process (Clock, Reset)
   begin
      if (Reset = '0') then
         HoldCout <= '0';
      elsif rising_edge(Clock) then
         if (EnableShiftAdd = '1') then
            HoldCout <= Cout;
         else
            HoldCout <= HoldCout;
         end if;
      end if;
   end process HOLD_COUT;
end architecture RTL;
```

```verilog
module ADD_SEQ
   (Clock, Reset, ParaLoad, CoeffData, SerialIn,
    EnableShiftAdd, ParallelOut);
   input       Clock, Reset;
   input       ParaLoad, SerialIn, EnableShiftAdd;
   input  (7:0) CoeffData;
   output (7:0) ParallelOut;

   reg       ShiftRegA_LSB;
   reg  (7:0) ShiftRegA, ShiftRegB;
   wire      Sum, Cout;
   reg       HoldCout;


   always @(posedge Clock)
      begin: REG_AB
         //---------------------
         // Shift register A
         //---------------------
         if (ParaLoad)
            ShiftRegA = CoeffData;
         else if (EnableShiftAdd)
            begin
               ShiftRegA_LSB = ShiftRegA(0);
               ShiftRegA = ShiftRegA >> 1;
               ShiftRegA(7) = ShiftRegA_LSB;
            end

         //---------------------
         // Shift register B
         //---------------------
         if (EnableShiftAdd)
            begin
               ShiftRegB = ShiftRegB >> 1;
               ShiftRegB(7) = Sum;
            end
      end
      assign ParallelOut = ShiftRegB;
   //------------------------------
   // Single bit full adder
   //------------------------------
   FULL_ADD FA1
      ( .A(SerialIn), .B(ShiftRegA(0)),
        .Cin(HoldCout),
        .Sum(Sum), .Cout(Cout));


   //---------------------------------------------
   // Hold carry out for next add
   //---------------------------------------------
   always @(posedge Clock or negedge Reset)
      begin: HOLD_COUT
         if (! Reset)
            HoldCout = 0;
         else if (EnableShiftAdd)
            HoldCout = Cout;
         else
            HoldCout = HoldCout;
      end

endmodule
```

Multipliers and Dividers

The area that combinational logic multiplier and divider circuits occupy on a chip often prohibits them from being used in many applications. This area increases exponentially with increasing bit widths. Instead, sequential multiplier and divider circuits are often implemented because of the substantial savings in chip area. Though sequential implementations do take a finite number of clock cycles in which to perform an operation, unless the design is for a *real time* critical system where speed is the essence, a sequential implementation is often the better compromise.

Combinational Circuits. Current synthesis tools do not synthesize combinational multiplier and divider circuits at all well using the "*" and "/" arithmetic operators. The resulting synthesized circuits are typically very large before optimization for input bit widths much above 4 or 5 bits. This makes the optimizer's job of optimizing the circuit particularly difficult, very CPU intensive, and most important of all, will probably not yield as optimal a circuit as could be achieved if a specific structure was modeled. A more efficient combinational multiplier circuit can be produced by modeling the structure of the shift and add multiplication algorithm. Similarly, for a divider circuit a more efficient circuit can be produced by modeling the structure of the shift, compare and subtract algorithm. These algorithms are described later in this section.

Synchronous Circuits. The two algorithms commonly used to model sequential multiplier circuits are, 1) the same shift and add algorithm used for combinational circuits, and 2) Booth's Algorithm. Booth's Algorithm is defined specifically to speed up sequential multiplication operations. Synchronous dividers are better modeled using the same shift, compare and subtract algorithm used for combinational dividers. There is no equivalent to Booth's algorithm for speeding up synchronous division.

Combinational versus synchronous

A comparison of typical combinational versus synchronous circuit implementations for different bit width multipliers and dividers, using a typical 0.5 micron ASIC library, is indicated in Figure 9.6. The area disadvantage of combinational circuits is clearly seen.

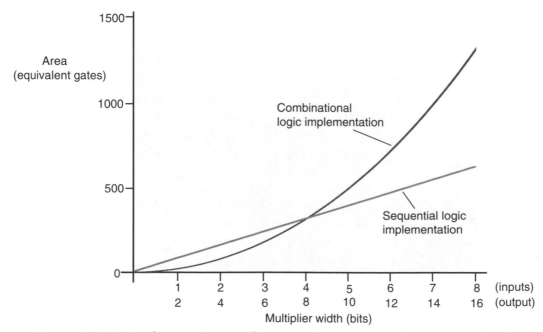

Figure 9.6 Typical area for combinational verses synchronous multipliers

Combinational logic multipliers are faster, but are significantly larger than their sequential counterpart for input bit widths of 4 or more. The area of the combinational circuit increases exponentially as the input and output bit widths increase. In contrast, circuits implemented sequentially are smaller but do take a finite number of clock cycles in which to perform an operation. Sequential multiplication takes up to twice the number of clock cycles as there are bits in the multiplier input; the actual number depends on the multiplier's binary value. Sequential division will take exactly twice the number of clock cycles as there are bits in the divisor. Due to the vast area differences the choice between modeling a combinational or sequential multiplier or divider circuit is usually fairly clear.

Algorithms for performing multiplication and division are described in the following section. Models showing their combinational or sequential implementation are included in Examples 9.8 through to 9.12. Notice that the sequential implementation of a multiplier or divider uses very similar data registers and so could be combined into one circuit that either multiplies or divides.

Multiplier and Divider Algorithms

The following algorithms are described: 1) Shift and add multiplication algorithm for combinational or sequential circuits, 2) Booth's multiplication algorithm for sequential circuits, 3) Shift and subtract division algorithm for combinational or sequential circuits.

Shift and add Multiplication Algorithm

The multiplication of two positive binary numbers is achieved with paper and pencil by a process of successive shift and add operations as illustrated in Figure 9.7a). Figure 9.7b) shows the multiplication using signed 2's complement numbers.

Decimal	Binary		5 x (-6) in 2's complement form.
39	1 0 1 1 1	multiplcand	0 1 1 0 (6)
49	1 1 0 0 1	multiplier	1 0 1 0 (-6 in 2's comp)
	1 0 1 1 1	partial product 1	0 1 0 1 (5)
	0 0 0 0 0	partial product 2	1 1 1 1 1 0 1 0 x (-6)
	0 0 0 0 0	partial product 3	0 0 0 0 0 0 0 0
	1 0 1 1 1	partial product 4	0 0 0 0 1 0 1
	1 0 1 1 1	partial product 5	0 0 0 0 0
1911	1 0 0 0 1 1 1 1 1 1	product = sum of partial products	0 0 1 0 1
			0 1 0 1
			1 0 1
	a)		0 1
			1
			1 1 1 0 0 0 1 0 (-30 in 2's comp)
			0 0 0 1 1 1 1 0 (+30)
			b)

Figure 9.7 Example of binary multiplication

The process consists of looking at each successive bit of the multiplier in turn, starting with the least significant bit. If the multiplier bit is a logic 1, the multiplicand is copied down; otherwise, zeros are copied down. The numbers copied down in successive lines are shifted one position to the left from the previous number. Finally, the numbers are added and their sum provides the product.

When multiplying two signed numbers together the algorithm is modified slightly to cope with the sign bits. The sign of the product is determined from the signs of the multiplicand and multiplier. If they are alike, the sign of the product is a plus. If they are not alike, the sign of the multiplier is a minus.

Example 9.8 shows this shift and add algorithm employed in the model of a 6x6 input combinational multiplier, while Example 9.9 shows it employed in the model of a generic (*n* x *m*) bit sequential multiplier.

Booth's Multiplication Algorithm

Booth's algorithm, like all multiplication schemes requires the examination of the multiplier bits and the shifting of partial products. Booth's algorithm is intended for a synchronous logic implementation of a multiplier circuit and works equally for positive and negative numbers. It treats positive and negative multipliers uniformly and is ideally suited for the multiplication of signed 2's complement numbers.

Booth's algorithm operates on two basic facts. The first is that strings of successive 0's in the multiplier require no addition, but just shifting. The second is that a string of successive 1's in the multiplier can be treated as $2^{up}+1 - 2^{lo}$ where "up" is the upper weighted bit and "lo" is the lower weighted bit. For example, if the multiplier is 001110 (+14), then up = 3 and lo = 1 and $2^4 - 2^1 = 14$. For this algorithm, the individual partial products determined from the multiplicand may be: added too, subtracted from, or may not change the final product at all based on the following rules:

- the multiplicand is subtracted from the partial product upon encountering the first 1 in a string of 1's in the multiplier,

- the multiplicand is added to the partial product upon entering the first 0 provided that there was no previous 1 in a string of 0's in the multiplier,

- the partial product does not change when the bit is identical to the previous multiplier bit.

This algorithm works equally for positive and negative multipliers in a 2's complement representation because a negative multiplier fills the most significant bits with a string of 1's and the last operation will be a subtraction of the appropriate weight. For example, a multiplier equal to -14 is represented as 110010 and treated as $-2^4 + 2^2 - 2^1 = -14$. A paper and pencil illustration of this algorithm is shown in Figure 9.8 for (-9) x (-13) = (+117).

```
2's complement of multiplicand 10111 is 01001

    9 8 7 6 5 4 3 2 1 0   bit weighting
        1 0 1 1 1   multiplicand  (-9)
        1 0 0 1 1   multiplier    (-13)        first 1
                                               first 0
                                               second 1

    0 0 0 0 0 0 1 0 0 1   1st  multiplier bit 1 - subtract (add 2's complement)
    0 0 0 0 0 0 0 0 0    2nd multiplier bit also 1 - no change so no add/subtract
    1 1 1 1 0 1 1 1      3rd multiplier bit changes to 0 so add. Note sign extension
    0 0 0 0 0 0 0        4th  multiplier bit also 0 - no change so no add/subtract
    0 0 1 0 0 1          5th multiplier bit changes to 1 so subtract (add 2's complement)

    0 0 0 1 1 1 0 1 0 1   product  (+117)
```

Note the overflow of adding the the partial products into the 11th bit (bit weighting10) of the product is ignored as it represents the original sign bit of the multiplier.

Figure 9.8 Paper and pencil illustration of Booth's algorithm

Division Algorithm

The division of two positive binary numbers is achieved with paper and pencil by a process of successive compare, shift and subtract operations. Binary division is simpler than decimal division because the quotient digits are either 0 or 1 and there is no need to estimate how many times the dividend or partial remainder fits into the divisor.

This division process is illustrated in Figure 9.9.

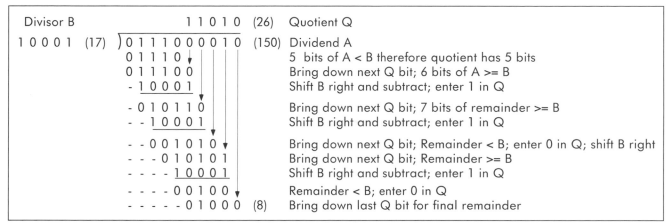

Figure 9.9 Example of binary division

The divisor B consists of five bits and the dividend A, of ten bits. The five most significant bits of the dividend are compared with the divisor. Since the 5-bit number is smaller than B, we try again by bringing down the sixth most significant bit and comparing the six most significant bits of A with the divisor B. The 6-bit number is now greater than B so we place a 1 for the first quotient bit in the sixth position above the dividend. The divisor is then shifted one place to the right and subtracted from the dividend. The difference is called a *partial remainder* because the division could have stopped here to yield a quotient of 1 and a remainder equal to the partial remainder. This process is continued by comparing a partial remainder with the divisor. If the partial remainder is greater than or equal to the divisor, the quotient bit is equal to 1. The divisor is then shifted right and subtracted from the partial remainder. If the partial remainder is smaller than the divisor, the quotient bit is 0 and no subtraction is needed. The divisor is shifted once to the right in any case. Note that the result gives both a quotient and a remainder.

Example 9.11 employs this division algorithm in the model of a combinational logic divider having a 10-bit dividend, divided by a 5-bit divisor and provides a resulting 5-bit quotient, with a 5-bit remainder. An overflow signal is also provided to indicate when the quotient wants to be more than 5-bits wide. Example 9.12 employs this same algorithm in the model of a generic *n*-bit, divide by *m*-bit sequential divider. It provides an (*n* minus *m*) bit quotient with an *m*-bit remainder and an overflow signal.

Example 9.8 Signed combinational multiplier using shift and add algorithm

A 7x7 bit combinational logic multiplier of signed-magnitude numbers is modeled according to the shift and add algorithm already described. It contains an exclusive OR of the input sign bits in order to generate the product's sign bit. The model's structure, Figure 9.10, consists of five adders in parallel, each with differing input and output bit widths.

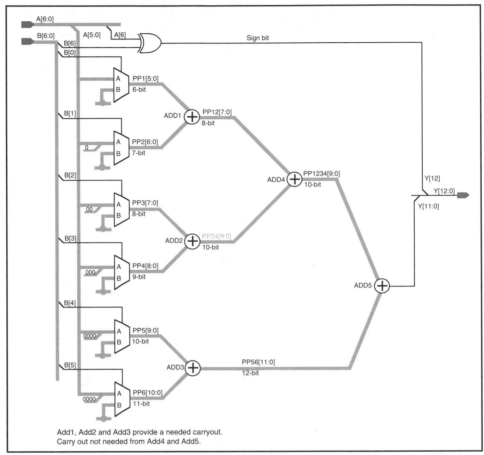

Figure 9.10 Structure of 7x7 signed combinational logic multiplier

The Verilog language has the advantage of allowing signals of one bit width to be assigned to signals of a different bit width, see Chapter 4. This means the left or right hand side of an assignment that has the least number of bits is automatically expanded to meet the size of the larger, and any unused bits are optimized away during synthesis. This is taken advantage of in two ways in the code of the Verilog model; one for how the partial products are generated, and the other for how the partial products are summed, and are described separately below.

Forming the partial products:

The six partial products are formed in accordance with the algorithm, that is, it is zero if the corresponding bit in the multiplier B is zero, or a shifted version of the multiplicand A if a logic 1. The partial products are generated using conditional signal assignments and do not infer any logic; it only specifies how the shifted multiplier input is connected to the adders.

Verilog. The Verilog model shows two different ways in which the multiplier can be shifted to form the partial products. The first method uses the concatenation of constant logic 0's to the least significant bit of the multiplier. The second uses the shift operator and is shown commented out in this particular model. The point to note about this commented out portion of code is that multiplicand A is shifted from 1 to 5 times, but is still effectively only 6-bits wide. The shifted bits are not lost because the assignments to PP1-PP6 have the exact number of bits necessary to take the shifted bits.

VHDL. Shifting using a shift operator or shift function is not possible in VHDL. As described in Chapter 4, VHDL assignments (<= and :=) <u>must</u> resolve to have equivalent bit widths on each side of the assignment operator. This means, that although that VHDL assignment operators can be overloaded on their data type, they cannot be overloaded on their size. This means, that if the Verilog assignments using the shift operator, were modeled to their VHDL equivalent, there would be unavoidable bit width mismatches.

Summing the partial products:

Five adders sum the six partial products to yield the multipliers product excluding the sign bit. Delay paths pass through either two or three adders and so are structured so that the delay paths are balanced and minimized. Adders with the largest bit widths will have the longest delay and so are placed in a path that passes through only two adders. This structuring could have been achieved with all partial products, PP1-PP6, defined as being 12-bits wide and using a single parenthesized statement, that is,

```
Y <= ((PP1 + PP2) + (PP3 + PP4)) + (PP5 + PP6);  -- VHDL
Y  = ((PP1 + PP2) + (PP3 + PP4)) + (PP5 + PP6);  // Verilog
```

This would work fine and the synthesis tool would optimize away unused most significant input and output bits connected to logic 0. However, a more explicit structure is modeled because three of the adders (ADD1, ADD2 and ADD3) must use a carry output while the other two (ADD4 and ADD5) need not. For example, adder ADD4 has a 10-bit input but only needs a 10-bit output because even if all bits of the partial products PP1, PP2, PP3 and PP4 were a logic 1, the maximum output from ADD4 is still only 10-bits, as indicated.

```
      1 1 1 1 1 1   PP1        6-bit
      1 1 1 1 1 1 0   PP2        7-bit
  1 0 1 1 1 1 0 1   PP1+PP2    8-bit

    1 1 1 1 1 1 0 0   PP3        8-bit
  1 1 1 1 1 1 0 0 0   PP4        9-bit
1 0 1 1 1 1 0 1 0 0   PP3+PP4    10-bit

    1 0 1 1 1 1 0 1   PP1+PP2    8-bit
1 0 1 1 1 1 0 1 0 0   PP3+PP4    10-bit
1 1 1 0 1 1 0 0 0 1   (PP1+PP2) + (PP3+PP4)  10-bit
```

This results in a slight reduction in the size of adders ADD4 and ADD5.

Verilog. Assignments for the adders needing a carry out are of the type PP12 = PP1 + PP2; where PP12 is defined as being one bit bigger than PP2, and which is one bit bigger that PP1.

VHDL. Assignments have a logic 0 concatenated to the most significant bit of the largest of the two adder operands solely for the purposes of matching the bit widths either side of the assignment for VHDL compliance. The port declarations; A, B and Y are of type unsigned because type signed is reserved for 2's complement signed numbers and not signed magnitude numbers as used in this example.

The addition of partial products is performed without regard to the magnitude bits of inputs A and B, that is, Am and Bm.

7x7 signed combinational logic multiplier

VHDL	Verilog
| ```vhdl
library IEEE;
use IEEE.STD_Logic_1164.all; IEEE.Numeric_STD.all;

entity MULT7X7SIGNED_COMB is
    port ( A, B:  in    unsigned(6 downto 0);
           Y:     out  unsigned(12 downto 0));
end entity MULT7X7SIGNED_COMB;

architecture COND_DATA_FLOW of MULT7X7SIGNED_COMB is
    signal Am,Bm: unsigned(5 downto 0); -- magnitude bits only
    signal PP1: unsigned(5 downto 0);
    signal PP2: unsigned(6 downto 0);
    signal PP3: unsigned(7 downto 0);
    signal PP4: unsigned(8 downto 0);
    signal PP5: unsigned(9 downto 0);
    signal PP6: unsigned(10 downto 0);

    signal PP12:    unsigned(7 downto 0);
    signal PP34:    unsigned(9 downto 0);
    signal PP1234: unsigned(9 downto 0);
    signal PP56:    unsigned(11 downto 0);
begin

    -- Generate the product's sign bit
    Y(12) <= A(6) xor B(6);

    -- Generate partial products
    Am  <= A(5 downto 0);
    Bm  <= B(5 downto 0);
    PP1 <= (    Am    )      when Bm(0)='1' else (others => '0');
    PP2 <= (  Am & '0')      when Bm(1)='1' else (others => '0');
    PP3 <= (  Am & "00")     when Bm(2)='1' else (others => '0');
    PP4 <= ( Am & "000")     when Bm(3)='1' else (others => '0');
    PP5 <= ( Am & "0000")    when Bm(4)='1' else (others => '0');
    PP6 <= (Am & "00000")    when Bm(5)='1' else (others => '0');

    -- Sum partial products
    PP12    <= PP1 + ('0' & PP2); -- Uses the carry out
    PP34    <= PP3 + ('0' & PP4); -- Uses the carry out
    PP56    <= PP5 + ('0' & PP6); -- Uses the carry out
    PP1234 <= PP12 + PP34;     -- Carry out not needed
    -- Carry out not needed for PP1234 + PP56
    Y(11 downto 0) <= PP1234 + PP56;

end architecture COND_DATA_FLOW;
``` | ```verilog
module MULT7X7SIGNED_COMB (A, B, Y);
    input  [6:0] A, B;
    output [12:0] Y;

    wire [5:0] Am, Bm;  // magnitude bits only
    wire [5:0] PP1;
    wire [6:0] PP2;
    wire [7:0] PP3;
    wire [8:0] PP4;
    wire [9:0] PP5;
    wire [10:0] PP6;

    wire [7:0] PP12;
    wire [9:0] PP34;
    wire [9:0] PP1234;
    wire [11:0] PP56;

// Generate the product's sign bit
assign Y[12] = A[6] ^ B[6];

// Generate partial products using concatination
assign Am = A[5:0];
assign Bm = B[5:0];
assign PP1 = Bm[0] ? Am        : 6'b 0;
assign PP2 = Bm[1] ? {Am, 1'b0}: 7'b 0;
assign PP3 = Bm[2] ? {Am, 2'b0}: 8'b 0;
assign PP4 = Bm[3] ? {Am, 3'b0}: 9'b 0;
assign PP5 = Bm[4] ? {Am, 4'b0}: 10'b 0;
assign PP6 = Bm[5] ? {Am, 5'b0}: 11'b 0;

// Generate partial products using shift
//assign PP1 = Bm[0] ? Am       : 6'b 0;
//assign PP2 = Bm[1] ? Am << 1 : 7'b 0;
//assign PP3 = Bm[2] ? Am << 2 : 8'b 0;
//assign PP4 = Bm[3] ? Am << 3 : 9'b 0;
//assign PP5 = Bm[4] ? Am << 4 : 10'b 0;
//assign PP6 = Bm[5] ? Am << 5 : 11'b 0;

// Sum partial products
assign PP12    = PP1 + PP2;    // Uses the carry out
assign PP34    = PP3 + PP4;    // Uses the carry out
assign PP56    = PP5 + PP6;    // Uses the carry out
assign PP1234 = PP12 + PP34;  // Carry out not needed
assign Y[11:0] = PP1234 + PP56; // Carry out not needed

endmodule
``` |

Concatenation or shift method of generating partial products.

Example 9.9 Generic sequential shift and add multiplier

A generic (n x m) bit sequential signed multiplier is modeled to the shift and add multiplication algorithm previously described, but with the addition of a sign bit. It is convenient to change the algorithm's process slightly for sequential hardware implementation.

- Instead of providing registers to simultaneously store and add as many binary numbers as there are bits in the multiplier, hardware is substantively reduced by using only one adder and successively accumulating the partial products in a register.
- Instead of shifting the multiplicand to the left the partial product is shifted to the right; this results in leaving the partial product and multiplicand in their required relative position.
- When the corresponding bit of the multiplier is 0, there is no need to add all zeros to the partial product as it will not alter its value.

The sequential implementation of the multiplication algorithm is shown graphically in the flow chart, Figure 9.11. The corresponding modeled hardware structure is indicated in Figure 9.12. Because the model is generic, the width of the multiplicand and multiplier can be specified when the model is instantiated from another model. This avoids having multiple versions of the same model with different width registers.

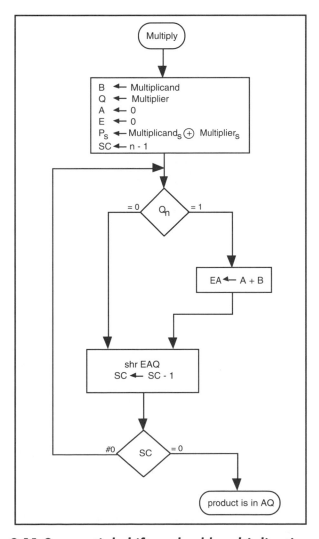

Figure 9.11 Sequential shift and add multiplication algorithm

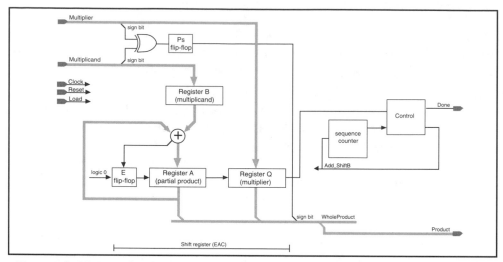

Figure 9.12 Hardware structure of sequential shift and add multiplier

The operation starts when Load is a logic 1 and causes the following register loading.

RegA   <- 0
RegB   <- multiplicand without the sign bit
RegQ   <- multiplier without the sign bit flip-flop
Ps   <- exclusive OR of the multiplicand and multiplier sign bits
SequenceCounter <- number of bits in the multiplier minus the sign bit

The products sign is the exclusive OR of the sign of the two inputs. Instead of storing the sign of each input, the exclusive OR of the two input sign bits is stored in a single flip-flop. This is the products sign bit and saves a flip-flop.

With the multiplicand minus its sign bit in register B, and the multiplier minus its sign bit in register Q, the operation proceeds. This consists of a sequence of consecutive test, possible add, and shift right operations. The control signal Add_Shiftb controls whether to add or shift.

When new data is loaded, the least significant bit of the Multiplier is loaded directly into the add/ shift control flip-flop producing Add_Shiftb. In this way, the Add_Shiftb is set ready for an immediate add if logic 1, or shift if logic 0.

When Add_Shiftb is a logic 1 the sum of registers A and B form a partial product that is transferred to EA (the concatenation flip-flop E and register A) as depicted in Figure 9.12. It is necessary to hold the carry out from the adder in flip-flop E so that it can be used in the generation of the next partial product summation. A shift right is of EAQ; the least significant bit of register A is shifted into the most significant bit of register Q; the bit from E is shifted into the most significant bit of register A; and logic 0 is shifted into E. The shift causes one bit of the partial product in register A to be shifted into register Q, pushing the multiplier bits one position to the right. In this manner, the right-most flip-flop in register Q, designated by Qn, will hold the bit of the multiplier which must be inspected next. If Qn is a logic 1 an addition is required before the next shift. This is a two clock cycles process; one for the partial product add, and one for the shift during which the counter is decremented. If Qn is a logic 0 no addition is required and so only one clock cycle is needed for shifting EAQ and decrementing the counter.

A single multiplication will take from between (WidthMultiplier - 1) and ((WidthMultiplier - 1) x 2) clock cycles to complete depending upon the logic 0's and 1's in the multiplier; it takes 2 cycles per magnitude bit if the multiplier bit is at logic 1 and 1 cycle per magnitude bit if at logic 0. When a multiplication is complete, that is, the sequence counter is zero, Done is set to a logic 1.

HDL Code

As this is a generic (n x m) bit multiplier, the input and output bit widths can be specified when the model is instantiated from another model. In VHDL, this is achieved using generics while in Verilog it is achieved by overloading parameter values. When this model is instantiated from a calling model, the following data must be passed to it.

WidthMultiplicand   - width of the input multiplicand
WidthMultiplier   - width of the input multiplier
WidthCount   - width of the counter where: (Verilog only)
$$2^{WidthCount} <= WidthMultiplier*2 - 1$$

Ignoring the sign bit, this particular model has been designed such that the width of the output magnitude does not need to be the width of the sum of the two input magnitude widths. This may not be necessary, but does mean there will not be any unused (unconnected) outputs in the calling model. For example, a 10-bit multiplicand and multiplier, each having 1 sign bit and 9 magnitude bits will yield a 19-bit product having 1 sign bit and 2 x 9 = 18 magnitude bits. Now, if for some reason you only want a 15-bit resolution output, including the sign bit, WidthProduct can be specified as being 15. In this case, the 15 most significant bits of the product are output and the 4 least significant bits are ignored. The model still computes a 19-bit signed product to maintain accuracy. This feature may be of use when designing DSP filters etc.

Suppose a (9 x 6) bit sign multiplier is required. The process for choosing to model a 9 x 6 (multiplicand x multiplier) or a (6 x 9) bit multiplier is as follows.

1. Magnitude bits of the multiplicand and multiplier will be 8 and 5, or 5 and 8, respectively.

2. Magnitude bits of (8 x 5) will be multiplied in 5 to 10 (2 x 5) clock cycles, will need 22 magnitude related flip-flops and an 8-bit adder.

3. Magnitude bits of (5 x 8) will be multiplied in 8 to 16 (2 x 8) clock cycles, will need 19 magnitude related flip-flops and a 5-bit adder.

4. Choose from 3 or 4 above depending upon the design criteria.

VHDL: The VHDL model has two variables defined, E_RegA and E_RegA_RegQ, that are not needed in the Verilog model. They are necessary to avoid data type mismatches, that is, a target aggregate of the form:

(E, RegA) <= RegB + RegA;

This does not become a one dimensional array of bits. It is a record with 2 fields; the first field being a 1-bit object of type std_logic and the second having a number of bits constituting an object of type unsigned. This is discussed in Chapter 4.

The addition statement in the VHDL model has a logic 0 concatenated onto the most significant bit, that is, '0' & Multiplicand. This ensures the output bit width matches that of the resolved expression on the right hand side of the assignment; a requirement of VHDL, but not Verilog.

Generic sequential shift and add multiplier

VHDL	Verilog

```vhdl
library IEEE;
use IEEE.STD_Logic_1164.all; IEEE.Numeric_STD.all;

entity MULT_SEQ is
    generic (WidthMultiplicand, WidthMultiplier,
             MaxCount: natural);
    port ( Clock, Reset, Load: in std_logic;
        Multiplicand:  in unsigned(WidthMultiplicand - 1
                            downto 0);
        Multiplier:    in unsigned(WidthMultiplier - 1
                            downto 0);
        Done:          out std_logic;
        Product:       out unsigned(WidthMultiplicand +
                            WidthMultiplier - 1
                            downto 0));
end entity MULT_SEQ;

architecture RTL of MULT_SEQ is
    signal ProductSign:  std_logic;
    signal RegA: unsigned(WidthMultiplicand - 1 downto 0);
    signal RegB: unsigned(WidthMultiplicand - 1 downto 0);
    signal RegQ: unsigned(WidthMultiplier - 1 downto 0);
    signal E:            std_logic;
    signal Add_Shiftb:   std_logic;
    signal SequenceCount: integer range 0 to MaxCount-1;
    signal WholeProduct:unsigned(WidthMultiplicand
                    + WidthMultiplier - 1downto 0);
begin


    ------------------------------------
    -- Shift and add multiplier
    ------------------------------------
    SHIFT_ADD_MULT: process (Clock)
        variable E_RegA: unsigned(WidthMultiplicand
                        downto 0);
        variable E_RegA_RegQ: unsigned(WidthMultiplicand
                            +WidthMultiplier downto 0);
        variable Done_v: std_logic;
    begin
        if rising_edge(Clock) then
            ----------------------------
            -- Synchronous reset
            ----------------------------
            if (Reset = '0') then
                ProductSign <= '0';
                RegA <= (others => '0');
                RegB <= (others => '0');
                RegQ<= (others => '0');
                E <= '0';
                Add_Shiftb <= '0';
                SequenceCount <= WidthMultiplier - 1;
                Done_v := '0';
            ------------------------------------------------
            -- Load new data & set control signal
            ------------------------------------------------
            elsif (Load = '1') then
                ProductSign <= Multiplicand
                        (WidthMultiplicand - 1)
                        xor Multiplier(WidthMultiplier - 1);
                RegA <=(others => '0');
                RegB <= Multiplicand(WidthMultiplicand - 2
                            downto 0);
                RegQ <=Multiplier(WidthMultiplier - 2 downto 0);
                E <= '0';
```

```verilog
module MULT_SEQ
    (Clock, Reset, Load, Multiplicand, Multiplier, Done, Product);
        parameter WidthMultiplicand = 5, // multiplicand
                  WidthMultiplier   = 8,   // multiplier
                  // 2**WidthCount<= (WidthMultiplier - 1) * 2
                  WidthCount        = 4;
    input    Clock, Reset, Load;
    input    [WidthMultiplicand - 1:0] Multiplicand;
    input    [WidthMultiplier - 1:0] Multiplier;
    output Done;
    output   [WidthMultiplicand+WidthMultiplier-1:0] Product;
    reg Done;

    reg ProductSign;
    reg [WidthMultiplicand-2:0] RegA;
    reg [WidthMultiplicand-2:0] RegB;
    reg [WidthMultiplier-2:0]  RegQ;
    reg E;
    reg Add_Shiftb;
    reg [WidthCount-1:0] SequenceCount;
    wire [WidthMultiplicand+WidthMultiplier-2:0]
                                    WholeProduct;




    //----------------------------------
    // Shift and add multiplier
    //----------------------------------
    always @(posedge Clock)
        begin: SHIFT_ADD_MULT




            //--------------------------
            // Synchronous reset
            //--------------------------
            if (! Reset)
                begin
                    ProductSign = 0;
                    RegA = 0;
                    RegB = 0;
                    RegQ = 0;
                    E = 0;
                    Add_Shiftb = 0;
                    SequenceCount = WidthMultiplier-2;
                    Done = 0;
                end
            //------------------------------------------------------
            // Load new data & set control signals
            //------------------------------------------------------
            else if (Load)
                begin
                    ProductSign = Multiplicand[WidthMultiplicand - 1]
                                ^ Multiplier[WidthMultiplier - 1];
                    RegA = 0;
                    RegB = Multiplicand[WidthMultiplicand - 2:0];
                    RegQ = Multiplier[WidthMultiplier - 2:0];
                    E = 0;
                    Add_Shiftb = Multiplier[0];
```

continued

Generic sequential shift and add multiplier

VHDL	Verilog
``` Add_Shiftb <= Multiplier(0); SequenceCount <= WidthMultiplier - 1; Done_v := '0'; ---------- -- Add ---------- elsif (Add_Shiftb = '1') then E_RegA := ('0' & RegB) + RegA; E <= E_RegA(WidthMultiplicand - 1); RegA <= E_RegA(WidthMultiplicand - 2 downto 0); Add_Shiftb <= '0'; ---------- -- Shift ---------- elsif (Done_v = '0') then E_RegA_RegQ := shift_left((E & RegA & RegQ), 1); E <= E_RegA(WidthMultiplicand-1); RegA <= E_RegA(WidthMultiplicand-2 downto 0); RegQ <= E_RegA(WidthMultiplicand-2 downto 0); if (RegQ(0) = '1') then -- multiplier bit Add_Shiftb <= '1'; else Add_Shiftb <= '0'; end if; if (SequenceCount = 0) then Done_v := '1'; else SequenceCount <= SequenceCount - 1; end if; end if; end if; Done <= Done_v; end process SHIFT_AADD_MULT; Product <= (ProductSign & RegA & RegQ); end architecture RTL; ```	``` SequenceCount = WidthMultiplier-2; Done = 0; end //-------- // Add //-------- else if (Add_Shiftb) begin {E, RegA} = RegB + RegA; Add_Shiftb = 0; end //-------- // Shift //-------- else if (! Done) begin {E, RegA,RegQ} = {E, RegA, RegQ} >> 1; if (RegQ[0]) // multiplier bit Add_Shiftb = 1; else Add_Shiftb = 0; if (SequenceCount == 0) Done = 1; else SequenceCount = SequenceCount - 1; end end assign Product = {ProductSign, RegA, RegQ}; endmodule ```

Example 9.10 Generic NxM sequential multiplier using Booth's Algorithm

A generic (n x m) bit sequential multiplier implementing Booth's algorithm is modeled to the hardware structure, Figure 9.13. The structure is very similar to that implemented for the standard shift and add algorithm of Example 9.9. The hardware differences needed to implement Booth's algorithm are:

1. An extra flip-flop, Q_{n+1}(Qnplus1), is appended to the least significant bit of register Q in order to facilitate double bit inspection of the multiplier.

2. The ability to subtract as well as add.

3. The E flip-flop that holds the carry out from the adder is not needed as an add will never cause an overflow. The flow chart, Figure 9.14, indicates how Booth's algorithm is implemented in this example. When Load is a logic 1 the sequential elements are initialized as follows:

RegA	<- 0	Shift_afterAddSub	<- 0
RegB	<- multiplicand	SequenceCounter	<- number of bits multiplier.
RegQ	<- multiplier	Done	<- 0
Qnplus1	<- 0		

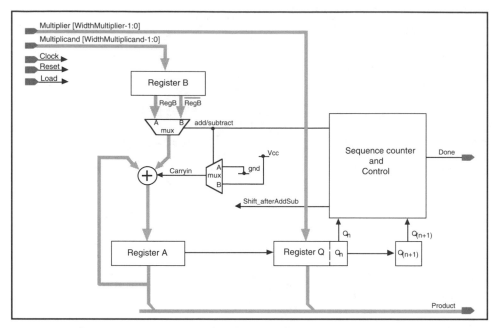

Figure 9.13 Hardware structure implied by multiplier model using Booth's algorithm

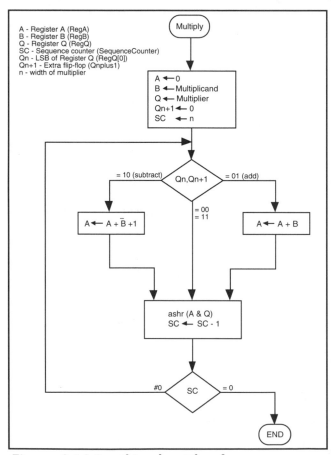

Figure 9.14 Booth's algorithm for multiplication of signed - 2's complement numbers

The flip-flop providing the output signal Done is implied by virtue of being assigned in the synchronous section of code and ensures it changes immediately after a clock edge along with the multiplied product. If a small delay of the Done signal after a clock edge is tolerable, it could be assigned in a combinational section of code, saving a flip-flop.

The operation begins by inspecting two bits of the multiplier Qn and Qnplus1, along with the control bit Shift_afterAddSub in a **case** statement. If the two bits Qn and Qnplus1 are equal to binary 10, the first 1 in a string of 1's has been encountered in the multiplicand. This requires a subtraction of the multiplicand from the partial product in the accumulator register (RegA). If the two bits are equal to binary 01, the first 0 in a string of 0's has been encountered. This requires the addition of the multiplicand to the partial product in RegA. If Qn and Qnplus1 are binary 00 or 11 no action is necessary and so the next shift occurs.

After an add or subtract, the control signal Shift_afterAddSub is set to logic 1 in order to guarantee a shift occurs during the next clock cycle, as defined by the algorithm. The shift is an arithmetic shift right of the partial product in RegA, the multiplier in RegQ and the Qnplus1 flip-flop. When the two bits are equal, the partial product does not change and so another shift follows. Following any shift, the two bits Qn and Qnplus1 are retested and the process repeated.

An arithmetic shift ensures that the most significant bit of Register A before the shift, is duplicated into the most significant bit of Register A after the shift; this ensures no sign change. When a shift operation occurs the control signal Shift_afterAddSub is set back to logic 0 ready to test the next Qn and Qn+1 values. The sequence counter is decremented during each shift and the computational loop is repeated as may times as there are bits in the multiplier.

HDL code

The VHDL model uses an extra variable, Shift_Q0_Q0plus1, to group (concatenate) the three signals Shift_afterAddSub, RegQ(0) and Q0plus1. This is not necessary in Verilog, as they can be concatenated in the **case** statement itself.

The VHDL model uses the arithmetic shift right operator, **asr**. Verilog has no equivalent and so a second assignment is used after the shift in order to copy the most significant bit but one, the original sign bit, to the new most significant bit, the new sign bit.

An overflow cannot occur because addition and subtraction operations alternate and the two numbers being added or subtracted always have opposite signs, a condition that excludes an overflow.

Table 9.5 shows a numerical example of data flowing through the registers as a multiplication operation is performed and uses the same numbers used in the description of Booth's algorithm.

Multiplicand in RegB = 10111
not B + 1 = 01001

multiplier

Clock cycle	Sequence counter	Qn	Qn+1	Shift_afterAddSub	RegA	RegQ	Done	Comments
1	5	1	0	0	00000	10011	0	Initial value after Load
2	5			1	01001			subtract (add Bbar + 1)
					01001			
3	4			0	00100	11001	1	arithmetic shift right
4	3	1	1	0	00010	01101	1	arithmetic shift right
5	3	0	1	1	10111			add
					11001			
6	2			0	11100	10110	0	arithmetic shift right
7	1	0	0	0	11100	10110	0	arithmetic shift right
8	1	1	0	1	01001			subtract (add Bbar + 1)
					00111			
9	0			0	00011	10101	1	arithmetic shift right

product

Table 9.5 Example register data flow for sequential multiplier using Booth's Algorithm

Generic Booth's algorithm multiplier

VHDL	Verilog

```vhdl
library IEEE;
use IEEE.STD_Logic_1164.all; IEEE.Numeric_STD.all;

entity MULT_SEQ_BOOTH is
    generic (WidthMultiplicand, WidthMultiplier,
            MaxCount: natural);
    port ( Clock, Reset, Load: in std_logic;
        Multiplicand:  in  unsigned(WidthMultiplicand - 1
                            downto 0);
        Multiplier:    in  unsigned(WidthMultiplier - 1
                            downto 0);
        Done:          out std_logic;
        Product:       out unsigned(WidthMultiplicand +
                            WidthMultiplier - 1
                            downto 0));
end entity MULT_SEQ_BOOTH;

architecture RTL of MULT_SEQ_BOOTH is
    signal Shift_afterAddSub: std_logic;
    signal RegA:   unsigned(WidthMultiplicand downto 0);
    signal RegB:   unsigned(WidthMultiplier downto 0);
    signal RegQ:   unsigned(WidthMultiplier downto 0);
    signal SequenceCount: integer range 0 to MaxCount;
    signal Qnplus1:  std_logic;
begin



    -----------------------------------------------
    -- Booth algorithm Shift and add multiplier
    -----------------------------------------------
    SHIFT_ADD_MULT: process (Clock)
        variable Shift_Q0_Q0plus1: unsigned(0 to 2);
        variable Reg_A_Q_Qn1: unsigned(WidthMutiplicand+
                            WidthMultiplier - 1 downto 0);
        variable Done_v;
    begin
        if rising_edge(Clock) then
            ------------------------------
            -- Synchronous reset
            ------------------------------
            if (Reset = '0') then
                RegA <= (others => '0');
                RegB <= (others => '0');
                RegQ <= (others => '0');
                Qnplus1 <= '0';
                Shift_afterAddSub <= '0';
                SequenceCount <= WidthMultiplier;
                Done_v := '0';

            --------------------------------------------
            -- Load new data to be multiplied & set control
            -- signals
            --------------------------------------------
            elsif (Load = '1') then
                RegA <= (others => '0');
                RegB <= Multiplicand;
                RegQ <= Multiplier;
                Qnplus1 <= '0';
                Shift_afterAddSub <= '0';
                SequenceCount <= WidthMultiplier;
                Done_v := '0';
```

```verilog
module MULT_SEQ_BOOTH
    (Clock, Reset, Load, Multiplicand, Multiplier,
    Done, Product);
        parameter WidthMultiplicand = 5,  // multiplicand
                    WidthMultiplier  = 5, // multiplier
                    WidthCount    = 3;    // 2**WidthCount <=
                                        WidthB * 2
    input  Clock,Reset,Load;
    input  [WidthMultiplicand - 1:0] Multiplicand;
    input  [WidthMultiplier - 1:0] Multiplier;
    output Done;
    output [WidthProduct - 1:0] Product;
    reg Done;

    reg                             Shift_afterAddSub;
    reg [WidthMultiplicand - 1:0] RegA;
    reg [WidthMultiplier - 1:0]   RegB;
    reg [WidthMultiplier - 1:0]   RegQ;
    reg [WidthCount - 1:0]        SequenceCount;
    reg                           Qnplus1;



//--------------------------------------------------------
// Booth algorithm Shift and add multiplier
//--------------------------------------------------------
always @(posedge Clock)
    begin: SHIFT_ADD_MULT



        //-------------------------
        // Synchronous reset
        //-------------------------
        if (!Reset)
            begin
                RegA = 0;
                RegB = 0;
                RegQ = 0;
                Qnplus1 = 0;
                Shift_afterAddSub = 0;
                SequenceCount = WidthMultiplier;
                Done = 0;
            end
//----------------------------------------------------------
// Load new data to be multiplied & set control
// signals
//----------------------------------------------------------
        else if (Load)
            begin
                RegA = 0;
                RegB = Multiplicand;
                RegQ = Multiplier;
                Qnplus1 = 0;
                Shift_afterAddSub = 0;
                SequenceCount = WidthMultiplier;
                Done = 0;
            end
```

continued

continued

Generic Booth's algorithm multiplier

VHDL	Verilog
| ```
--------------------------------------------
-- Add, subtract or arithmetic shift depending
-- upon Qn and Qn+1
--------------------------------------------
elsif (Done = '0') then
    Shift_Q0_Q0plus1 := Shift_afterAddSub &
                        RegQ(0) &
                        Qnplus1;
        case (Shift_Q0_Q0plus1) is
            when "010" =>
                RegA <= RegA + not RegB + 1;
                Shift_afterAddSub <= '1';
            when "001" =>
                RegA <= RegA + RegB;
                Shift_afterAddSub <= '1';
            when others =>
                Reg_A_Q_Qn1 := (RegA & RegQ &
                               Qnplus1) sra 1;
                RegA <= Reg_A_Q_Qn1(WidthMultiplicand
                    +WidthMultiplier-2 downto
                    WidthMultiplier);
                RegQ    <= Reg_A_Q_Qn1(Width
                        Multiplicand downto 1);
                Qnplus1 <= Reg_A_Q_Qn1(0);
                SequenceCount <= SequenceCount - 1;
                Shift_afterAddSub <= '0';
                if (SequenceCount = 0) then
                    Done_v := '1';
                end if;
        end case;
    end if;
end if;
    Done <= Done_v;
end process SHIFT_ADD_MULT;

    Product <= RegA & RegQ;
end architecture RTL;
``` | ```
//------------------------------------------------
// Add, subtract or arithmetic shift depending upon
// Qn and Qn+1
//------------------------------------------------
else if (! Done)
    case ( {Shift_afterAddSub, RegQ[0], Qnplus1} )
        3'b 010 : begin
                RegA = RegA + ~ RegB + 1;
                Shift_afterAddSub = 1;
            end
        3'b 001 : begin
                RegA = RegA + RegB;
                Shift_afterAddSub = 1;
            end
        default : begin
                {RegA, RegQ, Qnplus1} =
                    ({RegA, RegQ, Qnplus1} >> 1);
                RegA[WidthMultiplicand - 1] =
                    RegA[WidthMultiplicand - 2];
                SequenceCount =
                    SequenceCount - 1;
                Shift_afterAddSub = 0;
                if (SequenceCount == 0)
                    Done = 1;
            end
    endcase
end


assign Product = {RegA, RegQ};

endmodule
``` |

Example 9.11 10-bit divide by 5-bit combinational logic divider

The divide algorithm is modeled for a 10-bit divide by 5-bit combinational logic divider. As with most algorithms, the process is changed slightly for hardware implementation. Instead of using consecutive sequences of shift, compare and subtract operations, it is convenient to use consecutive sequences of shift and add a 2's complement number. This process applies equally for combinational or sequential circuit implementations. By adding a 2's complement number instead of subtracting, a single adder is able to perform both the compare and subtract operations. The carry out from the adder indicates which of the two inputs is the greater. For example A - B becomes A + (! B + 1), and the carry out, if a logic 1, indicates that A is greater than or equal to B. This principle is shown in the model's structure, Figure 9.15.

In the combinational implementation of the multiplier algorithm, Example 9.8, the individual partial products could be derived directly from the inputs. This is not possible for the divider; individual partial remainders must be derived from the previously computed partial remainder in a chain. This chain of successive shift, compare and subtract (shift and add 2's complement) operations, causes the circuit to exhibit much longer delays than multipliers of equivalent bus widths. This somewhat reduces the primary advantage of using combinational circuit dividers over sequential ones.

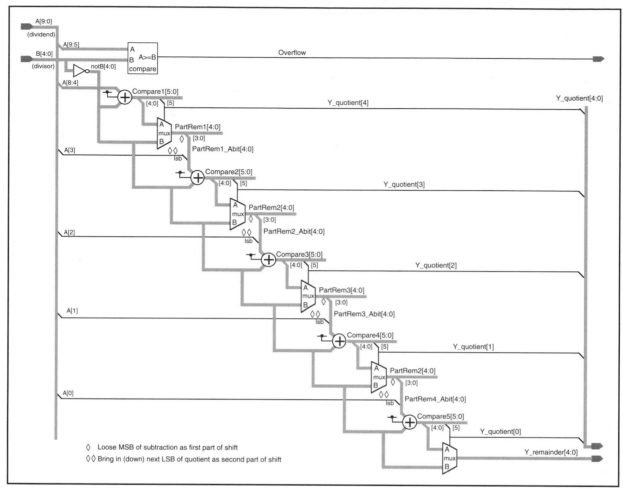

Figure 9.15 Inferred structure of 10-bit divide by 5-bit combinational logic divider

The first compare is of the upper 5-bits of the dividend A and the 5-bit divisor B. If A[9:5] is greater than, or equal to B[4:0] it means the division will result in a number that is greater than 5-bits wide. As only 5-bits have been allocated to hold the quotient Quotient an overflow signal is generated, that is, Overflow is set to logic 1. No subtraction is required because if A[9:5] >= B an overflow condition exists. For this reason, the first stage in the chain uses a comparator and not an adder.

The next stage in the chain of add, compare and shift operations continues with A[8:4]. Each partial remainder that is generated, is a remainder in its own right; the required resolution of the quotient determines which partial remainder is the output remainder. For example, the first partial remainder, PartRem1, would be the output remainder for a single bit quotient, but would be 9-bits wide instead of 5. The second remainder would be the output for a 2-bit quotient, etc.

HDL Code. There is nothing unusual about the coding style; only continuous signal assignments and **if** statements are used. The code is self-documenting and sufficiently commented for easy comprehension.

Table 9.6 shows by example, signal values resulting from using the same dividend and divisor numbers as used in the description of the algorithm.

Signal name	Binary value	Operation
A (dividend) B (divisor)	0111000010 (450) 10001 (17)	
2's comp B	01111	
Overflow	0	
Compare1[5:0] Quotient[4] PartRem1[4:0]	101011 1 01011	A[8:4] + 2's comp B Compare1[4:0]
PartRem1_Abit[4:0]	10110	Bring down dividend bit 3
Compare2[5:0] Quotient[3] PartRem2[4:0]	100101 1 00101	Compare1_Abit + 2's comp B Compare2[4:0]
PartRem2_Abit[4:0]	01010	Bring down dividend bit 2
Compare3[5:0] Quotient[2] PartRem3[4:0]	011001 0 01010	Compare2_Abit + 2's comp B Compare2_Abit
PartRem3_Abit[4:0]	10101	Bring down dividend bit 1
Compare4[5:0] Quotient[1] PartRem4[4:0]	100100 1 00100	Compare3_Abit + 2's comp B PartRem3_Abit - B
PartRem4_Abit[4:0]	01000	Bring down dividend bit 0
Compare5[5:0] Quotient[0]	010111 0	Compare4_Abit + 2's comp B
Quotient[4:0] Remainder[4:0]	11010 (26) 01000 (8)	

Table 9.6 Example signal values for the 10-bit divide by 5-bit combinational divider

10-bit divide by 5-bit combinational logic divider

VHDL	Verilog

`library` IEEE;
`use` IEEE.STD_Logic_1164.`all`; IEEE.Numeric_BIT.`all`;
 	
`entity` DIV10BY5_COMB `is`
   `port` (A: `in` unsigned(9 `downto` 0); -- dividend
          B: `in` unsigned(4 `downto` 0); -- divisor
          Overflow: `out` std_logic;
          Quotient,
          Remainder: `out` unsigned(4 `downto` 0));
`end entity` DIV10BY5_COMB;
 	
`architecture` RTL `of` DIV10BY5_COMB `is`
`begin`
   `process` (A, B)
      `variable` notB: unsigned(4 `downto` 0);
      `variable` Compare1, Compare2,
                                     continued
	`module` DIV10BY5_COMB
	   (A, B, Overflow, Quotient, Remainder);
	      `input` [9:0] A; // dividend
	      `input` [4:0] B; // divisor
	      `output` Overflow;
	      `output` [4:0] Quotient, Remainder;
	      `reg` Overflow;
	      `reg` [4:0] Quotient, Remainder;
	
	      `reg` [4:0] notB;
	      `reg` [5:0] Compare1, Compare2,
	                Compare3, Compare4,
	                Compare5;
	      `reg` [4:0] PartRem1, PartRem2, PartRem3, PartRem4,
	                PartRem1_Abit, PartRem2_Abit,
	                PartRem3_Abit, PartRem4_Abit;
	                                       continued

10-bit divide by 5-bit combinational logic divider

VHDL	Verilog
| ```
              Compare3, Compare4,
              Compare5:       unsigned(5 downto 0);
    variable PartRem1, PartRem2,
              PartRem3, PartRem4,
              PartRem1_Abit, PartRem2_Abit,
              PartRem3_Abit, PartRem4_Abit:
                          unsigned(4 downto 0);
begin
    ----------------------------------------------------
    -- Subtract upper 5-bits of quotient from divisor (B)
    -- and test for a Quotient bit overflow.
    ----------------------------------------------------
    if (A(9 downto 5) >= B) then
        Overflow <= '1';   -- an overflow has occured
                           -- Quotient & Remainder void
    else
        Overflow <= '0';   -- no overflow
                           -- Quotient & Remainder valid
    end if;



    ---------------
    -- Invert B
    ---------------
    notB := not B;
    ----------------------------------------------------
    -- Ignore MSB of A and test if next 5 MSB bits of
    -- A >= divisor (B). Quotient(4)=1 if A(8:4)>= B.
    ----------------------------------------------------
    Compare1 := A(8 downto 4) + ('0' & notB) + 1;
    if (Compare1(5) = '1') then   -- A[8:4] >= B
        PartRem1 := Compare1(4 downto 0);
        Quotient(4) <= '1';
    else
        PartRem1 := A(8 downto 4);
        Quotient(4) <= '0';
    end if;




    ------------------------------------------
    -- Bring down next dividend bit (bit 3)
    ------------------------------------------
    PartRem1_Abit := PartRem1(3 downto 0) & A(3); -- shift
    ------------------------------------------------
    -- Subtract if first remainder >= divisor (B)
    ------------------------------------------------
    Compare2 :=  PartRem1_Abit(4 downto 0) + ('0' &
                         notB) + 1;
    if (Compare2(5) = '1') then  -- PartRem1_Abit >= B
        PartRem2 := Compare2(4 downto 0);
        Quotient(3) <= '1';
    else
        PartRem2 := PartRem1_Abit(4 downto 0);
        Quotient(3) <= '0';
    end if;
``` | ```
always @(A or B)
  begin



    //----------------------------------------------------
    // Subtract upper 5-bits of quotient from divisor (B)
    // and test for a Quotient bit overflow.
    //----------------------------------------------------
    if (A[9:5] >= B)
        begin
            Overflow = 1;  // an overflow has occured
                           // Quotient & Remainder void
        end
    else
        begin
            Overflow = 0;  // no overflow
                           // Quotient & Remainder valid
        end
    //------------
    // Invert B
    //------------
    notB = ~ B;
    //----------------------------------------------------
    // Ignore MSB of A and test if next 5 MSB bits of
    // A >= divisor (B). Quotient[4]=1 if A[8:4]>=B.
    //----------------------------------------------------
    Compare1 = A[8:4] + notB + 1;
    if (Compare1[5])  // A[8:4] >= B
        begin
            PartRem1 = Compare1[4:0];
            Quotient[4] = 1;
        end
    else
        begin
            PartRem1 = A[8:4];
            Quotient[4] = 0;
        end

    //--------------------------------------------------
    // Bring down next dividend bit (bit 3)
    //--------------------------------------------------
    PartRem1_Abit = {PartRem1[3:0], A[3]};  // shift
    //--------------------------------------------------
    // Subtract if first remainder >= divisor (B)
    //--------------------------------------------------
    Compare2 = PartRem1_Abit[4:0] + notB + 1;
    if (Compare2[5])  // PartRem1_Abit >= B
        begin
            PartRem2 = Compare2[4:0];
            Quotient[3] = 1;
        end
    else
        begin
            PartRem2 = PartRem1_Abit[4:0];
            Quotient[3] = 0;
        end
``` |

continued   continued

10-bit divide by 5-bit combinational logic divider

VHDL	Verilog

```vhdl
--------------------------------------
-- Bring down next quotient bit (bit 2)
--------------------------------------
PartRem2_Abit := PartRem2(3 downto 0) & A(2); -- shift
--------------------------------------
-- Subtract if second remainder 2 >= divisor (B)
--------------------------------------
Compare3 := PartRem2_Abit(4 downto 0) + ('0' & notB) + 1;
if (Compare3(5) = '1') then   -- PartRem2_Abit >= B
    PartRem3 := Compare3(4 downto 0);
    Quotient(2) <= '1';
else
    PartRem3 := PartRem2_Abit(4 downto 0);
    Quotient(2) <= '0';
end if;




--------------------------------------
-- Bring down next quotient bit (bit 1)
--------------------------------------
PartRem3_Abit := PartRem3(3 downto 0) & A(1); -- shift
--------------------------------------
-- Subtract if third remainder >= divisor (B)
--------------------------------------
Compare4 := PartRem3_Abit(4 downto 0) + ('0' & notB) + 1;
if (Compare4(5) = '1') then   -- PartRem3_Abit >= B
    PartRem4 := Compare4(4 downto 0);
    Quotient(1) <= '1';
else
    PartRem4 := PartRem3_Abit(4 downto 0);
    Quotient(1) <= '0';
end if;




--------------------------------------
-- Bring down last quotient bit (bit 0)
--------------------------------------
PartRem4_Abit := PartRem4(3 downto 0) & A(0); -- shift

--------------------------------------
-- Subtract if fourth remainder >= divisor (B)
--------------------------------------
Compare5 := PartRem4_Abit(4 downto 0) + ('0' & notB) + 1;
if (Compare5(5) = '1') then   -- PartRem4_Abit >= B
    Remainder <= Compare5(4 downto 0);
    Quotient(0) <= '1';
else
    Remainder <= PartRem4_Abit(4 downto 0);
    Quotient(0) <= '0';
end if;
  end process;

end architecture RTL;
```

```verilog
//--------------------------------------
// Bring down next dividend bit (bit 2)
//--------------------------------------
PartRem2_Abit = {PartRem2[3:0], A[2]}; // shift
//--------------------------------------
// Subtract if second remainder >= divisor [B]
//--------------------------------------
Compare3 = PartRem2_Abit[4:0] + notB + 1;
if (Compare3[5]) // PartRem2_Abit >= B
    begin
        PartRem3 = Compare3[4:0];
        Quotient[2] = 1;
    end
else
    begin
        PartRem3 = PartRem2_Abit[4:0];
        Quotient[2] = 0;
    end


//--------------------------------------
// Bring down next dividend bit (bit 1)
//--------------------------------------
PartRem3_Abit = {PartRem3[3:0], A[1]}; // shift
//--------------------------------------
// Subtract if third remainder >= divisor (B)
//--------------------------------------
Compare4 = PartRem3_Abit[4:0] + notB + 1;
if (Compare4[5]) // PartRem3_Abit >= B
    begin
        PartRem4 = Compare4[4:0];
        Quotient[1] = 1;
    end
else
    begin
        PartRem4 = PartRem3_Abit[4:0];
        Quotient[1] = 0;
    end


//--------------------------------------
// Bring down last dividend bit (bit 0)
//--------------------------------------
PartRem4_Abit = {PartRem4[3:0], A[0]}; // shift

//--------------------------------------
// Subtract if fourth remainder >= divisor (B)
//--------------------------------------
Compare5 = PartRem4_Abit[4:0] + notB + 1;
if (Compare5[5]) // PartRem4_Abit >= B
    begin
        Remainder = Compare5[4:0];
        Quotient[0] = 1;
    end
else
    begin
        Remainder = PartRem4_Abit[4:0];
        Quotient[0] = 0;
    end
  end
endmodule
```

Example 9.12 Generic sequential divider

A generic (n x m) bit sequential shift, compare and subtract divider is modeled to the same division algorithm described earlier. Like multiplication, it is convenient to change the algorithm's process slightly for hardware implementation. Instead of shifting the divisor to the right, the dividend, or partial remainder is shifted to the left. This leaves the two numbers in their required relative position. As in the case for the combinational divider in the previous example, subtraction is better achieved by taking the 2's complement and adding so that information about their relative magnitude is available from the most significant (carry out) end. In this way, a single adder can perform both the compare and subtract functions.

The sequential process of the division algorithm, as modeled in this example, is indicated by flow chart, Figure 9.16. The hardware structure inferred by the model is in Figure 9.17; notice the data register structure is again very similar to the sequential multipliers in Examples 9.9 and 9.10.

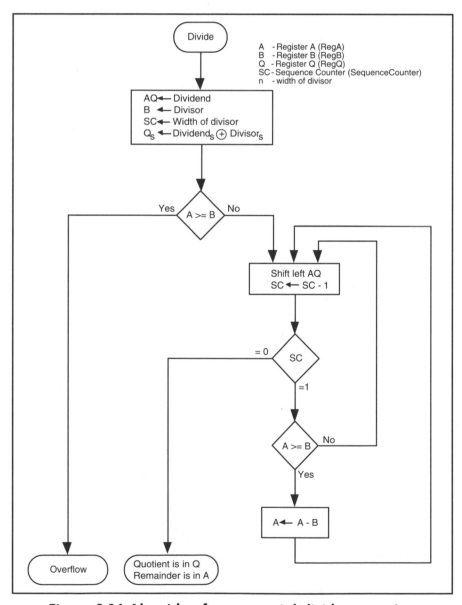

Figure 9.16 Algorithm for sequential divide operation

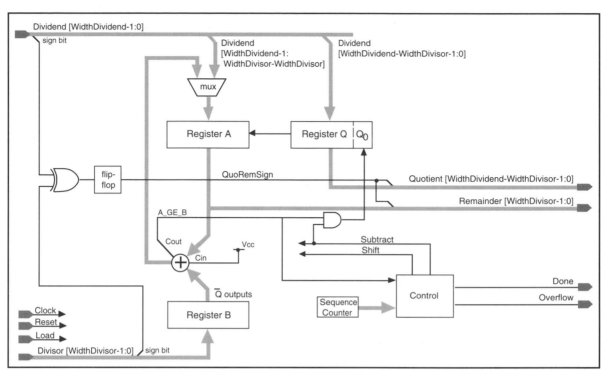

Figure 9.17 Hardware structure implied by sequential divider

Because this model is generic, the width of the dividend and divisor can be specified when the model is instantiated from another model and avoids having multiple versions of the same model, but with different width registers. The control block uses a finite state machine to provide; Shift and Subtract control signals, and Done and Overflow output signals. Its state diagram is shown in Figure 9.18.

The state machine controller is initialized and stays in state ST_WaitLoad until Load is a logic 1 whereupon division starts with the following register loading.

RegA   - Upper bits of dividend equal to number of divisor bits (ignoring sign bit)
RegB   - divisor (ignoring sign bit)
RegQ   - lower bits of the dividend equal to dividend bits minus divisor bits (ignoring sign bit)
QuoRemSign   - sign bit of dividend XOR'ed with sign bit of divisor
SequenceCounter   - VHDL: number of bits in the divisor (including the sign bit) times two. Verilog: bit width of counter. 2 x WidthCount <= (WidthDivisor - 1) x 2

The sign of the quotient (Quotient) and remainder (Remainder) are always the same, that is, QuoRemSign and is set when data is loaded.

Initially, a divide overflow condition is tested by subtracting the divisor in RegB from the upper n bits of the quotient in RegA, where n is the number of bits in the divisor. Subtraction is achieved from: RegA plus the 2's complement of RegB. If RegA is greater than, or equal too, RegB, that is, A_GE_B is a logic 1, an overflow condition exists and the state machine traverses to state ST_Overflow and Overflow is set to logic 1. Overflow remains set until either a reset or subsequent load occurs. An overflow means division would result in a quotient that requires more bits than there are bits in RegQ to hold it.

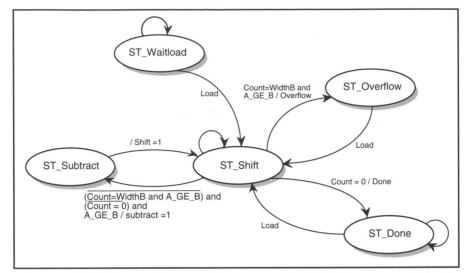

Figure 9.18 State diagram for sequential divider control block

If RegA is less than RegB, that is, A_GE_B is a logic 0, there is no overflow, so the process continues by shifting left RegA and RegQ, ready for the next test. The most significant bit of RegQ is shifted into the least significant bit of RegA.

The flow chart, Figure 9.16, shows a loop which shifts left and either transfers RegA - RegB back to RegA if A_GE_B = 1, or leaves RegA unchanged if A_GE_B = 0. If A_GE_B is at logic 1, the divisor will "go into" the bits of the quotient or partial remainder in RegA. The corresponding quotient bit is, therefore, at logic 1 and is inserted into Qn. This can also be seen in the model's state diagram, Figure 9.18. If A_GE_B is a logic 0, the bits of the quotient or partial remainder in RegA is less than the divisor. The corresponding quotient bit is therefore at logic 0 and is inserted into Qn. This looping process continues until the counter is zero, that is, there has been as many shifts as there are bits in the divisor. When the counter reaches zero the magnitude bits of the quotient resides in RegQ and the magnitude bits of the remainder resides in RegA.

Table 9.7 demonstrates the flow of data through the registers during a divide operation and uses the same numbers used in the description of the algorithm.

HDL Code: The following VHDL generics and Verilog parameters are used to customize the bit widths of this generic divider:

WidthDividend   - bit width of the dividend
WidthDivisor   - bit width of the divisor

MaxCount (VHDL)   - number of magnitude bits in the divisor
WidthCount (Verilog) - bit width of the sequence counter according to:
$$2^{WidthCount} <= (WidthDivisor-1) * 2$$

This divider operates on signed-magnitude numbers, and not 2's complement numbers. For this reason, the VHDL model uses unsigned data types and not signed data types. The signed data type, as defined in the IEEE 1076.3 synthesis packages, are intended for 2's complement operations.

Divisor B = 10001
notB + 1 = 01111

Clock cycle	State	Count	A	Q	A_GE_B	RegA_minus_RegB	Comments
1	ST_WaitLoad	5	0 1 1 1 0	0 0 0 1 0		0 1 1 1 0 (A) + 0 1 1 1 1 (notB + 1)	Load dividend AQ, divisor B
					0	1 1 1 0 1	A_GE_B = 0. No overflow.
2	ST_Shift	4	1 1 1 0 0	0 0 1 0 0		1 1 1 0 0 (A) + 0 1 1 1 1 (notB + 1)	Shift left AQ
					1	0 1 0 1 1	A_GE_B = 1. Q[0] = 1. Subtract needed.
3	ST_Subtract	4	0 1 0 1 1	0 0 1 0 1			A <- A - B. 1 in Q[0].
4	ST_Shift	3	1 0 1 1 0	0 1 0 1 0		1 0 1 1 0 (A) + 0 1 1 1 1 (notB + 1)	
					1	0 0 1 0 1	A_GE_B = 1. Q[0] = 1. Subtract needed.
5	ST_Subtract	3	0 0 1 0 1	0 1 0 1 1			A <- A - B. 1 in Q[0].
6	ST_Shift	2	0 1 0 1 0	1 0 1 1 0		0 1 0 1 0 (A) + 0 1 1 1 1 (notB + 1)	Shift left AQ
					0	1 1 0 0 1	A_GE_B = 1. Q[0] = 0. Subtract not needed.
7	ST_Shift	1	1 0 1 0 1	0 1 1 0 0		1 0 1 0 1 (A) + 0 1 1 1 1 (notB + 1)	Shift left AQ
					1	0 0 1 0 0	A_GE_B = 1. Q[0] = 1. Subtract needed.
8	ST_Subtract	1	0 0 1 0 0	0 1 1 0 1			A <- A - B. 1 in Q[0].
9	ST_Shift	0	0 1 0 0 0	1 1 0 1 0			Shift left AQ

remainder   quotient

dividing line between partial remainder or remainder, and the quotient

Table 9.7 Example of binary division with sequential divider

Generic n-bit sequential divider

VHDL	Verilog
| ```
library IEEE;
use IEEE.STD_Logic_1164.all; IEEE.Numeric_STD.all;

entity DIV_SEQ is
  generic (WidthDividend,WidthDivisor,MaxCount: natural);
  port (Clock, Reset, Load: in std_logic;
        Dividend: in unsigned(WidthDividend-1 downto 0);
        Divisor:  in unsigned(WidthDivisor - 1 downto 0);
        Overflow: out std_logic;
        Done:     out std_logic;
        Quotient: out unsigned(WidthDividend -
                           WidthDivisor - 1 downto 0);
        Remainder: out unsigned(WidthDivisor - 1
                           downto 0));
end entity DIV_SEQ;

architecture RTL of DIV_SEQ is
  type StateType is (ST_WaitLoad, ST_Shift, ST_Overflow,
               ST_Subtract, ST_Done);
  signal CurrentState, NextState: StateType;

  signal CurrentCount, NextCount: integer range 0 to
                         MaxCount;
  signal Shift,Subtract,A_GE_B: std_ulogic;

  signal QuoRemSign:   std_logic;
  signal RegA:  unsigned(WidthDivisor - 2 downto 0);
  signal RegQ:  unsigned(WidthDividend - WidthDivisor - 1
                    downto 0);
  signal RegB, notRegB:  unsigned(WidthDivisor - 2
                    downto 0);
  signal RegA_minus_RegB: unsigned(WidthDivisor - 2
                    downto 0);
begin
  ----------------------------------------------------------
  -- FSM Controller with integrated counter
  ----------------------------------------------------------
  FSM_COMB: process ( Load, A_GE_B, CurrentCount,
                     CurrentState)
  begin
    Shift <= '0';
    Subtract <= '0';
    Overflow <= '0';
    Done <= '0';
    NextCount <= CurrentCount;
    case (CurrentState) is
      when ST_WaitLoad =>
        NextCount <= MaxCount;
        if (Load = '1') then
          Shift <= '1';
          NextState <= ST_Shift;
        else
          NextState <= ST_WaitLoad;
        end if;
      when ST_Shift =>
        if (CurrentCount = WidthDivisor and
          A_GE_B ='1') then
          Overflow <= '1';
          NextState <= ST_Overflow;
        elsif (CurrentCount = 0) then
          Done <= '1';
          NextState <= ST_Done;
        elsif (A_GE_B = '1') then
          Subtract <= '1';
``` | ```
module DIV_SEQ
  (Clock, Reset, Load, Dividend, Divisor, Overflow,
   Done, Quotient, Remainder);
    parameter WidthDividend = 11, // dividend
              WidthDivisor  = 6,  // divisor
              WidthCount    = 3;  // From:
              // 2**WidthCount <= (WidthDivisor-1)*2
    input  Clock, Reset, Load;
    input  (WidthDividend - 1:0) Dividend;
    input  (WidthDivisor - 1:0) Divisor;
    output Overflow, Done;
    output (WidthDividend - WidthDivisor - 1:0) Quotient;
    output (WidthDivisor - 1:0) Remainder;
    reg    Overflow,Done;

    // FSM states
    parameter ST_WaitLoad = 0,
              ST_Shift    = 1,
              ST_Overflow = 2,
              ST_Subtract = 3,
              ST_Done     = 4;
    reg (2:0)                CurrentState, NextState;
    reg (WidthCount - 1:0)  CurrentCount, NextCount;
    reg Shift, Subtract, A_GE_B;

    reg QuoRemSign;
    reg (WidthDivisor - 2:0)  RegA;
    reg (WidthDividend - WidthDivisor - 1:0) RegQ;
    reg (WidthDivisor - 2:0)  RegB, notRegB;
    reg (WidthDivisor - 2:0)  RegA_minus_RegB;

  //----------------------------------------------------------
  // FSM Controller with integrated counter
  //----------------------------------------------------------
  always @(Load or A_GE_B or CurrentCount or
                  CurrentState)
  begin: FSM_COMB
    Shift = 0;
    Subtract = 0;
    Overflow = 0;
    Done = 0;
    NextCount = CurrentCount;
    case (CurrentState)
      ST_WaitLoad: begin
                 NextCount = WidthDivisor - 1;
                 if (Load)
                   begin
                     Shift = 1;
                     NextState = ST_Shift;
                   end
                 else
                   NextState = ST_WaitLoad;
                 end

      ST_Shift:    if ((CurrentCount == (WidthDivisor - 1))
                     && A_GE_B)
                   begin
                     Overflow = 1;
                     NextState = ST_Overflow;
                   end
                 else if (CurrentCount == 0)
``` |
| *continued* | *continued* |

Generic n-bit sequential divider

VHDL	Verilog

``
            NextState <= ST_Subtract;
        else
            Shift <= '1';
            NextCount <= CurrentCount - 1;
            NextState <= ST_Shift;
        end if;
 	
    when ST_Overflow =>
        if (Load = '1') then
            Shift <= '0';
            NextCount <= MaxCount;
            NextState <= ST_Shift;
        else
            Overflow <= '1';
            NextState <= ST_Overflow;
        end if;
 	
    when ST_Subtract =>
        Shift <= '1';
        NextCount <= CurrentCount - 1;
        NextState <= ST_Shift;
 	
    when ST_Done =>
        if (Load = '1') then
            Shift <= '1';
            NextCount <= MaxCount;
            NextState <= ST_Shift;
        else
            Done <= '1';
            NextState <= ST_Done;
        end if;
 	
    when others => NextState <= CurrentState;
    end case;
end process FSM_COMB;
 	
FSM_SEQ: process (Clock)
begin
    if rising_edge(Clock) then
        if (Reset = '0') then
            CurrentCount <= MaxCount;
            CurrentState <= ST_WaitLoad;
        else
            CurrentCount <= NextCount;
            CurrentState <= NextState;
        end if;
    end if;
end process FSM_SEQ;
``
	``
	                begin
	                    Done = 1;
	                    NextState = ST_Done;
	                end
	            else if (A_GE_B)
	                begin
	                    Subtract = 1;
	                    NextState = ST_Subtract;
	                end
	            else
	                begin
	                    Shift = 1;
	                    NextCount = CurrentCount - 1;
	                    NextState = ST_Shift;
	                end
	ST_Overflow: if (Load)
	                begin
	                    Shift = 0;
	                    NextCount = WidthDivisor-1;
	                    NextState = ST_Shift;
	                end
	            else
	                begin
	                    Overflow = 1;
	                    NextState = ST_Overflow;
	                end
	ST_Subtract: begin
	                    Shift = 1;
	                    NextCount = CurrentCount - 1;
	                    NextState = ST_Shift;
	                end
	ST_Done: if (Load)
	                begin
	                    Shift = 1;
	                    NextCount = WidthDivisor - 1;
	                    NextState = ST_Shift;
	                end
	            else
	                begin
	                    Done = 1;
	                    NextState = ST_Done;
	                end
	    default: NextState = CurrentState;
	    endcase
	end
	
	always @(posedge Clock)
	    begin: FSM_SEQ
	        if (! Reset)
	            begin
	                CurrentCount = WidthDivisor-2;
	                CurrentState = ST_WaitLoad;
	            end
	        else
	            begin
	                CurrentCount = NextCount;
	                CurrentState = NextState;
	            end
	    end
	end
	``

continued

Generic n-bit sequential divider

VHDL	Verilog

<pre>--- 	
-- Compare (RegA - RegB)
-- (RegA + 2's complement of RegB with overflow
--- 	
A_SUB_B: process (RegA, RegB)
    variable AddOut: unsigned(WidthDivisor downto 0);
begin
    notRegB <= notRegB;
    AddOut := RegA + notRegB + 1;
    A_GE_B <= AddOut(WidthDivisor);
    RegA_minus_RegB <= AddOut(WidthDivisor - 1
                                  downto 0);
end process A_SUB_B;
 	
----------------------- 	
-- Data registers
----------------------- 	
REGISTERS: process (Clock)
    variable RegAQ: unsigned(WidthDividend-1 downto 0);
begin
 	
    --------------------------- 	
    -- Synchronous reset
    --------------------------- 	
    if (Reset = '0') then
        RegA <= (others => '0');
        RegQ <= (others => '0');
        RegB <= (others => '0');
 	
    --- 	
    -- Load new data to be divided
    --- 	
    elsif (Load = '1') then
        QuoRemSign <= Dividend(WidthDividend - 1) xor
                        Divisor(WidthDivisor - 1);
        RegA <= Dividend(WidthDividend - 2 downto
                      WidthDividend - WidthDivisor);
        RegQ <= Dividend(WidthDividend - WidthDivisor - 1
                        downto 0);
        RegB <= Divisor(WidthDivisor - 2 downto 0);
    ----------- 	
    -- Shift
    ----------- 	
    elsif (Shift = '1') then
        RegAQ := shift_left((RegA & RegQ), 1);
        RegA <= RegAQ(WidthDividend - 2 downto
                      WidthDividend - WidthDivisor);
        RegQ <= RegAQ(WidthDividend - WidthDivisor - 1
                        downto 0);
 	
    ---------------- 	
    -- Subtract
    ---------------- 	
    elsif (Subtract = '1') then
        RegQ(0) <= A_GE_B;
        RegA   <= RegA_minus_RegB;
    end if;
  end process REGISTERS;
 	
  Quotient <= QuoRemSign & RegQ;
  Remainder <= QuoRemSign & RegA;
 	
end architecture RTL ;</pre>
	<pre>//---
	// Compare (RegA - RegB)
	// (RegA + 2's complement of RegB with overflow
	//---
	always @(RegA or RegB)
	    begin: A_SUB_B
	        notRegB = ~ RegB;
	        {A_GE_B,RegA_minus_RegB} = RegA + notRegB + 1;
	    end
	
	//---------------------
	// Data registers
	//---------------------
	always @(posedge Clock)
	    begin: REGISTERS
	
	        //---------------------------
	        // Synchronous reset
	        //---------------------------
	        if (! Reset)
	            begin
	                RegA = 0;
	                RegQ = 0;
	                RegB = 0;
	            end
	        //---
	        // Load new data to be divided
	        //---
	        else if (Load)
	            begin
	                QuoRemSign = Dividend[WidthDividend - 1] ^
	                               Divisor[WidthDivisor - 1];
	                {RegA,RegQ} =Dividend[WidthDividend - 2:0];
	                RegB = Divisor[WidthDivisor - 2:0];
	            end
	
	        //--------
	        // Shift
	        //--------
	        else if (Shift)
	            {RegA, RegQ} = {RegA, RegQ} << 1;
	
	        //--------------
	        // Subtract
	        //--------------
	        else if (Subtract)
	            begin
	                RegQ[0] = A_GE_B;
	                RegA = RegA_minus_RegB;
	            end
	    end
	
	  assign Quotient = {QuoRemSign, RegQ};
	  assign Remainder = {QuoRemSign, RegA};
	
	endmodule</pre>

Tri-State Buffers

Chapter 10 Contents

Modeling Tri-State Buffers

Data with multiple sources that need to be connected to one or more destination points in a circuit may be implemented using either multiplexers or tri-state buffers. This chapter shows the different ways in which tri-state buffers may be modeled for inference by synthesis tools.

Tri-State buffers are modeled using any of the multi-way branch statements:

> **if** statements,
> **case** statements,
> conditional signal assignments (VHDL),
> conditional continuous assignments (Verilog).

A tri-state buffer is inferred by assigning a high impedance value (Z) to a data object in a particular branch of a multi branch statement. The main point to note about modeling tri-state buffers is that multiple buffers that are connected to the same output <u>must</u> be modeled in separate <u>concurrent</u> statements, see examples.

Example 10.1 models three tri-state buffers connected to the same tri-state output signal using either concurrent or sequential assignment statements. Example 10.2 has a tri-state buffer inferred from a **case** statement and indicates how it inhibits use of a "don't care" default assignment. Example 10.3 has five mutually exclusive busses connect to the same output bus via tri-state buffers. Example 10.4 is similar to Example 10.3, but has synchronously clocked enable signals for minimal skew between switching tri-state buffers.

Example 10.1 Modeling tri-state buffers

Two different models of the same circuit are shown. It consists of tri-state buffers whose outputs are connected together. The operation is such that only one of the three enable signals EnA, EnB and EnC are at logic 1 at any one time.

TRI_STATE_1A. This first model version has three conditional assignments. Each assignment assigns a value to the output concurrently, and infers a tri-state buffer by virtue of the **else** clause defining a default assigned value for Y of "Z" (high impedance). Because each assignment is concurrent, successive assignments to Y do not overwrite each other as they would if they were sequential assignments in a **process** (VHDL) or sequential **always** block (Verilog).

Tri-state buffers from conditional signal assignments

VHDL	Verilog	Syn. Circuit

library IEEE;
use IEEE.std_logic_1164.**all**;
entity TRI_STATE_1A **is**
   port (A, B, C: **in** std_logic;
    EnA, EnB, EnC: **in** std_logic;
    Y: **out** std_logic);
end entity TRI_STATE_1A;
 	
architecture LOGIC **of** TRI_STATE_1A **is**
begin
  Y <= A **when** (EnA = '1') **else** 'Z';
  Y <= B **when** (EnB = '1') **else** 'Z';
  Y <= C **when** (EnC = '1') **else** 'Z';
end architecture LOGIC;
	module TRI_STATE_1A
	  (A, B, C, EnA, EnB, EnC, Y);
	   input A, B, C, EnA, EnB, EnC;
	   output Y;
	
	  assign Y = EnA ? A : 1'b Z;
	  assign Y = EnB ? B : 1'b Z;
	  assign Y = EnC ? C : 1'b Z;
	
	endmodule	

TRI_STATE_1B. This second model version uses three **process** statements (VHDL) or three **always** statements (Verilog). Each is a separate concurrent statement containing an **if** statement that infers a single tri-state buffer. The synthesis tools from VeriBest Incorporated allow WIRE-OR or WIRE-AND logic to be synthesized. These options should not be used when tri-state buffers are required. The synthesized circuit shows what happens if the WIRE-OR logic option is used.

Tri-state buffers from separate process statements

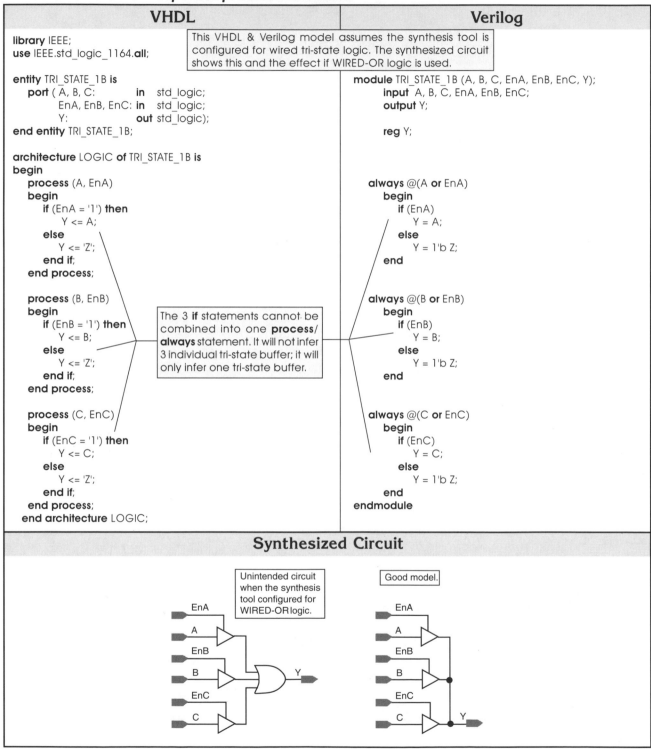

VHDL	Verilog
| ```
library IEEE;
use IEEE.std_logic_1164.all;

entity TRI_STATE_1B is
    port ( A, B, C:       in   std_logic;
           EnA, EnB, EnC: in   std_logic;
           Y:             out  std_logic);
end entity TRI_STATE_1B;

architecture LOGIC of TRI_STATE_1B is
begin
    process (A, EnA)
    begin
        if (EnA = '1') then
            Y <= A;
        else
            Y <= 'Z';
        end if;
    end process;

    process (B, EnB)
    begin
        if (EnB = '1') then
            Y <= B;
        else
            Y <= 'Z';
        end if;
    end process;

    process (C, EnC)
    begin
        if (EnC = '1') then
            Y <= C;
        else
            Y <= 'Z';
        end if;
    end process;
end architecture LOGIC;
``` | ```
module TRI_STATE_1B (A, B, C, EnA, EnB, EnC, Y);
    input A, B, C, EnA, EnB, EnC;
    output Y;

    reg Y;

    always @(A or EnA)
    begin
        if (EnA)
            Y = A;
        else
            Y = 1'b Z;
    end

    always @(B or EnB)
    begin
        if (EnB)
            Y = B;
        else
            Y = 1'b Z;
    end

    always @(C or EnC)
    begin
        if (EnC)
            Y = C;
        else
            Y = 1'b Z;
    end
endmodule
``` |

This VHDL & Verilog model assumes the synthesis tool is configured for wired tri-state logic. The synthesized circuit shows this and the effect if WIRED-OR logic is used.

The 3 **if** statements cannot be combined into one **process/always** statement. It will not infer 3 individual tri-state buffer; it will only infer one tri-state buffer.

Synthesized Circuit

Unintended circuit when the synthesis tool configured for WIRED-OR logic.

Good model.

Example 10.2 Tri-state buffers from case and VHDL selected signal assignment

Tri-state buffers are modeled using the **case** statement and VHDL selected signal assignment. Only five of the eight **case** choice values are explicitly defined for each of the five enable signals. The remaining three **case** choice values leave the output in a high impedance state. The problem is that the default branch of a **case** statement, **others** (VHDL) or **default** (Verilog), cannot be used to both assign a "don't care" output value to reduce logic, and assign a high impedance output value to infer a tri-state buffer.

Two sets of functionally equivalent models are shown. The first set of models below assigns a high impedance default output value and does not use a "don't care" default assigned value. The second set of models on the following page use a "don't care" default assigned output value to ensure the inferred logic is minimized. It has a separate conditional assignment to assign a high impedance output value to infer the tri-state buffer. It so happens that a logic 0 default for the **case** statement yields a minimum circuit and both sets of models yield the same synthesis circuit as shown.

Tri-state signals but no don't care default

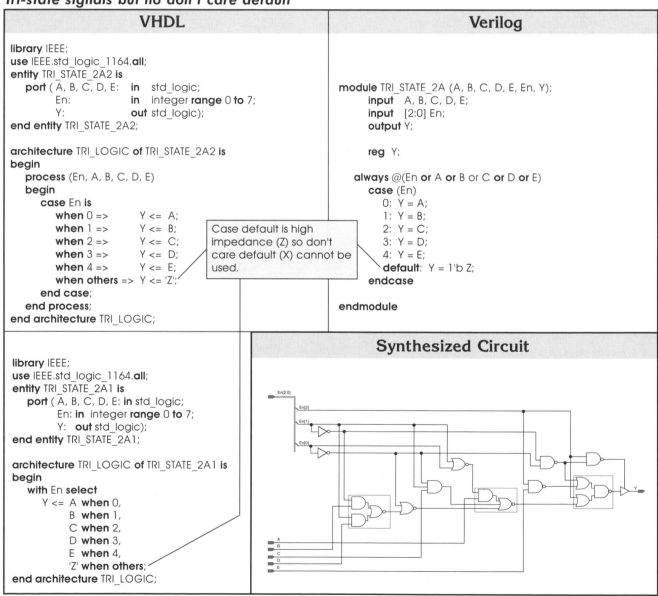

VHDL	Verilog
library IEEE; **use** IEEE.std_logic_1164.**all**; **entity** TRI_STATE_2A2 **is** 　　**port** (A, B, C, D, E:　**in**　std_logic; 　　　　　En:　　　　　**in**　integer **range** 0 **to** 7; 　　　　　Y:　　　　　　**out** std_logic); **end entity** TRI_STATE_2A2; **architecture** TRI_LOGIC **of** TRI_STATE_2A2 **is** **begin** 　　**process** (En, A, B, C, D, E) 　　**begin** 　　　**case** En **is** 　　　　**when** 0 =>　　Y <= A; 　　　　**when** 1 =>　　Y <= B; 　　　　**when** 2 =>　　Y <= C; 　　　　**when** 3 =>　　Y <= D; 　　　　**when** 4 =>　　Y <= E; 　　　　**when others** => Y <= 'Z'; 　　　**end case**; 　　**end process**; **end architecture** TRI_LOGIC;	module TRI_STATE_2A (A, B, C, D, E, En, Y); 　　**input**　A, B, C, D, E; 　　**input**　[2:0] En; 　　**output** Y; 　　**reg**　Y; 　　**always** @(En **or** A **or** B **or** C **or** D **or** E) 　　　**case** (En) 　　　　0: Y = A; 　　　　1: Y = B; 　　　　2: Y = C; 　　　　3: Y = D; 　　　　4: Y = E; 　　　　**default**: Y = 1'b Z; 　　　**endcase** endmodule

> Case default is high impedance (Z) so don't care default (X) cannot be used.

Synthesized Circuit

```
library IEEE;
use IEEE.std_logic_1164.all;
entity TRI_STATE_2A1 is
   port ( A, B, C, D, E: in std_logic;
          En: in  integer range 0 to 7;
          Y:  out std_logic);
end entity TRI_STATE_2A1;

architecture TRI_LOGIC of TRI_STATE_2A1 is
begin
   with En select
      Y <= A when 0,
           B when 1,
           C when 2,
           D when 3,
           E when 4,
           'Z' when others;
end architecture TRI_LOGIC;
```

Tri-state signals with a don't care default

VHDL	Verilog
| ```
library IEEE;
use IEEE.std_logic_1164.all;

entity TRI_STATE_2B1 is
    port (A, B, C, D, E:  in   std_logic;
          En:            in   integer range 0 to 7;
          Y:             out std_logic);
end entity TRI_STATE_2B2;

architecture TRI_LOGIC of TRI_STATE_2B2 is
    signal Y_ABCDE: std_logic;
begin

    process (En, A, B, C, D, E)
    begin
      case En is
        when 0 =>      Y_ABCDE <=  A;
        when 1 =>      Y_ABCDE <=  B;
        when 2 =>      Y_ABCDE <=  C;
        when 3 =>      Y_ABCDE <=  D;
        when 4 =>      Y_ABCDE <=  E;
        when others => Y_ABCDE <= '-';
      end case;
    end process;

    Y <= Y_ABCDE when (En >= 0 and En <= 4) else 'Z';

end architecture TRI_LOGIC;
``` | ```
module TRI_STATE_2B (A, B, C, D, E, En, Y);
    input   A, B, C, D, E;
    input   (2:0) En;
    output Y;

    reg  Y_ABCDE;
    wire Y;

    always @(En)
      case (En or A or B or C or D or E)
        0: Y_ABCDE = A;
        1: Y_ABCDE = B;
        2: Y_ABCDE = C;
        3: Y_ABCDE = D;
        4: Y_ABCDE = E;
        default: Y_ABCDE = 1'b X;
      endcase

    assign Y = (En >= 0 && en <= 4) ? Y_ABCDE : 1'b Z;

endmodule
``` |

> Not a true "don't care" in terms of logic reduction.

> Separate don't care (X) and high impedance (Z) states assigned. In this particular model:
> 1. the synthesis tool chooses a default logic 0 for a reduced logic implementation,
> 2. The tri-state buffer is inferred in a separate continuous assignment.

```
library IEEE;
use IEEE.std_logic_1164.all;

entity TRI_STATE_2B2 is
    port ( A, B, C, D, E:  in   std_logic;
           En:            in   integer range 0 to 7;
           Y:             out std_logic);
end entity TRI_STATE_2B1;

architecture TRI_LOGIC of TRI_STATE_2B1 is
    signal Y_ABCDE: std_logic;
begin

    with En select
      Y_ABCDE <=  A  when 0,
                  B  when 1,
                  C  when 2,
                  D  when 3,
                  E  when 4,
                  '-' when others;

    Y <= Y_ABCDE when (En>=0 and En<=4) else 'Z';

end architecture TRI_LOGIC;
```

Synthesized Circuit

Circuit the same as the previous model which does not use a "don't care" default assigned output value for this particular model.

Example 10.3 Tri-state buffers using continuous signal assignments

One of five 3-bit input busses (BusA to BusE) can drive the 3-bit tri-state output bus, BusY. The five enable inputs, (En_A to En_E), one for each bus, are guaranteed to be mutually exclusive in that only one can be active high at any one time. When no bus is enabled, BusA defaults to drive BusY. This ensures one, and only one, input bus is always driving the output bus, and that it is not left in the high impedance state assuming there are no pull-up resistors in the cells of the inferred tri-state buffer. If pull-up resistors are connected to the tri-state bus then it is not necessary to ensure the bus is always driven in this way. The five assignments to BusY cannot be modeled using **if** statements and combined in the same process.

Tri-state buffers from continuous signal assignments

VHDL	Verilog

library IEEE;
use IEEE.std_logic_1164.all; IEEE Numeric_STD.all;
entity TRI_STATE_3 is
  port (BusA, BusB, BusC,
       BusD, BusE: in unsigned(2 downto 0);
       En_A, En_B, En_C, En_D, En_E: in std_logic;
       BusY: out unsigned(2 downto 0));
end entity TRI_STATE_3;
 	
architecture TRI_LOGIC of TRI_STATE_3 is
begin
  BusY <= BusA when En_A = '1' or (En_B = '0' and En_C = '0'
             and En_D = '0' and En_E = '0')
             else "ZZZ";
  BusY <= BusB when En_B else "ZZZ";
  BusY <= BusC when En_C else "ZZZ";
  BusY <= BusD when En_D else "ZZZ";
  BusY <= BusE when En_E else "ZZZ";
end architecture TRI_LOGIC;
	module TRI_STATE_3 (BusA, BusB, BusC, BusD, BusE,
	                En_A, En_B, En_C, En_D, En_E, BusY);
	  input [2:0] BusA, BusB, BusC, BusD, BusE;
	  input En_A, En_B, En_C, En_D, En_E;
	  output [2:0] BusY;
	
	  assign BusY = En_A | (!En_B & !En_C & !En_D & !En_E) ?
	             BusA : 3'b Z;
	  assign BusY = En_B ? BusB : 3'b Z;
	  assign BusY = En_C ? BusC : 3'b Z;
	  assign BusY = En_D ? BusD : 3'b Z;
	  assign BusY = En_E ? BusE : 3'b Z;
	
	endmodule

Example 10.4 Synchronously clocked tri-state buffers from concurrent and sequential statements

This example is similar to Example 10.3 in that there are five 3-bit busses connected to a single 3-bit output bus using tri-state buffers. The difference is that all enable signals to the tri-state buffers are clocked through a flip-flop at the same time to minimize skew between switching tri-state buffers. The tri-state buffers for BusA and BusB are inferred using concurrent conditional signal assignments. The tri-state buffers for BusC, BusD and BusE are inferred from sequential conditional signal assignments. Data from bus signals BusD and BusE are shown clocked through a register.

Synchronously clocked enables to tri-state buffers

VHDL	Verilog

library IEEE;
use IEEE.STD_Logic_1164.all, IEEE.Numeric_STD.all;
entity TRI_STATE_4 is
  port (Clock: in std_logic;
      BusA, BusB, BusC, BusD, BusE: in unsigned(2 downto 0);
      En_A, En_B, En_C, En_D, En_E: in std_logic;
      BusY: out unsigned(2 downto 0));
end entity TRI_STATE_4;
 	
architecture TRI_LOGIC of TRI_STATE_4 is
  signal En_A_sync, En_B_sync, En_C_sync,
      En_D_sync, En_E_sync: std_logic;
begin
  process (Clock)   continued
	module TRI_STATE_4
	  (Clock,
	  BusA, BusB, BusC, BusD, BusE,
	  En_A, En_B, En_C, En_D, En_E,
	  BusY);
	
	  input Clock,En_A, En_B, En_C, En_D, En_E;
	  input [2:0] BusA, BusB, BusC, BusD, BusE;
	  output [2:0] BusY;
	
	  reg En_A_sync, E n_B_sync, En_C_sync,
	      En_D_sync, En_E_sync;
	  reg [2:0] BusY_reg;
	                          continued

Synchronously clocked enables to tri-state buffers

VHDL	Verilog
| ```vhdl
  begin
    if rising_edge(Clock) then
      En_A_sync <= En_A or (not En_B and not En_C and
                            not En_D and not En_E);
      En_B_sync <= En_B;
      En_C_sync <= En_C;
      En_D_sync <= En_D;
      En_E_sync <= En_E;
    end if;
  end process;

  BusY <= BusA when En_A_sync = '1' else (others => 'Z');
  BusY <= BusB when En_B_sync = '1' else (others => 'Z');

  process (En_C_sync, BusC)
  begin
    if (En_C_sync = '1') then
      BusY <= BusC;
    else
      BusY <= (others => 'Z');
    end if;
  end process;
  process (Clock)
  begin
    if rising_edge(Clock) then
      if (En_D_sync = '1') then
        BusY <= BusD;
      else
        BusY <= (others => 'Z');
      end if;
    end if;
  end process;
  process (Clock)
  begin
    if rising_edge(Clock) then
      if (En_E_sync = '1') then
        BusY <= BusE;
      else
        BusY <= (others => 'Z');
      end if;
    end if;
  end process;
end architecture TRI_LOGIC;
``` | ```verilog
always @(posedge Clock)
  begin
    En_A_sync = En_A | (! En_B & ! En_C &
                        ! En_D & ! En_E);
    En_B_sync = En_B;
    En_C_sync = En_C;
    En_D_sync = En_D;
    En_E_sync = En_E;
  end

assign BusY = En_A_sync ? BusA : 3'b Z;
assign BusY = En_B_sync ? BusB : 3'b Z;

always @(En_C_sync or BusC)
  if (En_C_sync == 1)
    BusY_reg = BusC;
  else
    BusY_reg = 3'b Z;

always @(posedge Clock)
  if (En_D_sync == 1)
    BusY_reg = BusD;
  else
    BusY_reg = 3'b Z;

always @(posedge Clock)
  if (En_E_sync == 1)
    BusY_reg = BusE;
  else
    BusY_reg = 3'b Z;

assign BusY = BusY_reg;

endmodule
``` |

Synthesized Circuit

Test Harnesses

Chapter 11 Contents

Introduction

This chapter describes the common methods of writing test harnesses. A test harness is often referred to as a *test bench* in the VHDL world and a *test fixture* in Verilog.

A test harness is a software program written in any language for the purposes of exercising and verifying the functional correctness of a hardware model during simulation in a simulation environment. As a result, test harness development should be driven by specification requirements which accurately reflect the system environment. Designers typically spend as much time writing test harnesses and verifying models as they do writing the hardware models themselves. The expressive power of both VHDL and Verilog means two things:

- a test harness is normally written in the same HDL language as the hardware model itself, the assumption made in this chapter, and contains no input or output ports,
- there is a wide variety of ways in which test harnesses may be coded.

The objectives of a test harness are to:

- instantiate the hardware model under test,
- generate stimulus waveforms and apply them to the hardware model in the form of functional test vectors during simulation,
- generate expected waveforms in the form of reference vectors and compare them with the output from the hardware model during simulation,
- possibly automatically provide a pass or fail indication,
- consider simulation efficiency for long test sequences. That is, reduce actual processes where possible and use *on-off* control of other stimulus and response mechanisms. For VHDL, access types are slow, use signals where possible as they are statiscally allocated at elaboration time.

The advantages of writing a test harness in the same HDL (VHDL or Verilog) as the hardware model are:

- there is no need to learn a special simulation tool or special language,
- VHDL and Verilog are IEEE standardized languages so models and their associated test harnesses should be transportable across different design tools,
- both languages have rich simulation semantics that can be exploited to the full in a test harness.

The structure of a test harness, Figure 11.1, shows its three constituent parts. It is sometimes convenient to include other parts of the modeled hardware system within the test harness itself, in order to aid the generation of stimulus vectors, reference vectors, or both.

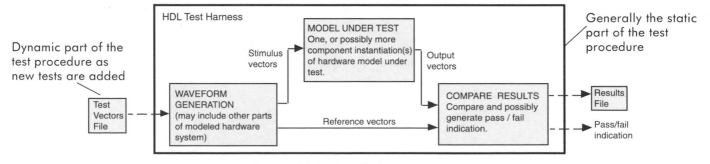

Figure 11.1 Test harness structure

There are both static and dynamic parts to a test procedure using a test harness. The static part reads test vectors, applies them to the model under test and controls where results will go. The dynamic part of a test harness is the part that changes when using the same test harness to perform new test sequences.

Configurations (VHDL)

A configuration is a separate *design unit* (see Figure 3.1) that allows different **architecture** and **component** bindings to be specified after a model has been analyzed and compiled, by a simulator for example. There are two types; the *configuration declaration* and the *configuration specification*.

Chapter 5 discussed configuration declarations and configuration specifications. Configurations are useful in test harnesses to configure different component (**entity-architecture** pair) bindings, and to bind a particular **entity** and **architecture** design units together.

Assertion Statement (VHDL)

The assertion, **assert** statement is used to conditionally display a text string message to the standard output, that is, the screen, during simulation. The **assert** statement checks the value of a boolean expression, and if true does nothing. If the expression evaluates false, the **assert** statement will **report** a user-specified text string. Note, this is the opposite from the branch expression of an **if** statement which executes the branch when the condition is true, not false. A designer can also specify one of four **severity** level messages with which the **assert** statement applies. They are "note", "warning", "error" and "failure", see Table 11.1. Do not over use as they slow simulation.

Severity level	Use
note	General information about the condition of a model
warning	Alert designers of potential problem conditions
error	Alert designers of conditions that will cause errors
failure	Alert designers of conditions that have disastrous effects

Table 11.1 Severity level in an assert statement

An example extracted from a model in this chapter is:

```
assert (AlarmEnable = '1')
    report "ALARM_CLOCK Error: Alarm not on at 07:00:00 am"
    severity failure;
```

Special Simulation Constructs - System Tasks & Functions (Verilog)

The Verilog LRM defines simulation specific system tasks and functions as part of the language. They perform activities such as monitoring and displaying simulation time and associated signal values at a specific simulation time. All system tasks and functions begin with a dollar sign, for example, $monitor. The Verilog standard permits tool vendors to define system tasks and functions unique to their particular tool using the programming language interface (PLI). However, to maintain portability between EDA tools only use the standard system tasks and functions defined as part of the Verilog language, see Appendix B. This chapter uses only these language defined system tasks and functions.

Hardware Model Under Test

Only one instantiation of the hardware under test is usually needed. However, with bus-orientated ASICs becoming more and more prevalent, it may be convenient to instantiate more than one instance of the model under test and use the extra models to aid vector generation. For instance, a model with both serial and parallel input and output ports, could be easily tested by instantiating two models and connecting the serial output from one back to the serial input of the other; and likewise for the parallel ports.

Vector Generation (Stimulus & Reference)

As previously mentioned, a test harness provides stimulus vectors to the model under test in order to exercise it during simulation. To automatically verify correct behavior, reference vectors must also be provided to compare output vectors from the model under test, with the reference vectors. In this case, an automatic pass or fail indication can be given. The extra time needed to write reference vectors is well worth spending; the model may need to be simulated several times before achieving the desired results. Another reason for generating reference vectors is that they can be used to verify the synthesized circuit operates correctly and that dynamic timing delays do not violate constraint specified timing. The synthesized circuit will include timing delays from cells in the targeted technology library. A test harness can be easily modified to instantiate the synthesized circuit, or possibly both the RTL model and synthesized circuit model at the same time, in which case their output vectors can be compared with the reference vectors during a single simulation. Automatic vector checking will save considerable time in the long run when compared to repeatedly checking simulation results manually.

There are three ways a test harness can provide test vectors:

1. generate them "on-the-fly" from within a test harness,
2. read vectors stored as constants in an array and
3. read vectors stored in a separate system file.

The following three sections describe these three methods. For complex models requiring many random type vectors, it may be better to store them in a separate system file. Adding extra vectors to the vector file is easy and different sets of vectors in different system files can be easily referenced as required from the same test harness.

1. Vectors generated "on-the-fly"

Test vectors that are generated "on-the-fly" are those that are not explicitly stored in an array or separate system file. Signal waveforms (functional test vectors) can be generated "on-the-fly" in many different ways from within a test harness as listed below and described in the following sections.

a) use continuous loops for repetitive signals, such as clocks,
b) use simple assignments for signals with few transitions, such as resets,
c) use relative or absolute time generated signals, not both,
d) use loop constructs for repetitive signal patterns,
e) use procedures to generate specific waveforms,
f) use tri-state buffers to both stimulate and monitor bidirectional signals.

This section covers these different ways and advises on when to use each method.

a) Generating clock signals

It is far easier to keep the generation of clock signal waveforms, and possibly reset signal waveforms, separate from other signal waveforms, even if all others are defined as vectors in a separate system file. This shortens the vector width, but more importantly avoids the necessity of having to define two vectors every single cycle of the clock signal. Clock signals can be generated in several different ways as illustrated below. The following models show how clock signals can be generated. Note that manufacturing test vectors, that have been automatically generated by an ATPG tool, will include any clock signals in the vector list.

Clock waveform generation in a test harness (VHDL)

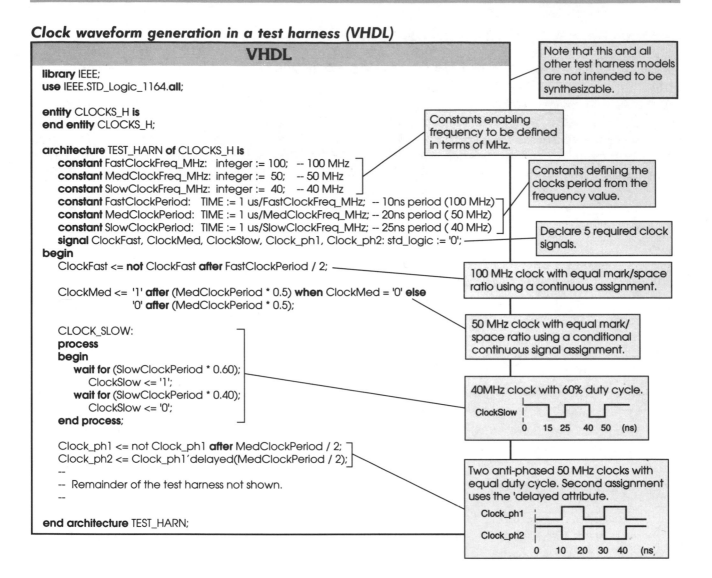

```
                        VHDL
library IEEE;
use IEEE.STD_Logic_1164.all;

entity CLOCKS_H is
end entity CLOCKS_H;

architecture TEST_HARN of CLOCKS_H is
   constant FastClockFreq_MHz:  integer := 100;   -- 100 MHz
   constant MedClockFreq_MHz:   integer := 50;    -- 50 MHz
   constant SlowClockFreq_MHz:  integer := 40;    -- 40 MHz
   constant FastClockPeriod:   TIME := 1 us/FastClockFreq_MHz; -- 10ns period (100 MHz)
   constant MedClockPeriod:    TIME := 1 us/MedClockFreq_MHz; -- 20ns period ( 50 MHz)
   constant SlowClockPeriod:   TIME := 1 us/SlowClockFreq_MHz; -- 25ns period ( 40 MHz)
   signal ClockFast, ClockMed, ClockSlow, Clock_ph1, Clock_ph2: std_logic := '0';
begin
   ClockFast <= not ClockFast after FastClockPeriod / 2;

   ClockMed <=  '1' after (MedClockPeriod * 0.5) when ClockMed = '0' else
                '0' after (MedClockPeriod * 0.5);

   CLOCK_SLOW:
   process
   begin
      wait for (SlowClockPeriod * 0.60);
         ClockSlow <= '1';
      wait for (SlowClockPeriod * 0.40);
         ClockSlow <= '0';
   end process;

   Clock_ph1 <= not Clock_ph1 after MedClockPeriod / 2;
   Clock_ph2 <= Clock_ph1'delayed(MedClockPeriod / 2);
   --
   -- Remainder of the test harness not shown.
   --

end architecture TEST_HARN;
```

Note that this and all other test harness models are not intended to be synthesizable.

Constants enabling frequency to be defined in terms of MHz.

Constants defining the clocks period from the frequency value.

Declare 5 required clock signals.

100 MHz clock with equal mark/space ratio using a continuous assignment.

50 MHz clock with equal mark/space ratio using a conditional continuous signal assignment.

40MHz clock with 60% duty cycle.

ClockSlow   0   15 25   40 50   (ns)

Two anti-phased 50 MHz clocks with equal duty cycle. Second assignment uses the 'delayed attribute.

Clock_ph1
Clock_ph2
             0   10   20   30   40   (ns)

Clock waveform generation in a test harness (Verilog)

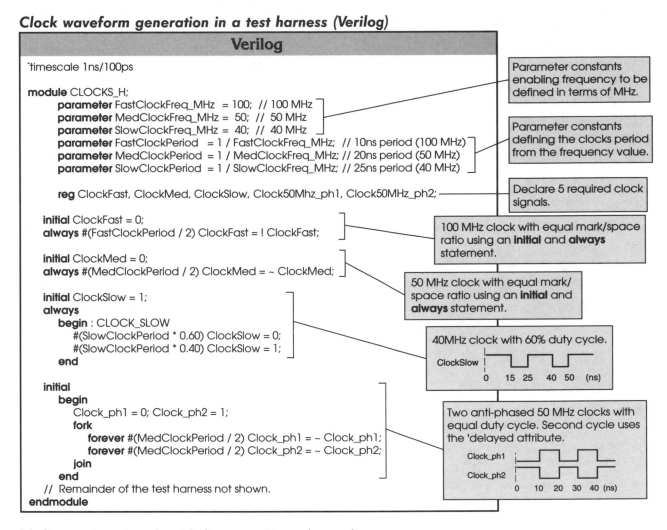

```
`timescale 1ns/100ps

module CLOCKS_H;
    parameter FastClockFreq_MHz = 100; // 100 MHz
    parameter MedClockFreq_MHz = 50;  // 50 MHz
    parameter SlowClockFreq_MHz = 40;  // 40 MHz
    parameter FastClockPeriod = 1 / FastClockFreq_MHz; // 10ns period (100 MHz)
    parameter MedClockPeriod = 1 / MedClockFreq_MHz; // 20ns period (50 MHz)
    parameter SlowClockPeriod = 1 / SlowClockFreq_MHz; // 25ns period (40 MHz)

    reg ClockFast, ClockMed, ClockSlow, Clock50Mhz_ph1, Clock50MHz_ph2;

    initial ClockFast = 0;
    always #(FastClockPeriod / 2) ClockFast = ! ClockFast;

    initial ClockMed = 0;
    always #(MedClockPeriod / 2) ClockMed = ~ ClockMed;

    initial ClockSlow = 1;
    always
        begin : CLOCK_SLOW
            #(SlowClockPeriod * 0.60) ClockSlow = 0;
            #(SlowClockPeriod * 0.40) ClockSlow = 1;
        end

    initial
        begin
            Clock_ph1 = 0; Clock_ph2 = 1;
            fork
                forever #(MedClockPeriod / 2) Clock_ph1 = ~ Clock_ph1;
                forever #(MedClockPeriod / 2) Clock_ph2 = ~ Clock_ph2;
            join
        end
    // Remainder of the test harness not shown.
endmodule
```

Parameter constants enabling frequency to be defined in terms of MHz.

Parameter constants defining the clocks period from the frequency value.

Declare 5 required clock signals.

100 MHz clock with equal mark/space ratio using an **initial** and **always** statement.

50 MHz clock with equal mark/space ratio using an **initial** and **always** statement.

40MHz clock with 60% duty cycle.

Two anti-phased 50 MHz clocks with equal duty cycle. Second cycle uses the 'delayed attribute.

b) Generating signals with few transitions (resets)

Waveforms for signals with few transitions, such as reset signals, are easily generated as shown below.

VHDL
Reset <= '1', '0' **after** 20 ns, '1' **after** 40 ns;

Concurrent signal assignment appearing in a test harness.

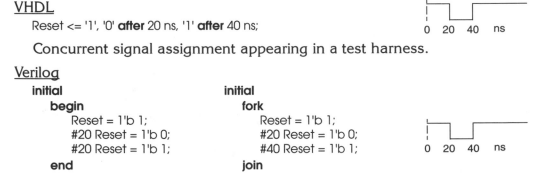

Verilog
```
initial                      initial
  begin                        fork
    Reset = 1'b 1;               Reset = 1'b 1;
    #20 Reset = 1'b 0;           #20 Reset = 1'b 0;
    #20 Reset = 1'b 1;           #40 Reset = 1'b 1;
  end                          join
```

Reset signal waveform generated from within an **initial** statement using a sequential **begin - end** block or concurrent **fork - join** block. Signal waveforms are usually generated in conjunction with other signal waveforms as shown in this chapter.

c). Relative or absolute time generated signals

The most straight forward method of generating "on-the-fly" stimulus is to implement procedural stimulus and specify waveform changes as needed.

Advantages of procedural stimulus are:

- easy to write,
- only input signals that change need to be listed at particular simulation times,
- can use relative or absolute simulation times for each input signal,
- input changes may be asynchronous, allowing different delays between each input signal change.

The disadvantages of procedural stimulus is that large amounts of input stimulus requires lengthy blocks of procedural code which can become unmanageable.

Procedural stimulus can specify waveform changes either relative or absolute to a specific simulation time.

- *Relative time.* Signal waveforms that are specified to change at simulation times relative to the previous time, in a time accumulated manner.
- *Absolute time.* Signal waveforms that are specified to change at simulation times absolute to a particular simulation time corresponding to the start of a particular section of code.

Time generated signal waveforms are shown in the following test harness using both relative and absolute specified timing. The test harnesses are for the alarm clock model shown in Chapter 12.

Relative time generated signal waveforms in a test harness (VHDL)

```
                                    VHDL

library IEEE;
use IEEE.STD_Logic_1164.all, IEEE.Numeric_STD.all;
use work.AM_PM_Package.all; ——————     Package shown in the code
                                        labeled "VHDL Alarm clock
                                        package for AM/PM type" on
entity ALARM_CLOCK_REL_TIME_H is        page 351.
end entity ALARM_CLOCK_REL_TIME_H;

architecture TEST_HARN of ALARM_CLOCK_REL_TIME_H is
    -- Data type and component declarations not shown

begin
    -- Clock waveform specification not shown


    ------------------------------------------------
    -- Instantiate RTL model under test
    ------------------------------------------------
    ALARM_CLOCK_1: ALARM_CLOCK
        port map ( Clock_1sec, Reset, LoadTime, LoadAlm,
                   SetSecs, SetMins, SetHours, Set_AM_PM,
                   AlarmMinsIn, AlarmHoursIn, Alarm_AM_PM_In,
                   AlarmEnable,
                   Secs, Mins, Hours, AM_PM, Alarm, Flashing);

    --------------------------------------------------     Statements are executed in sequence
    -- Relative time specified signal changes             at a time relative to previous
    --------------------------------------------------     statements and determined by the
    process                                                accumulated delay from the wait
    begin                                                  statements.
        Passed <= '1';
        -- Set all hardware model inputs to zero at time 0
        ----------------------------------------------------------
        Reset <= '0';
        LoadTime <= '0'; SetHours <= 0; SetMins <= 0; SetSecs <= 0; Set_AM_PM <= AM;
        LoadAlm <= '0'; AlarmHoursIn <= 0; AlarmMinsIn <= 0; Alarm_AM_PM_In <= AM;
        AlarmEnable<='0';

        -- Perform reset
        ------------------------
        wait for ClockPeriod_1sec;
```

continued

Relative time generated signal waveforms in a test harness (VHDL)

```
                                            VHDL

          Reset <= '1';
     wait for ClockPeriod_1sec;
          Reset <= '0';

     -- Set the time for the alarm clock (06:59:50 am)
     --------------------------------------------------
     wait for ClockPeriod_1sec;
          LoadTime <= '1'; SetHours <= 6; SetMins <= 59; SetSecs <= 50; Set_AM_PM <= AM;   -- time = 6:59:50 am
     wait for ClockPeriod_1sec;
          LoadTime <= '0'; SetHours <= 0; SetMins <= 0; SetSecs <= 0; Set_AM_PM <= AM;       -- time = 6:59:51 am

     -- Set the alarm time for the alarm clock (07:00 am)
     ----------------------------------------------------------------------
     wait for ClockPeriod_1sec;
          LoadAlm <= '1'; AlarmHoursIn <= 7; AlarmMinsIn <= 0; Alarm_AM_PM_In <= AM;  -- time = 6:59:52 am
     wait for ClockPeriod_1sec;
          LoadAlm <= '0'; AlarmHoursIn <= 0; AlarmMinsIn <= 0; Alarm_AM_PM_In <= AM;  -- time = 6:59:53 am

     -- Wait for 9 seconds and check alarm is turned off
     ----------------------------------------------------------------------
     wait for (ClockPeriod_1sec * 6);                                    -- time = 6:59:59 am
          if (AlarmEnable /= '0') then
               Passed <= '0';
          end if;
          assert (AlarmEnable = '0')
               report "ALARM_CLOCK Error: Alarm already on at 06:59:59 am"
               severity failure;

     -- Wait a further 1 second and check alarm turns on
     ----------------------------------------------------------------------
     wait for ClockPeriod_1sec;                                          -- time = 7:00:00 am
          if (AlarmEnable /= '1') then
               Passed <= '0';
          end if;
          assert (AlarmEnable = '1')
               report "ALARM_CLOCK Error: Alarm not on at 07:00:00 am"
               severity failure;

     --
     -- Further testing not shown
     --
     end process;

end architecture TEST_HARN;
```

> May want to use TEXTIO to report error message in order to improve simulation speed. Usually better to only use **assert** when stopping a simulation.

Relative time generated signal waveforms in a test harness (Verilog)

```
                                           Verilog

`timescale 1ns/100ps
module ALARM_CLOCK_REL_TIME_H;

     // Data type declarations and clock waveform specification not shown
     //-------------------------------------------------
     // Instantiate RTL model under test
     //-------------------------------------------------
     ALARM_CLOCK ALARM_CLOCK_1
          ( Clock_1sec, Reset, LoadTime, LoadAlm,
            SetSecs, SetMins, SetHours, Set_AM_PM,
            AlarmMinsIn, AlarmHoursIn, Alarm_AM_PM_In,
            AlarmEnable,
            Secs, Mins, Hours, AM_PM, Alarm, Flashing);
```

continued

Relative time generated signal waveforms in a test harness (Verilog)

Verilog

```
//----------------------------------------------------
// Relative time specified signal changes
//----------------------------------------------------
initial
    begin
        Passed = 1;
        // Set all hardware model inputs to zero at time 0
        // -----------------------------------------------------------
        Reset = 0;
        LoadTime = 0; SetHours = 0; SetMins = 0; SetSecs = 0; Set_AM_PM = 0;
        LoadAlm = 0; AlarmHoursIn = 0; AlarmMinsIn = 0; Alarm_AM_PM_In = 0;
        AlarmEnable = 0;

        // Perform reset
        // --------------------
        #ClockPeriod_1sec Reset = 1;
        #ClockPeriod_1sec Reset = 0;

        // Set the time for the alarm clock (06:59:50 am)
        // -----------------------------------------------------------------
        #ClockPeriod_1sec LoadTime = 1; SetHours = 6; SetMins = 59; SetSecs = 50; Set_AM_PM = 0; // time = 6:59:50 am
        #ClockPeriod_1sec LoadTime = 0; SetHours = 0; SetMins = 0; SetSecs = 0; Set_AM_PM = 0;    // time = 6:59:51 am

        // Set the alarm time for the alarm clock (07:00 am)
        //-------------------------------------------------------------------
        #ClockPeriod_1sec LoadAlm = 1; AlarmHoursIn = 7; AlarmMinsIn = 0; Alarm_AM_PM_In = 0; // time = 6:59:52 am
        #ClockPeriod_1sec LoadAlm = 0; AlarmHoursIn = 0; AlarmMinsIn = 0; Alarm_AM_PM_In = 0; // time = 6:59:53 am

        // Wait for 9 seconds and check alarm is turned off
        //-------------------------------------------------------------------
        #(ClockPeriod_1sec * 6)                                    // time = 6:59:59 am
            if (AlarmEnable != 0)
                begin
                    Passed = 0;
                    $fdisplay (SimResults,
                            "ALARM_CLOCK Error: Alarm already on at 06:59:59 at simulation time %d",
                            $time);
                end

        // Wait a further 1 second and check alarm turns on
        // -----------------------------------------------------------------
        #ClockPeriod_1sec                                          // time = 7:00:00 am
            if (AlarmEnable != 1)
                begin
                    Passed = 0;
                    $fdisplay (SimResults,
                            "ALARM_CLOCK Error: Alarm not on at 07:00:00 at simulation time %d",
                            $time);
                end

        // Further testing not shown
    end
endmodule
```

> The **begin** - **end** reserved words designate a "sequential" procedural block. Each delay is relative to the previous delays and time accumulates.

Absolute time generated signal waveforms in a test harness (VHDL)

VHDL

library IEEE;
use IEEE.STD_Logic_1164.**all**, IEEE.Numeric_STD.**all**;
use work.AM_PM_Package.**all**;
 	
entity ALARM_CLOCK_ASB_TIME_H **is**
end entity ALARM_CLOCK_ASB_TIME_H;
 	
architecture TEST_HARN **of** ALARM_CLOCK_ASB_TIME_H **is**
  -- Data type and component declarations not shown
begin
  -- Clock waveform specification not shown
  --- 	
  — Instantiate RTL model under test
  --- 	
  ALARM_CLOCK_1: ALARM_CLOCK
    port map (Clock_1sec, Reset, LoadTime, LoadAlm,
          SetSecs, SetMins, SetHours, Set_AM_PM,
          AlarmMinsIn, AlarmHoursIn, Alarm_AM_PM_In,
          AlarmEnable,
          Secs, Mins, Hours, AM_PM, Alarm, Flashing);
 	
  --- 	
  -- Relative time specified signal changes
  --- 	
 	
  process
  begin
    Passed <= '1';
    -- Set all hardware model inputs to zero at time 0
    -- 	
 	
    --Reset
    ---------- 	
    Reset <= '0',   -- simulation time = 0
    '1' **after** ClockPeriod_1sec,   -- simulation time = 1
    '0' **after** (ClockPeriod_1sec * 2); -- simulation time = 2
 	
    -- LoadTime
    ------------------ 	
    LoadTime <= '0',   -- simulation time = 0
          '1' **after** (ClockPeriod_1sec * 3), -- simulation time = 3
          '0' **after** (ClockPeriod_1sec * 4); -- simulation time = 4
 	
    -- SetHours
    ------------------ 	
    SetHours <= 0;   -- simulation time = 0
          6 **after** (ClockPeriod_1sec * 3),   -- simulation time = 3
          0 **after** (ClockPeriod_1sec * 4);   -- simulation time = 4
 	
    -- SetMins
    ---------------- 	
    SetMins <= 0,   -- simulation time = 0
          59 **after** (ClockPeriod_1sec * 3), -- simulation time = 3
          0 **after** (ClockPeriod_1sec * 4);   -- simulation time = 4
 	
    -- SetSecs
    ---------------- 	
    SetSecs <= 0,   -- simulation time = 0
          50 **after** (ClockPeriod_1sec * 3), -- simulation time = 3
          0 **after** (ClockPeriod_1sec * 4);   -- simulation time = 4
 	
    -- Set_AM_PM
    ---------------------- 	
    Set_AM_PM <= AM;
 	
                                     continued

> Waveforms generated for each signal separately starting from the same absolute time when the process is activated, which is at time zero in this example.

Absolute time generated signal waveforms in a test harness (VHDL)

```
                           VHDL
        -- LoadAlm
        ----------------
        LoadAlm <= '0';                              -- simulation time = 0
                    '1' after (ClockPeriod_1sec * 5),   -- simulation time = 5
                    '0' after (ClockPeriod_1sec * 6);   -- simulation time = 6

        -- AlarmHoursIn
        ---------------------
        AlarmHoursIn <= 0;
                        7 after (ClockPeriod_1sec * 5),  -- simulation time = 5
                        0 after (ClockPeriod_1sec * 6);  -- simulation time = 6

        -- AlarmMinsIn
        --------------------
        AlarmMinsIn <= 0;                            -- simulation time = 0

        -- Alarm_AM_PM_In
        ----------------------------
        Alarm_AM_PM_In <= AM;                        -- simulation time = 0

        -- AlarmEnable
        ---------------------
        AlarmEnable <= '0';                          -- simulation time = 0
        --
        -- Further testing not shown
        --
    end process;


    -----------------------------------------------------
    -- Check alarm is still "off" at 6:59:59 am
    -----------------------------------------------------
    process
    begin
        wait for (ClockPeriod_1sec * 12);            -- simulation time = 12
            if (AlarmEnable /= '0') then
                Passed <= '0';
            end if;
            assert (AlarmEnable = '0')
                report "ALARM_CLOCK Error: Alarm already on at 06:59:59 am"
                severity failure;
    end process;


    ------------------------------------------------
    -- Check alarm is "on" at 7:00:00 am
    ------------------------------------------------
    process
    begin
        wait for (ClockPeriod_1sec * 13);            -- simulation time = 13
            if (AlarmEnable /= '1') then
                Passed <= '0';
            end if;
            assert (AlarmEnable = '1')
                report "ALARM_CLOCK Error: Alarm not on at 07:00:00 am"
                severity failure;
    end process;
    --
    -- Further testing not shown
    --

end architecture TEST_HARN;
```

Absolute time generated signal waveforms in a test harness (Verilog)

Verilog

```
`timescale 1ns/100ps
module ALARM_CLOCK_ABS_TIME_H;

    // Data type declarations and clock waveform specification not shown
    //--------------------------------------------
    // Instantiate RTL model under test
    //--------------------------------------------
    ALARM_CLOCK ALARM_CLOCK_1
        ( Clock_1sec, Reset, LoadTime, LoadAlm,
          SetSecs, SetMins, SetHours, Set_AM_PM,
          AlarmMinsIn, AlarmHoursIn, Alarm_AM_PM_In,
          AlarmEnable,
          Secs, Mins, Hours, AM_PM, Alarm, Flashing);
    //--------------------------------------------
    // Relative time specified signal changes
    //--------------------------------------------
    initial
        fork
            Passed = 1;
            // Set all hardware model inputs to zero at time 0
            // ----------------------------------------------------------------
            Reset = 0;                                                            // simulation time = 0
            LoadTime = 0; SetHours = 0; SetMins = 0; SetSecs = 0; Set_AM_PM = 0;  // simulation time = 0
            LoadAlm = 0; AlarmHoursIn = 0; AlarmMinsIn = 0; Alarm_AM_PM_In = 0;   // simulation time = 0
            AlarmEnable = 0;                                                      // simulation time = 0

            // Perform reset
            // --------------------
            #ClockPeriod_1sec Reset = 1;                                          // simulation time = 1
            #(ClockPeriod_1sec * 2) Reset = 0;                                    // simulation time = 2

            // Set the time for the alarm clock (06:59:50 am)
            // ----------------------------------------------------------------
            #(ClockPeriod_1sec * 3) LoadTime = 1; SetHours = 6; SetMins = 59; SetSecs=50; Set_AM_PM=0; // simulation time = 3
            #(ClockPeriod_1sec * 4) LoadTime = 0; SetHours = 0; SetMins = 0; SetSecs=0; Set_AM_PM=0;   // simulation time = 4

            // Set the alarm time for the alarm clock (07:00 am)
            // ----------------------------------------------------------------
            #(ClockPeriod_1sec * 5) LoadAlm = 1; AlarmHoursIn = 7; AlarmMinsIn=0; Alarm_AM_PM_In=0;   // simulation time = 5
            #(ClockPeriod_1sec * 6) LoadAlm = 0; AlarmHoursIn = 0; AlarmMinsIn=0; Alarm_AM_PM_In=0;   // simulation time = 6

            // Check alarm is "off" at 6:59:59 am
            // ----------------------------------------------
            #(ClockPeriod_1sec * 12)                                              // simulation time = 12
                if (AlarmEnable != 0)
                    begin
                        Passed = 0;
                        $fdisplay (SimResults,
                            "ALARM_CLOCK Error: Alarm already on at 06:59:59 at simulation time %d",
                            $time);
                    end

            // Check alarm turns on at 7:00:00 am
            // ----------------------------------------------
            #(ClockPeriod_1sec * 13)                                              // simulation time = 13
                if (AlarmEnable != 1)
                    begin
                        Passed = 0;
                        $fdisplay (SimResults,
                            "ALARM_CLOCK Error: Alarm not on at 07:00:00 at simulation time %d",
                            $time);
                    end
            // Further testing not shown
        join
endmodule
```

> The **fork** - **join** reserved words designate a "parallel" procedural block. Each delay is absolute to the start of the block, which is at time zero in this example.

d. Repetitive stimulus using loops

Loop statements in both VHDL and Verilog provide a powerful means of generating stimulus that has some form of repetitive sequence. The advantages are:

- easy to write,
- code is compact and avoids having to store large vector files,
- reduces simulation virtual memory requirements substantially.

The following example shows part of a test harness that generates a gray-code sequence for a 16-bit data bus. Gray-coded patterns are particularly useful in test applications as only one bit changes between adjacent values in the sequence. This means specific errors are more easily identified in either the hardware model or its physical implementation. In the code below, each pattern in the sequence is held for 7 clock cycles. This means that if the sequence was modeled as test vectors, including the clock signal, there would be at least 917504 (2^{16} x 7 x 2) test vectors instead of the few statements shown in this test harness.

Repetitive stimulus using loops

VHDL	Verilog

`library IEEE;`
`use IEEE.STD_Logic_1164.all, IEEE.Numeric_STD.all;`
 	
`entity GRAY_SCALE_LOOP_H is`
`end entity GRAY_SCALE_LOOP_H;`
 	
`architecture TEST_HARN of GRAY_SCALE_LOOP_H is`
 	
`  -- Data type and component declarations not shown`
 	
`begin`
 	
`  -- Hardware model instantiation not shown`
 	
`  Clock <= not Clock after ClockPeriod / 2;`
 	
`  -- 16-bit gray scale sequence`
`  ------------------------------------------`
`GRAY_SCALE:`
`process`
`begin`
`    DataBus_16 <= (others => '0');`
`    for N in 0 to 65535 loop`
`      DataBus_16_var <= to_unsigned(N, 16) xor`
`                       shift_right(to_unsigned(N, 16), 1);`
`      for M in 1 to 7 loop`
`        wait until rising_edge(Clock);`
`      end loop;`
`      wait until falling_edge(Clock);`
`    end loop;`
 	
`    --`
`    -- Remainder of the test harness, including`
`    -- output verification procedure, not shown`
`    --`
 	
`  end process GRAY_SCALE;`
`end architecture TEST_HARN;`
	`` `timescale 1ns/100ps ``
	
	`module GRAY_SCALE_LOOP_H;`
	
	`  // Data type declarations not shown`
	
	`  // Hardware model instantiation not shown`
	
	`  initial Clock = 0;`
	`  always #(ClockPeriod / 2) Clock = ! Clock;`
	
	`  // 16-bit gray scale sequence`
	`  //-----------------------------------------`
	`  initial`
	`    begin: GRAY_SCALE`
	`      integer N;`
	`      DataBus_16 = 0;`
	`      for (N = 0; N < 65535; N = N + 1)`
	`        begin`
	`          DataBus_16 = (N ^ (N >> 1));`
	`          repeat(7) @(posedge Clock);`
	`          @(negedge Clock);`
	`        end`
	
	`      //`
	`      // Remainder of the test harness not shown.`
	`      //`
	
	`    end`
	
	`  //`
	`  // Output verification procedure not shown`
	`  //`
	
	`endmodule`

e. Tri-state buffers for bidirectional signals

Designs often have bidirectional ports which a test harness must both drive and read. In such a case, the hardware model under test will have a means of controlling its direction. The model may drive the signal as an output, or read it as an input, in which case the output driver is tri-stated. The directional control signal is often not accessible as an output from the hardware model at the (top) chip level. The test harness must contain bidirectional control code to fully exercise the model under test.

There are many ways bidirectional logic can be modeled. The test harness below illustrates one of the more common methods.

Bidirectional bus control in a test harness

VHDL	Verilog
| ```
library IEEE;
use IEEE.STD_Logic_1164.all, IEEE.Numeric_STD.all;

entity ALU_BIDIR_H is
end entity ALU_BIDIR_H;

architecture TEST_HARN of ALU_BIDIR_H is
   component ALU_BIDIR
      port ( A, B:    in   unsigned(15 downto 0);
             Y_bidir:  out unsigned(15 downto 0));
   end component ALU_BIDIR;
   signal OutputEnable: std_logic;
   signal A, B, Y_in, Y_out, Y_bidir: unsigned(15 downto 0);
begin


   -----------------------------------
   -- Bidirectional bus control
   -----------------------------------

   Y_bidir <= Y_in when (OutputEnable = '1') else
              (others => '0');


   --------------------------------------------------
   -- Instantiate the RTL model to be simulated
   --------------------------------------------------
   ALU_BIDIR_1: ALU_BIDIR
      port map (A, B, OutputEnable, Y_bidir);


   --------------------------------------------
   -- Apply stimulus to model under test
   --------------------------------------------
   process
   begin
      -- Drive bidirectional port
      ---------------------------------

      OutputEnable <= '1';
      A <= 16#A5A5#, B <= 16#5A5A#;
      wait for 25 ns;

      -- Tri-state bidirectional port
      ---------------------------------

      OutputEnable <= '0';
      wait for 25 ns;
      assert (Y_bidir = 16#25D6#)
         report "ALU_BIDIR Error: A = A5A5, B = 5A5A,
               Y /= 25D6."
         severity failure;
      --
      -- Remainder of test harness not shown
   end process;
end architecture TEST_HARN;
``` | ```
`timescale 1ns/100ps

module ALU_BIDIR_H;

   // Inputs to RTL hardware model
   // -------------------------------------
   reg OutputEnable;
   reg (15:0) A, B, Y_in;

   // Outputs from RTL hardware model
   // -------------------------------------
   wire (15:0) Y_bidir;



   //-------------------------------------
   // Bidirectional bus control
   //-------------------------------------
   assign Y_bidir = (OutputEnable == 1) ? Y_in : 16'b Z;



   //----------------------------------------------------
   // Instantiate the RTL model to be simulated
   //----------------------------------------------------
   ALU_BIDIR ALU_BIDIR_1
      (A, B, OutputEnable, Y_bidir);


   //-----------------------------------------------------
   // Apply stimulus to model under test
   //-----------------------------------------------------
   initial
      begin
         // Drive bidirectional port
         // ---------------------------------

         OutputEnable = 1;
         A = 16'h A5A5, B = 16'h 5A5A;

         // Tri-state bidirectional port
         // ---------------------------------

         #25 OutputEnable = 0;
         if (Y_bidir != 16'h 25D6)
            $diplay ("ALU_BIDIR Error: A = A5A5, B = 5A5A,
                  Y != 25D6");
         //
         // Remainder of test harness not shown
         //
      end

endmodule
``` |

> Notice VHDL **assert** uses "=" while the Verilog **if** uses "!=".

f) Example where all vectors are generated "on-the-fly"

The following example shows a test harness for the sequential Booth multiplier shown in Chapter 9. It is similar to the other test harnesses in this chapter, except that all test vectors are generated "on-the-fly" from within the test harness. Pseudo-random test data is generated by using the algorithm for a linear feedback shift register and Booth's algorithm is modeled within the test harness in order to generate reference test vectors. Specific points of note for the VHDL and Verilog test harnesses are summarized below.

VHDL test harness:

- A dedicated function called to_bitvector is declared (overloaded), and used to convert data objects of type unsigned to type bit_vector. The purpose of this is to enable simulation result data to be written to a text file using the VHDL package, TEXTIO, that is defined as part of the IEEE 1076 standard; see Appendix A. Fuction to_bitvector is already declared in STD_LOGIC_1164 for std_logic_vector. As unsigned is "closely related" to std_logic_vector a cast to std_logic_vector would preclude this overloading. (See also page 328.)

- True random data could be automatically generated using the random number generator package called "rnd2", which has been released to the public domain by McDonnell Douglas Aerospace. This package is useful for automatically generating test vectors in a test harness.

Verilog test harness:

- True random data could be automatically generated using the $random system function.

All stimulus and reference vectors generated "on-the-fly"

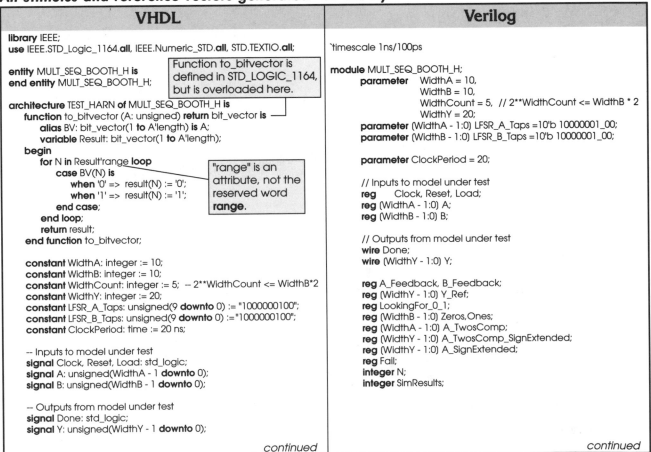

All stimulus and reference vectors generated on-the-fly

VHDL	Verilog

file SimResults: text **open** write_mode **is** "mult_seq_booth.simres";
 	
signal Y_Ref: unsigned(WidthY - 1 **downto** 0);
 	
component MULT_SEQ_BOOTH
  generic (WidthA, WidthB, WidthCount, WidthY: integer);
  port (Clock, Reset, Load: **in** std_logic;
    A: **in**   unsigned(WidthA - 1 **downto** 0);
    B: **in**   unsigned(WidthB - 1 **downto** 0);
    Done: **out** std_logic;
    Y: **out** unsigned(WidthY - 1 **downto** 0));
end component MULT_SEQ_BOOTH;
begin
 	
--- 	
-- Instantiate the RTL model to be simulated
--- 	
MULT_SEQ_BOOTH_1: MULT_SEQ_BOOTH
  generic map (WidthA, WidthB, WidthCount, WidthY)
  port map (Clock, Reset, Load, A, B,
       Done, Y);
 	
--------------------------------------- 	
-- Set up free running clock
--------------------------------------- 	
Clock <= **not** Clock **after** ClockPeriod / 2;
 	
--- 	
-- Apply stimulus to model under test
--- 	
process
  variable A_Feedback, B_Feedback: std_logic;
  variable LookingFor_0_1: std_logic;
  variable Zeros,Ones: unsigned(WidthB - 1 **downto** 0);
  variable A_TwosComp: unsigned(WidthA - 1 **downto** 0);
  variable A_TwosComp_SignExtended:
               unsigned(WidthY - 1 **downto** 0);
  variable A_SignExtended: unsigned(WidthY - 1 **downto** 0);
  variable Fail: std_logic;
  variable BufLine: line;
begin
  -- SimResults <= $fopen("booth_mult16x16.simres");
  Fail := '0';
 	
  Clock<='0'; Reset<='1'; Load<='0'; A <= (**others** => '0');
                  B <= (**others** => '0');
  wait for ClockPeriod; Reset <= '0';
  wait for ClockPeriod; Reset <= '1';
  -- for pseudo random data generation
  A_Feedback := '0'; B_Feedback := '0';
  A(0) <= '1'; -- so A & B will always be different
  for N **in** 0 **to** 99 **loop**
  --------------------------------------- 	
  -- Generate random data
  --------------------------------------- 	
  -- Use the Random Number Generator package "rnd2"
  -- that has been released for public use by:
  -- McDonnell Douglas Aerospace.
 	
  --------------------------------------- 	
  -- Generate pseudo-random data
  --------------------------------------- 	
  A_Feedback := '0';
  for N **in** 0 **to** (WidthA - 2) **loop**
    A_Feedback := A_Feedback **nor** A(N);
  end loop;
  A_Feedback := A_Feedback **xor** A(WidthA - 1);
  for N **in** (WidthA - 1) **to** 1 **loop**
    if (LFSR_A_Taps(N - 1) = '1') **then**
      A(N) <= A(N - 1) **xor** A_Feedback;
    else
      A(N) <= A(N - 1);
 	
continued
	//---
	// Instantiate the RTL model to be simulated
	//---
	MULT_SEQ_BOOTH
	  #(WidthA, WidthB, WidthCount, WidthY) MULT_SEQ_BOOTH_1
	  (Clock, Reset, Load, A, B,
	   Done, Y);
	
	//---------------------------------------
	// Set up free running clock
	//---------------------------------------
	initial Clock = 0;
	always
	    #(ClockPeriod / 2) Clock = ! Clock;
	
	//---
	// Apply stimulus to model under test
	//---
	initial
	  begin
	    SimResults = $fopen("booth_mult.simres");
	    Fail = 0;
	
	    Clock = 0; Reset = 1; Load = 0; A = 0; B = 0;
	    #ClockPeriod Reset = 0;
	    #ClockPeriod Reset = 1;
	    A_Feedback = 0; B_Feedback = 0; // for pseudo random
	                            // data generation
	    A(0) = 1; // so A & B will always be different
	
	    for (N = 0; N < 100; N = N + 1)
	      begin
	        //---
	        // Generate random data
	        //---
	        //A = $random; B = $random;
	
	        //---
	        // Generate pseudo-random data
	        //---
	        A_Feedback = ~
		A(WidthA - 2:0) ^A(WidthA - 1);
		        for (N = WidthA - 1; N >= 1; N = N - 1)
		          if (LFSR_A_Taps(N - 1) == 1)
		            A(N) = A(N - 1) ^ A_Feedback;
		          else
		            A(N) = A(N - 1);
		        A(0) = A_Feedback;
		
		        B_Feedback = ~
			B(WidthB - 2:0) ^ B(WidthB - 1);
			        for (N=WidthB - 1; N >= 1; N = N - 1)
			
			continued

Random number generator disabled.

Models shown with pseudo-random number generation enabled.

All stimulus and reference vectors generated on-the-fly

VHDL	Verilog

```vhdl
        end if;
    end loop;
    A(0) <= A_Feedback;

    B_Feedback := '0';
    for N in 0 to (WidthB - 2) loop
        B_Feedback := B_Feedback nor B(N);
    end loop;
    B_Feedback := B_Feedback xor B(WidthB - 1);
    for N in (WidthB - 1) to 1 loop
        if (LFSR_B_Taps(N - 1) = '1') then
            B(N) <= B(N - 1) xor B_Feedback;
        else
            B(N) <= B(N - 1);
        end if;
    end loop;
    B(0) <= B_Feedback;

    ------------------------------------------------------
    -- Use Booth's algorithm to compute reference product
    ------------------------------------------------------
    Y_Ref <= (others => '0');
    LookingFor_0_1 := '1';
    Zeros := (others => '0');
    Ones := (others => '1');
    A_TwosComp := not A + 1;

    -- Sign extend
    -- -----------------
    if (A_TwosComp(WidthA - 1) = '1') then
        A_TwosComp_SignExtended := Ones & A_TwosComp;
    else
        A_TwosComp_SignExtended := Zeros & A_TwosComp;
    end if;
    if (A(WidthA - 1) = '1') then
        A_SignExtended := Ones & A;
    else
        A_SignExtended := Zeros & A;
    end if;

    -- Perform Booth's algorithm
    ----------------------------------------
    for N in 0 to (WidthB - 1) loop
        if (LookingFor_0_1 = '1' and B(N) = '1') then
            Y_Ref <= Y_Ref + A_TwosComp_SignExtended;
            LookingFor_0_1 := '0';
        elsif (LookingFor_0_1 = '0' and B(N) = '0') then
            Y_Ref <= Y_Ref + A_SignExtended;
            LookingFor_0_1 := '1';
        else
            Y_Ref <= Y_Ref;
        end if;
        if (N < WidthB - 1) then
            A_TwosComp_SignExtended :=
                shift_left(A_TwosComp_SignExtended, 1);
            A_SignExtended := shift_left(A_SignExtended, 1);
        end if;
    end loop;

    ------------------------------------------------
    -- Test product on hardware model
    ------------------------------------------------
    wait for ClockPeriod; Load <= '1'; -- load A and B
    wait for ClockPeriod; Load <= '0';
    while (Done /= '1') loop
        wait for ClockPeriod;
    end loop;
    if (Y /= Y_Ref) then -- i.e. has failed
        Fail := '1';
        write(BufLine, string'("Error at time "));
```
continued

```verilog
    if (LFSR_B_Taps(N - 1) == 1)
        B(N) = B(N - 1) ^ B_Feedback;
    else
        B(N) = B(N - 1);
    B(0) = B_Feedback;

    //------------------------------------------
    // Use Booth's algorithm to compute
    // reference product
    //------------------------------------------
    Y_Ref = 0;
    LookingFor_0_1 = 1;
    Zeros = 0;
    Ones = ~ 0;
    A_TwosComp = ~ A + 1;
    // Sign extend
    // ----------------
    if (A_TwosComp(WidthA - 1) == 1)
        A_TwosComp_SignExtended = {Ones,
                                   A_TwosComp};
    else
        A_TwosComp_SignExtended = {Zeros,
                                   A_TwosComp};
    if (A(WidthA - 1) == 1)
        A_SignExtended = {Ones, A};
    else
        A_SignExtended = {Zeros, A};

    // Perform Booth's algorithm
    // ------------------------------------
    for (N = 0; N < WidthB; N = N + 1)
        begin
            if (LookingFor_0_1 == 1 && B(N) == 1)
                begin
                    Y_Ref = Y_Ref +
                        A_TwosComp_SignExtended;
                    LookingFor_0_1 = 0;
                end
            else if (LookingFor_0_1 == 0 && B(N) == 0)
                begin
                    Y_Ref = Y_Ref + A_SignExtended;
                    LookingFor_0_1 = 1;
                end
            else
                Y_Ref = Y_Ref;
            if (N < WidthB - 1)
                begin
                    A_TwosComp_SignExtended =
                        A_TwosComp_SignExtended << 1;
                    A_SignExtended = A_SignExtended << 1;
                end
        end
    //------------------------------------------
    // Test product on hardware model
    //------------------------------------------
    #ClockPeriod Load = 1; // load A and B
    #ClockPeriod Load = 0;
    while (Done != 1)
        #ClockPeriod;
    if (Y != Y_Ref) // i.e. has failed
        begin
            Fail = 1;
            $fdisplay (SimResults,
```
continued

All stimulus and reference vectors generated on-the-fly

VHDL	Verilog
| ```
        write(BufLine, now);
        write(BufLine, string'(": "));
        write(BufLine, (to_bitvector(A)));
        write(BufLine, string'(" x "));
        write(BufLine, (to_bitvector(B)));
        write(BufLine, string'(" not equal to "));
        write(BufLine, (to_bitvector(Y_Ref)));
        write(BufLine, string'(". Should be "));
        write(BufLine, (to_bitvector(Y)));
        writeline(SimResults, BufLine);
      end if;
      wait for ClockPeriod * 3;
    end loop;
    if (Fail = '0') then  -- Sim results are the same
      write(SimResults, string'("MULT_SEQ_BOOTH passed"));
    end if;
    wait;
  end process;
end architecture TEST_HARN;
``` | ```
                "Error at %d: %d x %d not equal to
                %d. Should be %d",
                $time, A, B, Y_Ref, Y);
          end
        repeat (3)
          #ClockPeriod;
      end
    if (Fail == 0) // Sim results are the same
      $fdisplay (SimResults, "MULT_SEQ_BOOTH passed");
    $fclose (SimResults);
    $stop;
  end
endmodule
```
Function to_bitvector is defined in STD_LOGIC_1164, but is defined and overloaded in this model. Could use : write(BufLine, to_bitvector(std_logic_vector(A))); and not use overloaded to_bitvector in this test harness. |

## 2. Vectors stored in an array

Test vectors may be conveniently stored as constants in an array and defined within the test harness itself rather than in a separate system file. Although this method is convenient for small numbers of test vectors, it soon becomes less manageable as the number of test vectors increase. For this reason, it is often better to put the vectors in a separate system file, see the following section which covers the reading of test vector files.

The following test harness contains vectors stored in an array and tests the error detection and correction model shown in Chapter 12.

### Test harness using vectors stored in an array

| VHDL | Verilog |
|---|---|
| ```
library IEEE;
use IEEE.STD_Logic_1164.all, IEEE.Numeric_STD.all, STD.TEXTIO.all;
use work.ERRDET_COR_PKG.all;

entity ERRDET_CORRECTION_H is
end entity ERRDET_CORRECTION_H;

architecture TEST_HARN of ERRDET_CORRECTION_H is
  function to_bitvector (A: unsigned) return bit_vector is
    alias BV: unsigned(1 to A'length) is A;
    variable Result: bit_vector(1 to A'length);
  begin
    for N in Result'range loop
      case BV(N) is
        when '1'    => Result(N) := '1';
        when others => Result(N) := '0';
      end case;
    end loop;
    return Result;
  end function to_bitvector;

  constant TestPeriod: time := 20 ns;
  constant TestCycles: integer := 5;

  -- Common inputs to RTL model
  signal ReadWrite_b: std_logic;

  -- Bidirectional ports to RTL model
  signal ProcData: unsigned(15 downto 0);
  signal MemData: unsigned(21 downto 0);

  -- Proc & Mem stimulus busses
  signal ProcWriteData: unsigned(15 downto 0);
  signal MemReadData: unsigned(21 downto 0);

  -- Reference data
                                    continued
``` | ```
`timescale 1ns/100ps

module ERRDET_CORRECTION_H;
  parameter   TestPeriod = 20,
              TestCycles = 5;

  // Common inputs to RTL model
  reg ReadWrite_b;

  // Bidirectional ports to RTL model
  wire (15:0) ProcData;
  wire (21:0) MemData;

  // Proc & Mem stimulus buses
  reg (15:0) ProcWriteData;
  reg (21:0) MemReadData;

  // Reference data
  reg (15:0) RefProcData;
  reg (21:0) RefMemData;

  // Outputs from RTL model
  wire (1:0) ErrorType;

  // Define array for Processor & Memory test and
  //  result data
  reg (15:0) ProcArr (TestCycles - 1:0);
  reg (21:0) MemArr  (TestCycles - 1:0);

  integer   N;
  reg       Fail,
            FailTime;
  integer   SimResults;
                                    continued
``` |

Test harness using vectors stored in an array

VHDL	Verilog

VHDL:

```
signal RefProcData: unsigned(15 downto 0);
signal RefMemData: unsigned(21 downto 0);

-- Outputs from RTL model
signal ErrorType: ErrorTypeType;

-- Define array for Processor & Memory test and result data
type MemVecArr is array (0 to TestCycles - 1) of
                              unsigned(21 downto 0);
type ProcVecArr is array (0 to TestCycles - 1) of
                              unsigned(15 downto 0);

----------------------------------------------
-- Assign test data to constant arrays
----------------------------------------------
-- Write data to memory is 1010 1011 1100 1101 bin (ABCD hex)

-- MEMORY Read data from memory. P=Parity bits.
constant MemArr: MemVecArr :=
-- parity bits: 22, 16, 8, 4, 2 & 1
    (0 => "0101011011110001100101", -- 15BC65 ABCD No error
     1 => "0100011011110001100101", -- 11BC65 8BCD
                              -- Single bit data error
     2 => "0101011011110011100101", -- 15BCE5 ABCD P3 error
     3 => "0100011011110011100101", -- 11BCE5 8BCD & P3 error
     4 => "1101011011110001100101"); -- 35BC65 Overall parity error

-- Verification data. PROCESSOR read data from memory.
constant ProcArr: ProcVecArr :=
    (0 => "1010101111001101", -- ABCD No error
     1 => "1010101111001101", -- ABCD Single bit corrected
                              -- data error
     2 => "1010101111001101", -- ABCD Single bit corrected
                              -- data error
     3 => "1000101111001101", -- 8BCD Double error uncorrectable
     4 => "1010101111001101"); -- ABCD P5 in error

signal Fail: std_logic;
-- Open simulation results file for appending pass/fail messages
file SimResults: text open write_mode is "errdet_correction.simres";

component ERRDET_CORRECTION
    port ( ReadWrite_b:  in    std_logic;
           ProcData:     inout unsigned(15 downto 0);
           MemData:      inout unsigned(21 downto 0);
           ErrorType:    out   ErrorTypeType);
end component ERRDET_CORRECTION;

begin
----------------------------------------------
-- Instantiate model to be simulated
----------------------------------------------
ERRDET_CORRECTION_1: ERRDET_CORRECTION
    port map (ReadWrite_b, ProcData, MemData, ErrorType);

----------------------------------------------
-- Assign tri states for device under test
----------------------------------------------
ProcData <= ProcWriteData when (ReadWrite_b = '1') else
            (others => 'Z');
MemData  <= MemReadData when (ReadWrite_b = '1') else
            (others => 'Z');

----------------------------------------------
-- Apply stimulus to RTL models under test
----------------------------------------------
process
    variable BufLine: line;
begin
    Fail <= '0';  -- Set to 1 if fails
    ProcWriteData <= (others => '0');  -- 16-bit
    MemReadData   <= (others => '0');  -- 22-bit
    RefProcData   <= (others => '0');  -- 16-bit
    RefMemData    <= (others => '0');  -- 22-bit
```

Verilog:

```
//------------------------------------------------
// Assign test data to memory arrays
//------------------------------------------------
initial
    begin
        // Write data to memory is 16'b 1010_1011_1100_1101
        // (ABCD hex)

        // MEMORY Read data from memory. P=Parity bits.
        // parity bits: 22, 16, 8, 4, 2 &1
        MemArr(0)=22'b 01_0101_1011_1100_0110_0101;
                              // 15BC65 ABCD No error
        MemArr(1)=22'b 01_0001_1011_1100_0110_0101;
                              // 11BC65 8BCD Single bit data error
        MemArr(2)=22'b 01_0101_1011_1100_1110_0101;
                              // 15BCE5 ABCD P3 error
        MemArr(3)=22'b 01_0001_1011_1100_1110_0101;
                              // 11BCE5 8BCD & P3 error
        MemArr(4)=22'b 11_0101_1011_1100_0110_0101;
                              // 35BC65 Overall parity error

        // Verification data. PROCESSOR read data from memory.
        ProcArr(0)=16'b 1010_1011_1100_1101;
                              // ABCD No error
        ProcArr(1)=16'b 1010_1011_1100_1101;
                              // ABCD Single bit corrected data error
        ProcArr(2)=16'b 1010_1011_1100_1101;
                              // ABCD Single bit corrected data error
        ProcArr(3)=16'b 1000_1011_1100_1101;
                              // 8BCD Double error uncorrectable
        ProcArr(4)=16'b 1010_1011_1100_1101;
                              // ABCD P5 in error
    end

//------------------------------------------------
// Instantiate model to be simulated
//------------------------------------------------
ERRDET_CORRECTION ERRDET_CORRECTION_1
    (ReadWrite_b, ProcData, MemData, ErrorType);

//------------------------------------------------
// Assign tri states for device under test
//------------------------------------------------
assign ProcData = ReadWrite_b ? 16'b Z : ProcWriteData;
assign MemData  = ReadWrite_b ? MemReadData :22'b Z;

//------------------------------------------------
// Apply stimulus to RTL models under test
//------------------------------------------------
initial
    begin
        Fail = 0;  // Set to 1 if fails
        ProcWriteData = 16'b 0;
        MemReadData = 22'b 0;
        RefProcData = 16'b 0;
        RefMemData  = 22'b 0;
        ReadWrite_b = 0;
```

Memory read test vectors; one vector for each error type.

Reference vectors used to compare against the error corrected memory read data to the microprocessor.

continued

continued

Test harness using vectors stored in an array

VHDL	Verilog

```vhdl
        ReadWrite_b <= '0';




        ------------------------------------------
        -- Write data to memory
        ------------------------------------------
        wait for TestPeriod;
        ProcWriteData <= "1010101111001101";
        RefMemData <= MemArr(0);
            if (RefMemData /= MemData) then  -- i.e. Has failed
                Fail <= '1';
                write(BufLine, string'("ERRDET_CORRECTION Write
                                    error at time "));
                write(BufLine, now);
                write(BufLine, string'("Should be equal to "));
                write(BufLine, (to_bitvector(RefMemData)));
                write(BufLine, string'(", but is equal to "));
                write(BufLine, (to_bitvector(MemData)));
                writeline(SimResults, BufLine);
            end if;
        wait for TestPeriod;
        ProcWriteData <= (others => '0');


        ------------------------------------------
        -- Read data from memory
        ------------------------------------------
        wait for TestPeriod;
        ReadWrite_b <= '1';
        for N in 0 to 7 loop
            wait for TestPeriod;
            MemReadData <= MemArr(N);
            RefProcData <= ProcArr(N);
            if (RefProcData /= ProcData) then  -- i.e. Has failed
                Fail <= '1';
                write(BufLine, string'("ERRDET_CORRECTION
                                    Read error at time "));
                write(BufLine, now);
                write(BufLine, string'(": Should be equal to "));
                write(BufLine, (to_bitvector(RefProcData)));
                write(BufLine, string'(", but is equal to "));
                write(BufLine, (to_bitvector(ProcData)));
                writeline(SimResults, BufLine);
            end if;
        end loop;

        if (Fail = '0') then  -- Sim results are the same
            write(BufLine, string'("ERRDET_CORRECTION passed"));
            writeline(SimResults, BufLine);
        end if;
        wait;
    end process;
end architecture TEST_HARN;
```

```verilog
    // Open simulation results file for appending
    // pass/fail messages
    SimResults = $fopen("errdet_correction.simres");
    //-------------------------------
    // Write data to memory
    //-------------------------------
    #TestPeriod ProcWriteData =16'b 1010_1011_1100_1101;
    RefMemData = MemArr(0);
        if (RefMemData != MemData)    // i.e. Has failed
            begin
                Fail = 1;
                $fdisplay (SimResults,
                            "ERRDET_CORRECTION
                            Write error at time %d:
                            Should be equal to %d, but
                            is = %d",
                            $time, RefMemData
                            MemData);
            end
    #TestPeriod ProcWriteData = 16'b0;


    //-------------------------------
    // Read data from memory
    //-------------------------------
    #TestPeriod ReadWrite_b = 1;
    for (N = 0; N < 8; N = N + 1)
        begin
            #TestPeriod;
            MemReadData = MemArr(N);
            RefProcData = ProcArr(N);
            if (RefProcData!=ProcData)   // i.e. Has failed
                begin
                    Fail = 1;
                    $fdisplay (SimResults,
                                "ERRDET_CORRECTION
                                Read error at time %d:
                                Should be equal to %d,
                                but is = %d",
                                $time, RefProcData,
                                ProcData);
                end
        end

    if (Fail == 0)   // Sim results are the same
        $fdisplay (SimResults, "ERRDET_CORRECTION passed");
    $fclose (SimResults);
    $stop;
    end
endmodule
```

3. Reading test vector system files

Both input vectors and reference output vectors may be stored in tabular form in a system file. Input vectors may be read from a system file and applied directly to the model under test during simulation. The reference output vectors are also read from the file, but are used to compare with the output vectors from the model under test. A benefit of writing a test harness that accesses system files is that only one, relatively simple, generic test harness need be written. Changing the tests being performed can be as simple as telling the test harness to read a different test vector file. In VHDL, this means telling the simulator to simulate a different configuration. In Verilog, it means supplying a different parameter name.

Repetitive signal waveforms, such as clock signals, and signals that only change once or twice, such as resets, are better left out of the vector files. Such signals are easy to implement directly in the test harness, will make the vector file less cluttered, and may reduce simulation time.

a) VHDL

Files in the host environment are referenced as VHDL objects and must be of type file.

> Example   **type** TestVectorFileType **is** file **of** unsigned;

A file of type TestVectorFileType contains a sequence of values of type unsigned.

A file can be opened, closed, read, written to, or tested for an end-of-file condition using special procedures and functions that are implicitly declared for every file type.

Package TEXTIO. This VHDL package is defined as part of the language and resides in a VHDL library called STD, see Appendix A. To use this package, the following use clause must be included at the top of a test harness.

> **use** STD.TEXTIO.**all**;

Package TEXTIO defines a single file type called TEXT to represent a file consisting of variable length strings. An access type, LINE, is also provided to point to such strings. Various overloaded procedures called "READ" and "WRITE" allow the reading and writing of data to or from an object of type LINE. All VHDL test harnesses shown in this chapter access system files using the types and procedures defined in package TEXTIO. The READ and WRITE procedures in this package use the vector data type bit_vector. If an equivalent package using unsigned and signed values is available it may be more convenient to use that instead, and avoid the possible need to use conversion functions between bit_vector and either signed or unsigned.

The following VHDL test harness illustrates a vector file being accessed using the "READ" function defined in TEXTIO in order to read each line of the input vector file.

b) Verilog

Files in the host environment are referenced and applied to the hardware model under test using one of two system tasks or a system function.

$readmemb	- This system task reads a system file containing test vectors stored in a <u>binary</u> format and which can be applied directly to the hardware model under test.
$readmemh	- This system task reads a system file containing test vectors stored in a <u>hexadecimal</u> format and which can be applied directly to the hardware model under test.
$getpattern	- This system function provides a fast means of propagating stimulus patterns to a large number of 1-bit wide (scalar) inputs. It reads stimulus patterns that have been loaded into a memory using the $readmemb or $readmemh system tasks. Except for exclusively long simulation runs, $getpattern is rarely needed to be used.

The following Verilog test harness illustrates vector file access using $readmemb. The test vectors file are in a format that can be read using $readmemb.

Vectors in separate system file

VHDL	Verilog
# Test vectors in file "tri_pipe_h.vhdl_vec". # 1 - InDataReady # 2 - A(1) # 3 - A(0) # 4 - B(1) ┌─────────────────┐ # 5 - B(0) │ Comments in a vector file will slow simulation time, use wisely. │ # 6 - C(1) └─────────────────┘	// Test vectors in file "tri_pipe_h.v_vec". // 1 - InDataReady // 2 - A(1) // 3 - A(0) // 4 - B(1) // 5 - B(0) // 6 - C(1)

Vectors in separate system file

VHDL	Verilog
# 7 - C(0) # [Comments not needed here.] #1233467 1011011 InDataReady = 1, A = 1, B = 2, C = 3 0100010 InDataReady = 0, A = 2, B = 0, C = 2 0111110 InDataReady = 0, A = 3, B = 3, C = 2 #Test vector file in a format that can be read using readline #function from package TEXTIO	// 7 - C(0) /* 1233467 */ 1011011 // InDataReady = 1, A = 1, B = 2, C = 3 0100010 // InDataReady = 0, A = 2, B = 0, C = 2 0111110 // InDataReady = 0, A = 3, B = 3, C = 2 //Test vector file in a format that can be read using //$readmemb.

Test harness that reads vectors in separate system file

VHDL	Verilog

VHDL

```vhdl
library IEEE, STD;
use IEEE.STD_Logic_1164.all, IEEE.Numeric_STD.all, STD.TEXTIO.all;

entity TRI_PIPE_H1 is
end entity TRI_PIPE_H1;
```
[IEEE 1076 TEXTIO package.]

```vhdl
architecture TEST_HARN of TRI_PIPE_H1 is

------------------------------
-- Specify vector file
------------------------------
file vectors: text open read_mode is "tri_pipe_h1.vhdl_vec";

------------------------------
-- Declare hardware model under test
------------------------------
component TRI_PIPE
    port (Clock, Reset, InDataReady: in std_logic;
          A, B, C: in unsigned(1 downto 0);
          OutDataReady: out std_logic;
          Y: out unsigned(2 downto 0));
end component TRI_PIPE;

constant ClockPeriod: time := 20 ns;
signal Clock: std_logic := '0';
signal Reset, InDataReady, OutDataReady: std_logic;
signal A, B, C, Y: unsigned(2 downto 0);
begin
------------------------------
-- Generate reset waveform
------------------------------
Reset <= '1', '0' after 20 ns, '1' after 20 ns;

------------------------------
-- Set up free running clock
------------------------------
Clock <= not Clock after ClockPeriod / 2;

------------------------------
-- Instantiate the hardware model under test
------------------------------
TRI_PIPE_1: TRI_PIPE
    port map (Clock, Reset, InDataReady, A, B, C,
              OutDataReady, Y);

------------------------------
-- Read vector file &apply test vectors to model under test
------------------------------
process
    variable VectorLine: line;
    variable InDataReady_Var: bit;
    variable A_Var, B_Var, C_Var: bit_vector(1 downto 0);
begin
```
[Notice type bit and bit_vector]

continued

Verilog

```verilog
`timescale 1ns/100ps

module TRI_PIPE_H1;
    parameter ClockPeriod = 20,
              TestCycles  = 3;

    // Inputs to RTL hardware model
    // ----------------------------------------
    reg     Clock, Reset, InDataReady;
    reg (1:0) A, B, C;

    // Outputs from RTL hardware model
    // ----------------------------------------
    wire     OutDataReady;
    wire (2:0) Y;

    // Set up register (memory) arrays to hold input data
    // -----------------------------------------------------
    reg  (7:1) ABC_Arr (1:TestCycles);

    integer N;
    reg     PassFail,
            FailTime;
    //-----------------------------------------------------
    // Instantiate the RTL model to be simulated
    //-----------------------------------------------------
    TRI_PIPE TRI_PIPE_1
        (Clock, Reset, InDataReady, A, B, C,
        OutDataReady, Y);
    //-----------------------------------------------------
    // Set up free running clock
    //-----------------------------------------------------
    initial Clock = 1;
    always
        #(ClockPeriod / 2) Clock = ! Clock;

    //-----------------------------------------------------
    // Apply stimulus to model under test
    //-----------------------------------------------------
    initial
        begin
            $readmemb("tri_pipe_h1.v_vec", ABC_Arr);

            //---------------------
            // Initial values
            //---------------------
            Clock = 0; Reset = 1;
            InDataReady = 0; A = 2'b 0; B = 2'b 0; C = 2'b 0;

            // ---------------------
            // Perform reset
            // ---------------------
```
[$readmemb loads the contents of the file "tri_pipe_h1.vec" into the vector array.]

continued

Test harness that reads vectors in separate system file

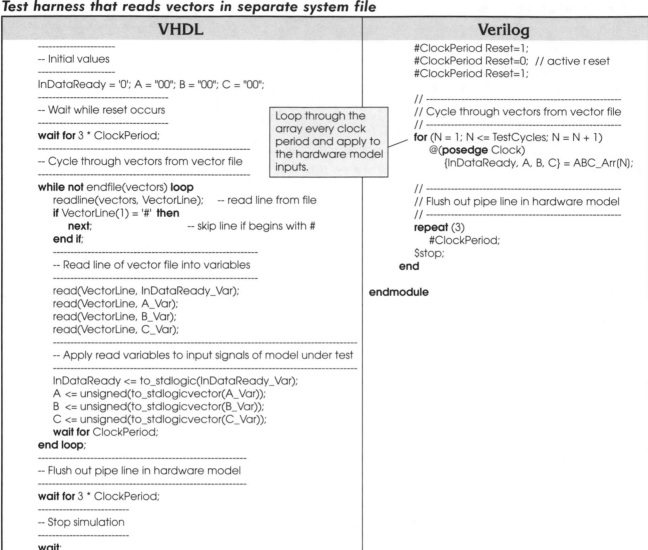

VHDL	Verilog
| ```
--------------------
-- Initial values
--------------------
InDataReady = '0'; A = "00"; B = "00"; C = "00";
--------------------------------------
-- Wait while reset occurs
--------------------------------------
wait for 3 * ClockPeriod;
----------------------------------------------------
-- Cycle through vectors from vector file
----------------------------------------------------
while not endfile(vectors) loop
    readline(vectors, VectorLine);    -- read line from file
    if VectorLine(1) = '#' then
        next;                        -- skip line if begins with #
    end if;
    ----------------------------------------------------------
    -- Read line of vector file into variables
    ----------------------------------------------------------
    read(VectorLine, InDataReady_Var);
    read(VectorLine, A_Var);
    read(VectorLine, B_Var);
    read(VectorLine, C_Var);
    ------------------------------------------------------------------
    -- Apply read variables to input signals of model under test
    ------------------------------------------------------------------
    InDataReady <= to_stdlogic(InDataReady_Var);
    A <= unsigned(to_stdlogicvector(A_Var));
    B <= unsigned(to_stdlogicvector(B_Var));
    C <= unsigned(to_stdlogicvector(C_Var));
    wait for ClockPeriod;
end loop;
----------------------------------------------------------
-- Flush out pipe line in hardware model
----------------------------------------------------------
wait for 3 * ClockPeriod;
------------------------
-- Stop simulation
------------------------
wait;
end process;
end architecture TEST_HARN;
``` | ```
#ClockPeriod Reset=1;
#ClockPeriod Reset=0;  // active r eset
#ClockPeriod Reset=1;

// --------------------------------------------------
// Cycle through vectors from vector file
// --------------------------------------------------
for (N = 1; N <= TestCycles; N = N + 1)
    @(posedge Clock)
        {InDataReady, A, B, C} = ABC_Arr(N);

// --------------------------------------------------
// Flush out pipe line in hardware model
// --------------------------------------------------
repeat (3)
    #ClockPeriod;
$stop;
end

endmodule
``` |

Loop through the array every clock period and apply to the hardware model inputs.

Comparing Actual and Expected Results

Comparing of actual and expected vectors at specific times during simulation is an important and often overlooked task. It is worth the extra effort of enhancing a test harness so that during simulation, the test harness automatically compares output vectors from the model being tested with expected reference vectors. A simple pass or fail indication will save lengthy manual checking of simulation results every time a change is made to either the test harness or the model under test, which necessitates resimulation. A fail indication should give the simulation time at which the failure occurred, the actual vectors from the model under test, and the expected results. This is achieved in VHDL using the **assert** statement to send messages to the screen, and the procedure write to send messages to a system file. In Verilog, the system task $display is used to send messages to the screen and the system task $fdisplay is used to send messages to a system file.

Examples incorporating automatic vector checking have been included in the test harnesses already shown in this chapter. Section 1c) showed an example (ALARM_CLOCK_H) where simulation results are sent to a separate system file. Section 1e) showed an example (ALU_BIDR_H) where simulation results are sent to the screen.

12
Practical Modeling Examples

Chapter 12 Contents

1. Tri-stated pipeline stage for area efficiency

Problem

Three 8-bit data busses A, B and C, have valid data arriving in three consecutive clock cycles. Design a model that computes the sum of the three pairs of busses, that is, (A + B), (A + C), and (B + C) and supply the results on a single 9-bit output bus in three consecutive clock cycles. A separate input signal is at logic 1 for one clock cycle to indicate when data on the first bus, A, is valid. Data on the other two busses, B and C, then become valid on the following two consecutive clock cycles.

An output control signal should be at logic 1 for one clock cycle to signify the start of the three clock cycles when the three summed output results are available.

Chip area is critical and must be kept to an absolute minimum. Timing and any latent delay is not an issue. Data on the input busses is arriving late in the clock cycle so must be stored in registers before being processed through any combinational logic.

Solution

As chip area is critical, it is necessary to use only one adder. Also, instead of multiplexing different input bus combinations to the single adder a single tri-stated bus and a single 2-1 multiplexer is used. The solution architecture is shown graphically in Figure 12.1.

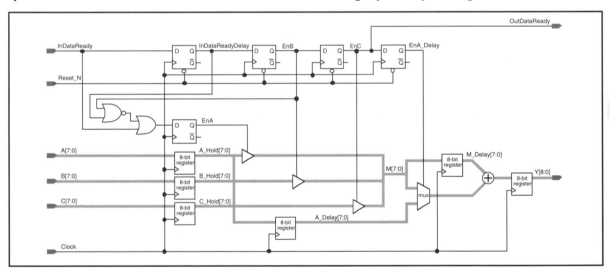

Figure 12.1 Modeled architecture for the tri-stated pipelined stage

The three input buses are first clocked into registers as required, for example, A to A_Hold. The control path provides the tri-state buffer enable signals EnA, EnB and EnC to allow each of the three pieces of stored data onto the internal tri-state bus in turn. Signal EnA is arranged so that it is always be at logic 1 when EnB and EnC are at logic 0 so that the tri-state bus is always driven. The enable signals are derived directly from the output of flip-flops in order to minimize skew.

The control path allows the three stored input busses, A_Hold, B_Hold and C_Hold onto the internal tri-state bus M in the order A, B, C. Bus M provides one input to the adder and M delayed one clock cycle, M_Delayed, provides the second input to yield the summations (A + B) and (B + C). In order to generate the last sum, (A + C), A_Hold must be delayed by one clock cycle, A_Delay, in order to allow the next new value of A from the start of a subsequent sequence of three values, to be passed to M and M_Delay.

Simulated signal waveforms, Figure 12.2, indicate how three sets of three back-to-back values are added in consecutive sequences of (A + B), (B + C) and (C + A). The pipe-lined arrangement means there is a latent delay of four clock cycles from valid data arriving on A to the first valid summed data, A + B, arriving on the output Y. Therefore, a four clock cycle delay exits between InDataReady switching to logic 1 and its corresponding output OutDataReady switching to logic 1.

HDL code. Inferred flip-flops for signals InDataReady_Delay, EnA, EnB, EnC and EnA_Delay are all inferred from within the same **process/always** statement. In VHDL, signals are used to feed data from one flip-flop to the next. In Verilog, non-blocking procedural assignments are used for the same reason. Similarly M_Delay and Y are generated from within a separate **process/always** statement. Two addition operators are used, but resource sharing ensures that only one adder is actually synthesized.

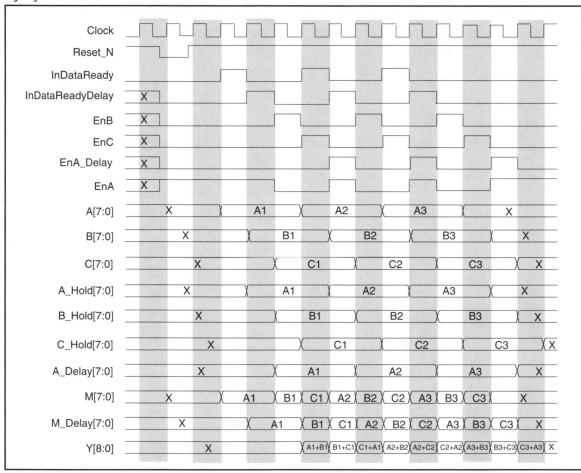

Figure 12.2 Signal waveforms for the tri-stated pipelined stage

Tri-stated pipeline stage for area efficiency

VHDL	Verilog
| ```
library IEEE;
use IEEE.STD_Logic_1164.all, IEEE.Numeric_STD.all;
 entity TRI_PIPE is
    port ( Clock, Reset_N, InDataReady: in std_logic;
        A, B, C:           in   unsigned(7 downto 0);
        OutDataReady:    out std_logic;
        Y:                 out unsigned(8 downto 0));
end entity TRI_PIPE;

architecture RTL of TRI_PIPE is
    signal InDataReady_Delay, EnA, EnB, EnC, EnA_Delay:
                                            std_logic;
    signal A_Hold, B_Hold, C_Hold, A_Delay,
        M,M_Delay: unsigned(7 downto 0);
begin
  CONTROL_PATH:
  process (Clock, Reset_N)
  begin
     if  (Reset_N = '0') then
        InDataReady_Delay <= '0';
        EnA <= '1'; -- So tri-state bus has a drive.
        EnB  <= '0';
        EnC <= '0';
        EnA_Delay <= '0';
     elsif rising_edge(Clock) then
        InDataReady_Delay <= InDataReady;
        EnA  <= InDataReady and
             (not InDataReady_Delay and not EnB);
        EnB  <= EnA;
        EnC  <= EnB;
        EnA_Delay <= EnC;
     end if;
  end process CONTROL_PATH;

  OutDataReady <= EnC;

  IP_BUS_REG:
  process (Clock)
  begin
     if rising_edge(Clock) then
        A_Hold  <= A;
        B_Hold  <= B;
        C_Hold  <= C;
        A_Delay <= A_Hold;
     end if;
  end process IP_BUS_REG;

  -- Tri-state bus drivers
  M <= A_Hold  when EnA  = '1' else (others => 'Z');
  M <= B_Hold  when EnB = '1' else (others => 'Z');
  M <= C_Hold  when EnC = '1' else (others => 'Z');

  OUT_STAGE:
  process (Clock)
  begin
     if rising_edge(Clock) then
        M_Delay <= M;
        if (EnA_Delay = '1') then
           Y <= ('0' & M_Delay) + A_Delay;
        else
           Y <= ('0' & M_Delay) + M;
        end if;
     end if;
  end process OUT_STAGE;
end RTL;
``` | ```
module TRI_PIPE
  (Clock, Reset_N, InDataReady, A, B, C, OutDataReady, Y);
    input      Clock, Reset_N, InDataReady;
    input [7:0] A, B, C;
    output     OutDataReady;
    output [8:0] Y;

    wire       OutDataReady;  // shown for clarification.
                              // Is default if not defined.

    reg      InDataReady_Delay,EnA,EnB,EnC,EnA_Delay;
    reg [7:0] A_Hold, B_Hold, C_Hold, A_Delay;
    wire [7:0] M;
    reg [7:0] M_Delay;
    reg [8:0] Y;

  always @(posedge Clock or negedge Reset_N)
    begin: CONTROL_PATH
       if (! Reset_N)
          begin
             InDataReady_Delay = 0;
             EnA        = 1; // So tri-state bus has a drive.
             EnB        = 0;
             EnC        = 0;
             EnA_Delay = 0;
          end
       else
          begin
             EnA        = InDataReady &
                          (! InDataReady_Delay & ! EnB);
             EnB        = EnA;
             EnC        = EnB;
             EnA_Delay = EnC;
          end
    end

  assign OutDataReady = EnC;

  always @(posedge Clock)
    begin: IP_BUS_REG
       A_Hold  = A;
       B_Hold  = B;
       C_Hold  = C;
       A_Delay = A_Hold;
    end

  // Tri-state bus drivers
  assign M = EnA ?  A_Hold : 8'b Z;
  assign M = EnB ?  B_Hold : 8'b Z;
  assign M = EnC ?  C_Hold : 8'b Z;

  always @(posedge Clock)
    begin: OUT_STAGE
       M_Delay <= M;
       if (EnA_Delay == 1)
          Y <= M_Delay + A_Delay;
       else
          Y <= M_Delay + M;
    end

endmodule
``` |

M_Delay assigned and used in same synchronous block.

Non-blocking signal assignment.

Resource shared adder.

2. Digital Alarm Clock

Problem

Design a digital alarm clock that has the following terminal (port) signals:

Inputs	Clock_1sec, Reset, LoadTime, SetHours, SetMins, SetSecs, Set_AM_PM, LoadAlm, AlarmHoursIn, AlarmMinsIn, Alarm_AM_PM_In, AlarmEnable
Outputs	Hours, Mins, Secs, Hours, AM_PM, Flashing, Alarm

The required characteristics of the digital alarm clock are:

- timing is to be controlled from a 1 second input clock, Clock_1sec,
- to operate on a 12 hour basis with separate am/pm control,
- the value of time to be set when LoadTime is high,
- the alarm time to be set when LoadAlm is high,
- the Alarm output should go high when the current value of time is equal to the alarm time. the alarm should stay on until either the AlarmEnable signal goes low, which equates to turning the alarm off, or after period of 1 minute has elapsed when left on.
- if power is lost, and then powered up again, it should display the time 00:00:00 and the "Flashing" signal should be activated high. This causes the display to flash and so indicate that the alarm clock's time needs to be set. The Flashing signal should stay high and the clock's time should increase from zero until a new time is set.

Solution

First, identify what storage elements are required. A total of 29 flip-flops are needed to hold the current clock time and set alarm time. The constituent flip-flops are listed in Table 12.1.

This problem is most easily solved by splitting the problem into two; one for the clock time and the other for the alarm time. The VHDL and Verilog models show this split. In the VHDL model, separate **process** statements model the clock time and alarm time generation. In the Verilog model, a single **always** statement is used to model the clock time, but two **always** statements are needed to implement the alarm time because both synchronous and combinational output logic is needed.

The first **process**/**always** statements instantiate the 18 flip-flops needed to hold the current value of time and compute its next incremental value. The word "time" in this context means hours, minutes, seconds plus the AM/PM indication. It uses nested **if** statements, the outermost of which waits for a rising edge on the 1 second clock signal Clock_1sec. If a rising edge has occurred, the time and Flashing signals are updated. Notice that no matter which branch is taken through the nested **if** statements, new values for Hours, Mins, Secs, AM_PM and Flashing are always defined and avoids extra unneeded latches being inferred.

	Function	Range	No. of bits
Clock Time			
	Clock time - Seconds	(range 0 to 59)	6
	Clock time - Minutes	(range 0 to 59)	6
	Clock time - Hours	(range 0 to 11)	4
	Clock time - AM/PM	(1 bit toggle)	1
	Time not set (Flashing)	(1 bit toggle)	1
			18 = Flip-flops needed
Alarm Time			
	Alarm time - minutes	(range 0 to 59)	6
	Alarm time - Hours	(range 0 to 11)	4
	Alarm time - AM/PM	(1 bit toggle)	1
			11 = Flip-flops needed
	Total flip-flops needed = 29		

Table 12.1 Constituent flip-flops for the alarm clock

The second part of the VHDL and Verilog models hold the alarm time (AlarmHours, AlarmMins and Alarm_ AM_PM) and checks to see if the current time is equal to the alarm time. Notice that seconds are not used for the alarm time. If the two time values compare and the AlarmEnable signal is at logic 1 the Alarm signal is activated. The alarm will stay on until turned off by the AlarmEnable changing to logic 0 or for a maximum of 1 minute if AlarmEnable stays at logic 1.

VHDL Alarm clock package for AM/PM type

VHDL	Verilog

package AM_PM_Package is
  type AM_PM_type is (AM, PM);
  function "not" (Value: AM_PM_type) return AM_PM_type;
end;
 	
package body AM_PM_Package is
  function "not" (Value: AM_PM_type) return AM_PM_type is
  begin
    if Value = AM then
      return PM;
    else
      return AM;
    end if;
  end "not";
end AM_PM_Package;
	Verilog does not support enumerated data types.

Digital alarm clock

VHDL	Verilog

```vhdl
library IEEE;
use IEEE.STD_Logic_1164.all, IEEE.Numeric_STD.all;
use work.AM_PM_Package.all;

entity ALARM_CLOCK is
  port ( Clock_1sec:        in    std_logic;
         Reset:             in    std_logic;
         LoadTime:          in    std_logic;
         SetHours:          in    integer range 0 to 11;
         SetMins, SetSecs:  in    integer range 0 to 59;
         Set_AM_PM:         in    AM_PM_type;
         LoadAlm:           in    std_logic;
         AlarmHoursIn:      in    integer range 0 to 11;
         AlarmMinsIn:       in    integer range 0 to 59;
         Alarm_AM_PM_In:    in    AM_PM_type;
         AlarmEnable        in    std_logic;
         Hours:             out   integer range 0 to 11;
         Mins, Secs:        out   integer range 0 to 59;
         AM_PM:             out   AM_PM_type;
         Flashing:          out   std_logic;
         Alarm:             out   std_logic);
end entity ALARM_CLOCK;

architecture RTL of ALARM_CLOCK is
  signal Hours_s:         integer range 0 to 11;
  signal Mins_s, Secs_s:  integer range 0 to 59;
  signal AM_PM_s:         AM_PM_type;
  signal Flashing_s:      std_logic;
```

> Signal names ending in "_s" are internal
> signals that are both read and written to.

```vhdl
begin
--***************************************************
-- Calculate the next value of time:
--       Secs, Mins, Hours, AM_PM & Flashing.
--***************************************************
TIMER: process (Clock_1sec)
begin
  if rising_edge(Clock_1sec) then
    -- Synchronous Reset
    if (Reset = '1') then
      Hours_s    <= 0;
      Mins_s     <= 0;
      Sec_s      <= 0;
      AM_PM_s    <= AM;
      Flashing_s <= '1';
    -- Set the time
    elsif (LoadTime = '1') then
      Hours_s    <= SetHours;
      Mins_s     <= SetMins;
      Sec_s      <= SetSecs;
      AM_PM_s    <= Set_AM_PM;
      Flashing_s <= '0';

    -- Increment time
    -------------------------
    else
      Flashing_s <= Flashing_s;           -- Unchanged
      if (Secs_s = 59) then               -- reached 59
        Secs_s <= 0;                      -- Reset secs
        if (Mins_s = 59) then             -- Reached 59
          Mins_s <= 0;                    -- Reset mins
          if (Hours_s = 11) then          -- Reached 11
            Hours_s <= 0;                 -- Reset hours
            AM_PM_s <= not AM_PM_s;       -- Toggle
                                          -- am_pm
          else
```

continued

```verilog
module ALARM_CLOCK
 ( Clock_1sec, Reset, LoadTime, LoadAlm, SetSecs,
   SetMins, SetHours, Set_AM_PM, AlarmMinsIn,
   AlarmHoursIn, Alarm_AM_PM_In, Secs, Mins, Hours,
   AM_PM, Alarm, Flashing);

   input          Clock_1sec, Reset;
   input          LoadTime, LoadAlm;
   input   [0:5]  SetSecs, SetMins;
   input   [0:3]  SetHours;
   input          Set_AM_PM;
   input   [0:5]  AlarmMinsIn;
   input   [0:3]  AlarmHoursIn;
   input          Alarm_AM_PM_In;
   input          AlarmEnable;
   output  [0:5]  Secs, Mins;
   output  [0:3]  Hours;
   output         AM_PM, Flashing, Alarm;

   reg     [0:5]  AlarmMins;
   reg     [0:3]  AlarmHours;
   reg            Alarm_AM_PM;
   reg     [0:5]  Secs, Mins;
   reg     [0:3]  Hours;
   reg            AM_PM, Flashing, Alarm;
```

```verilog
//***************************************************
// Calculate the next value of time:
//       Secs, Mins, Hours, AM_PM & Flashing.
//***************************************************
always @ (posedge Clock_1sec)
  // Synchronous Reset
  //----------------------------
  if (Reset)
    begin
      Secs     = 0;
      Mins     = 0;
      Hours    = 0;
      AM_PM    = 0;
      Flashing = 1;
    end
  //  Set the time
  else if (LoadTime)
    begin
      Secs     = SetSecs;
      Mins     = SetMins;
      Hours    = SetHours;
      AM_PM    = Set_AM_PM;
      Flashing = 0;
    end
  // Increment time
  else
    begin
      Flashing = Flashing;                // Unchanged
      if (Secs == 59)                     // Reached 59
        begin
          Secs = 0;                       // Reset secs
          if (Mins == 59)                 // Reached 59
            begin
              Mins = 0;                   // Reset mins
              if (Hours == 11)            // Reached 11
```

continued

Digital alarm clock

VHDL	Verilog

<pre>   Hours_s <= Hours_s + 1; -- Increment
            AM_PM_s <= AM_PM_s;   -- unchanged
        end if;
      else
          Mins_s <= Mins_s + 1;   -- Increment
          Hours_s <= Hours_s;   -- unchanged
          AM_PM_s <= AM_PM_s;   -- unchanged
        end if;
      else
          Secs_s <= Secs_s + 1;   -- Increment
          Mins_s <= Mins_s;   -- unchanged
          Hours_s <= Hours_s;   -- unchanged
          AM_PM_s <= AM_PM_s;   -- unchanged
      end if;
    end if;
  end if;
  Hours   <= Hours_s;
  Mins   <= Mins_s;
  Secs   <= Secs_s;
  AM_PM <= AM_PM_s;
end process TIMER;</pre>
	<pre> begin
	              Hours = 0; // Reset hours
	              AM_PM = ! AM_PM; // Toggle AM_PM
	          end
	        else
	          begin
	              Hours = Hours + 1; // Increment
	              AM_PM = AM_PM; // Unchanged
	          end
	        end
	      else
	        begin
	            Mins = Mins + 1; // Increment
	            Hours = Hours; // Unchanged
	            AM_PM = AM_PM; // Unchanged
	        end
	      end
	    else
	      begin
	          Secs = Secs + 1; // Increment
	          Mins = Mins; // Unchanged
	          Hours = Hours; // Unchanged
	          AM_PM = AM_PM; // Unchanged
	      end
	  end</pre>

<pre>---*** 	
--- Store set alarm time when "LoadAlm" active and
--- compare current time with set alarm time.
---*** 	
ALARM_LOAD_AND_TEST:
process (Clock_1sec)
    variable AlarmMins: integer range 0 to 59;
    variable AlarmHours: integer range 0 to 11;
    variable Alarm_AM_PM: AM_PM_type;
begin
  --- Store set alarm time when "LoadAlm" active.
  if rising_edge(Clock_1sec) then
    if (Reset = '1') then
      AlarmMins   := 0;
      AlarmHours   := 0;
      Alarm_AM_PM := AM;
    elsif (LoadAlm ='1') then
      AlarmMins   := AlarmMinsIn;
      AlarmHours   := AlarmHoursIn;
      Alarm_AM_PM := Alarm_AM_PM_In;
    else
      AlarmMins   := AlarmMins;
      AlarmHours   := AlarmHours;
      Alarm_AM_PM := Alarm_AM_PM;
    end if;
  end if;
  --- Compare current time with set the alarm time.
  --- Sets alarm for 1 minute (ignores seconds).
  if (Mins_s = AlarmMins and
      Hours_s = AlarmHours and
      AM_PM_s = Alarm_AM_PM and
      AlarmEnable = '1') then
      Alarm <= '1';
  else
      Alarm <= '0';
  end if;
  end process ALARM_LOAD_AND_TEST;
end architecture RTL;</pre>
	<pre>//***
	// Store set alarm time when "LoadAlm" active.
	//***
	always @(posedge Clock_1sec)
	  if (Reset)
	    begin
	      AlarmMins = 0;
	      AlarmHours = 0;
	      Alarm_AM_PM = 0;
	    end
	  else if (LoadAlm)
	    begin
	      AlarmMins = AlarmMinsIn;
	      AlarmHours = AlarmHoursIn;
	      Alarm_AM_PM = Alarm_AM_PM_In;
	    end
	  else
	    begin
	      AlarmMins = AlarmMins;
	      AlarmHours = AlarmHours;
	      Alarm_AM_PM = Alarm_AM_PM;
	    end
	
	//***
	// Compare current time with the set alarm time.
	// Sets alarm for 1 minute (ignores seconds).
	//***
	always @(Hours or Mins or AM_PM or AlarmEnable or
	            AlarmHours or AlarmMins or Alarm_AM_PM)
	  if (Hours== AlarmHours && Mins== AlarmMins &&
	      AM_PM == Alarm_AM_PM && AlarmEnable ==1)
	      Alarm = 1;
	  else
	      Alarm = 0;
	
	endmodule</pre>

3. Three-Way Round-Robin Arbiter

Problem

Three independent microprocessors (A, B and C) are required to share access to the same synchronous RAM. The memory is 1024 x 8-bits in size and requires a single read/write signal. The following data is therefore needed from each microprocessor.

Address	-	12-bits
Write Data	-	8-bits
Read Data	-	8-bits
Read/write	-	1-bit

Design an arbiter that accepts data from each microprocessor and arbitrates which one is granted access to the RAM at any one time. Each microprocessor will initiate a RAM request signal when it wants access to the RAM and will deactivate it when finished. If more than one microprocessor requests the bus at the same time, access should be granted on a "round robin" basis so that no one microprocessor is locked out while another has continuous access. Continuous access is granted to any one microprocessor for a period of time, up to a number of clock cycles separately programmable from microprocessor A data bus. When a programmable "watch dog" time has not been set, a 64 clock cycle delay should default.

Tri-state buffers, not multiplexers, are needed for speed purposes.

Solution

The "round robin" priority access to the RAM, from each microprocessor, is easiest modeled using a state machine. A "watch dog" timer (counter) is used to deny a microprocessor RAM access when it has had access for more than 64 clock cycles or a number of clock cycles stored in TimeOutClockPeriods.

Figure 12.3 shows the arrangement of microprocessors, arbiter and RAM; it also shows the modeled structure of the arbiter. The state machine, see Figure 12.4, has four states: Idle, Grant_A, Grant_B and Grant_C. The "round robin" priority access is Grant_A, Grant_B, Grant_C and back to Grant_A again should more than one microprocessor request access at the same time. The structure of the state machine, Figure 12.5, shows the enable signals EnA1, EnA2, EnB1, EnB2, EnC1 and EnC2 generated separately from the microprocessor acknowledge signals AckA, AckB and AckC. The enable signals are generated directly from the next state logic through extra, non-state machine flip-flops, and drive the enable inputs to the tri-state buffers directly with no extra loading; this reduces skew. Each pair of enable signals, for example EnA1 and EnA2, are identical, but are derived from separate flip-flops. Enable signals with a number 1 suffix (EnA1, EnB1 and EnC1) are used to enable the tri-state buffers for the address busses, while enable signals with a number 2 suffix (EnA2, EnB2 and EnC2) are used to enable the tri-state buffers for the data busses and read/write signals. This reduces the loading on each enable signal and so also reduces skew.

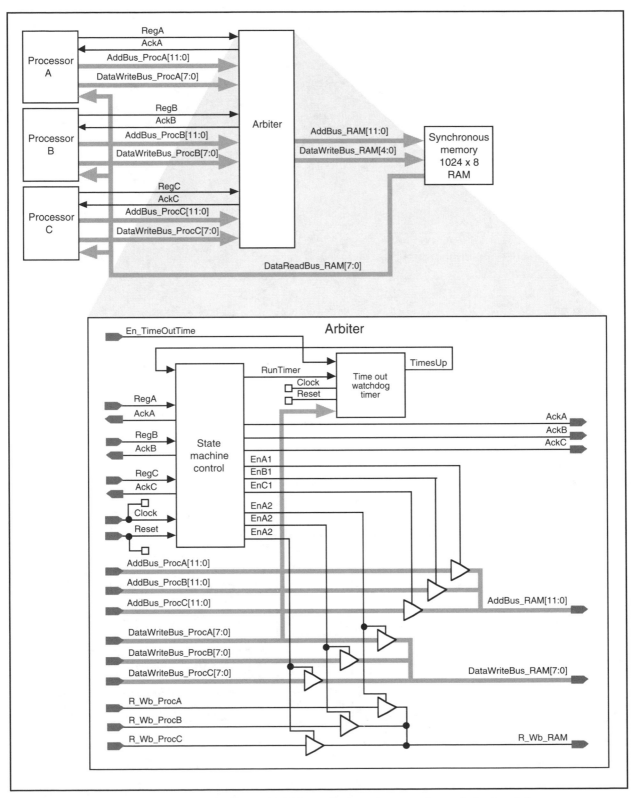

Figure 12.3 Microprocessor/arbiter/RAM configuration and modeled arbiter structure

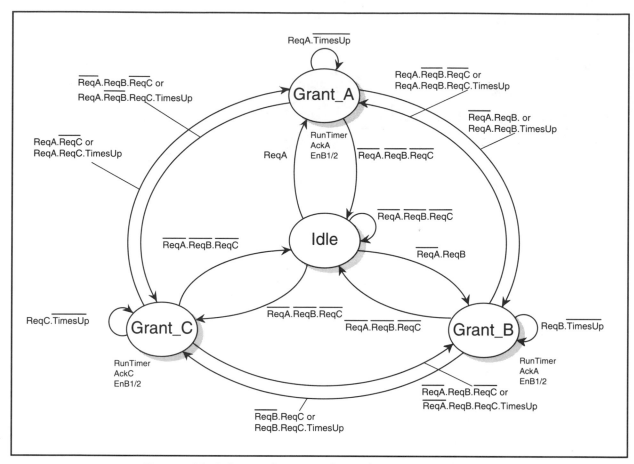

Figure 12.4 State diagram for arbiter control logic

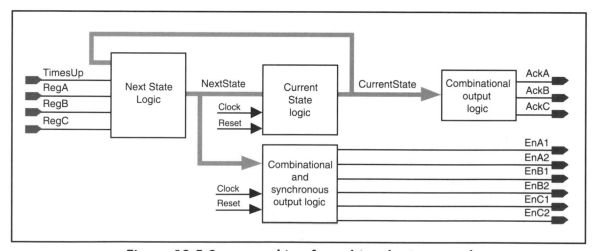

Figure 12.5 State machine for arbiter logic control

Three-way round-robin arbiter

VHDL	Verilog
| ```vhdl
library IEEE;
use IEEE.STD_Logic_1164.all, IEEE.Numeric_STD.all;

entity ARBITER is
  port ( Clock, Reset:          in std_logic;
         En_TimeOutTime:        in std_logic;
         ReqA, ReqB, ReqC:      in std_logic;
         R_Wb_ProcA, R_Wb_ProcB,
         R_Wb_ProcC:            in std_logic;
         AddBus_ProcA,
         AddBus_ProcB,
         AddBus_ProcC:          in  unsigned(11 downto 0);
         DataWriteBus_ProcA,
         DataWriteBus_ProcB,
         DataWriteBus_ProcC:    in  unsigned(7 downto 0);
         AckA, AckB, AckC:      out std_logic;
         R_Wb_RAM:              out std_logic;
         AddBus_RAM:            out unsigned(11 downto 0);
         DataWriteBus_RAM:      out unsigned(7 downto 0) );
end entity ARBITER;

architecture RTL of ARBITER is
  constant DefaultTimeOut: integer := 64;
  signal TimeOutClockPeriods: unsigned(7 downto 0);
  signal RunTimer, TimesUp: std_logic;
  signal Count: unsigned(5 downto 0);

  -- Define 4 states of arbiter state machine.
  type ARB_STATE_TYPE is (Idle,Grant_A,Grant_B,Grant_C);

  signal CurrentState, NextState: ARB_STATE_TYPE;

  signal EnA1, EnA2, EnB1, EnB2, EnC1, EnC2: std_logic;
begin


------------------------------------------------------------
-- Process:  TIMEOUT_COUNT
-- Purpose:  Hold En_TimeOutTime and time how long a
--           microprocessor has had access to the RAM.
-- Inputs:   Clock, Reset, RunTimer.
-- Outputs:  TimesUp.
------------------------------------------------------------
TIMEOUT_COUNT:
process (Clock, Count, TimeOutClockPeriods)
begin
  if rising_edge(Clock) then
    if (Reset = '1') then
      TimeOutClockPeriods <=
                to_unsigned(DefaultTimeOut, 8);
    elsif (En_TimeOutTime = '1') then
      TimeOutClockPeriods <= DataWriteBus_ProcA;
    end if;
  end if;

  if rising_edge(Clock) then
    if (Reset = '1' or RunTimer = '0') then
      Count <= (others => '0');
    else
      Count <= Count + 1;
    end if;
  end if;
  if (Count = TimeOutClockPeriods) then
``` | ```verilog
module ARBITER
  (Clock, Reset, En_TimeOutTime, ReqA, ReqB, ReqC,
   R_Wb_ProcA, R_Wb_ProcB, R_Wb_ProcC,
   AddBus_ProcA, AddBus_ProcB, AddBus_ProcC,
   DataWriteBus_ProcA, DataWriteBus_ProcB,
   DataWriteBus_ProcC,
   AckA, AckB, AckC,
   R_Wb_RAM, AddBus_RAM, DataWriteBus_RAM);

  input        Clock,Reset,En_TimeOutTime,ReqA,ReqB,ReqC;
  input        R_Wb_ProcA, R_Wb_ProcB,
               R_Wb_ProcC;
  input (11:0) AddBus_ProcA,
               AddBus_ProcB,
               AddBus_ProcC;
  input (7:0)  DataWriteBus_ProcA,
               DataWriteBus_ProcB,
               DataWriteBus_ProcC;
  output       AckA, AckB, AckC;
  output       R_Wb_RAM;
  output (11:0) AddBus_RAM;
  output (7:0) DataWriteBus_RAM;
  reg          AckA, AckB, AckC;

  reg (7:0) TimeOutClockPeriods;
  reg       RunTimer, TimesUp;
  reg (5:0) Count;

// Define 4 states of arbiter state machine.
parameter Idle = 0,Grant_A = 1,Grant_B = 2,Grant_C = 3;

reg (1:0) CurrentState, NextState;

reg       EnA1, EnA2, EnB1, EnB2, EnC1, EnC2;


//---------------------------------------------------------
// Process:  TIMEOUT_COUNT1 and TIMEOUT_COUNT2
// Purpose: Hold En_TimeOutTime and time how long a
//          microprocessor has had access to the RAM.
// Inputs:   Clock, Reset, RunTimer.
// Outputs: TimesUp.
//---------------------------------------------------------
always @(posedge Clock)
  begin: TIMEOUT_COUNT1
    if (Reset == 1)
      TimeOutClockPeriods = 64;
    else if (En_TimeOutTime == 1)
      TimeOutClockPeriods = DataWriteBus_ProcA;

    if (Reset == 1 || RunTimer == 0)
      Count = 6'b 0;
    else
      Count = Count + 1;
  end

always @(Count or TimeOutClockPeriods)
  begin: TIMEOUT_COUNT2
    if (Count == TimeOutClockPeriods)
      TimesUp = 1;
    else
      TimesUp = 0;
  end
``` |
| *continued* | *continued* |

Three-way round-robin arbiter

VHDL	Verilog

<pre>   TimesUp <= '1';
    else
        TimesUp <= '0';
    end if;
end process TIMEOUT_COUNT;
 	
--- 	
-- Process: ARBITER_COMB
-- Purpose: Arbiter's combinational logic which
--   computes next state and output signal
--   values. Does not include tri-state buffers.
-- Inputs: ReqA, ReqB, ReqC, TimesUp CurrentState,
-- Outputs: AckA, AckB, AckC, RunTimer.
--- 	
ARBITER_COMB:
process (ReqA, ReqB, ReqC, TimesUp, CurrentState)
begin
 	
    -- Initialize to default values to save the need
    -- to define every output in every case branch.
    --- 	
    AckA   <= '0';
    AckB   <= '0';
    AckC   <= '0';
    RunTimer <= '0';
    case (CurrentState) is
        -- Idle
        --------- 	
        when Idle =>
            if (ReqA = '1') then
                AckA   <= '1';
                NextState <= Grant_A;
            elsif (ReqB = '1') then
                AckB   <= '1';
                NextState <= Grant_B;
            elsif (ReqC = '1') then
                AckC   <= '1';
                NextState <= Grant_C;
            else
                NextState <= Idle;
            end if;
 	
        -- Grant_A
        --------------- 	
        when Grant_A =>
            if (ReqA = '1' and TimesUp = '0') then
                -- Processor A allowed continued access.
                RunTimer <= '1';
                AckA   <= '1';
                NextState <= Grant_A;
            else
                -- Processor A voluntarily releases access
                -- request or has had access too long.
                if (ReqB = '1') then
                    NextState <= Grant_B;
                elsif (ReqC = '1') then
                    NextState <= Grant_C;
                else
                    NextState <= Idle;
                end if;
            end if;</pre>
	<pre>//---
	// Module: ARBITER_COMB
	// Purpose: Arbiter's combinational logic which
	// computes next State and output signal
	// values. Does not include tri-state buffers.
	// Inputs: ReqA, ReqB, ReqC, TimesUp, CurrentState.
	// Outputs: NextState, AckA, AckB, AckC, RunTimer.
	//---
	always @ (ReqA or ReqB or ReqC or TimesUp or
	          CurrentState)
	    begin: ARBITER_COMB
	
	    // Initialize to default values to save the need
	    // to define every output in every case branch.
	    // ---
	    AckA = 0;
	    AckB = 0;
	    AckC = 0;
	    RunTimer = 0;
	    case (CurrentState)
	        // Idle
	        // -------
	        Idle:
	            if (ReqA == 1)
	                begin
	                    AckA = 1;
	                    NextState = Grant_A;
	                end
	            else if (ReqB == 1)
	                begin
	                    AckB = 1;
	                    NextState = Grant_B;
	                end
	            else if (ReqC == 1)
	                begin
	                    AckC = 1;
	                    NextState = Grant_C;
	                end
	            else
	                NextState = Idle;
	
	        // Grant_A
	        //-------------
	        Grant_A:
	            if (ReqA == 1 && TimesUp == 0)
	                // Processor A allowed continued access.
	                begin
	                    RunTimer = 1;
	                    AckA = 1;
	                    NextState = Grant_A;
	                end
	            else
	                // Processor A voluntarily releases access
	                // request or has had access too long.</pre>

continued	*continued*

Three-way round-robin arbiter

VHDL	Verilog

```vhdl
        -- Grant_B
        ----------------
        when Grant_B =>
            if (ReqB = '1' and TimesUp = '0') then
                -- Processor B allowed continuing access.
                RunTimer  <= '1';
                AckB      <= '1';
                NextState <= Grant_B;
            else
                -- Processor B voluntarily releases access
                -- request or has had acces too long.
                if (ReqC = '1') then
                    NextState <= Grant_C;
                elsif (ReqA = '1') then
                    NextState <= Grant_A;
                else
                    NextState <= Idle;
                end if;
            end if;


        -- Grant_C
        ----------------
        when Grant_C =>
            if (ReqC = '1' and TimesUp = '0') then
                -- Processor C allowed continuing access.
                RunTimer  <= '1';
                AckC      <= '1';
                NextState <= Grant_C;
            else
                -- Processor C voluntarily releases access
                -- request or has had acces too long.
                if (ReqA = '1') then
                    NextState <= Grant_A;
                elsif (ReqB = '1') then
                    NextState <= Grant_B;
                else
                    NextState <= Idle;
                end if;
            end if;
    end case;
end process ARBITER_COMB;
```

```verilog
            if (ReqB == 1)
                NextState = Grant_B;
            else if (ReqC == 1)
                NextState = Grant_C;
            else
                NextState = Idle;

    // Grant_B
    // ------------
    Grant_B:
        if (ReqB == 1 && TimesUp == 0)
            // Processor B allowed continued access.
            begin
                RunTimer  = 1;
                AckB      = 1;
                NextState = Grant_B;
            end
        else
        // Processor B voluntarily releases access
        // request or has had access too long.
        if (ReqC == 1)
            NextState = Grant_C;
        else if (ReqA == 1)
            NextState = Grant_A;
        else
            NextState = Idle;

    // Grant_C
    // ------------
    Grant_C:
        if (ReqC == 1 && TimesUp == 0)
            // Processor C allowed continued access.
            begin
                RunTimer  = 1;
                AckC      = 1;
                NextState = Grant_C;
            end
        else
        // Processor C voluntarily releases access
        // request or has had access too long.
        if (ReqA == 1)
            NextState = Grant_A;
        else if (ReqB == 1)
            NextState = Grant_B;
        else
            NextState = Idle;

        endcase
    end
```

```vhdl
--------------------------------------------------
-- Process:  ARBITER_SEQ
-- Purpose:  Arbiter's state machine state register.
-- Inputs:   Clock, Reset, NextState.
-- Outputs:  CurrentState.
--------------------------------------------------
ARBITER_SEQ:
process (Reset, Clock)
begin
    if (Reset = '1') then
        CurrentState <= Idle;
    elsif rising_edge(Clock) then
        CurrentState <= NextState;
    end if;
end process ARBITER_SEQ;
```
continued

```verilog
//------------------------------------------------
// Module:  ARBITER_SEQ
// Purpose: Arbiter's state machine state register.
// Inputs:   Clock, Reset, NextState.
// Outputs: CurrentState.
//------------------------------------------------
always @ (posedge Reset or posedge Clock)
    begin: ARBITER_SEQ
        if (Reset)
            CurrentState = Idle;
        else
            CurrentState = NextState;
    end
```
continued

359

Three-way round-robin arbiter

VHDL	Verilog
| ```
---------------------------------------------
-- Process:  SYNC_TRI_STATE_ENS
-- Purpose: Synchronize tri-state enable signals
--              to minimize swithing skew.
--              Async reset ensures EnA1/2, EnB1/2
--              and EnC1/2 all 0 for safe (no multiple
--              drives) tri-state start condition.
--              Inputs:  NextState.
-- Outputs:  EnA1/2, EnB1/2 EnC1/2.
---------------------------------------------
SYNC_TRI_STATE_ENS:
process (Reset, Clock)
begin
    if (Reset = '1') then
        EnA1 <= '0'; EnA2 <= '0';
        EnB1 <= '0'; EnB2 <= '0';
        EnC1 <= '0'; EnC2<= '0';
    elsif rising_edge(Clock) then
        EnA1 <= '0'; EnA2 <= '0';
        EnB1 <= '0'; EnB2 <= '0';
        EnC1 <= '0'; EnC2 <= '0';
        case NextState is
            when Grant_A =>   EnA1 <= '1'; EnA2 <= '1';
            when Grant_B =>   EnB1 <= '1'; EnB2 <= '1';
            when Grant_C =>   EnC1 <= '1'; EnC2<= '1';
            when others  =>   EnA1 <= '0'; EnA1 <= '0';
                              EnB1 <= '0'; EnB1 <= '0';
                              EnC1 <= '0'; EnC1<= '0';
        end case;
    end if;
end process SYNC_TRI_STATE_ENS;




---------------------------------------------
-- Process: No process name - concurrent statements.
-- Purpose: Infer tri-state buffers for RAM access
-- Inputs:  EnA1/2, EnB1/2, EnC1/2,
-- AddBus_ProcA, AddBus_ProcB, AddBus_ProcC,
-- DataWriteBus_ProcA, DataWriteBus_ProcB,
-- DataWriteBus_ProcC.
-- Outputs: AddBus_RAM, DataWriteBus_RAM.
---------------------------------------------
AddBus_RAM <= AddBus_ProcA when (EnA1 = '1') else
                (others => 'Z');
AddBus_RAM <= AddBus_ProcB when (EnB1 = '1') else
                (others => 'Z');
AddBus_RAM <= AddBus_ProcC when (EnC1 = '1') else
                (others => 'Z');

DataWriteBus_RAM <= DataWriteBus_ProcA when
                        (EnA2 = '1') else
                (others => 'Z');
DataWriteBus_RAM <= DataWriteBus_ProcB when
                        (EnB2 = '1') else
                (others => 'Z');
DataWriteBus_RAM <= DataWriteBus_ProcC when
                        (EnC2 = '1') else
                (others => 'Z');
R_Wb_RAM <= R_Wb_ProcA  when (EnA2 = '1') else 'Z';
R_Wb_RAM <= R_Wb_ProcB  when (EnB2 = '1') else 'Z';
R_Wb_RAM <= R_Wb_ProcC  when (EnC2 = '1') else 'Z';

end architecture RTL;
``` | ```
//---------------------------------------------
// Module:  SYNC_TRI_STATE_ENS
// Purpose: Synchronize tri-state enable signals
//              to minimize swithing skew.
//              Async reset ensures EnA1/2, EnB1/2
//              and EnC1/2 all 0 for safe (no multiple
//              drives) tri-state start condition.
// Inputs:    NextState.
// Outputs: EnA1/2, EnB1/2 EnC1/2.
//---------------------------------------------
always @(posedge Reset or posedge Clock)
    begin: SYNC_TRI_STATE_ENS
        if (Reset)
            begin
                EnA1 = 0;  EnA2 = 0;
                EnB1 = 0;   EnB2 = 0;
                EnC1 = 0;  EnC2 = 0;
            end
        else
            begin
                EnA1 = 0;  EnA2 = 0;
                EnB1 = 0;   EnB2 = 0;
                EnC1 = 0;  EnC2 = 0;
                case (NextState)
                    Grant_A:  begin EnA1 = 1;EnA2 = 1; end
                    Grant_B:  begin EnB1 = 1; EnB2 = 1; end
                    Grant_C:  begin EnC1 = 1;EnC2 = 1; end
                    default:
                        begin
                            EnA1 = 0; EnA2 = 0;
                            EnB1 = 0; EnB2 = 0;
                            EnC1 = 0; EnC2 = 0;
                        end
                endcase
            end
    end
//---------------------------------------------
// Module:  No model name - concurrent statements.
// Purpose: Infer tri-state buffers for RAM access.
// Inputs: EnA1/2, EnB1/2, EnC1/2,
//         AddBus_ProcA, AddBus_ProcB, AddBus_ProcC,
//         DataWriteBus_ProcA, DataWriteBus_ProcB,
//         DataWriteBus_ProcC.
// Outputs: AddBus_RAM, DataWriteBus_RAM.
//---------------------------------------------
assign AddBus_RAM = EnA1 ? AddBus_ProcA : 12'b Z;
assign AddBus_RAM = EnB1 ? AddBus_ProcB : 12'b Z;
assign AddBus_RAM = EnC1 ? AddBus_ProcC : 12'b Z;

assign DataWriteBus_RAM = EnA2 ? DataWriteBus_ProcA
                                        : 8'b Z;
assign DataWriteBus_RAM = EnB2 ? DataWriteBus_ProcB :
                                        : 8'b Z;
assign DataWriteBus_RAM = EnC2 ? DataWriteBus_ProcC
                                        : 8'b Z;

assign R_Wb_RAM = EnA2 ? R_Wb_ProcA : 1'b Z;
assign R_Wb_RAM = EnB2 ? R_Wb_ProcB : 1'b Z;
assign R_Wb_RAM = EnC2 ? R_Wb_ProcC : 1'b Z;

endmodule
``` |

4. Greatest Common Divisor (GCD)

Problem

The problem consists of three parts:

1. Design three algorithmic level models of an algorithm that finds the Greatest Common Divisor (GCD) of two numbers in the software programming language, "C", and the two hardware description languages, VHDL and Verilog. Use common test data files to test the algorithm where practically possible. Neither the VHDL nor Verilog models need to contain timing. All three models should automatically indicate a pass or fail condition.

2. Model the GCD algorithm at the register transfer level for synthesis in both VHDL and Verilog. The model must be generic so that it can be instantiated with different bit widths. A signal called Load should indicate when input data is valid, and a signal called Done should be provided to signify when valid output data is available. The generic model should be verified with 8-bit bus signals.

3. Write VHDL and Verilog test harnesses for the two models that 1) use the same test data files used by the algorithmic level models, and 2), instantiates both the RTL and synthesized gate level models so that they are simulated and tested at the same time.

Solution

The solution is broken into three parts corresponding to those of the problem.

1. Designing algorithmic level models in C, VHDL and Verilog

The algorithm used to find the greatest common divisor between two numbers is indicated by the flow chart; Figure 12.6.

The algorithm operates by continually subtracting the smaller of the two numbers, A or B, from the largest until such point the smallest number becomes equal to zero. It does this by continually subtracting B from A while A is greater than or equal to B, and then swapping A and B around when A becomes less than B, so that the new value of B can once again be continually subtracted from A. This process continues until B becomes zero.

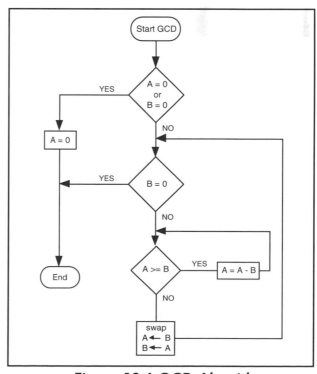

Figure 12.6 GCD Algorithm

C model

The C model first declares integer values for the two inputs A and B, the computed output of the algorithm Y, and the reference output Y_Ref. Integer Y_Ref is the expected GCD result and is used to compare with the computed result from the algorithm. The integer Swap is also declared and used in the algorithm to swap the two inputs A and B. A final integer, Passed, is used to indicate a pass (1) or fail (0) condition.

A file pointer (file_pointer) is defined in order to access the test data file "gcd_test_data.txt". It is opened for read mode only. Integer Passed is initially set to 1 and only set to 0 if the algorithm fails.

Reading test data file. The test data file contains three numbers on each line corresponding to values of A, B and Y_Ref, respectively. A **while** loop is used to 1) read each line of the test data file, 2) assign the three values to A, B and Y_Ref, respectively, 3) use A and B to compute the GCD output Y, and 4) compare Y with Y_Ref. This **while** loop continues while there is test data in the test data file.

Algorithm implementation. The initial **if** statement is an extra check that both A and B are not zero. The algorithm is then modeled using two **while** statements. The first, outermost, **while** statement checks to see if B has reached zero; if it has, the GCD has been found. The second, innermost **while** statement checks to see if A is greater than or equal to B; if it is, it continually subtracts A from B and puts the result back in A. When A becomes less than B the innermost **while** loop completes, A and B are swapped using Swap, and the outer most **while** statement rechecks B to see if it has reached zero.

Testing the result. The algorithm is tested using an **if** statement which tests to see if the computed result Y is the same as the expected result Y_Ref. If they are different an error message is printed to the screen and Passed assigned the value 0. Finally, when all tests have completed and Passed is still equal to 1 a passed message is printed to the screen.

VHDL Model

The VHDL model follows exactly the same principle as defined for the C model above. When reading the integer values from the test date file they must be read and assigned to a variable; they cannot be read and assigned to a signal. As this is an algorithmic level model defined in a single entity it contains no inputs or outputs, nor does it contain any internal signals or associated timing. All computations use variables; variables are read from the test data file, the algorithm computes the result and variables are written to a results file.

Verilog Model

The Verilog model also follows the same principle as defined above for the C model. A major difference in this model is that Verilog cannot read decimal integer values from a system file. Data read from a system file <u>must</u> be: 1) read using one of the two language define system tasks, $readmemh or $readmemb and 2) stored in a memory, which has specific width and depth. This limits any read data to being in either hexadecimal or binary format. In this case, a separate test data file is used "gcd_test_data_hex.txt" which has the test data specified in hexadecimal format.

GCD test data files

file: gcd_test_data.txt			file: gcd_test_data_hex.txt								
21	49	7	15	31	7	//	Decimal	21	49	7
25	30	5	19	1E	5	//	Decimal	25	30	5
19	27	1	13	1B	1	//	Decimal	19	27	1
40	40	40	28	28	28	//	Decimal	40	40	40
250	190	10	FA	6E	A	//	Decimal	250	190	10
5	250	5	5	FA	5	//	Decimal	5	250	5

GCD modeled at the algorithm level

C

```c
#include <stdio.h>

main ()
  {
  int A_in, B_in,A,B, Swap, Y, Y_Ref, Passed;
  FILE *file_pointer;
  file_pointer =
      fopen("gcd_test_data.txt", "r");

  Passed = 1;

  while (!feof(file_pointer))
    {
    /*-----------------------*/
    /* Read test data from file */
    /*-----------------------*/
    fscanf (file_pointer, "%d %d
        %d\n", &A_in, &B_in, &Y_Ref);

    /*-----------------------*/
    /* Model GCD algorithm */
    /*-----------------------*/
    A = A_in;
    B = B_in;
    if (A != 0 && B != 0)
      {
      while (B != 0)
        {
        while (A >= B)
          {
          A = A - B;
          }
        Swap = A;
        A = B;
        B = Swap;
        }
      }
    else
      {
      A = 0;
      }
    Y = A;

    /*-----------------------*/
    /* Test GCD algorithm */
    /*-----------------------*/
    if (Y != Y_Ref)
      {
      printf ("Error. A = %d B = %d
          Y = %d Y_Ref = %d\n",
          A_in, B_in, Y, Y_Ref);
      Passed = 0;
      }
    }

  if (Passed == 1)
    printf ("GCD algorithm test passed
        ok\n");

  }
```

VHDL

```vhdl
library STD;
use STD.TEXTIO.all;

entity GCD_ALG is
end entity GCD_ALG;

architecture ALGORITHM of GCD_ALG is

---------------------------------------
-- Declare test data file and results file
---------------------------------------
file TestDataFile: text open
    read_mode is "gcd_test_data.txt";
file ResultsFile: text open write_mode is
    "gcd_alg_test_results.txt";
begin

GCD: process
  variable A_in, B_in, A, B, Swap, Y, Y_Ref:
          integer range 0 to 65535;
  variable TestData: line;
  variable BufLine: line;
  variable Passed: bit := '1';
begin
  while not endfile(TestDataFile) loop

    ---------------------------------------
    -- Read test data from file
    ---------------------------------------
    readline(TestDataFile, TestData);
    read(TestData, A);
    read(TestData, B);
    read(TestData, Y_Ref);

    ---------------------------------------
    -- Model GCD algorithm
    ---------------------------------------
    A := A_in;
    B := B_in;
    if (A /= 0 and B /= 0) then
      while (B /= 0) loop
        while (A >= B) loop
          A := A - B;
        end loop;
        Swap := A;
        A    := B;
        B    := Swap;
      end loop;
    else
      A := 0;
    end if;
    Y := A;

    ---------------------------------------
    -- Test GCD algorithm
    ---------------------------------------
    if (Y /= Y_Ref) then  -- has failed
      Passed := '0';
      write(Bufline, string '("GCD Error: A="));
      write(Bufline, A_in);
      write(Bufline, string '(" B="));
```

continued

Verilog

```verilog
module GCD_ALG;
  parameter Width = 16;
  reg (Width - 1:0) A_in,B_in,A,B, Y, Y_Ref;

  parameter TestPeriod = 20,
            GCD_tests = 6:

  integer N, M;
  reg     Passed,
          FailTime;
  integer SimResults;

  // Declare memory array for test data
  // -----------------------------------
  reg  (Width - 1:1) AB_Y_Ref_Arr
                  (1:GCD_tests * 3);

  //-----------------------------------
  // Model GCD algorithm
  //-----------------------------------
  always @(A or B)
    begin: GCD
      A = A_in;
      B = B_in;
      if (A != 0 && B != 0)
        while (B != 0)
          begin
            while (A >= B)
              A = A - B;
            Swap  = A_reg;
            A = B;
            B = Swap;
          end
      else
        A = 0;
      Y = A;
    end

  //-----------------------------------
  // Test GCD algorithm
  //-----------------------------------
  initial
    begin
      // Load contents of
      // "gcd_test_data.txt" into array.
      $readmemh("gcd_test_data_hex.txt",
          AB_Y_Ref_Arr);

      // Open simulation results file
      SimResults = $fopen("gcd.simres");

      Passed = 1;  // Set to 0 if fails

      for (N = 1; N <= GCD_tests; N = N + 1)
        begin
          A_in = AB_Y_Ref_Arr((N * 3) + 1);
          B_in = AB_Y_Ref_Arr((N * 3) + 2);
          Y_Ref = AB_Y_Ref_Arr((N * 3) + 3);
          #TestPeriod
```

continued

GCD modeled at the algorithm level

C	VHDL	Verilog

	write(Bufline, B_in);
	write(Bufline, string'(" Y="));
	write(Bufline, Y);
	write(Bufline, string'(" Y_Ref="));
	write(Bufline, Y_Ref);
	writeline(ResultsFile, Bufline);
	   end if;
	  end loop;
	  if (Passed = '1') **then** -- has passed
	   write(Bufline, string'
	     ("GCD algorithm test has passed"));
	   writeline(ResultsFile, Bufline);
	  end if;
	  wait;
	 end process GCD;
	
	end architecture ALGORITHM;
		if (Y != Y_Ref) // has failed
		   begin
		    Passed = 0;
		    $fdisplay (SimResults,
		     "GCD Error: A = %d
		     B=%d Y=%d. Y should be %d",
		     A_in, B_in, Y, Y_Ref);
		   end
		  end
		  if (Passed == 1) // has passed
		   $fdisplay (SimResults,
		    "GCD algorithm test has passed");
		   $fclose (SimResults);
		   $finish;
		 end
		endmodule

2. Designing RTL level hardware models in VHDL and Verilog

The RTL level models infer the architectural structure illustrated in Figure 12.7. The models have additional inputs and outputs over and above that of the algorithmic models. They are inputs Clock, Reset_N and Load, and the output Done. When Load is at logic 1 it signifies input data is available on inputs A and B, and are loaded into separate registers whose output signals are called A_hold and B_hold. The extra output signal, Done, switches to a logic 1 to signify the greatest common divisor has been computed. It takes a number of clock cycles to compute the GCD and is dependent upon the values of A and B.

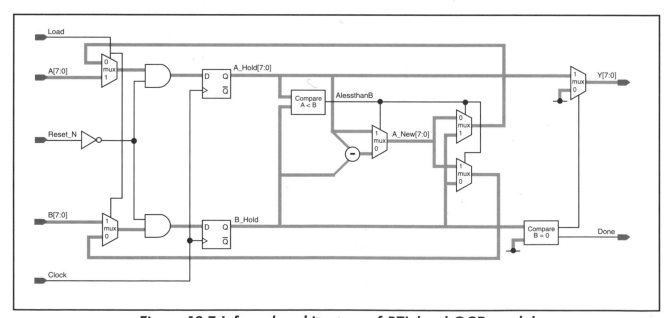

Figure 12.7 Inferred architecture of RTL level GCD model

The models are broken down into three **process/always** statements.

First **process/always** *statement* LOAD_SWAP. This statement infers two registers which operate as follows:

1) When Reset_N is at logic 0, A_hold and B_hold are set to zero.
2) When not 1) and Load is at logic 1, data on A and B is loaded into A_hold and B_hold.
3) When not 1) or 2) and A_hold is less than B_hold, values on A_hold and B_hold are swapped, that is, A_hold and B_hold are loaded into B_hold and A_hold respectively.
4) When not 1), 2) or 3), A_hold is reloaded, that is, it keeps the same value. The value of A_hold - B_hold, from the second **process/always** statement, is loaded into B_hold.

Second **process/always** *statement* SUBTRACT_TEST. The first **if** statement tests to see if A_hold is greater than or equal to B_hold. If it is, the subtraction, (A_hold - B_hold), occurs and the result assigned to A_New ready to be loaded into B_hold on the next rising edge of the clock signal. If A_hold is less than B_hold, then subtraction cannot occur and A_New is assigned the value B_hold so that a swap occurs after the next rising edge of the clock signal. The second **if** statement checks to see if the value of B_Hold has reached zero. If it has, signal Done is set to logic 1 and the value of A_Hold is passed to the output Y through an inferred multiplexer function.

It is a requirement of the problem to synthesize the generic model with 8-bit bus signals. This is easily achieved in the Verilog model by setting the default parameter value Width to 8. This means it does not need to be separately instantiated before it can be synthesized and have the correct bit width. This is not the case in VHDL, which uses a generic. The value of the generic is only specified when the model is instantiated. Although the VHDL model will be instantiated in the test harness, the test harness is not synthesized. Therefore, in order to synthesize an 8-bit GCD circuit a separate synthesizable model must be used which instantiates the RTL model so that it can assign the generic, Width, to be 8. This extra model only contains one component instantiation and is not included in this text. The simulation test harness does not need to use this extra model, as it too will specify the generic, Width, to be 8.

GCD modeled at the RTL level

VHDL	Verilog
``
library IEEE;
use IEEE.STD_Logic_1164.all, IEEE.Numeric_STD.all;

entity GCD is
    generic (Width: natural);
    port (Clock, Reset, Load: in std_logic;
           A, B: in   unsigned(Width - 1 downto 0);
           Done: out std_logic;
           Y: out unsigned(Width - 1 downto 0));
end entity GCD;

architecture RTL of GCD is
    signal A_New,A_Hold,B_Hold: unsigned(Width-1 downto 0);
    signal A_lessthan_B: std_logic;
begin

    -- Load 2 input registers and ensure B_Hold < A_Hold

    LOAD_SWAP: process (Clock)
    begin
        if rising_edge(Clock) then
            if (Reset = '0') then
                A_Hold <= (others => '0');
``` *continued* | ```
module GCD (Clock, Reset, Load, A, B, Done, Y);
    parameter Width = 8;
    input  Clock, Reset, Load;
    input  (Width - 1:0) A, B;
    output Done;
    output (Width - 1:0) Y;

    reg A_lessthan_B, Done;
    reg (Width - 1:0) A_New, A_Hold,B_Hold, Y;
//--------------------------------------------------
// Load 2 input registers and ensure B_Hold < A_Hold
//--------------------------------------------------
always @(posedge Clock)
    begin: LOAD_SWAP
        if (Reset)
            begin
                A_Hold = 0;
                B_Hold = 0;
            end
        else if (Load)
            begin
                A_Hold = A;
                B_Hold = B;
            end
``` *continued* |

GCD modeled at the RTL level

VHDL	Verilog

<pre>   B_Hold <= (others => '0');
    elsif (Load = '1') then
        A_Hold <= A;
        B_Hold <= B;
    elsif (A_lessthan_B = '1') then
        A_Hold <= B_Hold;
        B_Hold <= A_New;
    else
        A_Hold <= A_New;
    end if;
  end if;
end process LOAD_SWAP;
 	
SUBTRACT_TEST: process (A_Hold, B_Hold)
begin
 	
    -- Subtract B_Hold from A_Hold if A_Hold >= B_Hold
    -- 	
 	
    if (A_Hold >= B_Hold) then
        A_lessthan_B   <= '0';
        A_New <= A_Hold - B_Hold;
    else
        A_lessthan_B   <= '1';
        A_New <= A_Hold;
    end if;
 	
    --- 	
    -- Greatest common divisor found if B_Hold = 0
    --- 	
    if (B_Hold = (others => '0')) then
        Done <= '1';
        Y <= A_Hold;
    else
        Done <= '0';
        Y <= (others => '0');
    end if;
  end process SUBTRACT_TEST;
 	
end architecture RTL;</pre>
	<pre> else if (A_lessthan_B)
	
	        begin
	            A_Hold = B_Hold;
	            B_Hold = A_New;
	        end
	    else
	        A_Hold = A_New;
	  end
	
	always @(A_Hold or B_Hold)
	  begin: SUBTRACT_TEST
	    //--
	    //Subtract B_Hold from A_Hold if A_Hold >= B_Hold
	    //--
	    if (A_Hold >= B_Hold)
	        begin
	            A_lessthan_B = 0;
	            A_New = A_Hold - B_Hold;
	        end
	    else
	        begin
	            A_lessthan_B = 1;
	            A_New = A_Hold;
	        end
	
	    //--
	    // Greatest common divisor found if B_Hold = 0
	    //--
	    if (B_Hold == 0)
	        begin
	            Done = 1;
	            Y = A_Hold;
	        end
	    else
	        begin
	            Done = 0;
	            Y = 0;
	        end
	  end
	endmodule</pre>

3. Designing VHDL and Verilog test harnesses for the RTL level models

The VHDL and Verilog test harnesses instantiate both the RTL and synthesized gate level models as required. The RTL model, called GCD, is instantiated with the instance name GCD_1. The synthesized gate level model, called GCD_GL, is instantiated with the instance name GCD_GL_1. Notice bus signals in the RTL model are expanded to individual signals in the gate level model and so are individually connected in its instantiation. The width of the bus signals are specified to be 8, that is, the generic Width in the VHDL test harness, and the overloaded parameter value Width in the Verilog test harness. Note, the default **parameter** value of Width in the Verilog RTL level model is already 8, so overloading it with a new value of 8, is not necessary in this particular instance, although it is shown in the example for completeness.

These test harnesses read the same test data files as the algorithmic models shown earlier. The common input signals to both the RTL and gate level instances, that is, Clock, Resset_N, Load, A and B, plus the separate output signals, Y from the RTL model, and Y_gl from the gate level model, are all declared and connected appropriately. A free running clock is defined and has period, ClockPeriod, defined to be 20ns.

The final **process**/**initial** statement, 1) applies the test data to the two models, 2) waits an unknown number of clock cycles until signal Done switches to a logic 1, and 3) tests that the signal Done_gl, is also at logic 1 and that both Y and Y_gl are the same as Y_Ref. If the signals are not as expected an error message is written to the system file "gcd_rtl_test_results.txt" together with the expected and actual results. If the signals are as expected, the next test is performed. When all tests are complete, and Passed still has a value of 1, a "passed" message is written to the system file "gcd_rtl_test_results.txt".

Test harness for RTL and synthesized gate level

VHDL	Verilog
| ```
library IEEE,STD;
use IEEE.STD_Logic_1164.all, IEEE.Numeric_STD.all;
use STD.TEXTIO.all;

entity GCD_H is
end entity GCD_H;

architecture TEST_HARN of GCD_H is
--------------------------------------
-- Declare test data file
--------------------------------------
file TestDataFile: text open read_mode is
    "gcd_test_data.txt";

file ResultsFile: text open write_mode is
    "gcd_rtl_test_results.txt";

constant Width: integer := 8;
constant ClockPeriod: time := 20 ns;
constant GCD_TestClockPeriods: integer := 100;

signal Clock, Reset, Load, Done: std_logic;
signal A, B, Y_Ref, Y, Y_gl: unsigned(Width - 1 downto 0);

  -- Declare RTL level model
component GCD
    generic (Width: integer);
    port( Clock, Reset, Load: in  std_logic;
          A, B:     in   unsigned(Width - 1 downto 0);
          Done:     out std_logic;
          Y:        out unsigned(Width - 1 downto 0));
end component;
-- Declare Gate level model
component GCD_GL
    port( Clock, Reset, Load: in  std_logic;
          A7, A6, A5, A4, A3, A2, A1, A0,
          B7, B6, B5, B4, B3, B2, B1, B0: in std_logic;
          Done: out std_logic;
          Y_gl7, Y_gl6, Y_gl5, Y_gl4,
          Y_gl3, Y_gl2, Y_gl1, Y_gl0: in std_logic);
end component;

begin

------------------------------------------------
-- Instantiate RTL & gate level models
------------------------------------------------
GCD_1: GCD
    generic map (8)
    port map (Clock, Reset, Load, A, B, Done, Y);

GCD_GL_1: GCD_GL
    port map (Clock, Reset, Load,
``` | ```
`timescale 1ns/100ps


module GCD_H;
    parameter Width = 8,
              ClockPeriod = 20,
              GCD_TestClockPeriods = 100,
              GCD_Tests = 5;

    reg Clock, Reset, Load;
    reg (Width - 1:0) A, B;

    wire Done, Done_gl;
    wire (Width - 1:0) Y, Y_gl;

    reg (Width - 1:0) Y_Ref;

    integer N, M;
    reg      Passed,
             FailTime;
    integer  SimResults;

    // Declare memory array for test data
    // ------------------------------------------------
    reg (Width - 1:1) AB_Y_Ref_Arr (1:GCD_Tests * 3);
``` |

Sub level components do not need to be separately declared before they can be instantiated in Verilog.

| | ```
//------------------------------------------------
// Instantiate the RTL & gate level models
//------------------------------------------------
GCD GCD_1 #(8)
    (Clock, Reset, Load, A, B, Done, Y);


GCD_GL GCD_GL_1
    (.Clock(Clock), .Reset(Reset), .Load(Load),
     .A7(A(7)), .A6(A(6)), .A5(A(5)), .A4(A(4)),
``` |

continued   *continued*

367
```

GCD modeled at the RTL level

VHDL	Verilog
A7=>A(7), A6=>A(6), A5=>A(5), A4=>A(4), A3=>A(3), A2=>A(2), A1=>A(1), A0=>A(0), B7=>B(7), B6=>B(6), B5=>B(5), B4=>B(4), B3=>B(3), B2=>B(2), B1=>B(1), B0=>B(0), Done_gl=>Done_gl, Y_gl7=>Y_gl(7), Y_gl6=>Y_gl(6),Y_gl5=>Y_gl(5), Y_gl4=>Y_gl(4), Y_gl3=>Y_gl(3), Y_gl2=>Y_gl(2), Y_gl1=>Y_gl(1), Y_gl0=>Y_gl(0));	.A3(A(3)), .A2(A(2)), .A1(A(1)), .A0(A(0)), .B7(B(7)), .B6(B(6)), .B5(B(5)), .B4(B(4)), .B3(B(3)), .B2(B(2)), .B1(B(1)), .B0(B(0)), .Done(Done), .Y_gl7(Y_gl(7)), .Y_gl6(Y_gl(6)), .Y_gl5(Y_gl(5)), .Y_gl4(Y_gl(4)), .Y_gl3(Y_gl(3)), .Y_gl2(Y_gl(2)), .Y_gl1(Y_gl(1)), .Y_gl0(Y_gl(0)),

```
VHDL

-------------------------------------
-- Set up free running clock
-------------------------------------
Clock <= not Clock after ClockPeriod / 2;


-----------------------------------------------
-- Apply stimulus to GCD models under test
-----------------------------------------------
STIM_GCD: process
    variable A_var,B_var,Y_Ref_var: integer range 0 to 255;
    variable TestData: line;
    variable BufLine: line;
    variable Passed: bit := '1';  -- Set to 0 if fails
begin
    Reset <= '0';
    Load  <= '0';
    wait for ClockPeriod; Reset <= '1';
    wait for ClockPeriod; Reset <= '0';
    while not endfile(TestDataFile) loop

        ---------------------------------------
        -- Read test data from file
        ---------------------------------------
        readline(TestDataFile, TestData);
        read(TestData, A_var);
        read(TestData, B_var);
        read(TestData, Y_Ref_var);

        A     <= to_unsigned(A_var, 8);
        B     <= to_unsigned(B_var, 8);
        Y_Ref <= to_unsigned(Y_Ref_var, 8);

        --------------------------------
        -- Test GCD algorithm
        --------------------------------
        wait for ClockPeriod; Load <= '1';
        wait for ClockPeriod; Load <= '0';
        for M in 0 to (GCD_TestClockPeriods - 1) loop
            wait for ClockPeriod;
            if (Done = '1') then
                if (Y /= Y_Ref or Y_gl /= Y_Ref or
                            Done_gl /= '1') then  -- has failed
                Passed := '0';
                write(Bufline, string'("Error: A="));
                write(Bufline, to_integer(A));
                write(Bufline, string'(" B="));
                write(Bufline, to_integer(B));
                write(Bufline, string'(" Y="));
                write(Bufline, to_integer(Y));
                write(Bufline, string'(" Y_Ref="));
                write(Bufline, to_integer(Y_Ref));
                writeline(ResultsFile, Bufline);
                end if;
            end if;
        end loop;
```

```
Verilog

//-------------------------------------
// Set up free running clock
//-------------------------------------
always
    #(ClockPeriod / 2) Clock = ! Clock;


//----------------------------------------------
// Apply stimulus to GCD under test
//----------------------------------------------
initial
    begin
        // Load contents of "gcd_test_data.txt" into array.
        $readmemh("gcd_test_data_h.txt", AB_Y_Ref_Arr);

        // Open simulation results file
        SimResults = $fopen("gcd_rtl_test_results.txt");

        Passed = 1;  // Set to 0 if fails

        Clock = 0;
        Reset = 0;
        Load  = 0;

        #ClockPeriod Reset = 1; #ClockPeriod Reset = 0;
        for (N = 0; N < GCD_Tests; N = N + 1)
            begin
                A = AB_Y_Ref_Arr((N * 3) + 1);
                B = AB_Y_Ref_Arr((N * 3) + 2);
                Y_Ref = AB_Y_Ref_Arr((N * 3) + 3);

                #ClockPeriod Load = 1; #ClockPeriod Load = 0;
                for (M=0; M<GCD_TestClockPeriods; M=M+1)
                    #ClockPeriod
                    if (Done == 1)
                        if (Y != Y_Ref || Y_gl != Y_Ref ||
                            Done_gl != 0)    // has failed
                            begin
                                Passed = 0;
                                $fdisplay (SimResults,
                                    "Error: Y_Ref=%d, Y=%d, Y_gl=%d
                                        at time %d",
                                    Y_Ref, Y, Y_gl, $time);
                            end
            end
        if (Passed == 1)  // has passed
            $fdisplay (SimResults,
                    "GCD RTL & gate level test passed");
        $fclose (SimResults);
        $finish;
    end

endmodule
```

GCD modeled at the RTL level

VHDL	Verilog

end loop;
  if (Passed = '1') **then** -- has passed
    write(Bufline, string'("GCD algorithm test has
                passed"));
    writeline(ResultsFile, Bufline);
  end if;
  end process;
 	
end architecture TEST_HARN;	

Simulated waveform

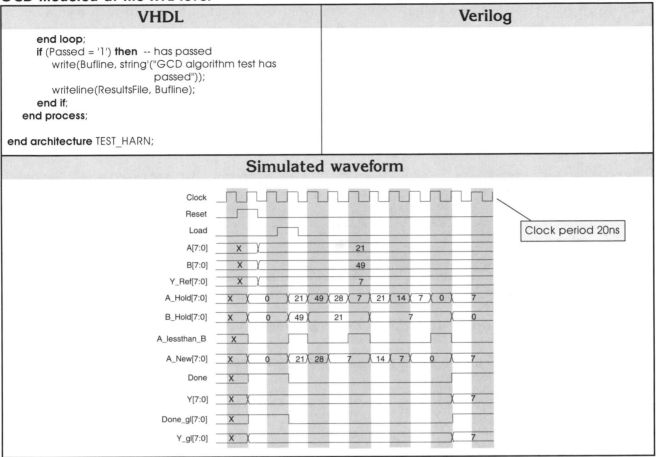

5. Error Detection And Correction (EDAC)

Problem

A microprocessor system that processes vital data needs to employ an automatic error detection and correction (EDAC) mechanism between the microprocessor and its associated memory in order to enhance reliability.

Design VHDL and Verilog models of a circuit that sits between the microprocessor and memory which performs *flow-through* error detection and correction of data written to, and read from the memory. Single bit errors should be detected and corrected. Two bit errors should be detected, but do not have to be corrected. A two bit status flag should be given to indicate the type of error, or if no error has occurred. This allows the microprocessor to take appropriate action in the extremely rare case of two bits being in error at the same time. There is a single read/write signal that should be used to control the direction of the two bidirectional data busses; microprocessor and memory. Ignore the address bus; model only the purely combinational EDAC logic between the bidirectional microprocessor and memory data busses. The vital data from the microprocessor is 16-bits wide.

Algorithm

A simple parity bit is the most common method of detecting errors, however, the erroneous bit is not known so cannot be corrected. Multiple parity check bits are needed which check the

369

parity of groups of bits, and which are stored along with the data in memory. When data is read back from memory, the associated parity bits are also read and compared with a new set of check bits that are generated from the read data. If the newly generated check bits do not compare with the stored parity bits, they generate a unique pattern called a SYNDROME and means an error has occurred. This syndrome can be used to identify the erroneous bit which can then be corrected.

For this model, we will use the modified Hamming code developed by R W Hamming*. Data which is N bits wide requires K parity bits to be stored along with the data where

$$N <= 2^K - 1 - K$$

If the bits are numbered in sequence, those bits that are a power of two are reserved for the parity bits. Figure 12.8 shows how the 16-bit data (D0-D15) is stored along with a total of 6 parity bits (P0-P5) to form a 22-bit word that is stored in memory.

Position number	22	21	20	19	18	17	16	15	14	13	12	11	10	9	8	7	6	5	4	3	2	1
Bit number	21	20	19	18	17	16	15	14	13	12	11	10	9	8	7	6	5	4	3	2	1	0
Data/Parity Bit	P5	D15	D14	D13	D12	D11	P4	D10	D9	D8	D7	D6	D5	D4	P3	D3	D2	D1	P2	D0	P1	P0

D = Data Bit
P = Parity Bit

Figure 12.8 Configuration of 16-bit data and 6 bit parity stored as a 22-bit word in memory

The five parity bits P0-P4 make up the parity check bits for single bit error detection and correction. They are generated as follows:

P0 = XOR of data bits (0, 1, 3, 4, 6, 8, 10, 11, 13, 15)
P1 = XOR of data bits (0, 2, 3, 5, 6, 9, 10, 12, 13)
P2 = XOR of data bits (1, 2, 3, 7, 8, 9, 10, 14, 15)
P3 = XOR of data bits (4, 5, 6, 7, 8, 9, 10)
P4 = XOR of data bits (11, 12, 13, 14, 15)

The term "modified Hamming code" refers to the addition of an extra parity bit (P5) that is used to detect double errors, but which cannot be corrected. It is an overall parity of the 16 data bits (D0-D15) and 5 parity bits P0-P4, that is,

P5 = XOR of (D0-D15,P0-P4)

When the 22-bit word is read from memory the syndrome word is formed by comparing (XORing) the original parity bits (P0-P4) stored in memory with the newly generated parity bits (P0-P4) from the stored data (D0-D15). If they compare, no error has occurred. If they are different, the value of the syndrome indicates the position number of the error bit in the 22-bit word as indicated in Figure 12.8.

Table 12.2 shows how the type of error is detected based on the value of the syndrome and overall parity bit, P5.

Syndrome (5-bits)	P5 (1-bit)	Error type	Comments
0	0	No error	
/= 0	1	Single error	Is Correctable. (Syndrome equal to erroneous bit position)
/= 0	0	Double error	Cannot be corrected
0	1	P5 error	Is Correctable.

Table 12.2 EDAC Error Type Detection

*Described in Computer Engineering Hardware Design by M. Morris Mano.

Solution

The architecture used to implement the algorithm is illustrated in Figure 12.8. When the microprocessor writes data to memory, this EDAC model generates the 6 parity bits (P0-P5) and stores them along with the data in a 22-bit word. When the 22-bit word is read back from memory, the same parity generation circuit is used to regenerate the parity bits. These parity bits are compared with the actual parity bits from memory in the "Generate Syndrome" block and the syndrome is generated. This syndrome is then used in the "Correct Data" block to correct any errors that may have occurred. The corrected 16-bit data is then read by the microprocessor. The syndrome, and overall parity check bit, is used to generate the two bit error type according to Table 12.2.

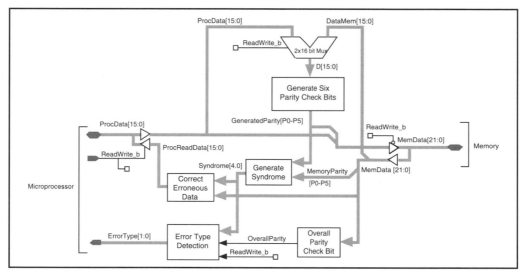

Figure 12.8 Implemented architecture for EDAC algorithim

Example of Corrected Data

Suppose the following 16-bit word is to be stored in memory.

Data Bit	15	14	13	12	11	10	9	8	7	6	5	4	3	2	1	0	
Value	1	0	1	0	1	0	1	1	1	1	0	0	1	1	0	1	= ABCD$_{HEX}$

The parity bits stored along with this data would be as indicated in Table 12.3.

	Microprocessor Data Bits (ABCD$_{HEX}$)																
Parity Bit	15 1	14 0	13 1	12 0	11 1	10 0	9 1	8 1	7 1	6 1	5 0	4 0	3 1	2 1	1 0	0 1	Parity Bit (No error)
P0 = XOR of	1	1			1	0		1		1		0	1		1	1	P0 = 1
P1 = XOR of		1		0		0	1			1		0	1	1		1	P1 = 0
P2 = XOR of	1	0				0	1	1	1				1	1	0		P2 = 0
P3 = XOR of						0	1	1	1	1	0	0					P3 = 0
P4 = XOR of	1	0	1	0	1												P4 = 1

Table 12.3 Parity bit generation for data of ABCD$_{HEX}$

Figure 12.9 shows the 22-bit data that is stored in memory and includes the overall parity bit (P5). Figure 12.9 indicates how this word is read back from memory, but with bit position number 19 in error.

Position Number	22	21	20	19	18	17	16	15	14	13	12	11	10	9	8	7	6	5	4	3	2	1
Bit Number	21	20	19	18	17	16	15	14	13	12	11	10	9	8	7	6	5	4	3	2	1	0
Data/Parity bits	P5	D15	D14	D13	D12	D11	P4	D10	D9	D8	D7	D6	D5	D4	P3	D3	D2	D1	P2	D0	P1	P0
Write Data (15BC65$_{HEX}$)	0	1	0	1	0	1	1	0	1	1	1	1	0	0	0	1	1	0	0	1	0	1
Read Data (11BC65$_{HEX}$)	0	1	0	0	0	1	1	0	1	1	1	1	0	0	0	1	1	0	0	1	0	1

Bit in error when data read back from memory

Figure 12.9 Memory write data (15BC65$_{HEX}$) and erroneous read data (11BC65$_{HEX}$)

The data bits (D0-D15) generate new parity bits and are compared with the parity bits from memory. The result is a syndrome value of 19 indicating that the bit in position number 19 is in error. This can be seen as 13$_{HEX}$ in the simulated waveforms, see Figure 12.10. Memory bit position 19 contains data bit D13 and means the value 8BCD$_{HEX}$ would have been read back by the microprocessor if it had not been corrected back to ABCD$_{HEX}$.

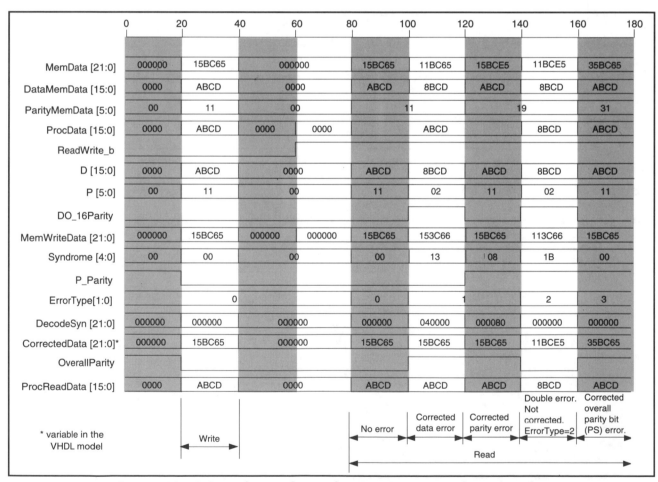

Figure 12.10 Signal waveforms for EDAC write and read cycles

HDL Code for EDAC

The HDL code is partitioned into **process/always** statements according to the architecture shown in Figure 12.8. There are 8 parts to the architecture, however there are 9 **process/always** statements in the HDL models. The reasons for the difference is summarized as follows.

1. Tri-state buffers are implied using continuous signal assignment statements and so are not contained in a **process/always** statement.
2. The two VHDL processes named PR_MemData and PR_MemWriteData and equivalent Verilog **always** blocks named BK_MemData and BK_MemWriteData do not imply logic, they simply reassign signal names.
3. The box in Figure 12.8 named "Correct Erroneous Data" represents two **process/always** statements.

Table 12.4 summarizes the link between the **process/always** statement in the code and the block in the structural diagram; Figure 12.8.

	process/always name	Block name from Figure 12.8
1	PR_MemData/BK_MemData	n/a
2	PR_Ham_Select/BK_HamSelect	2x1 16-bit multiplexer
3	PR_GenParity/BK_GenParity	Generate 6 parity check bits
4	PR_OverallParity/BK_OverallParity	Overall parity check bit
5	PR_MemWriteData/BK_MemWriteData	n/a
6	PR_GenSyndrome/BK_GenSyndrome	Generate syndrome
7	PR_GenErrorType/BK_GenErrorType	Error type detection
8	PR_DecodeSyndrome/BK_DecodeSyndrome	Correct erroneous data (1)
9	PR_CorrectErrors/BK_CorrectErrors	Correct erroneous data (2)
10	n/a	Tri-state buffers for microprocessor and memory busses.

Table 12.4 Link between HDL code and block diagram Figure 12.8

The different multiple input XOR operations needed in this model are defined using separate function statements.

VHDL Specific. Uses a VHDL package to define the enumerated data type for the type of EDAC error, ErrorTypeType, and the XOR function definitions. These functions make the code in the EDAC model shorter and easier to comprehend.

Verilog Specific. Four `define compiler directives are used to represent the four EDAC error type conditions. The XOR function definitions are placed in a separate system file and referenced using the `include compiler directive. When the model is synthesized the file pointed to by the `include compiler directive is replaced by the `include statement itself, so like the VHDL code, it makes the main body of the model shorter and easier to comprehend.

373

Common XOR functions used in the EDAC model

VHDL	Verilog
| ```
library IEEE;
use IEEE.std_logic_1164.all, IEEE.Numeric_STD.all;
package ERRDET_COR_PKG is
  type ErrorTypeType is (NoError, SingleError, DoubleError, OverallParityError);
  function XOR5    (A0, A1, A2, A3, A4: std_logic) return std_logic;
  function XOR6    (A0, A1, A2, A3, A4, A5: std_logic) return std_logic;
  function XOR7    (A0, A1, A2, A3, A4, A5, A6: std_logic) return std_logic;
  function XOR9    (A0,A1,A2,A3,A4,A5,A6,A7,A8,A9: std_logic) return std_logic;
  function XOR10   (A0,A1,A2,A3,A4,A5,A6,A7,A8,A9: std_logic) return std_logic;
  function XOR16   (A: unsigned(15 downto 0)) return std_logic;
end package ERRDET_COR_PKG;

package body ERRDET_COR_PKG is
  function XOR5 (A0, A1, A2, A3, A4: std_logic) return std_logic is
  begin
      return (( A0 xor A1 ) xor
            ( A2 xor A3 )) xor
            ( A4 );
  end function XOR5;

  function XOR6 (A0, A1, A2, A3, A4, A5: std_logic) return std_logic is
  begin
      return (( A0 xor A1 ) xor
            ( A2 xor A3 )) xor
            ( A4 xor A5 );
  end function XOR6;

  function XOR7 (A0, A1, A2, A3, A4, A5, A6: std_logic) return std_logic is
  begin
      return( ( A0 xor A1 ) xor
            ( A2 xor A3 )) xor
            (( A4 xor A5 ) xor
            ( A6 ));
  end function XOR7;

  function XOR9 (A0, A1, A2, A3, A4, A5, A6, A7, A8: std_logic) return std_logic is
  begin
    return    (( A0 xor A1 ) xor
            ( A2 xor A3 )) xor
            (( A4 xor A5 ) xor
            ( A6 xor A7 )) xor
            ( A8 );
  end function XOR9;

  function XOR10 (A0,A1,A2,A3,A4,A5,A6,A7,A8,A9: std_logic) return std_logic is
  begin
    return    (( A0 xor A1 ) xor
            ( A2 xor A3 )) xor
            (( A4 xor A5 ) xor
            ( A6 xor A7 )) xor
            ( A8 xor A9 );
  end function XOR10;

  function XOR16 (A: unsigned(15 downto 0)) return std_logic is
  begin
    return    ((( A(0) xor A(1) )   xor
            ( A(2) xor A(3) )) xor
            (( A(4) xor A(5) )   xor
            ( A(6) xor A(7) ))) xor
            ((( A(8) xor A(9) )   xor
            ( A(10) xor A(11) )) xor
            (( A(12) xor A(13) ) xor
            ( A(14) xor A(15) )));
  end function XOR16;
end package body ERRDET_COR_PKG;
``` | ```
function XOR5;
  input A0, A1, A2, A3, A4;
  XOR5 = (( A0 ^ A1 )   ^
        ( A2 ^ A3 ))   ^
        ( A4 );
endfunction

function XOR6;
  input A0, A1, A2, A3, A4, A5;
  XOR6 = (( A0 ^ A1 )   ^
        ( A2 ^ A3 ))   ^
        ( A4 ^ A5 );
endfunction

function XOR7;
  input A0, A1, A2, A3, A4, A5, A6;
  XOR7 = (( A0 ^ A1 )   ^
        ( A2 ^ A3 ))   ^
        (( A4 ^ A5 )   ^
        ( A6 ));
endfunction

function XOR9;
  input A0,A1,A2,A3,A4,A5,A6,A7,A8;
  XOR9 = (( A0 ^ A1 )   ^
        ( A2 ^ A3 ))   ^
        (( A4 ^ A5 )   ^
        ( A6 ^ A7 ))   ^
        ( A8 );
endfunction

function XOR10;
  input A0,A1,A2,A3,A4,A5,A6,A7,A8,A9;
  XOR10 = ( ( A0 ^ A1 )   ^
        ( A2 ^ A3 ))   ^
        ( ( A4 ^ A5 )   ^
        ( A6 ^ A7 ))   ^
        ( A8 ^ A9 );
endfunction

function XOR16;
  input [15:0] A;
  XOR16 = ( (( A[0] ^ A[1] )   ^
        ( A[2] ^ A[3] ))   ^
        (( A[4] ^ A[5] )   ^
        ( A[6] ^ A[7] )))  ^
        ( (( A[8] ^ A[9] )   ^
        ( A[10] ^ A[11] ))  ^
        (( A[12] ^ A[13] )   ^
        ( A[14] ^ A[15] )));
endfunction
``` |

Error Detection and Correction (EDAC)

VHDL	Verilog
| ```
library IEEE;
use IEEE.std_logic_1164.all, IEEE.Numeric_STD.all;
use work.ERRDET_COR_PKG.all;

entity ERRDET_CORRECTION is
    port ( ReadWrite_b:  in     std_logic;
           ProcData:     inout  unsigned(15 downto 0);
           MemData:      inout  unsigned(21 downto 0);
           ErrorType:    out    ErrorTypeType);
end entity ERRDET_CORRECTION;

architecture RTL of ERRDET_CORRECTION is
    signal ProcReadData, D, DataMemData:
                         unsigned(15 downto 0);
    signal MemWriteData, DecodeSyn:
                         unsigned(21 downto 0);
    signal D0_16Parity, OverallParity, P_Parity: std_logic;
    signal P,  -- Ham Parity
           ParityMemData: unsigned(5 downto 0);
    signal Syndrome: unsigned(4 downto 0);
begin
``` | ```
`define NoError             2'b 00
`define SingleError         2'b 01
`define DoubleError         2'b 10
`define OverallParityError  2'b 11

module ERRDET_CORRECTION
    (ReadWrite_b,ProcData,MemData,ErrorType);
    input        ReadWrite_b;
    inout  (15:0) ProcData;
    inout  (21:0) MemData;
    output (1:0)  ErrorType;

    wire  (15:0) ProcData;
    wire  (21:0) MemData;
    reg   (1:0)  ErrorType;

    integer N;
    reg  (15:0) ProcReadData, D, DataMemData;
    reg  (21:0) MemWriteData,DecodeSyn,CorrectedData;
    reg         D0_16Parity, OverallParity, P_Parity;
    reg  (5:0)  P,  // Ham Parity
                ParityMemData;
    reg  (4:0)  Syndrome;

//-----------------------------
// Function Definitions
//-----------------------------
`include "errdet_cor_fns.v"
``` |
| ```
---------------------------------------------------
-- Assign separate 16-bit data and 6-bit
-- parity from combined 22-bit memory
-- read data bus.
-- No physical logic synthesized.
---------------------------------------------------
PR_MemData: process (MemData)
begin
    DataMemData(0)  <= MemData(2);
    DataMemData(1)  <= MemData(4);
    DataMemData(2)  <= MemData(5);
    DataMemData(3)  <= MemData(6);
    DataMemData(4)  <= MemData(8);
    DataMemData(5)  <= MemData(9);
    DataMemData(6)  <= MemData(10);
    DataMemData(7)  <= MemData(11);
    DataMemData(8)  <= MemData(12);
    DataMemData(9)  <= MemData(13);
    DataMemData(10) <= MemData(14);
    DataMemData(11) <= MemData(16);
    DataMemData(12) <= MemData(17);
    DataMemData(13) <= MemData(18);
    DataMemData(14) <= MemData(19);
    DataMemData(15) <= MemData(20);

    ParityMemData(0) <= MemData(0);
    ParityMemData(1) <= MemData(1);
    ParityMemData(2) <= MemData(3);
    ParityMemData(3) <= MemData(7);
    ParityMemData(4) <= MemData(15);
    ParityMemData(5) <= MemData(21);
end process PR_MemData;
``` | ```
//----------------------------------------------------
// Assign separate 16-bit data and 6-bit
// parity from combined 22-bit memory
// read data bus.
// No physical logic synthesized.
//----------------------------------------------------
always @(MemData)
  begin: BK_MemData
    DataMemData(0)  = MemData(2);
    DataMemData(1)  = MemData(4);
    DataMemData(2)  = MemData(5);
    DataMemData(3)  = MemData(6);
    DataMemData(4)  = MemData(8);
    DataMemData(5)  = MemData(9);
    DataMemData(6)  = MemData(10);
    DataMemData(7)  = MemData(11);
    DataMemData(8)  = MemData(12);
    DataMemData(9)  = MemData(13);
    DataMemData(10) = MemData(14);
    DataMemData(11) = MemData(16);
    DataMemData(12) = MemData(17);
    DataMemData(13) = MemData(18);
    DataMemData(14) = MemData(19);
    DataMemData(15) = MemData(20);

    ParityMemData(0) = MemData(0);
    ParityMemData(1) = MemData(1);
    ParityMemData(2) = MemData(3);
    ParityMemData(3) = MemData(7);
    ParityMemData(4) = MemData(15);
    ParityMemData(5) = MemData(21);
  end
``` |

continued   *continued*

375

Error Detection and Correction (EDAC)

VHDL	Verilog
| ```
----------------------------------------
-- Select 16-bit processor (write) or
-- memory (read) from which to generate
-- Hamming code parity bits.
----------------------------------------
PR_HamSelect: process (ReadWrite_b, ProcData,
                       DataMemData)
begin
    if (ReadWrite_b = '0') then
        D <= ProcData;
    else
        D <= DataMemData;
    end if;
end process PR_HamSelect;


----------------------------------------
-- Generate Hamming Code parity bits
----------------------------------------
PR_GenParity: process (D)
begin
    -- Five bit parity for single error detection
    P(0) <= XOR10(D(0), D(1), D(3), D(4), D(6),D(8), D(10),
            D(11), D(13), D(15));

    P(1) <= XOR9(D(0), D(2), D(3), D(5), D(6),D(9), D(10),
            D(12), D(13));

    P(2) <= XOR9(D(1), D(2), D(3), D(7), D(8),D(9), D(10),
            D(14), D(15));

    P(3) <= XOR7(D(4), D(5), D(6), D(7),D(8), D(9), D(10));

    P(4) <= XOR5(D(11), D(12), D(13), D(14), D(15));

    -- Parity of 16-bit data
    D0_16Parity <= XOR16(D);

    -- Additional parity bit required for double error
    -- detection
    P(5) <= XOR6(D0_16Parity, P(0), P(1), P(2), P(3), P(4));
end process PR_GenParity;


-----------------------------------------------------
-- Generate overall parity bit from 22-bit memory read
-- data (Needed for error type)
-----------------------------------------------------
PR_OverallParity: process (ParityMemData, D0_16Parity)
begin
    P_Parity <= XOR6(ParityMemData(0),
                ParityMemData(1),
                ParityMemData(2),
                ParityMemData(3),
                ParityMemData(4),
                ParityMemData(5));
    OverallParity <= D0_16Parity xor P_Parity;
end process PR_OverallParity;
``` | ```
//----------------------------------------
// Select 16-bit processor (write) or
// memory (read) from which to generate
// Hamming code parity bits.
//----------------------------------------
always @(ReadWrite_b or ProcData or DataMemData)
    begin: BK_HamSelect
        if (ReadWrite_b == 0)
            D = ProcData;
        else
            D = DataMemData;
    end




//----------------------------------------
// Generate Hamming Code parity bits
//----------------------------------------
always @(D)
    begin: BK_GenParity
        // Five bit parity for single error detection
        P[0] = XOR10( D[0], D[1], D[3], D[4], D[6], D[8], D[10],
               D[11], D[13], D[15]);

        P[1] = XOR9( D[0], D[2], D[3], D[5], D[6], D[9], D[10],
               D[12], D[13]);

        P[2] = XOR9( D[1], D[2], D[3], D[7], D[8], D[9], D[10],
               D[14], D[15]);

        P[3] = XOR7(D[4], D[5], D[6], D[7], D[8], D[9], D[10]);

        P[4] = XOR5(D[11], D[12], D[13], D[14], D[15]);

        // Parity of 16-bit data
        D0_16Parity = XOR16(D);

        // Additional parity bit required for double error
        // detection
        P[5] = XOR6(D0_16Parity, P[0], P[1], P[2], P[3], P[4]);
    end


//-----------------------------------------------------
// Generate overall parity bit bit from 22-bit memory read
// data (Needed for error type)
//-----------------------------------------------------
always @(ParityMemData or D0_16Parity)
    begin: BK_OverallParity
        P_Parity = (( ParityMemData[0] ^
                    ParityMemData[1] ) ^
                    ( ParityMemData[2] ^
                    ParityMemData[3] )) ^
                    ( ParityMemData[4] ^
                    ParityMemData[5] );
        OverallParity = D0_16Parity ^ P_Parity;
    end
``` |
| continued | continued |

Error Detection and Correction (EDAC)

VHDL	Verilog
| ```
-----------------------------------------------------
-- Assign 22-bit memory write data
-- from 16-bit processor data and 6 bit parity.
-- No physical logic synthesized.
-----------------------------------------------------
PR_MemWriteData: process (P, ProcData)
begin
   MemWriteData(0)  <= P(0);
   MemWriteData(1)  <= P(1);
   MemWriteData(2)  <= ProcData(0);
   MemWriteData(3)  <= P(2);
   MemWriteData(4)  <= ProcData(1);
   MemWriteData(5)  <= ProcData(2);
   MemWriteData(6)  <= ProcData(3);
   MemWriteData(7)  <= P(3);
   MemWriteData(8)  <= ProcData(4);
   MemWriteData(9)  <= ProcData(5);
   MemWriteData(10) <= ProcData(6);
   MemWriteData(11) <= ProcData(7);
   MemWriteData(12) <= ProcData(8);
   MemWriteData(13) <= ProcData(9);
   MemWriteData(14) <= ProcData(10);
   MemWriteData(15) <= P(4);
   MemWriteData(16) <= ProcData(11);
   MemWriteData(17) <= ProcData(12);
   MemWriteData(18) <= ProcData(13);
   MemWriteData(19) <= ProcData(14);
   MemWriteData(20) <= ProcData(15);
   MemWriteData(21) <= P(5);
end process PR_MemWriteData;


------------------------------------------------
-- Generate syndrome
-- XOR of HAM code parity bits from memory
-- and actual parity bits from memory
------------------------------------------------
PR_GenSyndrome: process (ParityMemData(4 downto 0),
                         P(4 downto 0))
begin
   Syndrome(4 downto 0) <=ParityMemData(4 downto 0)
                      xor P(4 downto 0);
end process PR_GenSyndrome;


---------------------------
-- Detect error type
---------------------------
PR_GenErrorType: process (ReadWrite_b, Syndrome,
                          OverallParity)
begin
   if (ReadWrite_b = '1') then
      if (Syndrome = "00000" and OverallParity = '0') then
         ErrorType <= NoError;
      elsif (Syndrome /= "00000" and OverallParity = '1') then
         ErrorType <= SingleError;
      elsif (Syndrome /= "00000" and OverallParity = '0') then
         ErrorType <= DoubleError;
      else
         ErrorType <= OverallParityError;
      end if;
   else
      ErrorType <= NoError;
   end if;
end process PR_GenErrorType;
``` | ```
//-----------------------------------------------------
// Assign 22-bit memory write data
// from 16-bit processor data and 6 bit parity.
// No physical logic synthesized.
//-----------------------------------------------------
always @(P or ProcData)
   begin: BK_MemWriteData
      MemWriteData(0)  = P(0);
      MemWriteData(1)  = P(1);
      MemWriteData(2)  = ProcData(0);
      MemWriteData(3)  = P(2);
      MemWriteData(4)  = ProcData(1);
      MemWriteData(5)  = ProcData(2);
      MemWriteData(6)  = ProcData(3);
      MemWriteData(7)  = P(3);
      MemWriteData(8)  = ProcData(4);
      MemWriteData(9)  = ProcData(5);
      MemWriteData(10) = ProcData(6);
      MemWriteData(11) = ProcData(7);
      MemWriteData(12) = ProcData(8);
      MemWriteData(13) = ProcData(9);
      MemWriteData(14) = ProcData(10);
      MemWriteData(15) = P(4);
      MemWriteData(16) = ProcData(11);
      MemWriteData(17) = ProcData(12);
      MemWriteData(18) = ProcData(13);
      MemWriteData(19) = ProcData(14);
      MemWriteData(20) = ProcData(15);
      MemWriteData(21) = P(5);
   end

//------------------------------------------------
// Generate syndrome
// XOR of HAM code parity bits from memory
// and actual parity bits from memory
//------------------------------------------------
always @(ParityMemData(4:0) or P(4:0))
   begin: BK_GenSyndrome
      Syndrome(4:0) = ParityMemData(4:0) ^ P(4:0);
   end
``` |

> Although only bits and (4:0) are used, a slice e.g. P(4:0) in the event list may not be supported.

```
//---------------------------
// Detect error type
//---------------------------
always @(ReadWrite_b or Syndrome or OverallParity)
   begin: BK_GenErrorType
      if (ReadWrite_b == 1)
         if (Syndrome == 5'b 0 && OverallParity == 0)
            ErrorType = `NoError;
         else if (Syndrome != 5'b 0 && OverallParity == 1)
            ErrorType = `SingleError;
         else if (Syndrome != 5'b 0 && OverallParity == 0)
            ErrorType = `DoubleError;
         else
            ErrorType = `OverallParityError;
      else
         ErrorType = `NoError;
   end
```

continued　*continued*

Error Detection and Correction (EDAC)

VHDL	Verilog

```vhdl
--------------------------------------------------------
-- Decode syndrome
-- Input: Syndrome (Number representing bit error position)
-- Output: Decoded syndrome. (If any of 22-bits is 1 an
--            error has occured in that bit position)
--------------------------------------------------------

PR_DecodeSyndrome: process (Syndrome)
begin
    for N in 1 to 22 loop       -- N = bit position
        if (Syndrome = to_unsigned(N, 22)) then
            DecodeSyn(N - 1) <= '1';
        else
            DecodeSyn(N - 1) <= '0';
        end if;
    end loop;
end process PR_DecodeSyndrome;


---------------------------------------------
-- Correct any errors in 22-bit read data
-- and assign processor read bits.
---------------------------------------------
PR_CorrectErrors: process (MemData, DecodeSyn)
    variable CorrectedData: unsigned(21 downto 0);
begin
    CorrectedData      := MemData xor DecodeSyn;
    ProcReadData(0)    <= CorrectedData(2);
    ProcReadData(1)    <= CorrectedData(4);
    ProcReadData(2)    <= CorrectedData(5);
    ProcReadData(3)    <= CorrectedData(6);
    ProcReadData(4)    <= CorrectedData(8);
    ProcReadData(5)    <= CorrectedData(9);
    ProcReadData(6)    <= CorrectedData(10);
    ProcReadData(7)    <= CorrectedData(11);
    ProcReadData(8)    <= CorrectedData(12);
    ProcReadData(9)    <= CorrectedData(13);
    ProcReadData(10)   <= CorrectedData(14);
    ProcReadData(11)   <= CorrectedData(16);
    ProcReadData(12)   <= CorrectedData(17);
    ProcReadData(13)   <= CorrectedData(18);
    ProcReadData(14)   <= CorrectedData(19);
    ProcReadData(15)   <= CorrectedData(20);
end process PR_CorrectErrors;


---------------------------------------------
-- Assign microprocessor and memory
-- tri-state busses.
---------------------------------------------
ProcData <=  ProcReadData when ReadWrite_b = '1' else
             (others => 'Z');
MemData  <= MemWriteData when ReadWrite_b = '0' else
             (others => 'Z');

end architecture RTL;
```

```verilog
//--------------------------------------------------------
// Decode syndrome
// Input: Syndrome (Number representing bit error position)
// Output: Decoded syndrome. (If any of 22-bits is 1 an
//            error has occured in that bit position)
//--------------------------------------------------------
always @(Syndrome)
    begin: BK_DecodeSyndrome
        for (N = 1; N <= 22; N = N + 1)  // N = bit position
            if (Syndrome == N)
                DecodeSyn(N - 1) = 1;
            else
                DecodeSyn(N - 1) = 0;
    end


//---------------------------------------------
// Correct any errors in 22-bit read data
// and assign processor read bits.
//---------------------------------------------
always @(MemData or DecodeSyn)
    begin: BK_CorrectErrors
        CorrectedData = MemData ^ DecodeSyn;
        ProcReadData(0)    = CorrectedData(2);
        ProcReadData(1)    = CorrectedData(4);
        ProcReadData(2)    = CorrectedData(5);
        ProcReadData(3)    = CorrectedData(6);
        ProcReadData(4)    = CorrectedData(8);
        ProcReadData(5)    = CorrectedData(9);
        ProcReadData(6)    = CorrectedData(10);
        ProcReadData(7)    = CorrectedData(11);
        ProcReadData(8)    = CorrectedData(12);
        ProcReadData(9)    = CorrectedData(13);
        ProcReadData(10)   = CorrectedData(14);
        ProcReadData(11)   = CorrectedData(16);
        ProcReadData(12)   = CorrectedData(17);
        ProcReadData(13)   = CorrectedData(18);
        ProcReadData(14)   = CorrectedData(19);
        ProcReadData(15)   = CorrectedData(20);
    end


//---------------------------------------------
// Assign microprocessor and memory
// tri-state buses.
//---------------------------------------------
assign ProcData   = ReadWrite_b ? ProcReadData : 16'bZ;
assign MemData    = ReadWrite_b ? 22'bZ : MemWriteData;

endmodule
```

Glossary

aggregate (VHDL)

A set of comma-separated elements enclosed within parentheses. Either elements of a record or array type may be grouped to form an aggregate which has a single composite value. Individual elements of an aggregate may be specified using either named or positional notation.

algorithmic level (VHDL & Verilog)

The level at which an HDL model is described. It describes the functional behavior hardware in terms of signals and their response to various stimulus. Hardware behavior is described algorithmically and has no regard to how it will be implemented structurally and so is not synthesizable by RTL synthesis tools.

algorithmic level synthesis

The process of converting an HDL model described at the algorithmic level to either the RTL level, or all the way down to the gate level. It includes such processes as scheduling, resource allocation, resource binding, etc.

allocation

A process performed by a synthesis tool that assigns a particular operation in an HDL model to a piece of hardware.

See also resource allocation.

Application-Specific Integrated Circuit (ASIC)

A device (chip) whose initial stages of manufacture are design independent and the final photographic mask process is design dependent.

architecture body (VHDL)

One of the five design units defined by VHDL. It contains the internal functional description (behavior), of a block using one of the following modeling styles:

Structural	- a set of interconnected components
Dataflow	- a set of concurrent assignment statements
RTL	- a set of sequential assignment statements
Combined	- combination of the above three.

array types (VHDL)

An array type (or array subtype) is one of two forms of a composite type, a record type being the other. Objects declared as being of an array type contain a collection of elements that are of the same type. The array types may be constrained (fixed number of elements) or unconstrained (generic number of elements). Any unconstrained array types must be constrained as subtypes in synthesizable models.

```
-- constrained array type
type Bus8 is array (7 downto 0) of unsigned;
type ROM is array (0 to 31) of Bus8;
-- unconstrained array type
type FIFO_Type is array (Bus8 range <>);
```

A constrained subtype array can be declared, which is of an unconstrained base type, and so is also supported for synthesis.

```
-- constrained subtype array of an unconstrained base
-- type
type FIFO_Type is array (Bus8 range <>);
subtype FIFO_Type64 is FIFO_Type (0 to 63);
```

ASIC

See Application-Specific Integrated Circuit.

assertion violation (VHDL)

Describes when the condition in an assertion statement evaluates false.

association list (VHDL & Verilog)

VHDL. Provides the mapping between formal or local: generics, port or subprograms parameter names and local or actual names or expressions.

Verilog. The same VHDL principle applies to Verilog though is not normally referred to as an association list.

ATPG

See automatic test pattern generator.

attribute (VHDL)

Attributes a particular characteristic to a named item. There are five kinds: function, range, signal, type and value. An attribute can be attributed to one of five kinds of item: type (scalar, composite or file), array, signal (scalar or composite), or entity. There are 36 predefined attributes, 10 of which are typically supported for synthesis; see Appendix A.

automatic test pattern generator (APTG)

The automatic generation of manufacturing test vectors by a CAE software tool.

base type (VHDL)

All type and subtype declarations have a base type. The base type of a type declaration is the type itself while the base type of a subtype declaration is the type of the type declaration of which it is a subtype.

Backus-Naur (VHDL)

Refers to a semi-algebraic notation for documenting the syntax of a programming language. The VHDL Language Reference Manual uses this notation; see Appendix A.

behavior

How an HDL model operates (behaves) functionally. The behavior of a model should be the same regardless of the abstract level at which it is modeled, i.e. algorithmic, RTL, data flow, logic, or gate level.

binary representation

The way in which binary numbers, positive and negative, are represented. When a binary number is positive, the sign is represented by 0 in the most significant bit and the magnitude by a positive binary number in the remaining bits. When the number is negative, the sign is represented by 1 in the most significant bit, but the remaining bits may be represented in one of three possible ways: signed-magnitude, signed-1's complement or signed-2's complement.

(*See signed-magnitude, signed-1's complement and signed-2's complement*)

BIST

See Built-In Self-Test.

block statements (Verilog)

Used to group two or more statements together so that they act syntactically like a single statement. There are two types of block statement; the sequential block which is supported by synthesis and delimited by the keywords **begin** and **end**, and the parallel block which is not supported by synthesis and delimited by the keywords **fork** and **join**.

blocking procedural assignment (Verilog)

An assignment that must be executed before subsequent statements may be executed within the same procedural flow of statements in a sequential **begin-end** block. A blocking procedural assignment uses the delimiter "=".

```
#3  Y1 = A1 + B1;
#1  Y2 = A2 + B2;  // Y2 assigned after 4 time units
```

Two dependent blocking signal assignments in a sequential always block will synthesize to a single flip-flop, i.e.

```
always @(posedge Clock)
begin
    Sig1    = A & B;
    Y1      = Sig1 & C;  // single flip-flop inferred
end
```

boolean algebra

Mathematical equations representing combinational logic.

Built-In Self-Test (BIST)

The extra circuitry added to a circuit that enables the circuit to test itself.

CDFG

See control-data flow-graph.

cell

A logic function in the cell library defined by the manufacturer of an ASIC or FPGA.

cell library

The collective name for a set of logic functions defined by the manufacturer of an ASIC or FPGA. A cell library defines the type of cells that can be used in the design of a particular device for which the library applies. Simulation and synthesis tools will use the information in a cell library when simulating and synthesizing a design's model.

character literal (VHDL)

A single ASCII symbol enclosed in single quotes ('). They are case sensitive, that is, 'Y' is not the same as 'y' despite VHDL being case insensitive to object names.

checksum

The final cyclic-redundant check value stored in a linear-feedback shift-register (or its software equivalent). Also known as a "signature" in functional test applications.

comment (VHDL & Verilog)

Phrases or sentences that are used within a model's code purely for documentation purposes. They make a model clearer and easier to read and are ignored by design tool compilers reading them unless it is a comment directive.

VHDL. Comments start with a double dash (--) on a per line basis. Any text appearing after the double dash, and the end of the line, is ignored by a compiler.

```
-- This is a comment
Y <= A + B;  -- This is a comment at the end of a line
```

Verilog. Comments can start with a double slash (//) on a per line basis like VHDL. Alternatively they can start with slash-star (/*) and carry over to multiple lines and ended with star-slash (*/).

```
/* This is a
   comment that crosses
   several lines */
// This is a comment
Y <= A + B;  // This is a comment at the end of a line
```

(*See also comment directive*)

comment directive (VHDL & Verilog)

Standard comments that are recognized by a particular design tool, or tools, in order to direct it how a certain statement, or statements, should be interpreted. For example, synthesis tools will typically recognize certain comments as directives to implement a carry-look-ahead or ripple-carry type adder.

```
Y <= A + B;  --$ RPL (Ripple carry adder - VHDL)
Y = A + B;   //$ RPL (Ripple carry adder - Verilog)
```

compiled simulation

A type of simulation where a model is compiled prior to being simulated; the other form of simulation is interpreted simulation. The compilation process means it takes longer for a simulator to prepare a model (build) ready for simulation, but means the simulation run time is faster than interpreted simulation.

(*See also interpreted simulation*)

complement numbers

See signed one's complement and signed two's complement.

component declaration (VHDL)

Declares both the name and the interface of a component. The interface specifies the mode and the type of parts. Component declarations are not necessary in Verilog.

composite type (VHDL)

A data type that is composed of elements of a single type and which are grouped together under a single identifier. The elements may be of a single type (an array type) or different types (a record type).

concatenation (VHDL & Verilog)

The combination of two or more elements into one larger element. VHDL elements include identifiers, arrays, etc., while Verilog elements are of any of the net data types (e.g. **wire**) or of type **reg**.

```
Y <= A & B;  -- VHDL concatenation
Y = {A,B};   // Verilog concatenation
```

concurrent statements (VHDL & Verilog)

Statements that are executed in parallel and so their textual order within a model has no effect on the implied behavior.

configuration declaration (VHDL)

Provides a means of deferring the binding of architecture bodies, and any components in the structural hierarchy of that architecture, to an entity.

configuration specification (VHDL)

Used to bind component instances to specific design entities.

constant declaration (VHDL)

One of four kinds of data object (signal, variable and file being the other three), that are declared to have a fixed value that cannot be changed by any statement during simulation or synthesis.
(*See also deferred constant*).

constraints

The desired area, speed and possibly power performance characteristics used by a synthesis tool during any level of optimization.

continuous assignment (VHDL & Verilog)

Assignments that are always driven during simulation.

VHDL. The syntax of continuous and conditional assignments are the same.

Verilog. The syntax of continuous assignments differ from procedural assignments in that they are preceded by the reserved word **assign**.

```
assign Y = A & B;
```

Control-Data Flow-Graph (CDFG)

A synthesis internally compiled graphical representation of a design. A control-data flow-graph represents design behavior and not circuit structure. Both algorithmic and RTL synthesis tools may use a control-data flow-graph technique. Algorithmic synthesis tools manipulate control-data flow-graphs when performing scheduling, allocation and high-level structural partitioning, etc.

control path

The path of intermediate control signals through control logic used to provide necessary control signals to a data path.

data object (VHDL & Verilog)

A place holder for holding data values of a specific type in an HDL model. A data object is created using an object declaration.

VHDL. There are four specific kinds of object; constant, variable, signal or file, and must be of a specific type; for example, integer, unsigned, etc.

Verilog. Data objects are any of the net data types (**wire**, **tri**, **wand**, etc.), **parameter**, register (**reg**) or **integer**.

data path

The path through which information (data) is processed through a circuit. A data path normally refers to the path through successive blocks of combinational and sequential logic, though can also mean the path through blocks of combinational logic only.

delta delay (VHDL)

The delay between two simulation cycles that occur at the same simulation time.
(*See also iteration*).

DeMorgan transformation

The transformation of boolean expressions, representing boolean logic, into an alternative, and often more convenient, form. For example, the boolean equation:

$$y = (a + b + c)$$

is transformed to:

$$y = (\overline{\overline{a}.\overline{b}.\overline{c}})$$

This technique is used extensively during logic optimization.

design constraints

See constraints.

design for test

Design for test (DFT) is the process of designing and adding extra hardware in an HDL model or its associated synthesized circuit for the purposes of improving the ability of manufacturing test vectors to stimulate all circuit nodes and monitor potential manufactured chip defects.

design unit (VHDL)

Any set of constructs that may be independently analyzed and inserted into a design library. The VHDL design units that may be declared are:

> entity
> architecture
> configuration
> package
> package body

DFT

See design for test.

discrete type (VHDL)

A discrete type is a data type whose elements consist of a one dimensional array, that is, an enumerated type or an array type.

driver (VHDL & Verilog)

Contains the projected output waveform for a data object. A data object can have multiple assignments which can each schedule values to be assigned an object at different simulation times. Each scheduled value is a driver.

dynamically reconfigurable hardware

A circuit, that when implemented in a chip, can be customized "on-the-fly" while remaining resident in the system. An example is a single circuit that can perform multiplication, division, addition or subtraction dynamically as needed.

elaboration (VHDL & Verilog)

A stage performed by a simulator or synthesizer when an HDL model is compiled. Elaboration consists of:
- expanding and linking the separately analyzed units, if any, and building the design hierarchy.
- allocating storage for the object's values etc. (simulation only).
- any other local specific preparation required for simulation or synthesis.

element

The constituent port of a type. This means the element of an array or record type (VHDL) or a vector or memory type (Verilog).

enumeration literal (VHDL)

One of the individual values of an enumeration type.

```
-- contains three enumeration literals Red, Green and
-- Blue
type Color is (Red, Green, Blue);
```

equation flattening

A logic optimization process that takes a group of hierarchical sum of product equations and merges them together. Generally, the process is constrained to avoid what is known as *combinational explosion*.

equivalent gates

The term "equivalent gates" is used as a guide to compare the size of circuits. The size of an equivalent gate is referenced to the size of a two input NAND gate. A two input NAND gate is normalized to the equivalent of one equivalent gate and all other cells in the library are given an equivalent gate size with reference to the two input NAND gate. A circuit's total equivalent gate size is the parameter often used by a synthesizer when performing gate-level area optimization.

event (VHDL & Verilog)

Refers to a change in a signals value in terms of simulation.

event scheduling

When a signal assignment contains a delay the assigned signal value is scheduled to occur at some simulation time in the future. This process is called *scheduling an event.*

```
Y <= A and B after 2ns;   -- VHDL
Y = #2 (A & B);           // Verilog
```

execute

To execute means to evaluate assignment statements in an HDL model.

expression (VHDL & Verilog)

The mathematical formula on the right hand side of an assignment statement, that is, after the assignment operator.

factorization

A process performed by a logic optimizer that identifies and removes one or more common factors from a set of one or more boolean equations to form a multilevel set of equations. The equations represent logic, so factorization means the sharing of logic which will reduce area. This area reduction may be at the expense of increasing the delay through the logic since the depth of logic from the input to output is increased. Factorization of the following two boolean equations produces four equations as shown.

```
y1 = a.b.c + a.b.d      n = c + d
y2 = a.b + c + d        m = a.d
                        y1 = n.m
                        y2 = n + m
```

fan-in

The input capacitance on the input to a cell as seen by the driving source of that signal.

fan-out

The output capacitance seen by the output driver from a cell.

Field Programmable Gate Array (FPGA)

A programmable logic device (chip) that can be programmed in the field for a particular application. All chip manufacturing processes are independent of the particular circuit being implemented, so it is more generic and cheaper than standard cell devices. Logic gates are laid out in a fixed and structured way on the silicon. This means circuit density will not be as high as standard cell devices.

(*See also gate array and standard cell*)

finite state machine

See state machine.

flip-flop

An edge-sensitive memory device (cell).

floorplan

This is the area on a silicon chip not including the input, output and bidirectional buffers around its periphery.

formal verification

A method of mathematically verifying the logic synthesized from a hardware model. Formal verification is the process of building an internal mathematical model of logic contained in an HDL model and comparing it with the actual synthesized logic using specialized algorithms. Especially useful in the verification of large complex systems where excessive functional verification vectors would be needed using a simulation verification technique.

FPGA

See Field Programmable Gate Array.

full scan

Where every flip-flop and latch in a design is transposed to being a scan type flip-flop or latch in order to improve the accessibility of internal nodes to manufacturing test vectors and the observability of nodes for monitoring possible manufacturing defects. Full scan makes writing manufacturing test vectors considerably shorter and easier to generate than if partial or no scan was used. Full scan manufacturing test vectors are easily generated automatically by test synthesis tools. The reduced number of test vectors, compared to those needed with no scan or partial scan, means the important test cycle per chip is shortened. In many cases full scan can be overly expensive in terms of extra area on the silicon chip.

function (VHDL & Verilog)

One of the two kinds of subprogram that is common to both VHDL and Verilog. A function can: only model combinational logic, must have a least one input, must not contain timing and returns a single value. Functions are called from operands within an expression. The function call operand is substituted with the returned value from the function.

functional test vectors

The input stimuli used during simulation to verify an HDL model operates functionally as intended.

gate array

An application-specific integrated circuit in which the manufacturer prefabricates uncustomized devices containing arrays of unconnected basic cells organized in groups. A designer specifies the function of the device in terms of cells from a cell library and their interconnection. The manufacturer then customizes the device by generating the masks used to create the metallization layers which form the interconnections.

gray code

A sequence of binary values where adjacent values change by only one bit; for example, 00, 01, 11, 10.

gate level

A low-level behavioral model of a circuit described in terms of gate primitives from a technology specific library, or possibly from some generic technology independent library of gates.

gate level optimization

Optimization performed on the model of a circuit described at the gate level.

generic (VHDL)

Used to pass static information of a particular type to any of the following. A generic is determinable at elaboration time.

- an entity declaration,
- a component declaration,
- a component instantiation,
- a configuration specification or
- a configuration declaration.

Generics are commonly used in synthesizable models to parameterize bus widths.

glue logic

Logic used to interface more complex circuits together.

Hardware Description Language (HDL)

A software computer language used for the purposes of modeling hardware circuits.

HDL

See Hardware Description Language.

heuristic

In general computing terms, this means proceeding to a solution by trial and error. Specifically, it relates to a logic optimizer's trial and error method of using different algorithms to iteratively improve a circuits structure in order to optimally fit desired specified constraints.

host environment

The computer and its resident CAE design tools. Used to design and store HDL models in system files and to store all appropriate compiled files.

identifier (VHDL & Verilog)

Used to give a name to a data object so that it may be easily referenced in an HDL model.

Identifiers consist of a continuous (contains no spaces) sequence of letters, numbers and underscores (_), and additionally for Verilog the dollar sign ($).

VHDL is not case sensitive so "ENABLE" and "enable" are regarded as being the same identifier; they are different in Verilog as it is case sensitive.

iteration

One of several delta cycles, or one cycle of an iterative statement.

iterative statement (VHDL & Verilog)

A repetitively executed statement. The loop statement (**for**) is the only statement that allows the repeated execution of a sequence of statements.

interpreted simulation

A type of simulation where a model's HDL code is directly simulated by the simulator, i.e., it is interpreted line by line during simulation. (The other form of simulation is compiled simulation.) Interpreted simulation prepares a model (builds) for simulation very fast, but then simulation run times will be longer.
(*See also compiled simulation*)

Johnson state encoding

A state encoding format for a state machine where only one bit changes between successive state values in a pattern of consecutive 1s and 0s from left to right.

                0000
                0001
                0011
                0111
                1111
                1110
                1100
                1000

Karnaugh map

Graphical means to represent and minimize a boolean equation.

latch

A level sensitive memory device (cell).

leaf cell

The lowest level hierarchical structure of a circuit that is decomposed by a particular CAE tool. For simulation and synthesis tools, leaf cells are the cells in an ASIC or FPGA technology specific library.

lexical element (VHDL & Verilog)

An individual item of text in an HDL model that is separated by a space or spaces.

LFSR

See Linear Feedback Shift Register.

library (VHDL)

This is a VHDL design library and facilitates the storage of analyzed VHDL design units. Design libraries are classified into two groups: working libraries and resource libraries. The working library is the library in which compiled design units are placed. There is only one working library during the compilation of a design. The resource library is a library that is referenced within a design unit when that design unit is compiled. Any number of resource libraries can be referenced from a design unit.

Linear Feedback Shift Register (LFSR)

A register with either XOR or XNOR feedback logic around it in such a way that causes it to pseudo-randomly sequence through up to 2^n values, where n is the number of bits in the register. Often used in BIST techniques.

literal (VHDL & Verilog)

A lexical element that represents itself in VHDL, Verilog or a boolean equation. In VHDL it can be a number, character or string; in Verilog it is simply a number. In a boolean equation a literal is a variable in either its true or false condition.

logic optimization

Covers the steps of conventional multilevel minimization, factorization and equation flattening in such way that fits area, timing and possibly power requirements (constraints) in the most optimal manner.
(*See also optimization*)

logic synthesis

The process of optimizing boolean equations at the logic level, mapping them to a technology specific library of cells and then optimizing at the gate level using timing and area information from the cells in the technology library.

LRM (VHDL & Verilog)

See Language Reference Manual.

Language Reference Manual (LRM)

The IEEE standardized manual defining the hardware description language for VHDL (IEEE 1076-1993) or Verilog (IEEE 1364-1995).

macro cell

Intermediately sized cells such as adders, comparators, counters, decoders etc.
(*See also cell, primitive and mega cell*)

385

manufacturing test vectors

The exhaustive input stimuli used to test the physically manufactured chips and which are designed to test and detect as near to 100% of the chip as practically possible.

maxterm

A boolean product in a boolean product-of-sum expression. A maxterm is represented by the boolean OR of all input signals,

e.g., (a or b or c).

mega cell

Large sized cells such as microprocessors and micro-controllers, etc.

(*See also cell, primitive and macro cell*)

memory declaration (Verilog)

Declares a group (array) of register variables which are used to model read only memories (ROMs), random access memories (RAMs) or simply an array of registers. Each element in such an array is addressed by a single array index.

reg [7:0] MemA [0:255];

minimization

A process of minimizing the numbers of literals in one or more boolean equations. Single output minimization relates to Karnaugh maps where the aim is to simplify and reduce the number of product terms in a single equation. This is also known as flat minimization as only one equation is minimized at a time. Minimization typically performed by a logic optimizer uses multilevel (multiple equations), multi-output minimization in order to achieve global minimization of a combinational logic function. Multilevel minimization includes logic (equation) flattening.

minterm

A boolean sum in a boolean sum-of-products expression. A minterm is represented by the boolean AND of all inverted input signals,

e.g., ($\overline{a}.\overline{b}.\overline{c}$) where "." is the boolean AND.

named association (VHDL & Verilog)

An association is considered named when an association element is matched by name from the actual port to the formal port.

VHDL.
```
ALU2: ALU port map (Operand2  => A(15 downto 8),
                    Operator   => Control(5 downto 3),
                    Result     => Y(15 downto 8),
                    Operand1   => B(15 downto 8));
```
Verilog.
```
ALU ALU2(.Operand2(A[15:8]),
         .Operator(Control[5:3]),
         .Result(Y[15:8]), .Operand1(B[15:8]));
```

net data type (Verilog)

Used to represent the physical connection of inferred hardware elements in a structural manner. The different kinds of net data types are: **wire, tri, wand, triand, trireg, tri0, tri1, supply0** and **supply1**. Not all net data types are supported by synthesis tools.

wire Net1, Net2;

netlist

A file containing the representation of a design at the cell level in VHDL, Verilog or EDIF, etc. The cell level is also the gate level if all cells are gate level cells. A netlist file contains a list of cells, usually from a technology specific library, and identifies how the cells are interconnected.

non-blocking procedural assignment (Verilog)

Non-blocking procedural assignment statements are found in a sequential **begin-end** block and use the assignment operator "<=". They are scheduled to occur without blocking the procedural flow from one statement to the next. Such assignments are used where more than one register assignment is required without regard to their order. In the example below, the addition in the first assignment is computed immediately and the assignment is scheduled for 3 time units later. This allows the second assignment to be executed independently of the first.

```
#3  Y1 <= A1 + B1;
#1  Y2 <= A2 + B2;  // Y2 assigned after 1 time unit
```

Two dependent non-blocking procedural assignments in a sequential **always** block will synthesize to two flip-flops, i.e.

```
always @(posedge Clock)
    begin
        Sig1    <= A & B;      // First flip-flop inferred
        Y1      <= Sig1 & C;   // Second flip-flop inferred
    end
```

object (VHDL & Verilog)

An object is a place holder for storing values in an HDL model.

(*See also data object*)

one's complement

See signed-1's complement.

optimization

A general term used to describe the process of improving the structural configuration of a circuit model given certain area, timing and possibly power constraints.

(*See also logic level optimization and gate level optimization*)

overloading (VHDL)

Describes the process of using the same name for two or more subprograms. If they have the same scope they are differentiated by having different enumeration literals or a different subprogram type (**function** or **procedure**).

```
type rainbow is (Red, Orange, Yellow, Green, Blue,
                 Indigo, Violet);
type rainbow is (Yellow, Magenta, Cyan, Indigo, Violet);
```

package (VHDL)

Provides a convenient means of grouping multiple declarations so that they are accessible across many design units. A package consists of a **package** declaration and an optional **package body**. A **package** declaration contains a set of declarations, for example types, constants and subprograms. In contrast, a **package body** contains the hidden details of a package, for example the bodies of subprograms.

parallel block statement (Verilog)

Uses the reserved words **fork** and **join** to group a series of statements that are to be executed concurrently. Control does not pass out of the block until the last time ordered statement has executed. It is not supported by synthesis tools.

parameter declaration (Verilog)

A declaration is used to declare a constant.

parameter Width = 16;

partial scan

A circuit where only a selection of flip-flops and latches are transposed to being scan type flip-flops or latches in order to improve the accessibility of specific internal nodes to manufacturing test vectors and the observability of specific internal nodes for the observability of possible manufacturing defects. Partial scan is a compromise between using full scan and keeping area to a practical minimum.

partitioning

The process of dividing a design into smaller pieces, either through the HDL code design of concurrent hardware modules or, by using a synthesis tool to automatically partition a flattened netlist.

physical synthesis

The process of taking a technology specific netlist of gates and physically laying them out on the floor plan of the chip. Typical processes include: partitioning, cell compaction, layout compaction, floor-planning, placement and routing. Physical synthesis is regarded as a back-end process normally performed by the chip vendor.

port (VHDL & Verilog)

VHDL. The word **port** in VHDL is a reserved word and defines the communication signals between interfacing sections of code. Each port has a name, a mode and type. The modes are:

in	- input only port
out	- output only port
inout	- bidirectional port
buffer	- bidirectional port that can only have one source and that can only be connected to another port signal of type buffer
linkage	- no defined semantics

Verilog. The word "port" is not a Verilog reserved word, but is a term often used to refer to the interconnection of modules, primitives and macro modules. Each **module** has ports declared in its body as follows:

input	- input only port
output	- output only port
inout	- bidirectional port

positional notation/positional association (VHDL & Verilog)

One of two ways of associating an actual port to a corresponding formal port without explicitly specifying which actual port matches a corresponding formal port. The association is made by the position of each element.

VHDL.

ALU1: ALU **port map** (Control(2 **downto** 0), A(7 **downto** 0), B(7 **downto** 0), Y(7 **downto** 0));

Verilog.

ALU ALU1(Control[2:0], A[7:0], B[7:0], Y[7:0]);

primitives

Simple logic gates such as BUF, NOT, AND, NAND, OR, NOR, XOR and XNOR plus flip-flops and latches. Such primitives are normally cells found in an ASIC or FPGA technology specific library.

procedural assignment (Verilog)

Assignments that are updated under the control of the procedural flow of constructs that surround them.

procedure (VHDL)

One of two kinds of VHDL subprogram; function being the other. Like the Verilog **task**, a **procedure** can contain timing, can enable other subprograms and can compute zero or more values. A VHDL **procedure** can be called concurrently as well as sequentially.

process (VHDL)

Is a passive or persistent concurrent statement. A passive process contains no signal assignment statement or any signal assignments in a called procedure and may appear in any **entity** declaration, but is not supported for synthesis. A persistent process is the more common type of process containing sequential statements. Once a persistent process has been elaborated, it exists for the duration of a simulation run.

propagation delay

The delay of a signal passing from one point in a circuit to another. A propagation delay may be: a delay passing along a wire in the physical circuit on the chip, the delay of a signal being passed through a cell, or the total delay through multiple cells and their associated wires. Propagation delays are determined by cell drive capability and capacitive loading. Capacitive loading consists of the input capacitances of cells connected to the drive cell and the total capacitance on the interconnecting wire network.

387

pseudo-random
A sequence of values that give the appearance of being random, but which is deterministic and hence repeatable.

Read Muller logic
Logic functions that are implemented using only XOR and XNOR gates, for example as used in the feedback path around registers in LFSRs.

reconfigurable hardware
Hardware designed to be used in many different ways.

record type (VHDL)
A composite type consisting of named elements.
```
type FloatPointType is
    record
        Sign: std_logic;
        Exponent: unsigned(23 downto 0);
        Fraction: unsigned(6 downto 0);
    end record;
```

reduction operator (Verilog)
An operator that operates on all bits of a multiple bit bus and that produces a single bit result. For example,
```
...
reg [5:0]A;
reg Y;
...
Y = & A;
```

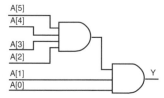

register
A memory device containing more than one latch or flip-flop that are all clocked from the same clock signal.

register (reg) data type (Verilog)
A data type used for the declaration of objects that need to hold their value over simulation cycles. They are used to describe objects that are assigned using blocking and non-blocking procedural assignments. A register data type should not be confused with a hardware register. The reserved word **reg** is used to signify a register data type.
```
reg Y;
reg [7:0] Bus1, Bus2;
```

Register Transfer Level
The model of a circuit described in a hardware description language that infers memory devices.

resource allocation
A process performed by algorithmic (high-level) synthesis tools which assigns each operational part of a design to a particular piece of hardware.

resource sharing
A process performed by RTL synthesis tools that allows specific circuit functions (resources) to be shared. For instance, if two independent additions are required in a circuit, and they do not need to be performed at the same time, the same physical adder could be used and the inputs to it, and outputs from it, multiplexed accordingly. This operation is performed automatically by synthesis as directed by the user.

reserved word (VHDL & Verilog)
A word that has been defined by the HDL language to have specific meaning and so cannot be used as basic identifiers. Certain characters such as the semicolon and parentheses could also be classified as reserved words. (All reserved words in the models and text of this book are shown emboldened.)

RTL synthesis
The process of converting an HDL model described at the register transfer level (RTL), to the logic level, and then to the gate level, performing combinational logic optimization at each stage. Register transfer level synthesis does not optimize (add or remove) registers. The definition of RTL synthesis encompasses logic level synthesis, logic level optimization and gate level optimization.

resolved signal (VHDL)
A signal whose type has an associated resolution function.

rol (VHDL)
Language defined rotate left operator.

ror (VHDL)
Language defined rotate right operator.

RTL
See Register Transfer Level.

scheduling
A process performed by algorithmic (high-level) synthesis tools which assigns each operational part of a design to a particular time step (clock cycle).

scope (VHDL & Verilog)
Refers to the region of code where a declaration has effect.

SDF
See Standard Delay Format.

sea-of-cells
Popular name for a channel-less gate array.

sea-of-gates
Popular name for a channel-less gate array.

388

semantics (VHDL & Verilog)

The rules that determine the meaning of language constructs as they relate to the description of hardware.

```
signal A:    unsigned(4 downto 0);
signal B:    unsigned(3 downto 0);
signal C:    unsigned(0 to 15);
signal Y:    unsigned(3 downto 0);
...
Y <= A;      -- correct syntax, incorrect semantics
Y <= B;      -- correct syntax, correct semantics
Y <= C;      -- correct syntax, incorrect semantics
```

separators (VHDL & Verilog)

Characters that separate lexical elements. Such characters are the space and end of line character, and non-printable characters such as: tab, line feed, form feed and carriage return.

sequential block statement (Verilog)

Groups a series of statements (blocking or non-blocking) between the reserved words **begin** and **end** such that they are executed one after the another in sequence. Control does not pass out of the block until the last statement has been executed. Sequential block statements are supported by synthesis tools and used extensively in synthesizable models.

sequential statements (VHDL & Verilog)

Statements that are executed in the order in which they are encountered.

VHDL. Statements within a **process** or **procedure**.
Verilog. Statements within a **begin-end** block.

signal (VHDL) & variable (Verilog)

A data object that has a current value and scheduled future values at future simulation times. In RTL synthesizable models they have direct hardware intent.

VHDL.	*Verilog.*
Y <= A;	Y = A;
Y <= A **after** 3.5 ns;	Y = #3.5 A;

In the second assignment the value of Y is calculated immediately and then assigned 3.5 ns later.

signed

Data objects whose value can be positive, 0 or negative.

signed-1's complement

One of three ways of representing binary numbers. Signed-1's complement is represented with a sign bit, followed by the magnitude with all bits, including the sign bit, complemented.
(*See also signed-magnitude and signed-2's complement*)

signed-2's complement

One of three ways of representing binary numbers. Signed-2's complement is represented with a sign bit, followed by the magnitude with all bits, including the sign bit, complemented and 1 added to the result.
(*See also signed-magnitude and signed 1's complement*)

signed-magnitude

One of three ways of representing binary numbers. Signed-magnitude is represented with a sign bit (0 for positive, 1 for negative), followed by the magnitude of the number.
(*See also signed 1's complement and signed 2's complement*)

skew

The difference in the time it takes a signal's transitions to travel from a single source point in a circuit to different destination points.

sla (VHDL)

Language defined shift left arithmetic operator.

slice (VHDL & Verilog)

Designates a portion of a one dimensional array that is created from another one dimensional array.

VHDL.

```
type FloatPoint is unsigned(31 downto 0);
Sign <= FloatPoint(31);  -- 1 bit slice
Exponent <= FloatPoint(30 downto 7];  -- 24 bit slice
Fraction <= FloatPoint(6 downto 0);  -- 7 bit slice
```

Verilog.

```
reg (31:0) FloatPoint;
Sign = FloatPoint;  // 1 bit slice
Exponent <= FloatPoint[30:7];  // 24 bit slice
Fraction <= FloatPoint[6:0];  // 7 bit slice
```

sll (VHDL)

Language defined shift left logical operator.

source code (VHDL & Verilog)

The HDL constructs that together constitute a model of hardware behavior and that is stored in a system file on the resident computer.

specification (VHDL)

Provides additional information associated with a model's description. There are three types: attribute, configuration and disconnection.

sra (VHDL)

Language defined shift right arithmetic operator.

srl (VHDL)

Language defined shift right logical operator.

standard cell

An application specific integrated circuit which, unlike a gate array, does not use the concept of a basic cell and does not have any prefabricated components, A chip manufacturer creates custom masks for every stage of the device's fabrication. This allows each function to be created using the minimum number of transistors in a more efficient layout than field programmable gate arrays.

Standard Delay Format

Standard Delay Format (SDF) is an industry standard notation for a file format. This format is used for the exchange of a circuits timing delay and constraint data between different tools. An IEEE group is working towards final standardization of SDF.

state assignment

The process of assigning states in a state machine to binary numbers used in the implementation of a state machine.

state diagram

A graphical representation of the operation of a state machine.

state machine

The model of a circuit, or its hardware implementation, that cycles through a predefined sequence of operations (states).

state table

The tabular representation of a state machine listing input, next state, current state and output values.

structural level (VHDL & Verilog)

The level at which an HDL model describes hardware as an arrangement of interconnected components.

subprogram (VHDL & Verilog)

VHDL subprograms are the **procedure** and **function** while Verilog subprograms are the **task** and **function**. The use of subprograms decomposes (portions) a design into models that are easier to read and maintain.

subtype (VHDL)

A subtype is a type with a constraint. The constraint specifies the subset of values of the base type for the subtype.

syntax

The syntax of an HDL model refers to the formal rules of how an HDL model should be constructed. The syntax specifies how constructs such as declarations and statements should be written. A VHDL or Verilog compiler will generate error messages if discrepancies are found.

```
Y <_ A + B    -- VHDL syntax incorrect, missing ";"
Y = A + B     -- VHDL syntax incorrect, "=" not valid for a
                 signal or variable
Y <= A + B    -- Verilog syntax incorrect, missing ";"
```

synthesis

A general term used to describe the process of converting the model of a design described in an HDL from one behavioral level of abstraction to a lower, more detailed, behavioral level.
(*See Algorithmic synthesis, RTL synthesis and logic synthesis*)

synthesis subset (VHDL or Verilog)

A subset of HDL constructs (VHDL or Verilog) that are supported for use with a particular synthesis tool.

technology library

A library of cells that are available for use in a particular type of ASIC or FPGA device.

technology mapping

The process of converting boolean logic equations into a netlist of logic gates from an ASIC of FPGA library.

test bench

See test harness.

test harness

Also known as a test bench in the VHDL world and a test fixture in Verilog. A test harness is an HDL model used to verify the correct behavior of a hardware model. Normally written in the same HDL language as the hardware model being tested. A test harness will:

- instantiate one or more instances of the hardware model under test,
- generate simulation input stimuli (test vectors) for the model under test,
- apply this input stimuli to the model under test and collate output responses (output vectors)
- compare output responses with expected values and possibly automatically give a pass or fail indication.

test fixture

See test harness.

test vectors

See functional test vectors and manufacturing test vectors.

test synthesis

The modification of circuits to make them more testable and the automatic generation of test vectors. Examples of how circuits can be modified include boundary scan, full or partial internal scan and built in self test (BIST) techniques.

timestep (VHDL & Verilog)

The unit of time corresponding to the smallest time increment in a simulator. A Verilog model can specify this simulation time by using the language defined compiler directive `timescale, e.g.
```
`timescale 1ns/1ps
```
where:

1ns is the unit of measurement for time and delay

1ps is the precision of time in the simulator

A VHDL simulator may provide a means whereby a model can specify a simulation time unit, but this is not part of the language.

transaction (VHDL)

Identifies a value to appear on a signal along with the time at which the value is to appear. This principle applies equally to VHDL and Verilog as shown, but the word "transaction" is normally only associated with VHDL models.

```
Y <= A after 10 ns;     -- VHDL transaction scheduled after 10 ns
Y = #10 A;              // Verilog equivalent of the VHDL transaction
```

tri-state

An HDL data object that is in its high-impedance (Z) state. This means it is not being driven. For VHDL this assumes the data object has at least three values, {0, 1, Z}.

tri-state buffer

A cell primitive whose output can adopt one of three states: logic 0, logic 1 and high-impedance (Z). The high-impedance state can be considered disconnected allowing other tri-state buffers to drive the same circuit node.

truth table

A convenient means of representing the operation of circuits as columns of input values and their corresponding output responses. The function of combinational logic and single level sequential logic circuits are often represented using truth tables, especially in ASIC and FPGA vendor technology library books.

two's complement

See signed-2's complement.

type (VHDL)

A type declaration defines all values that objects of that type can take. Objects of a particular type must be one of four kinds: constant, signal, variable or file.

```
-- From package Numeric_STD
type unsigned is array (natural range <>) of std_logic;
type op_code is (Inc, Dec, Load, Store, Shift, Add);
```

unconstrained array type (VHDL)

An array type in which the type of the indices are specified, but whose range is not. The box symbol "<>" is used in place of specifying the range. In this way many arrays of the same type, but with a different range may be declared. The range can be specified when a subtype is declared (supported for synthesis), or when an object of the type is declared (not supported for synthesis). Objects of an unconstrained array type may be passed to and from subprograms.

```
-- The "<>" symbol is called "box".
type DataWordWidth is array (0 to 31) of unsigned;
type FIFO_buffer_type is array (integer range <>) of
DataWordWidth;
-- Subtype defining range
subtype FIFO_buffer is FIFO_buffer_type (0 to 127);
-- Object defining range
variable FIFI_1: FIFO_buffer_type (0 to 127);
```

unsigned

Data objects whose value can only be positive or 0.

variable (VHDL)

A class of data object that only has a current value associated with it and that is changed in a variable assignment statement using the delimiter "=:". It has no history and so only holds its current value across simulation time steps, and not any scheduled values.

VeriBest Synthesis

The synthesis tool suite supplied by VeriBest Incorporated.

VHDL

VHSIC Hardware Description Language used to describe discrete hardware systems.

VHDL Initiative Toward ASIC Libraries

Normally abbreviated VITAL, this is an industry consortium for the purpose of generating a standard for writing models of the cells in a technology library which can be used with VHDL. This standard has been adpoted by the IEEE as IEEE 1076.4.

VHSIC

Very High Speed Integrated Circuit. A program of the United States Department of Defense from which the VHDL language derived.

visible (VHDL & Verilog)

Refers to the region of code where a declaration is visible.

VITAL

See VHDL Initiative Toward ASIC Libraries.

wire (Verilog)

A Verilog net data type used to declare objects that are to be driven by a single driver or from a continuous assignment. Like the register (**reg**) and **parameter** data types, they are four valued {0, 1, X, and Z}.

APPENDIX

A

VHDL

Appendix A Contents

Reserved Words

The following identifiers are reserved words in the VHDL language and so cannot be used as basic identifiers in a VHDL model. A reserved word is a keyword that has specific meaning in the language.

VHDL Reserved Words				
abs	else	map	register ‡	variable
access ‡	elsif	mod	reject Δ ‡	wait
after ‡	end		rem	when
alias ‡	entity	nand	report ‡	while
all ‡	exit	new ‡	return	with ‡
and		next	rol Δ	
architecture	file ‡	nor	ror Δ	xnor Δ
array	for	not		xor
assert ‡	function	null	select ‡	
attribute			severity ‡	
	generate	of	shared Δ ‡	
begin	generic	on ‡	signal	
block	group Δ	open ‡	sla Δ	
body	guarded ‡	or	sll Δ	
buffer		others	sra Δ	
bus ‡	if	out	srl Δ	
	impure Δ ‡		subtype	
case	in	package		
component	inertial Δ ‡	port	then	
configuration	inout	postponed Δ ‡	to	
constant	is	procedure	transport ‡	
		process	type	
disconnect ‡	label ‡	pure Δ ‡		
downto	library		unaffected Δ ‡	
	linkage ‡	range	units ‡	
	literal Δ	record	until	
	loop		use	

‡ Constructs not supported by synthesis tools.
Δ Constructs in the current version of the VHDL language, IEEE 1076 '93, and that are not in the old version of VHDL language, IEEE 1076 '87.

Predefined Attributes

An attribute is a value, function, type, range, signal or constant that can be associated (attributed) with certain names within a VHDL model. These names could be among others, an entity name, an architecture name, a label or a signal. The VHDL language has predefined attributes that may be attributed to various names. These attributes are listed in Table A.1, using the following notations.

1. **Type.** The type of entity to which the attribute is attributed.

Type	-	An attribute of a type (Denoted by T')
Array	-	An attribute of an array object (Denoted by A')
Signal	-	An attribute of a signal object (Denoted by S')
Entity	-	An attribute of an entity (Denoted by E')

2. **Kind.** The attribute "kind", which can be:

Value	-	attributes that returns a constant value.
Type	-	attributes that returns a type value.
Range	-	attributes that returns a range.
Function	-	attributes that calls a function which returns a value.
Signal	-	attributes that creates a new signal

3. **Prefix.** The object or "prefix" to which the attribute is attributed.

T1	-	Any type or subtype T
T2	-	Any scalar type or subtype T
T3	-	Any discrete or physical type or subtype T
A	-	Any array object or alias thereof, or a constrained array subtype.
S	-	Any signal.
E	-	Any named entity.

4. **Parameter.** Some predefined attributes require a "Parameter" value to be supplied when being used. These are denoted as follows:

(X)	-	An expression whose type or subtype is of type T1, T2 or T3.
(N)	-	An expression of type integer that does not exceed the dimensionality of the array "A".
(Ti)	-	An expression of type TIME. Must not be negative. Defaults to 0 ns if omitted.

5. **Result Type.** This is the result type, if applicable, of evaluation the attribute. These are defined implicitly in Table A.1.

6. **Result.** This is the result of evaluating the value, type, range, function or signal attributed to a named VHDL object. These are defined implicitly in Table A.1.

Attributes grouped by type	Kind	Prefix	Para-meter	Returned Result Type	Returned Result
Type Related					
T'base	value	T1		same base as T	
T'left ‡	value	T2		same base as T	the left bound of T
T'right ‡	value	T2		same base as T	the right bound of T
T'high ‡	value	T2		same base as T	the upper bound of T
T'low ‡	value	T2		same base as T	the lower bound of T
T'ascending	value	T2		boolean	true if T defined with ascending range
T'image(X)	function	T2	(X)	string	string representation of (X).
T'value(X)	function	T2	(X)	same base as T	value of T whose string representation is given by (x).
T'pos(X)	function	T2	(X)	universal integer	position number of X in list T.
T'val(X)	function	T3	(X)	same base as T	value of the type corresponding to position X.
T'succ(X)	function	T3	(X)	same base as T	value of the parameter whose position is one greater than the parameter.
T'pred(X)	function	T3	(X)	same base as T	value of the parameter whose position is one less than the parameter.
T'leftof(X)	function	T3	(X)	same base as T	value of the parameter to the left of X in type T.
T'rightof(X)	function	T3	(X)	same base as T	value of the parameter to the right of X in type T.
Array Related					
A'left[(N)]	function	A	(N)	type of Nth index range of A	left bound of the Nth index range of A.
A'right[(N)]	function	A	(N)	type of Nth index range of A	left bound of the Nth index range of A.
A'high[(N)]	function	A	(N)	type of Nth index range of A	upper bound of the Nth index range of A.
A'low[(N)]	function	A	(N)	type of Nth index range of A	lower bound of the Nth index range of A.
A'range[(N)] ‡	function	A	(N)	type of Nth index range of A	range A'left(N) to A'right(N) of values in Nth index range of A.
A'reverse_range[(N)] ‡	function	A	(N)	type of Nth index range of A	range A'right(N) to A'left(N) of values in Nth index range of A.
A'length[(N)] ‡	function	A	(N)	universal integer	number of values in the Nth index range.
A'ascending[(N)]	function	A	(N)	boolean	TRUE if Nth index range of A has an ascending range.
Signal Related					
S'delayed[(Ti)]	signal	S	(Ti)	same base as S	signal S delayed by T units of time.
S'stable[(Ti)] ‡	signal	S	(Ti)	boolean	TRUE when event has not occurred on signal S for T units of time.
S'quiet[(Ti)]	signal	S	(Ti)	boolean	TRUE when signal S has been quiet for T units of time.
S'transaction	signal	S		bit	signal whose value toggles when S is active.
S'event ‡	function	S		boolean	TRUE if an event has just occurred on signal S.
S'active	function	S		boolean	TRUE if signal S is active during current simulation delta cycle.
S'last_event	function	S		time	time elapsed since the last event on signal S.
S'last_active	function	S		time	time since signal S was last active.
S'last_value	function	S		same base as T	previous value of signal S immediately before last change of S.
S'driving	function	S		boolean	false if, in the enclosing process the driver for signals is disconnected. True otherwise.
S'driving_value	function	S		same base as T	the current value of S.
Entity Related					
E'simple_name	value	E		string	the name of a named entity.
E'instance_name	value	E		string	the name of a named entity including the design hierarchy path.
E'path_name	value	E		string	the design hierarchy path to the entity excluding the entity name.

‡ Typically support for synthesis

Table A.1 VHDL Attributes

Package STANDARD - language defined types and functions

Package STANDARD is defined in the VHDL LRM so is part of the language and does not need to be referenced with a **use** clause. It contains predefined definitions for the types and functions of the language.

STANDARD	STANDARD

```
package STANDARD is
  -- Predefined enumeration types:
  type BOOLEAN is (FALSE, TRUE);
  type BIT is ('0', '1');
  type CHARACTER is (
    NUL,  SOH,  STX,  ETX,  EOT,  ENQ,  ACK,
    BEL,  BS,   HT,   LF,   VT,   FF,   CR,
    SO,   SI,   DLE,  DC1,  DC2,  DC3,  DC4,
    NAK,  SYN,  ETB,  CAN,  EM,   SUB,  ESC,
    FSP,  GSP,  RSP,  USP,

    ' ',  '!',  '"',  '#',  '$',  '%',  '&',
    ''',  '(',  ')',  '*',  '+',  ',',  '-',
    '.',  '/',  '0',  '1',  '2',  '3',  '4',
    '5',  '6',  '7',  '8',  '9',  ':',  ';',
    '<',  '=',  '>',  '?',

    '@',  'A',  'B',  'C',  'D',  'E',  'F',
    'G',  'H',  'I',  'J',  'K',  'L',  'M',
    'N',  'O',  'P',  'Q',  'R',  'S',  'T',
    'U',  'V',  'W',  'X',  'Y',  'Z',  '[',
    '\',  ']',  '^',  '_',

    '`',  'a',  'b',  'c',  'd',  'e',  'f',
    'g',  'h',  'i',  'j',  'k',  'l',  'm',
    'n',  'o',  'p',  'q',  'r',  's',  't',
    'u',  'v',  'w',  'x',  'y',  'z',  '{',
    '|',  '}',  '~',  DEL,

    -- Plus other characters from the ISO 8859-1:1987(E)
    -- standard.
    );

  type SEVERITY_LEVEL is (NOTE, WARNING, ERROR, FAILURE);
  -- Predefined numeric types:
  type INTEGER is range implementation_defined;
  type REAL is range implementation_defined;
```

```
  -- Predefined physical type TIME:
  type TIME is range implementation_defined;
    units
      fs;                    -- femtosecond
      ps   =1000fs;          -- picosecond
      ns   = 1000ps;         -- nanasecond
      us   = 1000ns;         -- microsecond
      ms   = 1000 us;        -- microsecond
      sec  = 1000 ms;        -- seconds
      min  = 60 secs;        -- minutes
      hr   = 60 min;         -- hours
    end units;

  -- Predefined physical subtype:
  subtype DELAY_LENGTH is TIME range 0 fs to TIME'HIGH;

  -- Function that returns the current simulation time:
  impure function NOW return DELAY_LENGTH;

  -- Predefined numeric subtypes:
  subtype NATURAL is INTEGER range 0 to INTEGER'HIGH;
  subtype POSITIVE is INTEGER range 1 to INTEGER'HIGH;

  -- Predefined array types:
  type STRING is array (POSITIVE range <>) of CHARACTER;
  type BIT_VECTOR is array (NATURAL range <>) of BIT;

  -- Predefined types for file operations:
  type FILE_OPEN_KIND is (READ_MODE, WRITE_MODE, APPEND_MODE);
  type FILE_OPEN_STATUS is (OPEN_OK, STATUS_ERROR,  MODE_ERROR);

  -- Attribute declaration:
  attribute FOREIGN: STRING;
end STANDARD;
```

Standard file manipulation package TEXTIO

The VHDL package, TEXTIO, is shown. It contains declarations of types and subprograms that support formatted input and output operations on text files. It contains read and write procedures for vector arrays of type bit. Therefore, when used with types like unsigned for example, type conversions are needed as shown in this book. If a different version of this package contains procedures that use data types, std_logic and unsigned, conversion functions would not be needed.

Standard file manipulation package TEXTIO

```
--
-- Package TEXTIO from the IEEE 1076 VHDL LRM.  Modifications have -
-- been made based on the recommendations in VASG issue #32.
-- Textio package body was re-written in C to improve performance.
-- The supporting routines have been added to sim_support in
--

package TEXTIO is
    -- Type Definitions for Text I/O
    type LINE is access STRING;  -- a LINE is a pointer to a STRING value
    type TEXT is file of STRING; -- a file of variable-length ASCII records
    type SIDE is (RIGHT, LEFT);  -- for justifying output data within fields
    subtype WIDTH is NATURAL; -- for specifying widths of output fields


    -- Input Routines for Standard Types
    procedure READLINE(variable F: in TEXT; L: inout LINE);

    procedure READ(L: inout LINE; VALUE: out BIT; GOOD: out
            BOOLEAN);
    procedure READ(L: inout LINE; VALUE: out BIT);

    procedure READ(L: inout LINE; VALUE: out BIT_VECTOR; GOOD: out
            BOOLEAN);
    procedure READ(L: inout LINE; VALUE: out BIT_VECTOR);

    procedure READ(L: inout LINE; VALUE: out BOOLEAN; GOOD: out
            BOOLEAN);
    procedure READ(L: inout LINE; VALUE: out BOOLEAN);

    procedure READ(L: inout LINE; VALUE: out CHARACTER; GOOD: out
            BOOLEAN);
    procedure READ(L: inout LINE; VALUE: out CHARACTER);

    procedure READ(L: inout LINE; VALUE: out INTEGER; GOOD: out
            BOOLEAN);
    procedure READ(L: inout LINE; VALUE: out INTEGER);

    procedure READ(L: inout LINE; VALUE: out REAL; GOOD: out
            BOOLEAN);
    procedure READ(L: inout LINE; VALUE: out REAL);
```

```
    procedure READ(L: inout LINE; VALUE: out STRING; GOOD: out
            BOOLEAN);
    procedure READ(L: inout LINE; VALUE: out STRING);

    procedure READ(L: inout LINE; VALUE: out TIME; GOOD: out
            BOOLEAN);
    procedure READ(L: inout LINE; VALUE: out TIME);

    -- Output Routines for Standard Types:
    procedure WRITELINE(F: out TEXT; L: inout LINE);

    procedure WRITE(L: inout LINE; VALUE: in BIT;
            JUSTIFIED: in SIDE := RIGHT; FIELD: in WIDTH := 0);

    procedure WRITE(L: inout LINE; VALUE: in BIT_VECTOR;
            JUSTIFIED: in SIDE := RIGHT; FIELD: in WIDTH := 0);

    procedure WRITE(L: inout LINE; VALUE: in BOOLEAN;
            JUSTIFIED: in SIDE := RIGHT; FIELD: in WIDTH := 0);

    procedure WRITE(L: inout LINE; VALUE: in CHARACTER;
            JUSTIFIED: in SIDE := RIGHT; FIELD: in WIDTH := 0);

    procedure WRITE(L: inout LINE; VALUE: in INTEGER;
            JUSTIFIED: in SIDE := RIGHT; FIELD: in WIDTH := 0);

    procedure WRITE(L: inout LINE; VALUE: in REAL;
            JUSTIFIED: in SIDE := RIGHT; FIELD: in WIDTH := 0;
            DIGITS: in NATURAL := 0);

    procedure WRITE(L: inout LINE; VALUE: in STRING;
            JUSTIFIED: in SIDE := RIGHT; FIELD: in WIDTH := 0);

    procedure WRITE(L: inout LINE; VALUE: in TIME;
            JUSTIFIED: in SIDE := RIGHT; FIELD: in WIDTH := 0;
            UNIT: in TIME := ns);

end TEXTIO;


-------------------------------------------------------
-- This package has no package body
-------------------------------------------------------
```

Standard logic Package STD_LOGIC_1164 (IEEE 1164)

This is the IEEE 1164 standard VHDL logic package called STD_LOGIC_1164.

Standard logic Package STD_LOGIC_1164 (IEEE 1164)

```
-- This package defines the portable constructs that were defined
-- by the IEEE VHDL Model Standards Group.
-------------------------------------------------------------------
--  Title       : std_logic_1164 multi-value logic system
--  Library     : This package shall be compiled into a library
--              : symbolically named IEEE.
--
--  Developers  : IEEE model standards group (par 1164)
--  Purpose     : This packages defines a standard for designers
--              : to use in describing the interconnection data types
--              : used in vhdl modeling.
--
--  Limitation  : The logic system defined in this package may
--              : be insufficient for modeling switched transistors,
--              : since such a requirement is out of the scope of this
--              : effort. Furthermore, mathematics, primitives,
--              : timing standards, etc. are considered orthogonal
--              : issues as it relates to this package and are
--              : therefore beyond the scope of this effort.
--              :
--  Note        : No declarations or definitions shall be included in,
--              : or excluded from this package. The "package
--              : declaration" defines the types, subtypes and
--              : declarations of std_logic_1164. The std_logic_1164
--              : package body shall be considered the formal
--              : definition of the semantics of this package. Tool
--              : developers may choose to implement
--              : the package body in the most efficient manner
--              : available to them.
-------------------------------------------------------------------
--  modification history :
--
--  version   | mod. date: |
--  v4.200    | 01/02/92   |
-------------------------------------------------------------------

library IEEE;

PACKAGE Std_logic_1164 is

    -- Built-in attribute for synthesis:    -- D
    attribute BUILT_IN: BOOLEAN;            -- D

    -- Logic State System (unresolved)
    -------------------------------------------------------------------
    TYPE std_ulogic is (  'U',   -- Uninitialized
                          'X',   -- Forcing Unknown
                          '0',   -- Forcing 0
                          '1',   -- Forcing 1
                          'Z',   -- High Impedance
                          'W',   -- Weak   Unknown
                          'L',   -- Weak   0
                          'H',   -- Weak   1
                          '-'    -- don't care);

    attribute unique : string;                                          -- D
    attribute unique of std_logic_1164 : package is "LOGIC_1164";       -- D
    attribute unique of std_ulogic : type is "LOGIC9_BASE";             -- D

    -------------------------------------------------------------------D
    -- These lines are added for synthesis: J. Bhasker, Feb 27, '92:    -- D
    -------------------------------------------------------------------D
    ATTRIBUTE enum_type_encoding: STRING;                               -- D
    ATTRIBUTE enum_type_encoding OF std_ulogic: TYPE IS "U D 0 1 Z D
                                                         0 1 D";        -- D

    -------------------------------------------------------------------
    -- Unconstrained array of std_ulogic for use with the resolution
    -- function
    -------------------------------------------------------------------
    TYPE std_ulogic_vector IS ARRAY ( NATURAL RANGE <> ) of
                                                        std_ulogic;

    attribute unique of std_ulogic_vector : type is
                                      "LOGIC9_BASE_VEC";     -- D

    -------------------------------------------------------------------
    -- Resolution function
    -------------------------------------------------------------------
    FUNCTION resolved ( s : std_ulogic_vector ) RETURN std_ulogic;

    -------------------------------------------------------------------
    -- *** Industry Standard Logic Type ***
    -------------------------------------------------------------------
    SUBTYPE std_logic IS resolved std_ulogic;

    attribute unique of std_logic : subtype is "LOGIC9_X";          -- D

    -------------------------------------------------------------------
    -- Unconstrained array of std_logic for use in declaring signal arrays
    -------------------------------------------------------------------
    TYPE std_logic_vector IS ARRAY ( NATURAL RANGE <> ) of std_logic;

    attribute unique of std_logic_vector : type is "LOGIC9_X_VEC";  --D

    -------------------------------------------------------------------
    -- Basic states + Test
    -------------------------------------------------------------------
    SUBTYPE X01    is resolved std_ulogic range 'X' to '1';
                      -- ('X','0','1')
    SUBTYPE X01Z   is resolved std_ulogic range 'X' to 'Z';
                      -- ('X','0','1','Z')
    SUBTYPE UX01   is resolved std_ulogic range 'U' to '1';
                      -- ('U','X','0','1')
    SUBTYPE UX01Z  is resolved std_ulogic range 'U' to 'Z';
                      -- ('U','X','0','1','Z')

    attribute unique of X01    : subtype is "LOGIC9_X01";       -- D
    attribute unique of X01Z   : subtype is "LOGIC9_X01Z";      -- D
    attribute unique of UX01   : subtype is "LOGIC9_UX01";      -- D
    attribute unique of UX01Z  : subtype is "LOGIC9_UX01Z";     -- D

    -------------------------------------------------------------------
    -- Overloaded Logical Operators
    -------------------------------------------------------------------
    FUNCTION "and"  ( l : std_ulogic; r : std_ulogic ) RETURN UX01;
    FUNCTION "nand" ( l : std_ulogic; r : std_ulogic ) RETURN UX01;
    FUNCTION "or"   ( l : std_ulogic; r : std_ulogic ) RETURN UX01;
    FUNCTION "nor"  ( l : std_ulogic; r : std_ulogic ) RETURN UX01;
    FUNCTION "xor"  ( l : std_ulogic; r : std_ulogic ) RETURN UX01;
    FUNCTION "xnor" ( l : std_ulogic; r : std_ulogic ) RETURN UX01;
    FUNCTION "not"  ( l : std_ulogic                 ) RETURN UX01;

    -------------------------------------------------------------------
    -- Vectorized Overloaded Logical Operators
    -------------------------------------------------------------------
    FUNCTION "and" ( l, r : std_logic_vector ) RETURN std_logic_vector;
    FUNCTION "nand" ( l, r : std_logic_vector ) RETURN std_logic_vector;
    FUNCTION "or" ( l, r : std_logic_vector ) RETURN std_logic_vector;
    FUNCTION "nor" ( l, r : std_logic_vector ) RETURN std_logic_vector;
    FUNCTION "xor" ( l, r : std_logic_vector ) RETURN std_logic_vector;
    FUNCTION "not" ( l    : std_logic_vector ) RETURN std_logic_vector;
    FUNCTION "and" ( l, r : std_ulogic_vector ) RETURN
                                              std_ulogic_vector;
    FUNCTION "nand" ( l, r : std_ulogic_vector ) RETURN
                                              std_ulogic_vector;
    FUNCTION "or" ( l, r : std_ulogic_vector ) RETURN std_ulogic_vector;
    FUNCTION "nor" ( l, r : std_ulogic_vector ) RETURN std_ulogic_vector;
    FUNCTION "xor" ( l, r : std_ulogic_vector ) RETURN std_ulogic_vector;
    FUNCTION "not" ( l    : std_ulogic_vector ) RETURN std_ulogic_vector;
```

> This is the case for VeriBest Incorporated. Extra lines are indicated with "--D" at the end of the line.

Standard logic package STD_LOGIC_1164 (IEEE 1164)

```
--  Note : The declaration and implementation of the "xnor" function
--  is specifically commented until at which time the VHDL language
--  has beenofficially adopted as containing such a function. At such
--  a point, the following comments may be removed along with this
--  notice without further "official" ballotting of this std_logic_1164
--  package. It is the intent of this effort to provide such a function
--  once it becomes available in the VHDL standard.

--  function "xnor" ( l, r : std_logic_vector ) return std_logic_vector;
--  function "xnor" ( l, r : std_ulogic_vector ) return std_ulogic_vector;
```

```
-- Conversion Functions
```

```
FUNCTION   To_bit         ( s : std_ulogic;        xmap : BIT := '0')
           RETURN BIT;
FUNCTION   To_bitvector ( s : std_logic_vector ;  xmap : BIT := '0')
           RETURN BIT_VECTOR;
FUNCTION   To_bitvector ( s : std_ulogic_vector; xmap : BIT := '0')
           RETURN BIT_VECTOR;

FUNCTION   To_StdULogic       ( b : BIT          )
           RETURN std_ulogic;
FUNCTION   To_StdLogicVector      ( b : BIT_VECTOR    )
           RETURN std_logic_vector;
FUNCTION   To_StdLogicVector      ( s : std_ulogic_vector )
           RETURN std_logic_vector;
FUNCTION   To_StdULogicVector( b : BIT_VECTOR     )
           RETURN std_ulogic_vector;
FUNCTION   To_StdULogicVector( s : std_logic_vector )
           RETURN std_ulogic_vector;
```

```
-- strength strippers and type convertors
```

```
FUNCTION To_X01 ( s : std_logic_vector ) RETURN std_logic_vector;
FUNCTION To_X01 ( s : std_ulogic_vector) RETURN
                                         std_ulogic_vector;
FUNCTION To_X01 ( s : std_ulogic ) RETURN X01;
FUNCTION To_X01 ( b : bit_vector) RETURN std_logic_vector;
FUNCTION To_X01 ( b : bit_vector) RETURN std_ulogic_vector;
FUNCTION To_X01 ( b : bit        ) RETURN X01;

FUNCTION To_X01Z ( s : std_logic_vector ) RETURN std_logic_vector;
FUNCTION To_X01Z ( s : std_ulogic_vector) RETURN
                                         std_ulogic_vector;
FUNCTION To_X01Z ( s : std_ulogic ) RETURN X01Z;
FUNCTION To_X01Z ( b : bit_vector) RETURN std_logic_vector;
FUNCTION To_X01Z ( b : bit_vector) RETURN std_ulogic_vector;
FUNCTION To_X01Z ( b : bit        ) RETURN X01Z;

FUNCTION To_UX01 ( s : std_logic_vector ) RETURN std_logic_vector;
FUNCTION To_UX01 ( s : std_ulogic_vector) RETURN
                                         std_ulogic_vector;
FUNCTION To_UX01 ( s : std_ulogic ) RETURN UX01;
FUNCTION To_UX01 ( b : bit_vector) RETURN std_logic_vector;
FUNCTION To_UX01 ( b : bit_vector) RETURN std_ulogic_vector;
FUNCTION To_UX01 ( b : bit        ) RETURN UX01;
```

```
attribute BUILT_IN of TO_BIT: function is TRUE;               -- D
attribute BUILT_IN of TO_BITVECTOR: function is TRUE;         -- D
attribute BUILT_IN of TO_STDULOGIC: function is TRUE;         -- D
attribute BUILT_IN of TO_STDULOGICVECTOR: function is TRUE;   -- D
attribute BUILT_IN of TO_STDLOGICVECTOR: function is TRUE;    -- D
attribute BUILT_IN of TO_X01: function is TRUE;               -- D
attribute BUILT_IN of TO_X01Z: function is TRUE;              -- D
attribute BUILT_IN of TO_UX01: function is TRUE;              -- D
```

```
-- Edge Detection
```

```
FUNCTION rising_edge  (SIGNAL s : std_ulogic) RETURN boolean;
FUNCTION falling_edge (SIGNAL s : std_ulogic) RETURN boolean;

-- synthesis built-in functions                              -- D
attribute BUILT_IN of rising_edge : function is TRUE;         -- D
attribute BUILT_IN of falling_edge : function is TRUE;        -- D
```

```
-- object contains an unknown
```

```
FUNCTION Is_X ( s : std_ulogic_vector ) RETURN  BOOLEAN;
FUNCTION Is_X ( s : std_logic_vector  ) RETURN  BOOLEAN;
FUNCTION Is_X ( s : std_ulogic        ) RETURN  BOOLEAN;

END Std_logic_1164;
```

```
-----------------------------------------------------------------
--                                                            --
--              Body of IEEE.Std_logic_1164                   --
--                                                            --
-----------------------------------------------------------------
```

```
--  Title      : std_logic_1164 multi-value logic system
--  Library    : This package shall be compiled into a library
--             : symbolically named IEEE.
--             :
--  Developers : IEEE model standards group (par 1164)
--  Purpose    : This packages defines a standard for designers
--             : to use in describing the interconnection data t
--             : types used in vhdl modeling.
--             :
--  Limitation : The logic system defined in this package may
--             : be insufficient for modeling switched transistors,
--             : since such a requirement is out of the scope of this
--             : effort. Furthermore, mathematics, primitives,
--             : timing standards, etc. are considered orthogonal
--             : issues as it relates to this package and are
--             : therefore beyond the scope of this effort.
--             :
--  Note       : No declarations or definitions shall be included in,
--             : or excluded from this package. The "package
--             : declaration" defines the types, subtypes and
--             : declarations of std_logic_1164. The std_logic_1164
--             : package body shall be considered the formal
--             : definition of the semantics of this package. Tool
--             : developers may choose to implement the
--             : package body in the most efficient manner
--             : available to them.
```

```
-- modification history :
-----------------------------------------------------------------
-- version | mod. date:|
-- v4.200  | 01/02/92  |
-----------------------------------------------------------------

PACKAGE BODY Std_logic_1164 is
```

```
-- Local Types
```

```
TYPE stdlogic_1d  is array (std_ulogic) of std_ulogic;
TYPE stdlogic_table is array (std_ulogic, std_ulogic) of std_ulogic;
```

```
-- Resolution Function
```

```
CONSTANT resolution_table : stdlogic_table := (
--    ----------------------------------------------------
--    |  U   X   0   1   Z   W   L   H   -         |  |
--    ----------------------------------------------------
      ( 'U', 'U', 'U', 'U', 'U', 'U', 'U', 'U', 'U' ), -- | U |
      ( 'U', 'X', 'X', 'X', 'X', 'X', 'X', 'X', 'X' ), -- | X |
      ( 'U', 'X', '0', 'X', '0', '0', '0', '0', 'X' ), -- | 0 |
```

Standard logic package STD_LOGIC_1164 (IEEE 1164)

```vhdl
        ( 'U', 'X', 'X', '1', '1', '1', '1', '1', 'X' ), — | 1 |
        ( 'U', 'X', '0', '1', 'Z', 'W', 'L', 'H', 'X' ), — | Z |
        ( 'U', 'X', '0', '1', 'W','W','W','W','X' ), — | W |
        ( 'U', 'X', '0', '1', 'L', 'W', 'L','W','X' ), — | L |
        ( 'U', 'X', '0', '1', 'H', 'W','W','H', 'X' ), — | H |
        ( 'U', 'X', 'X', 'X', 'X', 'X', 'X', 'X', 'X' ) — | - |
    );

    FUNCTION resolved ( s : std_ulogic_vector ) RETURN std_ulogic IS
        VARIABLE result : std_ulogic := 'Z'; -- weakest state default
    BEGIN
        -- the test for a single driver is essential otherwise the
        -- loop would return 'X' for a single driver of '-' and that
        -- would conflict with the value of a single driver unresolved
        -- signal.
        IF  (s'LENGTH = 1) THEN  RETURN s(s'LOW);
        ELSE
            -- Iterate through all inputs
            FOR i IN s'RANGE LOOP
                result := resolution_table (result, s(i));
            END LOOP;
            -- Return the resultant value
            RETURN result;
        END If;
    END resolved;


--------------------------------------------------------------
-- Tables for Logical Operations
--------------------------------------------------------------


-- truth table for "and" function
CONSTANT and_table : stdlogic_table := (
--            -------------------------------------------
--            | U  X  0  1  Z  W  L  H  -   | |
--            -------------------------------------------
        ( 'U', 'U', '0', 'U', 'U', 'U', '0', 'U', 'U' ), — | U |
        ( 'U', 'X', '0', 'X', 'X', 'X', '0', 'X', 'X' ), — | X |
        ( '0', '0', '0', '0', '0', '0', '0', '0', '0' ), — | 0 |
        ( 'U', 'X', '0', '1', 'X', 'X', '0', '1', 'X' ), — | 1 |
        ( 'U', 'X', '0', 'X', 'X', 'X', '0', 'X', 'X' ), — | Z |
        ( 'U', 'X', '0', 'X', 'X', 'X', '0', 'X', 'X' ), — | W |
        ( '0', '0', '0', '0', '0', '0', '0', '0', '0' ), — | L |
        ( 'U', 'X', '0', '1', 'X', 'X', '0', '1', 'X' ), — | H |
        ( 'U', 'X', '0', 'X', 'X', 'X', '0', 'X', 'X' ) — | - |
    );

-- truth table for "or" function
CONSTANT or_table : stdlogic_table := (
--            -------------------------------------------
--            | U  X  0  1  Z  W  L  H  -   | |
--            -------------------------------------------
        ( 'U', 'U', 'U', '1', 'U', 'U', 'U', '1', 'U' ), — | U |
        ( 'U', 'X', 'X', '1', 'X', 'X', 'X', '1', 'X' ), — | X |
        ( '1', 'X', '0', '1', 'X', 'X', '0', '1', 'X' ), — | 0 |
        ( 'U', '1', '1', '1', '1', '1', '1', '1', '1' ), — | 1 |
        ( 'U', 'X', 'X', '1', 'X', 'X', 'X', '1', 'X' ), — | Z |
        ( 'U', 'X', 'X', '1', 'X', 'X', 'X', '1', 'X' ), — | W |
        ( 'U', 'X', '0', '1', 'X', 'X', '0', '1', 'X' ), — | L |
        ( '1', '1', '1', '1', '1', '1', '1', '1', '1' ), — | H |
        ( 'U', 'X', 'X', '1', 'X', 'X', 'X', '1', 'X' ) — | - |
    );

-- truth table for "xor" function
CONSTANT xor_table : stdlogic_table := (
--            -------------------------------------------
--            | U  X  0  1  Z  W  L  H  -   | |
--            -------------------------------------------
        ( 'U', 'U', 'U', 'U', 'U', 'U', 'U', 'U', 'U' ), — | U |
        ( 'U', 'X', 'X', 'X', 'X', 'X', 'X', 'X', 'X' ), — | X |
        ( 'U', 'X', '0', 'X', '1', 'X', '0', '0', 'X' ), — | 0 |
        ( 'U', 'X', '1', '1', '0', 'X', '1', '1', 'X' ), — | 1 |
        ( 'U', 'X', 'X', '1', 'X', 'X', 'X', 'X', 'X' ), — | Z |
        ( 'U', 'X', 'X', '1', 'X', 'X', 'X', 'X', 'X' ), — | W |
        ( 'U', 'X', '0', '1', '1', 'X', '0', '1', 'X' ), — | L |
```

```vhdl
        ( 'U', 'X', '1', '1', '0', 'X', '1', '0', 'X' ), — | H |
        ( 'U', 'X', 'X', 'X', 'X', 'X', 'X', 'X', 'X' ) — | - |
    );
-- truth table for not function
CONSTANT not_table : stdlogic_1D :=
--            -------------------------------------------
--            | U  X  0  1  Z  W  L  H  -  |
--            -------------------------------------------
        ( 'U', 'X', '1', '0', 'X', 'X', '1', '0', 'X' ),


--------------------------------------------------------------
-- Overloaded Logical Operators ( with optimizing hints )
--------------------------------------------------------------

FUNCTION "and"  ( l : std_ulogic; r : std_ulogic ) RETURN UX01 IS
BEGIN
    RETURN (and_table(L, R));
END "and";

FUNCTION "nand"  ( l : std_ulogic; r : std_ulogic ) RETURN UX01 IS
BEGIN
    RETURN (not_table (and_table(L, R)));
END "nand";

FUNCTION "or"   ( l : std_ulogic; r : std_ulogic ) RETURN UX01 IS
BEGIN
    RETURN (or_table(L, R));
END "or";

FUNCTION "nor"  ( l : std_ulogic; r : std_ulogic ) RETURN UX01 IS
BEGIN
    RETURN (not_table (or_table(L, R)));
END "nor";

FUNCTION "xor"  ( l : std_ulogic; r : std_ulogic ) RETURN UX01 IS
BEGIN
    RETURN (xor_table(L, R));
END "xor";

FUNCTION "xnor"  ( l : std_ulogic; r : std_ulogic ) RETURN UX01 IS
BEGIN
    RETURN not_table(xor_table(l, r));
END "xnor";

FUNCTION "not"  ( l : std_ulogic ) RETURN UX01 IS
BEGIN
    RETURN (not_table(L));
END "not";


--------------------------------------------------------------
-- Vectorized Overloaded Logical Operators (resolved vectors)
--------------------------------------------------------------

FUNCTION "and"  ( L,R : std_logic_vector ) RETURN std_logic_vector
                                                               IS
    ALIAS LV : std_logic_vector ( 1 to L'length ) IS L;
    ALIAS RV : std_logic_vector ( 1 to R'length ) IS R;
    VARIABLE result : std_logic_vector ( 1 to L'length );
begin
    if ( L'length /= R'length ) then
        assert false
        report "Arguments of overloaded 'and' operator are not of
                the same length"
        severity FAILURE;
    else
        for i in  result'range loop
            result(i) := and_table (LV(i), RV(i));
        end loop;
    end if;
    return result;
end "and";
```

Standard logic package STD_LOGIC_1164 (IEEE 1164)

```vhdl
FUNCTION "nand"  ( L,R : std_logic_vector ) RETURN
                                           std_logic_vector IS
    ALIAS LV : std_logic_vector ( 1 to L'length ) IS L;
    ALIAS RV : std_logic_vector ( 1 to R'length ) IS R;
    VARIABLE result : std_logic_vector ( 1 to L'length );
begin
    if ( L'length /= R'length ) then
        assert false
        report "Arguments of overloaded 'nand' operator are not
                of the same length"
        severity FAILURE;
    else
        for i in  result'range loop
            result(i) := not_table(and_table (LV(i), RV(i)));
        end loop;
    end if;
    return result;
end "nand";
```

```vhdl
FUNCTION "or"  ( L,R : std_logic_vector ) RETURN std_logic_vector IS
    ALIAS LV : std_logic_vector ( 1 to L'length ) IS L;
    ALIAS RV : std_logic_vector ( 1 to R'length ) IS R;
    VARIABLE result : std_logic_vector ( 1 to L'length );
begin
    if ( L'length /= R'length ) then
        assert false
        report "Arguments of overloaded 'or' operator are not of
                the same length"
        severity FAILURE;
    else
        for i in  result'range loop
            result(i) := or_table (LV(i), RV(i));
        end loop;
    end if;
    return result;
end "or";
```

```vhdl
FUNCTION "nor"  ( L,R : std_logic_vector ) RETURN std_logic_vector
                                                              IS
    ALIAS LV : std_logic_vector ( 1 to L'length ) IS L;
    ALIAS RV : std_logic_vector ( 1 to R'length ) IS R;
    VARIABLE result : std_logic_vector ( 1 to L'length );
begin
    if ( L'length /= R'length ) then
        assert false
        report "Arguments of overloaded 'nor' operator are not of
                the same length"
        severity FAILURE;
    else
        for i in  result'range loop
            result(i) := not_table(or_table (LV(i), RV(i)));
        end loop;
    end if;
    return result;
end "nor";
```

```vhdl
FUNCTION "xor"  ( L,R : std_logic_vector ) RETURN std_logic_vector IS
    ALIAS LV : std_logic_vector ( 1 to L'length ) IS L;
    ALIAS RV : std_logic_vector ( 1 to R'length ) IS R;
    VARIABLE result : std_logic_vector ( 1 to L'length );
begin
    if ( L'ength /= R'length ) then
        assert false
        report "Arguments of overloaded 'xor' operator are not of
                the same length"
        severity FAILURE;
```

```vhdl
    else
        for i in  result'range loop
            result(i) := xor_table (LV(i), RV(i));
        end loop;
    end if;
    return result;
end "xor";
```

```vhdl
FUNCTION "xnor"  ( l,r : std_logic_vector ) RETURN std_logic_vector IS
    ALIAS lv : std_logic_vector ( 1 to l'length ) IS l;
    ALIAS rv : std_logic_vector ( 1 to r'length ) IS r;
    VARIABLE result : std_logic_vector ( 1 to l'length );
begin
    if ( l'length /= r'length ) then
        assert false
        report "arguments of overloaded 'xnor' operator are not of
        the same length"
        severity failure;
    else
        for i in result'range loop
            result(i) := not_table(xor_table (lv(i), rv(i)));
        end loop;
    end if;
    return result;
end "xnor";
```

```vhdl
FUNCTION "not"  ( L : std_logic_vector ) RETURN std_logic_vector IS
    ALIAS LV : std_logic_vector ( 1 to L'length ) IS L;
    VARIABLE result : std_logic_vector ( 1 to L'length ) :=
                                          (Others => 'X');
begin
    for i in  result'range loop
        result(i) := not_table(LV(i));
    end loop;
    return result;
end "not";
```

```vhdl
-- Vectorized Overloaded Logical Operators (unresolved  vectors)
```

```vhdl
FUNCTION "and"  ( L,R : std_ulogic_vector ) RETURN
                                        std_ulogic_vector IS
    ALIAS LV : std_ulogic_vector ( 1 to L'length ) IS L;
    ALIAS RV : std_ulogic_vector ( 1 to R'length ) IS R;
    VARIABLE result : std_ulogic_vector ( 1 to L'length );
begin
    if ( L'length /= R'length ) then
        assert false
        report "Arguments of overloaded 'and' operator are not of
                the same length"
        severity FAILURE;
    else
        for i in  result'range loop
            result(i) := and_table (LV(i), RV(i));
        end loop;
    end if;
    return result;
end "and";
```

```vhdl
FUNCTION "nand"  ( L,R : std_ulogic_vector ) RETURN
                                 std_ulogic_vector IS
    ALIAS LV : std_ulogic_vector ( 1 to L'length ) IS L;
    ALIAS RV : std_ulogic_vector ( 1 to R'length ) IS R;
    VARIABLE result : std_ulogic_vector ( 1 to L'length );
begin
    if ( L'length /= R'length ) then
        assert false
```

Standard logic package STD_LOGIC_1164 (IEEE 1164)

```vhdl
        report "Arguments of overloaded 'nand' operator are not
                of the same length"
        severity FAILURE;
    else
        for i in  result'range loop
            result(i) := not_table(and_table (LV(i), RV(i)));
        end loop;
    end if;
    return result;
end "nand";

------------------------------------------------------------

FUNCTION "or"  ( L,R : std_ulogic_vector ) RETURN
                                    std_ulogic_vector IS
    ALIAS LV : std_ulogic_vector ( 1 to L'length ) IS L;
    ALIAS RV : std_ulogic_vector ( 1 to R'length ) IS R;
    VARIABLE result : std_ulogic_vector ( 1 to L'length );
begin
    if ( L'length /= R'length ) then
        assert false
        report "Arguments of overloaded 'or' operator are not of
                the same length"
        severity FAILURE;
    else
        for i in  result'range loop
            result(i) := or_table (LV(i), RV(i));
        end loop;
    end if;
    return result;
end "or";

------------------------------------------------------------

FUNCTION "nor"  ( L,R : std_ulogic_vector ) RETURN
                                    std_ulogic_vector IS
    ALIAS LV : std_ulogic_vector ( 1 to L'length ) IS L;
    ALIAS RV : std_ulogic_vector ( 1 to R'length ) IS R;
    VARIABLE result : std_ulogic_vector ( 1 to L'length );
begin
    if ( L'length /= R'length ) then
        assert false
        report "Arguments of overloaded 'nor' operator are not of
                the same length"
        severity FAILURE;
    else
        for i in  result'range loop
            result(i) := not_table(or_table (LV(i), RV(i)));
        end loop;
    end if;
    return result;
end "nor";

------------------------------------------------------------

FUNCTION "xor"  ( L,R : std_ulogic_vector ) RETURN
                                    std_ulogic_vector IS
    ALIAS LV : std_ulogic_vector ( 1 to L'length ) IS L;
    ALIAS RV : std_ulogic_vector ( 1 to R'length ) IS R;
    VARIABLE result : std_ulogic_vector ( 1 to L'length );
begin
    if ( L'length /= R'length ) then
        assert false
        report "Arguments of overloaded 'xor' operator are not of
                the same length"
        severity FAILURE;
    else
        for i in  result'range loop
            result(i) := xor_table (LV(i), RV(i));
        end loop;
    end if;
    return result;
end "xor";
```

```vhdl
FUNCTION "xnor"  ( l,r : std_ulogic_vector ) RETURN std_ulogic_vector IS
    ALIAS lv : std_ulogic_vector ( 1 to l'length ) IS l;
    ALIAS rv : std_ulogic_vector ( 1 to r'length ) IS r;
    VARIABLE result : std_ulogic_vector ( 1 to l'length );
begin
    if ( l'length /= r'length ) then
        assert false
        report "arguments of overloaded 'xnor' operator are not of
                the same length"
        severity failure;
    else
        for i in result'range loop
            result(i) := not_table(xor_table (lv(i), rv(i)));
        end loop;
    end if;
    return result;
end "xnor";

------------------------------------------------------------

FUNCTION "not"  ( L : std_ulogic_vector ) RETURN std_ulogic_vector
                                                            IS
    ALIAS LV : std_ulogic_vector ( 1 to L'length ) IS L;
    VARIABLE result : std_ulogic_vector ( 1 to L'length ) :=
                                            (Others => 'X');
begin
    for i in  result'range loop
        result(i) := not_table(LV(i));
    end loop;
    return result;
end "not";

------------------------------------------------------------
-- Conversion Tables
------------------------------------------------------------
TYPE logic_x01_table  is array (std_ulogic'low to std_ulogic'high) of
                                                            X01;
TYPE logic_x01z_table is array (std_ulogic'low to std_ulogic'high) of
                                                            X01Z;
TYPE logic_ux01_table is array (std_ulogic'low to std_ulogic'high) of
                                                            UX01;

------------------------------------------------------------
-- table name    : cvt_to_x01
--
-- parameters    :
--    in         : std_ulogic  -- some logic value
-- returns       : x01        -- state value of logic value
-- purpose       : to convert state-strength to state only
--
-- example       : if (cvt_to_x01 (input_signal) = '1' ) then ...
--
------------------------------------------------------------
CONSTANT cvt_to_X01 : logic_x01_table := (
        'X', -- 'U'
        'X', -- 'X'
        '0', -- '0'
        '1', -- '1'
        'X', -- 'Z'
        'X', -- 'W'
        '0', -- 'L'
        '1', -- 'H'
        'X'  -- '-'
        );

------------------------------------------------------------
-- table name    : cvt_to_x01z
--
-- parameters    :
--    in         : std_ulogic  -- some logic value
-- returns       : x01z        -- state value of logic value
-- purpose       : to convert state-strength to state only
--
-- example       : if (cvt_to_x01z (input_signal) = '1' ) then ...
```

Standard logic package STD_LOGIC_1164 (IEEE 1164)

```
CONSTANT cvt_to_x01z : logic_x01z_table := (
        'X',  -- 'U'
        'X',  -- 'X'
        '0',  -- '0'
        '1',  -- '1'
        'Z',  -- 'Z'
        'X',  -- 'W'
        '0',  -- 'L'
        '1',  -- 'H'
        'X'   -- '-'
        );


--- table name   : cvt_to_ux01
--
-- parameters    :
--        in      : std_ulogic  -- some logic value
-- returns        : ux01       -- state value of logic value
-- purpose        : to convert state-strength to state only
--
-- example        : if (cvt_to_ux01 (input_signal) = '1' ) then ...
--

CONSTANT cvt_to_ux01 : logic_ux01_table := (
        'U',  -- 'U'
        'X',  -- 'X'
        '0',  -- '0'
        '1',  -- '1'
        'X',  -- 'Z'
        'X',  -- 'W'
        '0',  -- 'L'
        '1',  -- 'H'
        'X'   -- '-'
        );


-- Conversion Functions

FUNCTION To_bit      ( s : std_ulogic; xmap : BIT := '0')
    RETURN BIT IS
BEGIN
        CASE s IS
            WHEN '0' | 'L' => RETURN ('0');
            WHEN '1' | 'H' => RETURN ('1');
            WHEN OTHERS => RETURN xmap;
            END CASE;
END;

FUNCTION To_bitvector ( s : std_logic_vector ; xmap : BIT := '0')
            RETURN BIT_VECTOR IS
    ALIAS sv : std_logic_vector ( s'LENGTH-1 DOWNTO 0 ) IS s;
    VARIABLE result : BIT_VECTOR ( s'LENGTH-1 DOWNTO 0 );
BEGIN
    FOR i IN result'RANGE LOOP
        CASE sv(i) IS
            WHEN '0' | 'L' => result(i) := '0';
            WHEN '1' | 'H' => result(i) := '1';
            WHEN OTHERS => result(i) := xmap;
            END CASE;
        END LOOP;
        RETURN result;
END;

FUNCTION To_bitvector ( s : std_ulogic_vector; xmap : BIT := '0')
            RETURN BIT_VECTOR IS
    ALIAS sv : std_ulogic_vector ( s'LENGTH-1 DOWNTO 0 ) IS s;
    VARIABLE result : BIT_VECTOR ( s'LENGTH-1 DOWNTO 0 );
BEGIN
    FOR i IN result'RANGE LOOP
        CASE sv(i) IS
            WHEN '0' | 'L' => result(i) := '0';
            WHEN '1' | 'H' => result(i) := '1';
            WHEN OTHERS => result(i) := xmap;
            END CASE;
```

```
    END LOOP;
    RETURN result;
END;

FUNCTION To_StdULogic  ( b : BIT)
            RETURN std_ulogic IS
BEGIN
    CASE b IS
        WHEN '0' => RETURN '0';
        WHEN '1' => RETURN '1';
    END CASE;
END;

FUNCTION To_StdLogicVector  ( b : BIT_VECTOR)
            RETURN std_logic_vector IS
    ALIAS bv : BIT_VECTOR ( b'LENGTH-1 DOWNTO 0 ) IS b;
    VARIABLE result : std_logic_vector ( b'LENGTH-1 DOWNTO 0 );
BEGIN
    FOR i IN result'RANGE LOOP
        CASE bv(i) IS
            WHEN '0' => result(i) := '0';
            WHEN '1' => result(i) := '1';
        END CASE;
    END LOOP;
    RETURN result;
END;


FUNCTION To_StdLogicVector  ( s : std_ulogic_vector )
            RETURN std_logic_vector IS
    ALIAS sv : std_ulogic_vector ( s'LENGTH-1 DOWNTO 0 ) IS s;
    VARIABLE result : std_logic_vector ( s'LENGTH-1 DOWNTO 0 );
BEGIN
    FOR i IN result'RANGE LOOP
        result(i) := sv(i);
    END LOOP;
    RETURN result;
END;

FUNCTION To_StdULogicVector ( b : BIT_VECTOR)
            RETURN std_ulogic_vector IS
    ALIAS bv : BIT_VECTOR ( b'LENGTH-1 DOWNTO 0 ) IS b;
    VARIABLE result : std_ulogic_vector ( b'LENGTH-1 DOWNTO 0 );
BEGIN
    FOR i IN result'RANGE LOOP
        CASE bv(i) IS
            WHEN '0' => result(i) := '0';
            WHEN '1' => result(i) := '1';
        END CASE;
    END LOOP;
    RETURN result;
END;


FUNCTION To_StdULogicVector ( s : std_logic_vector )
            RETURN std_ulogic_vector IS
    ALIAS sv : std_logic_vector ( s'LENGTH-1 DOWNTO 0 ) IS s;
    VARIABLE result : std_ulogic_vector ( s'LENGTH-1 DOWNTO 0 );
BEGIN
    FOR i IN result'RANGE LOOP
        result(i) := sv(i);
    END LOOP;
    RETURN result;
END;


-- strength strippers and type convertors

-- to_x01

FUNCTION To_X01  ( s : std_logic_vector ) RETURN std_logic_vector
                                                                IS
    ALIAS SV : std_logic_vector ( 1 to s'length ) IS s;
    VARIABLE result : std_logic_vector ( 1 to s'length );
BEGIN
```

Standard logic package STD_LOGIC_1164 (IEEE 1164)

```
      for i in result'range loop
          result(i) := cvt_to_x01 (SV(i));
      end loop;
      return result;
   END;


   FUNCTION To_X01  ( s : std_ulogic_vector ) RETURN
                                              std_ulogic_vector IS
      ALIAS SV : std_ulogic_vector ( 1 to s'length ) IS s;
      VARIABLE result : std_ulogic_vector ( 1 to s'length );
   BEGIN
      for i in result'range loop
          result(i) := cvt_to_x01 (SV(i));
      end loop;
      return result;
   END;


   FUNCTION To_X01  ( s : std_ulogic ) RETURN X01 IS
   BEGIN
      return (cvt_to_x01(s));
   END;


   FUNCTION To_X01  ( b : bit_vector ) RETURN std_logic_vector IS
      ALIAS BV : bit_vector ( 1 to b'length ) IS b;
      VARIABLE result : std_logic_vector ( 1 to b'length );
   BEGIN
      for i in result'range loop
          case BV(i) is
              when '0' => result(i) := '0';
              when '1' => result(i) := '1';
          end case;
      end loop;
      return result;
   END;


   FUNCTION To_X01  ( b : bit_vector ) RETURN std_ulogic_vector IS
      ALIAS BV : bit_vector ( 1 to b'length ) IS b;
      VARIABLE result : std_ulogic_vector ( 1 to b'length );
   BEGIN
      for i in result'range loop
          case BV(i) is
              when '0' => result(i) := '0';
              when '1' => result(i) := '1';
          end case;
      end loop;
      return result;
   END;


   FUNCTION To_X01  ( b : bit ) RETURN X01 IS
   BEGIN
      case b is
          when '0' => return ('0');
          when '1' => return ('1');
      end case;
   END;


   ----------------------------------------------------
   -- to_x01z
   ----------------------------------------------------


   FUNCTION To_X01Z  ( s : std_logic_vector ) RETURN std_logic_vector
                                              IS
      ALIAS SV : std_logic_vector ( 1 to s'length ) IS s;
      VARIABLE result : std_logic_vector ( 1 to s'length );
   BEGIN
      for i in result'range loop
          result(i) := cvt_to_x01z (SV(i));
      end loop;
      return result;
   END;


   FUNCTION To_X01Z  ( s : std_ulogic_vector ) RETURN
                                              std_ulogic_vector IS
      ALIAS SV : std_ulogic_vector ( 1 to s'length ) IS s;
      VARIABLE result : std_ulogic_vector ( 1 to s'length );
```

```
   BEGIN
      for i in result'range loop
          result(i) := cvt_to_x01z (SV(i));
      end loop;
      return result;
   END;


   FUNCTION To_X01Z  ( s : std_ulogic ) RETURN X01Z IS
   BEGIN
      return (cvt_to_x01z(s));
   END;


   FUNCTION To_X01Z  ( b : bit_vector ) RETURN std_logic_vector IS
      ALIAS BV : bit_vector ( 1 to b'length ) IS b;
      VARIABLE result : std_logic_vector ( 1 to b'length );
   BEGIN
      for i in result'range loop
          case BV(i) is
              when '0' => result(i) := '0';
              when '1' => result(i) := '1';
          end case;
      end loop;
      return result;
   END;


   FUNCTION To_X01Z  ( b : bit_vector ) RETURN std_ulogic_vector IS
      ALIAS BV : bit_vector ( 1 to b'length ) IS b;
      VARIABLE result : std_ulogic_vector ( 1 to b'length );
   BEGIN
      for i in result'range loop
          case BV(i) is
              when '0' => result(i) := '0';
              when '1' => result(i) := '1';
          end case;
      end loop;
      return result;
   END;


   FUNCTION To_X01Z  ( b : bit ) RETURN X01Z IS
   BEGIN
      case b is
          when '0' => return ('0');
          when '1' => return ('1');
      end case;
   END;


   ----------------------------------------------------
   -- to_ux01
   ----------------------------------------------------


   FUNCTION To_UX01  ( s : std_logic_vector ) RETURN
                                              std_logic_vector IS
      ALIAS SV : std_logic_vector ( 1 to s'length ) IS s;
      VARIABLE result : std_logic_vector ( 1 to s'length );
   BEGIN
      for i in result'range loop
          result(i) := cvt_to_ux01 (SV(i));
      end loop;
      return result;
   END;


   FUNCTION To_UX01  ( s : std_ulogic_vector ) RETURN
                                              std_ulogic_vector IS
      ALIAS SV : std_ulogic_vector ( 1 to s'length ) IS s;
      VARIABLE result : std_ulogic_vector ( 1 to s'length );
   BEGIN
      for i in result'range loop
          result(i) := cvt_to_ux01 (SV(i));
      end loop;
      return result;
   END;


   FUNCTION To_UX01  ( s : std_ulogic ) RETURN UX01 IS
   BEGIN
```

Standard logic package STD_LOGIC_1164 (IEEE 1164)

```
    return (cvt_to_ux01(s));
END;

FUNCTION To_UX01  ( b : BIT_VECTOR ) RETURN  std_logic_vector IS
    ALIAS bv : BIT_VECTOR ( 1 TO b'LENGTH ) IS b;
    VARIABLE result : std_logic_vector ( 1 TO b'LENGTH );
BEGIN
    FOR i IN result'RANGE LOOP
        CASE bv(i) IS
            WHEN '0' => result(i) := '0';
            WHEN '1' => result(i) := '1';
        END CASE;
    END LOOP;
    RETURN result;
END;

FUNCTION To_UX01  ( b : BIT_VECTOR ) RETURN  std_ulogic_vector IS
    ALIAS bv : BIT_VECTOR ( 1 TO b'LENGTH ) IS b;
    VARIABLE result : std_ulogic_vector ( 1 TO b'LENGTH );
BEGIN
    FOR i IN result'RANGE LOOP
        CASE bv(i) IS
            WHEN '0' => result(i) := '0';
            WHEN '1' => result(i) := '1';
        END CASE;
    END LOOP;
    RETURN result;
END;

FUNCTION To_UX01  ( b : BIT ) RETURN  UX01 IS
BEGIN
    CASE b IS
        WHEN '0' => RETURN('0');
        WHEN '1' => RETURN('1');
    END CASE;
END;

----------------------------------------------
-- Edge Detection
----------------------------------------------

Function rising_edge  (SIGNAL s : std_ulogic) RETURN boolean is
begin
    return  (s'event and (To_X01(s) = '1') and
            (To_X01(s'last_value) = '0'));
end;

Function falling_edge (SIGNAL s : std_ulogic) RETURN boolean is
begin
    return  (s'event and (To_X01(s) = '0') and
            (To_X01(s'last_value) = '1'));
end;

----------------------------------------------
-- object contains an unknown
----------------------------------------------

FUNCTION Is_X ( s : std_ulogic_vector ) RETURN  BOOLEAN IS
BEGIN
    FOR i IN s'RANGE LOOP
        CASE s(i) IS
            WHEN 'U' | 'X' | 'Z' | 'W' | '-' => RETURN TRUE;
            WHEN OTHERS => NULL;
        END CASE;
    END LOOP;
    RETURN FALSE;
END;

FUNCTION Is_X ( s : std_logic_vector ) RETURN  BOOLEAN IS
BEGIN
    FOR i IN s'RANGE LOOP
        CASE s(i) IS
            WHEN 'U' | 'X' | 'Z' | 'W'| '-' => RETURN TRUE;
            WHEN OTHERS => NULL;
        END CASE;
```

```
    END LOOP;
    RETURN FALSE;
END;

FUNCTION Is_X ( s : std_ulogic) RETURN  BOOLEAN IS
BEGIN
    CASE s IS
        WHEN 'U' | 'X' | 'Z' | 'W' | '-' => RETURN TRUE;
        WHEN OTHERS => NULL;
    END CASE;
    RETURN FALSE;
END;

END Std_logic_1164;
```

Standard synthesis package NUMERIC_STD (IEEE 1076.3)

The IEEE 1076.3 VHDL synthesis package NUMERIC_STD is shown. Although this is a draft standard, the final approval is imminent and only comments are expected to change. Package NUMERIC_STD is one of two standard synthesis packages being defined in IEEE 1076.3; NUMERIC_BIT is the other. NUMERIC_STD uses the multivalued data type, std_logic, defined in package STD_LOGIC_1164. Array types of type std_logic are defined in this package and are named signed and unsigned. These are the types used by the VHDL models throughout this book. Package NUMERIC_BIT has identical functions, but instead uses the two valued data type, bit and bit_vector.

Standard synthesis Package NUMERIC_STD (IEEE 1076.3)

```
-- ---------------------------------------------------------
-- Copyright © 1996 by IEEE. All rights reserved.
-- This source file is an essential part of IEEE Draft Standard P1076.3,
-- Standard VHDL Synthesis Packages.
--
-- This source file represents a portion of IEEE Draft Standard P1076.3 and is
-- unapproved and subject to change.
--
-- This package may be modified to include additional data required by tools,
-- but it must in no way change the external interfaces or simulation behavior of
-- the description. It is permissible to add comments and/or attributes to the
-- package declarations, but not to change or delete any original lines of the
-- package declaration. The package body may be changed only in
-- accordance with the terms of 7.1 and 7.2 of this draft standard.
--
-- Title       : Standard VHDL Synthesis Packages  (1076.3,NUMERIC_STD)
-- Library     : This package shall be compiled into a library symbolically
--             : named IEEE.
-- Developers  : IEEE DASC Synthesis Working Group, PAR 1076.3
-- Purpose     : This package defines numeric types and arithmetic functions for
--             : use with synthesis tools. Two numeric types are defined :
--             : -- > UNSIGNED: represents UNSIGNED number in vector form -- >
--             : SIGNED: represents a SIGNED number in vector form. The base
--             : element type is type STD_LOGIC. The leftmost bit is treated as
--             : the most significant bit. Signed vectors are represented in
--             : two's complement form. This package contains overloaded
--             : arithmetic operators on the SIGNED and UNSIGNED types. The
--             : package also contains useful type conversions functions.
--
--             : If any argument to a function is a null array, a null array
--             : is returned (exceptions, if any, are noted individually).
-- Note        : No declarations or definitions shall be included in, or excluded
--             : from this package. The "package declaration" defines the types,
--             : subtypes and declarations of NUMERIC_STD. The NUMERIC_STD
--             : package body shall be considered the formal definition of the
--             : semantics of this package. Tool developers may choose to
--             : implement the package body in the most efficient manner
--             : available to them.
-- ---------------------------------------------------------
-- modification history :
-- ---------------------------------------------------------
-- Version:  2.4
-- Date   :  12 April 1995
-- ---------------------------------------------------------
library IEEE;
use IEEE.STD_LOGIC_1164.all;

package NUMERIC_STD is
    constant CopyRightNotice: STRING
        := "Copyright © 199X IEEE. All rights reserved.";
    --=====================================================
    Numeric array type definitions
    --=====================================================
    type UNSIGNED is array (NATURAL range <>) of STD_LOGIC;
    type SIGNED is array (NATURAL range <>) of STD_LOGIC;
    --=====================================================
    -- Arithmetic Operators:
    --=====================================================
    -- Id: A.1
    function "abs" (ARG: SIGNED) return SIGNED;
    -- Result subtype: SIGNED(ARG'LENGTH-1 downto 0).
    -- Result: Returns the absolute value of a SIGNED vector ARG.

    -- Id: A.2
    function "-" (ARG: SIGNED) return SIGNED;
    -- Result subtype: SIGNED(ARG'LENGTH-1 downto 0).
    -- Result:    Returns the value of the unary minus operation on a
    --            SIGNED vector ARG.
    --=====================================================

    -- Id: A.3
    function "+" (L, R: UNSIGNED) return UNSIGNED;
```

```
    -- Result subtype: UNSIGNED(MAX(L'LENGTH, R'LENGTH)-1 downto 0).
    -- Result: Adds two UNSIGNED vectors that may be of different lengths.

    -- Id: A.4
    function "+" (L, R: SIGNED) return SIGNED;
    -- Result subtype: SIGNED(MAX(L'LENGTH, R'LENGTH)-1 downto 0).
    -- Result: Adds two SIGNED vectors that may be of different lengths.

    -- Id: A.5
    function "+" (L: UNSIGNED; R: NATURAL) return UNSIGNED;
    -- Result subtype: UNSIGNED(L'LENGTH-1 downto 0).
    -- Result: Adds an UNSIGNED vector, L, with a non-negative INTEGER, R.

    -- Id: A.6
    function "+" (L: NATURAL; R: UNSIGNED) return UNSIGNED;
    -- Result subtype: UNSIGNED(R'LENGTH-1 downto 0).
    -- Result: Adds a non-negative INTEGER, L, with an UNSIGNED vector, R.

    -- Id: A.7
    function "+" (L: INTEGER; R: SIGNED) return SIGNED;
    -- Result subtype: SIGNED(R'LENGTH-1 downto 0).
    -- Result: Adds an INTEGER, L(may be positive or negative), to a SIGNED
    --         vector, R.

    -- Id: A.8
    function "+" (L: SIGNED; R: INTEGER) return SIGNED;
    -- Result subtype: SIGNED(L'LENGTH-1 downto 0).
    -- Result: Adds a SIGNED vector, L, to an INTEGER, R.
    --=====================================================

    -- Id: A.9
    function "-" (L, R: UNSIGNED) return UNSIGNED;
    -- Result subtype: UNSIGNED(MAX(L'LENGTH, R'LENGTH)-1 downto 0).
    -- Result: Subtracts two UNSIGNED vectors that may be of different lengths.

    -- Id: A.10
    function "-" (L, R: SIGNED) return SIGNED;
    -- Result subtype: SIGNED(MAX(L'LENGTH, R'LENGTH)-1 downto 0).
    -- Result: Subtracts a SIGNED vector, R, from another SIGNED vector, L,
    --         that may possibly be of different lengths.

    -- Id: A.11
    function "-" (L: UNSIGNED;R: NATURAL) return UNSIGNED;
    -- Result subtype: UNSIGNED(L'LENGTH-1 downto 0).
    -- Result: Subtracts a non-negative INTEGER, R, from an UNSIGNED vector, L.

    -- Id: A.12
    function "-" (L: NATURAL; R: UNSIGNED) return UNSIGNED;
    -- Result subtype: UNSIGNED(R'LENGTH-1 downto 0).
    -- Result: Subtracts an UNSIGNED vector, R, from a non-negative INTEGER, L.

    -- Id: A.13
    function "-" (L: SIGNED; R: INTEGER) return SIGNED;
    -- Result subtype: SIGNED(L'LENGTH-1 downto 0).
    -- Result: Subtracts an INTEGER, R, from a SIGNED vector, L.

    -- Id: A.14
    function "-" (L: INTEGER; R: SIGNED) return SIGNED;
    -- Result subtype: SIGNED(R'LENGTH-1 downto 0).
    -- Result: Subtracts a SIGNED vector, R, from an INTEGER, L.

    --=====================================================

    -- Id: A.15
    function "*" (L, R: UNSIGNED) return UNSIGNED;
    -- Result subtype: UNSIGNED((L'LENGTH+R'LENGTH-1) downto 0).
    -- Result: Performs the multiplication operation on two UNSIGNED vectors
    --         that may possibly be of different lengths.

    -- Id: A.16
    function "*" (L, R: SIGNED) return SIGNED;
    -- Result subtype: SIGNED((L'LENGTH+R'LENGTH-1) downto 0)
```

Standard synthesis Package NUMERIC_STD (IEEE 1076.3)

-- Result: Multiplies two SIGNED vectors that may possibly be of
--   different lengths.

-- Id: A.17
 function "*" (L: UNSIGNED; R: NATURAL) return UNSIGNED;
-- Result subtype: UNSIGNED((L'LENGTH+L'LENGTH-1) downto 0).
-- Result: Multiplies an UNSIGNED vector, L, with a non-negative
--   INTEGER, R. R is converted to an UNSIGNED vector of
--   SIZE L'LENGTH before multiplication.

-- Id: A.18
 function "*" (L: NATURAL; R: UNSIGNED) return UNSIGNED;
-- Result subtype: UNSIGNED((R'LENGTH+R'LENGTH-1) downto 0).
-- Result: Multiplies an UNSIGNED vector, R, with a non-negative
--   INTEGER, L. L is converted to an UNSIGNED vector of
--   SIZE R'LENGTH before multiplication.

-- Id: A.19
 function "*" (L: SIGNED; R: INTEGER) return SIGNED;
-- Result subtype: SIGNED((L'LENGTH+L'LENGTH-1) downto 0)
-- Result: Multiplies a SIGNED vector, L, with an INTEGER, R. R is
--   converted to a SIGNED vector of SIZE L'LENGTH before multiplication.

-- Id: A.20
 function "*" (L: INTEGER; R: SIGNED) return SIGNED;
-- Result subtype: SIGNED((R'LENGTH+R'LENGTH-1) downto 0)
-- Result: Multiplies a SIGNED vector, R, with an INTEGER, L. L is converted to a
--   SIGNED vector of SIZE R'LENGTH before multiplication.

--==
--
-- NOTE: If second argument is zero for "/" operator, a severity level of ERROR
-- is issued.
--

-- Id: A.21
 function "/" (L, R: UNSIGNED) return UNSIGNED;
-- Result subtype: UNSIGNED(L'LENGTH-1 downto 0)
-- Result: Divides an UNSIGNED vector, L, by another UNSIGNED vector, R.

-- Id: A.22
 function "/" (L, R: SIGNED) return SIGNED;
-- Result subtype: SIGNED(L'LENGTH-1 downto 0)
-- Result: Divides an SIGNED vector, L, by another SIGNED vector, R.

-- Id: A.23
 function "/" (L: UNSIGNED; R: NATURAL) return UNSIGNED;
-- Result subtype: UNSIGNED(L'LENGTH-1 downto 0)
-- Result: Divides an UNSIGNED vector, L, by a non-negative INTEGER, R.
--   If NO_OF_BITS(R) > L'LENGTH, result is truncated to L'LENGTH.

-- Id: A.24
 function "/" (L: NATURAL; R: UNSIGNED) return UNSIGNED;
-- Result subtype: UNSIGNED(R'LENGTH-1 downto 0)
-- Result: Divides a non-negative INTEGER, L, by an UNSIGNED vector, R.
--   If NO_OF_BITS(L) > R'LENGTH, result is truncated to R'LENGTH.

-- Id: A.25
 function "/" (L: SIGNED; R: INTEGER) return SIGNED;
-- Result subtype: SIGNED(L'LENGTH-1 downto 0)
-- Result: Divides a SIGNED vector, L, by an INTEGER, R.
--   If NO_OF_BITS(R) > L'LENGTH, result is truncated to L'LENGTH.

-- Id: A.26
 function "/" (L: INTEGER; R: SIGNED) return SIGNED;
-- Result subtype: SIGNED(R'LENGTH-1 downto 0)
-- Result: Divides an INTEGER, L, by a SIGNED vector, R.
--   If NO_OF_BITS(L) > R'LENGTH, result is truncated to R'LENGTH.

--==
-- NOTE: If second argument is zero for "rem" operator, a severity level
--   of ERROR is issued.

-- Id: A.27
 function "rem" (L, R: UNSIGNED) return UNSIGNED;
-- Result subtype: UNSIGNED(R'LENGTH-1 downto 0)
-- Result: Computes "L rem R" where L and R are UNSIGNED vectors.

-- Id: A.28
 function "rem" (L, R: SIGNED) return SIGNED;
-- Result subtype: SIGNED(R'LENGTH-1 downto 0)
-- Result: Computes "L rem R" where L and R are SIGNED vectors.

-- Id: A.29
 function "rem" (L: UNSIGNED; R: NATURAL) return UNSIGNED;
-- Result subtype: UNSIGNED(L'LENGTH-1 downto 0)

-- Result: Computes "L rem R" where L is an UNSIGNED vector and R is a
--   non-negative INTEGER. If NO_OF_BITS(R) > L'LENGTH, result is
--   truncated to L'LENGTH.

-- Id: A.30
 function "rem" (L: NATURAL; R: UNSIGNED) return UNSIGNED;
-- Result subtype: UNSIGNED(R'LENGTH-1 downto 0)
-- Result: Computes "L rem R" where R is an UNSIGNED vector and L is a
--   non-negative INTEGER.
--   If NO_OF_BITS(L) > R'LENGTH, result is truncated to R'LENGTH.

-- Id: A.31
 function "rem" (L: SIGNED; R: INTEGER) return SIGNED;
-- Result subtype: SIGNED(L'LENGTH-1 downto 0)
-- Result: Computes "L rem R" where L is SIGNED vector and R is an INTEGER.
--   If NO_OF_BITS(R) > L'LENGTH, result is truncated to L'LENGTH.

-- Id: A.32
 function "rem" (L: INTEGER; R: SIGNED) return SIGNED;
-- Result subtype: SIGNED(R'LENGTH-1 downto 0)
-- Result: Computes "L rem R" where R is SIGNED vector and L is an INTEGER.
--   If NO_OF_BITS(L) > R'LENGTH, result is truncated to R'LENGTH.

--==
-- NOTE: If second argument is zero for "mod" operator, a severity level
--   of ERROR is issued.

-- Id: A.33
 function "mod" (L, R: UNSIGNED) return UNSIGNED;
-- Result subtype: UNSIGNED(R'LENGTH-1 downto 0)
-- Result: Computes "L mod R" where L and R are UNSIGNED vectors.

-- Id: A.34
 function "mod" (L, R: SIGNED) return SIGNED;
-- Result subtype: SIGNED(R'LENGTH-1 downto 0)
-- Result: Computes "L mod R" where L and R are SIGNED vectors.

-- Id: A.35
 function "mod" (L: UNSIGNED; R: NATURAL) return UNSIGNED;
-- Result subtype: UNSIGNED(L'LENGTH-1 downto 0)
-- Result: Computes "L mod R" where L is an UNSIGNED vector and R
--   is a non-negative INTEGER.
--   If NO_OF_BITS(R) > L'LENGTH, result is truncated to L'LENGTH.

-- Id: A.36
 function "mod" (L: NATURAL; R: UNSIGNED) return UNSIGNED;
-- Result subtype: UNSIGNED(R'LENGTH-1 downto 0)
-- Result: Computes "L mod R" where R is an UNSIGNED vector and L
--   is a non-negative INTEGER.
--   If NO_OF_BITS(L) > R'LENGTH, result is truncated to R'LENGTH.

-- Id: A.37
 function "mod" (L: SIGNED; R: INTEGER) return SIGNED;
-- Result subtype: SIGNED(L'LENGTH-1 downto 0)
-- Result: Computes "L mod R" where L is a SIGNED vector and
--   R is an INTEGER.
--   If NO_OF_BITS(R) > L'LENGTH, result is truncated to L'LENGTH.

-- Id: A.38
 function "mod" (L: INTEGER; R: SIGNED) return SIGNED;
-- Result subtype: SIGNED(R'LENGTH-1 downto 0)
-- Result: Computes "L mod R" where L is an INTEGER and
--   R is a SIGNED vector.
--   If NO_OF_BITS(L) > R'LENGTH, result is truncated to R'LENGTH.

--==
-- Comparison Operators
--==

-- Id: C.1
 function ">" (L, R: UNSIGNED) return BOOLEAN;
-- Result subtype: BOOLEAN
-- Result: Computes "L > R" where L and R are UNSIGNED vectors possibly
--   of different lengths.

-- Id: C.2
 function ">" (L, R: SIGNED) return BOOLEAN;
-- Result subtype: BOOLEAN
-- Result: Computes "L > R" where L and R are SIGNED vectors possibly
--   of different lengths.

-- Id: C.3
 function ">" (L: NATURAL; R: UNSIGNED) return BOOLEAN;
-- Result subtype: BOOLEAN
-- Result: Computes "L > R" where L is a non-negative INTEGER and
--   R is an UNSIGNED vector.

409

Standard synthesis Package NUMERIC_STD (IEEE 1076.3)

-- Id: C.4
function ">" (L: INTEGER; R: SIGNED) **return** BOOLEAN;
-- Result subtype: BOOLEAN
-- Result: Computes "L > R" where L is a INTEGER and
--   R is a SIGNED vector.

-- Id: C.5
function ">" (L: UNSIGNED; R: NATURAL) **return** BOOLEAN;
-- Result subtype: BOOLEAN
-- Result: Computes "L > R" where L is an UNSIGNED vector and
--   R is a non-negative INTEGER.

-- Id: C.6
function ">" (L: SIGNED; R: INTEGER) **return** BOOLEAN;
-- Result subtype: BOOLEAN
-- Result: Computes "L > R" where L is a SIGNED vector and
--   R is a INTEGER.

--===

-- Id: C.7
function "<" (L, R: UNSIGNED) **return** BOOLEAN;
-- Result subtype: BOOLEAN
-- Result: Computes "L < R" where L and R are UNSIGNED vectors possibly
--   of different lengths.

-- Id: C.8
function "<" (L, R: SIGNED) **return** BOOLEAN;
-- Result subtype: BOOLEAN
-- Result: Computes "L < R" where L and R are SIGNED vectors possibly
--   of different lengths.

-- Id: C.9
function "<" (L: NATURAL; R: UNSIGNED) **return** BOOLEAN;
-- Result subtype: BOOLEAN
-- Result: Computes "L < R" where L is a non-negative INTEGER and
--   R is an UNSIGNED vector.

-- Id: C.10
function "<" (L: INTEGER; R: SIGNED) **return** BOOLEAN;
-- Result subtype: BOOLEAN
-- Result: Computes "L < R" where L is an INTEGER and
--   R is a SIGNED vector.

-- Id: C.11
function "<" (L: UNSIGNED; R: NATURAL) **return** BOOLEAN;
-- Result subtype: BOOLEAN
-- Result: Computes "L < R" where L is an UNSIGNED vector and
--   R is a non-negative INTEGER.

-- Id: C.12
function "<" (L: SIGNED; R: INTEGER) **return** BOOLEAN;
-- Result subtype: BOOLEAN
-- Result: Computes "L < R" where L is a SIGNED vector and
--   R is an INTEGER.

--===

-- Id: C.13
function "<=" (L, R: UNSIGNED) **return** BOOLEAN;
-- Result subtype: BOOLEAN
-- Result: Computes "L <= R" where L and R are UNSIGNED vectors possibly
--   of different lengths.

-- Id: C.14
function "<=" (L, R: SIGNED) **return** BOOLEAN;
-- Result subtype: BOOLEAN
-- Result: Computes "L <= R" where L and R are SIGNED vectors possibly
--   of different lengths.

-- Id: C.15
function "<=" (L: NATURAL; R: UNSIGNED) **return** BOOLEAN;
-- Result subtype: BOOLEAN
-- Result: Computes "L <= R" where L is a non-negative INTEGER and
--   R is an UNSIGNED vector.

-- Id: C.16
function "<=" (L: INTEGER; R: SIGNED) **return** BOOLEAN;
-- Result subtype: BOOLEAN
-- Result: Computes "L <= R" where L is an INTEGER and
--   R is a SIGNED vector.

-- Id: C.17
function "<=" (L: UNSIGNED; R: NATURAL) **return** BOOLEAN;
-- Result subtype: BOOLEAN
-- Result: Computes "L <= R" where L is an UNSIGNED vector and
--   R is a non-negative INTEGER.

-- Id: C.18
function "<=" (L: SIGNED; R: INTEGER) **return** BOOLEAN;
-- Result subtype: BOOLEAN
-- Result: Computes "L <= R" where L is a SIGNED vector and
--   R is an INTEGER.

--===

-- Id: C.19
function ">=" (L, R: UNSIGNED) **return** BOOLEAN;
-- Result subtype: BOOLEAN
-- Result: Computes "L >= R" where L and R are UNSIGNED vectors possibly
--   of different lengths.

-- Id: C.20
function ">=" (L, R: SIGNED) **return** BOOLEAN;
-- Result subtype: BOOLEAN
-- Result: Computes "L >= R" where L and R are SIGNED vectors possibly
--   of different lengths.

-- Id: C.21
function ">=" (L: NATURAL; R: UNSIGNED) **return** BOOLEAN;
-- Result subtype: BOOLEAN
-- Result: Computes "L >= R" where L is a non-negative INTEGER and
--   R is an UNSIGNED vector.

-- Id: C.22
function ">=" (L: INTEGER; R: SIGNED) **return** BOOLEAN;
-- Result subtype: BOOLEAN
-- Result: Computes "L >= R" where L is an INTEGER and
--   R is a SIGNED vector.

-- Id: C.23
function ">=" (L: UNSIGNED; R: NATURAL) **return** BOOLEAN;
-- Result subtype: BOOLEAN
-- Result: Computes "L >= R" where L is an UNSIGNED vector and
--   R is a non-negative INTEGER.

-- Id: C.24
function ">=" (L: SIGNED; R: INTEGER) **return** BOOLEAN;
-- Result subtype: BOOLEAN
-- Result: Computes "L >= R" where L is a SIGNED vector and
--   R is an INTEGER.

--===

-- Id: C.25
function "=" (L, R: UNSIGNED) **return** BOOLEAN;
-- Result subtype: BOOLEAN
-- Result: Computes "L = R" where L and R are UNSIGNED vectors possibly
--   of different lengths.

-- Id: C.26
function "=" (L, R: SIGNED) **return** BOOLEAN;
-- Result subtype: BOOLEAN
-- Result: Computes "L = R" where L and R are SIGNED vectors possibly
--   of different lengths.

-- Id: C.27
function "=" (L: NATURAL; R: UNSIGNED) **return** BOOLEAN;
-- Result subtype: BOOLEAN
-- Result: Computes "L = R" where L is a non-negative INTEGER and
--   R is an UNSIGNED vector.

-- Id: C.28
function "=" (L: INTEGER; R: SIGNED) **return** BOOLEAN;
-- Result subtype: BOOLEAN
-- Result: Computes "L = R" where L is an INTEGER and
--   R is a SIGNED vector.

-- Id: C.29
function "=" (L: UNSIGNED; R: NATURAL) **return** BOOLEAN;
-- Result subtype: BOOLEAN
-- Result: Computes "L = R" where L is an UNSIGNED vector and
--   R is a non-negative INTEGER.

-- Id: C.30
function "=" (L: SIGNED; R: INTEGER) **return** BOOLEAN;
-- Result subtype: BOOLEAN
-- Result: Computes "L = R" where L is a SIGNED vector and
--   R is an INTEGER.

--===

-- Id: C.31
function "/=" (L, R: UNSIGNED) **return** BOOLEAN;
-- Result subtype: BOOLEAN

Standard synthesis Package NUMERIC_STD (IEEE 1076.3)

```
-- Result: Computes "L /= R" where L and R are UNSIGNED vectors possibly
--         of different lengths.

-- Id: C.32
function "/=" (L, R: SIGNED) return BOOLEAN;
-- Result subtype: BOOLEAN
-- Result: Computes "L /= R" where L and R are SIGNED vectors possibly
--         of different lengths.

-- Id: C.33
function "/=" (L: NATURAL; R: UNSIGNED) return BOOLEAN;
-- Result subtype: BOOLEAN
-- Result: Computes "L /= R" where L is a non-negative INTEGER and
--         R is an UNSIGNED vector.

-- Id: C.34
function "/=" (L: INTEGER; R: SIGNED) return BOOLEAN;
-- Result subtype: BOOLEAN
-- Result: Computes "L /= R" where L is an INTEGER and
--         R is a SIGNED vector.

-- Id: C.35
function "/=" (L: UNSIGNED; R: NATURAL) return BOOLEAN;
-- Result subtype: BOOLEAN
-- Result: Computes "L /= R" where L is an UNSIGNED vector and
--         R is a non-negative INTEGER.

-- Id: C.36
function "/=" (L: SIGNED; R: INTEGER) return BOOLEAN;
-- Result subtype: BOOLEAN
-- Result: Computes "L /= R" where L is a SIGNED vector and
--         R is an INTEGER.
--
-- ==============================================================
-- Shift and Rotate Functions
-- ==============================================================

-- Id: S.1
function SHIFT_LEFT (ARG: UNSIGNED; COUNT: NATURAL) return UNSIGNED;
-- Result subtype: UNSIGNED(ARG'LENGTH-1 downto 0)
-- Result: Performs a shift-left on an UNSIGNED vector COUNT times.
--         The vacated positions are filled with '0'.
--         The COUNT leftmost elements are lost.

-- Id: S.2
function SHIFT_RIGHT (ARG: UNSIGNED; COUNT: NATURAL) return UNSIGNED;
-- Result subtype: UNSIGNED(ARG'LENGTH-1 downto 0)
-- Result: Performs a shift-right on an UNSIGNED vector COUNT times.
--         The vacated positions are filled with '0'.
--         The COUNT rightmost elements are lost.

-- Id: S.3
function SHIFT_LEFT (ARG: SIGNED; COUNT: NATURAL) return SIGNED;
-- Result subtype: SIGNED(ARG'LENGTH-1 downto 0)
-- Result: Performs a shift-left on a SIGNED vector COUNT times.
--         The vacated positions are filled with '0'.
--         The COUNT leftmost elements are lost.

-- Id: S.4
function SHIFT_RIGHT (ARG: SIGNED; COUNT: NATURAL) return SIGNED;
-- Result subtype: SIGNED(ARG'LENGTH-1 downto 0)
-- Result: Performs a shift-right on a SIGNED vector COUNT times.
--         The vacated positions are filled with the leftmost
--         element, ARG'LEFT. The COUNT rightmost elements are lost.

-- ==============================================================

-- Id: S.5
function ROTATE_LEFT (ARG: UNSIGNED; COUNT: NATURAL) return UNSIGNED;
-- Result subtype: UNSIGNED(ARG'LENGTH-1 downto 0)
-- Result: Performs a rotate-left of an UNSIGNED vector COUNT times.

-- Id: S.6 function ROTATE_RIGHT (ARG: UNSIGNED; COUNT: NATURAL) return
--         UNSIGNED;
-- Result subtype: UNSIGNED(ARG'LENGTH-1 downto 0)
-- Result: Performs a rotate-right of an UNSIGNED vector COUNT times.

-- Id: S.7
function ROTATE_LEFT (ARG: SIGNED; COUNT: NATURAL) return SIGNED;
-- Result subtype: SIGNED(ARG'LENGTH-1 downto 0)
-- Result: Performs a logical rotate-left of a SIGNED
--         vector COUNT times.

-- Id: S.8 function ROTATE_RIGHT (ARG: SIGNED; COUNT: NATURAL) return
--         SIGNED;
-- Result subtype: SIGNED(ARG'LENGTH-1 downto 0)
-- Result: Performs a logical rotate-right of a SIGNED
--         vector COUNT times.
```

```
-- ==============================================================
-- ==============================================================

-- Note : Function S.9 is not compatible with VHDL 1076-1987. Comment
--        out the function (declaration and body) for VHDL 1076-1987 compatibility.

-- Id: S.9
function "sll" (ARG: UNSIGNED; COUNT: INTEGER) return UNSIGNED;
-- Result subtype: UNSIGNED(ARG'LENGTH-1 downto 0)
-- Result: SHIFT_LEFT(ARG, COUNT)

-- Note : Function S.10 is not compatible with VHDL 1076-1987. Comment
--        out the function (declaration and body) for VHDL 1076-1987 compatibility.

-- Id: S.10
function "sll" (ARG: SIGNED; COUNT: INTEGER) return SIGNED;
-- Result subtype: SIGNED(ARG'LENGTH-1 downto 0)
-- Result: SHIFT_LEFT(ARG, COUNT)

-- Note : Function S.11 is not compatible with VHDL 1076-1987. Comment
--        out the function (declaration and body) for VHDL 1076-1987 compatibility.

-- Id: S.11
function "srl" (ARG: UNSIGNED; COUNT: INTEGER) return UNSIGNED;
-- Result subtype: UNSIGNED(ARG'LENGTH-1 downto 0)
-- Result: SHIFT_RIGHT(ARG, COUNT)

-- Note : Function S.12 is not compatible with VHDL 1076-1987. Comment
--        out the function (declaration and body) for VHDL 1076-1987 compatibility.

-- Id: S.12
function "srl" (ARG: SIGNED; COUNT: INTEGER) return SIGNED;
-- Result subtype: SIGNED(ARG'LENGTH-1 downto 0)
-- Result: SIGNED(SHIFT_RIGHT(UNSIGNED(ARG), COUNT))

-- Note : Function S.13 is not compatible with VHDL 1076-1987. Comment
--        out the function (declaration and body) for VHDL 1076-1987 compatibility.

-- Id: S.13
function "rol" (ARG: UNSIGNED; COUNT: INTEGER) return UNSIGNED;
-- Result subtype: UNSIGNED(ARG'LENGTH-1 downto 0)
-- Result: ROTATE_LEFT(ARG, COUNT)

-- Note : Function S.14 is not compatible with VHDL 1076-1987. Comment
--        out the function (declaration and body) for VHDL 1076-1987 compatibility.

-- Id: S.14
function "rol" (ARG: SIGNED; COUNT: INTEGER) return SIGNED;
-- Result subtype: SIGNED(ARG'LENGTH-1 downto 0)
-- Result: ROTATE_LEFT(ARG, COUNT)

-- Note : Function S.15 is not compatible with VHDL 1076-1987. Comment
--        out the function (declaration and body) for VHDL 1076-1987 compatibility.

-- Id: S.15
function "ror" (ARG: UNSIGNED; COUNT: INTEGER) return UNSIGNED;
-- Result subtype: UNSIGNED(ARG'LENGTH-1 downto 0)
-- Result: ROTATE_RIGHT(ARG, COUNT)

-- Note : Function S.16 is not compatible with VHDL 1076-1987. Comment
--        out the function (declaration and body) for VHDL 1076-1987 compatibility.

-- Id: S.16
function "ror" (ARG: SIGNED; COUNT: INTEGER) return SIGNED;
-- Result subtype: SIGNED(ARG'LENGTH-1 downto 0)
-- Result: ROTATE_RIGHT(ARG, COUNT)

-- ==============================================================
-- RESIZE Functions
-- ==============================================================

-- Id: R.1
function RESIZE (ARG: SIGNED; NEW_SIZE: NATURAL) return SIGNED;
-- Result subtype: SIGNED(NEW_SIZE-1 downto 0)
-- Result: Resizes the SIGNED vector ARG to the specified size.
--         To create a larger vector, the new (leftmost) bit positions
--         are filled with the sign bit (ARG'LEFT). When truncating,
--         the sign bit is retained along with the rightmost part.
```

Standard synthesis Package NUMERIC_STD (IEEE 1076.3)

-- Id: R.2
function RESIZE (ARG: UNSIGNED; NEW_SIZE: NATURAL) **return** UNSIGNED;
-- Result subtype: UNSIGNED(NEW_SIZE-1 downto 0)
-- Result: Resizes the SIGNED vector ARG to the specified size.
--   To create a larger vector, the new (leftmost) bit positions
--   are filled with '0'. When truncating, the leftmost bits are dropped.

--==
-- Conversion Functions
--==

-- Id: D.1
function TO_INTEGER (ARG: UNSIGNED) **return** NATURAL;
-- Result subtype: NATURAL. Value cannot be negative since parameter is an
--   UNSIGNED vector.
-- Result: Converts the UNSIGNED vector to an INTEGER.

-- Id: D.2
function TO_INTEGER (ARG: SIGNED) **return** INTEGER;
-- Result subtype: INTEGER
-- Result: Converts a SIGNED vector to an INTEGER.

-- Id: D.3
function TO_UNSIGNED (ARG, SIZE: NATURAL) **return** UNSIGNED;
-- Result subtype: UNSIGNED(SIZE-1 downto 0)
-- Result: Converts a non-negative INTEGER to an UNSIGNED vector with
--   the specified SIZE.

-- Id: D.4
function TO_SIGNED (ARG: INTEGER; SIZE: NATURAL) **return** SIGNED;
-- Result subtype: SIGNED(SIZE-1 downto 0)
-- Result: Converts an INTEGER to a SIGNED vector of the specified SIZE.

--==
-- Logical Operators
--==

-- Id: L.1
function "not" (L: UNSIGNED) **return** UNSIGNED;
-- Result subtype: UNSIGNED(L'LENGTH-1 downto 0)
-- Result: Termwise inversion

-- Id: L.2
function "and" (L, R: UNSIGNED) **return** UNSIGNED;
-- Result subtype: UNSIGNED(L'LENGTH-1 downto 0)
-- Result: Vector AND operation

-- Id: L.3
function "or" (L, R: UNSIGNED) **return** UNSIGNED;
-- Result subtype: UNSIGNED(L'LENGTH-1 downto 0)
-- Result: Vector OR operation

-- Id: L.4
function "nand" (L, R: UNSIGNED) **return** UNSIGNED;
-- Result subtype: UNSIGNED(L'LENGTH-1 downto 0)
-- Result: Vector NAND operation

-- Id: L.5 **function** "nor" (L, R: UNSIGNED) **return** UNSIGNED;
-- Result subtype: UNSIGNED(L'LENGTH-1 downto 0)
-- Result: Vector NOR operation

-- Id: L.6
function "xor" (L, R: UNSIGNED) **return** UNSIGNED;
-- Result subtype: UNSIGNED(L'LENGTH-1 downto 0)
-- Result: Vector XOR operation

-- Note : Function L.7 is not compatible with VHDL 1076-1987. Comment
-- out the function (declaration and body) for VHDL 1076-1987 compatibility.

Id: L.7
function "xnor" (L, R: UNSIGNED) **return** UNSIGNED;
-- Result subtype: UNSIGNED(L'LENGTH-1 downto 0)
-- Result: Vector XNOR operation

-- Id: L.8
function "not" (L: SIGNED) **return** SIGNED;
-- Result subtype: SIGNED(L'LENGTH-1 downto 0)
-- Result: Termwise inversion

-- Id: L.9
function "and" (L, R: SIGNED) **return** SIGNED;
-- Result subtype: SIGNED(L'LENGTH-1 downto 0)
-- Result: Vector AND operation

-- Id: L.10
function "or" (L, R: SIGNED) **return** SIGNED;

-- Result subtype: SIGNED(L'LENGTH-1 downto 0)
-- Result: Vector OR operation

-- Id: L.11
function "nand" (L, R: SIGNED) **return** SIGNED;
-- Result subtype: SIGNED(L'LENGTH-1 downto 0)
-- Result: Vector NAND operation

-- Id: L.12
function "nor" (L, R: SIGNED) **return** SIGNED;
-- Result subtype: SIGNED(L'LENGTH-1 downto 0)
-- Result: Vector NOR operation

-- Id: L.13
function "xor" (L, R: SIGNED) **return** SIGNED;
-- Result subtype: SIGNED(L'LENGTH-1 downto 0)
-- Result: Vector XOR operation

-- Note : Function L.14 is not compatible with VHDL 1076-1987. Comment
-- out the function (declaration and body) for VHDL 1076-1987 compatibility.

-- Id: L.14
function "xnor" (L, R: SIGNED) **return** SIGNED;
-- Result subtype: SIGNED(L'LENGTH-1 downto 0)
-- Result: Vector XNOR operation

--==
-- Match Functions
--==

-- Id: M.1
function STD_MATCH (L, R: STD_ULOGIC) **return** BOOLEAN;
-- Result subtype: BOOLEAN
-- Result: terms compared per STD_LOGIC_1164 intent

-- Id: M.2
function STD_MATCH (L, R: UNSIGNED) **return** BOOLEAN;
-- Result subtype: BOOLEAN
-- Result: terms compared per STD_LOGIC_1164 intent

-- Id: M.3
function STD_MATCH (L, R: SIGNED) **return** BOOLEAN;
-- Result subtype: BOOLEAN
-- Result: terms compared per STD_LOGIC_1164 intent

-- Id: M.4
function STD_MATCH (L, R: STD_LOGIC_VECTOR) **return** BOOLEAN;
-- Result subtype: BOOLEAN
-- Result: terms compared per STD_LOGIC_1164 intent

-- Id: M.5
function STD_MATCH (L, R: STD_ULOGIC_VECTOR) **return** BOOLEAN;
-- Result subtype: BOOLEAN
-- Result: terms compared per STD_LOGIC_1164 intent

--==
-- Translation Functions
--==

-- Id: T.1
function TO_01 (S: UNSIGNED; XMAP: STD_LOGIC := '0') **return** UNSIGNED;
-- Result subtype: UNSIGNED(S'RANGE)
-- Result: Termwise, 'H' is translated to '1', and 'L' is translated to '0'. If a value
-- other than '0' | '1' | 'H' | 'L' is found, the array is set to (others => XMAP), and
-- a warning is issued.

-- Id: T.2
function TO_01 (S: SIGNED; XMAP: STD_LOGIC := '0') **return** SIGNED;
-- Result subtype: SIGNED(S'RANGF)
-- Result: Termwise, 'H' is translated to '1', and 'L' is translated
--   to '0'. If a value other than '0' | '1' | 'H' | 'L' is found, the array is set to
--   (others => XMAP), and a warning is issued.

end NUMERIC_STD;

VHDL Constructs

This is a quick reference guide to the different kinds of constructs used in VHDL. The symbol "‡" is used to identify constructs that are <u>not</u> supported by present synthesis tools. For each construct the following is shown:

      - the formal syntax definition,
      - an indication of where it may be used in a Verilog model,
      - a brief description,
      - in most cases, a simple example.

The formal syntax is shown in Backus Naur Form (BNF). The following conventions are used:

Symbol/Notation	Description	Meaning
	One or more spaces, tabs or carriage returns.	Separator between lexical elements.
<>	Sharp pointed angle brackets	Surround any non-literal symbols.
module (for example)	A word in bold print.	A Verilog keyword.
<name>	Name is in lower case.	A syntax construct item.
<NAME>	Name in upper case.	A lexical term.
<name><,<name>>*	Name is in lower case.	A comma separated list of items.
<name> ::=	Name is in lower case.	The syntax definition of an item.
|	Vertical line.	Alternative syntax definition.

entity - primary design unit declaration (design entity port list)

Used to define the interface (inputs & outputs) of a given design unit plus the environment in which it is used.

```
entity ENT1 is
    use work.SPECIAL_FNS;
    generic (N: in natural);
    port (A, B: in    std_logic;
          Y:    out  unsigned(N downto 0));
    type BUS_N is unsigned(N downto 0);
begin
    report "ERROR" severity ERROR;
end entity ENT3;
```

```
entity identifier is
    (generic (generic_list);)
    (port (port_list);)
    ( subprogram_declaration | subprogram_body
    | type_declaration | subtype_declaration
    | constant_declaration | signal_declaration
    | shared_variable_declaration
    | file_declaration | alias_declaration
    | attribute_declaration | attribute_specification
    | use_clause | disconnection_specification
    | group_template_declaration | group_declaration)
begin
    ( concurrent_assertion_statement
    | passive_concurrent_procedure_call
    | passive_process_statement)
end (entity)(entity_name);
```

```
entity ENT1 is
    }.....
begin
    }.....
end enity ENT1;
```

```
architecture ARC1 of ENT1 is
    }.....
begin
    }.....
end architecture ARC1;
```

```
BLK1: block (...) is
    }.....
begin
    }.....
end block BLK1;
```

```
PS1 : process (...)
    }.....
begin
    }.....
end process PS1;
```

```
procedure PD1 (...) is
    }.....
begin
    }.....
end procedure PD1;
```

```
function FN1 (...) return TP is
    }.....
begin
    }.....
end function FN1;
```

```
package PCK1 is
    }.....
end package PCK1;
```

```
package body PCK1 is
    }.....
end package body PCK1;
```

```
configuration CF1 of ENT1 is
    }.....
end configuration CF1;
```

architecture - secondary design unit declaration (design entity functional body)

Defines the functionality of a design unit i.e., the relationship between inputs and outputs of a given design unit. More than one **architecture** body may be associated with the same entity.

```
architecture RTL of MULT is
    }...declaration area
begin
    }.... statement area
end architecture RTL;
```

```
architecture identifier of entity_name is
    ( subprogram_declaration | subprogram_body
    | type_declaration | subtype_declaration
    | constant_declaration | signal_declaration
    | shared_variable_declaration
    | file_declaration | alias_declaration
    | attribute_declaration | attribute_specification
    | use_clause | disconnection_specification
    | group_template_declaration | group_declaration)
begin
    (concurrent_statement)
end (architecture)(architecture_name);
```

package - primary design unit declaration (common design data)

Defines the interfaces (inputs & outputs) of common design information that may be made visible to many other designs.

```
package PKG1 is
    constant Coeff1: integer;
    type Mem1 is array(1 to Coeff1) of
                                 natural;
    signal Bus1: bit_vector(7 downto 0);
    function MAX (L, R integer) return
                                 integer is
    component OR5_GATE
        port (A, B, C, D, E: in bit; Y: out BIT);
    end component;
end package PKG1;
```

```
package package_name is
    ( subprogram_declaration
    | type_declaration | subtype_declaration
    | constant_declaration | signal_declaration
    | shared_variable_declaration
    | file_declaration | alias_declaration
    | component_declaration
    | attribute_declaration | attribute_specification
    | disconnection_specification | use_clause
    | group_template_declaration | group_declaration)
end (package) (package_name);
```

package body - secondary design unit declaration (common design data)

Declares the functional bodies of subprograms (procedures and functions) that may be made visible to many designs. Also defines the values of any deferred constants declared in the interface within the package declaration.

```
package body package_name is
    ( subprogram_declaration | subprogram_body
    | type_declaration | subtype_declaration
    | constant_declaration | shared_variable_declaration
    | file_declaration | alias_declaration
    | use_clause |
    | group_template_declaration | group_declaration)
end (package_body) (package_name);
```

configuration - primary design unit declaration

A configuration specification binds component instances to design entities. A configuration declaration is similar except it allows component binding to be deferred and is specified separately in the declarative part of a design unit.

```
library TechLib1;
configuration OR8_AND8_Bind of
BitManipulation is
    for Gates
        for Comp1: OR8
            use entity TechLib1.OR_Gate;
        end for;
        for Comp2: AND8
            use entity TechLib1.OR_Gate;
        end for;
    end for;
end configuration OR8_AND8_Bind;
```

```
configuration identifier of entity_name is
    ( use_clause
    | attribute_specification
    | group_declaration)
    for ( architecture_name
        | block_statement_label
        | generate_statement_label ( discrete_range
                                 | static_expression)
    {use_clause}
    ( block_configuration
    | component_configuration)
    end for;
end (configuration) (configuration_name);
```

```
entity ENT1 is
}.....
begin
}.....
end enity ENT1;
```

```
architecture ARC1 of ENT1 is
}.....
begin
}.....
end architecture ARC1;
```

```
BLK1: block (...) is
}.....
begin
}.....
end block BLK1;
```

```
PS1 : process (...)
}.....
begin
}.....
end process PS1;
```

```
procedure PD1 (...) is
}.....
begin
}.....
end procedure PD1;
```

```
function FN1 (...) return TP is
}.....
begin
}.....
end function FN1;
```

```
package PCK1 is
}.....
end package PCK1;
```

```
package body PCK1 is
}.....
end package body PCK1;
```

```
configuration CF1 of ENT1 is
}.....
end configuration CF1;
```

415

library - context clause

A design library is used to store previously analyzed designs. These designs are made visible to new designs by preceding the new design with the library clause. (A library may contain one or more packages.)

library IEEE, Macros;

library identifier {, identifier}; — ①

① ② entity ENT1 is
② }.....
begin
}.....
end entity ENT1;

① ② architecture ARC1 of ENT1 is
② }.....
begin
}.....
end architecture ARC1;

② BLK1: **block** (...) **is**
}.....
begin
}.....
end block BLK1;

② PS1 : **process** (...)
}.....
begin
}.....
end process PS1;

use - context clause

Usually comes after a library clause and before a new design entity. It causes previously declared declarations within a library to be made directly visible within a new design provided they are visible in a library defined by the library statement.

use IEEE.STD_logic_1164.**all**;

use selected_name {, selected_name}; — ②

② **procedure** PD1 (...) **is**
}.....
begin
}.....
end procedure PD1;

② **function** FN1 (...) **return** TP **is**
}.....
begin
}.....
end function FN1;

① ② **package** PCK1 **is**
② }.....
end package PCK1;

① ② **package body** PCK1 **is**
② }.....
end package body PCK1;

① ② **configuration** CF1 **of** ENT1 **is**
② }.....
end configuration CF1;

attribute - specification

Used to specify an attribute which is a value, function, type, constant, signal or range that is attributed to a particular item in a model. An item is an entity name, architecture name, label or signal.
The attributes name and the name of one of more named objects and their value are defined.

attribute Capacitance of Clock1, Clock2: **signal is** 25 pf
attribute DELAY_TIME **of** Clock: **signal is** 2.3 ns;
attribute MAX_AREA **of** ASIC1: real **is** 25000 gates;

attribute attribute_designator **of**
(entity_designator {, entity_designator}
| **others**
| **all**):
(**entity** | **architecture** | **configuration**
| **procedure** | **function** | **package**
| **type** | **subtype** | **constant**
| **signal** | **variable** | **component**
| **label** | **literal** | **units**
| **group** | **file**)
is expression; — ③

③ entity ENT1 is
}.....
begin
}.....
end entity ENT1;

③ ④ architecture ARC1 of ENT1 is
}.....
begin
}.....
end architecture ARC1;

③ ④ BLK1: **block** (...) **is**
}.....
begin
}.....
end block BLK1;

③ PS1 : **process** (...)
}.....
begin
}.....
end process PS1;

configuration - specification

Used to bind particular component instantiations to specific entities that have been precompiled into the same or a different library. Appear in the same architecture or block declaration area as the instantiated components.
It is useful for managing multiple design projects where commonly used subblocks of the same name may need to use different precompiled versions from different libraries. For example, if you have multiple adder defined (e.g., ripple carry, or carry look ahead) in a library you can use a configuration to define which kind of adder to use in a particular instance.

for ADD1: ADDER **use configuration** Proj1Lib.ADDER_CONF;

for (instantiation_llabel {, instantiation_label}
| **others**
| **all**)
((**use** (**entity** entity_name ((architecture_identifier))
| **configuration** configuration_name
| **open**))
(**generic map** (generic_association_list))
(**port map** (port_association_list))); — ④

③ **procedure** PD1 (...) **is**
}.....
begin
}.....
end procedure PD1;

④ ③ **function** FN1 (...) **return** TP **is**
}.....
begin
}.....
end function FN1;

③ **package** PCK1 **is**
}.....
end package PCK1;

package body PCK1 **is**
}.....
end package body PCK1;

③ **configuration** CF1 **of** ENT1 **is**
}.....
end configuration CF1;

disconnect - specification

Defines the time delay to be used in the implicit disconnection of drivers of a guarded signal within a guarded signal assignment. Is used to model the delay times of signals being switched off i.e., tri-stated by a null driver.
Ignored by synthesis tools.

disconnect Bus1: wired_or **after** 4.0 ns;

```
disconnect
    ( guarded_signal_name {,guarded_signal_name}
    | others
    | all )
    after time_expression;
```

⑤

⑤

⑤

⑤

```
entity ENT1 is
}.....
begin
}.....
end enity ENT1;
```

```
architecture ARC1 of ENT1 is
}.....
begin
}.....
end architecture ARC1;
```

```
BLK1: block (...) is
}.....
begin
}.....
end block BLK1;
```

```
PS1 : process (...)
}.....
begin
}.....
end process PS1;
```

```
procedure PD1 (...) is
}.....
begin
}.....
end procedure PD1;
```

```
function FN1 (...) return TP is
}.....
begin
}.....
end function FN1;
```

⑤
```
package PCK1 is
}.....
end package PCK1;
```

```
package body PCK1 is
}.....
end package body PCK1;
```

```
configuration CF1 of ENT1 is
}.....
end configuration CF1;
```

alias - declaration

Declares an alternative name for an existing named object or part of an object. A compiler transposes an alias name with the text that is defined in the alias and allows named objects to be referenced in a more convenient manner.

variable TimeInSeconds integer **range** 0 **to** 59;
alias Secs: integer **range** 0 **to** 59 **is** TimeSeconds;

```
alias (identifier | character_literal |
    operator_symbol)
    (:subtype_indication)
    is name (signature);
```

⑥⑦

⑥

⑥⑦

```
entity ENT1 is
}.....
begin
}.....
end enity ENT1;
```

```
architecture ARC1 of ENT1 is
}.....
begin
}.....
end architecture ARC1;
```

⑥⑦
```
BLK1: block (...) is
}.....
begin
}.....
end block BLK1;
```

attribute - declaration

A value, function, type, range, signal or constant that may be associated with one or more named items in a description. There are two categories; predefined and user-defined. Predefined attributes are defined by the language, as shown earlier in this appendix. User-defined attributes are shown below. Software tools may have their own defined attributes that the designer can use. For synthesis only, use the VHDL predefined attributes supported by the synthesis tools plus any synthesis specified attributes.

attribute ENUM_TYPE_ENCODING; string;
type is (Red, Orange, Yellow, Green, Blue);
attribute color ENUM_TYPE_ENCODING **of** color: **type is** ("010 110 11 011 00");

```
attribute identifier: type_mark;
```

⑥⑦

⑦

```
PS1 : process (...)
}.....
begin
}.....
end process PS1;
```

⑥⑦
```
procedure PD1 (...) is
}.....
begin
}.....
end procedure PD1;
```

⑥⑦
```
function FN1 (...) return TP is
}.....
begin
}.....
end function FN1;
```

⑥⑦
```
package PCK1 is
}.....
end package PCK1;
```

⑥⑦
```
package body PCK1 is
}.....
end package body PCK1;
```

⑥
```
configuration CF1 of ENT1 is
}.....
end configuration CF1;
```

type - declaration

Used to declare a data type. It's name is associated with a set of values defined within the definition part of the type declaration.

```
type identifier is type definition;
```

type Rainbow **is** (Red, Orange, Yellow, Green, Blue, Indigo, Violet);
type Matrix **is array** integer **range** 1 **to** 16;

subtype - declaration

Similar to the type declaration, it is a type with a constraint that specifies a subset of values from the parent type. Predefined subtypes NATURAL and POSITIVE declared in package STANDARD are example subtypes of the parent type integer.

```
subtype identifier is subtype definition;
```

type Rainbow **is** (Red, Orange, Yellow, Green, Blue, Indigo, Violet);
subtype MidRainbow **is** Rainbow **range** Yellow **to** Blue;
subtype Byte **is** unsigned (7 **downto** 0);

constant - declaration

Declares a constant of a particular type. Can be explicitly declared or maybe deferred; see "constant (deferred)".

```
constant identifier_list: subtype_indication := expression;
```

constant BusMess: string := "Bus **is** 32 bits long";
constant StartVec: bit_vector (3 **downto** 0) := "1010";
constant Coefficient: bit_vector (15 **downto** 0) := (15 **downto** 8 => '0', 7 | 6 => '1', **others** => '0');

constant (deferred) - declaration

Deferred constants are only used in VHDL packages. Their declaration is split into two parts. The name and type of a constant is defined in a package while the actual value of the constant is specified in a package body.

```
constant identifier_list: subtype_indication;
```

The motivation for using deferred constants is that if the value of the constant needs to changed then only the package body need be recompiled and not the package itself and all models that use it.

constant NO_MSBs: integer;   -- Deferred constant in a package
constant NO_MSBs: integer := 3;   -- Value of deferred constant specified in a package body.

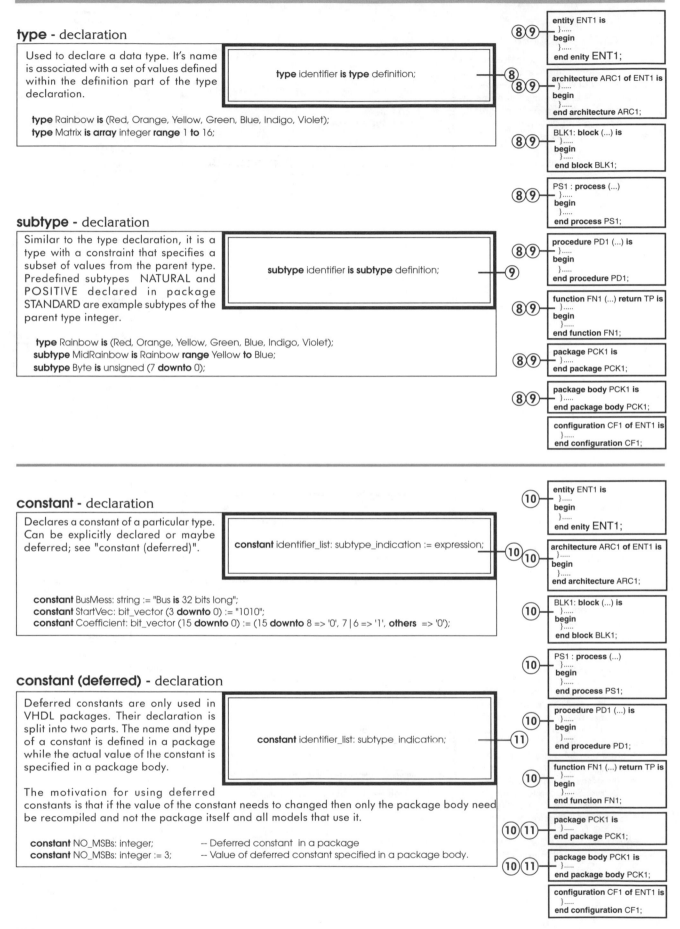

```
entity ENT1 is
  }.....
begin
  }.....
end enity ENT1;
```

```
architecture ARC1 of ENT1 is
  }.....
begin
  }.....
end architecture ARC1;
```

```
BLK1: block (...) is
  }.....
begin
  }.....
end block BLK1;
```

```
PS1 : process (...)
  }.....
begin
  }.....
end process PS1;
```

```
procedure PD1 (...) is
  }.....
begin
  }.....
end procedure PD1;
```

```
function FN1 (...) return TP is
  }.....
begin
  }.....
end function FN1;
```

```
package PCK1 is
  }.....
end package PCK1;
```

```
package body PCK1 is
  }.....
end package body PCK1;
```

```
configuration CF1 of ENT1 is
  }.....
end configuration CF1;
```

signal - declaration

Declares a signal of a particular type. Can have initial values for simulation purposes only. Initial values have no physical hardware meaning and are ignored by synthesis tools.

```
signal identifier_list: subtype_indication
    (register | bus) (:= expression);
```

```
signal Clock, Reset: std_logic;
signal Bus1: unsigned(7 downto 0);
signal TrackDelay1: time := 5 ns;
signal FSM_State: unsigned(2 downto 0);
```

variable - declaration

Declares a variable of a particular type and generally only declared and used within a particular process. Global variables should be used with caution so that not more than one process drives a variable at the same time. Can have initial values for the purposes of simulation, but as with signals, no physical hardware meaning and are ignored by synthesis tools.

```
(shared) variable identifier_list:
    subtype_indication (:= expression);
```

```
variable Count8: integer range 0 to 7 := 0;
```

group - declaration

Declares a group name for a collection of named objects. A separate group template can be declared which defines the allowable classes of named objects that can appear within a particular group.

```
group identifier: group_template name
    (name | character_literal) (, (name | character_literal));
```

```
group MixedGroup: AllData (Entity1, Signal1, Variable1);
```

group template - declaration

Declares a group template for groups. It defines the allowable classes of named objects that may appear within a particular group.

```
group identifier is
    (object_class (< >) (,object_class (< >) ))

object_class ::=
        entity          | architecture    | configuration
        | procedure      | function         | package
        | type           | subtype          | constant
        | signal         | variable         | component
        | label          | literal          | units
        | groups         | file
```

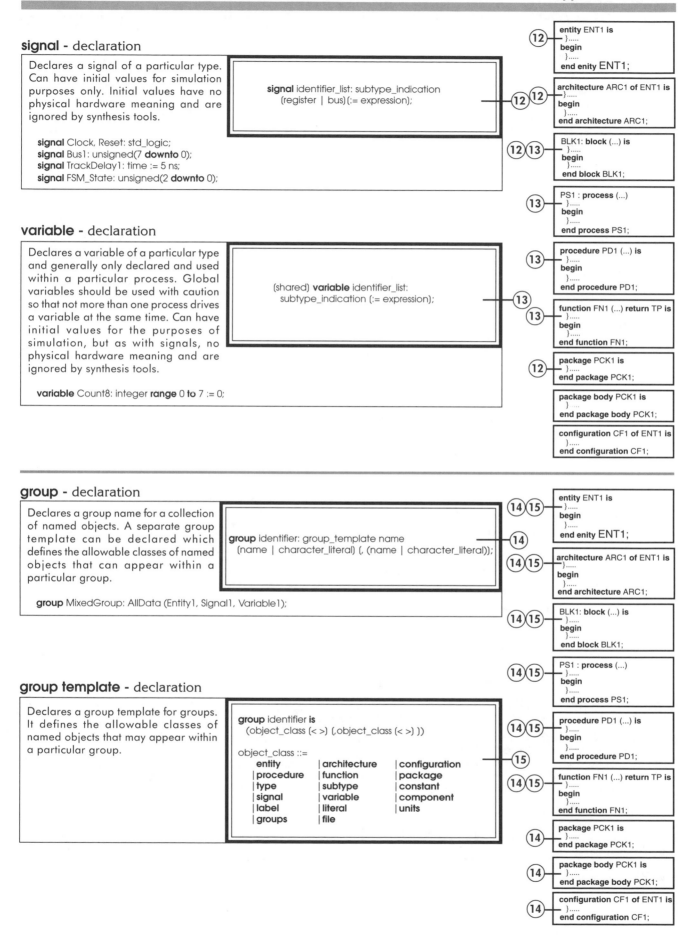

```
(12)  entity ENT1 is
          }.....
      begin
          }.....
      end enity ENT1;

(12)(12)  architecture ARC1 of ENT1 is
          }.....
      begin
          }.....
      end architecture ARC1;

(12)(13)  BLK1: block (...) is
          }.....
      begin
          }.....
      end block BLK1;

(13)  PS1 : process (...)
          }.....
      begin
          }.....
      end process PS1;

(13)  procedure PD1 (...) is
          }.....
      begin
          }.....
      end procedure PD1;

(13)  function FN1 (...) return TP is
          }.....
      begin
          }.....
      end function FN1;

(12)  package PCK1 is
          }.....
      end package PCK1;

      package body PCK1 is
          }
      end package body PCK1;

      configuration CF1 of ENT1 is
          }.....
      end configuration CF1;

(14)(15)  entity ENT1 is
          }.....
      begin
          }.....
      end enity ENT1;

(14)(15)  architecture ARC1 of ENT1 is
          }.....
      begin
          }.....
      end architecture ARC1;

(14)(15)  BLK1: block (...) is
          }.....
      begin
          }.....
      end block BLK1;

(14)(15)  PS1 : process (...)
          }.....
      begin
          }.....
      end process PS1;

(14)(15)  procedure PD1 (...) is
          }.....
      begin
          }.....
      end procedure PD1;

(14)(15)  function FN1 (...) return TP is
          }.....
      begin
          }.....
      end function FN1;

(14)  package PCK1 is
          }.....
      end package PCK1;

(14)  package body PCK1 is
          }.....
      end package body PCK1;

(14)  configuration CF1 of ENT1 is
          }.....
      end configuration CF1;
```

file - declaration

Explicitly declares a file in the host environment and its type. A file type declaration must be used to define the "subtype_indication" before declaring a file. If the **open** clause is omitted it defaults to opening a file in READ_MODE. A file may be opened in the file declaration with an implicit call to FILE_OPEN.

type vectors **is file of** unsigned;
file DataFile1: vectors is "testvecs.dat");

file identifier_list: subtype_indication
(**open** READ_MODE | WRITE_MODE
expression) **is** file_logical_name;

component - declaration

Declares the name and interface of a specific design unit (a sublevel of hierarchy or library primative) that is to be used within the calling design unit. A component configuration or configuration specification can be used to associate a particular component instance with a specific design unit.

component OR5_GATE
generic (N: positive);
port (A, B, C, D, E: **in** std_logic; Y: **out** std_logic);
end component;

component identifier **is**
(logical_generic_clause)
(local_port_clause)
end component (component_name);

procedure/function (subprogram) - declaration

Declares the inputs and outputs of a sub-program (procedure or function). Most often declared in a package body so that they may be shared by many design units. Procedure declarations may have any number of inputs and outputs declared. Functions have exactly one return value. A function declaration defines the inputs plus their type and just the type of the return value.

procedure PRD1 (**variable** A: **in** unsigned(4 **downto** 0);
constant B: **in** unsigned(4 **downto** 0);
signal Y: **out** unsigned(4 **downto** 0));
function "and" (L, R: Apples) **return** Apples;

procedure (identifier | string_literal)
((**constant** | **variable** | **signal** | **file**))

|

(**pure** | **impure**)
function designator ((**constant** | **variable** | **signal** | **file**))
return type_mark

procedure/function (subprogram body) - declaration

Declares the functional body part of a subprogram (procedure or function). The declaration of a subprogram body is optional. If the subprogram body is not declared the subprogram declaration acts as the subprogram body declaration as well. Each subprogram body declaration must have a corresponding subprogram declaration. A procedure returns zero or more values. A function returns a single value specified by the return statement.

subprogram_specification **is**
(subprogram_declaration | suprogram_body
| type_declaration | subtype_declaration
| constant_declaration | variable_declaration
| file_declaration | alias_declaration
| attribute_declaration | attribute_specification
| use_clause
| group_template_declaration | group_declaration)
begin
sequential_statement
end (subprogram_kind) (designator);

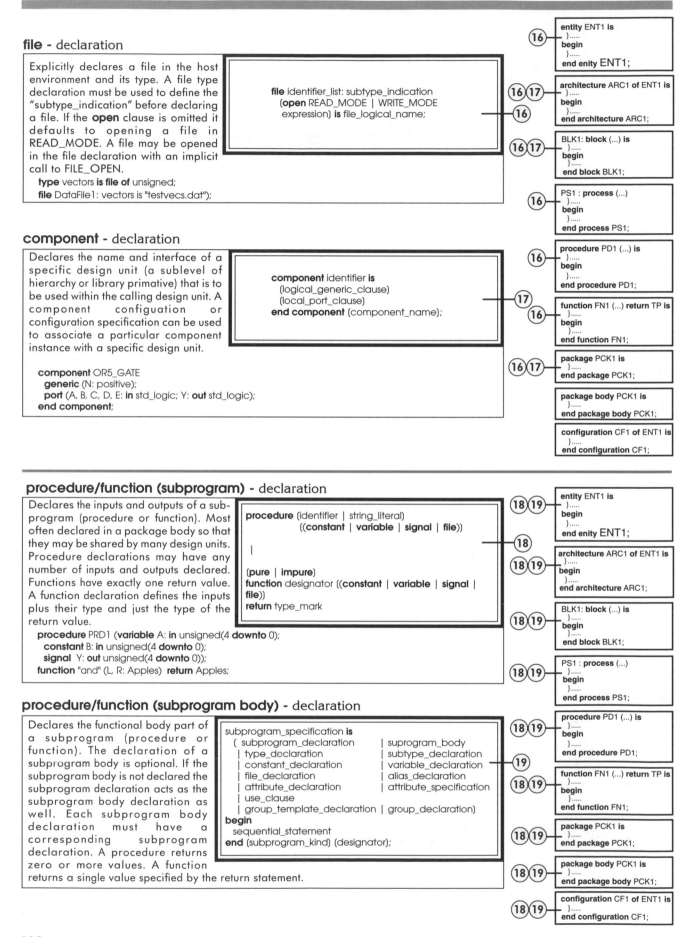

block - concurrent statement

Defines an internal block that represents a portion of a design within an architecture body. Blocks may be hierarchically nested to support design decomposition. The operation of statements within the block may be controlled by the guard expression which must be of type boolean.

```
label: block ((guard_expression)) (is)
        (generic_clause (generic_map_aspect;))
        (port_clause (port_map_aspect;))
        (block_declarative_item)
    begin
        (concurrent_statement)
    end block (label);
```

process - concurrent statement

Is the primary concurrent statement used to design synthesizable models. It defines a set of sequential statements within the process which in turn represents some portion of a design. Operates independently and concurrently with other processes.

A process is allowed within an entity statement although it must be passive like the rest of the entity statement i.e., it must not contain signal assignments.

```
(label:)
process ((sensitivity_list)) (is)
    (   subprogram_declaration  | subprogram_body
      | type_declaration        | subtype_declaration
      | constant_declaration     | variable_declaration
      | file_declaration        | alias_declaration
      | attribute_declaration    | attribute_specification
      | use_clause
      | group_type_declaration   | group_declaration)
begin
    (sequential_statement)
end (postponed) process (label);
```

This may be useful in simulation models to check for particular conditions. Passive processes do not represent hardware and so are not supported by synthesis tools.

procedure call - concurrent statement

Is concurrent by virtue of being called from within an entity, architecture or a block. As with the process statement a procedure call from within an entity statement must be passive, represents no hardware and so is not supported by synthesis tools.

```
(label:) (postponed) procedure_name
        ((formal_part =>) actual_part)
        {,formal_part=>) actual_part));
```

A concurrent procedure call can be represented with an equivalent process containing the same sequential statements from the procedure i.e., there is an equivalent process for each concurrent procedure call statement.

    Proc1(A,B,C,Y);

function call - concurrent statement

Invokes the execution of a function body and is called from within an expression of a concurrent statement. Is concurrent by virtue of the expression from where it is called being within the body of an architecture or a block.

```
function_name ((parameter_association_list))
```

    Y <= Fn1(A,B,C)

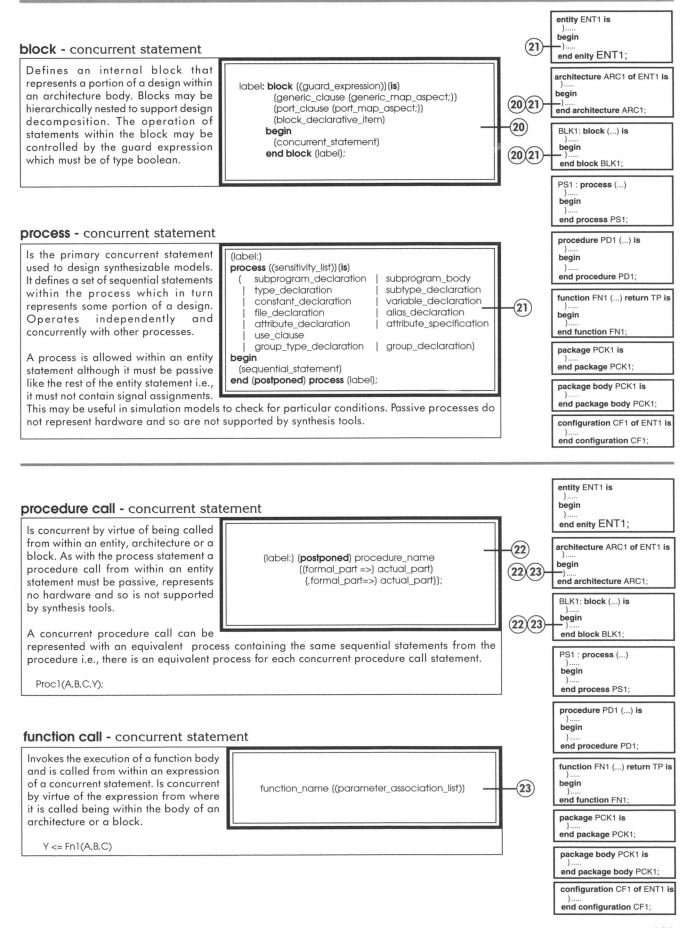

```
entity ENT1 is
    }.....
begin
    }.....
end enity ENT1;
```
(21)

```
architecture ARC1 of ENT1 is
    }.....
begin
    }.....
end architecture ARC1;
```
(20)(21)

```
BLK1: block (...) is
    }.....
begin
    }.....
end block BLK1;
```
(20)(21)

```
PS1 : process (...)
    }.....
begin
    }.....
end process PS1;
```

```
procedure PD1 (...) is
    }.....
begin
    }.....
end procedure PD1;
```

```
function FN1 (...) return TP is
    }.....
begin
    }.....
end function FN1;
```

```
package PCK1 is
    }.....
end package PCK1;
```

```
package body PCK1 is
    }.....
end package body PCK1;
```

```
configuration CF1 of ENT1 is
    }.....
end configuration CF1;
```

(20) (21)

```
entity ENT1 is
    }.....
begin
    }.....
end enity ENT1;
```

```
architecture ARC1 of ENT1 is
    }.....
begin
    }.....
end architecture ARC1;
```
(22)(23)

```
BLK1: block (...) is
    }.....
begin
    }.....
end block BLK1;
```
(22)(23)

```
PS1 : process (...)
    }.....
begin
    }.....
end process PS1;
```

```
procedure PD1 (...) is
    }.....
begin
    }.....
end procedure PD1;
```

```
function FN1 (...) return TP is
    }.....
begin
    }.....
end function FN1;
```
(23)

```
package PCK1 is
    }.....
end package PCK1;
```

```
package body PCK1 is
    }.....
end package body PCK1;
```

```
configuration CF1 of ENT1 is
    }.....
end configuration CF1;
```

421

assertion - concurrent statement

Is concurrent by virtue of residing in an entity, architecture or block. Represents a passive process containing a specified assertion statement. Is used during simulation to check a signals timing, range or value. A simulator then takes appropriate action if the assertion statement is true. Forms no functional description of a model and so is not supported by synthesis tools.

```
(label:) (postponed) assert condition
          (report expression)
          (severity expression);
```

assert Reset = '1' and Set = '1'

signal assignment - concurrent statement

Is concurrent by virtue of residing in the body of an architecture or block. Assigns values to signals. Signals may be guarded and include a delay mechanism.
A guarded signal assignment must be associated with a guard defined in a block statement. The action of a guard is similar to the sensitivity list in a process statement.
The delay mechanism using the after clause are ignored by synthesis, although the assignment still holds true but for zero time.

```
(label:) (name | aggregate)
      (transport | reject time_expression) inertial)
      waveform_element {, waveform_element}
      | unaffected
```

Y <= (A and B) or (C and D);

component instantiation - concurrent statement

Instantiates a subcomponent of a design from where the instantiation appears. It associates signals or values with the ports of the subcomponent. It can also associate constants with the generics of the subcomponent.

```
(label:) ( component ) component_name
      | entity entity_name ((architecture_identifier))
      | configuration configuration_name
          (generic_map_aspect)
          (port_map_aspect);
```

```
Add8: AddN
    generic map (8)
    port map (A,B,Y);
```

generate - concurrent statement

Is a concurrent statement in its own right like the process and block statements. Used for structurally replicating multiple parts of a design model. If the **for** statement is used concurrent statements are replicated a predetermined number of times. If the **if** statement is used concurrent statements are conditionally selected for execution. Both **for** and **if** generate statements are supported by synthesis tools. The "condition" part of the **if** clause must have static values at compile time in order for synthesis tools to generate a defined amount of logic.

```
(label:) for generate_parameter_specification
      | if condition
      generate
          ({block_declarative_item}
      begin
          {concurrent_statement}
      end generate (label);
```

```
GEN_1:      for N in 0 to 7 generate
GEN_2:          if N < 4 generate
                    Unit1: AND2 port map (A(N),B(N),Y(N));
                end generate;
GEN_3:          if N >= 4 generate
                    Unit2: OR2 port map (A(N),B(N),Y(N));
                end generate;
            end generate;
```

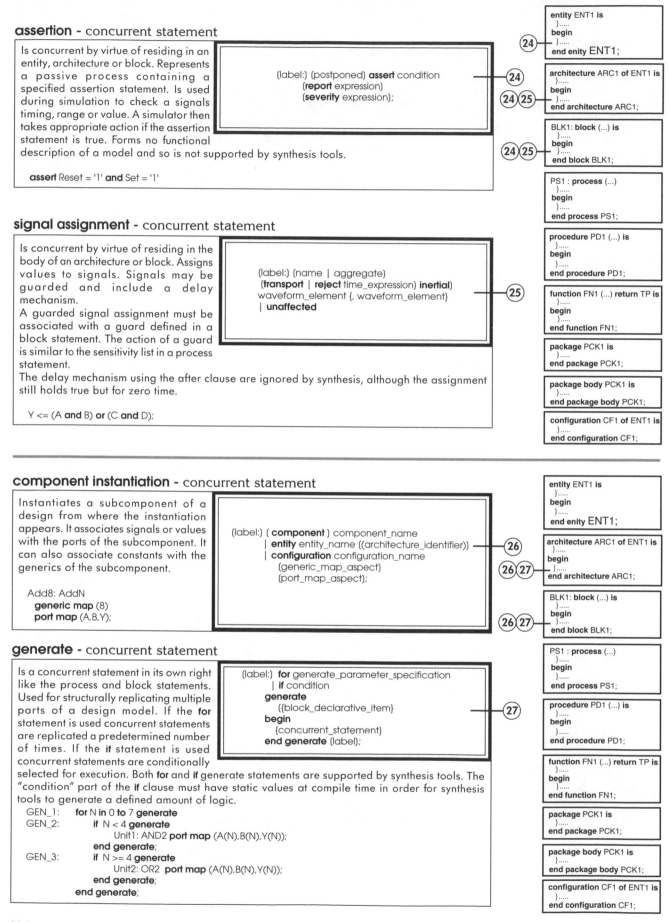

Right margin reference boxes:

```
entity ENT1 is
}.....
begin
}.....        (24)
end enity ENT1;

architecture ARC1 of ENT1 is
}.....          (24)
begin
}.....        (24)(25)
end architecture ARC1;

BLK1: block (...) is
}.....          (24)(25)
begin
}.....
end block BLK1;

PS1 : process (...)
}.....
begin
}.....
end process PS1;

procedure PD1 (...) is
}.....
begin
}.....
end procedure PD1;

function FN1 (...) return TP is
}.....          (25)
begin
}.....
end function FN1;

package PCK1 is
}.....
end package PCK1;

package body PCK1 is
}.....
end package body PCK1;

configuration CF1 of ENT1 is
}.....
end configuration CF1;

entity ENT1 is
}.....
begin
}.....
end enity ENT1;

architecture ARC1 of ENT1 is
}.....          (26)
begin
}.....        (26)(27)
end architecture ARC1;

BLK1: block (...) is
}.....          (26)(27)
begin
}.....
end block BLK1;

PS1 : process (...)
}.....
begin
}.....
end process PS1;

procedure PD1 (...) is
}.....          (27)
begin
}.....
end procedure PD1;

function FN1 (...) return TP is
}.....
begin
}.....
end function FN1;

package PCK1 is
}.....
end package PCK1;

package body PCK1 is
}.....
end package body PCK1;

configuration CF1 of ENT1 is
}.....
end configuration CF1;
```

wait - sequential statement

Causes the suspension of a process or procedure. A list of signal names define the sensitivity list to which the wait statement is sensitive. Each signal in the sensitivity list must be statically defined. Is used to infer registered elements when used with synthesis using **wait until**. The statements beginning **wait on** and **wait for** relate to timing and are not supported by synthesis tools.

```
label: wait    (on (signal_name {, signal_name}))
               | (until boolean_expression)
               | (for time_expression);
```
(28)

wait until (Enable = '1');

assertion - sequential statement

Is sequential by being in the statement area of a process or procedure.
Checks if a specified boolean condition is true during simulation. If it is not true an error message and a severity expression may be

```
label: assert condition
       (report expression)
       (severity expression);
```
(28)(29)
(29)
(28)(29)

given. If the **report** clause is present it must include an expression of predefined type STRING that specifies the message to be reported. If the **severity** clause is present it must specify an expression of predefined type SEVERITY_LEVEL that specifies the severity level of the assertion. The enumerated type SEVERITY_LEVEL is defined in package STANDARD and has the values NOTE, WARNING, ERROR AND FAILURE. Does not imply hardware so not supported by synthesis tools; are useful in test harnesses.

assert SystemReset = '1'
  report "System reset **signal** active!"
  severity WARNING;

assert Set = '1' **and** Reset = '1'
  report "Set & reset active at the same time!"
  severity error;

assert (Now - LastEvent) >= HoldTime
  report "Hold time violation"
  severity Failure;

signal assignment - sequential statement

Modifies the projected output of drivers of one or more signals. Is sequential by virtue of being positioned within the statement (body) of a concurrent process or procedure. A signal assignment is

```
label:
  name | aggregate <=
  (transport | (reject time_expression) inertial)
  waveform_element {, waveform_element} | unaffected;
```
(30)

not allowed within a function body. Signal assignments are scheduled to happen concurrently at a particular simulation delta cycle at any given simulation time. (There are as many scheduled simulation delta cycles as needed to schedule all signal assignment events at a particular simulation time.)
The **reject**, **inertial** and **after** clauses are ignored by synthesis tools.

```
--The following 3 assignments are equivalent
Y <= A after 10 ns;
Y <= inertial A after 10 ns;
Y <= reject 10 ns inertial A after 10 ns;

--Pulse rejection limit less than time expression.
Y <= reject 5 ns inertial A after 10 ns;
```

```
Reset <= TRUE, FALSE after 20 ns;
Clk <= '1' after ClkPeriod/2, '0' after
                              ClkPeriod;

Y <= A and B;
Secs <= Secs + 1;
AM_PM <= not AM_PM;
```
(30)(31)

variable assignment - sequential statement

Replaces the current value of a variable with a new value specified by the expression instantaneously. They are not scheduled like signals. The named

```
(label:) target := expression;
```
(31)
(31)

variable and the right hand side expression must be of the same type. Are used in synthesizable models.

Y := Y + 1;

Right margin syntax boxes (top group):

```
entity ENT1 is
  }.....
begin
  }.....
end enity ENT1;
```

```
architecture ARC1 of ENT1 is
  }.....
begin
  }.....
end architecture ARC1;
```

```
BLK1: block (...) is
  }.....
begin
  }.....
end block BLK1;
```

```
PS1 : process (...)
  }.....
begin
  }.....
end process PS1;
```

```
procedure PD1 (...) is
  }.....
begin
  }.....
end procedure PD1;
```

```
function FN1 (...) return TP is
  }.....
begin
  }.....
end function FN1;
```

```
package PCK1 is
  }.....
end package PCK1;
```

```
package body PCK1 is
  }.....
end package body PCK1;
```

```
configuration CF1 of ENT1 is
  }.....
end configuration CF1;
```

Right margin syntax boxes (bottom group):

```
entity ENT1 is
  }.....
begin
  }.....
end enity ENT1;
```

```
architecture ARC1 of ENT1 is
  }.....
begin
  }.....
end architecture ARC1;
```

```
BLK1: block (...) is
  }.....
begin
  }.....
end block BLK1;
```

```
PS1 : process (...)
  }.....
begin
  }.....
end process PS1;
```

```
procedure PD1 (...) is
  }.....
begin
  }.....
end procedure PD1;
```

```
function FN1 (...) return TP is
  }.....
begin
  }.....
end function FN1;
```

```
package PCK1 is
  }.....
end package PCK1;
```

```
package body PCK1 is
  }.....
end package body PCK1;
```

```
configuration CF1 of ENT1 is
  }.....
end configuration CF1;
```

procedure call - sequential statement

Is sequential by virtue of being called from within a process or another procedure. Invokes the execution of a procedure body. The "procedure_name" specifies the particular procedure to be invoked. The "actual_parameter_part", if present, specifies any inputs to and outputs from the procedure.

A procedure call acts like an in-line process. The body of the procedure is effectively inserted wherever it is called. This helps to partition large sections of code which makes it easier to read and debug.

```
-- Positional notation parameter list
PD1: Inc1(A, B, C);
-- Named notation parameter list
PD2: ClkFn1(Clk50MHz => CLK, A => X, B => Y, C => Z);
```

```
(label:) procedure_name
        ((formal_part =>) actual_part)
        (,formal_part=>) actual_part));
```
(32)

function call - sequential statement

Invokes the execution of a function body and is called from within an expression. Is sequential by virtue of the expression from where it is called being within the body of a process or a procedure.

The "function_name" specifies the name of the function to be invoked. The "parameter_association_list" lists only the input parameters to the function.

```
function_name ((parameter_association_list));
```
(33)

```
-- Positional notation parameter list
Y <= A and FN1(A1, A2, A3, A4)
-- Named association parameter list
Y <= A and FN1(F3=>A3, F4=>A4, F1=>A1, F2=>A2)
```

if - sequential statement

Selects for execution one or no sets of sequential statements depending on the value of one or more corresponding conditions. Maybe be nested within other **if** statements.

```
if (Select = '1') then
  Y <= A + B;
else
  Y <= C + A;
end if;
```

```
(label:) if condition then
           sequence_of_statements
        (elsif condition then
           sequence_of_statements)
        (else
           sequence_of_statements)
        end if (label);
```
(34)

case - sequential statement

Selects one of several branches within the **case** statement to execute based on the value of the expression. Each **case** statement considers the signal value of the expression. Cannot consider more than one expression at a time. All **case** expression values must have a **when** choice branch.

Maybe be nested within other case statements.

```
case Number is
  when "00" => Y <= A;
  when "01" => Y <= A + 1;
  when "10" => Y <= A + 2;
  when "11" => Y <= A + 3;
end case;
```

```
(label:) case expression is
           when choices =>
             sequence_of_statements
           (when choices =>
             sequence_of_statements)
        end case (label);
```
(35)

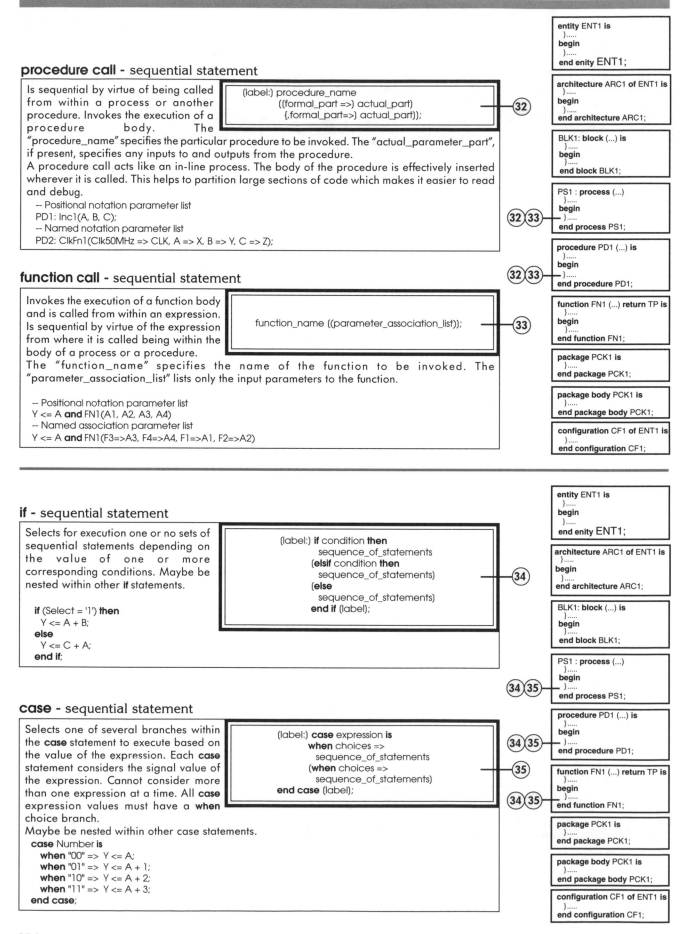

Side reference boxes:
```
entity ENT1 is
}.....
begin
}.....
end enity ENT1;

architecture ARC1 of ENT1 is
}.....
begin
}.....
end architecture ARC1;

BLK1: block (...) is
}.....
begin
}.....
end block BLK1;

PS1 : process (...)
}.....
begin
}.....
end process PS1;                (32)(33)

procedure PD1 (...) is
}.....
begin
}.....
end procedure PD1;              (32)(33)

function FN1 (...) return TP is
}.....
begin
}.....
end function FN1;               (33)

package PCK1 is
}.....
end package PCK1;

package body PCK1 is
}.....
end package body PCK1;

configuration CF1 of ENT1 is
}.....
end configuration CF1;

entity ENT1 is
}.....
begin
}.....
end enity ENT1;

architecture ARC1 of ENT1 is
}.....
begin
}.....
end architecture ARC1;

BLK1: block (...) is
}.....
begin
}.....
end block BLK1;

PS1 : process (...)
}.....
begin
}.....
end process PS1;                (34)(35)

procedure PD1 (...) is
}.....
begin
}.....
end procedure PD1;              (34)(35)

function FN1 (...) return TP is
}.....
begin
}.....
end function FN1;               (34)(35)

package PCK1 is
}.....
end package PCK1;

package body PCK1 is
}.....
end package body PCK1;

configuration CF1 of ENT1 is
}.....
end configuration CF1;
```

loop - sequential statement

Encompasses a sequence of other sequential statements to be executed repeatedly, zero or more times. May be nested within other loop statements. Do not use the **while** loop with synthesis. Synthesis needs a **for** loop with a statically defined range (known at compiled time) in order to synthesis a defined amount of logic.

```
AND_BIT_LOOP: for N in A'range loop
                  Y := Y and A(N);
              end loop;
```

```
(label:) {while condition
         |
         for loop_parameter_specification} loop
             sequence_of_statements
         end loop (label);}
```
(36)

next - sequential statement

Can only reside inside a loop, it completes the execution of an iteration of the enclosing loop. Causes the execution to jump out of the loop with the current loop parameter and begin the loop again with the next loop parameter. The completion of the current loop is conditional if the statement includes a **when** condition. Is normally supported by synthesis tools.

```
TestAB:         for (N in 1 to 12) loop
                    next when (A=B):
Test_A_less_B:      if (A < B) then
                        Y := C1;
                    else
                        Y := C2;
                    end if;
                end loop;
```

```
(label:) next (loop_label) (when condition);
```
(36) (36)(37)

exit - sequential statement

Can only reside inside a loop. Used to completely stop any further execution of the inner most enclosing loop. The completion of the loop is conditional if the statement includes a **when** condition. Is normally supported by synthesis tools.

```
AND_BIT_LOOP: for N in A'range loop
                  Y := Y and A(N);
                  exit when Y = '0';
              end loop;
```

```
(label:) exit (loop_label) (when condition);
```
(38)

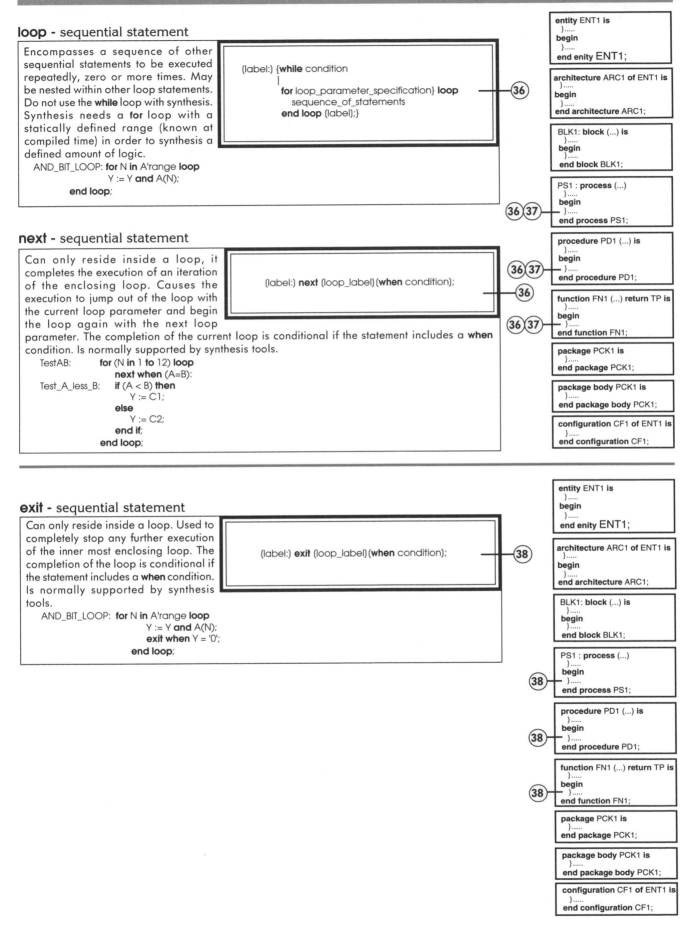

```
entity ENT1 is
  }.....
begin
  }.....
end entity ENT1;
```

```
architecture ARC1 of ENT1 is
  }.....
begin
  }.....
end architecture ARC1;
```

```
BLK1: block (...) is
  }.....
begin
  }.....
end block BLK1;
```

```
PS1 : process (...)
  }.....
begin
  }.....
end process PS1;
```
(36)(37)

```
procedure PD1 (...) is
  }.....
begin
  }.....
end procedure PD1;
```
(36)(37)

```
function FN1 (...) return TP is
  }.....
begin
  }.....
end function FN1;
```
(36)(37)

```
package PCK1 is
  }.....
end package PCK1;
```

```
package body PCK1 is
  }.....
end package body PCK1;
```

```
configuration CF1 of ENT1 is
  }.....
end configuration CF1;
```

```
entity ENT1 is
  }.....
begin
  }.....
end entity ENT1;
```

```
architecture ARC1 of ENT1 is
  }.....
begin
  }.....
end architecture ARC1;
```

```
BLK1: block (...) is
  }.....
begin
  }.....
end block BLK1;
```

```
PS1 : process (...)
  }.....
begin
  }.....
end process PS1;
```
(38)

```
procedure PD1 (...) is
  }.....
begin
  }.....
end procedure PD1;
```
(38)

```
function FN1 (...) return TP is
  }.....
begin
  }.....
end function FN1;
```
(38)

```
package PCK1 is
  }.....
end package PCK1;
```

```
package body PCK1 is
  }.....
end package body PCK1;
```

```
configuration CF1 of ENT1 is
  }.....
end configuration CF1;
```

return - sequential statement

Can only appear in a subprogram (procedure or function). Is used to complete the execution of the innermost enclosing subprogram body.

(label:) **return** (expression); — 39

A return statement is optional within a procedure and must not have an expression. A function must have a return statement and an associated expression which may simple be a single data object.

```
-- For procedures
return;
-- For functions
return A;
return A + B;
return AddFunction(A, B);
```

null - sequential statement

Performs no action. Has no other effect other than to pass execution on to the next sequential statement.

(label:) **null**; — 40

```
case SEL_INT is
  when 0 =>
    YN <= not A(0);
  when 1 =>
    YN <= not A(1);
  when others =>
    null;
end case;
```

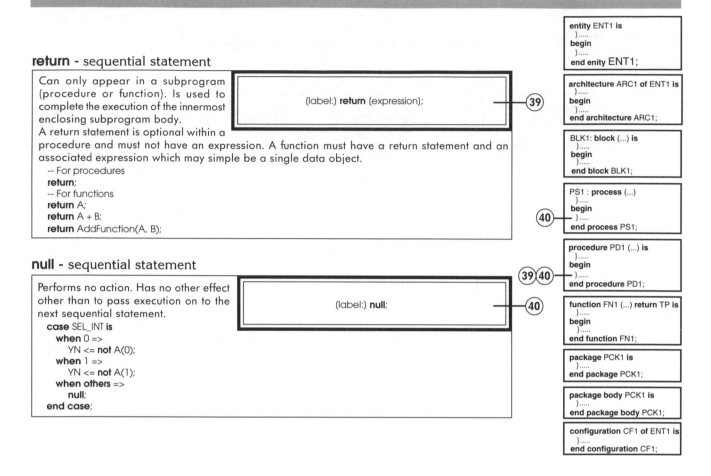

```
entity ENT1 is
  }.....
begin
  }.....
end enity ENT1;
```

```
architecture ARC1 of ENT1 is
  }.....
begin
  }.....
end architecture ARC1;
```

```
BLK1: block (...) is
  }.....
begin
  }.....
end block BLK1;
```

```
PS1 : process (...)
  }.....
begin
  }.....
end process PS1;
```
40

```
procedure PD1 (...) is
  }.....
begin
  }.....
end procedure PD1;
```
39 40

```
function FN1 (...) return TP is
  }.....
begin
  }.....
end function FN1;
```

```
package PCK1 is
  }.....
end package PCK1;
```

```
package body PCK1 is
  }.....
end package body PCK1;
```

```
configuration CF1 of ENT1 is
  }.....
end configuration CF1;
```

Appendix B Contents

Reserved Words

The following identifiers are reserved words in the Verilog language and so cannot be used as basic identifiers in a Verilog model. A reserved word is a keyword that has specific meaning in the language.

Verilog Reserved Words				
always	event ‡	not	small ‡	while
and		notif0	specify ‡	wire
assign	for	notif1	specparam ‡	wor
	force ‡		strength ‡	
begin	forever ‡	or	strong0 ‡	xnor
buf	fork ‡	output	strong1 ‡	xor
bufif0	function		supply0	
bufif1		parameter	supply1	
	highz0 ‡	pmos ‡		
case	highz1 ‡	posedge	table ‡	
casex		primitive ‡	task	
casez	if	pull0 ‡	time ‡	
cmos ‡	ifnone ‡	pull1 ‡	tran ‡	
	initial ‡	pullup ‡	tranif0 ‡	
deassign ‡	inout	pulldown ‡	tranif1 ‡	
default	input		tri	
defparam ‡	integer	rcmos ‡	tri0 ‡	
disable ‡		real ‡	tri1 ‡	
	join ‡	realtime ‡	triand ‡	
edge ‡		reg	trior ‡	
else	large	release ‡	trireg ‡	
end		repeat		
endattribute ‡	macromodule	rnmos ‡	unsigned ‡	
endcase	medium	rpmos ‡		
endmodule	module	rtran ‡	vectored ‡	
endfunction		rtranif0 ‡		
endprimitive ‡	nand	rtranif1 ‡	wait	
endspecify ‡	negedge		wand	
endtable ‡	nmos	scalared ‡	weak0 ‡	
endtask	nor	signed ‡	weak1 ‡	

‡ Constructs not supported by synthesis tools.

Verilog Compiler Directives

This chapter describes the Verilog language defined compiler directives. All such directives are preceded by the " ` " (accent grave) character often referred to as *tick*. They are listed in Table B1 and typically only the `define (pronounced tick define) and the `include compiler directives are supported by synthesis tools. Except for these two, the word compiler in the text below implies a simulator's compiler.

`resetall	`include
`define	`celldefine
`undef	`endcelldefine
`timescale	`default_nettype
`ifdef	`unconnected_drive
`else	`nounconnected_drive
`endif	

Table B1 Verilog Compiler Directives

`resetall

Resets all compiler directives to their default values when encountered during compilation.

`define/`undef

Tick define creates macros for text substitutions. Can be used both inside and outside **module** definitions. After a text macro is defined, it can be used in the source description by using the "`" character followed by the macro name. The compiler will substitute the text of the macro for the sting `macro_name.

```
`define State0 2'b 00
`define State1 2'b 01
`define State2 2'b 10
`define State3 2'b 11
...
case (State)
   `State0 : Y = A0;
   `State1 : Y = A1;
   `State2 : Y = A2;
   `State3 : Y = A3;
endcase
...
```

Tick undef is used to undefine a previously defined macro.

`timescale

Specifies the unit of time and the precision of time of the models that follow.

```
`timescale 1ns / 1ps
```

All time values are in multiples of 1 ns with a precision of 1 ps.

`ifdef/`else/`endif

These are conditional compilation compiler directives that are used to optionally include lines of Verilog source code for compilation. As such, they perform a similar function to VHDL configurations, although in Verilog the whole module must be recompiled each time.

The directive `ifdef checks for the definition of a variable name. If the variable name is defined then the lines following the `ifdef are included. If the variable name is not defined and an `else directive exists then the source code is compiled.

```
`ifdef <text_macro_name>
<first_group_of_lines>
`else
<second_group_of_lines>
`endif
```

These directives can be nested.

`include

Used to insert the entire contents of a source file in another file during compilation. The result is the same as though the contents of the included file were to appear in place of the `include directive. Is useful in defining global or commonly used definitions, tasks or functions, without having to repeat the code in every module boundary.

It can be nested, that is, an included file may itself contain an included file.

`celldefine/`endcelldefine

Used to tag a module as being a cell.

`default_nettype

Used to control the net type created for implicit net types. The default type is **wire** and should not be changed to anything else in synthesizable models.

```
`default_nettype <type_of_net>
where:
```

type_of_net can be: **wire, wand, wor, tri, triand, trior, tri0, tri1** or **trireg**.

`unconnected_drive/`nounconnected_drive

Pulls all input ports to a logic 0 or logic 1 instead of leaving them floating to the high impedance value Z.

Verilog System Tasks and Functions

All Verilog system tasks and functions defined in the Verilog LRM as being part of the Verilog language are listed along with a description of those that are typically used in test harnesses. They are not needed in synthesizable models, nor are they supported by synthesis tools.

Verilog system tasks and functions are used to perform simulation related operations such as monitoring and displaying simulation time and associated signal values at a specific time during simulation. All system tasks and functions begin with a dollar sign, for example, $monitor.

The Verilog LRM also describes other system tasks and functions in a separate appendix that does not form part of the standard Verilog language, but that is included in the LRM for information. These, and any tool specific system tasks and functions, should not be used if a Verilog model is to maintain portability between different design tools. (These tools specific system tasks and functions are defined by using the Peripheral Language Interface (PLI) which is also defined as part of the Verilog language.)

As a result of the previous discussion, only use the standard system tasks and functions defined by the Verilog language. These are listed in Table B-2, and their description's follow.

Display tasks	$fstrobeb	$async$nand$array	Conversion functions for reals
	$fstrobeh	$async$or$array	
$display	$fstrobeo	$async$nor$array	
$displayb	$fwrite	$async$and$plane	$bitstoreal
$displayh	$fwriteb	$async$nand$plane	$itor
$displayo	$fwriteh	$async$or$plane	$readtobits
$monitor	$fwriteo	$async$nor$plane	$rtoi
$monitorb	$readmemh	$sync$and$array	
$monitorh		$sync$nand$array	**Probablistic distribution functions**
$monitoro	**Timescale tasks**	$sync$or$array	
$monitoroff		$sync$nor$array	
$strobe	$printtimescale	$sync$and$plane	$random
$strobeb	$timeformat	$sync$nand$plane	$dist_chi_square
$strobeh		$sync$or$plane	$dist_exponential
$strobeo	**Simulation control tasks**	$sync$nor$plane	$dist_poisson
$write			$dist_uniform
$writeb	$finish	**Stochastic analysis tasks**	$dist_erlang
$writeh	$stop		$dist_nornal
$writeo			$dist_t
$monitoron	**Timing check tasks**	$q_initialize	
		$q_remove	**Value change dump file**
File I/O tasks	$hold	$q_exam	
	$period	$q_add	
$fclose	$setup	$q_full	$comment
$fdisplay	$skew	$q_random	$date
$fdisplayb	$nochange		$enddefinitions
$fdisplayh	$recovery	**Simulation time functions**	$scope
$fdisplayo	$setuphold		$timescale
$fmonitor	$width		$upscope
$fmonitorb		$realtime	$var
$fmonitorh	**PLA modeling tasks**	$time	$version
$fmonitoro		$stime	$dumpall
$readmemb	$async$and$array		$dumpoff
$fopen			$dumpon
$fstrobe			$dumpvars

Note. System tasks differing by only a "b", "h" or "o" at the end refer to binary, hexidecimal and octal, respectively.

Table B-2 Verilog language defined system tasks and functions

Display tasks

$display/$write.

Displays a formatted message to the screen. They are identical except $display adds a newline character to the end of its output whereas $write does not. They can display a quoted string, an expression that returns a value, or a null argument. They are displayed in the order in which they appear in the argument list.

```
$display ("ERRDET_CORRECTION Write error at time
        %d: Should be equal to %d, but is = %d",
        $time,RefMemData,MemData);
```

$strobe.

Provide the ability to display simulation data at a selected time and has the same argument list format as $display and $write.

$monitor.

Displays a formatted message to the screen when any variables or expressions specified as arguments to the system task, change. Again, it has the same argument list format as $display and $write.

Displays a formatted message to the screen when any signal in the monitor list changes.

```
initial
    $monitor ("ERRDET_CORRECTION Write error at
            time %d: Should be equal to %d, but
            is = %d",
            $time, RefMemData, MemData);
```

431

File I/O tasks

$fopen.

Opens a system file for reading and writing.

    SimResults = $fopen("errdet_correction.simres");

$fclose.

Closes a system file that has previously been opened using $fopen.

    $fclose(SimResults);

$fdisplay/$fwrite/$fmonitor/$fstrobe.

Correspond to $display, $write, $monitor and $strobe, but writes to specific files as apposed to the standard output; normally the monitor.

    $fdisplay(SimResults,
        "ERRDET_CORRECTION Write error at time
        %d: Should be equal to %d, but is = %d",
        $time, RefMemData, MemData);

$readmemb/$readmemh.

Used to read and load data from a specified file into a specified memory.

    $readmemb("mem8x5.dat", Mem8x5);

Timescale tasks

$printtimescale.

Displays the unit of simulation time and its precision. A specific module name can be given as an argument to display the time unit and precision of a particular module.

    $printtimescale   // No name so uses module
                        name with current scope.
    $printtimescale <hierarchical_name>;

$timeformat.

Specifies how time will be displayed when using: $write, $display, $strobe, $monitor, $fwrite, $fdisplay, $fstrobe and $fmonitor. See Verilog LRM for details.

Simulation control tasks

$finish.

Finishes a simulation and passes control back to the host system.

$stop.

Halts simulation at the current simulation time and enters an interactive debug mode where values can be interactively changed or break points set-up etc.

Timing check tasks

Used primarily in technology library cells. See Verilog LRM for details.

PLA modeling tasks

These system tasks are provided for modeling PLA devices. See Verilog LRM for details.

Stochastic analysis tasks

These system tasks and functions manage queues and generate random numbers with specific distributions. See Verilog LRM for details.

Simulation time functions

These system functions provide access to the current simulation time.

$time.

Returns a 64-bit integer value scaled to the timescale value of the **module** from which it was invoked.

$stime.

Returns a 32-bit integer value scaled to the timescale value of the module from which it was invoked.

$realtime.

Returns a real number scaled to the timescale value of the module from which it was invoked.

Conversion functions for reals

$rtoi.

Converts a real value to an integer value through truncation, for example, 29.95 becomes 29.

$itor.

Converts an integer value to a real value, for example, 29 becomes 29.0.

$readtobits.

Used to convert real numbers to a 64-bit vector representation so that they can be passed across module ports.

$bitstoreal.

Used to convert bit patterns to real numbers.

Probablistic distribution functions

$random.

System function for generating random numbers and returns a new 32-bit signed integer value each time it is called. A "seed" argument can be used to control the random numbers that are generated.

> $random %64 // will generate numbers between
> -63 and 63.

$dist_chi_square/$dist_exponential/ $dist_poisson/$dist_uniform/$dist_erlang/ $dist_nornal/$dist_t.

Used to generate random number to a specific probabilistic distribution. See Verilog LRM for details.

$comment/$date/$enddefinitions/$scope/ $timescale/$upscope/$var/$version/$dumpall

$dumpoff/$dumpon/$dumpvars

A change dump file is a file that contains information about value changes on selected variables for a design using the value change dump system tasks. See Verilog LRM for details.

Verilog Constructs

This is a quick reference guide to the different kinds of constructs used in the Verilog language. The symbol "‡" is used to identify constructs that are <u>not</u> supported by synthesis tools. For each construct the following is shown:

- the formal syntax definition,
- an indication of where it may be used in a Verilog model,
- a brief description,
- in most cases, a simple example.

The formal syntax is shown in Backus Naur Form (BNF). The following conventions are used:

Symbol/Nomenclature	Description	Meaning
<>	One or more spaces, tabs or carriage returns.	Separator between lexical elements.
	Sharp pointed angle brackets	Surround any non-literal symbols.
module (for example)	A word in bold print.	A Verilog keyword.
<name>	Name is in lower case.	A syntax construct item.
<NAME>	Name in upper case.	A lexical term.
<name><,<name>>*	Name is in lower case.	A comma separated list of items.
<name> ::=	Name is in lower case.	The syntax definition of an item.
|	Vertical line.	Alternative syntax definition.

A summary of the described constructs are listed below with corresponding page numbers.

module - design entity

The **module** is the only design unit in the Verilog language and as such is also the design entity. Ideally, it should reside in its own system file, although multiple declarations may reside in a single file. Hierarchy is created when higher level modules create instances of lower level declared modules and connects their port signals appropriately. **Module** declarations cannot be nested.

```
module_declaration ::=
        module_keyword module_identifier ( list_of_ports); { module_item}
        endmodule
module_keyword ::= module | macromodule
list_of_ports ::= (port { , port})
port ::=  (port_expression)
        | .port_identifier ((port_expression))
port_expression ::=
        port_reference
        | {port_reference {, port_refernce}}
port_reference ::=
        port_identifier
        | port_identifier (constant_expression)
        | port_identifier (msb_constant_expression : lsb_constant_expression)
module_item ::=
        module_item_declaration
        | parameter_override          | continuous_assign
        | gate_instantiation          | udp_instantiation
        | module_instantiation        | specify_block
        | initial_construct           | always_construct
module_item declaration ::=
        parameter_declaration
        | input_declaration           | output_declaration
        | inout_declaration           | net_declaration
        | reg_declaration             | integer_declaration
        | real_declaration            | time_declaration
        | realtime_declaration        | event_declaration
        | task_declaration            | function_declaration
parameter_override ::= defparam list_of_param_assignments;
```

```
module MOD1 (...);
}.....
endmodule
```

```
initial                    ‡
.....
```

```
always
.....
```

```
begin : SeqBLK1;
}.....
end
```

```
fork: ConcBLK1;           ‡
}.....
join
```

```
task: TSK1;
}.....
endtask
```

```
function: FN1;
}.....
endfunction
```

parameter data type - declaration

A **parameter** is used to define parameter constants for specifying bit widths, loop variables etc. They are commonly used in synthesizable models. The **defparam** statement which modifies a parameter is not normally supported by synthesis tools.

```
parameter_declaration ::= parameter list_of_param_assignments;      ①
list_of_param_assignments ::= param_assignement {,param_assignment}   ①②
param_assignment ::= parameter_identifier = constant_expression
```

parameter PI = 3.14159; **parameter** CycleTime = 100; **parameter** TrackDelay = 5;
parameter byte_size = 8; **parameter** StartVec = 4'b 1010;

```
module MOD1 (...);
}.....
endmodule
```

```
initial                    ‡
.....
```

net data types - declaration

Used to model hardware structure that has a close correlation to the structure of the circuit being modeled. There are various kinds of net data types for which declarations may be made. The optional "drive_strength" and "delay" should not be used in synthesizable models. This information should always come from the primitives of the actual technology being used.

```
net_declaration ::=
        net_type (vectored | scalared) (range) (delay3) list_of_net_identifiers;
        | treg (vectored | scalared) (charge_strength) (range) (delay3)
                                        list_of_net_identifiers;
        | net_type (vectored | scalared) (drive_strength) (range) (delay3)
                                        list_of_net_decl_assignments;            ②
net_type ::= wire | tri | tri1 | supply0 | wand | triand | tri0
                | supply1 | wor | trior
range ::= (msb_constant_expression : lsb_constant_expression)
drive_strength ::=
        (strength0, strength1) | (slrength1, strength0) | (strength0, highz1)
        | (strength1, highz0) | ( highz1, strength0) | ( highz0, strength1)
strength0 ::= supply0 | strong0 | pull0 | weak0
strength1 ::= supply1 | strong1 | pull1 | weak1
charge_strength ::= (small) | (medium) | (large)
delay3 ::= #delay_value | (delay_value (,delay_value (,delay_value)))
delay_value ::= unsigned_number | parameter_identifier |
                                constant_mintypmax_expression
list_of_net_decl_assignments ::= net_decl_assignment {,net_decl_assignment}
net_decl_assignment ::= net_identifier = expression
list_of_net_identifiers ::= net_identifier {, net_identifier}
```

wire (7:0) Bus1, Bus2, Bus3;

```
always
.....
```

```
begin : SeqBLK1;     ①
}.....
end
```

```
fork: ConcBLK1;       ①     ‡
}.....
join
```

```
task: TSK1;          ①
}.....
endtask
```

```
function: FN1;        ①
}.....
endfunction
```

```
Key
}..... Both declaration and
       statement areas
.....  Single statement or block
‡      not for synthesis
```

register data type - declaration

The keyword for a register data type is **reg** and is used to declare data objects that will be asigned procedurally in procedural assignment statements. It is important to note a Verilog register data type does not mean that a flip-flop is inferred from a synthesis tool, although it is used for this purpose. A **reg** data type means it stores its value from one assignment to the next in the procedural flow of constructs that surround it.

```
reg_declaration ::= reg (range) list_of_register_identifiers;
time_declaration ::= time list_of_register_identifiers;
integer_declaration ::= integer list_of_register_identifiers;
real_declaration ::= real list_of_real_identifiers;
realtime_declaration ::= realtime list_of_real_identifiers;
list_of_real_identifiers ::= register_name {,register_name}
register_name ::=
        register_identifier
        | memory_identifier (upper_limit_constant_expression :
                             lower_limit_constant_expression)
list_of_real_identifiers ::= real_identifier {,real_identifier}
```

③

```
reg (3:0) CurrentState, NextState;
reg (15:0) ProcArr(TestCycles - 1:0);
```

③ module MOD1 (...);
   }.....
   endmodule

initial   ‡
   .....

always
   .....

③ begin : SeqBLK1;
   }.....
   end

③ fork: ConcBLK1;   ‡
   }.....
   join   .

③ task: TSK1;
   }.....
   endtask

③ function: FN1;
   }.....
   endfunction

task (sub program) - declaration

Declares a task so that it may be called from other parts of a models description. It provides a means of executing common subsections of a model's description. A task is used to improve a model's structure and make it easier to both read and debug. Task declarations may not be nested. A **task** is similar to a VHDL procedure. It can have zero or more inputs and outputs of different types. When using with synthesis, outputs must be of type **reg** or **integer,** that is, types **time** and **real** cannot be used. Any timing information will be ignored by synthesis tools.

```
task_declaration ::=
        task task_identifier;
        {task_item_declaration}
        statement_or_null
        endtask
task_item_declaration ::=
        block_item_declaration
        | input_declaration | output_declaration
        | inout_declaration
block_item_declaration ::=
        | reg_declaration | integer_declaration
        | real_declaration | time_declaration
        | realtime_declaration | event_declaration
```

④

④⑤ module MOD1 (...);
   }.....
   endmodule

initial   ‡
   .....

always
   .....

begin : SeqBLK1;
   }.....
   end

function (sub program) - declaration

Declares a function so that it may be called from within the expressions of assignment statements in other parts of a module's description. Like the task, a function improves code and hence design structure.
A function must not contain timing control, and must execute in one simulation time unit. Function declarations cannot be nested, must have at least one input, and always returns a single value.

```
function_declaration ::=
        function (range_or_type) function_identifier;
        function_item_declaration {function_item_declaration}
        statement
        endfunction
range_or_type ::= range | integer | real | realtime | time
function_item_declaration ::=
        input_declaration | block_item_declaration
block_item_declaration ::=
        | parameter_declaration | reg_declaration
        | integer_declaration | real_declaration
        | time_declaration | realtime_declaration
        | event_declaration
```

⑤

fork: ConcBLK1;   ‡
   }.....
   join

task: TSK1;
   }.....
   endtask

function: FN1;
   }.....
   endfunction

Key
}..... Both declaration and
       statement areas
..... Single statement or block
‡   not for synthesis

435

component instantiation - concurrent statement

Use to build course grain structure hierarchy within a design. Modules are instantiated within other modules by using component instantiations. Module statements are not nested. The instantiation specifies signal connections to the instantiated block within the calling module.

```
module_instantiation ::=
        module_identifier (parameter_value_assignment)
                        module_instance{, module_instance};
parameter_value_assignment ::= # (expression {,expression})
module_instance ::= name_of_instance ((list_of_module_connections))
name_of_instance ::= module_instance_identifier (range)
list_of_module_connections ::=
        ordered_port_connection {,ordered_port_connection}
        | named_port_connection {,named_port_connection}
ordered_port_connection ::= (expression)
named_port_connection ::=.port_identifier ((expression))
```
⑥

```
LFSR  LFSR_1 (A1, B1, Y1),
      LFSR_2 (A2, B2,Y2);
```

⑥ | **module** MOD1 (...);
) .....
endmodule

initial ‡
.....

always
.....

begin : SeqBLK1;
) .....
end

fork: ConcBLK1; ‡
) .....
join

task: TSK1;
) .....
endtask

function: FN1;
) .....
endfunction

initial - concurrent statement

Is only executed once at the beginning of a simulation, unlike the **always** statement which is executed continuously throughout simulation. The **initial** statement, like the **always** statement may incorporate **begin**-**end** and **fork**-**join** procedural blocks.

```
initial_construct::=                           ‡
        initial statement
```
⑦

⑦⑧ | **module** MOD1 (...);
) .....
endmodule

initial ‡
.....

Is used to initialize variables at the start of simulation and the specification of waveform signals in test harnesses for example. No hardware is implied and is not supported by synthesis tools.

```
initial
   begin
      RegA =0;
      for (N=0; N<8; N=N+1;)
         MemA(N) =0;
   end
```

always
.....

begin : SeqBLK1;
) .....
end

fork: ConcBLK1; ‡
) .....
join

always - concurrent statement

Is the primary construct used in RTL modeling. It may contain **begin**-**end** and **fork**-**join** blocks to group statements. Is similar to the **process** statement in VHDL. Used extensively in models which are to be synthesized, in which case only **begin**-**end** procedural blocks may be used.

```
always_construct::=
        always statement
```
⑧

task: TSK1;
) .....
endtask

function: FN1;
) .....
endfunction

```
always @(posedge Clock)
   begin
      Y1 = ! (A & B);
      Y2 = ! (A | B);
   end
```

Key
) ..... Both declaration and
statement areas
..... Single statement or block
‡ not for synthesis

continuous assignment - concurrent statement

Resides inside a **module** but not within any of the subblocks. It is concurrent with all other assignments in the **module**.
Is used to continuously assign drive values onto net data types. These nets may be a bit (scalar) or group of bits (vector). Whenever the right hand side of the assignment statement (the expression) changes the left hand side is automatically updated. The expression may contain function calls and may also be conditional.
Drive strength and delay values should not be used in synthesizable models.

```
procedural_continuous_assignments ::=
        assign reg_assignment; | deassign reg_lvalue;
      | force reg_assignment; | force_net_assignment;
      | release reg_lvalue; | release net_lvalue;
reg_assignment ::=
        reg_lvalue = expression
net_assignment ::=
        net_lvalue = expression
```

⑨ ⑩
⑨

```
module MOD1 (...);
}.....
endmodule
```

```
initial                    ‡
.....
```



```
    assign Y = !(A & B);
    assign Y = (Time != Timeout) ? Y+1 : Zero;
```

```
always
.....
```

function call - concurrent statement

Is called call from within an expression in a continuous concurrent assignment statement. The computed value returned by the function replaces the function call within the expression. Must execute in one simulation cycle so can only imply combinational logic. Cannot be nested, but functions can call other functions. Must have at least one input and returns a single value output.

```
function_call ::= function_identifier (expression {,expression});
```

⑩

```
begin : SeqBLK1;
}.....
end
```

```
fork: ConcBLK1;       ‡
}.....
join
```

```
task: TSK1;
}.....
endtask
```

```
function: FN1;
}.....
endfunction
```

fork-join - concurrent procedural block

Is a means of grouping two or more procedural assignments together so that they act like a single group of concurrent statements. The individual statements within a **fork-join** block execute concurrently with each other, that is, when simulating, each statement starts at the same time when control is passed to the block.
Is used when all variable delays within a block need to be relative to a particular simulation time which is the time when simulation control enters the block.
As timing for hardware models to be synthesized should come from technology library primitives, the **fork-join** block is not supported by synthesis tools. Use the **always** statement for concurrent blocks in synthesizable models.

```
par_block ::=                          ‡
        fork (: block_identifier
             { block_item_declaration})
        {statement} join
```

⑪

```
module MOD1 (...);
}.....
endmodule
```

⑪⑫
```
initial                    ‡
.....
```

⑪⑫
```
always
.....
```

⑪⑫
```
begin : SeqBLK1;
}.....
end
```

begin-end - sequential procedural block

Is a means of grouping two or more procedural assignments together so that they act like a single group of sequential statements. Individual statements within a **begin**-**end** block are executed sequentially.
Used extensively in synthesis models.

```
seq_block ::=
        begin(: block_identifier { block_item_declaration})
                              {statement} end
block_item_declaration ::=
        parameter_declaration
      | reg_declaration | integer_declaration
      | real_declaration | time_declaration
      | realtime_declaration | event_declaration
```

⑪⑫
⑫

⑪⑫
```
fork: ConcBLK1;       ‡
}.....
join
```

⑪⑫
```
task: TSK1;
}.....
endtask
```

```
    always @ (S or A or B)
        begin: TestAB
            if (S)
                begin
                    Y1 = A and B;
                    Y2 = A or B;
                end
        end
```

⑪⑫
```
function: FN1;
}.....
endfunction
```

```
Key
}..... Both declaration and
           statement areas
..... Single statement or block
‡   not for synthesis
```

blocking procedural assignment - sequential statement

This is one of two types of procedure assignment. It uses the equality operator (=) and is blocking in nature. This means assignments with timing delays in a sequential **begin-end** block will not be executed until all delays in the previous assignments in the same block, have completed. This means, only when one blocking procedural assignment in a **begin-end** block has been executed by a simulator, will control pass to the next assignment.

This blocking of the next statement does not apply in concurrent **fork-join** blocks as all statements within the block are executed concurrently. Synthesis ignores all timing.

```
always @(posedge Clock)
    begin: BLOCK_SYNCH
    #3 M3 = A3 & B3;
    #1 Y3 = M3 | C3;
    end
```

```
blocking assignment ::=
        reg_lvalue = (delay_or_event_control) expression
delay_or_event_control ::=
        delay_control
        | event_control | repeat (expression) event_control
reg_lvalue ::=
        reg_identifier
        | reg_identifier (expression)
        | reg_identifier (msb_constant_expression:
                        lsb_constant_expression)
.       | reg_concatenation
delay_control ::=
        # delay_value | # (mintypmax_expr ession)
event_control ::=
        @ event_identifier | @ (event_expression)
event_expression ::=
        expression | event_identifier | posedge expression
        | negedge expression | event_expression or
        event_expression
```

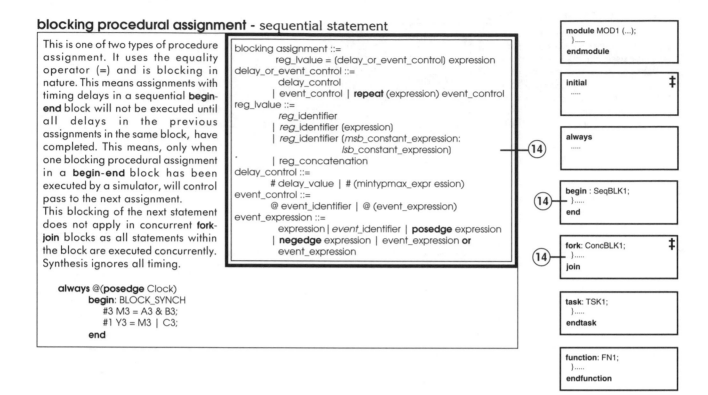

non-blocking procedural assignment - sequential statement

The non-blocking procedure assignment statements use the "<=" operator and allows assignments to be scheduled without blocking the procedural flow of constructs that surround them, as the blocking procedure assignment does. Can be used to make several assignments within the same time step without regard to their order, or dependence upon each other.

```
always @(posedge Clock)
    begin: NON_BLOCK_SYNCH
    #3 M4 <= A4 & B4;
    #1 Y4 <= M4 | C4;
    end
```

```
non_blocking assignment ::=
        reg_lvalue <= (delay_or_event_control) expression
```

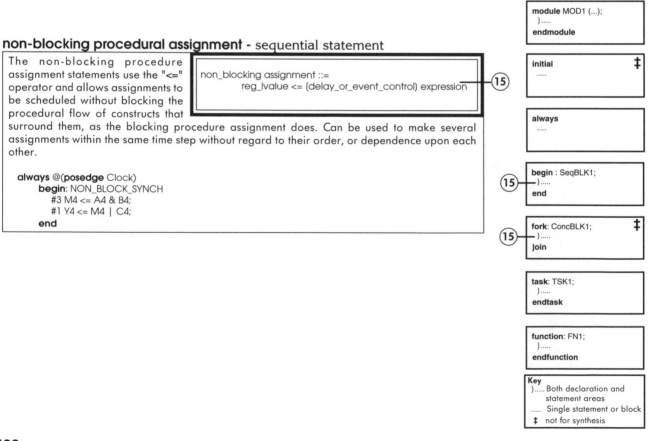

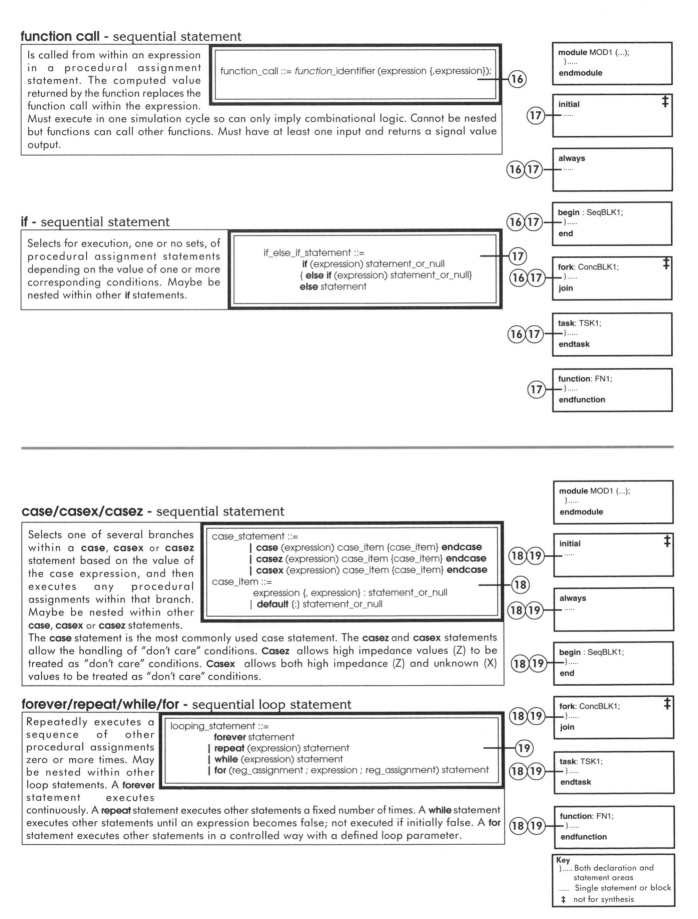

function call - sequential statement

Is called from within an expression in a procedural assignment statement. The computed value returned by the function replaces the function call within the expression.

```
function_call ::= function_identifier (expression {,expression});
```

Must execute in one simulation cycle so can only imply combinational logic. Cannot be nested but functions can call other functions. Must have at least one input and returns a signal value output.

if - sequential statement

Selects for execution, one or no sets, of procedural assignment statements depending on the value of one or more corresponding conditions. Maybe be nested within other **if** statements.

```
if_else_if_statement ::=
        if (expression) statement_or_null
    { else if (expression) statement_or_null}
        else statement
```

case/casex/casez - sequential statement

Selects one of several branches within a **case**, **casex** or **casez** statement based on the value of the case expression, and then executes any procedural assignments within that branch. Maybe be nested within other **case**, **casex** or **casez** statements.

```
case_statement ::=
    | case (expression) case_item {case_item} endcase
    | casez (expression) case_item {case_item} endcase
    | casex (expression) case_item {case_item} endcase
case_item ::=
        expression {, expression} : statement_or_null
    | default (:) statement_or_null
```

The **case** statement is the most commonly used case statement. The **casez** and **casex** statements allow the handling of "don't care" conditions. **Casez** allows high impedance values (Z) to be treated as "don't care" conditions. **Casex** allows both high impedance (Z) and unknown (X) values to be treated as "don't care" conditions.

forever/repeat/while/for - sequential loop statement

Repeatedly executes a sequence of other procedural assignments zero or more times. May be nested within other loop statements. A **forever** statement executes continuously. A **repeat** statement executes other statements a fixed number of times. A **while** statement executes other statements until an expression becomes false; not executed if initially false. A **for** statement executes other statements in a controlled way with a defined loop parameter.

```
looping_statement ::=
        forever statement
    | repeat (expression) statement
    | while (expression) statement
    | for (reg_assignment ; expression ; reg_assignment) statement
```

Key
}..... Both declaration and statement areas
..... Single statement or block
‡ not for synthesis

439

Index

ORDER FORM

Please send .... copies of HDL Chip Design ($65 each) at a total cost of $..............plus $6.00 postage and handling within the U.S. If I am not completely satisfied I can return the book for a full refund within 15 days of delivery.

A disk containing all the examples in the book is available at a cost of $15 each including postage. Please send .... copies of the disk.

Name ....
Company ....
Address ....
City ....
State ....
Zip ....
Daytime phone no. ....

☐ check or money order enclosed

charge my
☐ visa   ☐ mastercard
Acc.no. ....
Expiration date ....
Signature ....

• All orders must be prepaid

• Al residents add 8% sales tax   • For orders of 3 or more request information on discounts

Fill and return or fax to:
Doone Publications
7950 Hwy 72W, #G106,
Madison AL 35758 USA
Tel: 1-800-311-3753
or
Tel:fax: USA 205-837-0580
e.mail: asmith@doone.com

ORDER FORM

Please send .... copies of HDL Chip Design ($65 each) at a total cost of $ .... plus $6.00 postage and handling within the U.S. If I am not completely satisfied I can return the book for a full refund within 15 days of delivery.

A disk containing all the examples in the book is available at a cost of $15 each including postage. Please send .... copies of the disk.

Name ....

Company ....　☐ check or money order enclosed

Address ....

City ....

State ....　charge my

　　　　　　　　　　　　　　　　　　　　　　　　　　　　☐ visa　　☐ mastercard

Zip ....　Acc.no. ....

Daytime phone no. ....　Expiration date ....

　　　　　　　　　　　　　　　　　　　　　　　　　　　　Signature ....

• All orders must be prepaid

• Al residents add 8% sales tax　　• For orders of 3 or more request information on discounts

Fill and return or fax to:

Doone Publications

7950 Hwy 72W, #G106,

Madison AL 35758 USA

Tel: 1-800-311-3753

or

Tel:fax: USA 205-837-0580

e.mail: asmith@doone.com